D1728907

Orientalism, Philology, and the Illegibility of the Modern World

Europe's Legacy in the Modern World

Series Editors: Martti Koskenniemi and Bo Stråth (University of Helsinki, Finland)

The nineteenth century is often described as Europe's century. This series aims to explore the truth of this claim. It views Europe as a global actor and offers insights into its role in ordering the world, creating community and providing welfare in the nineteenth century and beyond. Volumes in the series investigate tensions between the national and the global, welfare and warfare, property and poverty. They look at how notions like democracy, populism, and totalitarianism came to be intertwined and how this legacy persists in the present-day world.

The series emphasizes the entanglements between the legal, the political, and the economic and employs techniques and methodologies from the history of legal, political, and economic thought, the history of events, and structural history. The result is a collection of works that shed new light on the role that Europe's intellectual history has played in the development of the modern world.

Published:
Historical Teleologies in the Modern World, Henning Trüper, Dipesh Chakrabarty, and Sanjay Subrahmanyam

Europe's Utopias of Peace, Bo Stråth

Political Reform in the Ottoman and Russian Empires, Adrian Brisku

European Modernity: A Global Approach, Bo Stråth and Peter Wagner

The Contested History of Autonomy, Gerard Rosich

Caesarism in the Post-Revolutionary Age: Crisis, Populace and Leadership, Markus J. Prutsch

Orientalism, Philology, and the Illegibility of the Modern World, Henning Trüper

Forthcoming:
Social Difference in Nineteenth-Century Spanish America: An Intellectual History, Francisco A. Ortega

Orientalism, Philology, and the Illegibility of the Modern World

Henning Trüper

BLOOMSBURY ACADEMIC
LONDON • NEW YORK • OXFORD • NEW DELHI • SYDNEY

BLOOMSBURY ACADEMIC
Bloomsbury Publishing Plc
50 Bedford Square, London, WC1B 3DP, UK
1385 Broadway, New York, NY 10018, USA

BLOOMSBURY, BLOOMSBURY ACADEMIC and the Diana logo are
trademarks of Bloomsbury Publishing Plc

First published in Great Britain 2020

Cover design: Tjaša Krivec
Cover image: Composition V, 1911. Artist: Kandinsky, Wassily Vasilyevich
(1866–1944) (© Heritage Image Partnership Ltd/Alamy Stock Photo)

A catalogue record for this book is available from the British Library.

A catalog record for this book is available from the Library of Congress.

ISBN: HB: 978-1-3501-1737-2
         ePDF: 978-1-3501-1738-9
         eBook: 978-1-3501-1739-6

Series: Europe's Legacy in the Modern World

Typeset by Integra Software Services Pvt. Ltd.
Printed and bound in Great Britain

To find out more about our authors and books visit www.bloomsbury.com
and sign up for our newsletters.

Contents

Illustrations

Acknowledgments

I owe a great debt of gratitude to many individuals and institutions that have supported this project over the rather many and peripatetic years of its incipience.

My research on matters of Orientalism and philology was first funded by the University Research Priority Program "Asia and Europe" at the University of Zurich, and I am grateful to various scholars, friends, and colleagues there for helping this project along in a variety of ways in its tentative early phase, in particular Wolfgang Behr, Jörg Fisch, Andreas Isler, Astrid Meier, Ulrich Rudolph, Roman Seidel, Ralph Weber, Christoph Uehlinger, and Paola von Wyss-Giacosa. The project was subsequently supported by the M4Human Program of the Gerda Henkel Foundation, on account of whose generosity I was able to spend a productive period at the *Ecole des Hautes Etudes en Sciences Sociales* in Paris, with Sabina Loriga as a stalwartly supportive host and patient and perceptive reader. I have presented my work in Paris on several occasions and still remember gratefully discussion in the *Atelier Usages de l'histoire* at EHESS and the intellectual history colloquium at Paris 8, with Cesare Cuttica, Will Slauter, Ann Thomson and others. I was able to continue work on the project in Princeton, where I remain particularly indebted to Danielle Allen, Didier Fassin, and Joan Wallach Scott, as well as to others who were at the Institute for Advanced Study 2013–2014, including Rainer Brunner, Bonnie Effros, Joe Hankins, Joe Masco, Ann McGrath, Naphtali Meshel, Matthew Mosca, Vanessa Ogle, Noah Salomon, and Yücel Yanıkdağ. In the following period in Berlin, I have repeatedly had the good fortune to be able to converse on matters of future philology with Islam Dayeh, and I remain indebted for the asylum and various opportunities to discuss my work, which I enjoyed thanks to Friedrich Steinle at *Technische Universität*. In Helsinki Ilkka Lindstedt and Arvind Rajagopal have been important interlocutors, as has Kaj Öhrnberg, who moreover contributed an extremely generous full reading of the first draft and offered uncounted corrections when I was preparing the manuscript for publication. During this process two anonymous reader reports also provided most helpful insights. The research on the volume has been helped along greatly by archival and library staff, especially in Berlin, Leiden, Princeton, and Tübingen.

Over the years, Dipesh Chakrabarty has been a friend and interlocutor for this project, as have been Faisal Devji and Jonathan Sheehan. Throughout, Mario Wimmer read and commented on parts of chapter drafts and acted as corrective to many, or at least some, of my worst propensities. A number of friends and colleagues have helped with linguistic or practical matters, among whom in particular Yonas Addise, Roman Benz, Maria Bulakh, Tobias Delfs, Tilly Fatke, Saleh Idris, Agnes Korn, Henk Looijesteijn, Gerhard Rammer, Fredrik Thomasson (conversations with whom sparked my initial interest in working on the history of Orientalism), and Jan Zutavern.

An earlier version of this work has been defended as a modern history *Habilitation* thesis at the University of Zurich. As a consequence of this procedure, I have had the privilege to profit from generous reader reports by Wolfgang Behr, Helge Jordheim, and Sabine Mangold-Will. I am also greatly obliged to Bo Stråth and Martti Koskenniemi for offering the hospitality of their series at Bloomsbury. For support of the publication, I moreover offer my sincere thanks to the Helsinki Collegium for Advanced Studies and its directors Minna Palander-Collin and Tuomas Forsberg. Alexia Grosjean helped immensely with straightening out at least some of the English, that forever elusive language. Last revisions were carried out during a stint as Visiting Fellow in the wonderful research environment at the School of History at Australian National University, Canberra. In the preparation of the manuscript for print, the publishers' staff, in particular Rhodri Mogford and Laura Reeves, assisted in numerous ways. I am deeply grateful for all help I have received.

Earlier versions of parts of Chapter 3 were published as "Wild Archives: Unsteady Records of the Past in the Travels of Enno Littmann," *History of the Human Sciences* 26.4 (2013), 128–148; and "Heteropsy and Autopsy in Nineteenth-Century Aksumite Epigraphy," *Storia della Storiografia* 66 (2015), 121–142. The last section of Chapter 4 is partly a translation and reworking of "Wie es uneigentlich gewesen: Zum Gebrauch der Fußnote bei Julius Wellhausen," *Zeitschrift für Germanistik*, n.s. 23.2 (2013), 329–342.

Translations of quotations are my own unless otherwise indicated. For the sake of offering chronological orientation, I have inserted philologists' life dates at first mention, where it seemed appropriate.

Helsinki, February 2019
Henning Trüper

Introduction: History in Meaning

1. Pigeon or Sandgrouse?

This book began as a general and vague befuddlement about reading as a method. I had previously worked on writing practice in historical scholarship and concluded that project with a sense of regret for omitting any sustained investigation of reading. Neither theories nor cultural histories of reading tend to focus much on the distinctness of scholarly knowledge from other bodies of knowledge, perhaps because it seems so obvious that the ability to read is not a domain exclusive to scholarship. Yet since, after all, many humanities disciplines subscribe to the notion that they dispose of methods of reading that yield otherwise unattainable knowledge, there is an epistemological lacuna at hand. Knowledge was, and is, regarded as scientific or scholarly if it is superior to ordinary knowledge in reliability, scope, cohesiveness, and similar regards. According to Gaston Bachelard, the relationship between scientific and other knowledge is even one of deliberate departure, of rejection and more or less radical rewriting of conventional convictions, a process of "epistemological rupture."[1] It appears hard to contest that his condition holds for the humanities, too. The penchant toward the formation of disciplinary bodies of knowledge, the use of specialized, non-ordinary language, the critical-revisionist tendency, the reliance on standards of argumentation and documentation—all of these function as markers of distinction.

What did the the distinctness of scholarly knowledge mean for "reading," though? How was expressly scholarly knowledge founded on something as humdrum as the explication of linguistic meanings? And what effects did scholarship have on meaning in turn, including more general understandings of what "meaning" meant? Method, needless to say, is not merely a matter of abstract and normative pronouncements—that is to say, methodology—but also one of practice. The concern for practice calls for a historical treatment, provided one intends to acknowledge the malleability of patterns of going about things. So it seemed logical to pursue my interest in the problem of reading-as-scholarship in the ambit of the history of philology, or philologies in the plural, the discipline, or disciplines, most exclusively built on reading practices and the ability to theorize these.

In this pursuit, the shifting ground of the singular and plural—of philology and philologies—presented itself first as a terminological nuisance, then as an intellectual problem. The overall field of philological scholarship has never been a model case of unity, neither in method nor in methodology. In fact, the disunity of philology came to appear more and more as the key to my questions concerning reading, and for that reason, I quickly found myself drawn to the area of philology where the plurality of subdisciplines accumulated most thickly. This area was, it seemed to me, Orientalism, in its manifestation as philological knowledge.

For the rest, perhaps my initial confusion was simply motivated by longstanding diffidence toward the official, even somewhat sterile tone of common hermeneutic theories and of the abstract and general critiques to which such theories have often been exposed. Was a general theory of reading—be it hermeneutic, or "reader-response," or deconstructionist, or media-theoretical, or otherwise—even plausible? If so, what had led scholars to believe that there was actually a methodology to reading, seeing as this belief implied that reading could also be unmethodical and therefore was not simply a unified monolith of mental activity but also not merely a sprawling plurality? Did theoretical efforts do enough to clear up ambiguities between the descriptive accounting for and the normative regulation of method?

Pushing ahead with my own uneasy readings of research literature and archives, my unease found something of a mark of orientation when I came across writings by a nowadays half-forgotten scholar, the Semitist and Turkologist Georg Jacob (1862–1937). Take, for instance, the following passage from a letter Jacob wrote to his longtime mentor, the Semitist Theodor Nöldeke (1836–1930), in the spring of 1914:

> Among the ancient poets, too, there are … good and bad observers. Al-Shanfara is among the former; among the latter are those who confuse sandgrouses with pigeons, which actually occurs. Brehm [i.e. the popular German zoological compendium on "animal lives"] regrettably now [in the heavily revised fourth edition, 1911ff.] arranges everything by embryonal development, which is entirely irrelevant for animal *lives*. The old structure—which did not yet assign the nocturnal birds of prey to a different volume than the diurnal ones, and did not scatter waterfowl across the most diverse volumes—was the only appropriate one for the stated task. [Added note:] In their outward habitus and their movements, pigeons and sandgrouses are *very* different.[2]

What struck me in these densely packed remarks is the question of why the problem at hand would be worth dwelling on not merely in correspondence but in several publications on the lexical distinction of two species of bird that even a layperson would not find difficult to tell apart.[3] In addition, this effort was hardly an isolated instance. Jacob and many other Orientalists devoted rather implausible amounts of page space to inquiries of this kind.

Admittedly, it seems easy—and is common—to dismiss such pursuits as precisely the mixture of excruciating pedantry and irksome eccentricity that contributed so much to the bad name of philology. Denis Sinor (1916–2011), a preeminent scholar of Central Asian matters, once recalled in vivid terms how he garnered all his courage to ask his master, the formidable Sinologist Paul Pelliot (1878–1945), why the latter spent so much time studying "matters of no consequence." Instead of taking offense, Pelliot "cheerfully answered: 'ça m'amuse, Sinor, ça m'amuse!'" Sinor suggests that his master lacked "the essential virtue necessary" for the vocation of the historian: "he was unable, or unwilling, to distinguish between the important and the unimportant."[4] This assessment captures the riddle that the pursuits of previous generations posed to their successors already in the interwar period. Sinor decides to limit his apprehension, even frustration, to Pelliot as an individual scholar in pursuit of a kind of intellectual egotism. "He did what he liked" (ibid.), Sinor states in conclusion of the anecdote.

Yet Pelliot's concerns were not so strictly a matter of private idiosyncrasy. In Sinor's disjunction—"unable, or unwilling"—there is a world of difference. Not least, this difference pertains to the territoriality of disciplines, in ways that are clearly often elusive to posterity. Probably, Pelliot would have been even more amused by the notion that his work ought to have satisfied the virtuous standards of historical synthesis his student came to hold so dear. The very sense of seriousness that informs Sinor's understanding of discriminating the important from the unimportant was a disciplinary standard that won out among twentieth-century philologists under the pressure of contemporary events: the world wars, exile, and resistance. In fact, it is precisely these topics that make up the bulk of his recollections about Pelliot before and during the Second World War. The notion of a tragic nadir of European history formed the backdrop against which Pelliot's egotist approach to philological study appeared alien and even frivolous. This perspective, however, made invisible an older, alternative standard of seriousness captured, one might say, in the Renaissance *topos* of *serio ludere*, playing in earnest.[5] Arguably, philology had previously distinguished itself from the gravitas of history by implicit alignment with a fading memory of this commonplace. Only, the Renaissance long over, the paradoxes of God and creation more of a dead memory than a living concern, the playful seriousness of nineteenth-century philologists relied on different points of reference than the theological ones of pre-modern scholarship.

Georg Jacob's letter to Nöldeke grants access to some of these points of reference. To begin with, Al-Shanfara, one of the most prominent authors in the corpus of Early Arabic poetry, was to be aesthetically *justified* by his exactitude.[6] This justification could be approximated by the modern philological reader who carefully sorted out the lexical evidence in order to recuperate the poet's acuity of observation. Poetry, in considerable measure, rested on the matching of language and nature; this was its value and tendency. In some sense, philology enjoyed a share in this foundation. In the preface to his translation of Al-Shanfara's most highly regarded poem, the *Lāmiyyāt 'al-arab*, Jacob reiterated the judgment of an older Austrian Orientalist and diplomat, Alfred von Kremer (1828–1889), according to whom the "significance of the Arab nation [*Arabertum*]" lay in its "empiricism."[7] Al-Shanfara's supposed precision in the description of nature illustrated this trait.

There was an echo, in the question of pigeons and sandgrouses, of the older metaphor of the "book of nature," the notion of a "legible" world, as Hans Blumenberg put it.[8] The book of nature was the totality of the world of divine creation, the companion piece to the book of revealed knowledge, scripture. The metaphor shaped a tremendous intellectual tradition of the structuring and balancing of different bodies of knowledge. This tradition rested on a notion of reading that was partly a practice but also partly a mere trope. Jacob's letter gestured toward the continuing relevance of this metaphorical meaning of "reading," even though the ascribed ability to read nature had already shifted from the scientist to the poet. What happened to the book of nature in this transfer had happened to the book of revelation earlier on, in a process in which the Bible became increasingly seen as a text the "truth" of which was poetic, not literal.[9] Alfred Brehm's (1829–1884) multi-volume compendium, which highlighted the "feelings" and "souls" of animals, appeared from 1863 onward in multiple editions, thus right after Darwin's 1859 *On the Origin of Species*. The novel notion of evolution had undercut the characterological anthropomorphism Brehm championed inasmuch as it produced a more temporalized and contextualized understanding of the differences of species.[10] Brehm's compendium arguably marks the moment of the poeticization of the book of nature when the traditional deployment of the metaphor—for the order of creation—was beginning to lose traction. Jacob's 1914 rejection of the scientifically revised fourth edition—which years after Brehm's death was issued under the tutelage of an academic zoologist—also bespeaks a sense of nostalgia for a past moment in which poeticized zoological "empiricism" had produced a "household" book so widely known that one could refer to it by the sole surname of its author.[11]

Yet, it is not this sense of nostalgia that actually matters in the quoted letter. Rather, the passage is a statement on poetics as such, for which the project of Brehm's animal lives is only a reminder: poetry itself is to be founded on "observation." Perhaps, in Jacob's notions, one can even hear a distant echo of Giambattista Vico's epoch-making assertions about the primacy of poetic signs and metaphors in the human appropriation of the world through language.[12] In any case, for Jacob, natural distinctions, such as those of avian species, were translatable into poetic language by way of assiduous observation. The task of philology was to realize that, and where, this translation took place, and where it did not. Philology thus read other people's readings and misreadings of the book of nature—their books about the book of nature, as one might say. So poetry functioned as a mediator between the reading of text and the reading of nature, and this mediation created an opening for philological argument. Jacob believed that confirming the naturalist exactitude of the poetic imagery around sandgrouses supplied evidence for authenticating Al-Shanfara's authorship of the poem. Only a poet deeply familiar with Bedouin life would have been able to adapt metaphor so closely to the behavior of birds. In this way, modern philology could resolve an age-old dispute in Islamic scholarship about whether the *Lamiyyāt* was merely the fabrication of a ninth-century (CE) Arab scholar. Jacob was convinced that a book-educated forger would have confused sandgrouses with pigeons and would perforce have failed to replicate the poetics of exactitude that informed Al-Shanfara's overall imagery.[13]

This also meant, however, that the modern philologist, who had no experience of the living sandgrouse, was still precisely in the position of a forger, always improving on his craft. The reading of the reading of reality was only a copy of poetic experience and could never attain the same level of authenticity. So what Jacob's remarks on

Al-Shanfara and the sandgrouse actually indicate is not so much a confident stance on the actual nature of authentic reading, but a sense of unease amid shifting, split meanings of "reading." The book of nature is not available to philology; the world is illegible to the philologist. The poeticization of the book of nature is just a sideways movement within the explication of the meaning of reading. This movement is the defensive positioning of a stand-in, poetry, for a proper explication of how nature might be regarded as an authoritative source of linguistic meaning.

The resulting sense of the illegibility of the world is the problem this book explores. The possibility of understanding the world as a whole, life as a whole, was condensed in the metaphor of the legible book, the decodable text, written by a secretive author whose ruses would eventually be uncovered by human ingenuity—or not. Indeed, many scholars, not least Vico himself, had traditionally regarded the prospect that natural reality would ultimately prove inscrutable as a comforting confirmation of divine superiority and omnipotence. From Blumenberg's point of view, therefore, those who insisted on the illegibility of the book of nature mainly expressed a hankering for theological reassurance. His analysis hardly focuses on notions of the illegibility of the world outside of its potential function as a comfort zone for Christian sentiment. Clearly, Blumenberg was more fascinated by the ways in which scientific and technological tools remain beholden to the metaphor of the legibility of the world while also constantly tending to undermine it.[14]

I contend, by contrast, that there is an interesting problem contained in philologists' widespread unease about, and in some cases outright denial of, the legibility of the world. I suggest analyzing the history of philology as a repository of variants of this unease, of different understandings of how language accesses reality, and of a lingering sense of the untenable and futile character of these understandings. Moreover, I argue that it is the history of Orientalism, in particular, that has been decisive for steering the history of philology in this direction. Sandgrouse or pigeon, easily clarified—the nature of meaning, not so much.

2. "Explication," "Meaning"

The concept of "reading," as it remains beset by figurative meanings, also functions as a synecdoche of the explication of meaning in general, that is to say, of semantics. The concept of "explication," as a term for the procedures one encounters in the production of knowledge about meaning, connotes an unsystematic, even gestural practice of unfolding something that coheres, an exegetic use of, mostly (but not exclusively), text for explaining language. The concept draws on a broad-minded approach to explanation that reaches beyond but includes a more narrowly causal understanding of what it means to explain something. The use of the concept of explication in this book also has to do with an eschewal of established models of "understanding" in the humanities, via Dilthey, the neo-Kantians, and Gadamer. These theories carry a burden of presuppositions about the nature of human phenomenal experience as the basis of linguistic understanding that will in many instances throughout this book play an adversarial role. "Explication," then, stands in for a notion of reading that is on the outside of hermeneutics: diffident of the latter's virtuous circle of establishing authority about authority. Hermeneutic theory is biased toward cognitive success; it is a lucky charm, rather than an explanation, of reading. By the same token, hermeneuticists embrace the tragic seriousness of the historical as a world of successes and failures, fortunes and misfortunes. Hermeneutic theory tends to subscribe to the autonomy of the subject of experience, the immediacy of the subject's grasp of what Dilthey, the great critic of a unified ontology that would have underpinned all scientific knowledge, called the "facts of consciousness."[15] This was a domain of facts categorically apart from those of "nature," but still a domain shared by all the varying humanities (*Geisteswissenschaften*), a unified ontology of all interpretation (*Auslegung*) of text and the understanding (*Verstehen*) of the "utterances of life."[16] The facts of the mind function as a level playing field for an athleticism of interpretation. One consequence of the positing of ontological unity within the ambit of humanist knowledge has been the tendency also to posit orderly relations and distinctions between written text and speech.[17] In the cultural disciplines, this has legitimized a practice of privileging writing, not just as the inevitable medium but also as the prime object of inquiry.[18] As a philosophical project, hermeneutics has always been about throwing all support behind specific ontological posits, and not about the question of what motivates such posits in the first place, whether they are inevitable, and what might be the alternative. For a history of philology, as I intend to show, these theoretical decisions *ex ante* are too limiting.

As for "semantics," even though the concept emerged already in the nineteenth century, it came into widespread use only after the period discussed in this study. For the most part, therefore, it serves as a concept of analysis, not as a concept that expresses the reflexivity of the sources under examination. The very basic point that the modern renewal of philology was centered on semantic explication has been rather neglected. One reason for this neglect, doubtless, is the diversity of forms that semantic inquiry and explication can assume. Another one is the fact that the explication of linguistic meanings is a feature of any natural language, and therefore seems at once too stably universal and too elastic to invite historical study. This finding appears to pose a steep challenge to historical research since meaning and its explication are hard to think of otherwise than as constant features of language. Even the most radical attempts at overturning traditional notions of semantics that emerged in the twentieth century, perhaps most prominently deconstruction, have arguably just replaced the previous constancy of plain textual meaning with the constancy of disruption and flux.

Philologists, too, both past and present, have tended toward embracing an ahistorical concept of linguistic meaning as such, although they have often been enthusiastic about tracking the histories of the meanings of individual words.[19] And yet, since the nineteenth century in particular, they have also been keen to suggest that they could improve on pre-given, non-scholarly modes of explicating meaning; that they could increase knowledge, not merely by accumulation but also by the pursuit of novel methods. Thus, they have constantly operated under a tacit assumption that semantics *are* capable of historical change. The significance of this assumption has been far-reaching. In natural languages, meaning never exists in isolation from the available procedures of its explication. There are indispensable linguistic tools in any such language that serve to clarify, or merely manipulate, the meanings of other expressions. That is to say, in natural languages there is no meaning without the explication of meaning. If philology is itself part of this universe of procedures for the explication of meaning, meaning itself is therefore, as a result of the historical development of philology, endowed with historicity (that is to say, the property of being historical, rather than merely past). In other words, the philological project of rendering semantics scientific, whether successful or not, entails that there is history in meaning as such. The philological assumption that semantic explication is historical renders it historical, in the manner of a self-fulfilling prophecy.

Relying on Ludwig Wittgenstein's respective remarks in *Philosophical Investigations*, I will assume that the field of semantics, at least in natural languages, consists of an open and only vaguely coherent set of "language games" that concern the explication of meaning. Wittgenstein plays through several of these games—often in the form of thought experiments—in the context of his discussion of referential relations between word and object, meaning as grounded in the ability of accounting for the use of linguistic expressions, and rule following as underpinning use. The upshot of his discussion appears to be that none of these games can claim priority or sovereignty over the others, not even the "pragmatist" perspective on use and its underlying rules, for these are always open to further semantic analysis. Where no agreement on meaning can be reached, explication breaks off, rather than being able to rely on a last instance of adjudicating the correctness of some understanding of a linguistic expression.[20]

In no small part beyond what Wittgenstein actually discusses, semantics as a set of language games is highly diverse and dependent on context. In order to explain, say, what a sandgrouse is, one can rely on gestural ostentation as the most basic form of referential explication (*that* bird over there is a sandgrouse). One can explain usage ("sandgrouse" is used for such and such birds), or vaguely paraphrase the meaning (a type of bird that lives in arid areas in Asia and Africa). One can rely on metaphoric transfers and other forms of figuration, as would be the case in a Brehm-style explication of the meaning of "sandgrouse" as characterized by anthropomorphic traits; in Jacob's words: "As the outcast only dares to sneak up to an outlying source of water in the dead of night ... thus the timid desert bird *pteroclidurus alchata* is wont to rest only shortly at night in the wasteland and from there, at dawn, flock to faraway waterholes to quench its thirst."[21] Semantics include naming, re-naming, and genealogy (sandgrouses belong to the *pteroclidae* family, but used to be classed as *galliformes*; they have only distant common ancestry); and etymology (named on account of their visual similarity to other grouses and their arid habitat). Semantics also includes theorization, systematization, and other explanatory procedures, including those that rely on mathematical means, e.g. statistics or modeling (in the example case of birds, "theory" perhaps applies less obviously than when one discusses the meaning of abstract concepts of the type of, say, "freedom"; yet analyses in terms of Linnaean classification or, nowadays, DNA, i.e. presupposing statistics, would actually pertain). Semantics also include translation into other natural languages ("sandgrouse" means *Flughuhn*), (partial) translation into formal languages, such as formal logic (sandgrouse as a predicate term of the form Fx that clarifies how it functions in calculus); transfer to literary form and from one literary form to another; and transfer to media other than text (e.g. images).

For more complex expressions—it would be a grave error to limit semantics to the explication of individual words—there are hermeneutic approaches, theory-guided or not, that entail the contextualization of meaning within text, textual genre, and the ambit of authorial intention (interpreting Jacob's discussion of the nocturnal habits of the sandgrouse as a statement, say, on his ideas about the relations between scholarship and poetics). Then, there are anti-hermeneutic approaches such as Foucault's "archaeology" (e.g. the discourse of animal lives in German Orientalism as a manifestation of imperial power), or, more recently, Franco Moretti's "distant reading"[22] (corpus linguistics of bird-mentions in the body of philological writings, perhaps?). These approaches highlight repetition and the possibility that meaning be flat and simple and beyond experience and intention. Moreover, there are historicizing approaches that seek to situate meaning within contexts of cultural practice and of historical singularities (synthetic account of e.g. Jacob's writings on Al-Shanfara as an intervention within a scholarly field, but also as determined by multiple forces on the outside of his texts).

Around 1800, philological scholarship, with its novel sense of epistemological rupture, emerged within this multitude of semantic language games. This entailed shifting balances within the overall set as well as adding expansions and imposing reductions on it. A selection of these processes will figure in subsequent chapters, most prominently the procedure of theorization as concerning the meaning of the name of "philology" and the staking off of disciplinary territory (Chapter 1); the procedure of aligning texts with the category of "world literature" (Chapter 2); the historicizing explication of inscriptions, both gnomic and monumental (Chapter 3); the referential semantics of the proper name and its relations with the meaning of divine revelation (Chapter 4); and the destabilization of the autonomy and agency of the subject of semantic explication as a last, if untenable resort for re-stabilizing the referential ontology of philology (Chapter 5). The chapters will present an account of the interlinkage of these procedures, in the attempt to constitute a particular semantic method of philology founded on relations of reference.

3. Philology, *Wissenschaft*, Reference

In a nutshell, I aim to show that philology since the early nineteenth century pursued a central project: rendering semantics, i.e. the explication of linguistic meanings, scientific. It did so by privileging certain semantic language games, especially those connected to referentiality. This process unleashed a powerful dynamic in which Orientalism gradually moved into a key position. For Orientalists, this was a role both new and unforeseen.

The dynamic in question was conditional on the specifics of the understanding of *Wissenschaft*—"science" in a broad sense—on the German academic scene around 1800. Arguably, it is in regard to the fine print, the intricacies of the meaning of "scientization," that the cliché of the preeminence of German philology in the nineteenth century is, relatively speaking, most justified. Admittedly, large bodies of significant "positive" knowledge were assembled there; yet this happened elsewhere, too. Unlike these bodies of knowledge, however, theoretical positions did not travel abroad in a straightforward manner, perhaps because the contexts of disciplines and of spontaneous and non-spontaneous philosophies of "science" varied across national contexts. The diligent young Americans training to be classicists in Germany around 1900, for instance, produced flawless transcripts of their professors' methodology lectures; but they never dropped their neutral, even indifferent, stance toward the contentious theoretical positions about which they had learned.[23] By 1900 "German method" was a brand as a whole, regardless of possible internal contradictions. Only through indirect reception processes did the provincial pursuits of German philology become significant abroad. When left implicit, though, they could even become influential on a large scale, as I will argue in the present book.

In general, if philology was to be *wissenschaftlich*, it had to appear just as capable as other disciplines of delivering preparatory work for the attainment of a general system of knowledge. The intimate linkage of systematicity and scienticity had emerged in the philosophical works of Christian Wolff in the first half of the eighteenth century, or indeed of the "rationalist"—Cartesian, Spinozist, Leibnizian—enlightenment in general. At least with hindsight, philology had symbolically been constituted as a discipline within the university by the young Friedrich August Wolf's (1759–1824) insistence, in 1777, to be inscribed at Göttingen as a student, not of any of the traditional faculties, but of philology (i.e. classics). Along with other emergent disciplines, philology was to be based on individual research and the constancy of criticism and reflexivity, as formulated by Kant in his argument about the nature of the university.[24] This novel understanding of *Wissenschaft* also found itself tied to the idea of *Bildung*, of the continuous, biographical self-cultivation of ingenuity that was regarded, in the educational politics of the "age of Goethe," as giving new meaning to scholarship.[25] In the reformist thought of the period, with Wilhelm von Humboldt (1767–1835) as the most prominent protagonist, philology was even assigned a potentially decisive role as the discipline in which language came to reflect on itself as the inevitable medium of knowledge.

Much of this account is, needless to say, semi-mythical.[26] One decisive aspect it leaves out even in terms of the symbolic self-understanding of philology in the nineteenth century is the pervasive sense of insufficiency, brittleness, and actual fragmentation. The requirement of future systematicity imposed further, more specific conditions of scienticity that were harder to meet and that established a contentious relationship with philosophy that was similarly engaged in defining its territory within the emerging order of novel disciplines. In order to amend its shortcomings, philology was required (1) to formulate a universally applicable method that was (2) to provide superior knowledge of a discrete domain of reality. It was in response to these conditions that philologists developed what they called a "theory" of their reformed endeavor. Philology, with its functionally discrete subfields of grammar, criticism, and hermeneutics, was to comprise the study of any document of the past productivity of the human mind, as F. A. Wolf's student August Boeckh (1785–1867) had it.

Yet the universal applicability of the supposed new method undermined the clear delimitation of the domain. Since the new philology was able to explore almost anything (as long as it had to do with meaning), the diversity of philological research increased dramatically. From outside the field, most menacingly perhaps on the part of the philosopher Hegel, philology was denigrated as "a mere aggregate" of knowledge, a collection of disunified pursuits of disunified ranges of objects.[27] Although theorists struggled to counter this charge, they only contributed to its dynamism, all the while the working practice of philology continued to expand aggregation. Throughout the century, this process of expansion was driven in particular by Orientalism, which engendered a superabundance of novel fields, objects, and even methods of study. The result was a self-defeating tendency within the project of rendering philology scientific, which found itself under a double bind of theorization and aggregation. Over the years, this tendency prompted a multitude of responses. None of these won universal acclaim, but together they complicated the understanding of how linguistic meanings related to reality. In the course of this process, the way in which the explication of meaning was settled into ordinary language also changed.

Since semantics was, and is, inescapably pluriform and at least provisionally had, and has, to be regarded as devoid of limits and foundation, philology could be rendered scientific only by privileging one procedure over others. Nineteenth-century philologists mostly opted to focus on relations of "reference," which they considered constitutive for linguistic meaning, i.e. the relations that supposedly held between "sandgrouse" and sandgrouse, words and entities, names and their bearers, concepts and classes, text and reality. Philological procedure would then be to explicate meanings primarily by showing how they related to things in the world, in the form of correspondences at multiple levels of generality. The most reference-oriented wing of the discipline came to label itself "philology of the real," *Realphilologie* or *Sachphilologie*, derived from the Latin *realia* (German *Sachen*), or things in the world. This group of scholars—some of whose representatives in German Orientalism are at the core of this book—viewed themselves in opposition to the mere "philology of words," *Wortphilologie*. Practitioners of the latter showed less interest in the cultural and natural realities underpinning linguistic meanings and remained within the ambit of canonical texts and, increasingly, the study of linguistics. The ambition to render scientific the referential explication of meaning involuntarily generated pressure to revise the understanding of how language accessed reality. This pressure contributed decisively to the dynamic development of philology over the nineteenth century and gave unprecedented significance to Orientalism.

The penchant toward referentiality formed part of an environment suggestively adumbrated in Michel Foucault's analysis of "words and things" (*les mots et les choses*) in the "human sciences," among which those of language.[28] Foucault asserts that there was an "epistemological" shift from the eighteenth to the nineteenth century, a shift concerning the very foundations, the "order" of scholarly knowledge in those scientific fields that were concerned with human matters. This shift turned natural languages into objects of knowledge in a novel way. Each language was to be studied in its own right, as it was endowed with its own lines of development and descent. No language was of greater proximity to the laws of thought than any other, nor was any of them closer to the origin of language as such. The question of a universal grammatical structure that would be in perfect representational correspondence with the order of nature receded to the background or disappeared altogether. The structure of any given natural language, its grids of concepts and modes of syntactic connection, lost its potential power to represent the structure of reality as such. The objectification of natural languages in their own right supposedly spawned a number of consequences. The first of these was a profound unease about the elusiveness of scientific language itself as its own object. Scientific language lacked a scientific grasp of the ways in which it was tied to particular natural languages. This reflexive deficiency prompted a desire for compensation, which was sought, on the one hand, in the familiar minimalist rhetoric of "clarity" and, on the other, in logical formalization. The second consequence was the endowment of any given natural language with an archive of expressive achievements that supposedly documented the expressive possibilities of that language. This notion gave rise to a tendency to drive further the exegesis of given texts in textual philology. Equally, it prompted novel structural analyses of the potentials of given languages in general, which developed into modern linguistics. The result was a hypostatization of the symbolic significance of language, which constituted the common ground, Foucault held, of phenomenology, structuralism, formal philosophies of language, and psychoanalysis. The third consequence, finally, was the emergence of a concept of literature as autonomous in its semantic expression and untethered from referential commitments.[29]

For the question of referential meaning, the upshot was puzzling. The breakdown of the notion of universal grammar as a representation of the relationship between mind and world as such discarded one previous sense of the referential character of language as such. Simultaneously, the rhetoric of scienticity focused attention on pared-down referential meanings: the worth of scientific language was to be strictly tied to its purported ability to refer to things in the world, if not the world as a whole. The idea of a purely referential language as the foundation of science became the target of most philosophical and logical attempts at formalizing language. The rise of the category of the historical also privileged other variants of referentiality, in which archives of texts could be read as traces of past reality. Yet, simultaneously, the notion that literary writing enjoyed full autonomy over all meanings in its discourse appeared to do away with the importance of referentiality altogether. As an account of relations between words and things, Foucault's analysis then appears to acknowledge contrary tendencies.

I believe that this acknowledgment remains a major breakthrough. Nonetheless, Foucault's categories, when applied to source material, often appear too schematic to come to terms with the varied fortunes of philological semantics. These fortunes emerged from philology's constant engagements with the given and irreducible multitude of semantic procedures. The epistemological underpinnings of the scientific study of language included a constant awareness of their own frailty, in keeping with Foucault's assumption of the lingering discomfort of scientific language with itself. Reconciling the resulting, more pluralist picture with a broader account of the ontology of philology is one of the aims of the present book.

4. Orientalism

Foucault's argument about "episteme," the discursive and practical infrastructures that determine how various disciplinary bodies of knowledge are ordered and arranged, is an argument about the way the category of the human, as the common denominator of disciplines, was understood. It is an argument that famously seeks to demonstrate the transitory and non-universal status of the human subject as it had been theorized by modern philosophers since Descartes as the carrier of reason as such. Instead, the subject appeared as a mere after-effect of reorganizations of societal power. This notion directly informed the emergence of the critical discourse about "Orientalism" that Edward Said (1935–2003) initiated with his 1978 landmark study of how scholarly knowledge and literary imagination aligned in the service of European imperial domination.[30] In the intellectual and affective constitution of western modernity, Orientalism has since been regarded as one of the most potent and least alterable articles. In the eighteenth century, Europe's more or less long-standing colonial undertakings, within their specific institutional and social spheres, increasingly generated strategies of the appropriation of linguistic and textual knowledge. This work then became integrated into the rapidly evolving apparatuses of higher education back home, as well as into the literary and artistic spheres. The result, for Said and many after him, was Orientalism as an imaginary, an instituted regime of fancy that governed those artistic, literary, and scholarly pursuits. As an ideological formation, Orientalism always expressed the pursuit of imperial domination and even intimated the perfectibility of otherwise "unfinished" structures of power.[31]

This imaginary supposedly functioned in the manner of a reading of code. The sounds and signs of Orientalism were a device for encrypting and, at the same time, communicating European dominance over the Orient, that is to say, Europe's progressive nature, historical futures, and exclusive ownership of historical time. Europe's Asian empires became reading operations.[32] They spelt out, interpreted, and applied the coded text Orientalism provided; and Orientalism became the obverse, a procedure of the encryption of power that was nonetheless perfectly transparent, provided the key was known. In a sense, what Said promised was precisely such a key. Behind the seemingly apolitical literary and pictorial aesthetics of nineteenth-century representations of, especially, the Middle East, behind the respectable and sober façade of pretend-objective scholarship, a monotonous pattern of imperial claims to, and practices of, domination was thus exposed. In this way, the reception of Foucault's argument on the part of the Orientalism debate made visible another problematic side of the schematism of *The Order of Things*: it was not useful for discussing something as fickle as reading under any other aspect than the decipherment of the code of power. If Foucault (and others) were beholden to what Paul Ricœur famously labeled a "hermeneutic of suspicion,"[33] the point, of course, is that this is still a hermeneutic. That is to say, it remains an attempt to privilege one procedure for the explication of meaning over others, in this case the uncovering and destruction of encoded pathological or malignant meanings. The lucky charm always scores.

This problem arguably continues to accompany debates on Orientalism. In what might well be the most radical and interesting recent attempt to move beyond Said's argument, Siraj Ahmed relies on Foucault as a resource for challenging what he sees as earlier shortcomings. He accepts the basic terms of Foucault's analysis of the epistemological shift in the study of language, in order to show that the root cause of the shift should be identified in the intellectual changes British scholar-administrators inaugurated in colonial India at the end of the eighteenth century. Specifically, in keeping with Foucault's schematism, Ahmed underlines the effects of the novel notion of literature as merely "expressive," non-referential, directly and universally accessible to readers. "Literature" in this sense was crucial for the European practice of comparing the merits of diverse traditions of writing. It fostered an understanding of text in terms of exact, immutable wording, reliant on the mediatic forms of print culture. This notion of textuality then spilled over into all readings of textual as well as oral traditions and became a prime vehicle of European notions of cultural superiority. The trigger for this process, according to Ahmed, had been a novel British colonial strategy of securing access to local traditions of jurisdiction, which had to be rigidly codified for the purpose. Literary translation and grammar flourished as tools for language acquisition and thus as practical instruments for colonial rule. The pressure imposed on traditions of writing to compete with what European learning around 1800 considered the expressive force of literature *tout court* suppressed divergent traditions of explicating the meaning of textual canons. It was from here that models of "Oriental" literature were disseminated in the European sphere of letters and created the modern world literary field.[34]

The problem with this assessment is, arguably, that it is reductive even for the notion of literature, let alone for that of scholarship. The further ranges of Foucault's schema, apart from the category of the literary, recede into obscurity. Philological writings, however, were not regarded as expressive in the same way as literary text. Rather, they were referential, and in multiple ways to boot. They were neither simply engaged in the hypostatization of the interpretive subject nor in the hypostatization of the autonomous history of languages, or else in the formalization of pure thought outside of language. Ahmed maintains that it is an "always colonial project to authorize one or another form of speech" over others.[35] Yet, the tendency to privilege one type of semantic procedure does not simply fall under the category of "authorizing one form of speech." It is also about establishing one procedure of explicating meanings as the site proper of scholarly discussion, including critique; and about the simultaneous awareness of the temporary character of this establishment and the frailty of the authority that can be derived from it. To be sure, the translation processes necessary to transform scholarly authority into political domination feature prominently in Ahmed's analysis. Yet, this perspective also endows philological pursuits with a teleological stringency they did not possess. In the perspective of Foucault's epistemological account and the postcolonial readings that draw on it, the plurality of forms philology and philologies adopted in practice and the wealth of pertinent contexts disappear from view. The problem of semantics and their historicization is eschewed.

Ahmed's study draws on Bernard Cohn's seminal discussion of the nexus of colonial rule with local jurisdiction and colonizer language acquisition in British India.[36] Cohn had stated his points mainly in terms of the practical choices of British administrator-scholars, without venturing further into the literary field. According to him, the British in India ignorantly invaded an "epistemological space" that was constituted by an understanding of speaking and writing within power relations that was incompatible to European political culture. In South Asia, according to Cohn, speech and writing were constitutively related to transformative acts of sharing and thus were based on transformations of "substances." This sense of the use of language was steamrolled by the European one of referential relations between signs and signifieds. A court ritual a British participant would describe as a symbolism of debasement actually was, according to Cohn, an act of inclusion, with the physical, bodily significance of incorporation. Gifts were not tokens of exchange, but transmissions of authority. Regal writs functioned in a similar way rather than merely as communications or bestowals of privilege; and listening to Brahman chant meant having "one's substance literally affected by the sound."[37]

Yet, the license to posit such "epistemological spaces" must acknowledge limits. Cohn's analysis stipulates that the British saw everything in terms of relations of monetary value, and that their sense of semantics was limited to individuated linguistic expressions and relations of reference between words and things. Similarly, the "substantial" sense of meaning imposed on the Indian scene is only spelled out in a system of hierarchical religious-political order that extends from the divine sphere over the monarch into the lower rungs of society. Natural language semantics, however, are irreducibly richer, anywhere. The practical-political symbolism of the Mughal-Indian order Cohn describes regulated something that must have appeared as only a small section of the possibilities of meaning, and its ultimate instability is documented precisely in the shifts colonialism induced. The European scholarly attempt to regulate semantics and submit it to epistemological rupture presupposes the givenness of the wealth of semantics and the instability of regulations. As a result, philology, as a practice rather than a methodological doctrine, requires a more variegated account. The story—to the extent that there is a discernible plotline—of the privileging of reference is one of makeshift, temporary solutions and instability, or so I will argue.

5. The "Crisis of Language"

This is not to say that the history of scholarship, in Germany or elsewhere, unfolded in a vacuum of learning talking only to itself. It is hard to deny that the debate on Orientalism has sometimes been short on the European contextualization of its objects of scrutiny, as many contributors have also pointed out. That said, any perspective that one-sidedly emphasizes the use of "the Other" for creating an identity—a particularly common theme in histories of nationalism and imperialism—will tend to marginalize the history of scholarly objectification and its efforts to break with what is common. For instance, the anxiety of autonomized male selfhood behind the process of nation-building that Nicholas Germana argues was the prime underlying concern of German philosophical uses of the category of "the Oriental" could latch on to multiple targets.[38] One might then wonder whether "the Oriental" was as privileged a category as that argument suggests; or perhaps, whether the tendency of scholarship to escalate the number of available and differentiated other Others remains under-appreciated and under-analyzed.[39] If "India" was an indispensable *topos* in philosophical argument since the times of Kant and Herder, as Germana suggests, "Jerusalem," to cite the most prominent example, also retained significance and, as it were, eigenvalue. It is hardly attractive to retreat to a history of Orientalism as a story of sheer enthusiasm and curiosity[40] that would have opened, as Raymond Schwab had it, the door to a truly cosmopolitan appreciation of the myriad cultural wonders of humankind.[41] Instead, it seems attractive to pursue a cautious examination of scholarly practice, with patience for such matters as that of pigeons and sandgrouses, in other words, a historicizing account that also acknowledges the alien and distant character of philology, next to its genealogical linkages to the present.

As far as such linkages are concerned, I follow the thrust of Tuska Benes's discussion, which pursues the descent of current theory debates from structural features of nineteenth-century philology, especially in the ambit of comparative linguistics.[42] It seems to me that the argument about reading and more broadly semantics pursued in the present study provides an important complementary lineage to the one Benes highlights. It can also offer correctives to the overall thought about modernity and the contribution of the German intellectual field to it. It is, or used to be, a commonplace especially of English-language intellectual histories that the nineteenth-century tradition of German thought suffered from a crisis of representation (i.e. of the access of linguistic mimesis to reality), or a "lack of realism."[43] This faultline subsequently would have expanded into French thought. In this way, it has been claimed, the lack of realism, in its various guises, helps to explain the particularity of so-called continental philosophy and provides a common infrastructure for the manifold of postmodern and poststructural "theory."[44] For those who wished to depart from what they perceived as a theoretical trap, the escape strategy then seemed clear: one only needed to re-embrace realism, a robust belief in the ontological unity and epistemological accessibility of the world and the forthcomingness of knowledge to the believer. Reconversion would rectify the intellectual aberration.

Yet the notion that the purported lack of realism could be reduced to a banal intellectual mistake—even if the mistake was then propped up by a philosophical tradition endowed with the force of an ideological apparatus—does not carry much historical plausibility. If one searches for manifestations of the lack of realism beyond the confines of philosophical discourse, for instance in the context of philology, one simply finds oneself cast into the aggregate practice of semantics. It might then seem attractive to relate the plotline of deficient realism to the subtle historical shifts the processing of referential meaning underwent in philological scholarship. The broader "loss of ontological security" in the epoch of modernity[45] has long become a matter settled into a purported "crisis of language" itself, as perhaps most famously—at least in a German-speaking context—expressed in Hugo von Hofmannsthal's *Chandos Letter*, in the aphasia condensed in the image of words and concepts that crumble in the speaker's mouth "like mouldy fungi."[46] Beyond the pale of the history of philosophical thought and literary writing, cultural-historical explanations of this "crisis" of the *fin-de-siècle* by reference to a broader history of political and technological innovation and the changing lifeworld of individuals abound.[47] Similarly, there is no scarcity of arguments about changes in meta-scientific expectations as to the security of knowledge—the shift from positivist, fact-based notions of the accumulation of knowledge to something more disruptive, under the impact of modern physics.[48] If the theory of scientific knowledge is granted participation in this putative cultural history, there cannot be objections to including the humanities in the picture as well. The possible contribution of philology, however, especially in terms of its quotidian practices and beyond the scope of canonized master thinkers, has received relatively short shrift. Yet it was here, in the unthinking iteration of semantic gestures, that the insecurity in question was expanded into language and began to undermine the very possibility of referential meaning.

The conditions of referential access to the world in philological semantics are the primary target of historicization the present study pursues. I aim to demonstrate that the loss or lack of realism was far from clear-cut, and that it instead consisted in a more intricate balancing of modes of access to, and senses of the elusiveness of, reality that marked the production of philological knowledge. The sense of elusive reference remains tied to the language of scholarship in general and "theory" in particular, an heirloom that, after having passed into new hands several times over, is no longer recognized as having once been in the possession of philology. Rather, it is regarded as a property shared across many disciplinary divisions of the humanities and social sciences. Yet, as I will argue, to understand the history of ownership is illuminating in this case. The problems of the practice as well as the theorization of philology in the nineteenth century became central components of the deliberately unsystematic abstractions that enframed humanities discourse in the latter half of the twentieth century. This can be demonstrated, I hold, in particular with regard to the theoretical positions of antihumanism, structuralism, and post-structuralism; the widespread opposition to so-called historicism and the related notion that histories occur in the plural rather than in the singular; and the theoretical and practical embrace of semantic absurdity. Even the theorization of the end of history in the form of nuclear cataclysm was, as I will argue, crucially dependent on the ways in which German Orientalist philology had processed its access to the world, or lack thereof.

6. Selectivity and the Status of Semitics

The book will focus on the exploration of working practices and research works within a more or less tightly-knit circle of Semitist Orientalists, who will be introduced at greater length within the text. The selection of these scholars follows, to some extent, the vagaries of archival documentation, but is mostly owed to the ways their works yield to specific lines of argument I found important to pursue. In a relatively informal manner, without any aspiration to exhaustive coverage, the period to be discussed stretches from the 1820s to the 1950s, although most of its material is concentrated in the narrower time slot of *c.* 1880–1930. The chosen scholars were, throughout, interested not merely in the study of linguistics, but of histories, cultures, folklores, artefacts, and religious forms. For the question of the worldliness of philology, these concerns have, after all, proved more helpful than those to be encountered among the scholars of mere phonetics, of mere syntax, or of mere classical texts. The selection is therefore not random, but nonetheless leaves out large portions of the overall fields under scrutiny.

There is an important methodological point to be made, however, about the sheer necessity of selectiveness in a line of research, the history of Orientalism, that has so far clung to a preference for national boundaries as primary selection criteria, and often sought to cover entire disciplines within these boundaries. Nowhere in the history of science does the writing of a history of, say, *all of* physics appear presentable as a research program nowadays. A separation of didactic synthesis from argumentative investigation is, I believe, urgently required in the history of the humanities in general and in the history of philologies in particular. Otherwise, a turn toward in-depth archival research, with the concomitant and indispensable openness to the serendipity of finds, will remain out of reach. The present study's inclination toward the concrete is also meant to demonstrate some of the potential of such a turn.

Two subsidiary hypotheses provide further help in making this target attainable. First, I hold that for the pursuit in question the study of mere doctrines, research programs, and institutions in the history of philology is insufficient. Rather it will be necessary to engage with a range of aspects that pertain to the practical and quotidian work of philologists. For this reason, the book will often cover seemingly odd material and follow somewhat uncommon targets. Behind these pursuits, there is a methodological rationale that is based on the analysis of the referential orientation of philology toward "the world," the objects of semantic knowledge, as a "historical ontology" of philology.[49] This notion—as referring to the way a scientific field alters the realities it studies, by its discursive and practical patterns that produce novel objects of inquiry and instruments—interlocks with the approach to semantics as hinged on access to "the real." It also intersects with a wider context of studying the infrastructural modes and conditions of the production, maintenance, and justification of scientific and scholarly knowledge that is often subsumed under the concept of a "historical epistemology."[50] The aim of such an approach is to uncover structural features rather than follow sequences of events such as, say, scholarly publications, research programs, or ideological mobilizations that are from today's perspective regarded as having shaped the development of particular fields. For this reason, the argument does not seek to establish a sequential order of periods, to be worked through in chronologically arranged chapters; and it only adheres to the periodization of political history when opportune.

Second, I hold that within the history of Orientalist philologies, it is in particular that of the study of Semitic languages and the broader Middle East that provides privileged access to the overall problem. German Orientalism throughout the nineteenth century had two main branches, Semitics and Indology. Central, East, or Southeast Asian as well as North African pursuits remained institutionally and epistemologically marginal undertakings, although they all existed. Semitics had been a longstanding tradition of European university scholarship, in the context of scriptural knowledge and theological-philosophical competition with Judaism as well as Islam.[51] Indology, by contrast, was a more upstart field, rather novel to German university scholarship around 1800, and, after an earlier history of especially missionary interest, propelled forward by the emerging institutional worlds of modern colonialism, to some extent French, but then above all British.[52] Indology's sudden advent, especially in Germany, where at least on the surface of things it was a perfectly useless field, continues to pose the more dazzling research questions. On account of its disruptive emergence, it has seemed to provide a particularly plausible laboratory for understanding the deep changes in philology after 1800 that are so very obvious as long as one does not try to actually make them explicit. As a result, Indology has attracted ample attention; and it is fair to say that debate on the intellectual history of German Orientalism has listed to the side of the Sanskritists.

Suzanne Marchand's synthetic account that covers both sides (as well as the more marginal fields) has emphasized intra- and interdisciplinary conflicts between classical philology and academic Orientalism in Germany, as centered on the status of the Old Testament, scriptural theology, the social and political status of the Jewish minority, and the rise of racist anti-Semitism.[53] This work has made an indispensable contribution to the filling of the lacuna, so often deplored in Said's account, of the historical particularities of German Orientalism. At the same time, Marchand's account also goes a long way toward establishing the importance of other historical contexts next to that of the British colonization of India. Doubtless, the Indological and Semitist subfields of Orientalist philology collaborated in their production of, or engagement with, concepts of human origins and race.[54] The construction of the dichotomy of "Aryans" and "Semites" is inconceivable without this pan-European history of collaboration.

Yet, in the case of Semitists, the broader context that devalued their object of study often prevented them from embracing the concept of "Aryanism" enthusiastically. The mere basis of shared contributions of different philologies to the history of racism arguably proves too thin to integrate the fields into a single formation of e.g. "German Orientalism." Different fields developed different structures of encounter, and conflict, with the traditions and institutions of learning whose materials and sources they studied. Semitics, for instance, both in theology and philology, generated vivid and institutionally proximate responses by, and sometimes actual exchanges with, Jewish scholarship in Europe. The resulting critiques of Orientalism sometimes appear to parallel more recent discussions about epistemic flaws and distortions, the neglect of bodies of knowledge from the outside of European Christian academia, and the subliminal violence of philology.[55] The emergence of the "science of Judaism," the *Wissenschaft des Judentums*, as a Jewish counter-appropriation of philology in response to Orientalist, Semitist research, was a result of this conflicted contiguity. In other parts of Semitics—as in other Orientalist fields—comprehensive counter-discourses also existed, for instance in Arabic studies.[56] Yet these remained institutionally more distant and even less acknowledged in Europe. Across the great variety of Orientalist philologies, there were different, sometimes very locally diverse landscapes of contact and conflict, engagement and disengagement that were significant for the norms and values scholarship observed.

The relative imbalance in favor of Indology has prompted two divergent tendencies to assert centers and peripheries in the meaning of the term "philology." The first of these is a rather one-sided emphasis on so-called textual criticism, and within this field, on the reconstruction of *Ur*-texts. This was a procedure applied across many fields and projects, for instance in editions of the Greek New Testament, the Vedic texts, medieval European vernacular epics, or indeed most of the textual heritage of classical antiquity. Semitics, by contrast, was built on a much stronger emphasis on the stratification and disassembling of given texts, as was the dominant procedure especially in Protestant Old Testament philology. This practice also shaped parts of classics, most prominently the philology of the Homeric epics. Moreover, within the Semitist field—as in classics, but not in Indology—epigraphy, the study of inscriptions, became one of the prime concerns. Inscriptions, however, since they often remain below even the threshold of a single sentence, tend to elude the straightforward, untheorized concept of "text" as a combination of sentences beyond a certain level of syntactic complexity that underpinned the dominant perspective on (written) texts as mere historical "documents" that Ahmed and also, from a different angle, Vishwa Adluri and Joydeep Bagchee excoriate.[57] Such a concept was certainly operative in nineteenth-century philological practice, in which written textuality did not, on the whole, become a target of theoretical curiosity. Perhaps it was for this reason that operative notions of "text" were rather practice-driven and diverged according to what scholars were aiming to accomplish. Referential semantics, however, were richer and can be grasped more fully only if one jettisons the exclusive concentration on written textuality.

Focusing on Semitics can help to avoid the bias in favor of a specific, hypostatized concept of textuality that unduly limits the scope of histories of philology. Epigraphy, in particular, opens a vista on relations between philology and theology that the historical study of textual criticism does not afford. Adluri and Bagchee, for instance, argue that textual critique was dependent on specific practices and notions of eighteenth-century Protestantism that required the return to an original text of scripture and the cutting away of subsequent interpretations. The resulting "historicization" of the text, its interpretation by a merely putative, often grotesquely speculative and skewed historical context, would have engendered longstanding hermeneutic distortions that were fortified by disciplinary and nationalist superiority claims on the side of German philologists. Significantly, Adluri and Bagchee almost entirely bypass the history of the textual criticism of the Old Testament and only discuss New Testament theologians, even though, or precisely because the operative notions of textuality were different in those fields.[58] Similarly, as I will argue in subsequent chapters, the reduction of philology to "historicism" is problematic. Paying attention to epigraphy helps to achieve a clearer picture of the ambivalent uses of historicity in philological scholarship.

The second imbalance the emphasis on Indology incurs is that of positing the centrality of comparative grammar, the field that later on became the discipline of linguistics. Admittedly, the comparison of the vocabularies and grammars of Sanskrit (and Persian) with various European languages gave rise to the most dynamic subfield within nineteenth-century philology, a subfield that grew ever more independent, both institutionally and epistemologically.[59] The founding legend of the field singles out as the sole discoverer of the interrelation—as usual, the story is more complicated—the famed William Jones (1746–1794), British scholar of languages, literatures, and the law; and judge, colonial administrator, and founder of educational institutions in Calcutta.

As many have pointed out, the biographical connections of bodies of knowledge in Jones's life provide initial evidence for the practical complexities in which comparative grammar emerged. Over a decades-long debate, the powerful impact of Foucault's arguments about the episteme of the human sciences—comparison of self-enclosed, developing, organic units that became the template of the era's historical approaches to language, nature, and society—has bolstered the status of comparative grammar. Tuska Benes's and Douglas McGetchin's works on the history of philology are particularly marked by according precedence to grammar and linguistics. The main pitfall of this assumption is not that it accords too much importance to the Indo-European field, although in the context of other language families comparative grammar remained a more ambivalent success.[60] Rather, though, the main pitfall is that the bias in favor of comparative grammar goes along with a reification of language that was produced by philology itself. The tendency is to treat grammar as a set of descriptive rules that has a natural language as a stable referent. By contrast, the interactions of partly normative grammatical discourses with the languages they describe do not figure prominently in accounts that take such discourses to be the centerpiece of modern histories of philology.

To be sure, political readings of grammatical traditions have emerged, once again especially in the context of Sanskrit, in the wake of Cohn's pioneering work. Sheldon Pollock's analysis of the long history of Sanskrit grammatical discourse as a symbolism of monarchical authority based on the ruler's proximity to the "language of the gods" has been a preeminent contribution to this line of argument.[61] Ahmed's intervention, sharply critical of Pollock's approach with regard to the merits of philology in general, also subscribes to the political import of grammar. In all relevant contexts, grammar is reduced to functioning as a tool, a means to a purpose, a solid stepping stone toward the exercise of power. Its interference in the supposed objects of its knowledge then becomes intelligible only in one respect, namely in terms of a rather top-down understanding of political rule. The problem that underlies the interrelation of grammatical knowledge and language itself remains sidelined, because even the most perceptive critics of Orientalist philology tend to treat western and non-western traditions of grammatical knowledge exclusively as competing infrastructures for political order. In sum, the Indological list of histories of German-language Orientalism then causes a grammatico-political bias that works against the study of semantics in philology.

In light of these tentative diagnoses, the study of Semitics in the history of Orientalism may serve as a balancing device that helps to better understand the workings of semantics.

7. Outline

In Chapter 1, I spell out in greater detail the book's basic line of argument, in terms of the central project of nineteenth-century philology, the rendering scientific of semantics; and in terms of the key dynamism that unfolded in the period, the double bind of theorization and aggregation. The chapter discusses a range of canonical authors from

Edward Said and Paul de Man via Nietzsche and Heidegger to the early nineteenth-century theorists of philology, Friedrich Schlegel, Schleiermacher, and August Boeckh. In this way, I provide a section of the layers of controversies about the meaning of the name of philology that obscure present-day uses of the term. The chapter also discusses relations between semantics and grammar, in order to demonstrate the inextricable interweaving of different fields in philology and the practical reasons for which referential meaning became important.

Chapter 2 explores philologists' agency in their relations with "the world" as a resource of referential meanings on the level of texts. It presents a case study of the practice of fieldwork on oral poetry that is particularly helpful for understanding the multiple facets, and the blind spots, of the Orientalist sense of what it meant to study meanings through access to reality. The case study is built on the documents that pertain to the suicide of a young Eritrean by the name of Naffaʿ wad ʿEtmân (c. 1882–1909), a rhapsodist and former mission pupil, who had spent the years 1907–1909 in Germany with the Orientalist Enno Littmann (1875–1958) in order to work on a collection of oral poetry in the Tigré language (a Semitic language of Eritrea and Northern Ethiopia). Naffaʿ committed suicide when the work was concluded and Littmann forced him to return to his native country. The chapter argues that recent debate on the prospects of a renewed "world philology" needs to develop an understanding of the world *of* philology, of what access to the world meant in terms of the central project of philological semantics, in a field of differentiated meanings of "world" in phrases such as world history or world literature. It turns out that the respective notions of access carried a strong sense of agency on the part of the Orientalist scholar, who was placed in a position to appropriate, if in subtle ways, forms of colonial violence. I argue that Naffaʿ's suicide was a correlate of this appropriation, thus a product of philological semantics. Yet, the violent underside of philological access to the world also destabilized the sense of semantic method. This also means that the referential relation between text and world does not exhaust the analysis of referential semantics as a method of scholarship.

Chapter 3 further explores philologists' agency in their relations with "the world" as a resource of referential meanings. For this purpose, I examine concrete practices of handling objects of philological knowledge, and the way in which these objects were treated as "given." There are good reasons, I argue, to analyze this quality of givenness through the notion of philological work as bound to "archives." Hence, the chapter pursues in detail the fieldwork of traveling "archival" philology in its privileged domain, epigraphy, the study of inscriptions. The chapter focuses on Enno Littmann's epigraphic work in Syria as well as in Ethiopia, in the years after 1900. It proceeds by rejecting various understandings of archival work through the notion of "order." It then shows that the practical work of explicating the meanings of epigraphic records remained indissolubly bound to situational conditions and "scenes" as constructed in the medium of travel writing. The chapter goes on to demonstrate that epigraphic work also served to charge philological semantics with ample surplus meanings. These surplus meanings provided further explanatory contexts in order to make the barren texts of ancient inscriptions legible as records of cultural history. Most importantly, the reading of inscriptions often entailed a context of monarchical politics and can be framed in terms of what Sanjay Subrahmanyam has labeled "courtly encounters," that is to say, cross-cultural contact in a shared framework of kingship and court life.[62] In the epigraphic variant of this type of encounter, the imperial-era situation was brought into uncanny symbolic connection with the long-defunct monarchies to which the inscriptions referred. The tendency to establish such a connection demonstrates that the semantic travails of philology interacted with the political theology of German monarchism itself. This interaction indicates a profound ambition on the part of Orientalist philologists to modify the meaning and self-understanding of state and society at large. This also underlines the disruptive potential of referential semantics that was tied to its situational instability and that engulfed the sense of scholarly agency as enframed in such situations, in "scenes" of knowledge.

Chapter 4 discusses one of the privileged objects of epigraphic knowledge, the meaning of the proper name, as a foundational case for the problems around reference. I show that Orientalist epigraphy was responsible for introducing a form of hypostatization into the analysis of proper names. In a momentous constellation of intellectual debates from the 1880s to the 1920s, following the lead of Semitist Orientalists, intellectuals of various backgrounds found new ways of tying together the names of deities, the concept of revelation, and the very notion of "being." This tendency emerged in 1880s Semitic philology specifically, namely in the context of the interference of epigraphic research with the philological deconstruction of the Old Testament, above all connected with the name of the theologian and Arabist Julius Wellhausen (1844–1918). Revelation was reducible, Wellhausen argued, to the moment in which a deity reputedly provided his or her name to some human addressee. Over time, in philosophical debate, this argument engendered novel understandings of metaphysics through an analysis of being itself as a "name." This analysis drew in particular on the burning bush episode in Hebrew scripture, in which the godhead explains his name as etymologically coinciding with a Hebrew root word for "being." Recourse to this topos was foundational in the tradition of "ontotheology" that brought together metaphysics and theological argument, and for which Spinoza's equation of the godhead with being-as-such perhaps provided the most powerful model. Semitic philology subtly changed the meaning of the philosophical *topos*. Arguments about the autonomy of philosophy became enmeshed with arguments about other things, such as Jewish-Gentile relations in Germany. The chapter focuses on select philosophical works by Hermann Cohen, Ernst Cassirer, and Franz Rosenzweig and discusses their interrelations with Wellhausen's biblical philology, as well as Wellhausen's, as it were, anti-philosophical responses to the beginnings of this debate. Alarmed by the philosophical consequences of the hypostatization of naming, Wellhausen grew increasingly skeptical about the possibility of generating secure knowledge about past referential meaning. He embraced a comprehensive ironizing of reference, of the access of words to things in general. This irony expressed a position of last resort regarding the explication of meaning on the part of an autonomous subject of semantic knowledge. It was precisely when Orientalist practice stumbled upon a novel resource for the explication of meaning that it triggered a latent crisis in the philological privileging of reference.

Chapter 5 examines how the fortunes of proper name reference and Wellhausenian irony informed a specific set of aesthetic debates that converged with modernism and provided basic positions that became formative for twentieth-century notions of "theory." The chapter analyzes the last, and arguably the most momentous, attempt of Orientalist philology to stabilize the uncertainty about referential meaning. This attempt entailed shifting uncertainty back from the objects of philological knowledge to its subjects. The retreat into irony would be blocked if there was no stable subject of philology left to stake a claim to sovereignty over the explication of meaning. The Semitist Georg Jacob, prime case study of this chapter, outlined such a position. Vociferously, he attacked the contemporary dominance of classicist humanism over the sphere of artistic ideals and over connected projects of societal education. Instead, Jacob—along with others—developed counter-positions that abandoned the integrity of human reason, representational realism, and the centrality of the human body. Precedence was to be accorded to dream, fantasy, non-human nature, and the unconscious. The resulting philological aesthetic amounted to a stance of antihumanism that entailed the ousting of earlier "humanist" notions of subjecthood. This gateway antihumanism constituted a decisive lineage in the genealogy of "theory," as the chapter shows by discussion of overt and covert Orientalist and philological motifs in the works of a variety of mid-twentieth-century German thinkers. Eventually, philology, Orientalism, and the rejection of humanism even played a significant role in the theorization of technological modernity, the mid-century perception of Japan, and the German philosophy of the atom bomb in the works of Martin Heidegger and Günther Anders. The transformation of the "last man" (Anders) into a shadow on a wall in Nagasaki indicated the transformation of the historical future into a reality that could not be represented anymore. The chapter shows that this "post-historical" end point was conceptualized by way of a transformation of philological semantics and aesthetics. The shadow of the stage was traded in for that of the nuclear blast. This exchange had been made possible by developments in the semantic theory and practice of philology.

What the book then develops is the notion of philological semantics as a field of interrelated positions on reference. These positions interlocked because they emerged through often subliminal responses to the limitations of one semantic mode of operation as seen from another one. If one takes the field as a whole, exclusively and aggressively referential semantic procedures inter-depend genetically with anti-referential ones. From the point of view of a history of scholarship, it is possible and attractive to regard philological method as co-extensive with the overall field, although the historical agents under examination monotonously identified method with only one particular position. The history of the field, rather than that of any of the individual positions, is not that of a collective, pre-programmed failure. Instead, one encounters an escalation of distinctions that pluralize and mobilize the understanding of philological method. As the concluding remarks adumbrate, this overall view of the scholarly explication of meaning is neither trivial nor is it a condition that mostly belongs to the past and from which it is easy to exit. Histories of Orientalism are often about departing from a burdensome, even unbearable past. The argument of beholdenness to the past, of a history of meaning that cannot simply be reversed or abandoned, is one possible reading of the present book. This argument might be regarded as sobering, perhaps even tragic. Yet another argument that is developed across the subsequent chapters concerns the tenacity of territoriality in scholarly disciplines and in this way highlights the inherited possibilities of plurality within the humanities. This result would appear to be less tragic; and perhaps it is also fitting that a historical study of the explication of meanings should not end in unambiguity.

1

After Philology, a Wild Goose Chase

1. Stratigraphy of a Name

Edward Said, in his landmark study, marginalized the history of philology as a constituent of Orientalism, which he regarded as dominated by patterns of imagination that followed a fantasmagoria of power. The scholarly and literary fields coincided. Many of the ensuing polemics followed his lead. This choice was in keeping with general tendencies. At the time of the publication of *Orientalism*, disdain of "philology" was widespread. The term had come to represent a misplaced and dated confidence in methodological objectivity and a narrow-mindedness in the choice of objects of research that was a prime target of criticism as well as ridicule. Not only did the methodological precepts of philology appear profoundly flawed, previous scholarship had also discredited itself from a political point of view, especially by the reckless promotion of nationalism, anti-Semitism, racism, and imperialism. To boot, philology seemed fatally entangled in the outdated ideal of politics as national education that had been the hallmark of nineteenth-century classicist "humanism," but had, in spite of its high-minded rhetoric, only ever produced authoritarian characters.

Nonetheless, a modicum of respect for philological tradition had never quite faded. Philological method, as it was criticized, was also refined and driven to new extremes, as for instance in the *critique génétique* movement that sought to disassemble the very notion of a finite text and shifted edition to all available manuscript stages.[1] Moreover, in certain institutionally smaller fields, such as indeed many "Orientalist" ones, the establishment of literary studies as an autonomous sub-discipline, in imitation of the secession of linguistics in the 1850s–70s,[2] never quite occurred. The messy commons of traditional philology always remained under the till, no matter the disregard of those who had fenced off sizable properties of their own. As an almost ironical outcome of these (and, no doubt, further) ambiguities, in an influential posthumous intervention from 2003, Edward Said, a representative of autonomized literary criticism, even saw fit to call for a "return" to philology, with a phrase that continues to resound in the textual disciplines.[3]

Leaving aside all the objections the discipline of history would traditionally raise against the very concept of "return"—the inexorability of change, the distastefulness of nostalgia—nonetheless, the volte-face in the overall debate also indicates that something about philology itself has remained in a dead angle. This defect of vision also impairs, I will seek to show, the historical understanding of Orientalism. Hence, as a first step, it appears imperative to explore the historical drift of the meaning of the concept of "philology." This exploration will pass through a veritable stratification of meanings. It will reveal, successively, why it is requisite, for understanding the modern history of philology, to look at the German context; at the referential meanings of names; at theorization in philology; at the role of Orientalism; and at semantics *tout court* and its relations with grammar.

This procedure requires a certain definitional openness. Decidedly, philology cannot be taken to be a stable set of procedures of such generality—say, comparison, contextualization, interpretation—that the epistemological side of the discipline is exiled into ahistoricity and its changes can only be grasped as externally induced forms of institutional or political differentiation.[4] At the same time, the exploration ought not to be satisfied by limiting itself to the history of the growth of a discipline, the emergence of a profession, or the often heinous political and cultural impact of philological discourse in the modern era. Certainly, these are important topics, but their prominence has often meant that discussion eschewed the basic question that concerns the history of the founding of a "science"—in the broader sense of German *Wissenschaft* or, also, French *science*—on the processing of linguistic meaning, that is to say, semantics.

2. Returning Returns

With what I think is best regarded as deliberate irony, for his lecture on the "return to philology," Said appropriated a title that had already been coined by Paul de Man (1919–1983) in 1982.[5] According to de Man, philology actually coincided with "theory": "[I]n practice, the turn to theory occurred as a return to philology, to an examination of the structure of language prior to the meaning it produces."[6] The enmity toward semantics here expressed, namely the deeply counter-hermeneutic notion that reading is about decoding something more fundamental than mere meaning, in this case the insurmountable semiotic instability of text itself, has a long and complex history, to which de Man here hardly alludes. His notion that philology coincides with a concern for linguistic "structure" (i.e. beyond textual meaning) constitutes a serious historical distortion since the very program of studying "structure" in language and text had emerged in the context of late-nineteenth-century aggressions against philology. The "return" de Man proposes therefore does not entail recurrence to past method by way of conscientious historicization. His notion of the instability, the "flight" of meaning aims to subvert historicity.[7] Similarly, he ought not to be credited with "the apparent advocacy of a new and improved form of philology,"[8] which would have been similarly subject to ironical displacement. Rather, the target of "return" was a biographical moment of epistemic and academic initiation. For de Man, theoretical interest in textuality was grounded, or so he maintained in 1982, in the experiences of Reuben A. Brower's (1908–1975) "slow-reading" exercises at Harvard in the 1950s. What was at stake, in other words, was a subtly ironized moment of personal nostalgia.

One may presume that it was less deliberately ironical of de Man to use the label of "philology" in order to mark this period of initiation. Brower, who had spent most of his teaching career at Amherst before eventually moving to Harvard, had received his academic training in England, at Cambridge, under the tutelage of I. A. Richards (1893–1979). Richards's own brand of "criticism"—indeed the very introduction of the label of "criticism" for literary studies in Britain—was driven by the desire that had emerged during the First World War, to purge literary studies from "philology." Philology as a label and, however vaguely, a practice had come to appear too German, too pedantic, too historical-contextual, too culturalist, too unable to understand the true, humane, psychological, transhistorical, and multivalent meanings of literary texts that were supposed to be read on their own account.[9] "Close reading," as advanced by Richards and others, was not a "text-immanent" existentialist hermeneutics, as e.g. proposed, in a distantly cognate move, by the Swiss *Literaturwissenschaftler* and *Heideggerisant* Emil Staiger in the 1950s.[10] Rather, the Cambridge program pursued a pragmatist-leaning, partly empirical-psychological study of what happened during the interpretation of texts, especially if these were stripped of contextual and para-textual information.[11] Richards removed titles and author names from poems and gave them to his students to read in this format, then published their responses. In its choice of opponent, this almost experimental-empiricist understanding of literary form corresponded to other, better-known interwar period trends of anti-historicism including, especially, multiple variants of structuralism.

Nonetheless, de Man failed to see, or so it seems, the threads connecting the various anti-philologies that had informed his education. When the British brand of criticism—fused with the contemporaneous American "new criticism" and toned down by a less polemical and more German-influenced academic environment in the United States—was imparted to de Man in the 1950s, apparently it was easy to mistake for "philology." Admittedly, it also seems possible that de Man deliberately sought to undermine the tradition to which he had been initiated at Harvard; and yet, the relative absence of a theorization or even just a problematization of "philology" from his oeuvre is remarkable. Philology, arguably, remained a blind spot for the theorist of "blindness" in reading.[12]

The implicit conflation of divergent traditions of "philology" and "literary criticism" may also have been due to one of the eternal returns of Nietzsche, whose works provided indispensable points of reference for de Man.[13] The "definition" of "philology" reproduced in the "Return" article was that of Roman Jakobson, who had stated that philology was simply the "art of reading slowly." This aphorism, which appears to have circulated orally rather than in written form, probably had originated in a Nietzschean "idea," as Sheldon Pollock has suggested.[14] In a famous passage at the end of the "Preface" of *Morgenröthe* (Daybreak), Nietzsche remarks:

> besides, both of us are friends of the *lento*, I and my book. One has not been a philologist in vain, and perhaps one still is, that is to say, a teacher of slow reading:—finally, one also writes slowly. At present it is not only part of my habits, but also part of my taste—a malicious taste perhaps?—to write Nothing that does not drive to despair any man who is "in a hurry." For, philology is that venerable art which exacts from its admirers one thing above all, to step aside, to take one's time, to grow silent, to become slow.[15]

The unsteadiness of Nietzsche's qualifications of the discipline in which he had himself been educated is admittedly notorious: philology, the life-throttling pursuit of irrelevant antiquarianism; philology, the relentless teacher of "Pyrrhonic" skepticism and epistemic reticence (*epokhe*); philology, the only possibility of uncovering the forgeries of "will" that make up so-called reality; philology, the author of such forgeries in turn.[16] In any case, in the *Morgenröthe* preface, what Nietzsche means by "slowness" is not the same as what the slow-reading "new critics" pursued, but rather a manipulation of the sense of time, of rhythm (*lento*),[17] of the malign provocation of an "age of 'work,' that is to say of haste, of indecent and sweaty alacrity, which wants to 'get done' with anything instantly."[18] This critique of hastiness in reading and writing could then appear as ultimately addressing a modern condition of alienated labor. Such a politicization of "slowness," though hardly an accurate reading, provided a way of identifying Nietzsche's "art"[19] of philology with the destination of an imagined return in the 1980s or the 2000s. In this process, perhaps abetted by the aphoristic abbreviation Jakobson had introduced, all the warning signs Nietzsche scattered over the passage were ignored: the personification of the book next to the author, the allegation of the impotence of philology-as-reading without philology-as-writing, the necessity of being contrarian and minoritarian, the need for manipulating the sense of time, the primacy of music and rhythm over text—it was not to any of these aspects that de Man proposed to return. Again, this was in keeping with his education. Brower, when describing his method as "reading in slow motion," used a cinematic metaphor rather than a musical one, thus emphasizing the readerly gaze over the holistic temporal sentience Nietzsche had pursued. De Man's overall aim, even in the short and, so to speak, popularizing "Return to Philology" article, was connected to his project of disabling the "aesthetic ideology"[20] of the modern period: the Kantian notion of the foundational character of aesthetics within systemic philosophy as a prime site of judgment that had to bridge the gulf between theoretical and practical reason; the autonomy of artistic play as a foundation for sociability, as found in Schiller's "aberrant" reading of Kantian aesthetics; the ensuing notion of aesthetic education; and its translation into projects of national disciplining and violent state-building that led de Man to conclude his lecture on Schiller's reception of Kant with a quotation by the failed literary writer and failed academic Germanist Joseph Goebbels.[21] After all, a subterranean similarity to Said's relative suppression of the history of philology in *Orientalism* may be discerned in de Man's political adumbrations. Both authors sought to salvage philology from the wreckage of modernity.

Said, who famously opposed deconstruction and its ideas about reading and "theory" and, as a literary critic, nurtured a certain degree of professional hostility toward de Man,[22] nonetheless shared the embrace of Nietzsche as well as the reliance on Jakobson's formula, and he, too, explained his attachment to the name of philology by reference to his own education: "Philology is, literally, the love of words, but as a discipline it acquires a quasi-scientific intellectual and spiritual prestige at various points in all of the major cultural traditions, including the Western and the Arabic-Islamic traditions that have framed my own development."[23] If philology is taken to be a goal-directed historical process, its *telos* is the production of readers, disciplinary and disciplined and "framed." Philology amounts to civilization through tradition, civilization as acquired through "acts of reading done more and more carefully."[24] Such reading forms

> the abiding basis for all humanistic practice. That basis is at bottom what I have been calling philological, that is, a detailed, patient scrutiny of and a lifelong attentiveness to the words and rhetorics by which language is used by human beings who exist in history: hence the word "secular," as I use it, as well as the word "worldliness."[25]

This basis is moral, it is the "humanism" Said advocates in the lectures collected in the volume, and it is biographically acquired and sustained, therefore a virtue, whose acquisition and sustenance is not merely a matter of one's own investment of time and effort, but a matter of initiation, a rite of passage, hence education in institutions. It is readerly "responsibility," the ethos of philology, that arguably marks the difference to de Man. For Said, the art of reading carefully promises the possibility of convergence across cultural boundaries. Reading is not an epistemic product of "the West." Further, it is not merely a technology of empire, but an escape. Indeed, it is hardly surprising that at least in such cultural contexts where the authoritative use of textual documents is of great importance, certain forms of textual study emerge. The circulation of encryptions and decryptions between imperial domination and Orientalism coincided with a kind of reading that was both technical and legal. Yet, at its best, if it halted on the details and figures of text, such reading practice allowed for its own subversion. Philology was to open an emergency exit to humanism.

Said, here and elsewhere, relied on the authority of Leo Spitzer (1887–1960) and Erich Auerbach (1892–1957), who over time, especially in American literary criticism, have come to be regarded as veritable embodiments of philology.[26] These scholars, however, pursued very specific, one might even say idiosyncratic, approaches to the study of literature that deliberately broke with procedures and practices that had previously been regarded as constitutive of philology. Spitzer, in particular, whose background was in linguistics and whose early studies concerned patterns of spoken discourse and its pragmatics, built much of his work on a rejection of standing procedures and values of philology, such as the prioritization of canonical writers and of classical antiquity. Auerbach's concerns for "figuration," for the theory of "representation" in literature, for the roles of detail and temporality, likewise have little to do with what was perceived, in Germany, as typically philological in the 1920s. Admittedly, their overall understandings of reading and interpretation drew on the notion of a circular movement between part and whole that had been a dominant theorem of German philological hermeneutics since the 1800s. Yet, in their explicit embrace of the modern, the aesthetic, and the semiotic, Spitzer's and Auerbach's positions initially were iconoclast and directed at the overcoming, or else the refoundation of philology on new theoretical terms.[27] The formula of "close reading," when applied to their practice, as Said did in his "Return" lecture,[28] is little more than a *passe-partout*. To be sure, this was entirely in accordance with the logic of his lecture, which posited a universalism of reading. Yet, in this way, Said was also forced to marginalize the historicity of reading, of scholarship, and thereby of meaning.

It seems clear then that recent "returns" to philology have taken place under the cover of a semantic smokescreen that obscured, deliberately or not, the wild divergence of a significant number of traditions. It seems hard to deny that the violent upheavals of the mid-twentieth century—if ever there was a crisis of the humanities, surely it was then?—destroyed much of the erstwhile transparency of such traditions. Understanding what it might mean to return to philology consequently remains a wild-goose chase. Both de Man and Said, when they pretended to return to something they regarded as "philology," wrote as expatriates alienated from their "mother tongues" and separated from the umbilical cord of tradition. Both were exiles who refashioned themselves as adherents of other exiles. These double ruptures with educational tradition bespeak a crisis of legitimacy in the meaning of philology. This is an ongoing development. In 2016 Sheldon Pollock, returning to something akin to the commonplace of close reading, declared that philology was "the practice of *making sense of texts.*" Philology, in the "large sense," is "the critical self-reflection of language. If mathematics is the language of the book of nature, philology is the language of the book of human being."[29] He goes on to invoke an ennobling nexus of philology with the domain of human freedom and envisages a mission of achieving a "philology of the anthropocene, the epoch of potential planetary consciousness."[30] Here, the division between the natural and the cultural is ultimately meant to disappear. At the end of the day, it appears that the most ambitious returns to philology entail re-establishing Blumenberg's *topos* of the legibility of the world.

It is a mere symptom of this uncertain terrain that philology continues to be understood one-sidedly in terms of reading, although a perspective that were to take seriously the history of philological scholarship would perforce include also the study of a system of writing.[31] This one-sided understanding has given rise to the exaltation of "close reading," which assumes the function of a surrogate foundational myth. As a side-product, this myth charges the notion of reading with the promise of moving beyond the automatism and banality of the decryption that is at the root of the common understanding of Orientalism. Texts, if scrutinized with sufficient care, will continue to reveal different meanings. In this way, ever so slowly, we can read our way out of Germany, out of nationalism and racism, out of historicism, out of empire; and we can read our way into "theory," or a novel, truly universalist "humanism." Yet, this weakly utopian scenario suffers from a lack of legitimacy that besets its genealogy. The shared desire to appropriate the historical lustre, the traditional legitimacy of the name of "philology" indicates that it is indeed the magpies and the cuckoos that are flying after the wild geese.

3. Genealogy and its Limits

In the attempt to elucidate the meaning of "philology," including its historical changes, it is no accident that the question of legitimacy and the presence of genealogy interlock. As I will argue, the reason for this mutual entanglement is that "philology" actually functions in the manner of a proper name, and a personal name to boot. "Philology" is not, or not primarily, a predicate expression, hence not a "concept," at least not as according to Gottlob Frege.[32] So perhaps the question as to the changing meanings of "philology" is not one that falls into the template of conceptual history as commonly understood. Admittedly, what is historically contested in "concepts," in the way that for instance Reinhart Koselleck thought was indispensable for the historicization of political language,[33] is usually not the application of a predicate. Rather, it is ownership of, or privileged attachment to, a name and the actual—Nietzsche says: "seigneurial"[34]— prerogative of naming. The point of the history of concepts precisely does not appear to have been the determination of a range of predications. When Koselleck discussed the concept of "history," for instance, he did not conduct a census of the things that were at a given time predicated to be history (or to be "historical" if the qualitative aspect is foregrounded).[35] Arguably, then, the history of concepts is to a large extent a history of names. And if so, it cannot be separated from a history of naming.

This latter history is non-trivial, for naming ought to be regarded as something quite different from what the analytic tradition in philosophy has made it out to be. It is not so much the referential, extensional, but rather the intensional aspect of naming that is of interest under the conditions of historicization: not the planet Venus, but the more peculiar territory of the semantics of morning star and evening star, to use Frege's famous example.[36] Frege had wondered why the assertion: "The morning star is (identical to) the evening star" was at all informative; for, since both expressions had the same object of reference, i.e. the planet Venus, the phrase was a mere tautology. His solution was to distinguish, within meaning, between reference (extension) and other meaning-giving circumstances ("sense," or intension). In natural language contexts, then, semantics always has to reckon with the compound character of meaning. And it is in the ambit of intension that all kinds of cultural and political trajectories peculiar to the use of names can be accommodated.[37] The intensional aspect of naming also allows for the condition that the name of "philology," which on the surface is anything but personal, could become subject to the trope of personification. It is this specific tropical meaning of names—as signifiers of (quasi-)persons, as carriers of anthropomorphism— that explains the particular importance of both autobiography and genealogy (and false genealogy) when it comes to determining the meaning of "philology."

Precisely by virtue of its embrace of genealogy, one of the most important historical attempts to explicate the meaning of "philology" remains Sebastiano Timpanaro's (1923–2000) account of "Lachmann's method."[38] Here, Timpanaro laid down two conditions for understanding philology, namely determining, in a genealogical fashion, its historical emergence; and defining it as a discrete "method." The second condition instantly attaches to a name, that of Karl Lachmann (1793–1851), a contemporary of the Brothers Grimm, who was hardly the first, but certainly one of the most accomplished specialists of editing texts according to *stemma*, the pedigree structure obtained by the collation of extant versions and the reconstruction of the earliest attainable underlying source text. Timpanaro shows that this practice was based in the history of the study of the New Testament, with Erasmus of Rotterdam and Richard Bentley as ancestral figures. Lachmann himself worked abundantly on the New Testament before turning his attention to the Middle High German epics.[39]

For all its merits, Timpanaro's account is reductionist in a problematic manner, both as regards the method of philology and its genesis. Another type of philology had already emerged before 1800, the aim of which was not to reconstruct an underlying *Ur*-text from which would have sprung a plethora of inferior variants, but that focused instead on the destruction of the unity of a given text by proving its composition from historically distinct vocabularies. This destructive approach focused in particular on the Old Testament on the one hand (with Johann Gottfried Eichhorn's 1780–3 *Historisch-kritische Einleitung in das Alte Testament* as key text); and on the Homeric epics on the other (with Friedrich August Wolf's 1795 *Prolegomena ad Homerum* as epoch-making work). Ancestral figures for this approach might have been the humanist Lorenzo Valla, who unmasked the post-classical vocabulary of the Constantinean Donation; and the eighteenth-century French polymath Jean Astruc, who had pioneered the deconstruction of the Pentateuch (as well as making a name for himself in the study of venereal diseases). The Astrucean argument was based on the different proper names the Pentateuch uses for the deity; and the interpretation of ancient Hebrew customs of naming has remained key to ascertaining the composite layers of the Old Testament. For, the notion that the Hebrews would have called their one god only by one name remained an assumption hard to prove. Shortly after 1800, the lexical orientation of this type of philology found another outlet in comparative linguistics, which emerged from the international reception of William Jones's observations about relations among Indo-European vocabularies and grammars. Moreover, philology included grammatical, antiquarian, archaeological, epigraphic, and ethnographic traditions. The boundary to natural history and other fields of science was blurred. A full genealogical account of the field would have to accommodate all of this diversity.

In addition, Timpanaro's account also poses another, quite significant problem: the genealogical perspective on philology reduces a phenomenon initially perceived as epitomizing the nineteenth century, as for instance "Lachmann's method," to something that was entirely in place long before 1800. What is left as the particular addition on the part of the nineteenth century is then, ultimately, just the "external" deployment of philology—as a method that, once established, remained unchanging—for the pursuit of certain ideals of "humanist" education, and for nationalism, imperialism, and racism. In other words, the change philology underwent in the nineteenth century would then have been induced by the political history of the period.[40] The rest is usurpation. "Lachmann's method" is not Lachmann's, but rather Bentley's or Erasmus'. It is only that, following the cycle of forgetting that marks the history of scholarship, from time to time a different person has his (always his) name attached to the method at hand.

The genealogical procedure makes visible the former carriers of the name. Arguably, this is one of the main techniques of conceptual history: to find out what were the previous carriers (or referents) of a name that is not obviously a name. The procedure does not even have to involve a personal name, such as Lachmann's. It is not much different in those cases where one poses a seemingly innocent semantic question such as, for instance, the one as to what was previously called "philology." Almost inevitably, however, such a question conjures up further inquiries that have to do, not with the history of individual proper names, but with the history of naming as a cultural practice. One thing that is perfectly clear in Timpanaro's procedure is that genealogy will not be concerned with, say, the sharing of a name in a patchwork family full of adoptions and transient unions (which is, arguably, what the history of philological method has been in structural terms).

With a side-glance at Nietzsche's thoughts on genealogy, it is clear that one of the most important traditional uses of the procedure is to prove or disprove legitimacy in the bearing of a name, or a title to rule. Arguably, the attraction of genealogy was tied to an underlying monarchical and aristocratic understanding of the political that bestowed additional significance on the privileging of naming. In any case, the transferring of names (and the transferring of "personal" rule, including the rule of symbolic quasi-personages such as "philology") carries a contingent distinction of the legitimate and the illegitimate. The exposing of illegitimacy can express either a desire to reinforce the underlying distinction or a desire to abandon it. In the disorder of history, though, naming practice is far richer, and there are also other practices than the "seigneurial" that have mostly been passed by as a result of the traditional, politically constrained understanding of genealogy as a method. As Foucault has suggested, this understanding ought to be broadened, into a fuller account of lines of descent without concern for origins.[41] As a crucial node in a non-aristocratic genealogy of philology, the 1872–1873 Wilamowitz-Rohde polemic about Nietzsche's *Birth of Tragedy* drew heavily on crude manipulations of the name of philology. Nonetheless, the penchant of genealogy toward the trope of personification prevailed.

4. Name Calling

The use of the personification of philosophical positions is a well-known feature of Nietzsche's works. His eagerness to speak through an ever-changing series of half-forgotten ancient masks, such as Democritus or, later on, Zarathustra, is part of the indispensable theatrics of his style of argument. This procedure also marks the indirect response, through his friend Erwin Rohde (1845–1898), to Ulrich von Wilamowitz-Moellendorff's (1848–1930) polemic against *Birth of Tragedy* in the summer of 1872. Rohde's intervention is often dismissed as an irrelevant piece of inferior polemics that failed to fully disarm Wilamowitz's attack. Embarrassment only appears to increase when scholars take into account the correspondence between Nietzsche and Rohde and come to the conclusion that Rohde's response was actually "orchestrated … down to the last detail" by Nietzsche, as James Porter has put it.[42] The inadequacy of the response then is Nietzsche's own when he is using Rohde as a mask in the struggle with Wilamowitz.

The situation, however, was more complicated. Rohde deliberately appropriated Nietzsche's personifying style of argument. It is clear from the correspondence that both Nietzsche and Rohde took Wilamowitz's pamphlet seriously as a manifestation of academic politics that questioned Nietzsche's status as a junior member of faculty. Nonetheless, it appears equally clear that for them the way in which the polemic was to be staged was comical in nature. The ridicule to which Wilamowitz had exposed

Nietzsche's study had to be outdone. It was primarily for the purpose of comical effect that Rohde offered to turn himself into a mouthpiece, a mask, and a dramatic role. Moreover, Wilamowitz was to be denied, not only Nietzsche's, but any direct response. Hence Rohde suggested framing the rebuttal as an open letter to Richard Wagner. This arrangement, of which Nietzsche approved, but which he had not himself devised,[43] was designed to mark Wilamowitz, not merely as an inferior intellect, but as a man whose honor was insufficient to be recognized by personal address. This, to be sure, was a conventional strategy in *Antikritik*. Less conventional were the finer points Rohde made about the exclusion of Wilamowitz from the conversation.

In numerous passages, Rohde alluded to a shared aesthetic (and more specifically, musical) sensibility that was the prerequisite of participating in the readership of Nietzsche's book. Aesthetic sentience translated directly into an affective bond. The most damaging shortcoming Rohde diagnosed in Wilamowitz's efforts was "anaesthesia," a lack of perceptivity, sensibility, and aesthetic judgment, which by necessity caused scientific failure:

> Precisely those who prefer to regard themselves as entirely neutral mirrors of true antiquity actually project the crude poverty of sentience, the bland vacuity of their own interior, the philistine narrowness of their own cast of mind, onto antiquity in the first place; and the prim, cheery rascal, as which they like to present to us the Greeks of the best epoch, in reality has about as much similarity to the archetype of a contemporary of Aeschylus as does the monkey to Heracles, nay, even less, about as much similarity as possesses the Dr. phil. von Wilamowitz to the model of "Socratic man," whom our friend [i.e. Nietzsche] calls the "noblest antagonist" of artistic culture, and by which moniker, amusingly, the Dr. phil. believes himself and his ilk to be denoted.[44]

Instead of reproducing contemporary commonplaces about the inevitability of "standpoint" Rohde makes a more subtle point about the scientific duty of being a sentient and always already aesthetic subject. This subject is not merely a socially given model of comportment, but a physical self with a sensory apparatus. Wilamowitz by contrast had reduced his sense of scholarly selfhood to an empty social façade, a "bland vacuity," which went under the name of "honor" and was crudely related to institutional initiation at the boarding school at Pforta. Decades later, Wilamowitz stated in his memoirs that his prime motive for attacking Nietzsche had been the sense that *Birth of Tragedy* had dishonored the institution from which they had both graduated.[45] Nietzsche and Rohde were less eager (to put it mildly) to accept an institutional threshold as a criterion for belonging to a community of honor. Rather, they suggested that such a threshold should consist in belonging to a community whose precondition was the embodiment of philology.

If one regards the quoted sentence at length—it is only one sentence—it becomes clear that Rohde's effective destruction of Wilamowitz's epistemic stance remains undeveloped and unsustained. Rather, the argument is submerged in a syntactic and lexical mess of surplus vilification. Here, the comical asserts itself. As a consequence, if the text is taken to exemplify philology as properly practiced, it fails, for it loses all poise and reticence and refuses to accommodate slow reading. The literary *polemos*, on the contrary, requires fast reading. Neither Rohde's nor Wilamowitz's pamphlets ever seem to dwell on a single thought. Every colon has to contain a new insult. Rohde's neat little summary of Nietzsche's critique of the blandness of contemporary classicism thus went unanswered in Wilamowitz's second polemic,[46] and among the classical philologists of Germany, none took notice of this crucial point. Rather, the declaration of Nietzsche's death as a scholar that Hermann Usener, one of Wilamowitz's teachers, emitted in his lectures and of which Nietzsche had received notice already in the fall of 1872,[47] summarized the reception of *Birth of Tragedy*. Wilamowitz, for the rest of his life, considered himself victorious.[48] In a sense then, the comical performance that was required by the genre of polemics defeated the aim of the reply to Wilamowitz's invective, provided the counter-critique was supposed to make an epistemological as well as semantic point about the meaning of "philology."

As a consequence of the unsustainability of substantial argument in the polemics, the key point of the controversy was reduced to a quarrel about the name of philology, and, at the end of the day, the actual titles of the polemical interventions. It was Nietzsche's friend and Basel housemate, the theologian Franz Overbeck (1837–1905), who came up with the title for Rohde's piece, *Afterphilologie*,[49] a title about which Rohde had misgivings ("the word, however fitting [*trefflich*], still is for my taste perhaps a little too Aristophanic"),[50] but with which he went along anyway. The term, a pun that is difficult to translate, dismisses Wilamowitz as a "representative of a 'false' philology," as Nietzsche put it in one of his letter instructions. The analogous term, on which it plays, is "the popular creation *Afterkunst*,"[51] a form of art that has been left so behind that it can only converse with the anus (it is left open whether the connotations are more on the side of excretion or of intercourse). The pun indicates a specific semantic undertaking, a manner of laying out the meaning of the name of "philology" by modifying it into a string of degrading nicknames and contaminating it with other names.

The lowly history of wordplay never seems to enter conceptual history, which in practice maintains, like many studies of past meaning, a commitment to a choric understanding of discourse as both commenting on and intervening in the tragedy of history. What makes the Wilamowitz-Rohde polemic interesting in a discussion of the history of the meaning of "philology" is precisely its transfer of the problem at hand to the field of ridicule and name-calling. For, this is a procedure that provides an alternative to, or if one follows Nietzsche, the actual aim of, genealogy. Admittedly, the tone of the correspondence between Nietzsche and Rohde on the polemic is multivalent and mixes scorn and melancholia, aggression and a surprising degree of tenderness for Wilamowitz, as "a seduced street urchin from Berlin." Yet, the outcome of the conversation anticipates some of the later Nietzschean opinions on "gay science" (*fröhliche Wissenschaft*), and indeed his pronouncements on the purpose of the "genealogy of morals" indicate that the latter was ultimately meant to relegate "our old morality" to comedy.[52]

Overbeck's invention responded to Wilamowitz's title *Zukunftsphilologie!*, "Philology of the Future!," which was itself a pun (adorned with a ridiculous exclamation point) that scorned the aesthetics underpinning Nietzsche's book as the breaking point of its scholarly argument (although Wilamowitz, under the same genre constraint as Rohde, failed to turn this into a more substantive critique in the text). *Zukunftsmusik*, "music of the future," had become a commonplace vilification of Wagner's compositions since around 1860. In his 1869 anti-Semitic treatise "On Jewry in Music," Wagner had berated a critic, Ludwig Bischoff, for ridiculing his aesthetic ideas regarding "the future work of art." Bischoff, who "disavowed being a Jew" (which indeed he was not), had allegedly transformed Wagner's serious theoretical intentions into the ridiculous notion of a "music of the future." By this notion one was to understand such a kind of music "that, even though at present it sounded awful, would in due time become much more enjoyable."[53] Previously, in an 1861 brochure, Wagner had actually attempted to appropriate the slogan, which had been around in the music criticism of the period for years.[54] The Nietzsche circle quickly developed a similarly ambivalent attitude toward Wilamowitz's witticism. Already on June 8, 1872, a mere day after Nietzsche had obtained a copy of Wilamowitz's pamphlet and roughly a month before Overbeck came up with the group's rejoinder, Nietzsche had addressed Rohde as *Geliebter Zukunftsphilolog*, "My beloved philologist of the future,"[55] signaling his intent to appropriate the term. Indeed, the phrase reoccurs in many passages of Nietzsche's subsequent oeuvre. The following year, Overbeck himself was working on a pamphlet that, in private conversation, was nicknamed *Zukunftstheologie*.[56]

As this wealth of private response indicates, Wilamowitz's title was based on a formidable intuition; it claimed ownership of the past and present of philology for the non-Nietzscheans. *Afterphilologie* responded by devaluing the past. Rohde, when he explained the title, protested:

> In reality the manner of such a dry-pedantic fellow [Wilamowitz ...] has so little to do with a true, soulful study of antiquity [*Alterthumskunde*], that in order to maintain the honor of our discipline one ought to refrain entirely from calling it a philology, *be it of the present or the future*, but only a parody of all true philology, an ugly caricature of one-sided criticism, a true *Afterphilologie*.[57]

Crucially, Rohde thus abandoned any claim on the past of philology. Nietzsche was driven in the same direction. In the unpublished fragments entitled "We Philologists," he even surpassed Rohde when he insisted "One believes philology has come to an end—and I believe it has not even started,"[58] and thus reneged on the claim even to own the present of philology. This was an almost logical step following the dominance over the present the *Afterphilologen* were clearly able to exercise. However, by renouncing ownership of the present, Nietzsche's aesthetic understanding of philological practice suffered serious damage. Like Wagner's *Zukunftsmusik*, *Zukunftsphilologie* would—perhaps—at best in future times yield the kind of sentience, the kind of interaction with the sensory world, on which the entire notion of superior philological method rested. By effecting a denial of a present time—almost a reverse type of "denial of coevalness"[59]—Wilamowitz exiled Nietzsche's work into a doubtful future the possibility of which was then in addition denied by Usener when he declared that Nietzsche was "dead as a scholar."

As a consequence, later Nietzschean pronouncements on the true meaning of "philology" ought not to be taken as supporting any imagination of "return" to past practice or submission to the present-time authority of tradition. Rather, his declarations indicate his attempts to break with traditional philology and to find a voice in exile from the discipline. The appeals to "slowness" have much to do with recuperating the present as a centerpiece of his understanding of "true" method. Since Nietzsche's position was determined less by autonomous choice than by the necessities of the *polemos* with classical philology in which he found himself, the notion that his writings, or in fact those of his opponents, might be taken to provide a philosophical foundation for an eternally valid clarification of "the" meaning of "philology" is hardly plausible. The upshot rather seems to be that philology was, in the 1870s, the symbolic, textual state of *polemos* that subsisted between the parties in question. This was a conflict about names; and a conflict about different appropriations and moblizations of temporality.[60] Since naming in this context was mockery, *uneigentlich*, it is hard to avoid the conclusion that philology, for the participants in this controversy, was not simply the side they championed, but rather the conflict itself. What was fought over was the temporality of staged performance, a mixture of the playful and the serious, a battle of stand-in champions, and not the actual pasts and futures the works of Nietzsche, Rohde, and Wilamowitz drew on or were to enjoy. Neither Nietzsche's writing nor his readership were actually altered by Wilamowitz. Although arguably the polemic contributed to the motives that induced Nietzsche to change his career path and writing, he was himself the author of these changes. So philology was the name of a conflict, and not merely the name of a party to the conflict.

5. The Father of All

Heidegger, in one of his eccentric etymologies, toiled over years—beginning, not accidentally, in 1933—to rework the meaning of Heraclitus' fragment 53, which had long become proverbial in the form: "War is the father of all things" (*Polemos panton men pater esti ...*). In full the fragment might be rendered as: "War is both father of all and king of all: it reveals the gods on the one hand and humans on the other, makes slaves on the one hand, the free on the other."[61] Heidegger, at the end of a series of translation attempts that demonstrate the semantic indeterminacy of the fragment, renders *polemos* by the German *Auseinandersetzung*—literally the setting apart of things or of people, a principle of differentiation and dissent. This principle is then the "progenitor" (*Erzeuger*, therefore perhaps also "sire," if one wishes to emphasize the physical-productive and sexual connotation, *pater* in the original) and "preserver" (*basileus*, i.e. king) of "all (that is present)."[62] The decision to translate kingship as a function of "preservation" is politically loaded and aligns Heidegger with the political conservatism of, say, Wilamowitz. At the same time, the translation suppresses the monarchical connotations of genealogy. Perhaps more importantly, the recourse to presence, which Heidegger bases (if flimsily) on the *panton*, the "of all" of the original, is a marker for the temporal dimensions one might discern in the Wilamowitz-Rohde polemic. If "philology" is a *polemos* in this sense, it can only be the progenitor of those that possess the quality of presence. *Polemos* does not generate the absent, the past, and the future. More importantly, however, the notion of fatherhood invested in the fragment does not merely connote the function of production and creation but also a custom of naming. "Philology," denoting a specific environment of *polemos*, may be understood as a slightly perverse type of patronym. It is perhaps this dimension (among others) that Heidegger seeks to capture through the use of "preserver" (*Bewahrer*), since it is among the prime functions of European personal names (and has been since antiquity) to stabilize individual identity and to mark (mostly patrilinear) descent. All in all, however, Heidegger does not seem keenly alert to the problem of naming. His translation of *pater* is reductive since fatherhood should have been taken as a cultural function with implications far beyond the physical contribution to procreation. Nonetheless, Heidegger's intuition—possibly triggered by Nietzsche[63]— that the *polemos* of an insurmountably polemical environment, such as that of 1870s philology, presents a serious semantic complication is of prime importance.

One of the basic tenets of Reinhart Koselleck's study of concepts was the notion, adapted from Carl Schmitt's understanding of "counter-concepts," that "political conflict" over meaning was the prime generator (the progenitor) of the historicity of concepts. Yet ultimately, conceptual historians clarified or differentiated neither the meaning of "political" nor that of "conflict." Mere disagreement within scholarly disciplines, such as the one that pitted Rohde against Wilamowitz in 1872, hardly appears to fit the bill. Neither do *Zukunftsphilologie* and *Afterphilologie* appear to qualify as Schmittian counter-concepts (such as the infamous pair friend/enemy), in part because they make a mockery of the very notion of counter-concepts. Heidegger's wordplay around *Auseinandersetzung* indicates a conviction that politics, or "the political" in Schmitt's terms, does not suffice for understanding the semantics of Heraclitus' fragment, and of any meaning-generating condition that was foundationally conflicted.

Significantly, Heidegger's first discussion of fragment 53 occurs in a letter of thanks for a complimentary copy of Schmitt's revised 1933 version of *On the Concept of the Political*, which includes a discussion of the fragment by which Heidegger apparently felt challenged.[64] In 1934–1935, he continued to translate *polemos* as *Kampf*, "struggle." This was in keeping, not only with the parlance (and one particularly unfortunate publication) of the time (Heidegger's notorious rectorate of Freiburg University, in the letter to Schmitt, also figured as an instance of *polemos*) but also with the Diels-Kranz edition of the fragment (a work of which Heidegger was generally critical, sometimes in philologically *outré* ways).[65] The shift to *Auseinandersetzung* then occurred in the 1935 introductory lectures on metaphysics. Both Diels and Kranz were closely connected to Wilamowitz, it bears mentioning, the former as a lifelong friend, the latter as a disciple. Heidegger's re-writing of their translation also rendered an oblique service to Nietzsche. The very questioning of the meaning of *polemos* entailed a partisan intervention into the conflicted terrain of philology itself. Therefore, clarifying the meaning of *polemos* was covertly circular since one was ineluctably drawn into philology and forced to take sides in its specific practice of *polemos*. Yet, one way of avoiding such circularity was to introduce additional internal differentiation into the term. The 1935 choice of *Auseinandersetzung* and its concomitant presentism arguably served to yield this surplus meaning and to seemingly extricate philosophy from philology.

Another pertinent aspect of Heidegger's re-translation is the result of a more conservative decision, quite in line with philological tradition. He retains the conventional notion that *panton*, "of all," refers to "everything (that is present)," "Auseinandersetzung ist allem (Anwesenden) Erzeuger." The fragment's use of *pater* would certainly have allowed, perhaps even called for, a reading of *panton* as "of everyone." Yet, Heidegger pulls away from the tendency toward implicit personalization that was so prominent a feature in the quarrel about the meaning of philology. The *Auseinandersetzung* at hand does not by necessity require personal protagonists and a theatrical set-up. Heidegger used Heraclitus and Hölderlin in ways very similar to Nietzsche's deployment of Democritus and Wagner (as implicit fathers-of-all). Nonetheless, at least after the *Kehre*—the "turn" in his philosophical thinking around 1930, in which he abandoned the foundational role of human existence for understanding ontology that had been the centerpiece of his previous departure from metaphysical tradition—Heidegger seems to have remained relatively immune to the temptation of making such a mechanism of personalization and dramatization *foundational* for his line of argument.

This immunity, however, did *not* constitute another ruse to avoid philological entanglement. Rather, it was part and parcel of precisely such an entanglement, for beyond the constellation of the 1870s conflict among Wilamowitz, Rohde, and Nietzsche, the very procedure of personification as pertaining to the name of philology was part of another line of polemical conflict. Therefore, personification does not provide a conclusive analysis of the historical semantics of "philology." This finding would also appear to explain Heidegger's reticence with regard to this procedure of figuration.

6. Philology of the Real

The Nietzsche-Rohde counter-critique heightened personalization, yet Wilamowitz also had his share in this dynamic. He, too, defined the understanding of philology by appeal to the names of the great dead fathers of the discipline (of everyone in philology).[66] In particular, these were Friedrich August Wolf, who had initiated a tradition of holding introductory lectures that theorized philology, under the title of "encyclopaedia";[67] and the antagonists of a previous 1820s polemic, August Boeckh and Gottfried Hermann (1772–1848). This was the polemic between Hermann's *Wortphilologie* (philology of words) and Boeckh's *Sachphilologie* or *Realphilologie* (philology of things),[68] which remained the central defining controversy of German philology throughout the nineteenth century, not only in classical studies but also in adjacent fields such as Orientalism. The confrontation of Boeckh and Hermann was a *locus classicus* of introductory lectures into the subject of philology until well after 1900, and in many partially mythified, partially reductive forms it was common knowledge among those trained in any of the philological subdisciplines.[69] Its use often seems to have lain in the confrontation between cultural-historical and linguistic approaches that structured many of the lesser philological controversies of the late nineteenth and early twentieth centuries.

Boeckh had refashioned philology as an infinitely approximative, always provisional, and thus hesitant and skeptical undertaking that amply practiced the virtue of *epokhe*, of withholding judgment. The aim of philology was not to acquire knowledge of that which was given in nature but of the full scope of the previous exercise of human reason, in Boeckh's formula *Erkenntnis des Erkannten*, a translation of the traditional humanist formula of *cognitio cogniti*, that is to say, the understanding of the (previously) understood, but in the broadest possible sense, as regarding all objects of human intentionality and all products of human agency.[70] Building on Friedrich August Wolf's discussion of classical philology as a "science" (*Wissenschaft*) of classical antiquity as a "whole," as a unified period, an epoch of history, Boeckh determined the task of this *Alterthumswissenschaft* as all-encompassing within the bounds of the epoch in question, only excluding those realities that had not passed, in some way, through the human mind. Evidently, this definition had the disadvantage of under-determining disciplinary division. While for Boeckh, text was the primary material with which philology had to operate, he insisted that there was no reason for limiting philology to the study of text, and he also expanded drastically the source base of classical philology by systematizing epigraphy. He thus collapsed philology and history into one, and openly and deliberately so. Continuing distinctions between the disciplines marked his failure. Hermann, by contrast, had insisted on the primacy of language as the basic object of philological knowledge of antiquity; all knowledge about the *realia* of antiquity had to be gained through the often difficult mediation of the ancient languages. This "grammatical" precondition—"grammar" meaning, at the time, the actual knowledge of a language[71]—ensured the disciplinary stability of classics against, for instance, the manifest absurdity that non-classical, and especially "Oriental," ancients might enjoy a claim to equal attention in Boeckh's totalizing pursuit. Orientalism threatened the stability of the *Gegenstandsbereich*, the range of objects foundational for the discipline of philology.

In his *Encyclopaedia of Philology* lectures, the prime site of his methodological work, Boeckh expressly attempted to achieve a new theory of philology.[72] The term "theory," in the parlance of the period, entailed, on the one hand, an abstract, weakly systematizing account of a given domain with explanatory force for the single component parts. On the other hand, less openly, the term also implied the makeshift and preliminary character of the abstract account in question. "Theory" suspended the obligation of establishing the exact position of a domain of abstraction within the supposedly consistent whole of systemic philosophy. Schleiermacher, for instance, used the term accordingly when he discussed the different "theories" of philology: the pragmatic, "applicable" and "useful" ones of the ancients and the "purely scientific" ones of "us Moderns," which "immerse themselves into abstruse discussions of the inner nature of art and its first causes."[73] Such uses of "theory" were even sanctioned by Kant.[74] The term was a deliberately vague placeholder that permitted shifting between the systematic and the practical. In this way, the philological theory of the period around 1800, into which Boeckh's attempt was one of the most influential entries, achieved exactly the move away from systematicity and applicability that Paul de Man considered characteristic for the twentieth-century formation of structural-linguistic and then literary theory. The meaning of "theory," then, has remained quite stable over more than 200 years.[75]

The overall theoretical environment of Boeckh's project consisted of several important component parts and constitutive challenges. Two of these are of particular significance for the present discussion since they ensured the ontological pertinence of philological theory. First, transmitted and modified by Schleiermacher, there was the novel notion of a hermeneutic circle, which at the time was regarded as a relationship of mutual presupposition between the knowledge of a whole and the knowledge of its parts (for knowing that and in what way something is a fragment one already needs an idea of the whole; for knowing the whole, one needs to have an idea of the parts). Following Schleiermacher, discussion has often credited the speculative romantic philologist Friedrich Ast as the one who first formulated the basic circle that troubled the study of antiquity.[76] This understanding of hermeneutics in terms of an inescapably paradoxical relationship between the parts and the whole, the scattered remnants and the unified history of antiquity, was still commonplace at the time of Nietzsche. Rohde, for instance, mentioned the circle in *Afterphilologie*, but with reference to Montaigne instead of Ast.[77] Only from the interwar period onward was it replaced with the Heidegger-Gadamer version of the hermeneutic circle as located in a phenomenological understanding of readerly interpretation. For Boeckh, who had studied with Schleiermacher, the parts-whole circle was an insurmountable condition that beset the archaeological knowledge of the ancient past and the reading of ancient texts alike. The unity, the ontological wholeness of the historical past was therefore a prerequisite of philological-historical knowledge; and yet such knowledge could never be more than an approximation.

Second, such approximation needed a theoretical underpinning that assured its unity. Otherwise, philology risked Hegel's much-cited verdict—codified in the authoritative *Encyclopaedia of the Philosophical Sciences* from 1830, but already foreshadowed in the opening remarks of *Phenomenology of the Spirit* from 1805— that philology constituted merely an "aggregate" of different and incoherent bodies of knowledge.[78] Curiously, this verdict appropriated, and turned into an unambiguously negative judgment, a formulation that had already appeared in Friedrich Schlegel's early writings. Here, in the context of an aesthetic of romantic, anti-classicist modernism that exalted fragmentation, being a "mere aggregate" potentially carried positive value, if only as a transitory stage in the process of history.[79] Schlegel suggested that being a "multitude of knowledges [is] one purpose of philology. Micrology."[80] Every "philologeme," every fragment of philological knowledge, was related "to a *boundless* number of bounded, indeed often most micrological, instances of knowledge. This is the philological *Absolute*."[81] In this way, Schlegel had inserted the problem of the unity and plurality of philology, as well as his tentative solution—unlimited fragmentation as a form of the absolute—into the emerging theorization of the field.

The semantic context of the discourse in which the metaphor of "aggregation" emerged was twofold. Significantly, there was a number of prominent remarks by Kant on the architectural "systemic unity" to be achieved by science as opposed to the "merely aggregate" nature of "common knowledge."[82] The more common use, however, was in the context of metaphysics and the philosophy of nature since

Leibniz.[83] In both Hegel's and Schlegel's cases, the underlying patterns were oriented toward chemistry. Chemical reactions were seen as based on the combinatory forces and the goal-directedness inherent in matter (and especially in the dualist structure of acids and bases). In this manner, one hoped to circumvent a merely mechanist understanding of natural philosophy where the only legitimate mode of explanation consisted in cause–effect relations within the realm of matter, but which seemed feeble in the explanation of non-material causation such as between mind and matter.[84] As a result of this entanglement with natural philosophy, the notion of aggregation thus placed the problem of philology's lack of unity, not merely in the epistemic but also in the ontological domain. Hegel's attack on philology in particular was not based on an epistemological criticism of philological knowledge. Nor was it by dint of methodological deficiency that philology supposedly lacked unity. Rather, the problem of philology was its diverse and disconnected *Gegenstandsbereich* of wildly different materials that did not cohere with each other to form a new superior unity.

Boeckh's response—it was demonstrably a response[85]—was to generate an ontological basis for philology from the notion of *cognitio cogniti*, which cleverly objectified mental content. In practice, Boeckh showed a predilection for such studies that sought unity not merely in the structure of the mind but in material reality itself. For instance, his oeuvre contained ample studies of Ancient Greek units of measurement the correct translations of which he intended to determine by correlating them to units of measurement in his own day. Measure had been produced by human reason in response to an underlying spatial reality, to things as they—unshakeably— were.[86] Philology thus required not only knowledge of the linguistic meanings involved in producing the textual record of antiquity but also the realities with regard to which these meanings had emerged. However, many of the meanings of texts were not fixed by referents in material reality, but rather (if at all) by the meanings of other texts. The grounding in physical reality Boeckh's procedure demanded was relatively easy to determine for units of measurement, but elusive when it came to, say, religious texts. Here, even the impulse to establish semantics from the *res extensa* of physical reality could be problematic, bordering on the naïve. Precisely the seeming naivety of such undertakings functioned (and continues to function) as indicator of the unity of a reality that steadily appeals to equally unified human reason. At the same time, the implicit refusal to permit further differentiation within the domain of the real betrays the controversial nature of the theoretical field such naïve realism attempts, with veiled polemical intent, to override.

The actual polemic between Boeckh and Hermann was arguably only a proxy for two semantically more decisive conflicts underpinning 1820s philology. First, the new philology—the new meaning invested in the term through the Boeckhian enterprise— was not going to be based on a principle of personification, but rather on a principle of objectification. Yet, as already indicated, Boeckh's ontological theorization ended in failure. The new theory was contested and, through the polemical constellation, became so connected to Boeckh's name—and the counter-position to Hermann's— that it was personified, or quasi-personified, through reception, against intention. This also means, however, that the confrontation between the personified antagonists Boeckh and Hermann was underpinned and preceded by a different *polemos*. This was the implicit conflict between mutually exclusive operations of personification and objectification in the semantic re-founding as well as the working practice of "philology" in and following the 1820s. It was precisely the search, deeply ingrained in academic custom, to find personal carriers for the name of this or that philology that counteracted the theorization of the field by way of the unification of its objects of study.

Second, objectification itself was also riven by internal division. The theorization of philology that Boeckh undertook did not even account for his own practice of objectification since his preference for the measurable and material remained out of theoretical focus. Instead, this focus was entirely on abstraction, since it aimed for objectification not in a pluralist sense, but in a monist one. The ultimate object of philology was to be one thing only, namely the unified totality of the human *cognitum*. In order to retain the conceptual possibility of this unity, Boeckh's *Encyclopaedia* lectures integrated the more concrete and diverse objects of philology into a "system."[87] Yet, outside the (seemingly) neatly ordered world of classicism, philological studies were transformed in manners that remained almost entirely outside the scope of the theorization of the discipline but nonetheless constituted an enormous effort of objectification.

This observation brings the argument back, finally, to the problem of Orientalism. Arguably the most important contribution of Orientalist research to the history of philology consisted in a tremendous expansion of the range of possible objects of study, of possible vistas of contextualization, and of possible inter-civilizational *Auseinandersetzungen*. This transformation challenged the purported historical self-sufficiency of Ancient Greece as well as the traditional dualist competition between "Athens and Jerusalem," of classical and biblical antiquity.[88] As a consequence, the overall constellation in which philology was practiced underwent a profound transformation over the course of the nineteenth century. The ontological productivity of philology was divided against itself. The unifying tendency of theorization—which spawned a corpus of systematizing handbook-style interventions—stood in a double bind with the practical diversification of objects philological Orientalism could not help producing.[89] While the Graecists struggled to overcome the condition of "mere aggregation," the Orientalists aggravated it. This is the second *polemos*, within objectification, that underpinned philology in the age of Boeckh and Hermann. The initial wonder as to why the name of philology became marginal in the critique of Orientalism may be regarded as a very late and indirect consequence of a clustering of scholarly *polemoi* from 150 years before. Philology was written out of Orientalism because the Orientalist philologies had subverted the earlier classicist theorization-by-objectification of philology; and in this respect, Said adhered to the party of isolationist classicists, much as de Man, in well-concealed agreement, had reproduced and simultaneously eclipsed the previous theorization of philology.

Contrary to the way it has rather consistently been treated, the history of the Orientalist subdisciplines was therefore central for the historical trajectory of the meaning of "philology." This centrality, however, cannot be grasped from a perspective that does not fully take into account the quotidian work of philological, and Orientalist, practice. Much work on the history of philologies, as well as on the history of philological theory, remains attached to the discussion of research programs and methodological declarations. This manner of writing the history of scholarship further tips the balance in favor of personification, of questions of intellectual descent and legitimate ownership of the name of philology. As long as historical studies of these fields do not readjust the one-sidedness of their attention, the history of philology and its layers upon layers of internal *Auseinandersetzungen* will remain out of sight. The development of linguistic theory and, later, literary theory both against and in emulation of (the failures of) the previous theorization of philology will remain obscured.

7. The Name of Semantics

The question as to what happens if Orientalism is returned into the meaning of philology is of considerable importance for clarifying "what is in" either name. As was the case with the Montagues and Capulets, it turns out, even from the few aspects sketched in the preceding pages, that the content in question was intricate; that it consisted of a historical series of quarrels, theorizations, and figurations none of which was fully erased at subsequent stages. The disorder of this history disables the pairing of writing and reading as encryption and decryption that has dominated much of the understanding of Orientalism. Any code drawn from such multivalent meanings would inevitably be ambiguous and therefore unworkable. At the same time, the semantic intricacy at hand disables the notion of philology as an escape, from the ills and woes of theory, into a territory of liberated universalist close reading. Something similar is the case for the de Manian assumption that philology, *qua* theory, might constitute a certain autonomy of reading, if only by surrendering to the undisturbed flight of meaning in the domain of written text. If theory remains bound up with the pre-given meanings inherited from the historical layering of *Auseinandersetzungen* that marked "philology," the autonomization de Man envisaged appears illusory. Theory, in this context, would be limited in its choice of objects by the previous meanings it ignores; and such ignorance cannot be amended. For, the very failure, or refusal, to take into account certain semantic layers of "philology" was part of the *polemos* constitutive of theorization. The situation, then, converges at a point of no return. We find ourselves, irrevocably, *after* philology, which remains an aggregate, migratory, and elusive meaning, a flock of wild geese departed, which to chase, across the continents, seems futile.

The hidden reason for the lasting attraction of philology is, I think, the notion that one single method, typically equated with "reading," could exercise stewardship over meaning. The elevation of "hermeneutics" to philosophical dignity has arguably also pivoted on this notion, as did the introduction of the concept of "semantics" in 1897, in the middle of the period here under consideration. The term was an invention by the Indo-Europeanist Michel Bréal (1832–1915), one of the most eminent teachers of Ferdinand de Saussure (1857–1913) in Paris. It was meant to denote the "science of significations," a novel subdiscipline within the system of scientific linguistics that would occupy itself with the explanation of changes of meanings.[90] Since change entails temporalization, this research program has a closer bond to the domain of historicity than one often appears to suspect. Bréal's implicit intention was, moreover, to claim privileged ownership of the territory of meaning for French linguistics and to supplant the German-coined concept of "semasiology," the study of the various things signified, over time, by a single signifier.[91] This antagonist of Bréal's *polemos* had emerged already in the 1820s, initially in the work of the short-lived classicist Karl Christian Reisig (1792–1829), a student of Gottfried Hermann's.[92] A complementary term, "onomasiology," the study of the varying signifiers signifying a single thing over time, was introduced only after Bréal's essay had appeared,[93] but to little avail: the success of the name of "semantics" could not be halted.

Bréal opposed naïve assumptions about "tendencies" toward change as inherent in mere words as well as in entire languages, which were often perceived as natural organisms by contemporary linguists. Instead, he aimed to reopen the explanation of linguistic and specifically semantic change to human intentionality, more precisely to the uncontrollable multitude of modest acts of will that constantly modified natural languages, and some of which, quite randomly, stuck·

> To permit will to intervene in the history of Language seems almost a heresy, so carefully has it been banished and excluded for forty years. But though men were justified in renouncing the puerilities of the ancient science, they contented themselves with an unduly simple psychology when they plunged into the opposite extreme. Between the actions of a consciously deliberate will, and the purely instinctive phenomenon, there is room for many intermediary states … .
>
> The child, for many months, exercises his tongue in uttering vowels, in articulating consonants. How many failures precede the clear pronunciation of a single syllable! Grammatical innovations are of a kindred nature, with the difference that in them a whole people collaborates. … In this long labour there is nothing that cannot be traced to the will.[94]

To the extent that there were regularities in such change, one could speak of "laws."[95] Yet this choice of term was not to occlude the fact that Bréal wanted to see meaning studied as a social phenomenon. The social was the anonymous collective, whose many short-sighted individual acts of will constantly manipulated linguistic expression. Language therefore had to be regarded as a repository of historical evidence, of the way in which humanity collectively perceived reality and put this perception into words, however insufficiently.

The very term "semantics" thus emerged in the context of the great *polemos* within philology that produced linguistics as an autonomous field, and that also fed into the even greater *polemos* between German and French scholarship, so important for the overall course of the modern humanities.[96] Bréal, a French scholar of German-Jewish origin, graduate of the *Ecole Normale*, had studied in the late 1850s with Berlin Indologists, among whom the illustrious Franz Bopp (1791–1867). Since 1864, he was professor of comparative grammar at the *Collège de France*. After 1870 he became increasingly opposed to what he considered the obscurantist organicism, the hypostatization of the natural in the history of language, and the concomitant one-sidedness of the focus on phonetics in the ambitiously scientific linguistics that had emerged especially in Germany since the 1850s. The new science of "semantics," by contrast, was to be a social science. Yet, as a result of this alignment, Bréal's formulation of the novel principle to underpin semantics tied meaning to a streamlined understanding of the historical. All change of meaning was to be located in a homogenous temporal space filled by the atomic speech acts of individual speakers who formed collectives that coincided with the national societies that provided the object of knowledge of historical writing as well as of the new sociology. To the extent that the fragmentation of temporality was actually part and parcel of semantic practice, as argued in this chapter with regard to the coining of *Zukunfts-* and *Afterphilologie*, Bréal's definition therefore narrowed the field. Hence, it does not provide a foundational model, but rather an opponent, for the manner in which the present study uses "semantics."

Foucault said of the "pataphysical saint" Jean-Pierre Brisset (1837–1919), a self-styled, delusional linguist celebrated by the absurdist writers around Jules Romains and Apollinaire in the 1910s, that he was the inheritor of all that the new science of linguistics had excluded in the second half of the nineteenth century:

> the rootedness of the signifier in the signified, the reduction of the synchronic to a primal state of history, the hieroglyphic secret of the letter (in the age of Egyptologists), the origin of phonemes in croaking pathos (descent, Darwin), the hermetic symbolism of signs: the immense myth of a word that was originary truth.[97]

"Croaking" because language, according to Brisset, had emerged in the descent of man from frog. In this manner, across his 1960s works on language, Foucault suggested that the history of linguistics, of which Bréal's "semantics" formed part, consisted in the clearcut shedding of figurative and mythical content from the understanding of language. This picture, however, remains incomplete. The expectation that one would be able to access things through their signs, even though these signs at the same time would continue to hold elusive secrets, certainly receded in the second half of the nineteenth century. No doubt Bréal's semantics also claim a role in this process. He, too, sought to discard an alleged secret; the diversity of the linguistic sign as an organic product of unified human nature was to be revealed as the consequence of the banal stutter of collective discourse.

Yet, if one takes, not linguistics, but rather philology more broadly to constitute the field of study for the alleged modernizing and rationalizing process in question, the picture becomes far more ambiguous than Foucault suggested. The "rootedness of the signifier in the signified," for instance, was precisely the key problem of academic *Realphilologie*; the obsession with "primal states" of history and language subsisted well into the twentieth century, and the expectation of secrets vested in ancient scripts or even individual words, such as the names of gods, retained a figurative presence even in the most arid of research programs. What Foucault proposed then, and what Bréal's work intended, gave excessive credit to the act of introducing theoretical stringency into the processing of linguistic meaning, by dint of the exclusion of seemingly aberrant components of the aggregate.

8. The Palimpsest Grammar of Arabic

In this context, it also seems opportune to return once more to the question of grammar, more precisely, the question of whether it was not actually grammatical knowledge, comparative or not, rather than semantics, that was the key pursuit of nineteenth-century philology. This question requires a discussion of grammar and semantics as discrete domains of philological knowledge and an examination of what "discrete" might actually mean in this context. Certainly, the "common sense" that allowed Bréal to introduce the name of semantics was marked by the notion that there was a clear distinction between grammatical knowledge and the previously nameless knowledge that pertained to linguistic meanings. The argument here pursued therefore has to show that such a distinction was artificial, and that the practice of grammar was inseparable from that of semantics. It is useful, in this context, to leave behind the Indo-European scene with its inbuilt bias toward grammar as established by the innovative prestige of comparative linguistics in the lineage of Jones and Bopp. Instead, I will turn to the case of Classical Arabic, which offers a particularly interesting context for European scholarly grammatization[20] in interaction with a longstanding tradition in the language of origin.

In general, in Semitics the distinction between linguistic and other pursuits remained far less certain than the history of Indo-European studies and the Francophone academic tradition would suggest. As a relatively small domain, Semitics was laggard in reproducing the fissure. Even if by 1900 many scholars had developed strong preferences for either the *Sachen* or the *Wörter* side, others strove to sustain the unity of philology. Especially those attracted to the party of realia typically also worked on linguistic matters, perhaps simply in order to demonstrate their competence for the academic teaching of languages. There was then a practice of comprehensive philology still in place that was receding in many other areas, not least Indological Orientalism.

Around 1900, from the perspective of German-language scholarship, the field of Arabic grammar was constituted by the mid-nineteenth-century contributions of Heinrich Leberecht Fleischer (1801–1888), William Wright (1830–1889), and, for teaching purposes, Albert Socin (1844–1899).[99] The working method of these scholars was similar throughout. Both Fleischer and Wright had assembled enormous arrays of fragmented grammatical notes which they arranged as revisions of previous works. Fleischer presented his grammatical "contributions" as a list of microscopic corrections to be inserted into the grammatical works of his teacher, the towering French romantic-era modernizer of Orientalism, Antoine-Isaac Silvestre de Sacy (1758–1838). Wright went even further in the submission of his work under a preceding tradition. He published his grammar under the name of a previous author, Fleischer's disciple, the Christiania-based Jewish-to-Lutheran convert and professor of theology Carl Paul Caspari (1814–1892), even though in the process of translation into English and after decades-long revisions, the work had changed beyond recognition. Wright reissued this grammar multiple times, and after his death it continued to be reworked by others, among whom his Cambridge successor William Robertson Smith (1846–1894). Already during his lifetime, Wright's grammar was also retranslated into German and independently revised during the process by August Müller (1848–1892), who also was a disciple of Fleischer's and also preserved Caspari's authorship.[100] Socin's grammar, while written for didactic purposes under omission of the baggage of scholarly tradition and excessive detail, was itself reissued numerous times and became a staple of language teaching especially since the fifth edition, revised by Theodor Nöldeke's former student Carl Brockelmann (1868–1956).[101] This tradition of interwoven grammar-writing arguably only ceased with the advent, or rather the return, of specialized single-author linguistic studies on Arabic that sought to cover full areas of grammar, such as for instance the works of Hermann Reckendorf (1863–1924) on syntax (Reckendorf, too, had been a student of Nöldeke's).[102] Already in 1897, Nöldeke himself had supplied a set of additional grammatical notes on selected problems of Arabic in the form of a standalone volume that proved significant enough to be reissued in an amplified version as late as 1963.[103]

Over the course of the nineteenth and well into the twentieth century, the writing of Arabic grammar in Europe had assumed an increasingly—rather than decreasingly—palimpsestic character. Yet the numerous re-editions under new authorship effectively occluded the recent history of the study of Arabic in Europe that had displayed different traits: marked authorship and divergent theoretical orientations. At the beginning of the nineteenth century, Arabic grammar had been a field of controversial positions. Silvestre de Sacy had written his monumental tomes (1810, re-edited 1831) in order to replace, not continue, the previous standard work. This was a grammar first published in 1613 in the late-humanist research context around Joseph Justus Scaliger (1540–1609) in Leiden, by Scaliger's student Thomas Erpenius (1584–1624).[104] Erpenius's grammar had been the common point of reference for European scholars, but by 1800 the work seemed bulky and faulty. It was written in Latin, which increasingly fell out of use. It was short on questions of syntax, and also shorter than one still needed to be on the grammatical discourses of the Arabic textual tradition itself, of what European scholars usually called the "national grammar" of the Arabs.[105] For Silvestre de Sacy, the question of how to work with, against, or around this "national" tradition became one of the key issues for his treatment of grammar. As he pointed out, before Erpenius, European scholars had studied Arabic merely in deference to the Arab tradition of adjudicating right and good usage in cases of obscurity and difficulty, for which Quranic language was both the prime resource and the ultimate standard. Erpenius, by contrast, had developed a more independent approach based on extant classicist models of European grammar-writing.

In the early nineteenth century, Silvestre de Sacy was not the only author attempting to come up with a replacement for Erpenius's work. A Scottish colonial scholar, Matthew Lumsden (1777–1835), professor at Fort William College in Calcutta, a new training facility for colonial officials that focused in particular on language education, published a volume of Arabic grammar that consisted almost wholly of excerpts from the national grammarians.[106] In the opening "advertisement" of the book to the reader, Lumsden dismissed the very possibility of a general grammar, on account of the arbitrariness of any systematization of the "parts of the speech" and of the abyss between contingent linguistic structures and necessary logic. Lumsden's attempt, then, though a non-starter in terms of publishing success, sought to abandon the makeshift

Europeanization Erpenius had introduced and to restore the purity of studying grammar out of a somewhat fictitious construction of the original, autonomous tradition.

As for Silvestre de Sacy, it was precisely the parts of speech, i.e. syntax, that prompted him to abandon the codifications of the national grammarians. Frustratingly, scholars in the Arab tradition had tended to disagree, sometimes even with themselves. Neither had they followed a unified system nor striven to take ordinary language use into account sufficiently. Instead, they had preferred to assert norms that were not actually followed. It seemed exceedingly hard to teach non-native speakers along the lines of this tradition. Already Erpenius, Silvestre de Sacy stated, had felt this pressure and "abandoned the ways of Oriental grammarians and adopted a less complicated system more analogous to the methods one usually follows in the study of learned languages."[107] Erpenius, that is to say, had adapted his account of Arabic to grammatical categories familiar from Latin and Greek, while also preserving some of the Arabic terminology; and he had structured his grammar in a European way, for didactic purposes. Silvestre de Sacy proposed to travel further down this road. Bolstered by the seventeenth-century linguistic philosophy of the *Grammaire générale et raisonnée* of Port-Royal (1660), his grammar was built on the notion that there was an underlying universal structure to all languages that predetermined the structure in which grammars ought to be written. This was precisely the line of argument Lumsden rejected.[108]

Another, somewhat later competitor in the effort to replace Erpenius was Heinrich Ewald (1803–1875)—Nöldeke's teacher—whose 1831 Arabic grammar had more traction in scholarship than Lumsden's.[109] Silvestre de Sacy had dealt with the divergence of Arab and European grammatical discourses by offering a dual account of syntax: one in accordance with his own Port-Royal-induced notions, the other one as according to the national grammarians. Ewald, by contrast, was prepared to discard the Arab tradition altogether, in the hope of achieving a unified system applicable to all Semitic languages at once. Paradoxically, however, he laid greater stress on the particularity of individual languages than Silvestre de Sacy (though less than Lumsden). In this regard, Ewald followed Wilhelm von Humboldt's radical recasting of the philosophy of language.

Humboldt had stressed the activity of language use as dynamic mediation between mind and world. He distinguished, and tentatively hierarchized, languages in accordance to the richness of their grammatical and otherwise expressive forms that permitted access to the "inner form," the worldview supposedly germane to a language.[110] For Humboldt, languages were subject to their own histories of development, on the basis of which they could also be compared. Classification yielded morphological groupings that provided irreducible and irreconcilable contexts for mental activity. This mode of comparison targeted integrated units of language and culture, so that philological study provided insight into something broadly speaking world-historical. This line of argument certainly displayed a sense of civilizational inequality, especially in Humboldt's notorious predilection for "inflective" languages, especially the Indo-European ones. Nonetheless, the argument was designed to counteract the notion of a uniform development of human civilization in stages, as put forward in many eighteenth-century philosophies of world history.

For Ewald, Arabic, "at the time it stepped into big history" had already followed its developmental course "toward ever more refined formation [*Ausbildung*]," containing "forms" (*Bildungen*) of which there was "as yet no trace" in the other Semitic languages, and which nonetheless

> perfect the entire linguistic structure [*Sprachbau*]: and one would expect as much from a country [i.e. Arabia] which has remained, for long millennia, far from the noise of the wider world, in that homely [*heimatlich*] childishness and calm wherein language is not yet regarded as a tool for higher purposes and therefore can truly develop itself further, for its own sake, in its mysterious workshop.[111]

This description of Arabic operates on several levels. Not least, it serves as an example for the normative charges vested in work on language as such, especially if conducted in a position relatively on the outside of history, toward a perfection of immanent poetic potential. Ideologically, Arabic here provided a mirror image of the supposed status of German among European languages. Not accidentally, Ewald preferred this opinion at the expense of the Hebrew language, which in his view lacked the "virtues" (ibid.) of Arabic because it was, precisely in its ancient manifestation, a more historical language, more muddled in political affairs. Perhaps most importantly, language functioned as an extension of something larger, of culture in general and thus the diversification of the "inner" life of humanity.

So where Silvestre de Sacy treated Arabic grammar as one among many representatives of universal *logos* (speech and thought), Ewald treated it as a representative of insurmountably particular *Kultur* (culture) and *Bildung* (formation, education). In the context of grammatical knowledge in the nineteenth century, however, Ewald's Humboldtian position was eccentric; he found only a few direct followers. In terms of Foucault's understanding of the "episteme" of linguistics after 1800, Humboldt's view of languages as organic cultural wholes should have been central, while Silvestre de Sacy's *Grammaire Générale* approach ought to have appeared as outdated, even anachronistic. In the ambit of Semitics, however, the opposite was the case. At least in this context, then, grammatical knowledge hardly matches the categories dominant in the research discussion on Orientalism. The theoretical orientation of Ewald's grammar constituted a disadvantage.

What happened in the following generation has repeatedly been described as a synthetization of both approaches. As Fleischer claimed, Caspari wrote his grammar, first published in 1848, with the aim of combining what was good, especially on the level of detail, in Silvestre de Sacy's and Ewald's respective works.[112] In its overall approach, though, Caspari's grammar rather followed Silvestre de Sacy's understanding of the field, which was in keeping with the education of Fleischer, who had been Caspari's teacher. Only, Caspari did not preserve Silvestre de Sacy's dual account of syntax. The resulting grammar, which became, by virtue of Wright's translation and ample reworking, the most influential work on the topic—although competing attempts based on the national grammarians continued to be published[113]—was one very predominantly on European terms. The palimpsestic grammar that started with Caspari expressed the conviction of European Arabists that they could work within an entirely European framework of scholarship that did not require references to outside authorities. On the established foundations, the work of grammar was one of collaborative empirical systematization. This work brought about a distinction between the study of grammar and the study of grammatical traditions, which continued as a subfield of European Arabic studies.[114] Grammar became a descriptive rather than prescriptive discourse the meaning of which was quite simply language, as both spoken and written.

Caspari-Wright's synthetization then went along with a dismissal of the larger philosophical frameworks of both Silvestre de Sacy's and Ewald's grammars. The point of grammatical discourse was no longer to uncover, be it national culture or universal structures of thought. Rather, such discourse sought to produce a scientific system that was meaningful because it referred to a given natural language as a set of utterances and formal rules. The individual natural language became an object of knowledge that gave meaning to its description without interference of further semantic procedures such as the explication of context or theoretical speculation about universal reason. Grammar itself, therefore, became entirely hinged on referential meanings; and these meanings were to be studied "empirically," namely from the language material. The normative notions of the Arab grammarians were dismissed; language was to be studied as a reality of its own. The shift in grammatical discourse was one toward its own referentiality. So in this general sense, the Arabic grammar of the palimpsestic period, from Caspari to Brockelmann, established the precedence of semantics. It did so by following a peculiar course of development that does not conform in the least with the clichés that dominate many accounts of the history of nineteenth-century philology. This finding suggests, then, that relations between grammar and semantics developed in divergent ways, in accordance with a smaller-scale topography of fields than commonly admitted. Nonetheless, the development of Arabic grammar would point to a conceptual shift of greater generality, the manner in which grammar became a text the referent of which was a given language itself. The generality lacking in the history of grammatical knowledge would then be recovered on the side of referential semantics. Or would it?

9. Nöldeke's Semantic Notes on Grammar

Indeed, the primacy of semantic over grammatical knowledge was not a matter of orderly procedure; rather, semantics, too, was a mess, as a foray into practice indicates. In this regard, it is of particular interest to consider Theodor Nöldeke's contributions to grammar, in which the problem comes to the fore with exceptional clarity.[115] Nöldeke was one of the intellectual dominants of German Orientalism whose associates and students by and large constitute the core group of Semitist *Realphilologie* scholars discussed in the present study.[116] His *chef-d'oeuvre* was the 1860 *History of the Quran*, written in response to a prize question of the Parisian *Académie des Inscriptions et Belles-Lettres*. In the revised version prepared by his student Friedrich Schwally (1863–1919), this work until recently remained the basic account on the textual stages the compilation of which supposedly produced Islamic scripture.[117] Nöldeke, a dogged agnostic, was hardly disposed to continue in this line of work, which would have entailed pursuing a philological historicization of Islam in the manner of the tradition of Old Testament textual criticism. Instead, he followed a dizzying number of trajectories and became a living emblem of philological aggregation. First a professor of Oriental Philology in Kiel from 1864, then in Strasbourg from 1872 onward until his retirement in 1906, he taught not only Hebrew but also Arabic, Syriac, Aramaic, Persian, and (in Kiel) Sanskrit, worked on Turkish themes for a number of years, and ventured as far as the Semitic languages of Ethiopia. Marginally, he discussed matters of Phoenician, Nabataic, and Sabaic. He worked on literatures and poetries, inscriptions, histories, and chronicles, and linguistic questions. In the latter respect, his contributions to Arabic linguistics and his (anything but) "short" grammars of the Syriac and Mandaic languages stand out. These grammatical works continue to be in use. To specialists in the field, their perceptivity for problems of detail is, it appears, hard to surpass; and being hard to outdo in detail remains the chief quality that constitutes the status of so many nineteenth-century Orientalist philologists as founding fathers of their fields.

The author of imposingly solid grammars of other Semitic languages, when it came to Arabic Nöldeke adapted effortlessly to the conditions of the palimpsest. His work took the form of interlinear commentary, written into the pages of his books and scribbled and posted on sheets and scraps of *Kollektaneen*, collected fragments of information.[118] More than any palpable theoretical decision, it was this interlinearity that established the referential character of grammatical discourse. The practice of commentary presupposed a stable text, and the stabilizer of the text of grammar-as-palimpsestic-account was the language-historical reality of Classical Arabic itself. This subtle transformation in the meaning of "grammar"—within the ambit of Arabic studies—had been prepared by the sequences of palimpsestic grammars from Fleischer and Caspari to Wright. Nöldeke's supplementary work then abstracted from the specific underlying books and covered the entire "ground," *the* grammar of Arabic (i.e. Arabic as such) rather than specific scholarly grammatical descriptions of Arabic. So it was arguably this intervention that completed the theoretical stance underlying Arabist practice.

In detail, however, the most significant fissure among the divergent available grammars was hard to forget. Given the normative force grammarians had exercised, a thousand years earlier, over a language whose Quranic purity they had regarded as slipping away a mere century after the Prophet's demise, the notion that the study of grammar did not influence its purported object of knowledge was hard to maintain. The best solution to this problem was what Silvestre de Sacy had adumbrated: not forgetting the national grammarians, but treating them as almost contemporary colleagues who were as insightful and prone to error as all other participants in the running commentary of grammar. Nöledeke and others therefore worked to project the palimpsest structure backward. Grammarians from the previous millennium had been after the same goals. In his discussion of the Arabic elative, for instance, Nöldeke remarked on the traditions of the schools of Kufa and Basra:

> The Kûfan grammarians at least allow for [a specific syntactic function that fulfills the function of the elative], see Košut, Fünf Streitfragen der Baṣrenser und

Kûfenser 12, but the Baṣrans reject this as well. And yet, their master, Sîbawaih, 2, 269 provides a series of such cases, which he nonetheless explains away in curious fashion.[119]

The passage hints at an underlying projection of continuity, from Nöldeke's contemporary puzzle to the times of the eighth-century Persian-born scholar Sibawayh, the most famous of the grammarians in the Arabic tradition. This projection raises a question about the temporality, the discursive order of time deployed when discussing European Orientalist and Arab national grammar, as it were, in the same breath. This question can only be tackled through indirect clues. For instance, to his coeval friend and colleague, the Dutch Arabist Michael Jan de Goeje (1836–1909), Nöldeke remarks: "The consolation that already the old philologists did not *really* understand most of the things we also do not understand is hardly great consolation."[120] The temporality at hand was not simply that of a progressive accumulation of scholarly knowledge, or of an infinitesimal approximation of the reality of grammar. Rather there appeared to be an inertia of development that made scholars equal in failure and need for consolation. If work on grammar consisted in correcting previous scholars' mistakes, these scholars were also commemorated by the emendations. The temporality in which Sibawayh and Nöldeke partook was that of a community of commemoration. Once the palimpsestic order of grammar had been introduced, it was maintained in the service of this community. It was a requirement of this service that there were hardly any efforts to write competing analyses of the system of a given language and that the names of previous authors were held in higher esteem than those of the actual, contemporary authors. The continuing longevity of Nöldeke's own grammars is in part a consequence of this pattern of backward reading of grammatical knowledge that still, to some extent, appears to constitute a commemorative community of grammarians.

The temporality of this community was (and remains) distinct from the temporality in which the history of the Arabic language was located. Language-historical time was anonymous and approached the rhythms of natural history:

If we were able to observe the development of Semitic languages in the millennia before the advent of script [*der Schriftlosigkeit*], we would certainly see how a large number of nouns with two radicals fully or at least halfway crossed over into the possession of three radicals.[121]

Nöldeke enjoyed declaring his predilection for Darwinism.[122] Indeed, there were important discursive parallels in place. As was the case with biological species, in spite or rather precisely on account of "mutations," the history of a language ensured its conceptual self-identity (Classical Arabic was still Arabic, even if contemporary Arabs required additional education in order to acquire fluency). Only when variation crossed a threshold—when procreation or communication failed—a new species, a new language emerged. Grammar was to capture the morphological and syntactic forms, which was supposed to constitute the mutable core of what preserved the identity of a language.

Yet, contrary to what significant numbers of late-nineteenth-century linguists believed,[123] the parallelism was gravely imperfect. While Darwinian evolution was based on the interplay of mutation within the species and the selective pressure of outer conditions, the discourse of language history did not dispose of a means by which a language would have interlaced seamlessly with its outside. Rather, the connection became something of an embarrassment. This embarrassment complicated the work that semantics did for grammar:

> As concerns the cause of the [missing] feminine end syllable in ḥāmil [pregnant], ṭāliq [divorced] etc. G. Meloni, Saggio di filologia semitica 247 highlights the intention that the woman be shielded from evil demonic powers by the pretense of male gender in such situations when she is particularly weak and requiring of protection. This may be correct.[124]

The decisive portion of this passage is the short last sentence. On one hand, Nöldeke found interest in the conjecture of the Italian Orientalist Meloni (1882–1912), who tried to explain a grammatical peculiarity by reference to cultural practice. On the other hand, Nöldeke was only too aware of the lack of a criterion for judging the correctness of the assumption. The passage reflects one of the later changes he made to his oeuvre. In the 1897 publication, he had written:

> The reason for the phenomenon that for so many female adjectives there is no feminine end syllable remains entirely obscure. For words with a female sexual meaning this might have to do with the fact that the Semitic nouns that denote exclusively natural Feminina originally all appear to have lacked a feminine ending [list of a number of Hebrew examples], since such endings were probably only attached to words that were male without them.[125]

The unchanging nature of the sexes for Nöldeke provided a domain in which meaning, as an expression of collective intentionality, could potentially interfere with grammatical morphology. Nonetheless, such interference was not founded in the source material. Instead, it was merely a matter of possibility and had to be located in the sphere of an elusive prehistory to the history of the Arabic language. This prehistory was not a legitimate concern of grammar; and the historicity inevitably vested in grammar was therefore split.

Importantly, the notion that the referential meaning of expressions for "naturally" feminine things "originally" required feminine grammatical forms made clear that the autonomous historical development of these grammatical forms did not originate in unbounded randomness. Rather, certain forms of knowledge about the world were a consequence of the manner in which this world was ordered by nature. Nonetheless, there remained a hiatus between knowledge about the natural order of the world and knowledge about the development of grammatical forms. Bridging this divide was clearly the purpose of Bréal's notion that "semantics" had to do with the anonymous multitude of individual acts of the production of meaning. Still, in this manner, he mainly offered a name for the hiatus. For, he was unable to offer a more solid, less speculative method for studying intersections of meaning and grammar, precisely because of the anonymous and untraceable character of the myriad manipulations of meaning that constituted, in his view, semantics.

The prehistoric character of the shaping of grammatical forms through natural meanings also entailed a surprising openness for entirely unsystematic comparative linguistic reasoning. Foucault—as enamored with the luster of innovation as most other historians of linguistics—took note only of the seemingly systematic forms of comparison that emerged in Indo-European studies at the time of Rasmus Rask, Jacob Grimm, and Franz Bopp.[126] Yet, the practice of unsystematic comparison, which did not generate "laws" and surprising genealogies of languages, remained a prominent preoccupation. Nöldeke, for instance, remarks in a footnote:

Barth, *Nominalbildung* 2, 256, 268 etc. (see also 1, 149) suggested that the identity of participle and abstract noun forms was only seeming; instead, two entirely different modes of formation would have come to coincide phonetically. However, I think he has meanwhile given up on this opinion. The phenomenon is not essentially different from the Greek, which, especially in the more ancient prose that as yet lacked command over a sufficient number of abstracta, uses the neuter form of the participle of the adjective for expressing the abstractum, as for instance διὰ τῆς πολιτείας τὸ κρυπτόν, "because they keep secret the matters of the state," Thuc. 5, 68 … Compare Latin *lētum*, "death," passive participle of **lēre*, the simplex of *dēlēre*.[127]

In this disagreement of Nöldeke's with his student Jakob Barth (1851–1914), both authors appealed to supposed interferences of nature and grammar. Since human knowledge is primarily given through the senses, thus the underlying assumption, access to abstract objects of knowledge is less primal, and natural languages fill the need for abstraction by re-purposing previously developed forms. Although Nöldeke drew on natural languages other than Arabic for illustration, the phenomenon was not limited to actual languages. Rather, it was situated in the sphere of the given linguistic competence of human beings in general. Around the same time, Bréal's student de Saussure began to seek capturing this distinction in the concepts of *langage* (language as such) and *langue* (actual language). The cogency of the distinction is hard to contest and appears to have remained firmly established in twentieth-century linguistics. Nonetheless, the passages from Nöldeke indicate that the distinction underdetermines the mess of practice. For, the notion of natural referential meaning and the semantic prehistory of the grammatical history of languages were bound up with the notion of human language as such as well as with the peculiarities of grammatical gender in the language history of Arabic. The history of grammatical knowledge then is a plural form also in regard to the hypostatization of referential semantics it produced. It is not only the general objectification of particular natural languages as referents of grammars that they produce but also a strange entanglement with questions of reference as at once underpinning particular aspects of particular languages and language-as-such. All this confusing wealth of distinctions was mediated, in the context of Arabic, by the tacit positing of the temporality of a community of scholarly commemoration that made it possible to disregard the impact of earlier grammar-writing on the history of the language.

The quotidian practice of philological grammar did not step in to provide the measure of stringency the theorization of philology had failed to provide. The relation between the work on meaning and other fields of philological work was not one between center and periphery. Still, the specific historicity with which grammar was bound up required the domain of natural meanings as a prehistory. In this manner, grammatical knowledge contributed to the privileging of referential meaning. And yet, reference was not a unified, unproblematic reality. As part of the broader practice of philological aggregation, the "grammatical microscopy"[128] that went into the furthering of the palimpsest accommodated categorically different objects of knowledge. The peculiar temporalities and historicities in place go along with different ontological orders of the realities to which they pertain. This inevitably pluralizes reference. The form and meaning of *ḥāmil*, in Nöldeke's discourse, refer to the natural ordering of sexual difference, the mediating cultural symbolisms around this difference, the features that concern abstract adjectives in language-as-such, and the inscrutable presumptive prehistory of the Arabic language, as well as its researchable history. All of these semantic options are bound up with each other. This interdependent pluralism does away, I think, with any perspective on past philology as a hierarchically ordered practice with tidily delimited and self-sufficient sections, with centers and peripheries. It is not as a matter of centers and peripheries that semantics become key to understanding the meaning of the name of "philology." If, in the practice of nineteenth-century philology, even grammar drew on referential semantics, not just in one, but in multiple ways, this finding only raises the stakes for an inquiry into the varieties of semantic method in the history of philology. This inquiry is what the following chapters will pursue.

2

The Suicide of Naffa ' wad 'Etmân

1. A Disappearance

In the Orientalist philologies, the basic *realphilologisch* assumption that temporally or spatially distant meaning could and should be explicated by recourse to matters in the world was widespread. Meanings, however, can only be distant in time and space on condition of the givenness of a world sizable and durable enough to allow for incomprehension. For this reason, the question of what notion of world underpinned philological practice in general and referential semantics in particular is not trivial. Since the conditions of semantic access to the world were marked by a condition of distance, such access required a subject endowed with a complicated, specialized agency. There was no imagination of scholarly subjecthood attainable that would have corresponded to the conceptually minimized, unified, and purified conscious subject of knowledge of the traditional empiricist and rationalist philosophies of scientific knowledge. At a distance, semantic access to the world was a matter of situatedness, productivity, order, mess, pleasure, dejection, play, and destruction. As I will argue in the present chapter, it was even a matter of violence. In terms of its archival traces, the problem of the world of philology is in many regards complicated by deceit and deflection. In the study of Orientalism as in the broader field of colonial and imperial histories, it is inevitable that one must go "along the archival grain," as Ann Laura Stoler had it,[1] to follow the sheer surface of a history of misdirections, in order to uncover them as such.

For the Orientalist Enno Littmann the First World War was a period of personal discontent. Unfit for active service, he sought repeatedly to be of military use. The Foreign Office eventually proposed to him to stoke unrest against the Entente powers in Abyssinia, but Littmann considered that a useless endeavor.[2] Unlike other Orientalists he only obtained a subservient position in the cartographic service of the army where he was in charge of identifying and harmonizing Middle Eastern place names on maps in preparation for operations that never came to pass. The post forced Littmann, then a professor in Göttingen, to reside in Berlin, a city he resented, "an anthill in a quarry," as he wrote to his mentor Nöldeke, then emeritus professor in Strasbourg.[3] Littmann's dissatisfaction grew to such proportions that he was moved to quit the Göttingen professorship he had held since 1914 for another one in Bonn before the war was even over. Politically, he gravitated ever more to the nationalist right. Having been employed as a lecturer at Princeton 1900–4, he had leaned toward an appreciation of democratic government ten years earlier; but by the end of the war, little was left of such sentiment.[4]

How strange, then, that in this period of fury and discord, at the very end of the war, when everybody was busy lambasting the failures of the imperial government or its opposition, he would also take the time to publish an obituary of sorts for a former collaborator who had died a full nine years earlier.[5] This piece is highly unusual since, to my knowledge, it is the only commemorative article a German Orientalist of this period ever devoted to a non-European collaborator.[6] The text treats the life and personality of Naffaʿ wad ʿEtmân (ነፋዕ፡ ወድ ፡ ዕትማን),[7] an Eritrean, son of a Muslim rhapsodist, Christian convert, and former pupil of the Swedish Lutheran mission at Geleb in the Italian colony of Eritrea. Littmann had traveled in the area on a primarily linguistic mission in the fall of 1905. His doctoral thesis, published in two parts over the course of 1898–9, had concerned the verb in the Tigré language, which he had never heard spoken.[8] In 1901 the Swedish missionary Richard Sundström (1869–1919) contacted him from Eritrea about linguistic matters.[9] Four years later, endowed with American funding, Littmann finally wanted to acquire fluency during a stay with the missionaries in Geleb. During the journey, an opportunity emerged to move south into uncolonized Abyssinia as head of a German-sponsored epigraphic and archaeological expedition to the ancient city of Aksum that was to take place in the spring of 1906. Littmann eagerly accepted. During the works in Aksum, he was then appointed to succeed Nöldeke at the University of Strasbourg. Since this swift sequence of events had forced Littmann to cut short his work in Eritrea, he arranged for Naffaʿ, who had acted as his language instructor in 1905, to travel to Europe at his expense. The young Eritrean spent the years 1907–9 in Strasbourg, mostly studying and working with Littmann. In the summer of 1908, Naffaʿ also visited Sundström, then in Sweden, and on the way there met with the Ethiopicist Eugen Mittwoch (1876–1942) in Berlin.

Naffaʿ's poetical knowledge was indispensable for the large philological project Littmann had decided to pursue, a comprehensive compilation and edition of oral poetry, as well as an array of prose texts of ethnographic and folklorist significance, in the Tigré language.[10] The more than 700 poems in the collection stemmed from four different sources, the largest of which was a compilation by the Swedish mission, carried out in the main by Sundström with the aid of other missionaries and mission pupils, among whom prominently Naffaʿ.[11] Another group Littmann received from Carlo Conti Rossini (1872–1949), the Italian Ethiopicist, who had published a selection already in 1903–6,[12] but disposed of surplus material he apparently was relieved to cede to someone else. A third cluster was provided by Naffaʿ during the sojourn in Strasbourg; and finally Littmann also obtained two further poems by another Eritrean interlocutor during a subsequent sojourn in Cairo, in 1911.[13]

Naffaʿ and Littmann shared extraordinary numbers of work hours in order to bring the oral tradition into written form and explain the poems. This was no easy feat. Littmann insisted that the corpus presented as many semantic and linguistic difficulties as the far more researched Early Arabic poetry that was the hallmark of scholarly competence in Arabic studies, both in Europe and in the Middle East. He repeatedly expressed his gratitude at having had Naffaʿ at his disposal as a "living commentary" during work on the collection: "While e.g. the Arab commentators often explain to us the most obvious things, but remain silent on the difficulties, I was now able always to ask questions exactly where I required enlightenment."[14] Littmann also meticulously acknowledged Naffaʿ's contributions in many of his explanatory annotations. He added a commemorative note to the preface of volume I and made further explicit mentions of Naffaʿ's contribution in those of volumes III and IV.[15] Volume III contains a Tigré-language introduction to the poems that was written "at my request and according to my instructions" by Naffaʿ himself.[16] The first tome Littmann dedicated to Naffaʿ's memory. By the standards of philological research practice it is hardly surprising that Littmann did not go so far as to put Naffaʿ's name on the cover of any of the volumes of the collection; yet it is perfectly conceivable that he might have. Since the obituary mentions that Naffaʿ "occasionally" wrote poetry himself,[17] one might perhaps even wonder whether the collection contained works of his own or his father's making. Yet, according to Littmann, this does not appear to be the case. Instead, Naffaʿ was represented in the collection mostly as a trasnmitter of national spirit. He was reduced to the role of what in ethnography would have been called a "native informant," a term problematic not least because of its obfuscation of co-authorship, but that I will use here because it captures most clearly the unequal relationship Littmann created. In fact, he came to use a German equivalent himself.[18]

After a period of strenuous work in the winter of 1908–9, the text and commentary of the poems was basically ready to print. Littmann, always tight for money, was now unwilling to further finance Naffaʿ, who nonetheless appears to have hoped to stay in Europe. It should be added that this hope was not entirely illusory, for another Ethiopian associated with the Swedish mission, Aleqa Taye Gebre-Maryam (1861–1924), had been working as language instructor at the Seminar for Oriental Languages in Berlin since 1905. Some form of academic employment for non-Europeans was certainly conceivable in Germany at the time. In April 1909, however, Littmann put an end to any designs Naffaʿ may have entertained, by purchasing a return ticket and sending his informant on his way back to Africa. Yet, when Naffaʿ's relatives came to collect him from the steamer *Birmania* in the port of Massawa, he was not there. The Swedish missionary Karl Gustav Rodén (1860–1943) wrote to Littmann on May 5 to make inquiries. Since it appeared that Naffaʿ had not been aboard the ship after Naples, the missionaries wondered, for a few weeks, whether for some reason, e.g. illness, Naffaʿ might have interrupted the journey there.[19] To be sure, communications appear to have been somewhat confused. Naffaʿ's father and another relative penned a letter to Littmann on May 19, relating what they had been told in Massawa by someone from the ship's crew: that Naffaʿ had definitely been aboard upon departure from Naples, and that upon arrival in Catania he could not be found; that his possessions had been left in Catania, and that one assumed that he had "fallen into the sea" unnoticed.[20] While this appears conclusive, and the letter does not express any hope that Naffaʿ might still be alive, the possibility of suicide is not mentioned, although it may simply have fallen victim to some indirectness in the authors' discourse. Littmann, at any rate, mobilized Italian contacts in order to find out whether anyone in the community of East African colonials in the Naples area had come across Naffaʿ. But as a letter from the Amharic scholar and literary writer Afework Gebre Yesus (1868–1947), dated May 1909, suggests, inquiries remained fruitless.[21] On May 20, Sundström, Littmann's closest friend among the missionaries, floated the idea that Naffaʿ might have been robbed and killed during the journey and wondered about the whereabouts of the young man's money supply.[22] A last message to Littmann, which Naffaʿ had sent from aboard the steamer[23] and the text of which Littmann had apparently summarized in a letter to his Swedish friend, seemed to have been written in the expectation of a response, as Sundström pointed out; perhaps Rodén's suspicion of an illness in Naples was plausible in spite of the lack of traces?[24] But Rodén had already come around to assuming that Naffa was dead.[25]

Further inquiries were made. On June 18, the Genoa-based shipping company *Navigazione Generale Italiana* supplied Littmann with a copy of a letter by the steamer's captain, Comandante Crespi, who confirmed, with reference to the ship's journal, that Naffaʿ had disappeared during the passage from Naples to Catania, and that the only plausible explanation was suicide: Naffaʿ must have jumped overboard unseen, at nighttime. His corpse was never recovered, or, if it was, never identified.[26] The crew had noted the passenger's absence in the morning and had inventoried and committed his belongings to the authorities in Catania, along with a report about the passenger's disappearance. Eventually, these effects were returned, via Rodén, to Naffaʿ's family in Eritrea.[27] Littmann's relations with the missionaries, which were important to him for aspects of his research, especially on Tigré grammar, were not permanently damaged. By contrast, he does not appear to have entertained further relations with Naffaʿ's relatives, although the rhapsodist father, the source of a considerable portion of the poetic knowledge Littmann had been using, lived for a number of years after these events.[28]

2. Voice and Guilt

Littmann's commemorative piece is almost entirely based, not so much on the work of recollection, but on a notebook in which he jotted down remarkable dicta Naffaʿ had uttered during his Strasbourg stay.[29] Mostly, these were humorous in nature. The keeping of this notebook may have been partly motivated by Littmann's curiosity as to how an African visitor perceived Europe and its inhabitants. This would then make the document the protocol of a cultural experiment in which Naffaʿ was the object submitted to tests and manipulations. At the same time, however, the notes also reverted to a well-known genre of European literature, the humorist Oriental mirror of Europe, as epitomized by Montesquieu's *Lettres persanes*.[30] Thus, from the moment it was started the notebook tended toward publication, and publication in a narrative form that was as smooth as it was implicit. The commemorative intention was only subsequently grafted onto an already extant writing project, which led to some wavering at the beginning:

> Since [Naffaʿ's] life and pursuits, his thoughts and sayings allow us to cast a glance into the soul of a talented and proficient son of the black continent and therefore have an interest for wider circles, some memories of him shall be shared with the public here.[31]

The "wider" curiosity about an African soul was founded, of course, in the putative imperialist interest of the German public in the attitudes and views of a stratum of "talented and proficient" colonial subjects. The war, which *de facto* had already led to the loss of the colonies, makes no appearance in Littmann's narrative. The imperialist framing, the appeal to political usefulness, no matter how out of joint with the context of 1918, served to reconcile Littmann's rival writing intentions, commemoration and the humorous mirror.

This also meant, however, that the genre standards of the scholarly obituary were distorted from the very outset of the text and that the question of what Naffa' represented could always be raised to eclipse the mere commemoration of his life, character, and scholarly pursuits; so, for instance, in the passage in which Littmann discusses "the meaning" of Naffa''s name:

> In German, Naffa' means "the useful one"; it is an Arabic word that has also found its way to Abyssinia. Names like "the useful one", but also the names of odorous herbs and valuable metals, are mostly used, among the Arabs, for slaves, while they give their own children the names of wild and dangerous animals … . Since names are inherited in the families, it seems possible that Naffa' too had received his name from an ancestor who had emerged from slavery.[32]

Naffa', like all the other informants on whom Littmann relied over the years, was not anonymous. In expedition diaries, for instance, Littmann recorded the names of his interlocutors quite scrupulously. It is also not remarkable that proper names became an object of philological knowledge since they constituted evidence of linguistic change as well as of cultural practices of naming, in which Littmann generally had an interest. This was "the meaning" of Naffa''s name Littmann opted to discuss: a semantic game that was not based on reference, but drew on etymology as cultural evidence. The fact that he required only one paragraph to connect the utility etymologically associated with the name to the issue of Islamic slavery, key to all African and Middle Eastern colonialist designs since the 1880s, entails the presence of something like poetic injustice in this carefully narrated and polished text, that is to say, an injustice produced by the mere artifice of text-making. Outside of Littmann's philological digression, and outside of the context of European racism, nothing associated this particular Eritrean with the institution of slavery any more closely than it did any of the German readers the article addressed. In addition, Littmann was keenly aware of the cultural implications of the association. In 1935 he published a small generalizing book on Abyssinia. With the impending Italian invasion, which Littmann as well as his peers found reprehensible,[33] the subject matter for once had some public traction. Early on, in his discussion of the "racial" features of the Abyssinian population, he pointed out: "For a free and proud, genuine Abyssinian it is a heavy insult when one calls him a Negro or even a slave, and this insult is compensated for by a heavy fine, or even avenged by manslaughter."[34] It was evidently hard to resist the temptation of crossing such lines. If the 1935 synthesis represents Littmann's understanding of Abyssinian culture, it is also clear that philological work had a subversive dimension *vis-à-vis* the cultural norms it professed to make accessible.

The 1918 obituary generally opts to speak in lieu, to subdue the voice, of the late Naffaʿ. When dialogue is rendered, it often looks as follows:

> When I once asked Naffaʿ how old he was, he replied to me that he had been born in the year in which Azzâzî had been killed. When I further asked him when that had been he responded that it had been two years after the fire had come from the earth, and one year before the cows of the tribe had suffered the great plague. In this primitive manner people there still calculate today; such chronologies are known to us from the Old Testament and from elsewhere in antiquity … ; in the year 1907 my friend M. Bartels, then a *Privatdozent* of ophthalmology in Strasbourg, ascertained, through an examination of Naffaʿ's eyes, that the latter had to be around 25 years of age.[35]

Naffaʿ's actual responses therefore were not properly responses, but evidence. The medical confirmation of philological reasoning was a welcome resource and demonstrated the superiority of European science over archaic African inexactitude. Littmann represented Naffaʿ as imperfectly self-aware, therefore less a subject than an object of knowledge. The account is based on a principle of infantilizing, and ultimately objectifying the interlocutor—a textbook case of "imperial eyes."[36]

With another sideglance at the 1935 account, it is, however, quite clear that Littmann thought he was, in his work, doing the opposite:

> For my purposes, the work by the Englishman C. H. Walker, *The Abyssinian at Home* (London 1933), has been of particular use. In this book the Abyssinians speak for themselves, and more precisely the inhabitants of southern Abyssinia, just as in my *Publications of the Princeton Expedition to Abyssinia* the North Abyssinians get to speak for themselves [*selbst zu Worte kommen*].[37]

The obvious, the standard point of critique—directed at the Orientalist who arrogates the representation of the Orientals since the latter cannot, allegedly, represent themselves—is appropriate, yet also curtailed. Depending on context, "representation" diverges in meaning. Authorship of a scholarly text requires the textual expression of a scholarly voice. Yet, the fact that this specific type of voice is reserved for the scholar alone by no means precludes the possibility of including other non-authorial and non-scholarly voices in the text. "Representation," in this context, is not merely about political participation through proxy or the manipulation of imagination through mimesis, but about the transfer from the spoken to the written. The genre of writing therefore matters. The respective *Zuwortkommen* of the scholar and the collective of Abyssinians resulted in different textual voices. Textual voice, in authorship, was (and is) one of the prime symbolic seats of scholarly selfhood. Tremendous complications around the theoretical constitution of the "subject" notwithstanding,[38] it may be helpful to shift, in the ambit of the history of scholarship, the problem of the "representation" of voice into the domain of scholarly selfhood, as opposed to selfhood *tout court*. The social exclusion effected by the restricted ownership of scholarly voice would then be tied in an interesting fashion to the existence of scholarly text. Interesting, because the exclusion would be transparent in text, yet opaque in practice.

In addition to the scriptural, there was also an oral side to this differentiation of voices. The European scholar, if he was to acquire speaking knowledge of a language, also had to *emulate* the native voice. This required a contribution on the part of a native speaker who functioned as a gatekeeper to the collective of, say, Tigré speakers. Yet, the Orientalist claimed some degree of control over the function of gatekeeping. In this case, for instance, the native enjoyed command over his language, but not over the philological analysis thereof. Irreducibly, mastery of the language was to be shared. According to Littmann, Naffa', in his role as language instructor, first had to learn the peculiarities of "grammatical thinking," the focus on forms and inflections and the suspension of semantics:

> At first it certainly happened that, when I used the paradigm form of "thou hast killed," he responded: "I haven't killed." Or, when I pronounced the form "I have killed" in order to know whether I was pronouncing it correctly, he asked "Whom have you killed?" ... Perhaps a little humor was involved as well, a trait he displayed also on other occasions later on.[39]

The concession that Naffa' may simply have sought to lighten up the dullness of the business of grammar cannot, perhaps, occlude the oddness of the choice of example. Something darkly comical almost seems to be working its way against Littmann throughout the obituary. It is the slippage of the "I have killed"—and Naffa''s poignant question as to who might have been the victim of this killing—that points in the direction of an admission Littmann was otherwise determined to avoid. Through the rule system of the game of grammatical analysis, he claimed sole control over the application and suspension of referential semantics; it was Littmann who decided when sentences were mere grammatical forms and when they were assertions. Only, such control eluded him.

When Naffa' wrote his last message to Littmann from aboard the *Birmania*, he intimated that he was considering killing himself. Yet, perhaps Littmann, in his conceit of semantic sovereignty, did not believe that this declaration might be regarded as referential; that the "I" in this paradigm was going to be the actual Naffa'. The message was scribbled in pencil on, apparently, at least four postcards—mailed according to the postal mark on April 14 from Livorno—whose picture side showed various, similar-looking steamers from the *NGI* fleet. Only two of these cards survive in Littmann's papers. On the first, Naffa' states that his "heart" blamed him "because of my going away from you." He speaks of a transfer of money to Rodén in Geleb and pleads: "I ought to return to you and to stay with you for two months." Then follows a fragmentary sentence containing a reference to the wife of one "Sokrates Emal" I cannot place. And the second fragment continues:

> Answer me by telegraph or by yourself, quickly, after one day. I have judged this in my mind, after I have lived until now like a Christian, and I have suffered like

Josef. He said "otherwise I shall kill myself, instead of dying in suffering at the hands of those." In truth, [follows a fragmentary sentence containing expressions for "death," "stopping," and "everything."][40]

Although he was already aboard an inexorably southbound vessel, Naffaʿ still asked to return to Strasbourg, if only for two months. The expectation of a response after one day may not have been realistic; it is uncertain whether Littmann replied to this message, but if so the message presumably did not arrive before Naffaʿ's death. Since something in the middle appears to be missing, it is not clear what concrete sufferings the second portion refers to. The contemplation of suicide, however, was certainly concrete. That an oblique reference to (it appears) biblical mythology would be used to motivate and legitimize suicide is, it seems, characteristic of the subtlety and indirectness of Naffaʿ's discourse. These qualities included the tendency to rely on opposite meanings, as seen, for instance, in the first portion of the message where Naffaʿ expressed feelings of guilt about "going away" from Strasbourg. Several of the anecdotes Littmann recorded follow a similar pattern. Irony epitomizes sovereignty over semantics since it conveys meaning and its negation at once; it entails a subject that is independent and free in its power of disposition over linguistic meanings. Littmann communicated some of the content of Naffaʿ's message to Sundström, as stated; but Sundström's reaction implies that he did not receive the entire text. Later on, Littmann seems to have made mention of the message only in order to mislead his readers about its content. For Naffaʿ's deathly serious ironical voice he had no use.

Littmann's account of the circumstances of Naffaʿ's death in the obituary begins with the claim that the latter had been eager to return to Eritrea. Littmann asserts that in Strasbourg the young Abyssinian, in addition to German, studied both Italian and Arabic, the first in order to be of service to his colonized nation; and the second in order to be able to study the Quran in the original so as to be able to participate, as a Christian, in religious polemics with Muslim clerics. In his life in Strasbourg he was supposedly timid and lonely and much relied on Littmann and the landlord for company.

It was as if a plant had been transferred to an entirely alien soil. This left him longing for home, although he knew that external living conditions there would be less favorable, and although he was perhaps also worried about returning to live among compatriots who had never left their country. And it was his tragic fate never to reach home again.[41]

This "fate" was Naffaʿ's premature demise, which was only possibly self-inflicted. Littmann's account stipulates that

he vanished in an as yet unexplained manner during the crossing from Naples to Catania. Only after a long period of time, following repeated warnings and a threat to publish the case in the newspapers, did the Italian shipping company provide information based on the ship's journal. Therein, it was stated that one assumed that Naffaʿ had committed suicide. He may have lost his senses as a result of the great joy that had overcome him at the outset of the return journey; his fellow passengers seem to have treated him very badly, as his last postcard to me indicated; among the Mänsa' [Naffa''s tribe], cases of suicide are frequent. So it is possible that the poor tortured spirit departed from life deliberately. But it is also possible that he was robbed and thrown overboard by his fellow passengers.[42]

This account, then, orientalizes suicide itself, by turning Naffa''s agency in the matter into a function of national (or more precisely tribal) spirit and the general lack of sensibility to be expected in an African tribesman helplessly exposed to the whims of his passions. The imputation of a "tragic fate" is also ominous in this respect, for the fate in question is then not merely individual, but collective: If the act even was suicide, it expressed national spirit rather than personal despair. The assumed interchangeability of the national and the psychological aspects of character underlay Littmann's narrative.

"Character," it is worth adding, was a complex term that connoted, not merely individuality and the "psychology of peoples"—a complex research program in nineteenth-century Germany[43]—but also dramatic theory. The admittedly unquestioning presence of the quality of the "tragic" in Littmann's obituary indicates the pertinence of dominant understandings of drama in nineteenth-century Germany, in which the quality in question resided in an entanglement of character, fate, and guilt. In the field of the study of Greek tragedy, which provided a prime arena for dramatic theory, it was only in the revolutionary dissertation of Wilamowitz's son Tycho (1885–1914) that an understanding of the tragic as a pure function of plot structure emerged. The younger Wilamowitz, who did not live to see his work in print as he died at the outbreak of the war, had proposed discarding all interpretive work on individual psychology and motivational plausibility by showing how little such considerations had mattered to the Ancient Greek dramatists. Notions of a national psychology of Ancient Greek drama thereby also became obsolete; plot structure was formal, not cultural.[44] Yet it is clear that Littmann's use of the category of the tragic continued to be informed by a sedimented literary theory from previous decades; individual psychology still reigned supreme and still implied full permeability for national spirit. The interplay of this permeability with the notion of guilt created ambiguities—did guilt rest more with the collective or the individual?—that had an attraction of their own. It was perhaps this attraction that induced Littmann, if ever so indirectly, to insert the notion of guilt into the obituary to begin with; his intimations of the tragic would then suggest that he sought to transfer his own sense of culpability on the deceased, or his nation.

The notion that Littmann felt some degree of guilt is, I think, undeniable if one pays attention to the fraudulent detail of his narrative. Naffa''s demise was not "as yet unexplained;"[45] Naffa' had indicated his intention; a different explanation than the one available was not forthcoming; and the Italians had actually responded quite swiftly and provided far more information than had been noted in the ship's journal. It was as clear a case of suicide as it could be under the circumstances, particulary since Naffa' had also initimated his worries in conversation with several fellow-passengers and the captain. Admittedly, there remains doubt about the exact anatomy and the qualia of such a course of action, which is indeed the case for all suicides. Even the factual uncertainty of whether Naffaʿ's death might have been, regardless of all evidence to the contrary, the result of some improbable crime or accident remains in place. Yet the forensic validity of the explanation Littmann had obtained was unassailable; and his manipulations indicate that he himself was not in any doubt about what he was seeking to conceal.

Since Littmann's deceits are documented in his own papers, the archive here works both as a repository of and a protection from guilt. It would seem that he preserved at least part of the counter-evidence to his claims in order not to add the second guilt of suppressing even the evidence of his dishonesty. This motive arguably marked all the texts in which Littmann commemorated Naffaʿ. The fact that this philological collaborator was not lost to oblivion—for, he is known today only on account of what Littmann wrote about him—would then be a mere side-effect of Littmann's strategies for assuaging his own conscience.

3. Testimony of a Sea Captain

As stated, the manner of Naffaʿ's death was already clarified to the maximal possible extent by the report Littmann obtained from the offices of *NGI* a mere two months after the event. His diffidence, it is true, prompted him—as well as the Swedes—to pursue the matter further. For this purpose Littmann eventually relied on the assistance of a German banker in Milan, Otto Joel (1856–1916), whose *Banca Commerciale Italiana* had close business ties to *NGI* and who managed to obtain further documentation, including in particular a lengthy protocol of the oral testimony of Comandante Crespi, written up in response to Littmann's inquests; and the inventory of Naffaʿ's possessions made aboard the ship and committed to the legal authority (*Autorità Giudiziaria*) in Catania.[46] The captain's report contains a degree of detail that should have been sufficient to dissipate lingering doubt.

Crespi's testimony reveals that Naffaʿ presented himself to the ship's authorities with a letter of recommendation from Littmann in which it was pointed out that this unusual passenger,

> although of Abyssinian origin, nonetheless possessed, as a result of having stayed for several years in Europe, a certain level of culture and education. Even though the Comandante did not know Professor Littmann, and also because the said Naffaʿ presented himself in an actually rather pleasant manner, he [the Comandante] complied with the desire that had been expressed to him, and in fact arranged with the chief steward [*Maestro di Casa*] that he [Naffaʿ] was to receive accommodation apart, although together with the other third class passengers.

According to the report, Naffaʿ spent most of his time, during the voyage, hidden away in his cabin, or on the afterdeck. At Naples, the captain talked to him a second time when he noticed that Naffaʿ was apparently staying on board instead of visiting the city. Continuing the conversation, the Comandante learned that he [Naffa'] had been attached from an early age to a Swedish mission in Eritrea that occupied itself with the education of indigenous youth, and that from this mission he had been recruited precisely by the Professor Littmann, in order to be brought to Europe for his [Littmann's] personal use and benefit in the study of the Amharic [!] language. He [Naffa'] had stayed in Strasbourg as a dependent of Littmann for several years, and now the said professor made him return to his home country [*lo faceva rimpatriare*]. Clearly, however, Naffa' was rather worried at this prospect, not knowing how he would be able to organize his future in Massawa, given that he felt that he would be absolutely out of place [*si sentiva ormai assolutamente spostato*] and unsuited to being a farmer or a baggage porter, after the years spent in Europe in rather different circumstances. It appears that he had expressed these concerns also to the ship's doctor and another passenger, the Professor Romolo Bertuzzi, with whom Naffa' had conversed a number of times in the German language.

Certainly Naffa' was still on board upon departure from Naples. His disappearance was noted in the morning. Although the night had been densely foggy, the sea had been quiet, so it was implausible that the young man had gone overboard accidentally on account of the swell. The Catanian authorities, after collecting testimony from the captain, the doctor, and four other crewmen, had also retained Littmann's letter of recommendation, for which reason Crespi, and, as he stressed once more, "because he did not know the Professor Littmann personally," had abstained from writing to Strasbourg himself.

The picture that emerges from this testimony suggests that a few casual and, it seems, moderately friendly conversations aboard the *Birmania* had revealed more about Naffa''s thoughts and worries than Littmann ever acknowledged. In light of the postcard message and Crespi's testimony, Littmann's claim in the obituary that Naffa' was looking forward to his return, and that he possibly "lost his senses" as a result of excessive joy, does not then appear just psychologically outlandish, but rather deliberately misleading. Clearly, Naffa' had been at a loss regarding his future life and livelihood in Eritrea and was anything but keen to return. It is also remarkable that he seems to have assumed that he would have had to make a living for himself without recourse to the Swedish mission. The alleged hopes of which Littmann writes in the obituary, that his former student would be enabled, through his European education, to contribute to the spread of Lutheranism in Eritrea, did not, it seems, preoccupy Naffa' during the last days of his life. In the obituary, Littmann mentions that Naffa', once his knowledge of German had become sufficient, had attended evangelical service regularly; but also, that one of his few enjoyments had been to go to the pub with his landlord afterwards.[47] Such habits were hardly condoned at the Swedish mission; it seems probable that the sojourn in Strasbourg had offered relief from a more narrowly religious life in Eritrea.

In his testimony, Crespi displays a curious tendency to distance himself from Littmann. The captain emphasizes twice that he does not personally know the German professor in question. In the particularly tangled sentence quoted previously, he sets store by pointing out that it was Naffa''s own *piuttosto simpatico* comportment rather than Littmann's letter that persuaded him, Crespi, to make special arrangements for the passenger aboard. In the captain's account of what Naffa' had purportedly told him in Naples, Littmann's course of action seems morally dubious, exploitative, egotistic, and unconcerned with Naffa''s future well-being. The unspoken question as to just what kind of person *il Professore Littmann a Strasburgo* was, a doubt as to the moral integrity of his character, looms large in the report. The captain's explicitly stated decision not to write to Littmann about the incident directly confirms the impression that he wanted nothing to do with this German academic.

The letter of recommendation that so irritated Crespi might, however, also be seen as a sign of Littmann's compliance with Abyssinian custom. 'Etmân's letter from May 19 expressed the worry that Littmann had sent Naffa' on his way negligently, without "entrusting" him properly into someone else's care.[48] The formalization of accompaniment in Ethiopia was generally a custom of which Littmann was aware and which he described repeatedly in connection with his expedition to Aksum.[49] This custom had far-reaching implications. 'Etmân in his letter underlined that Naffa', by dint of his sojourn in Strasbourg, had become Littmann's "son," and he therefore offered his condolences for Littmann's loss. It is uncertain whether the latter had understood these implications of his hosting of Naffa' fully; if he did, he certainly rejected them since he consistently referred to Naffa' as a servant and assistant and never let on that their relationship could have been regarded as familial. Not unlike Naffa''s last message, 'Etmân's letter is characterized by an indirect, *uneigentlich* discourse that qualifies as a form of serious irony and was presumably lost on Littmann. Ultimately, Naffa''s last journey was shrouded in several layers of cultural opacity in which Crespi's testimony also became caught up. It does not seem to have occurred to the captain that some culpability might actually lie with the *Birmania* crew into whose care Littmann had "entrusted" Naffa' through his letter.

For Littmann, the documents were easy to stow away; but the fact that he did not make any mention of them later on rather suggests that Crespi's, and perhaps even 'Etmân's, doubts about his, Littmann's, character registered with their addressee. The blame the testimony and the letter implied had the potential of tarnishing Littmann's honor and reputation. It was potentially something that colleagues could say about him with disapproval—that he had driven his informant into suicide—and he wanted to prevent this kind of judgment. In this, he was rather successful. Even during Naffa''s stay in Strasbourg, Littmann had already been somewhat careful about mentioning, in correspondence, the presence of the Eritrean. He was even apprehensive about mentioning Naffa''s name and tended to refer to him as "my Tigré-man" or "my Abyssinian."[50] Select friends and colleagues learnt about the suicide, but apparently mostly through oral conversation. Littmann controlled knowledge about everything involved. By November 1909, his colleague Carl Heinrich Becker (1876–1933), for instance, had only heard "vague rumors ... about the misfortune of your Ethiopian."[51] Only once during Naffa''s stay, as far as I have been able to see, did Littmann let down his guard, when he, in March 1909, complained bitterly about Naffa''s financial demands in a letter to his friend Friedrich Veit (1871–1913), a Tübingen-based Persianist.[52] Conflict with Naffa' at this time must have been far more acute than Littmann later on admitted.

4. Pleasure and Dejection Shared

Naffa''s effects were listed as follows:

> 1 overcoat, 2 blankets, 4 shirts, 1 towel, 1 shirt-front, 4 pairs of underpants, 2 aprons (one white, one colored), two pairs of trousers, two jackets, two vests, 1 pair of linen shoes, 5 handkerchiefs, 1 felt hat, 1 white hat, 1 bag containing 2 razors, soap, 2 medals, 1 pair of scissors, 2 collars, 1 pair of suspenders, 2 ties, 1 notebook containing various manuscripts, 8 different books, 1 razor strop, 1 tin bowl, 1 small mirror, 1 tin cup containing sweets, 1 notebook, 1 suitcase.

A visual impression of the listed or similar articles of clothing can be glimpsed from an amateur portrait of Naffa' with the children of his host family in Strasbourg (Figure 1). Nothing in the austere inventory indicates that these were the possessions of someone from Eritrea. Quite literally, all of Naffa' possessions were European in origin. The absence of money or any other valuables (I am uncertain what the *2 medaglie* are) may indeed appear suspicious; but it is conceivable that Naffa' was simply carrying his valuables on his person when he threw himself into the sea. His last message also mentions that money for his use had been transferred directly to Rodén.[53] Since Littmann had quarreled with him over funding that winter it does

Figure 1. Naffa' in Strasbourg seated center, "with the children of the landlady" (dorsal mark by Elsa Littmann); undated, *c.* 1909, photographer unknown. NL Littmann, K. 97, folder *Kollegen, Freunde 3.*

not seem, anyway, that Naffaʿ would have been in possession of a noteworthy sum in compensation for his services to philological scholarship. It is regrettable that the inventory does not give the books' titles; but it is clear that Naffaʿ, when packing his belongings, set greater store by immaterial goods and his attachment to, and hopes of continuing in, scholarship than by the rather minimal set of articles of clothing and personal grooming he possessed. The only hint to personal pleasure beyond reading is the cup of unspecified *dolci*.

The second portion of Littmann's obituary, by contrast, is dominated by the theme of pleasure. After concluding the sad task of accounting for Naffaʿ's premature death, Littmann provides a paragraph of summary appraisal and then changes gears abruptly:

> His death is a great loss for science. He had the ability to see what mattered in researching his own language; he also had still intended to collect and note down a great number of things for me. Had he remained alive, he could have contributed much to our knowledge of his people and his home country.
>
> His sense of humor and his quick perceptiveness were frequently revealed during the time he spent in Germany.
>
> In November 1907 I told him that Sirius was 500,000 times as far from Earth as the sun, and the sun, if it were in Sirius' place, would look like the dead star of the "Seven" (i.e. the middle star of Ursa Major, which is a star of the third magnitude). Naffaʿ remarked: "That has got to be very far." I continued: "If you wanted to walk there you would have to travel 1,000 million years." Naffaʿ: "Then I would grow old along the way!"[54]

In this mood, the text continues for several pages. The anecdotes Littmann renders here are in fact the contents of his Strasbourg notebook, in the sequence in which he had originally penned them. He copied this material into the obituary verbatim and added only a few tidbits of ethnological information (some of which he reused, without mentioning Naffaʿ's name, in the 1935 *Abessinien*).[55] Here is a comical African with an accent in full light: Naffaʿ telling off the landlady in a humorous fashion, Naffaʿ jesting about the grammatical gender of birds and the talkativeness of women, and so on. The text eventually closes with a longer anecdote about religious polemics in Abyssinia that Naffaʿ had related to Littmann, and which once more serves to illustrate the purposeful and deliberate nature of the young man's return.[56] This second portion of the obituary has a distinctly convivial tone. It conjures up sweetened memories of shared life in Strasbourg. The anecdotes are only of the vaguest philological significance; they no longer constitute much of a scholarly use of Naffaʿ's knowledge. The notebook moreover contains a structural sketch of the first portion of the obituary, with Naffaʿ's approximate life dates, and the concluding note "Great loss," as if Littmann had to remind himself of the aim of his commemorative narrative. And indeed he had to, for it was precisely in the logic of Naffaʿ's usefulness to "science" that it was uncertain why the loss was so great. Obviously, Naffaʿ had yielded the main portion of what Littmann had hoped to obtain from him. The "loss" was one that was intimate; that is to say, it was connected to his own sense of self and to the attachments to others that defined it. The shift, in the obituary, to the humorous matters of the second part is designed to restore, through the emphasis on the convivial aspects of Littmann's attachment to Naffaʿ, the integrity of this sense of self.

In this period, for Littmann, selfhood was frequently burdensome. In 1914 he took the opportunity to quit Strasbourg when he was offered the succession of Julius Wellhausen in Göttingen. The preceding years had been marked by conflict with other faculty members and bouts of dejection. He had developed a relatively close friendship at this time with the short-lived Persian scholar Veit in nearby Tübingen. Veit, due to illness and various other travails, was similarly dejected. Repeatedly in his letters, Littmann writes of his own state of mind in order to console and encourage his friend. Attempting to cheer Veit up was Littmann's way of dealing with his own low spirits; for "gaiety [*Fröhlichkeit*] is the essence [*Wesen*] of life, and the only way of coping with the sorrow [*Leid*] of existing."[57] In another letter, Veit was warned that he should prepare for Littmann's visit by drinking a glass of schnapps beforehand in order to brace himself for the latter's jokes.[58] The *fröhliche Wissenschaft* pursued here drew on basic physical delights in order to fight the *Schwermut*, the melancholia that had famously been the antagonist of much of Nietzsche's oeuvre. Already in his early work on tragedy, Nietzsche had insisted that the comical was a reaction to the absurdity of existence, and the tragic, to its suffering. To be sure, Littmann had read Nietzsche, although somehow he never commented much on what texts he had perused, and to what effect. He mentions, in a letter to Georg Jacob, one of his teachers, that Nietzsche had appeared in one of his dreams and played a tune on the piano for him. The dream had been so vivid and clear that Littmann "had retained the melody in my head for quite some time, but then forgot it."[59] This episode signals, indirectly, that the complex of dejection was not merely an emotional tangle, but a key portion of an intellectual and discursive infrastructure that served to process—to recognize and contain—the absurdity and the suffering of selfhood.

It is the articles of ambition and pleasure listed in the inventory of Naffa''s possessions, the books and the sweets, that indicate his integration into this infrastructure. This integration was, it seems to me, mimetic in character. Presumably, after two years in Strasbourg, Naffa' was inadvertently emulating the patterns of pleasure and dejection in Littmann's life; and conversely, Littmann's dejection may also have fed on Naffa''s, even if there were other factors involved, such as two rejected marriage proposals,[60] and Littmann's social sphere was wider than Naffa''s. If Jonathan Lamb, in his study of selfhood in South Seas exploration, is correct, encounters across cultural divides destabilized selves on all sides of the situation. Such destabilization was a well-established literary trope as well as a cultural practice in which seemingly stable contractual forms of socialization and of the exchange of goods were voided.[61] Arguably, this pattern was not by necessity limited to the vast spaces of the Pacific Ocean, which Lamb discusses, but also extended into the small-scale and decidedly post-romantic environment of encounter in which Littmann struck a bargain with Naffa' to exchange poetry for something else that did not remain stable. Littmann's guilt might also be understood as a debt incurred in a rigged exchange of gifts. The ability of philology to posit the objects of this exchange and to generate its own terms of justice and injustice signal the extent of the claim to ontological productivity inherent in its practice.

In the documents in Littmann's archives that relate to Naffa''s years in Strasbourg, a peculiar structure of anticipation can be discerned. The little notebook with Naffa''s dicta, for instance, anticipates a moment when Naffa' will be a distant memory to Littmann, when there will be no spatial proximity, when large stretches of their lives will have passed without renewed contact. The poetry will long have been separated from Naffaʿ's recitations and explanations and transferred into the secure, stable ownership of the Tigré nation, if under the tutelage of German philology. The writing work with which the encounter was shot through—and which constituted it as a specifically *philological* encounter[62]—strove for the restoration of stability upon exit from a destabilizing situation. The extent to which Naffaʿ's suicide corresponded to this requirement is remarkable. Littmann's notebook, already a document of anticipated recollection, could be, and was, seamlessly transformed into a draft (yet another anticipation) of the obituary article.

While it is perhaps not morally fair to press this point, it nonetheless appears that in a sense, namely on the level of philological writing, Littmann transferred death to Naffaʿ; that the latter, among other things, also emulated the former's own dejection; that Naffaʿ realized what had been written for him on the wall, as in the Belshazzar poem by Heine, which Littmann jestingly misquoted to Veit, substituting Babylon with Strasbourg.[63] It is a legitimate, perhaps necessary, if unanswerable, question, whether Naffaʿ's suicide was a form of what Homi Bhabha has labeled "mimicry" in the colonial (or quasi-colonial) situation; that is to say, a partial and parodistic emulation, a form of camouflage, ultimately menacing, that upset and upended a claim to authority in the assertion of distinction.[64] Littmann's decision to send Naffaʿ back to Eritrea was as clear an articulation of difference, racial and intellectual, as one could imagine. In his letters to Veit, by contrast, Littmann articulated equality, when, relying on contemporary eugenic vocabulary, he pointed out that he and Veit alike should be "looking into the future with courage: in this way we show that we are capable of life [*lebensfähig*], and therefore have a right to live [*lebensberechtigt*]."[65] Equality, as manifest in the exchange of letters, was then the antidote to the destabilization of self Littmann had recognized as a matter of existential legitimacy. When this legitimacy was lost, in a situation where the participants of communication were unequal and all alone in their inability to live, suicide could be a legitimate solution. It was perhaps not by accident that this vocabulary proliferated in Littmann's discourse after Naffaʿ's demise. And of course, here, too, the fates of individuals and the fates of nations could be translated into each other. Clearly, multiple sign relations held between the event of Naffaʿ's suicide and the philological practice that preceded and then surrounded it. These relations grant access to the manner in which philology related to the world as the precondition of meaning; and in which it altered, intruded into, and even produced events in this world as a precondition of its own self-explication. For this reason, it is necessary to examine the philological project at hand in some more detail.

5. The Abyssinian Laocoön

The Tigré poetry Littmann and Naffaʿ assembled forms a peculiar corpus. Many of the poems are commemorative, for instance of those who died in battle, or of settlements, or regions, that were destroyed or abandoned. They often sing the praise of the powerful but also report their downfall. War and revenge are frequent topics. Tone and content are often plaintive. The poems, especially when they address the poet's condition, also speak of guilt, illness, despair, or poverty. In general, the songs are replete with proper names and constantly refer to the features, conditions, and doings of very concrete individuals. In order to make sense of the referents, one needed to know something about the actual people concerned. For instance, one needed to know that Masmar wad ʿAddāla had a son Teġār, who was the addressee of "A Song He Sang About Himself," and that this son had a crippled arm that was alluded to in the concluding distich (10): "But you are crippled:/Else I would call on you for every chore."[66] The poets, too, and their next of kin, were in this manner named. Indeed, for the vast majority of the songs, authorship was specified and part of the tradition. The commentary needed to be "living" simply because the meaning of this poetry was irreducibly referential and often tied to concrete historical circumstances. When Naffaʿ explained that he was born in the year in which ʿAzzāzi was killed he alluded to events that, sure enough, were preserved in a poem he knew, by Yiddatīt wad Taklēs, entitled: "The Son of His Brother Was Killed in a Quarrel; and Since He Was Unable to Conduct Blood Revenge, He Sang This Song, Shaming Himself."[67] It does not appear exaggerated to suggest that Littmann, instead of being confronted with a naïve system of dating that required ophthalmological confirmation (as he claimed in the obituary), had actually received an answer that was contiguous with an elaborate system of poetic references. And this system was hardly the same as encountered "in the Old Testament or elsewhere in antiquity,"[68] as Littmann claimed in the obituary.

To be sure, he did go a long way toward understanding this system. *PEA*, in spite of the inherent problems of transferring an oral tradition into written and printed text, remains a remarkable monument of philological scholarship and a chief source of information for Tigré literary history. Littmann's ethnographic work also surpassed by far what other scholars of Semitic languages had until then accomplished in the area. For instance, as he pointed out in his preliminary expedition report, his study of the naming system of the Tigré language was indispensable for his reading of the poems.[69] Through the ethnological studies accounted for in the first two volumes of *PEA*, Littmann went far beyond Conti Rossini, who in his translations of Tigré poetry had simply dropped all the names he possibly could (especially the author names), left the others unexplained, and grouped the poems according to themes. If one casts a merely casual glance at the dense and difficult material, it becomes immediately clear why the Italian scholar was content to be rid of the surplus of poems he had collected; and equally, why the missionaries were not in a position to fully work out the complex meanings, either. The knowledge rendered in Littmann's annotations is indeed to an overwhelming extent Naffaʿʾs and could not have come from any other source, for it had the character of familial and regional lore and relied, not on a single one, but on two or three generations of lived life in the region. For this reason, the poems also fail to share key features of what was usually called folk poetry, or song, in European scholarship: The authors were not anonymous; the esprit was not that of an amorphous national collectivity extended over a vast territory of time, but of small communities in a rather recent period. The use of the poetry, it seems, was not directed primarily at the rehearsal of eternal meanings, but gave an aesthetic form to the social memory of individuals. While perhaps a degree of formal stability over time was to be expected of the overall genre (though even this notion was hard to substantiate, given the lack of earlier traditions), the intelligibility of the poems eroded with the social memory in question, and presumably the texts fell out of use and were replaced with different ones rather constantly, in spite of the presence of a "rhapsodist" culture that functioned as a preserve of the oral texts. In short, the poetry was *historical* in kind and function. Historicization—i.e. inclusion into a particular semiotic nexus of past objects, actors, events, structures, and so on—appears to have been carried out primarily by way of inclusion of events and personalities into the corpus of poetic and musical memory. This also means that Naffaʿ's role as a quasi-rhapsodist and (occasional) poet was simultaneously that of a historian.

Yet, to a considerable extent, Littmann's philological edition depletes the corpus of its historical meaning. There are two levels of structure imposed on the material: tribal affiliation (although it is not quite clarified what exactly constitutes a tribe) and author names. The logic of an event-based structure—that connected poems through protagonists and their deeds and fates and made it possible that a poem about, say, one particular ruler could be responded to by another one about the same person or events connected to his tenure—was eclipsed by the edition. Similarly, possibilities of music-based structure—for instance by identity and difference of tune or rhythm—were not explored in Littmann's and Naffaʿ's work, which remained exclusively linguistic and textual. Instead, Littmann's expectation, as commentator as well as translator, was to find, not even entire poems, but rather passages, individual distichs (the poems were arranged in couplets) that displayed affinity to a European corpus. In Masmar's aforementioned poem about himself, for instance, two distichs reminded Littmann of a couplet of Goethe's, which he rendered in the commentary.

Masmar states (6f.) "But so we continue to work the field/with ploughs and drawbars on the yoke./For the body requires feeding/As the hero does dying and killing."[70] Littmann explains:

> Distich 6: This is his chagrin and the reproach he addresses to himself, that he calmly continues ploughing and consuming food in spite of his grief; one thinks automatically [*unwillkürlich*] of Goethe's "Nowhere can I forget her/and yet I calmly eat" [*Nirgends kann ich sie vergessen,/und doch kann ich ruhig essen*], even though here the "bliss of distance" is described.

Indeed then, it occurs to Littmann that the connotation of Goethe's *Glück der Entfernung* is a bit far-fetched.[71] It is also remarkable that he leaves the seventh distich unannotated, although it clearly pertains to the question of defining the precise target of Masmar's complaint (one might be tempted to think: placement in an unchanging order of things that requires the body to be nourished as much as it demands warfare of the hero). It is clear that these lines appealed to Littmann because, especially if viewed in isolation, they were less concerned with the rather barren environment and the peasant and warrior existences of poetic cowherds in the hinterland of Geleb in Eritrea than the remainder of the poem. Therefore, the distich could be read as drawing on a European model of poetic meaning: eternal and universal moral-psychological truths instead of specific references to individuals through tangles of proper names. The procedure of philological commentary, which highlighted one distich after another, promoted this perspective on the texts; arguably, Littmann's attention never quite settled on the poems as complete pieces, but only on lines and passages.

On the Orientalist side, the backdrop to Littmann's reading of the Tigré poems was provided especially by Early Arabic, pre-Islamic poetry. He frequently pointed out that, as the Arab poets reached the peak of their sublimity in the poetic rendering of individual camels, for the Eritreans something quite similar was the case with respect to cattle. In order to grapple with the lexical difficulties of the translation, he partly relied on a Low German dialect vocabulary he suggested he had picked up as a child on his grandparents' farm in the environs of Oldenburg (Grand-Duchy).[72] Precision in the observation of nature was a feature Littmann had learned to appreciate from the philological works of Georg Jacob who had based his 1897 standard work *Early Arabic Bedouin Life* above all on the pre-Islamic poets' perceptiveness for the natural world (Littmann had collaborated on this work as a student).[73] For Jacob, the underlying poetics far outdid what he viewed as the artificial, abstract, and formalist humanism of Ancient Greek literature. Littmann, more irenic in temperament, saw in the heightened sensibility to the linguistic representation of animal life an equivalent to the plastic sensibility for the human body in classical sculpture.

In a letter to Nöldeke, about the reading of pre-Islamic poetry, he explained:

As Bedouins, the Arabs were unable to develop visual arts; these require a sedentary way of life. Therefore, poetry had to stand in for painting and sculpture. This makes things much more understandable. An Arab, who was *listening* to an anatomically correct description of a camel, underwent—mutatis mutandis—the same aesthetic sensation we have when *seeing* a statue. At some point, I would love to expand on all this and write an "Arab and Abyssinian Laocoön", but I will probably never get around to it.[74]

This half-ironical plan of updating Lessing's discussion—one of the chief contributions to the aesthetic theory of eighteenth-century German classicism—of the Vatican sculpture of Laocoön and his sons[75] signals that Littmann's perception of matters was far more informed by literary and philosophical tradition than one might assume at first glance. Lessing's discussion was a contribution to the longstanding tradition of *paragone*, the competitive discussion of the relative virtues, merits, and advantages of different forms of art. Littmann's fleeting remarks indicate that his interest aligned with Lessing's with regard to the specific comparison of poetry on the one hand and the visual arts on the other; and with regard to the problem of the divergence of the possible means of expression that were dictated by the different material environments of these forms of art. The environments in question not only consisted of the means of expression deployed; but also of the "sensations" and, by implication, of the objects represented; and, moreover, of the "ways of life," the totality of cultural habits in which artistic exertion formed only a part. The carefully sculpted anatomy of Laocoön and the carefully poeticized anatomy of a camel were equivalent, though not equal. An aesthetic theory on the basis of the plurality and foundational inequality of forms staked a non-normative claim to the existence of an underlying reality that exerted an unshakeable control over sensory perception and its artistic emulation. It was this reality that generated the distinctions of form. In addition, indirectly, it subverted the claim to the autonomy of individual artistic expression over any given material environment, a claim that had been central to aesthetic theory since the period of romanticism and which embodied more than any other aesthetic theorem the surpassing of the arts of the ancients on the part of modernism.[76] As predicted, Littmann never wrote the work in question, though the central idea he mentioned to Nöldeke resurfaced occasionally.[77] The attraction of the reference to *Laocoön* was partly Lessing's irenicism in the discussion of the unique features of the different forms of art. The way in which European philology was to make legible foreign poetries was supposedly peaceable and, at least on the surface, avoided inimical *Auseinandersetzung*.

Yet it was not only in the realm of aesthetic theory that specific European, or German, traditions shaped Littmann's reading of the Tigré corpus; in addition, it was also the genre tradition of pastoral and the idyllic that informed his translations.[78] This tradition was entirely able to accommodate both the melancholic tone in much of the Tigré collection and the references to concrete features of landscape and even concrete pieces of cattle that marked some (though far from all) of the songs. What the genre of the pastoral, however, in its modern understanding, was unable to accommodate was the wealth of historical connotations and the bent of the Tigré corpus toward record-keeping for a complex, if obscure, world of social relations. Genre entails that the diegesis of a pattern of narration draws on a particular set of ontological resources; and in the case of pastoral, historicity was decidedly not among these resources. If Littmann's aesthetic theory was built on an irenicism that aimed to include the different modes in which different forms of art accessed an ultimately unified reality, his recourse to genre in the actual explication of poetic meanings undermined this aim. While in the case at hand pastoral acted as a stabilizing factor in the interpretation of the poems, this stabilization then required suppressing the historical dimension of the meaning of the texts, and it left no place for the poet, nor the rhapsodist, as historians. Naffa´'s readiness to submit his own poetic knowledge to European philology therefore entailed an act of profound self-abnegation that arguably went further than mere "mimicry." It seems quite plausible that he felt this abnegation was part of an exchange in which he would be able, in return, to become a philologist in the European mold. Yet Littmann denied him this transformation. The poetry could become, by way of philology, literature; but the rhapsodist's son could not become a philologist.

Legibility and translatability have been prime concerns of postcolonial analysis. The fortunes of the semantics of the sign-systems encountered across cultural distances were deeply formative for cultural practice in modern history generally. Marie-Louise Pratt, leaning on the notion of a "contact language" as a linguistic hybrid emerging in areas of cultural overlap, proposed the concept of "contact zone" for the spaces of encounter and improvised hybridization that marked colonial histories.[79] Homi Bhabha contributed a complex theoretical account in order to lay open further layers in the production of fragmented subjects and symbolic orders in the locations of encounter in question.[80] In particular, drawing on Lacanian psychoanalysis, Bhabha emphasized a structure of fetishization in the production of stereotypes and articulations of differences in the stringing together of substitutable signifiers that constituted the "othering" of the colonial situation.[81] Hybridization was then productive of objects in combination with a manipulation, an equivocation, of signs. Overall, this is a plural, but streamlined, coordinated semantic operation that generates, through the game of the substitution of signs, a nexus of concepts, and thereby classes of objects, and embodied individuals within these classes. This approach would entail according the peculiarities of encounter primacy over the ontological productivity, and thereby the semantic preferences, of Orientalism.

The history of philology, though, in at least a number of significant respects, does not quite appear to coincide with this theoretical analysis of hybridization. Following the inexorable pull of aggregation, philological objectification rather resulted in an incoherent scattering of signs than in the cohesion arguably required for fetishization. For instance, the orientation of the field toward the ancient world was so heightened that entire cohorts of Orientalists underwent extensive situations of colonial encounter without integrating the actual people encountered, and stereotyped as others, with those distant dead they had opted to study and invested with different meanings. In a similar vein, the manner in which Littmann objectified Naffa' differed from the manner in which the actual poetry was objectified in philological work. Littmann's use of Naffa' was transient. The poetry, by contrast, was eternalized. It was inserted into the world—the ontological order—of world literature in which the rhapsodist-son informant did not actually figure. Naffa''s suicide constituted an additional, even redundant, sign for the point at which philological knowledge-production simply renounced objectifying the colonial-Oriental subject. In a sense, the world that was the object of philological knowledge was built on a tacit decision to depart from the mode of fetishizing objectification that was prominent in the sphere of actual colonialism. This departure marks the epistemological rupture, once more with Bachelard's term for the willing departure of scientific knowledge from other types of knowledge, that was, in spite of everything, to distinguish Orientalist philology from humdrum colonialist knowledge. The rupture, Bachelard was careful to point out, was active and ongoing.[82] It thereby generated a present temporality of its own, which was not identical to that of the zone of colonial encounter.

In Littmann's edition of the Tigré poems, it was clear to all concerned that what one might call the philologization of the corpus entailed incurring certain losses of meaning. If his transfer, even appropriation, of the corpus through philology created a cultural hybrid, this hybrid was highly controlled, hardly spontaneous, and entirely asymmetrical. For, Tigré poetry did not change anything in the patterns of world literature, the genre of pastoral, German aesthetic theory, and anthropological assumptions about rhapsodic culture, which were the elements that chiefly informed the transfer of the poems into script. By contrast, this transfer process had a profound effect on the status of personhood accorded to Naffa'. Clearly, it is speculative to claim that his suicide also took place in the service of the stability of the edition; and that it thereby constituted a way of retaining his usefulness for philology, of remaining what he had never been, a philologist; and of avoiding becoming what he had never been, say, a native baggage porter in an Italian colonial port.

6. Reading Anonymity into the Tigré Poems

Among contemporary philologists, the collection found only one serious reader, namely Nöldeke, who had been constantly present in Strasbourg and also met Naffaʿ on several occasions. In 1918 Nöldeke published a lengthy review essay in order to report on his reading experience, which had been daunting:

> After I had found my way back into this strange … language by renewed reading of the entire prose portion [i.e. *PEA* I and II; Nöldeke's annotation: "Some material I have read repeatedly."] and several other Tigré pieces, I went through all the songs word by word under constant use of the translation and the annotations. This was very time-consuming … and I would have had to go through everything three or four times in order to arrive at a point at which I would have been able to read the whole more or less smoothly, without constant recourse to the translation. So for the purpose of generating a living understanding of the nature of the single pieces as well as of this poetry as a whole, I made do simply with re-reading, afterwards, the entire translation, but under frequent use of the [original] text.[83]

Throughout his review, he emphasized the many difficulties the material presented, including also that of grasping the poems as wholes. The elusiveness of their form was in part the result of linguistic challenges that sabotaged continuous perusal, but in part also due to the "abrupt" changes of topic, "without even the pretended transitions we find in Early Arabic poetry."[84] In a hierarchy of national poetries, the Tigré poems were therefore inferior to the Arabic, "let alone the Old-Hebrew," corpora, but not without "force and beauty"; "and if Herder, who granted us access to the enjoyment of simple poetry, had known them, he would certainly have included specimens in his 'Voices of the Peoples.'"[85] Supposedly then, now that it was put in writing and translated, the Tigré corpus had gained a place of its own within the hierarchy of world literature.[86] This place was, however, so marginal that the world literary career of the poems remained imaginary. A few years later, Carl Heinrich Becker praised Littmann for having "given an entire nation its literature."[87] Since this also implied that in actuality the Tigré corpus was entirely irrelevant to the rest of the "world," the praise contained a sting Littmann quite certainly felt. This literature did not make it onto the world stage, nor was it world-making in any other sense. The only thing at stake was an unmaking of the specific worldliness, the specific way of interacting with reality, the corpus contained.

This unmaking was not merely the result of philological blundering into a domain of "untranslatability."[88] Rather, it was a matter of conscious decisions about what was to be omitted from the translation. More clearly than Littmann, Nöldeke understood the historical character of the poems.[89] Littmann had thought to use the material for a comparative study of Semitic poetries; he was disappointed that "everybody" found the poems boring and Nöldeke was their only serious reader: "And yet the Hebrews, 3,000 years ago, must have had a poetry very similar to that of those tribes; and here one can actually demonstrate matters on the living object. Of course one has to disregard names and everything that is temporally and spatially particular."[90] To Nöldeke, by contrast, the particulars gave reason for pause. He did not dismiss them so easily, but pointed out that "we," i.e. the European readers of the publication, "do not know the particular circumstances of which the poems treat." Moreover, he also noted that not even Naffaʿ had always known "all persons named, all circumstances referred to, in the poems."[91] So the condition of being occasionally lost in references also applied to native audiences, but was not apparently an obstacle to reception. Nöldeke was aware that the poems were all recent, that, more or less imperfectly, they served to transmit knowledge about past personages and events, and therefore were part of a system of historicization, a feature Conti Rossini had also stressed with reference to the poems he had published that treated the Italian invasion.[92] Nöldeke also noted that none of the poems could be regarded as older than the middle of the nineteenth century, and most were more recent. The system of historicization at hand entailed that the knowledge contained in the poetic corpus was as fleeting as the corpus itself.

Subtly, Nöldeke went on to determine the precise difference between the European and the Tigré system of historicization. He speculated that no matter if

> occasionally modern expressions and modern thoughts appear: the entire manner [*Art*] is archaic [*altertümlich*], and the poems sung in the area many generations ago were certainly similar in nature to the ones of which we dispose today. The influence of European rule [footnote: prepared for by Egyptian rule], which diminishes the old robbery and murder, but also diminishes the naivety and causes quite a few novel damages, and on the other hand Islam, which appears to be expanding slowly somewhat, will presumably soon finish off the old poetic art. For it is, as stated, not improbable that the Tigré language itself will eventually be superseded by Arabic.[93]

This poetry, then, along with its very language, was subjected to a history it could not fully grasp itself. As already expressed by Schiller's theorization of this category—which was decisive for its German uses—the naïve was an anomaly in the modern epoch. Nöldeke's casual attribution departed from Schiller's insistence that the naïve had emerged "only among the Greeks."[94] He even criticized Littmann for "smoothening"[95] the poems in translation and thus reducing their naïveté. As elsewhere in philology, the category gave rise to an implicit structure of comparison and competition at work. Schiller himself had contrasted Greek antiquity with Ossian (that the latter corpus was not genuine had not yet been common knowledge in German literary circles). Orientalism, with its constant uncovering of further poetic traditions, amplified this structure. Thanks to Littmann's exploration of Tigré literature, by 1916 one could compare the Greeks with the Mänsaʿ. Nöldeke's assessment echoes Schiller's remark about Ossian, whose naivety was supposedly thwarted by his sense of the "decline of humankind" (*Verfall der Menschheit*) and the resulting "elegiac tone."[96] Something similar befell the naivety of the Tigré poets, some of whom were aware, according to Nöldeke, that their art form would not last: "Some of the poems cast a melancholic look back on a happier prehistory [*Vorzeit*], as even before the advent of entirely foreign rule a consciousness makes itself known that the vital force [*Lebenskraft*] of the nation is broken—in accordance with what Munzinger observed."[97] This type of argument— supported here by reference to the authority of the Swiss Orientalist Werner Munzinger

(1832–1875), who had spent much of the 1860s and 70s in Eritrea, since 1871 as general governor on behalf of the Egyptian *khedive*[98]—used the melancholy of Tigré poetry as evidence for the insufficiency of Tigré historical consciousness. The Tigré noticed the historical decline of their "vital force"—significantly, the vocabulary Littmann had used for the description of individual dejection here returned on the level of nations—but could not fully explain it. In this way, for Nöldeke, the poetic corpus overrode the validity of its own historical knowledge. The Tigré "tribes" turned out to be a people not only without much of a future but also without a (proper) history, which really was only a *Vorzeit*. This, to be sure, was a hermeneutic move of high traditional prestige: to prove that the texts contained a semantic surplus beyond their authors' intentions; and to prove that Orientalist reading was superior to native reading.

By a slight, if decisive, quantum, Nöldeke was less bent than Littmann merely on interpreting the corpus in terms of its proximity to or distance from European poetry, and more inclined to recognize the particularity of its poetics. This recognition took a peculiar form: the better Nöldeke managed to read the corpus the more opportunities he found for reading it against its own poetics, and for reading the individual poets against their intention. Thus, the historical-commemorative melancholy of the poetic corpus was turned into the melancholy of a dying "nation" depleted of *Lebenskraft*. Naffaʿ's suicide may have appeared to Nöldeke as simply another symptom of precisely this underlying pathology of poetic, national, and individual character alike.

The natural history of national character was a type of problem in which Littmann, too, was highly interested. In a letter to Nöldeke, he gave his own views on the matter:

> It is correct, the Abyssinian heroes are braver than the Arab ones, but also less noble. Among those people, on the one hand, a primitive, naïve crudeness and lack of inhibition [*Schrankenlosigkeit*] is dominant (in spite of the often so peculiar minute detail in the determination of and compliance with custom in social and religious matters …); but on the other hand the race is degenerated, as Sundström has also rightly emphasized. Syphilis is, after all, endemic in Abyssinia.[99]

Yet, the difference to Nöldeke's point is clear: Littmann did not start out from the *reflexive* knowledge the Tigré nation possessed about its own situation in history, but from a purported unconscious of moral and indeed physical degeneration. In Littmann's account, the aesthetic category of the naïve struggled with the medical one of the syphilitic, a pollution of categories Nöldeke avoided.

The historicity that hinged on the names in the Tigré corpus disturbed the ordinary mode of functioning of the system that made possible the translation of, say, an individual suicide into a trait of national character, a lack of cultural and physical "vital force." This disturbance occurred because the system of literary expression that was to supply the idiom of translation did not fully work for the Tigré poems. Nöldeke's hermeneutic move to localize a surplus meaning in the poems was to restore the ordinary pattern, but at the same time highlighted its fragility. It does seem significant that the tentative notion of the unhistorical character of the Tigré "nation" here emerged as a mere side-effect of a system in which a timeless notion of psychology in literature was key to a philological stabilization of texts. It was precisely because the

Tigré speakers failed, in Nöldeke's view, to be sufficiently ahistorical in their literary expression that they ended up in the position of possessing neither historical self-awareness nor a historical future.

To some extent, the process here is that of an imposition of European historicity that suppresses the non-European model of historicity at hand. In both cases, what is at stake is basically a nexus of component parts that generate historicity through semiotic interrelations. Things from the past are marked as historical by integration into this nexus, which is accomplished not by sticking a label on them, but by turning them into signs for each other. The European model privileges indexical sign relations, of the kind where one thing is the causal indicator of another (smoke, fire, with Peirce's standard example).[100] The notion of a sign, in the semiotic tradition, is uneven; there are different kinds. The Tigré model, as presented in the Littmann-Naffa' collection, rather used the signification of poetic likeness and symbols and the referentiality of the proper names of a society marked by personal interrelations. The persons commemorated by Tigré poetry would not have been easily included into historicization in a European context. One can also discern that by the 1900s, the Tigré model had already taken on traits through which it actively responded to and antagonized the European regime of historicity, as e.g. the poems about the Italian invasion in Conti Rossini's collection indicate. Structurally, this is quite similar to the conflict of historicities that Dipesh Chakrabarty analyzed in detail in *Provincializing Europe*: the imposition, on the part of colonizers and colonial elites, of the category system of a "history 1" with a focus on modernity, secularity, European supremacy, and so on; and local forms of "history 2," traditions in defiance of the newly imposed categories.[101] However, in the case of Tigré poetry, the empty, homogenous, secular, progressive time that was constitutive of the dominant European model of "historicism" was arguably not the main imposition. As far as Naffa' is concerned, it rather seems that he strove to transfer Tigré poetry, via philology, into the European system of literature, where writing and print meant, among other things (e.g. prestige, recognition) deliverance from a type of historical time that was going to decompose the poetic compositions, the living corpus of knowledge, the living commentary.

It seems significant that "world literature" could produce the same effect as so-called historicism, although it did not seek to replace the historical knowledge it eclipsed with a comprehensive system of historical knowledge of its own. This is signaled in Nöldeke's vague apprehension that it would be the Italian influence *as well as* the Islamic one that would destroy the Tigré language and nation. This possible destruction was not simply a matter of European progress and world historical dominance, but something more open, inconclusive, and complicated. Although Littmann was endlessly admiring of Nöldeke's "historical sense,"[102] the quality of the latter's historical judgment was mercurial and tentative. There was no very palpable history 1 to the Tigré poets' history 2. For the philologists, when it came to determining the nature of things Oriental, world literature appears to have been preferable over world history. If push came to shove, though, "endemic syphilis" also served.

World literature then, and world philology alongside it, entailed a different kind of world than world history. Admittedly, Erich Auerbach's 1952 coining of the concept of a "world philologist" passes over these distinctions quickly. For him it was, with a *topos* inherited from the nineteenth century, the emergence of "the historical-perspectival sense" since the times of Vico and Herder that had allowed the formation of the very notion of "world literature." The constitutive aim of a world philology continued to be the understanding of "the idea of the human as unified in its diversity."[103] The world of the "world philologist" was, in a recognizably Boeckhian vein, "the inner history of the last millennia ... the history of humankind as it succeeded to express itself."[104] The *topoi* here deployed were familiar to the philologists of 1909, and perfectly compatible with their aims and procedures. Nonetheless, the divergence of the "world" of historicity and that of literature in Nöldeke's discourse suggests that there is something unresolved about the question of what "world" may have meant in relation to philology.[105] It seems clear that Auerbach's distinction of an "inner" and "outer" history of humanity—the former subject to literary representation and its philological study, the latter to that of history—did not suffice to distinguish the worlds available to, and in fact shaped by, the disciplines of philology and history, respectively. For, Auerbach's distinction posits a unified reality of humanity, but does not show that such a reality was indeed part of the ontology of philological knowledge. It is for this reason that the historical examination of the world-making activity, the practical ontological productivity of philology, cannot be eschewed.

The event of Naffa''s suicide indicates some of the contestation to which the notion of the *humanum*, the essence and unity of humanity, was subjected in the world of world philology. The ability, precisely of Orientalism, in the imperialist period, to establish the insufficiency of the "humanism" Auerbach would later undeterredly continue to defend was historically non-negligible. The genealogy of antihumanism is more varied and more unsettling than commonly recognized.[106] The pairing of humanism and antihumanism is most intimately related to the history of German philologies and provides one of the key themes that accompanied their efforts at imposing new methods on the explication of meaning. The twisted relation between world literature and philology on the one hand and world history on the other implies that there was an underlying *polemos* at work, or even multiple ones. In this context, the question raised by the interrelation of Naffa''s suicide with philological practice is that of the place of the violation of the *humanum* in philology, which in turn appears bound up with the problem of violence.

7. The Violence of Philology

Undeniably, the present chapter is about violence; not so much simply the physical violence of suicide (if there is anything simple about it), but rather the manner in which the epistemic work of philology was entwined with this violence, as a form of ontological production that made possible specific forms of semantic explication. The danger in this thematic is that the connection in question might appear, after all, unproblematic. The intimate linkage Foucault established between violence and what he called *episteme* has certainly provided the prime critical tool for interpreting the place of scholarly knowledge in colonial history. His use of the concept of episteme to some extent followed the terminology of Bachelard, who had posited that "epistemology" was to denote a theory of scientific knowledge apart. The particularity of scientific knowledge emerged by means of a constant, active rupture with quotidian knowledge. Foucault then inserted a further distinction into the concept of scientific knowledge, between disciplinary doctrine and its "unconscious," that is to say, the enabling discursive conditions that underpinned not merely one, but a plural ensemble of disciplinary orders of knowledge. It was this second level that he labeled episteme, in a very liberal *Umbesetzung* of the Ancient Greek concept for theoretical knowledge. This semantic shift facilitated the cross-disciplinary study of taxonomies, categorizations, and ordering systems Foucault proposed in *The Order of Things*. These sets of enabling conditions disposed of histories of their own, which formed a "historical a priori."[107] Since it was a specific episteme that first and foremost made possible the very ascription of historical knowledge, properly historical knowledge about episteme-in-the-plural was not attainable. Past episteme could only be understood through a type of inquest that was different from historical research and that Foucault labeled "archaeology." Particularly in his 1960s works, he also located power, subject-formation, and violence in the repetitive discursive patterns of episteme. In a way, the unconscious of "empirical" scholarly knowledge, the production of concepts of kinds always already within a broader taxonomic order, colonized the domain of quotidian knowledge, of which the knowledge of political power formed part. The Bachelardian rupture was thereby tacitly turned on its head.

Foucault's introduction of the episteme/doctrine distinction within scientific knowledge was loosely mapped on that of the conscious and unconscious in psychoanalysis. It restricted the range of application still available to epistemological rupture in Bachelard's sense of a conscious, if also irreducibly affective and social process in actual scientific and scholarly practice. For Foucault, the decisive component of scientific knowledge was the epistemic, and this part of knowledge enjoyed an uninterrupted connection with power. Effectively, the Bachelardian critique of the positivist assumption of the unity of all knowledge was then disabled. For, it became at least practically superfluous to assume that there were domains of scientific knowledge unaffected by episteme and that differences of doctrine mattered. Foucault was far too cautious to claim that he was putting forward a general theory of knowledge. Nonetheless, he excluded those forms of scientific knowledge that supposedly did not fall under his model for empirical bodies of knowledge (for instance, mathematics— *The Order of Things* explicitly leaves out the "formal" sciences and also has little to say on the theoretical status of their knowledge). Episteme was to have its own epochal ruptures. Yet, since the archaeological method to unearth these ruptures consisted in a discontinuous description of plain findings, the discontinuity of method and the discontinuity of the object under scrutiny became difficult to distinguish. In a very considerable portion of the reception of Foucault's historical-epistemological work, it appears that his intervention was treated as having served the end of reuniting scientific knowledge with power. In this way, the interpretation of Foucault reaffirmed the linkage that had animated the philosophies of history of the period of Kant and Hegel, namely the linkage between power (as positive freedom, agency) and knowledge that had established humankind as the subject of the historical process.

This criticism arguably aligns to some extent with Gayatri Spivak's in "Can the Subaltern Speak?" where she took Foucault (and Deleuze) to task for having retained, behind a mere smokescreen of pluralism, a notion of unified subjecthood, of a privileged, unified, and "transparent" knowing agent of the historical process. Transparency in this context was to entail that the subject in question neither required nor enabled any form of further representation. This unburdened its theoretical analysts from having to ask, reflexively, for the effects their own representational efforts produced. Yet, it is noteworthy that Spivak's text addresses Foucault and Deleuze as public intellectuals, participants in a common sphere of political thought and discourse, and only secondarily as scholars, or *Wissenschaftler*. Thereby her analysis appears to eschew the question of where its account stands with regard to the basic Bachelardian posit that scientific knowledge is different from quotidian knowledge simply because it constitutively seeks to be. That is to say, the connection between scientific knowledge in a broad sense on the one hand and power and violence on the other remains theoretically adrift. The Spivakian exhortation to maximize theorists' reflexivity about the work of representation they invest in the upholding of a unified subject of the historical process almost appears to set a trap in which knowledge is reduced to speaking about itself, and only about itself, endlessly. Inasmuch as the Foucaultian understanding of episteme was designed precisely to limit the possibility of such reflexivity—there cannot be a history of what makes history possible, only an archaeology—it even disposes of an inbuilt safeguard against this entrapment.

This also means, however, that from a certain point of view these—crudely simplified!—Foucault and Spivak positions indeed cancel each other out. Starting from the point of the epistemological rupture of Orientalist philology, its specificity as scholarly, *wissenschaftlich* knowledge might open a divergent perspective. Only, the immediate link between knowledge/power and violence would then be lost. Since the case of Naffaʿ illustrates why it is nonetheless important to be able to track such a linkage, recuperating a more mediated connection then becomes a substantial challenge. This challenge also entails addressing the additional problems that beset the work of bringing together what Spivak calls, and Foucault might call, the "macrological [and] micrological texture of power."[108] These problems inform the assertion that indeed Naffaʿ's suicide constituted a "case" of something, that the peculiar constellation of power between Littmann and him would intersect with, even be a function of, much larger forces. To be sure, there is an intimacy to Naffaʿ's act and its conditions that precludes endowing it with statistically representative qualities. Yet it may well be that, when it comes to the violence of philology, the particulars will always be decisive; and that it is precisely for this reason that the question involves the "world" of philology as a field of knowledge that is oriented toward concretion, if at various degrees of ambiguity and confusion.

In the manner in which history is written today, the access of violence to the sphere of the historical is immediate. The past act of violence requires neither justification nor explanatory mediation to gain admittance into the semiotic nexus of things historical, and even to be of exalted importance within it. Or, more straightforwardly:

if someone dies a death of unnatural causes, at the hands of a human being, even if it is their own hand, this is where history starts; not with Adam and Eve, but with Cain and Abel. Various theoreticians have even submitted that violence is among the very conditions of the possibility of historicity. Frantz Fanon, for instance, insisted that there was an inextricable connection between violence and emancipation. In a still distantly Hegelian understanding of history, this position entailed that only violence allowed colonial subjects to overcome their alienation, reverse the "dead time" of colonialism, and acquire historical agency.[109] Nothing easier, perhaps, and perhaps also nothing more appropriate, than relating Naffa''s suicide to the pathological acts of psychological internalization and redirection Fanon described as part of the violence essential to the colonial condition.

Yet this type of account would entail not only placing violence at the center of the historical event at hand but also suppressing the intimate detail of the case. Naffa''s European clothes and toiletries, the vests and hats and razors, can be taken as signs of the bodily impact of domination. The fact that he did not possess, or at least leave behind, a single material object that he had brought from home can be read as a symptom of deprivation and alienation. Yet the question as to his own pleasures and desires would then be suppressed, and his aesthetic and intellectual work on the Tigré poems sidelined. Philology would function as a merely secondary manifestation of the primary system of violent domination; which is arguably also the place assigned to the compound of scholarship and literature in Said's *Orientalism*.

In this type of analysis it is not clear what constitutes violence, or what necessitates that violence inexorably requires counterviolence. For Fanon it is the inevitably somatic realization of colonial domination that requires an equally bodily response. By way of tacit assumption, it is this physical manifestation that is then presumed to be constitutive of violence. Therefore, the concept of violence, which is meant to provide a foundation to historicity, is itself organized around another center, physical violence, from which other, less-physical forms are meant merely to be derived. It may be helpful at this point to refer to the criticism Derrida raised against a theorization of "structure" in terms of an organizing center, since any presumptive center, in spite of itself, continues to be unstable and to require the positing of ever further, equally untenable centers.[110] While this deconstructive manoeuver certainly carries problems of its own, it opens the field for another, less static arrangement of concepts.

In the archival record at hand, the symbolic place of violence is mobile; it is worth tracing it across the documents. The correspondence of Littmann and Nöldeke, for instance, touches upon colonial violence in a characteristically skewed manner. In the spring of 1912 Littmann wrote from Cairo, where he was teaching classes at the new international university:

> Several times over the last couple of days I have met with Dr. Carl Peters, as one meets the most interesting people here generally. He wants to conquer Somaliland with me, I almost feel like doing so [*ich hätte beinahe Lust dazu*]. Just upon arrival here, he received letters by Somali chiefs, who invite him to come. They want to recognize him and throw out the Italians, the time being favorable.[111]

And a few days later he added:

> For me, the months in Egypt have principally been a time of psychic healing
> [*psychische Kur*]. I have finished with the bitter years, in which, inwardly, I tore
> myself up. In spite of all outward success and constant hard work, I have endured
> years the misery of which I do not wish upon my worst enemy. The voyages of
> the last years, the complete transformation, the colorful, diverse life, the sun and
> the blue sky have finally made me *lebensfähig* again. I am very glad about that. Of
> course, by the bye, I have also learned a lot.[112]

He further mentioned the two rejected marriage proposals as the main source of his
dejection and did not accept Nöldeke's advice to simply continue trying. He also asked
his mentor to destroy the letter, which obviously Nöldeke failed to do, as did Littmann
himself when he reobtained the correspondence after Nöldeke's demise. At any rate,
the fantasy of violence, the lust for colonial conquest the encounter with Carl Peters
(1856–1918) had begot, was then part of an overall program of psychological healing,
of reattaining the capability to live.

Peters repeatedly appeared as a matter of discussion in Littmann's and Nöldeke's
correspondence. Already the previous year, Littmann had sent clippings of articles
from the press that concerned novel and ever more phantasmatic designs Peters, the
personification of German colonial violence, was proposing to the public.[113] Nöldeke,
however, was less favorably impressed than Littmann:

> Peters is, for all I know, a very smart and brutal-energetic man. Kiepert already
> wanted nothing to do with him when he [i.e. Peters] still enjoyed high public
> esteem. His [Peters's] judgment of British policy in his article is certainly right. But
> the project to drain Lake Victoria, considered possible [in the article], is starkly
> reminiscent of the old fantasies of the diversion of the Nile into the Red Sea, in
> order to ruin Egypt for the heathen Turks. And even if the plan could be carried
> out, would not the very first step toward its realization *force* England to declare
> war on Germany? Whoever touches England's position in Egypt, this Empire *must*
> confront him by all means.[114]

Susanne Zantop held that German colonial history started in the sphere of imperialist
phantasmagorias long before the actual acquisition of colonies;[115] and surely, as
Littmann's letters show, such fantasies had not ceased thirty years into the reality of
German imperialism. As Christian Geulen has argued, the idiom of eternal struggle,
boundless conquest, and being *lebensfähig* and therefore *lebensberechtigt*—the
entwinement of force and legitimacy—was interwoven with the manner in which
especially Peters theorized German colonialism.[116] In the 1890s Peters had been
denounced in national parliament and in the progressive and Social Democratic
press as "Henchman Peters" (*Hängepeters*) due to his "excessive," arbitrary use of
hanging as a method of punishment. In response to this campaign, the government
had decided to discharge him dishonorably. None of this, however, had durably
disqualified him as a political figure. His academic credentials—he held a doctoral

degree in history and a *Habilitation* in philosophy—remained intact, and as a prime animator of the Pan-German League he retained high public visibility.[117] By 1905 the Kaiser had transformed Peters's discharge into an honorable retirement. Nöldeke's disapproval was less directed at the brutality of Peters's comportment than at the phantasmatic quality of his designs. Although Nöldeke did not share Littmann's lust for colonial conquest—in fact, he had expressed doubts about the prudence of Germany's colonial expansion ever since the 1880s[118]—this was not a moral inhibition motivated by concern for the fate of the colonized. Rather, it was an argument about the instrumental rationality of German foreign policy in which fantasy was not to occupy a place. The professional ethos of philology then could serve to reject fantasies of violence, but primarily because these were fantasies, not because violence *per se* posed a problem.

In September 1911 Nöldeke, who in his correspondence was in the habit of commenting on the news, remarked on the recent lynching of an African American laborer, Zachariah Walker (whose name was not mentioned in the letter), in Coatesville, Pennsylvania:

> I would not have thought that even in the northern United States such disgusting acts of lynching could occur. In the South, yes, and at most *in the wild West* [orig. English], but in the state of the late Penn of blessed memory! True, a large amount [*großer Fonds*] of barbarism probably underpins all of civilized [*gebildeten*] Europe, and especially in the large cities. The sins that were committed, in the old times, against the Jews, who admittedly, in particular by their dissociation from the goyim, had themselves provoked the latters' revulsion—matters of this kind are committed over there against the Negroes, who as a particular race occupy, against their will, a special position. Still, how much "white" blood must run in the veins of those [orig. English racist expletive, omitted]! For, pure-race Africans purportedly do not even exist in America. In any case, the Negro problem is the most difficult the U.S. face, and will face. By contrast, as I read somewhere recently, the racial problems of European states are child's play. I do not know whether North America would have become so great without Negro slavery, but the bane of this atrocity will continue to haunt even the very distant posterity of American whites.[119]

The implicit message in this analysis was for Littmann to reject a job offer from Princeton.[120] Again, what is striking in the passage is the non-centrality of violence to the assessment of political constellations. Nöldeke was much more concerned with broader matters of civilization and barbarism as well as "racial mixing," in the overall framework of some kind of societal justice and the accommodation of contrary interests. If one follows the passage at length the meandering quality and hard contrasts that mark Nöldeke's idiosyncratic pattern of political discourse are conspicuous. While he abhorred lynching and considered slavery an atrocity, at the same time he did not, it seems, believe in the equality of races, whose "mixing" only caused additional degeneration.[121] Nonetheless, to the anti-anti-Semite Nöldeke, the Jews were not a distinct race. He had repeatedly been called upon as expert witness for the defense during several of the ritual murder trials Jewish communities periodically faced in Wilhelmine Germany.[122] Until his very old age he continued to chide colleagues for the expression of anti-Semitic views,[123] and he also had considerable influence on softening Littmann's prejudices in this regard.[124] Nöldeke's premonitions about the barbarism of Europe had the potential to subvert and ironize his put-downs of the United States. Yet, the self-critical perspective somehow lost out to a spate of topical points about America, among which his emphasis on what W. E. B. Du Bois so famously called the "color line" is perceptive, though in context hardly surprising.[125] For, as Andrew Zimmerman has shown, German academic discourse about race around 1900—not merely about Africans but also about Poles and Jews—was closely entangled with North American politics of race as well as the practical realities of German colonialism in Africa.[126] In the end, fitting the pattern, Nöldeke's concern, in the American context, is only for "white" posterity.

The casualness with which violence figured in these instances of Nöldeke's and Littmann's correspondence might be read as a broader, structural feature of enhancing European sovereignty over acts of this nature. Not only did it naturally fall to Europeans to commit violence; it also did not matter much to them; and neither did the victims. Violence left no lasting trace on the body of the perpetrators; in their lives, it mattered at most as a fleeting source of passing lust, a fancy that came and went and was compatible with, perhaps even complemented by, an equally fleeting compassion for the victims. In an odd reversal of meanings, the casual phenomenal blandness that among the dominants of society marked the discursive representation of violence would actually indicate its opposite, a twisted, indirect exaltation. Something rather similar would have been the case with such structures of exclusion and discrimination as anti-Semitism or racism, whose differentiation and horizontal, unhierarchical sprawl—in the sense of Judith Butler's analysis of "et cetera"[127]—would simply be another function of their casualness. In fact, Nöldeke's easy associative drift from North American lynchings to European pogroms indicates as much.

This overall reading, however, would also entail that violence, in Nöldeke's and Littmann's discourse, did not enjoy a position as gatekeeper for the nexus of things historical. The tendency to enhance ownership of violence by making it seem peripheral actually limited the ability of the term to align with others, to function as an organizing, hierarchical center of discourse. Violence was then very much part of Orientalist philology; but precisely because of the equivocal manner in which it was interwoven with the practice of historicization, it could not serve as the sovereign force that organized, or streamlined, this practice. For philology, violence was then not a key constituent of its object of knowledge, and a target of fetishization, as it arguably is for present-day historical writing. Nonetheless, Orientalist philology had succeeded in making violence its own, if in a different manner than was the case in the production of historical knowledge. And perhaps establishing this difference was the decisive motivation for this appropriation. The violence of philology could align with, and perhaps become a foundational component of, the rejection of a humanist perspective as implied in Auerbach's world philology. By deploying and appropriating violence in a different manner, the world of philology could be distinguished from that of history. In this manner, the violence of philology was then tied to the epistemological rupture that constituted the field.

8. The Land of Poetic Toys

There is, in the archive of Naffa''s disappearance, yet another document that contributes to grasping the divide of humanism and antihumanism and its significance for the world of philology, and thereby philology's practice of the explication of meaning. It appears, however, that a profound shift of the overall frame of discourse was necessary to grant the notion of the human an explicit presence in the documents at all. Among Littmann's philologist friends, Georg Jacob, too, had read the collection of Tigré poetry with a considerable degree of attention, but, lacking the necessary language skills, he did not peruse the volumes in the same manner as Nöldeke and focused only on the translations. As a response to his readings, on May 26, 1917 incidentally his 55th birthday –Jacob composed a poem about Naffa''s death in which he imitated the form of Littmann's translations of the Tigré songs and adapted some of the cultural detail and names from the Princeton Expedition volumes.[128] Jacob mailed the piece to Littmann, in whose papers it has been preserved; an accompanying letter appears to be missing, and any discernible response from the recipient is likewise absent. In general, Littmann was not overly appreciative of his friend's poetic efforts; the gift may have been quite unwanted.[129] In any case, Jacob made an effort to recover the inner history of Naffa''s death and to insert it, along with the Tigré poems, into the world of literature in a manner that would have been more recognizable to Auerbach than Littmann's or Nöldeke's hierarchizing interpretation.

The poem's main conceit, its scene, is an assembly of so-called *malak* (or *Mäläk* in Littmann's alternative transcription). The term denotes a type of Abyssinian mythical creature Littmann rendered into German as *Todesengel*, "angel of death." These creatures had been brought to his attention by Naffa', who had explained that, regardless of whether they were Muslim or Christian, Tigré speakers tended to believe that upon death each soul was met by an individual spirit-like companion—benign or malign, according to merit—who acted as a guide into the hereafter. Littmann pre-published this myth from his Abyssinian material in 1911 in a separate article, but at the same time dismissed it as an expression of "rather low-ranking syncretistic religious notions" and as the last reflex of the myth of the *ka*, the notion of soul or doppelganger that figured prominently in the Old-Egyptian cult of the dead.[130] The malak recur in a number of the Tigré poems of the collection.[131]

For his own poem, Jacob carefully borrowed the various traits accorded to the malak in the Tigré corpus. The first verse sets the scene of a nightly gathering and roll call of these mythical creatures, who seem to operate in a Prussian bureaucracy of sorts. For them, as Jacob explains in a footnote, there is no greater misfortune than losing the connection with their assigned human soul. This explanation was his own poetic invention, beyond the myth as Littmann had rendered it.

Nacht ists; es schlummern die Mâskalit,
Die ʿAd-Termâryâm und die Mänsaʿ;
Sieh jetzt im Kreise die Malak,
Den Aufruf mitsammen zu halten.[1)]

'Tis night; the Mâskalit are sleeping,
The ʿAd-Temâryâm and the Mänsaʿ;
See now in the circle the malak,
To hold the roll call together.[1)]

1) Es handelt sich augenscheinlich um eine Art abessinischen Malak giebt es kein größeres Unglück, als den Zusammenhang mit der ihm zugewiesenen Menschenseele zu verlieren. Alle [gestr: Schlafenden] im Lande scheinen gezählt zu werden, und für jeden Einzelnen wird der betreffende Malak sich melden müssen.

1) Apparently, this is a sort of control meeting. For the Abyssinian Malak there is no greater misfortune than to lose connection with his assigned human soul. All [deleted: who are sleeping] in the country appear to be counted, and for every single one the respective malak will have to report.

5   Sieh, wie Geschriebnes sie lesen
Kein Wort giebts, das sie nicht richten;
"Mir ist sie bestimmt", sagt der Malak,
Gott gab ihm die Seele zu hüten.

Look how they read what is written
There is no word they do not adjust;
"It is assigned to me," says the malak,
God gave him the soul to look after.

Heute war eitel Verwirrung.
10 Gieng denn ein Malak verloren?
Nie irrte zuvor, der sie zählte;
Heut war zuviel eine Seele.

Tonight there was pure confusion,
Has then a malak been lost?
Never before the counter has erred;
Tonight there was a soul too many.

Hin stoben wie Vögel die Malak
Hin zu den schlummernden Mänsaʿ.
15 Ins Bergland hin und ins Tiefland.
Die ledige Seele zu finden.

Like a flock of birds the malak swooped
Toward the slumbering Mänsaʿ.
In the mountains and the valleys
To find the solitary soul.

Sieh jetzt, wie ums Zelt sie hocken:
Sie fanden ihn bald, den Fremdling,

Now see them crouch around the tent:
Soon they had found him, the
                        strangeling,

Den der Rücken des Dampfers getragen,
20 Von weit her führt' ihn das Stahlroß.

Whom the back of the steamer had
                        carried,
From far away the iron horse brought
                        him.

Nur Schweigen umgibt ihn und Bücher.
Er wendet das Antlitz nicht aufwärts.
Sieh wie er schreibt, was nicht Sinn hat,

Only silence surrounds him and books.
He does not turn his face upward.
See how he writes what does not make
                        sense,

Doch sieh die glückbringende Stirne.

Yet see the luck-bearing forehead.

25 Nicht schaut sein Auge die Hundert,
His eye does not see the one-hundred,
Die tausend unheimlicher Gäste.
The one-thousand eerie guests.
Nicht weiß er um ihre Beratung;
He knows nothing of their council;
Sein Ohr fängt keins ihrer Worte.
His ear does not catch any of their words.

"Den fragte ich nicht die Frage"
"I would not ask him the question"
30 Spricht der mit dem Stab und der Rute.
Says the one with the staff and the rod,
"Der ist als hätt' er zwölf Herzen,
"It is as if he had twelve hearts,
Ich fürchte den Pfeffer der Rede."
I'm afraid of the pepper of his speech."
…

Zuletzt sprach der Malak des Naffaʿ,
Finally, the malak of Naffaʿ spoke,
Er hatte lange geschwiegen,:
For a long time he had been silent,:
'Ich künde euch kürzeste Rede,
'I announce to you the shortest of
speeches,

Doch salbt euch zuvor mit der Butter.
But first anoint yourselves with butter,

45 Bekümmert ihn nicht, den Faranǧî.
Do not concern yourselves with the
Faranǧî.

Seine Seele ist von ihm gegangen,
His soul has parted from him,
Sein Gott ists, der ihn gesendet,
It's his god who has sent him,
Verlornes kommt er zu suchen.
He comes to seek what is lost.

Die man herumreicht mit Händen,
That which one passes from hand to
hand,
50 Die dem Kinde vertraut wie dem Greis,
As familiar to a child as to an old man,
Die uns ward zum Trost und zur Klage,
Which holds for us solace and lament,
Die [gestr.: Unsre] Rede hat er verloren.
Speech [deleted: our] he has lost.

Spricht er, so ist es viel Mühe,
When he speaks, it is heavy toil,
Er stammelt und sucht auch vergeblich,
He stammers and also searches in vain,
55 Er sucht bei Nacht und bei Tage.
He searches night and day,
Siedend gleichwie ein Kessel.
As hot as a boiling cauldron.

Wie nie einer suchte, so sucht er.
He searches like no one ever sought.
Er ist nur selbst seines Gleichen,
He is only alike to himself.
"Hilf du mir" spricht er zu Naffaʿ;
"You help me," he says to Naffaʿ;
60 Sie schluckten die Kieselsteine.
They swallowed the pebbles.

Nun öffneten sie die Bücher
Now they opened the books
Und lasen dabei die Lektionen,
And read the lessons,
Nicht eher zieht er von hinnen,
No sooner will he go thither,
Bis daß er die Rede gefunden.
Until he has found speech.

65 Bis er die Rede gefunden,
Until he has found speech,
Läßt er sich an Garsa genügen,
He contents himself with Garsa,

Bis er die Rede gefunden,	Until he has found speech,
Lebt er auch wie ein Takrur.	He lives also like a Takrur.

	Bis er die Rede gefunden	Until he has found speech
70	Ist fern aller Freude sein Herz,	His heart is far from all joy.
	Seine Wagschale ist bei ihm selber,"	His scales are with himself,"
	Spricht der Malak des Naffaʿ ʿEtmân.	Says the Malak of Naffaʿ ʿEtmân.

	Sieh, wie sie horchen im Kreise,	Look how they listen in the circle,
	Die tausend unheimlicher Gäste,	The thousand eerie guests,
75	Sie wie er sucht, der Farangî.	See how he searches, the Farangî.
	Ihn umgiebt nur Schweigen und	All that surrounds him is silence and
	Bücher.	books.

Nicht einer fragt ihn die Frage,	Not one of them asks him the question,
Greift keiner zum Stab und zur Rute,	Not one of them reaches for his staff and rod,

	Sie schwirren davon wie die Vögel,	They soar away like birds,
80	Gad. Gad klingt tönend die Luft.	Gad. Gad resounds in the air.

The poem requires at least rudimentary commentary in order to become intelligible. Following Littmann's work, the names mentioned in the first verse refer to Eritrean tribes; *Garsa* (l. 66) was a treefruit consumed only by those too poor to find other nourishment;[132] the *Takrur* (l. 68) were a nomadic tribe reputed for their strict piousness;[133] and *Gad* (l. 80) which I have not retrieved in the actual poems, as a component of Tigré proper names, meant "good luck."[134] As is well known, *Farangî*, derived from "Frank," is the Arabic as well as Ethiopian term for European. In his description of Eritrean customs, Littmann refers to the swallowing of pebbles (l. 60) as pledges for an indissoluble bond of friendship.[135] Anointment with butter (l. 44) he mentions in the context of the description of wedding customs.[136] Staff and rod (l. 30, 78) were attributes of a punitive malak.[137] The notion of a "lucky forehead" Littmann brought up as a figure of speech in the context of a superstition about "unlucky hair."[138] The lines (58, 71) about exclusive self-sameness and scales (*Wagschale*) Jacob adapted from one of the poems, as he did with the metaphor of "the pepper of his speech" (l. 32).[139] The poem arguably has a number of weaknesses, among which perhaps the gravest is the failure to sufficiently clarify, around line 60, whether this passage is still to be read as part of the speech of Naffaʿ's malak. If so, line 59 must perhaps be understood as a conversation of Naffaʿ with himself, and the swallowed pebbles would mark a bond of friendship within his split personality; but this complicated interpretation is possibly not what Jacob intended.

In any case, it is clear that the motifs of the poem are opaque unless the reader has intimate knowledge of Littmann's publications. Given the dearth of serious readers of the Tigré collection, Jacob's attempt can only have been intended for an audience of one person, Littmann himself, who also most probably was the only recipient of a copy of the poem. Jacob may well have been attempting to offer a sort of consolation to—and in the process may also have projected his own need for consolation on—his friend. At the same time, the poem may have been intended as a corrective to Littmann's pronouncedly dismissive attitude toward the myth of the malak in particular and the aesthetic value of his Eritrean findings in general. Jacob ostentatiously exhibited the appeal of strange names and odd customs. His poetic effort was meant to demonstrate the world-literary potential of the collection. Where Littmann translated malak with "angel of death," Jacob reverted to the original expression and retrieved particularity as well as transcultural significance in the myth. His readiness to treat Naffa''s demise as an extraordinary matter, even a unique one, ran counter to Littmann's assessment. No matter whether suicide was "frequent" among the Mänsa', in Jacob's poem Naffa''s suicide was incommensurate with other such acts. And although suicide is not mentioned in the poem, the exclusive emphasis on Naffa''s dejection and forlornness does not allow for other explanations of his death. Admittedly, Jacob's poetic interpretation preceded Littmann's obituary by a number of months. Littmann possibly viewed the poem, even though it did not assign any blame in the event, as a token of the type of explication he wished to eschew. Jacob's portrayal of Naffa' as a person caught between Orient and Occident (a "Frank" from the perspective of the malak), as a troubled searcher who sought to regain the gift, and more precisely the community of speech he had lost, provided stark images of despair. In his sanguine obituary, Littmann studiously avoided broaching Naffa''s dejection.

While responsive to the melancholy of the overall situation, Jacob appears to have remained relatively blind to the structure of exclusion that weighed heavily on Naffa''s existence in Germany. In the cumbersome repetition, bordering on poetic crudeness, of the motif of lost "speech," Jacob deplores Naffa''s deprivation of voice; but the question of what agency had machinated this deprivation does not arise. Jacob's hunch, channeled through one of the punitive malaks (lines 29ff., see also the motif of the boiling cauldron l. 56), that Naffa''s speech, had it been recovered, might have been exuberant and angry, was acute. Nonetheless, the poem does not intimate a critique of Orientalism along Saidian lines. Rather, it is a document of compassion and of insurmountable individuation in the perception of Naffa''s plight. In his own work with Asian scholars, Jacob, at a later point in his life, was more supportive than Littmann. In the early thirties, for instance, he worked with a Chinese student of literature on questions of silhouette theater. This student, Chen Quan (1905–1969), whom a colleague in Kiel had actually recruited from an American college, was not only awarded a doctorate in 1933 but also enjoyed a distinguished career as a scholar of German literature in China.[140] Granted, the cases may have been quite different: The times were changing rapidly and the conditions in East Asia, where universities existed, unlike in colonial Eritrea, were more favorable. And yet, the collegial manner of Jacob's reliance on Chen forms a contrast.

In Jacob's poem, Naffaʻ's search is both cause and consequence of his loss of speech. This is correlated with a heavy presence of books and reading, a presence that also marks the activities of the malak. A reading practice that resembles that of philology is discernible with reference to both Naffaʻ and the spirit companions. The malak are assiduous students and emendators of the divine bookkeeping of human souls. Naffaʻ for his part, while impaired in his use of speech to the point where he stammers, and in his use of writing to a point where his scribblings do not make sense, nonetheless seems to be able to read. His affliction is related to the dissociation of reading from other uses of language. In this way, a modicum of philology is retained even in a condition of aphasia. This appears to be, in Jacob's eyes, an irreducible remainder of agency, which cannot be stripped from the unfortunate searcher; it is as a reader, surrounded by books, that Naffaʻ, in the poem, disappears from view (l. 76). The violence of his departure is reversed, in the last verse, into the abrupt departure of the malak from Naffaʻ. Given that it falls to the malak to interpret the mute, and given their overall philological preoccupations, the poem inadvertently associates the angels of death with the professors that helplessly, it seems, hover over the young man entrusted into their care. Their silent and distraught departure also appears to be an abandonment. For once the poetry, then, admitted more than the prose. The aggregate of philology was also a hapless, insufficient, and broken thing. It was marked by a futility that removed it from a context of use and made it into, at best, a toy.

According to Littmann, Naffaʻ, when returning "deeply impressed" from a visit to the circus in May 1908, had remarked that the "science of play in Germany is even greater than serious science."[141] In a sense, Jacob's poetic appropriation of Littmann's Tigré work supports Naffaʻ's humorous intuition that there was a competition at hand between the playful and the serious forms of scholarship. The analysis of this competition arguably profits from recourse to Giorgio Agamben's 1978 discussion of the "playland," or land of toys, in Collodi's *Pinocchio*.[142] Agamben's argument starts out from the manner in which Lévi-Strauss and Emile Benveniste had brought into connection ritual and play. Whereas ritual serves to make events steady, to integrate them into a stable structure of synchrony, play does the opposite; it extracts elements from a synchronous structure and transforms them into unique events or objects that are marked by their removal from previous deployment and subjection to novel uses that exhibit a high degree of spontaneity and contingency. Discarded or even produced for the purpose, for instance through miniaturization, toys symbolize the loss of structural significance and thereby acquire temporal significance in the sense of "once, no longer."[143] In their constitutive departure from synchrony, or so Agamben claims, the things of play are prime indicators of the cultural shaping of diachrony, that is to say of historicity.

Nonetheless, the departure from synchronous structural meaning can never be complete. Hence, play and ritual remain entwined. If to wildly varying degrees, forms of play remain moored to stable behavioral patterns that resemble ritual, but lack the latter's function of integrating practice with mythical meaning for the constitution of a stable, sanctified, repetitive temporality of the holy that embraces a total social collective. The balance, or rather the imbalance, of ritual and play is the key, as Lévi-Strauss argued, to the gradual differentiation of "warm" and "cold" societies, where the latter appear particularly tied to valuing stable cultural forms and ritual, whereas the former exalt change and play. It is for this reason, Agamben holds, that Collodi describes his Cockaigne of toys as a place marked by extreme rapidity in the passing of phenomenal time. Lévi-Strauss had noted the tendency, widespread through cultural systems around the world, to locate the divine in an imaginary space of total synchrony where time does not pass. This space also usually assumes the function of receiving the dead. The passage of the recently deceased into this space is difficult to negotiate, whence the tendency, across a wide range of cultural forms, to assign the dead a transitory ghostly status. Children, the recently born, are the mirror image of the recently deceased. Tainted by their proximity to the passage from non-life into life, children are located in a symbolic space of heightened diachrony and must pass into the state of relative equilibrium that is the dwelling place of the fully human. Collodi's "playland" is therefore, according to Agamben, a perfect negative image of the abode of the dead. Historicity, if seen as resting on the signification of the difference between past and present, therefore enjoys a cultural affinity with infancy. The historical is prominent in such social environments— the "warm societies" of Lévi-Strauss's work—that place particular emphasis on change, and on youth. In "cold societies" that stress the timeless eternity of the dead, historicity is a more marginal quality. In its hypertrophic varieties, the historical then bespeaks, in the manner of Nietzsche's diagnostic of the overpowering of modern life by history, an extreme cultural imbalance and negligence in the processing of the dead.

The perfect symmetry and rigid categories of this schema are, needless to say, suspicious. Their undifferentiated generality is not exactly of help in the interpretation of a cultural encounter—if it deserves such a euphemistic name—as that of Naffaʿ with the German Orientalists. Nonetheless, Agamben's theoretical effort suggests a valuable vista of interpretation. Jacob's decision to date his poem—which is presumably, on account of its sheer length, the result of more than a day's work—on his own birthday underlines the text's symbolic affinity to the passage of birth. The proximity between "serious science" and the "science of play"—which expresses itself in Jacob's embrace of poetic toys in lieu of serious reading exercises such as the ones conducted by Nöldeke— increases. That is to say, Jacob's playful appropriation becomes related to other symbolic functions. Therefore, it is not merely a random procedure of objectification that renders the corpus of Tigré poetry into a miniature toy for no apparent reason other than the author's amusement. Much rather, Jacob's choice of motif, his concern for the Eritrean facilitators of the passage between life and death, appears to indicate that the very philological work on the motif of the malak, along with Naffaʿ's actual passing, had run into an impasse. In a way, the precincts of philology were haunted by the specter of one of their dead who had not been properly transferred into the hereafter. Yet, philology, like history, appeared to belong to the sphere of play. It did not dispose of a proper ritual for accommodating (some of) the dead. If the malak—after all an outside, even exotic, and in Jacob's case, borrowed institution for the processing of the deceased—failed, philology was left with a task it could not perform. Naffaʿ's suicide was an event *of* philology, but not *for* it: It was not an object of philological knowledge, but nonetheless a reality to the production of which philology had contributed. For this reason, the event resisted the assignation of meaning through the rituals that accompanied the deaths of "proper" scholars. The response to this impasse was to transform the ritual into a plaything; and this was accomplished by the very act of the writing of the poem.

Jacob's recourse to poetry indicates something unresolved about temporal structure as a main constituent of the world of philology. The epistemic practice at hand remained suspended between maturity and immaturity, between earnestness and play. Poetic discourse entailed that the understanding of human nature, the *humanum* Jacob evoked also remained suspended between these poles. In order to banish the specter, Naffaʿ was marked with the possibility of eternal infancy, a term that, as Agamben points out, etymologically means the period in life before the acquisition of speech. Naffaʿ's muteness in Jacob's poem is then not so much that of a general subalternity deprived of voice, but rather a symbol of his infantilization through poetic play, as the only response philology provided for processing the memory of his actual, violent death. And yet, in this response, philology could not help speaking primarily about itself. The fact that Littmann eventually used a draft for his own funeral speech to make one final attempt at putting to rest Naffaʿ's ghost along with his own suggests that Jacob's attempt had been as unsuccessful as Littmann's own infantilizing obituary from 1918. The poeticization of philology hardly provides an easy route into humanism. Rather on the contrary, it just adds another blockade.

The malak were unable to restore justice to Naffaʿ because the preconditions for such a restoration remained elusive. Justice hinged on admission to the status of full subjecthood in philology; so justice could not be restored even to the dead when they were mere playthings. In this regard, while Jacob clearly sought to express regret over Naffaʿ's fate, the poem worked against its writer's intentions and turned the very notion of the pertinence of justice to the dead—or at least some dead—of philology into a category mistake. Philology, as an epistemic field, was perfectly capable of operating a system of norms that pertained to the objects it appropriated or created (for instance in situations of exchange); and equally to its subjects, for instance through notions of "character" or virtue. Yet such moral norms were deliberately limited in their sphere of application. When it came to issues of life and death, they did not apply; but the broader, supposedly "universal" morality that covered those issues had little authority over matters of philology, such as for instance the ownership of a batch of poetry and the question of what constituted just compensation in its transfer.

The Archive of Epigraphy

1. A Primal Scene

Since the late 1960s—with Foucault's *Archaeology of Knowledge* as the most important catalyst—"the archive" has come to connote a particular field of inquiry into the production, maintenance, and justification of historical knowledge. This field is marked by a deliberate clustering of problems: The rules of the language games in which the documents emerged, the conditions of storage in terms of filing and indexing, the material aspects of archival work, and the working practices of historical research are all discussed in the form of an integrated praxeology.[1] The archive has come to represent, by way of metonymy, the overall practice of perusing the written record of the past for the purpose of generating historical knowledge; it provides a figuration of the entire set of semantic procedures, the procedures responding to questions about meaning, that mark the philological and historical disciplines. At the same time, since semantics have to operate over meaning-bearing material, the archive is also a trope that colligates diverse senses of the givenness of such material. The archive stands in for the structure of classes of objects and individuals of these classes that underpins the explication of meaning. The term thus symbolizes the ontology of semantic knowledge and forms part of it at the same time. To boot, the archive is among the objects of research it contains; archives archive themselves. In a sense, such an entanglement of trope, research object, and reflexivity is hardly new. It already marked the methodological discourse that emerged in the nineteenth century and in which the reliance on archival documents symbolized as well as substantiated the newly scientific nature of, primarily, historical writing. The position of a merely empirical, document-based history of archival practice is therefore illusory from the outset. The very methodology espoused by such an undertaking relies on a symbolic meaning that is futile to suppress. Already in the nineteenth century the concept of the archive, as a result of its semantic overdetermination, had evolved into an amphibian with habitats in the medium of theory and concrete historical as well as philological practice.

Debates on the knowledge produced by Orientalism have eschewed recognizing the field as archival, perhaps because it has predominantly been perceived as reliant on the study of widely circulated literary texts on the one hand and of anthropological fieldwork on the other. Yet, in the period covered in the present inquiry, the unique manuscript text, especially in the form of the epigraphic record, was the paramount condition of the material of Orientalist philology. Making the archival character of

Orientalist knowledge explicit is indispensable for further determining the ensemble, the aggregate of objects of research, the world of Orientalist philology; and for further developing the theoretical notions required in this undertaking. This is the objective of the present chapter, which moves from notions of "world" to a more concrete analysis of philological objectification, and from a focus on literary textuality to one on archival practice as an alternative, and more ample, reservoir of philological semantics.

In terms of pertinence to the problem of the ontology of philology, it is essential that the archive is not only a trope of aggregation but also one of ordering. The archive makes its contents accessible by providing them with addresses, and addresses are determined through categorization, grouping, and hierarchization. Archival practice yields the classes of objects and individuals of such classes that constitute an identifiable order of kinds. In accordance with philosophical tradition, the presence of such an order is the condition of possibility for any ontology; and the plurality of such orders, their partial nature, pluralizes ontology itself.

For Foucault, the archive was a seat of order, an enabler of repetition, an extra-temporal mechanism that determined the sayable and the unsayable.[2] "The archive"—in Foucault's idiom a monolithic singular deviating from the plural form that is the norm in French—stood in for the apparatus of statal power and its rationality. At the same time, this apparatus also provided the possible manners, as well as the limits, of its subversion.[3] Reprising an older vocabulary,[4] Foucault proposed a terminological and epistemological shift from history to what he called an "archaeology" of knowledge that would entail regarding the "documents" as "monuments."[5] This proposal may have owed more than it admitted to the aesthetics of modern statehood, according to which the edifice of the state is designated for sublime greatness even after it will have fallen (future perfect) into ruins. Arguably, Foucault's partisanship for archaeology as opposed to history also bespoke a desire to repudiate the state's archive as "our" heritage, an almost impatient desire for the (Marxist-Leninist) withering away of the state. The contrast implicit in the terminology is clear: the archive as seen in terms of documents was conceived as "ours." The shift to its perception in terms of "monuments" accomplished a project of self-expropriation. "We," whoever we are, seek reassurance of at least the possibility of our own future alterity, of not having to remain "us" forever. So far, according to Foucault's implicit contention, such rupture of modernity with itself has yet to occur.

In the theoretical habitat then, the archive is (1) the written record of the past of a polity that (2) belongs to a social formation (a *Verband*, using a Weberian term) of which the producer of knowledge about the past forms a part. It is thus an epistemic-legal compound. Since the mere presence of social formations is a necessary as well as, arguably, a sufficient condition for the emergence of power, the archive is then a privileged site for exploring the entanglement of knowledge about the past with power. It is hardly necessary to mention that the paradigm case for this type of theoretical deployment of the archive is the nation state and the national archive. In the history of modern archival practice, the role of the French revolutionary government of the 1790s in the establishment of the first national archive with allegedly universal public access is rarely left out, even though the reality of the revolutionary archives was more complex.[6] Yet, the critical potential of the concept of the societal-statal grounding of "the archive" is far more extensive. If one accepts the possibility that the polity in question is that of all human association in its global web of political organizations, any knowledge that is based on the written record of the past of humanity is, potentially, "ours." The critical understanding of the archive in the singular, since it aimed to criticize the dominance inherent in record-keeping, sought to undermine this possibility of a universally human ownership of the archive, a concept quite present for instance in the notion of "world heritage" and similar institutional embodiments of twentieth-century global-political humanism. Therefore, the respective critics sought to develop a consistently antihumanist perspective. Yet, arguably they accepted the humanist notion of the history of the archive and focused on the normative cure to be provided by a future antihumanist rupture with the past. They were content with the Nietzschean position of "future philologist," so to speak.

In his 1995 *Mal d'archive*, Derrida laid out a surprisingly cognate account that allows sharpening the contours somewhat further. He conceived of "the archive" in terms of what one might call an ironical primal scene, in variation of a Freudian theme, a paradigmatic constellation of such force that it inflicts the wound of trauma and usurps the position of, and determines the search for, origins.[7] Engaging the etymology of "archive," Derrida draws on the Ancient Greek double meaning of *arché* to mark "the archive" as shaped by the principles both of beginnings in general and of rule by means of the setting and interpretation of law. Uncontrollably, this initial double meaning disintegrates into further distinctions. The archive—its very name deriving from the house of the archon where Athenian democracy stored its governmental documents—always already implies the mutual translatability of knowledge and power (and violence). It comprises the functions of spatial localization, supervised access, and instituted competence of interpretation. Through these functions, the archive exteriorizes memory so that it can be revisited and reproduced. It should be added that "exteriorization" does not entail the primacy of a purely "interior" memory; rather, that the archiving of meanings that are already bound up with systems and "scenes" of writing[8] means *further* semantic departures. Archiving requires technological means, which in turn require order.[9]

In order to keep the archive on shifting ground, Derrida emphasizes the ambiguity of "order," as command and categorization. Yet in his account, the notion of technology seems to underpin the archive equally as a seat of power and a seat of discretely categorized contents. For, the technical procedures of archiving determine what can be archived in the first place, and it is this technological determination of "the archive" that constitutes its proximity to power and its peculiar form of violence. The house of the archon, as the primal scene of such archiving, is thus more solidly constructed than Derrida lets on. His ironical insistence on the instability of meaning inherent in the scene, the insistence even on the self-destructive Freudian "death drive" inhabiting the archive as a site of compulsive repetition—all these manoeuvers, arguably, are sleight of hand. They obscure the rather straightforward notion of "order," and the rather unambiguous primal scene, with which Derrida operates. The specific archival exteriorization of memory is a function of statal powers of categorization and command; archival order is a function of dominance through classificatory agency that silences even the afterlives of the dominated.

The Athenian primal scene suggests that the archive is (always already) "our" exteriorized memory, the memory of the political system, primal democracy, that in western political thought still often figures as the original seed of European modernity. Certainly, Derrida seeks to undermine the modern identity politics connected to this first person plural. Nonetheless, he emphasizes that the archive is always open to the future.[10] In this way, the archive is capable of striking a connection to the structure of messianic promise, which crucially is always a promise made to "us," a form of address that constitutes and reconstitutes identity. It is not by accident that the other "primal scene" of cultural inscription Derrida discusses in *Mal d'Archive* is the Jewish ritual of circumcision as a primal bodily injury that institutes belonging. This is a way of contrasting a feigned origin in ancient Greece with one in ancient Hebrew law. The sting of this contrast is the lack of functional difference, which ironizes the mobilization of the competition of Athens and Jerusalem that was the prime organizing principle of the confrontation of Classicism and Orientalism. Derrida ironized and thereby destabilized Athens and Jerusalem in unison; but it was precisely this symmetric arrangement that caused him to circumvent, and perhaps even to fail to notice, the challenges nineteenth-century Orientalism had posed to the sanitized dichotomy of Greek and Hebrew antiquities. Indeed, preserving the dichotomy as such had gradually become a tactical device of beleaguered Classicism and as such survived especially in philosophical discourse throughout the twentieth century. The structure of Derrida's analysis of the archive is therefore yet another distant heir to nineteenth-century Classicism. Structurally, any account of archival practice that privileges the identitarian aspect of the nation state archive falls in line.

Recent theories of the archive, then, have committed two tacit conflations. On the one hand, they have merged the epistemic conditions of archival work with the institutional conditions of what is merely one specific type of twentieth-century European state archive: the ordered, legally accessible record of the workings of the constitutional organs of "our" state and of select societal appendices. This is what is captured in the widespread formula according to which the archive is a form of social memory. On the other hand, the theories in question have ensured the continuity of a classicist framework within the notion of the primal scene that frames the critical analysis of the archive. This second conflation corroborates the settlement that in effect cedes past and present to humanism and only reserves the use of irony and the possibility of a different future for antihumanism. In order to grapple with the archival character of Orientalist philological knowledge, however, it is necessary to revisit this overall arrangement. The intention of this revisitation—an intention continuous, I think, with the important points about the discontinuity and intricacy of the political foundations of archival practice Carolyn Steedman has contributed to this debate[11]— is to suspend the primal nexus of archival order and statal violence that eclipses the inherent disorder and transgressive violence that mark the Orientalist archive.

For practical purposes, this body of material mostly coincided with what Ernst Posner—using a phrase that did not resonate in theoretical debate—once labelled the "archives of the ancient world."[12] The exclusion of these archives, and the development of the theoretical account exclusively along the lines of the archives of the modern nation state, is not justified. A better-founded historical account has to establish the permeability of the distinction between the statal-institutional archive of modern Europe and the haphazard preservation of the debris of ancient writings. By necessity, this argument takes a variety of forms. To begin with, the "archival turn"[13] that symbolizes the onset of modernity in historical writing was genetically entwined with the turn toward epigraphy and archaeology in philology. This turn, central to the practice of classics since the 1810s and 20s, sought to eclipse and replace the earlier antiquarian tradition.[14] Leopold Ranke's propagation of archival historical research took one of its main cues from the new philology, especially the work of Barthold Georg Niebuhr, whose father Carsten, during his famous voyage across West and South Asia, had emerged as a pioneering collector of Oriental, especially ancient Persian, inscriptions.[15] The novel approach to classics was from its beginnings inextricably interlinked with the collection of Oriental inscriptions. The veritable explosion of Egyptian research in the early nineteenth century, after the Napoleonic invasion and the decipherment of the hieroglyphs, only added to this situation.[16] The methodological promises of epigraphy were in principle the same as those of, say, the study of medieval charters. The slow rise of the study of charters to the actual center of historical method during the second half of the nineteenth century generated a novel body of procedural precepts, technologies, and practical intuitions.[17] In the study of the ancient world, epigraphy had arguably supplied the model for this development. With Theodor Mommsen as chief research organizer, the study of Latin epigraphy and of medieval documents even shared a personal and institutional center.[18]

To be sure, European medieval charters had been relegated to institutional archives, that is to say, state-owned collections of documents. In the process, the charters had been removed from the chip boxes in which, folded, sealed, and unopened, often for centuries, they had been stowed away. The documents were opened, spread, inventoried, marked up with numerical signatures, and inserted into folders, files, and standardized boxes. In this way, archival order was established; the documents were indexed and hierarchized, and repeat access was made possible. Inscriptions, by contrast, especially those outside Europe, remained scattered in space, and the more or less precise description of their location was the basic indexing system that existed for them. *Epistemic* conditions, however, were not fundamentally different. Spatial location sufficed for indexing documents in such fashion that they could, at least in principle, be revisited. Similarly, the condition of hierarchization was fulfilled given that inscriptions were organized into collections with distinct elements such as, say, "the inscriptions of the ruined city of Sî'," which Littmann described in his diary and report.[19] Spatial indexing of this kind also permitted positing and exploring interrelations between individual documents. Inscriptions, to be sure, have always remained difficult material. They tend to be brief and marred by such fragmentation and incompleteness that many of them remain only barely legible. Yet exhaustive legibility is not a condition for being archived; and neither are the actual discreteness, completeness, and reliability of the indexing system created during this process. For scholarly users—as any self-interrogation will reveal[20]—the most attractive archives are often those that are imperfectly and not very intrusively indexed and thus accord space to serendipity.

This said, in nineteenth-century epigraphy, the difficulties of spatial indexing remained bedeviling. The stones kept moving in ways archival documents supposedly do not. Inscribed stones were used in various ways, e.g. for construction or for religious purposes. Smaller rocks with graffiti could be shifted around randomly. Moreover, the local population often resented European scholars and tended to remove inscribed stones so as to hide them from scholarly recording. European expeditions had acquired a track record of appropriating objects and by 1900 often found themselves under suspicious scrutiny. In Syria, Ottoman authorities and part of the local arabophone population opposed some practices of research, especially archaeological digging and the removal of artefacts that carried significance in communal life.[21] Other locals— or sometimes the same ones—sought profit from selling off archaeological objects. The economy of the epigraphic archive, as resulting from the specific and competing property claims with which the inscriptions were saddled, was thus seemingly different from much that constituted legally regulated archival storage in Europe at the time. Then again, the somewhat shady market that existed—and continues to exist—for European autographs[22] suggests that the institutional European archive was hardly free from the possessive desires that marked the hunt for epigraphic trophies.

Nonetheless, if it is the legal regulation of the property claims on, and modes of access to, documents that constitute the state archive as an institution, it might appear attractive to make not epistemic but legal order central to the notion of the archive in the singular. Yet, legal order, especially as concerning the regulation of access, remained spotty over the course of the nineteenth century.[23] Besides, great numbers of archival documents continued (and continue) to be in private property; and for centuries, written records of the past were regularly treated as military loot, in Europe as well as beyond. Therefore, the legal settlement of the ownership of the written record of the past historically underdetermines the notion of the archive. Much of the fine-print of inconsistency concerning the legal-institutional "order" of "the archive" appears to apply to the epigraphic enterprise just as well; and as already implied, epigraphy did not operate in a legal vacuum either. There were always social and political formations around that held some kind of property claim over the material. Supposed ruptures between modern European archives and epigraphic archives, on closer inspection, tend to transform into matters of degree at most.

This conclusion also holds for the most obvious difference, namely that of the actual material collected by the types of archives in question. This difference seems to be one mainly of the material substance that carries the writing. Otherwise, on either side, archival objects are predominantly written (and sometimes pictorial) records of the past. Every further specification presents complications not entailed by the concept of an archive. As I will argue in the present chapter, the objects are not ultimately determinable; on the contrary, they are protean. Any individual inscription, or set of inscriptions, could become an object of knowledge in a great variety of ways. Various disciplinary habits of objectification crisscrossed through epigraphy. In practice, archaeology and history did not stand apart. The expectation that they should might account for the intuition that the lithic objects of epigraphy ought not to be ascribed the same epistemic status as the parchment and paper objects of the ordinary state archive. Yet, the shifting of ontological type is hardly a privilege of inscriptions. It rather seems to be common to all the kinds of object-evidence that are used in order to gain knowledge about the past. The written record of the past can always be an object of research in many ways. It is quite thinkable that this is a consequence of the quality of being written, which might be taken to entail the presence of diverse semiotic structures, an uncontrollable variety of pragmatic interpretations, an exasperating variety of material carriers, and a vexing habit of semantic displacement between writing and reading.

Not infrequently, it has been held that the concept of "inscription" might be used to denote the one ontological aspect—a basic state of pure writtenness—that might serve as a foundation for all the others.[24] Inscription would then be transformed into a theory-metaphor in its own right. However, this appears to entail an unnecessary multiplication of entities, seeing as the state of writtenness would coincide with the state of being, in specific ways, ontologically protean, that is to say, shifting through different kinds of object. To begin with, "Inscription" does not appear to be a semantic amphibian in the same way as "the archive," for the actual inscriptions of epigraphy do not function as an empirical correlate for the metaphorical use. As evidenced by the deployment of "inscription" in theoretical context, there is no effort to draw on the history of epigraphy for furthering abstract analysis. In addition, if a foundational ontological determination of being merely written were discernible, a conclusive system of ordering archival documents in accordance with ontological type ought to be attainable. Given a foundation, one would have to be able to work up a system of discrete object-types. Yet the ordering system that has prevailed in the history of institutional state archives is the principle of provenience that orders archival documents under the contextual aspect of *where* they have been produced; thus not with regard to what, purportedly, they are as objects. Of course, the epigraphic corpora of inscriptions also arrange their material according to the location of origin. So what one is left with: indexing and provenience, provides a minimal concept of archival address that does not quite suffice to constitute order in the stronger sense of the theoretical debate, and does not at all suffice to exclude the epigraphic record.

The difference that remains between the state archive of European history and the epigraphic archive is merely one of degree. The distinction is perhaps most palpable in the function of regulating access to the archive. For the epigraphic record, in most cases there was no *central* power granting or denying access to the record of the past. The office of gatekeeping, indispensable for the European national archive, was absent, or perhaps rather more widely dispersed, in the archive of epigraphy. Again, this was a matter of degree; the Ottoman and Egyptian governments, over the course of the nineteenth century, established institutions for regulating access; but in fringe areas, such as the Syrian desert where government control was feeble, or even in Ethiopia, access was more situational. The absence of a keeper, and of an *Einhegung*, an enclosure of the documents, permits the application of a metaphor that in my view captures the gradual distinction at hand: the archives of epigraphy displayed a form of "wildness" that shaped the epistemic situations of Orientalist philology. This metaphor allows for a more than merely negative determination of what the study of the history of epigraphy, as an archival field, can contribute to both the theory and the history of the production of historical knowledge.

In ordinary usage "wild" seems to serve primarily as a counter-concept,[25] applying variously—and often by degree—to the undomesticated, uncultivated, uncontrolled, unrestrained, transgressive, uncivilized, or counter-civilized, and the non-human, merely creaturely. It is charged with associations of the spontaneous, the exhilarating, and the threatening. More to the point of the present discussion, wildness also connotes the, or a, state of nature. In order to understand this term with its complex and not necessarily inviting intellectual heritage, it seems useful to rely on the work of Philippe Lacoue-Labarthe, who mounted an intriguing argument as to the roots of Rousseau's ideas of the state of nature in an oblique reading of Aristotle's poetics of tragedy. According to Lacoue's Rousseau, the imitation of other creatures in compassion and fear would be constitutive of "savage" human nature and of the "nobility" so notoriously connected with it.[26] The making of scenes, as a function of empathy, would thereby enjoy conceptual primacy over the ability to generate political order.

As Thomas Laqueur has argued, there is reason to assume that a nexus between emotive response and the processing of "empirical" detail emerged in the eighteenth century to create a specific cultural regime of empathy for distant suffering.[27] In European contexts, the cultural history of epigraphic practice has heavily leaned toward interpretation in political terms, the use of inscriptions in the affirmation and contestation of power and status.[28] Approaching the problem from a different angle, however, Jonathan Lamb has shown, in his careful reconstruction of eighteenth-century religious, political, and moral controversies concerning the exegesis of the Book of Job, that the fluidity of the understanding of suffering, lament, and compassion was connected to the very notion of epigraphy. This connection rested on Job's desire for an epitaph (Job 19:23–4): "Oh that my words were now written! oh that they were printed in a book!/That they were graven with an iron pen and lead in the rock for ever!" Lamb points out that there was a specific investment in the symbol of the inscribed stone, as a trace that would stabilize, even perpetuate, the complaint of the otherwise elusive suffering self, and its reception.[29] In yet another important contribution, Davide Rodogno has moreover argued that for nineteenth-century Orientalism, humanitarian empathy was an indispensable component in the framing of the political perception of the Ottoman Empire. In this framework, attachment to Christians in the Middle East was still the prime, but not the only, field of application; a general sense of Orientalist moral empathy emerged that underpinned early designs of humanitarian military intervention.[30]

The question as to what suffering the epitaphs of the past indicated was connected with this regime of empathy, as the case of Johann Gottfried Wetzstein (1815–1905) demonstrates. As Prussian consul in Damascus, he was very actively engaged in raising awareness, both in the Prussian political apparatus and the broader German public, of the 1860 massacres of Syrian Christians, one of the cases Rodogno discusses. At the same time, Wetzstein carried out private research into epigraphic questions on a large scale. He even pioneered the inclusion, in the ambit of *realphilologisch* research, of the analysis of popular theater and oral storytelling.[31] This pattern of the aggregation of research objects appears to underscore the epistemic relevance of the problem of empathy. Significantly, by the time of the First World War, this overall nexus—the scene of research in which inscription, mimesis, empiricism, and empathy were tied together—had ceased to exist. For the most part, German Orientalists, even and especially those on site, failed to respond in public to the Armenian genocide.[32] Arguably, this shift in meaning was facilitated by an erosion of the symbolic connection of inscriptions with suffering. The conditions of this erosion are a prime question not only as regards the history of epigraphy in the nineteenth century but also as regards the theoretical potential of the epigraphic archive. I will argue that the wild archive was not reined in by the pathos of tragic suffering, and that not only empathetic engagement but also dispassionate disengagement have to be taken into account for a historical epistemology of epigraphy.

Wildness or savagery then refers to a field of diverse positions of situation, event, mimesis, and spectatorship whose distribution is unsteady and subject to spontaneous emergence. The wildness of archives is a historically specific metaphor whose intertwining with a particular enlightenment poetics, a specific regime of textual representation, cannot be disentangled. The epistemology of the archive would then still be a distinctly historical phenomenon, but not because of its association with the nation state and a history by necessity to be considered "ours," but rather because of its ties to a specific form of mimesis. In Lacouе's Rousseau, the function of catharsis is to provide a bridge between the different positions in play, between performance and spectatorship, between scene and action.[33] This function arguably cannot be limited to the poetic regime of prompting fear and pity by means of the tragic. I will argue that the comical, which often drew on a hostile form of empathy, was quite able to fulfill the same function; and that it was for this reason that in the epistemic framework shaping epigraphic practice the comical, as contained in the scenes of travel, was prevalent. It should also be noted that the comical, just as much as the tragic, was a highly fluent, time-bound pattern. Thus, in the last instance, there is no tension between the wild and the sphere of the historical; wildness does not stand outside or before history.

In order to establish this line of argument, the present chapter will rely on a micro-historical reading of the epigraphic work of Enno Littmann during the expeditions of 1899–1900 and 1904–5 in Syria and 1905–6 in Ethiopia. Over the course of the nineteenth century, Syria had progressed from being a peripheral to a central site of classics, especially in the wake of Melchior de Vogüé's (1829–1916) and William Waddington's (1826–1894) travels in the 1850s and 60s.[34] The young American scholar of the history of architecture, Howard Crosby Butler (1872–1922), when he developed the initiative for the Princeton expeditions, intended to retrace de Vogüé's itinerary and to broaden the documentation of ancient ruins and inscriptions in Syria. Ethiopia by contrast remained a peripheral site of classics. Aksum, the capital of an East African Empire from the third century CE until its disappearance from the historical record some time in the eighth or ninth centuries, and still the clerical center of the Ethiopian Church, was a known but only intermittently explored site of Semitic epigraphy.

2. Indiscrete Inscriptions

One of Littmann's achievements in the expeditions to Ottoman Syria was the documentation of a large number of Semitic inscriptions in the *Harra*, the volcanic desert located to the southeast of the *Ḥaurān* mountains in the south of present-day

Syria. The inscriptions allowed Littmann to propose a new reading of the so-called Safaitic alphabet, a distinct writing system used for an old North Arabian dialect in the first centuries CE, and exclusively preserved in the form of scratched rock graffiti. He was able to drastically increase the number of inscriptions known to western scholarship; and he made suggestions as to their decipherment that proved sound.[35] The first Safaitic inscriptions had only been seen by a western scholar, the British traveler Cyril C. Graham (1834–1895), in 1857. Wetzstein had then collected a larger number in 1858, but published only a few.[36] The first publication of a noteworthy number, without any attempt at decipherment, had been undertaken by de Vogüé and Waddington.[37] On the basis of their figure plates, the Ottoman-born French epigrapher Joseph Halévy (1827–1917) had identified sixteen of the twenty-eight letters of the alphabet in 1882, and Franz Praetorius (1847–1927), in a review of this attempt, had added another five.[38] In the period from 1899 to 1905, the Princeton expeditions and a series of French voyages conducted by René Dussaud (1868–1958) and Frédéric Macler (1869–1938) brought the count of known inscriptions up to more than 2,000. Littmann was able to identify the missing seven letters (and to determine variant letters) in 1901,[39] although he published the bulk of his material only in 1943.[40] In the meantime, Hubert Grimme (1864–1942) had published Wetzstein's copies, and other collectors had also added to the total.[41]

As an archive, the Semitic inscriptions of the *Harra* presented an assembly of multiple documents, naturally preserved, created by shared social practice. As was typical for epigraphic archives, the inscriptions were provided with an address, an archival index, by means of their spatial location. While the exact spatial limits of this archive remained fuzzy, the boundaries between individual texts were clear, so that the inscriptions could not count as a unified document. There were different alphabets at work, e.g. next to the Safaitic the Kufic, an early form of Arabic script, and occasionally, if rarely, younger inscriptions were written on top of older ones, as epigraphic palimpsests. In general, however, younger inscriptions were applied to as yet unmarked rock surfaces, so that the collection was also cumulative. The spatial indexing principle, however, could be reversed when rocks were moved. Orientalists participated in these reshufflings when they filed inscription-bearing objects into institutions with (as they thought) more reliable systems of addressing. In this practice, Orientalists did not categorically distinguish themselves from those locals who displaced inscribed stones. In the process of displacement the spatial-archival index and the information it contained as such—no matter how sparse—was destroyed. In such cases, the documenting practices of epigraphy did not establish what one might label a meta-archive, an archive of an archive; but only a new system of addresses for an unvarying set of documents—a new archive, replacing the old. In his 1943 publication, Littmann revised readings he had provided in the publication of the first set of a mere 134 inscriptions published after the 1900 expedition.[42] In the revision, he used the numbers assigned to the inscriptions in the earlier publication.

Undoubtedly, the inscriptions were a record, not merely of the past, but the *historical* past. When Littmann finally got to see the Safaitic rock carvings in 1900, he was at first no more able to fully decipher them than any of the previous European travelers who had examined the material. Nonetheless, on the spot, he interpreted the graffiti historically, that is to say, as to their mode of production and their position in historical time. From the extant literature, he had learned that since Wetzstein, scholars had classified inscriptions of this type as "earlier" and "later." Upon inspection on site, he attempted to explain the distinction:

> The difference is that between thick and thin script, and it results from the distinctiveness of the writing material, that is to say, of the stones used for writing. Many inscriptions are very thin-lined and carved in an elongated shape; others are thick and short, for the most part scraped in (if it is possible to say so) in a somewhat blurry fashion. Now, in some stones inscriptions are written on top of each other; and there it seems to me that the thicker one, even though often less clear, is the younger one.[43]

It is worth noting that this was the most superficial reading of the material possible; clearly an expression of the embarrassment of not being able to fully identify the single letters of the inscriptions. Historical explanation started *before* the legibility of the source was fully achieved;[44] or perhaps more precisely: legibility was not merely a technical matter of identifying characters and of steadily proceeding from this foundation. Historical meaning—placement in a nexus of events, circumstances, and epochs regarded as historical—was part of the very *semantics* of epigraphy. The meaning of a given inscription could not be reduced to an alphabetic-lexical exercise. Reading was an intricate affair that did not rest on a procedure sufficiently regulated to count as technological and thus ordered.

For instance, in spite of the failure to decipher the inscriptions immediately, Littmann was able to conjecture about the mode and the motives of their production and thus their content. One day, while he was working, one of the guides came up to him

> and asked what it was [that I was copying]. I said: Names from ancient times, of soldiers or of Bedouins, who were moving through here. Triumphantly he told me that he, too, had just carved his name (upon a subsequent question as to what with? Answer: "With a rock"). This is the solution to the entire question ... The Bedouins who have made camp here at these water holes since the old times, and also the inhabitants of the *Hauran* when going to the *Ruḥbe* and *Nemara* wrote, when they took a break here for half a day (it is only half a day from *Nemara* and from the *Hauran*, but still too far to use only for a lunch break when traveling with larger caravans), their names and possibly other remarks into the rocks with the help of smaller, pointed stones.[45]

When the decipherment was accomplished, actual translations—as, in particular, submitted by Dussaud and also Littmann—suggested that these conjectures were correct. The inscriptions were indeed mostly graffiti of proper names, often in genealogical sequence. Littmann dubbed them "memorial inscriptions" and distinguished a variety of other categories by reference to content, including burial, votive, and sales contract inscriptions.[46] Dussaud and most other scholars in this small field broadly concurred with Littmann's categorization of the record. Similar notions were also advanced for use in other epigraphic fields, for instance the South Arabian (Yemeni) one, which contained the oldest known Semitic inscriptions. Nonetheless the record remained hard to read. Hubert Grimme proposed a theory that roundly rejected Littmann's and Dussaud's memorial theory and sought to ascribe to the Safaitic archive a consistently religious meaning, an interpretation Littmann in turn dismissed.[47]

As this typical history of scholarly contestation indicates, the question of whether the proper names denoted persons, gods, or animals remained difficult to decide. The underlying semantics, the various means and modes of explaining meaning, could not be reduced to the simple identification of referents (neither in the form of types nor of tokens of individuals). Epigraphers required more abstract interpretive frameworks. Littmann's conjectures about the meaning of the inscriptions relied on a mingling of different kinds of evidence, along with orienting posits. In the quoted passage, this mixture is represented by his assumption of continuity between the habits of the ancient Bedouins and those of the modern Bedouin guide; and the on-site reconnoitering of the topographic situation around this specific set of inscriptions, in a place that forced passing travelers to rest for half a day as they could not make it to the next source of water before nightfall. Grimme, by contrast, relied on a highly speculative theory about ancient Semitic religion, the holiness of the *Harra* as a sacred "district" (*Bezirk*) and the supposition of a profound rupture between ancients and moderns. This latter notion targeted the concealed speculative element in Littmann's ostentatiously sober reading; the decision as to whether the Bedouins of 1900 had anything to do with the authors of the Safaitica on the fringes of the Roman Empire almost remained a mere matter of taste.

Littmann's mode of speculation entailed being present at the site, in the unfolding of a scene, to which Grimme could not stake a claim.[48] However, Littmann's reading also relied on procedures of a comparative nature that had nothing to do with presence on site. This was for instance the case for his notions about the "public character" of some of the graffiti, as documents of contracts analogous to those the Greek-Ottoman-born Austrian Orientalist Nicolaus Rhodokanakis (1876–1945) claimed to have recognized in the South Arabian corpus in 1915.[49] His argument, which combined legal history and archaeology, provided an important semantic resource that emerged neither from presence on site nor from the Safaitic corpus itself. The semantic procedure of decipherment thus drew on a variety of resources, which it brought together in an effort that contained an irreducibly situational component, but only next to others.

Frequently, the dispersion and incompleteness of the epigraphic record impaired Littmann's reading efforts. For instance, on November 7, 1899, in a different area, he happened on a stone with a Syriac inscription, which was merely a fragment,

> but the characters were carved very beautifully and appear to indicate a period of blossoming in Syriac epigraphy in this area. Among the abundantly scattered stones, certainly there are still more with Syriac inscriptions; yet, to examine them all and to conduct excavations would require a long time. I ordered digging around the stone the next day and the one after (November 8–9), regrettably without success.[50]

The individual object commanded attention, even if this command was not forceful. Numerous other contingencies impeded the perusal of the record of the past. Above all, the time pressure of the expedition made dispersion a prime challenge for legibility. Other intermittent difficulties that arose just in November 1899 were: nightfall, rain, the destruction of monuments and squeezes by angry locals, and crowds of spectators disturbing the works.[51] The record of the past was part of an intricate natural and social environment. The archive with which Littmann struggled was a holistic phenomenon that included an indeterminate number of materials of different kinds.

In order to contain the element of chance in its findings, the Princeton expeditions followed an itinerary quite literally composed of epigraphic commonplaces.[52] The great collective enterprises of European epigraphy, as developed by the German collections of the Greek and Latin inscriptions, initiated in 1815 and 1847, respectively, provided the most prominent symbol of the research agenda of *Realphilologie*. Mommsen's Latin inscriptions were remarkable for also comprising information on archaeological context, which Boeckh's older enterprise of collecting the Greek inscriptions had omitted. Mommsen had also established the principle of "autopsy," of visual inspection, as a pre-condition for actually editing an inscription.[53] Autopsy was meant to function as a rite of passage: An inscription that had undergone this procedure would henceforth not require revisiting on site. Autopsy also replaced the office of gatekeeper. In the absence of an agency with disciplined control over access to the documents, access was to be made redundant. Yet the ineradicable presence of imperfections in the procedure ensured that the original documents were never made entirely irrelevant. In classics, all material—the texts, the grammars, the inscriptions, the archaeological sites—was shared property, potentially known to the entire field. However, the need to revisit the same places again and again arose from the insufficiency of the disciplinary parcours: the inability of any single expedition, under the pressure of disorderly conditions, to "exhaust" any site completely. Always, the aim was to correct and exceed the predecessors.

As is commonly the case with methodological precepts, autopsy profoundly influenced practice, yet at the same time underdetermined it. The scholarly eye, however trained, was irredeemably fallible. On March 9, 1900, for instance, Littmann began work on an inscription he considered Safaitic; shortly after, William Kelly Prentice (1871–1964), the expedition's classical epigrapher, pointed out to him that it was a Greek one, bottom-up.[54] Less trivially, the eye was flawed because it relied on a changing and often half-improvised toolkit of technical means to at once document inscriptions and enhance their legibility. Certainly, Littmann still copied a significant number of inscriptions by hand, a procedure to which earlier epigraphers had also been partial. Admittedly, for some of these, such as Nöldeke's longtime Strasbourg associate Julius Euting (1845–1914), this work had also been a calligraphic exercise, an aesthetic pastime for which Littmann had less talent and patience. For the most part, he and his peers employed the methods of squeeze (*Abklatsch*) and photography. Photography remained secondary; the technology was less reliable and the results could not be checked against the original immediately. As for the squeezes, the expedition used a special paper developed by Euting, with whom Littmann had undergone practical training before departure.[55] Nonetheless, on repeated occasions, Littmann recorded that squeezes had failed to develop when there was no time left to repeat the procedure. Legibility was not simply a matter of the eye but also of the technical devices that on the one hand documented what had been read, and on the other also aided the feeble gaze. Reading required not only the original document but also the various kinds of technical reproduction.

Another flaw of the eye was its failure to reliably find the inscriptions on location and, when found, to keep them in focus. Even in places that were well-documented in the scholarly literature, the assistance of additional local guides was often required. Littmann was hired for the expedition because of his knowledge of Arabic, presumed active by the organizers. In the beginning of his travel notes, he admitted to considerable difficulties with conversation and relied, as did the other participants, on the help of interpreter-servants they had hired in Palestine.[56] Subsequently, however, Littmann's knowledge of the vernacular appears to have improved so that he became independent of translators. Retrieving objects already known to the research literature on site was often a matter of negotiation. As a result, reading the epigraphic record presupposed a type of dialogue entirely different from the one envisaged by hermeneutic theory, namely one that often went along with economic exchanges and was prone to shifting focus. The study of Semitic inscriptions was marginal in the Princeton expedition. In his fragmentary autobiography Littmann dryly remarked that during the first Syrian journey he had found a total of only twenty-four until then uncatalogued Syriac inscriptions; hence, there remained plenty of time for assisting Prentice with the Greek monuments, and other activities.[57] Frequently, Littmann's attention went even further astray. He neglected the expedition's prime mission of pursuing the documents of antiquity, in order to converse with native staff or local guides. He collected folk poetry— one of his abiding scholarly interests—and on occasion described at length the quotidian habits of the locals.[58] This range of interests followed the catalogue of objects of *Realphilologie* and, in its random sequential combination, the genre model of the Orientalist travel diary. The production of scholarly knowledge on site was interconnected with the literary form in which it was recorded. As a result, the reading of the archive shifted comfortably among various kinds of objects. The inscriptions as well as the habits of the guides belonged to the range of kinds of objects on which the traveling scholar's perception focused, but there were other kinds in play, and epigraphic procedure remained unsteady.

The reading of objects by way of their inclusion in a class or kind was clearly indispensable for Littmann's work. Even when inscriptions could not be fully deciphered as individual units of meaning—as was the case in his 1899 autopsy of the *Harra* material—they could be identified as graffiti of proper names in the Safaitic script. This identification also allowed for the ascription of historical meaning. In the overall semantic operation, other kinds of objects also figured, for instance, the behavior of the guide carving his own name into the rocks. For any given material, there were numerous ways in which it could become *gegenständlich*, that is to say, identifiable in terms of classes of objects of knowledge. In this sense, archival *Gegenständlichkeit* defied unequivocal predication; it was unsteady.[59] The unsteadiness of this ontological operation entailed that semantic explication was also unsteady.

Reading was disunified among divergent modes of relating signs to things, events, or other signs. Discreteness was possible, but it appears to have figured only within those modes, within the kinds of theoretical objects they posited. Thus, the Safaitic alphabet was distinct from the Thamudic or the Kufic Arabic, and inscriptions were a different object of knowledge than the behavior of Bedouins. Yet at the level of the actual individuals, of inscriptions, locations, ruins, persons, this discreteness was insufficient. It did not constitute the legibility of the given documents, the record of the past. Therefore, at least in the context of the reading procedures through which the meaning of the record of the past is deciphered, the notion of a comprehensive and discrete archival order proves a dead end.

3. The Archival State of Nature

In his preparation for the Syrian journey, Littmann had set high hopes on the possibility of visiting the Safaitic material Waddington and de Vogüé had seen in the *Ruḥbe* oasis in the 1860s, and of which the surrounding volcanic desert promised much greater quantities. The area, which formed the northern edge of what geographers then labeled "Inner Arabia," was Bedouin territory on which, according to Littmann's estimation, the Ottoman Empire did not have an actual hold. Therefore, the expedition entered into extended interaction with a local Druze sheikh, *Ḥasan Sallâm* of *Tarbâ*, to assure safe passage. Because of sickness in the expedition and the expected danger, the bulk of the caravan and the other scholars broke off while Littmann continued with his personal servant and a party of locals, both Bedouin and Druze, including Sheikh *Ḥasan*.

Just as in many other instances of scholarly travel writing, a specific set of aesthetic notions—which framed scholarly agency as adventure[60]– was connected with the passage into a territory beyond Empire. Already at the beginning of this passage, in his entry for May 16, 1900, Littmann included a portrayal of a guide, the Bedouin *Ḥalîl Abu Selîm*, "a magnificent fellow, stoutly and handsomely built, he had distinctive features and piercing eyes, a long beard one might call Old-Germanic. His language was entirely that which we know from the old Bedouin songs; full of similes and tropes, but also boastful and proud." And merely a few lines further he added another portrait: "Immediately, the wondrously beautiful face of a young man caught my eye; I believed I had never seen such beauty in a man: it was *Sallâm*, *Ḥasan*'s oldest son."[61] For Littmann, the attraction of these Bedouins and Druzes, while possibly also libidinous, resulted from their proximity to a cliché of originality, of a noble state of nature, and natural manhood, as connected with the origins of the Germans themselves. The adjective "proud" recurs throughout the following pages of the diary. In context, the "pride" with which, the very next day, the Bedouin guide recounts how he has just inscribed his own name with a rock acquires a new connotation, as do the inscriptions themselves: they are not merely proper names and sources for Semitic writing systems but also documents of a particular affective regime in Bedouin culture that expresses proximity to nature. For Littmann, the inscriptions themselves thus were a function of a mimetic operation in which

the pride of original man was performed. It was this understanding of pride—
subtly connected to gender and desire—that framed Littmann's interpretation of
the Safaitica as inscriptions that were to preserve the "memory" of self-confident
individuals, in contrast with the subordination under norms of religious exaltation
Grimme's interpretation entailed.

During the 1900 excursion to the *Ruḥbe* oasis, Littmann's epigraphic work was
hasty, even sloppy. The sheer number of inscriptions—which according to Littmann far
surpassed anything that could be found in the classical sites of Syria[62]—overwhelmed
the capacities of a single epigrapher. Moreover, Littmann once again grew distracted.
His attention wandered to a different kind of epistemic object, the Bedouins themselves.
When Littmann's group met a party of relatives of one of his guides, he asked them to
perform a "war dance" for him. After a lengthy description of the performance he
concluded:

> The entire dance is very exciting; the monotonous singing of the men, the eternally
> repeated movements, the sight of the sword which the dancing girl often passed
> closely in front of their faces, the war songs of the women: everything comes
> together to drive the men to an almost senseless fury before battle. I myself
> instinctively groped for my revolver whenever the dancers came near; although
> I could have felt entirely secure, nonetheless I had a vague, unsettling feeling
> that perhaps one of the people might jump at me in a fanatic rage. As long as I
> kept watching the dance, at any rate, my revolver stayed close to my hand. Then,
> however, I fell asleep, overwhelmed by fatigue, just where I was lying.[63]

Littmann, as spectator, testified to the authenticity of the performance, not by dint
of comparison with other such dances, but by dint of the intensity of the emotional
reaction the spectacle induced in him. To be sure, his claims as to this reaction were of
a somewhat spurious nature since the performance actually sent him to sleep. Toward
the beginning of the description of the dance, Littmann averred: "They wanted to
perform it exactly as if they were going to battle."[64] Thus, with the outside spectator
present, the performance was the imitation of a performance, mimesis of mimesis.
Watching the dance, Littmann consulted a *record* of past and present practice. For the
past loomed large in the performance; or at least in Littmann's description of it, since
in his understanding the dance clearly expressed Bedouin customs transmitted from
antiquity. The performance was of a piece with the poetics of the "old Bedouin songs"
Littmann referred to in the portrait of *Ḥalîl Abu Selîm*. The dance was part of the
world of world poetry that a few years later would also frame Littmann's reading of the
Eritrean corpus. Epigraphic sources, ethnographic description, and the philological
reading of poetry communicated intimately, if indirectly, by virtue of being materials
in the same archive.

The mimetic nature of the material was narrowly connected to the festive character
of occasions such as the Bedouin dance. In his travel diaries, Littmann repeatedly
described, in great detail and with palpable literary ambition, performances in his
honor. In January 1906, when the Aksumite church conducted elaborate services in
order to celebrate the arrival of the German expedition, Littmann noted:

When the trombones fell silent, the singing of the priests began; at first simple and solemn with the peculiar Abyssinian cadences: they sang, in Ancient Ethiopian: "Aksum is an exceedingly honored site and the Great of the Earth have come to her. The people of Jerusalem (= Europe) have honored us with their visit. Far away from Germania they have come to us". When the priests paused, the trombones blew. The priests' song grew ever more lively, the precentor sounded his voice ever more loudly, and the choir fell in with greater force. Then also the dance of worship commenced. The two dancers, in the rhythm of the singing, and swinging their rattles (sistra), moved toward each other, retreated, exchanged places. While we were sitting up there [on top of the stages leading to the church] we could not but think: as if we were sitting with King Salomon in front of his Temple, watching the dance of the Israelite priests and listening to the sound of the horns and trombones of the Old Testament: it seemed as if we had been transported 3,000 years back in history.[65]

The clerics of Aksum celebrated the "honor" bestowed upon them by their visitors. Their celebration intensified so as to affect the emotions, as far as that went, of the foreign spectators. In his account Littmann included a variety of references to antiquity. He noted that the chants were sung in Old Ethiopian (Ge'ez), and he included allusions to both Hebrew and Graeco-Roman antiquity (the latter linguistically present in the mention of *sistra*). The service of the Ethiopian Church was magnified by the millennia of time it had allegedly withstood. However, Littmann was aware that his remarks were a historical fabrication. Everything was, once again, given in the mimetic mode of "as if." In this case, though, the fabrication was not meant to be exclusively his own but also referred to the Ethiopian monarchy's genealogical myth of origin in the legendary Menelik, son of Salomon and the Queen of Sheba.

Littmann's "as if" marks the implicit presence of the hermeneutic problematic that had dominated the Germanophone humanities since the time of Schlegel and Schleiermacher: The reading of the source text required empathy and distance at the same time. A standard of realistic plausibility, a sort of common sense that was not derived from the textual corpus at hand was to function as the arbiter of textual meaning and the limiting condition of empathy. The liturgical performance was the mimetic enactment of "Ancient Israelite" service. The performance in question did not distinguish clearly between performers and spectators since the liturgy was celebrated by the congregation as a whole. The ritual was able to incorporate distanced, barely participating, and learned spectators. Possibly, the liturgy had even provided the concealed paradigm for the hermeneutic event as such. The incomprehensibility of Latin mass to vernacular audiences was a master *topos* of the Protestant tradition. The subsequent collapse of the intelligibility of key liturgical events such as the Eucharist could provide a prime motivation on the path toward becoming a philologist, as the case of Nöldeke testifies who liked to tell the story of how he lost his faith as an adolescent when he realized that the Lutheran ritual symbolized an act of cannibalism.[66] In any case, Littmann's ostentatious readiness to go along with the Abyssinian "as if," in compliance with the role of a marginal participant and spectator at once, was entirely compatible with the methodology of empathy and distance that formed part of *realphilologisch* training. The Aksumite service became a source; and its legibility as a source hinged on its being both intelligible and elusive, its being accessible to the empathetic as well as distancing process of *Verstehen*, to use Dilthey's momentous term.

Quite in line with Dilthey, what the case of Littmann's description suggests is that *Verstehen* was not merely an epistemic operation, an autonomous way of generating knowledge. The reason for its distinctness is that it requires mimesis and—this beyond Dilthey and arguably the older philological tradition—the spectatorial reactions of attraction and repulsion, of fear and trembling and relief, and the serene indifference of the comical. These reactions are not supplied by the circular movement—into which Heidegger and Gadamer developed the older philological notion of hermeneutics— within a common stock of lived experience informing both the authoring and the reading of the source. Rather, the range of spectatorial reactions hinges on the disunified variety of semantic operations and the mimetic unfolding of events in the archival scene on which the disunity of semantics unfolds. If anything, it is this constellation that marks the archival state of nature, a liminal state that departs from itself in the consciousness of an "as if."

The festive character of the events Littmann highlighted provides a crucial hint that in his perception the liminal state in question constituted what one might call a particular temporality.[67] The quality of festiveness requires the exclusion of the everyday, of the temporality of quotidian routine. Temporality is to be understood as the product of such a particularizing distinction within time. The overall pattern is quite analogous to the way in which for instance historical time is established as a temporality apart: a semiotic interconnection of representations of *realia* as signs for each other. The interconnection functions as a mechanism of order and simultaneously of exclusion, since it ensures that historical time does not simply coincide with past time as such. The liturgical celebration was sacred time for the clerics of Aksum. From Littmann's perspective, however, it was historical time (or almost: *as if*). If historical time was dependent, in this case, on the observation of congregational community in festive liturgical time, Littmann's reading of Aksumite documents in terms of their historical meaning leaned on the institution of the communal feast (with another nod to Lacoue-Labarthe's Rousseau and the *fête populaire*). To be sure, this was not a prerequisite in the absence of which Littmann would have failed to conduct a historical reading of, say, the inscriptions of Aksum. Rather, the Aksumites supplied an additional semantic resource of historical meaning Littmann then exploited over the following weeks in his handling of the historical record.

The supply was welcome. Orientalist of his period, Littmann yearned to be "transported back in history 3,000 years." The archival state of nature was itself a fragile combination of historically given components, emerging along the lines of a specific period-bound poetics that shaped Littmann's prose with its peculiar blend of impassioned and comically denigrating observation. These poetics permitted wildness to oscillate between the ridiculous and the historical sublime;[68] and this oscillation offered highly specific, even situation-bound, resources for setting up historical time and historical meaning. Littmann thus established highly particular modes of ascribing historicity, which coexisted alongside other regimes of historical time and yet further, non-historical types of particularized semiotic temporality. For this reason, it would be rash to ascribe to the archive a single mode of temporality—historical or other—as an insurmountable principle of order. Temporality was (and remains) more plural; it does not provide a unified ontological form, or a mode of discrete ordering, e.g. by sequence, to the archival material.

In Aksum, the archival situation as a whole—with regard to the mere state of preservation of the record of the past, its administration, and its consultation—was insecure and erratic. Even under optimal conditions, outsiders who wanted to access the records found themselves in a complicated situation. The expedition in practice required the support of the provincial governor, the *Dedschasmatsch Garasellase* or Gabra-Sellāsē (1872–1930).[69] Thus, the everyday work of archival research did not merely consist of the scholar's undisturbed confrontation with the material as envisaged by methodological handbooks of source study. Rather, such work was a situation in which several components of the archival state of nature intersected. Moreover, the actorial and spectatorial positions did not remain entirely stable. The following episode, which also involved the expedition's chief archaeologist, Daniel Krencker (1874–1941), and the attending medical officer, Erich Kaschke (1873–1910), provides an example:

> In the afternoon, Kaschke and I went to the *Dedj.*, I as substitute for Krencker—who had taken a laxative—to inspect the [newly excavated royal] tombs. After some *Tedsch* [Ethiopian mead], Kaschke bade farewell, and I rode alone, accompanied by more than 300 people, soldiers and petitioners, with the *Dedj.* and Passerini to *Enda Kaleb*. There we quickly entered the newly uncovered tomb, the large chambers and sarcophaguses, which enticed a series of cries of amazement: *woi gərrūm, woi gūd, 'amlāka 'əsrā'ēl, madhanä 'ālam, woi gara-səllāsä, Māryām 'Akhᵘsəm* and so on. He [that is, the *Dedj.*] had to measure the length of the chambers, the sarcophaguses, the great covering stone in the main chamber himself, and so on. He was certain that the longest sarcophagus (2.20m on top) had to be that of *Ḥaṣai Gabra Masqal*, who had been, according to tradition, very tall. The diverse stone mason signs were admired, and the *Dedj.* expressed the very appropriate idea that they might be the initials of proper names. ... Likely, these are indeed the signs of the masons who had delivered the stones; but full words also occur ...—Upon return, there was again much clamoring. The *Dedj.* virtually apologized that there were always so many people around him; but he had to have all his trusted servants and his best soldiers around him, since otherwise the crowd [of petitioners] would not let him pass.[70]

This passage demonstrates that given the conditions in Aksum, as in the *Harra* desert, different kinds of sources, different modes of *Gegenständlichkeit*, were present simultaneously. The governor's symbolic politics—perfectly compatible with genuine interest—demanded that he keep himself informed about the works. He visited the expedition camp and the archaeological sites frequently, often joining Littmann in attempted readings of Ge'ez inscriptions and manuscripts (Littmann consistently presents his own readings of the material as superior). None of this, however, exempted the governor from becoming a source himself. Thus, his exclamations of admiration were diligently transcribed by Littmann as part of the linguistic research conducted in Aksum. Moreover, Littmann also observed the governor from other perspectives, namely in terms of his knowledge of tradition (as opposed to history proper), and in his social and political role. Accordingly, Littmann, although moving in a sizeable crowd and accompanied by the governor, as well as one of the hired Italian guards (Passerini), "rode alone" to the site. This formulation not only stressed the earlier departure of Kaschke but also highlighted that Littmann *alone* was the scholarly observer to whom the cryptic signs of the stone cutters, the phraseology of the governor, and the social phenomenon of the petitioners were all equally sources, equally *gegenständlich*, and equally legible. Yet, the aligning of these different kinds of objects, as if in a sort of conversation, did not emerge by dint of some pre-given natural order in the material, but rather as a result of the spontaneous unfolding of events on site. The archive enacted both the individuation and the line-up of objects, and the archival scholar was a spectator of this enactment.

These considerations are not to be understood as a clear-cut ascription of agency to the archival record. Rather, they mean to illustrate the highly contingent event-structure of the archival situation as constituting the *Gegenständlichkeit* without which no archive would be legible. As a consequence of this structure, the semantics of the archival situation cannot be simply pragmatist in kind; the meaning of the written record of the past cannot be exclusively based on any interpreter's classification of the material; and neither can it be based solely on an author's intentions. In light of the mimetic character of the archival record, its meaning cannot solely reside in the material or in an order imposed on the material. Moreover, the event-structure of the archival situation is to a considerable degree spontaneous, as the example of the interactions with Gabra-Sellāsē indicates. Certainly, this structure drew on a large variety of external sources of meaning, for instance language, cultural and political customs, the positions of rocks, inscriptions, and archaeological sites. However, there remains a presence of spontaneity significant enough to defy the idea that the archival situation, under the aspect of mimesis, displays a discrete order. The Aksumite record of the historical past, as examined by Littmann, was a wild archive also from this point of view.

4. Revisiting the Safaitica

The argument as to the fluid ontological order of the epigraphic archive can even be carried further, into the very problem of the identity of the individual textual objects of research with themselves. In the terms set by Foucault, one of the most crucial aspects of archival order was that its structural nature enabled the repetition of discursive events. All the respective concepts aligned around the trope of the pre-given order of discourse, which supplied the condition of possibility of studying a historical a priori. Iterability was therefore to be constitutive of the novel "archaeological" approach to the archive since this approach entailed the identification of repetition in the written record of the past. This notion of iterability, and its concomitant hypostatization of order, can be challenged by scrutinizing episodes in which the archive was revisited; and a case in point is supplied by Littmann's second Syrian expedition, during which, in December 1904, he revisited the Safaitica.

At the time of the outing into the *Harra* desert in May 1900, Littmann had been palpably euphoric about the sheer number of inscriptions, of which he had only been able to record a tiny fraction due to the temporal and material constraints of his presence on site. A high priority of the 1904 expedition was to return to the area and achieve more complete documentation. Thus, the expedition, which at this point comprised—apart from hired staff—Littmann, Butler, and, as surveyor and keeper of the official diary, Frederick A. Norris (1872–1948),[71] returned to the Ḥaurān village of *Tarbā* and Sheikh *Ḥasan Sallâm*. The plan was to lodge the caravan—mules and camels and their accompanying staff—in *Tarbā*. Butler would ride off to Damascus to take care of correspondence and a few other matters; and Littmann and Norris, together with two of the more privileged expedition aides, *Butrus* and *Bshara* (once again Christian servants, hired in Palestine with the help of American missionaries), would set out for the desert with *Ḥasan Sallâm* and a few other Druzes for protection.

Littmann's visit to the desert in 1900 had been in late spring. In 1904, the caravan arrived in *Tarbā* on November 30. Heavy winds and snowfall on December 1 forced the expedition members to abandon their tents and seek refuge in the house of *Ḥasan Sallâm*. Littmann was irritated from the start. *Ḥasan* assigned the scholars a single room where he also insisted on sleeping during the night, so as to demonstrate his hospitality. Butler managed to set off in spite of the weather, yet the trip to the desert was delayed until December 4. Littmann, who unlike Norris was conversant in Arabic, passed the time by joining the Druzes for lengthy sessions of coffee-drinking and noting down a series of stories from quotidian Druze life, about feuds and wars and the Ottoman government. Although he recorded these stories diligently, he also annotated them with occasional doubt and ironical asides. The only thing he seemed to find enjoyable was the scenery:

> Saturday morning, the sky cleared and we had a most picturesque landscape before us. The mountains glistened in their white winter dress; here and there, black houses peeked out of the snow. The peaks north of *Tarba*, with their pointed summits looked especially splendorous. Then beneath the snowline, the black desert extended, and east of that, under a blue veil, the cragged *Ṣafā* mountains.[72]

Littmann's landscape descriptions were repetitive and contiguous with the patterns that characterize a widely shared poetic discourse. The "blue veil" for instance returns several times in the diary; revisiting a landscape was altogether unproblematic; conditions of identity were obviously different, presupposing a mingling of constancy and change from which textual documents were meant to be exempt. The passage draws on a reservoir of the idyllic and the sublime. The mixture of attraction and repulsion— the little houses in the snow and the cragged peaks—are important markers for the aesthetics informing the epigraphic archive, the socially instituted regime of perception, emotion, and judgment that framed Littmann's gaze and governed his attention.

In the diary of the 1899–1900 expedition, Littmann had registered only the best of impressions regarding *Ḥasan Sallâm*. Here was a sharp mind, a skillful handler of his environment, with clever and handsome sons, and exhibiting a somewhat uncultivated but impressive near-natural nobility: "He is only a short man, but his demeanor, his gaze, and his speech demonstrate that he is much superior to the common village dwellers"[73] (Figure 2). Most importantly, *Ḥasan* was not greedy: "He really seemed serious when betraying a certain embarrassment that he would have to accept a present before he had rendered us actual services."[74] Yet, in 1904, on second glance, everything was different. *Ḥasan Sallâm*, emerging victorious, though financially damaged, from a lawsuit in Damascus and, having entered a difficult feud with a neighboring village, had fallen on hard times:

> For the Druzes of *Tarbā* and surroundings our trip was easy prey. They all wanted to join, and *Ḥasan*, whose influence has by now been greatly undermined and who, in addition, required manpower to protect his own honorable person from blood avengers, could not deny anyone their wishes. When we left *Tarba* we had c. 14 Druzes with us, and in *Kusêb* [the neighboring village], another 6 joined. Originally, only 6 had been agreed, and even those would have been, as became apparent later on, superfluous.[75]

The Druzes quickly became a burden as Littmann grew apprehensive of being exploited. His dismissive attitude toward the protection the Druzes provided could not contrast more strongly with that of the 1900 diary, in which he described the outing into the same desert as a dangerous endeavor only made possible by the competent protection

Figure 2. Sheikh *Hasan Sallam*. Princeton University, Department of Art and Archaeology—Visual Resources, Archaeological Archives, Howard C. Butler Archive—Syria, image no. A7.

Ḥasan was kind enough to provide. Yet in 1904, the area had lost this specific aesthetic appeal; it was no longer the site of anticipated adventure. Revisiting the archive was not the same thing as visiting it for the first time. The sense of disappointment, disillusionment, and discontent was enhanced, or even made possible, by re-visitation. The scene was irrevocably changed.

On December 6, heavy rains forced the group to stop at a deserted Bedouin resting site that went by the name of *il-Mrôšan*:

> Here, there is a large number of camp sites (ṣîre, ṣiyar) in decent state; the Bedouins call the fenced sites *rasm (rusûm)*. Usually, they are covered by a comprehensive layer of sheep dung (*da'Þ*, Bedouin), which has gathered over centuries and quickly soaks up the rain, so that there it is much drier during rainfall than at other places, though it also reeks. But what were we supposed to do? Our Druzes had trusted their horses into the care of the two Bedouins accompanying us (both were called *Raġa* from the il-Ḥasan tribe) and squatted, packed as sardines, in the kitchen tent, where they, the great heroes, hardened against wind and weather, stayed all day and night as long as it rained. A few, however, especially *Selâme* from Tarbā, helped to look for inscriptions and turned over a great number of stones they presumed to be inscribed, and often correctly so. Many of those were from modern fences, others from modern ruġûm, which in part had been piled up by the Druzes as guideposts (*'alâme's*) during their most recent feuds (with the government and the Bedouins). This was especially indicated to me regarding the stone piles at il-Mrôšan. Admittedly it goes without saying that the old rusûm and ruġûm, the stones of which of course had their inscriptions on the side facing the onlooker, fell apart over time and that later generations simply piled inscribed and non-inscribed stones together as they happened to come across them.[76]

This lengthy passage illustrates once more the shifting of ontological types in the use of the epigraphic archive, which turned out to supply evidence for a considerable variety of things that stood in tentative explanatory relations with each other. The inscribed stones were viewed particularly under the aspect of their practical uses in the construction of fences and signposts. Littmann was careful, in this passage, to collect the vocabulary; and he was careful to explain such modern-day practices that led to the de-contextualization and scattering of inscribed rocks. At the same time, he was eager to name those who contributed to his work; and to provide a narrative account of the journey; to poke fun at the hydrophobic Druzes; and to point to the bizarre sponginess of the sheep manure carpeting, as the tactile and olfactory side effect of the herding life of the Bedouins. Once again, then, the epigraphic archive thus comprised all kinds of contextual objects that were not part of the text but rather of their spatial arrangement. In addition, these objects were aesthetically regimented; they were comical or even disgusting.

At any rate, in the situation at hand, the inscriptions were the primary record to be examined. The decision of what was to be classified as archival text, and what as context, was then perhaps mainly one of situational hierarchization. If one type of object did not yield results, another one moved to the foreground. Contemporary precepts of historical methodology tended to distinguish between "external" and "internal" critique of sources; and external critique comprised all kinds of considerations concerning the material state of the object as well as a variety of indirect readings of the text as evidence of something not contained in its literal meaning.[77] This type of critique was often associated with questions as to what a specific document was—that is to say, privileging a particular line of objectification, a particular determination of ontological type. Littmann's remarks about sheep dung are coextensive with this kind of procedure. The trouble with the Safaitic inscriptions was that they had been made by "primitive" nomads and mostly in pre-Islamic times. Their authors' actual uses for script required further explanation. Hence, all kinds of objectification came to seem attractive; and what in the end was the "external" and the "internal," the preliminary and the conclusive in a teleological process of research that was to penetrate from the outside to the inside of the object of knowledge, became an almost insubstantial question. Littmann's actual diary also appears to have fulfilled the purpose of not so much documenting but representing the drift of objectification in the day-to-day process of epigraphic exploration. Hence his lack of interest in establishing a rigid hierarchical order, in his narrative, among the objects he investigated. Neither the material nor the situation nor the order of the material remained stable between the first and second visit. One could not step twice into the same archive.

It is only on the basis of this instability of the written record of the past that Littmann's scholarly effort of classifying the inscriptions during publication, of ordering them in other than merely spatially determined groups, can be fully understood. The contrast between the fluidity of the collection on site and the transformations the inscriptions underwent in publication was stark. As mentioned, Littmann developed a grid of seemingly well-defined and exhaustive categories of meaning that served to group the inscriptions. Spatial proximity became a secondary criterion of address. Yet, the insecurities of content remained considerable, as the disagreements with Grimme suggested. The very status of the semantic categories remained tentative and tied to the problem of the overall interpretation of the Safaitic archive. Littmann's categorization aimed for dispersion; there was no recognizable system, no cultural unity discernible, beyond the "pride" of natural individuality. The relative prevalence of genealogical inscriptions indicated that the authors had been "nomads or semi-nomads."[78] Eritrean custom could serve for comparison.[79] In accordance with Rhodokanakis's legal theory, some inscriptions were to be regarded as public record of private law transactions. In some cases, the inscriptions contained, as had to be conceded to Grimme, prayers, and the importance of religious content was more prominent than often presumed in nineteenth-century Bedouin ethnography, as could be seen from the widespread presence of "theophoric" proper names that both epigraphers agreed expressed some form of attachment to a deity.[80] Yet elsewhere, the inscriptions had to be read as jocular. Littmann proposed distinguishing between the functions of literate scribe and illiterate author and identified at least one case in which the scribe had apparently ridiculed the author.[81] In this inscription as well as in others, the meaning could be read as scatological, with references to excretion as well as sexual intercourse that were so crude they only suffered Latin translation.[82] These inscriptions in particular were meant to prove that the archive was incompatible with Grimme's notion that the alleged unity of Safaitic religious sentiment had been translated into the spatial unity of the *Harra* as a holy district. At the same time, it was meant to retain some of the crudeness and incivility that had marked Littmann's revisiting of the inscriptions with the Druzes of *Tarbā*. Even Grimme conceded that the Safaitic pantheon did not make sense as a unified system the like of, for instance, the Homeric gods. Rather the authors of the inscriptions had offered hospitality to a random aggregation of foreign gods.[83] The religion Grimme believed he was investigating also turned out to be in flux. The seemingly stable, if divergent categories he and Littmann both used to generate the appearance of order among the published inscriptions thus subtly served to transfer the ontological fluidity of the objects of epigraphic archival research into the published format. Under the guise of classification, the categories actually practiced philological *epokhé*; and *epokhé* was a term that expressed recognition and acceptance of wildness.

5. The Aesthetics of *Realphilologie*

Littmann's parcours of objectifications resulted from the particularities of the Oriental philology he had studied at university. Repeatedly dissatisfied with his environment of study, he had changed university several times (Berlin, Greifswald, Halle, then postgraduate work with Nöldeke in Strasbourg) and had studied with professors from a considerable variety of disciplines, not only theology and several Semitic languages (he had especially focused on Arabic and Ge'ez) but also German linguistics and philosophy. While he had written his Ethiopicist dissertation under the supervision of the linguist Franz Praetorius, subsequently the *realphilologische* lectures and works of Georg Jacob became more important for the orientation of his research interests particularly in expedition travel.

Jacob, then an unsalaried *Privatdozent*, arrived at Halle in 1896 to assume the position of librarian of the *Deutsche Morgenländische Gesellschaft*, the association of German Orientalists that had been founded in 1845. Within a short period, he developed a visceral hatred of Praetorius, on both personal and scholarly grounds. Littmann found it at times difficult to navigate the tension between his masters.[84] Jacob abhorred the narrow historical-linguistic research championed by Praetorius and other Semitists of the period who were increasingly gravitating toward the new linguistics of the *Junggrammatiker*, the "neogrammarians." Since the 1870s this group had formed a forceful cartel of innovation especially in the Germanist and Indo-Europeanist fields. Their research was heavily dominated by the comparative study of cognate languages and the historical-empirical study of individual languages, with a focus on phonetics extending as far as the physiology of the voice. The aim of this approach was to achieve a novel scientific footing on which to formulate phonetic laws that would permit the reconstruction of genealogies and prehistorical states of languages. The model was descriptive-empirical natural science; and language was rigorously theorized as an autonomous domain whose history stood equally distinct from other forms of history as natural history.[85] Roughly at the same time, Indo-Europeanist scholars abroad, especially Ferdinand de Saussure, who had been educated in part by the neogrammarians in Leipzig, sought to depart from the model in the direction of novel "structuralist" notions of language—as determined by synchronous systemic differences rather than merely by phonetic change as diachronic center—that would come to mark twentieth-century linguistic research especially in France as well as Eastern Europe.[86] In the remote field of Semitic philology, an older, less theoretically positioned style of grammar—based on the stolid collection of data from ancient texts, arranged according to the structural schema of traditional grammar, and conducted in combination with lexical work on the vocabulary—continued to be practiced alongside the seemingly more innovative, more "scientific" approach. Nöldeke was a chief representative of this descriptive, empirical tradition.

Other scholars, such as Jacob, developed an understanding of philology in opposition to linguistics. It was in this context that the terminology of the old Graecist polemic between *Wortphilologie* and *Realphilologie* re-emerged. Jacob consistently understood philology in Boeckhian terms, as a research program interested in text as testimony to the manifold of the human appropriation of (natural) reality. In this way, he aligned himself with a partly invented tradition against a partly invented phalanx of linguists. To be sure, Jacob was not alone in the general thrust of his work, but marginal. He appropriated an older position he did not care to think through in theoretical terms, and his orientation was arguably out of tune with the trends of the period and, in its understanding of "nature," fed on the literary aesthetics of a bygone age, the period around 1800 and its complicated engagement with anti-mechanist natural philosophy and cultural autochthony. It was only a few years later, *c.* 1910, that Carl Heinrich Becker began formulating a research program for Islamic studies that in Germany became highly influential for the reorganization of the entire field. Yet for Becker, more strongly influenced by the studies of Islamic religion from Arabic sources that Ignaz Goldziher (1850–1921) and Christiaan Snouck Hurgronje (1857–1936) had pioneered since around 1880,[87] the religious determination of culture was to become the core problem of a renewed *Realphilologie*. This orientation remained alien to Jacob in spite of the considerable work he had conducted in particular on Sufism in the Ottoman Empire.[88] Littmann, Becker's coeval, worked in the line of Jacob's concerns.

The dichotomy of *Wort-* and *Realphilologie* could be variably mapped on other past antagonisms. Jacob frequently reprised Herderian phrasing when declaring his aim of attaining "full understanding of national character [*Volkstum*]."[89] In the preface to his *Early Arabic Bedouin Life*—which exerted a particularly strong influence on Littmann's perception of Bedouin matters in 1900–4[90]—Jacob attacked the normative aesthetics of "classicism," which "as everyone who has outgrown it knows, takes away infinitely more than it is able to give; for, in its one-sided and fanatical manner, it kills all receptivity for the beautiful in its natural diversity."[91] Orientalist philology—in alliance with Germanic studies—was to widen and transform the historical-philological disciplines in such a way as to reconstruct "the natural nexus of the phenomena" and ultimately to integrate philology into natural science proper.[92] In this fashion, the Jacobean project aimed for nothing less than the reappropriation of the model of natural science that marked the work of the opposing camp. This reappropriation was to be accomplished by recuperating the eighteenth-century amalgam of vitalist physics and aesthetic theorizing that had marked German reprisals of the *Querelle des anciens et des modernes* since the 1750s.[93] Jacob was staunchly on the side of the "moderns," which had also been that of the "romantics" and of those generally who had championed "the Orient" in some form or other. Indeed, Littmann, with a pinch of kindly irony, often referred to his teacher as a romantic.[94]

Jacob also relied on a romantic-era understanding of scientific method where knowledge was to draw above all on individual vision.[95] For this reason, aesthetics, as a regime of perception, pertained to everything in scientific reasoning. The traveling philologist was to expose the relatedness of culture to an overwhelmingly diverse natural reality; but "nature" and its "diversity" were poetic in kind, that is to say, geared to an aesthetically regimented phenomenal intentionality endowed with creative agency. In fact, Jacob's dichotomy of nature and classical antiquity still echoed the way in which Winckelmann had contrasted learning from nature and learning from classical sculpture in his foundational treatise on the imitation of the ancients.[96]

For Jacob, "nature" meant rejecting the centrality of the human form with which Greek art—both in literature and in sculpture—and its classicist imitation were chiefly associated. Winckelmann had argued that the "neglects" (*Nachlässigkeiten*) of the ancient sculptors were aesthetically legitimate since they concerned only accessories external to the human body that were of no concern to the ancient gaze.[97] In a letter to Littmann, written in July 1914, Jacob broke into one of his characteristic tirades:

> How incredibly stupid is the scene of Faust with the garment of Helena! By relying on the same recipe, the hideous, rattling hexameter, Goethe completely bungled *Hermann und Dorothea*, which if written in plain prose might have developed into a German folk epic [*Volksbuch*]; and as regards the Rostock Blücher [monument], in the design of which Goethe pushed for the cudgel of Hercules and the lion hide, he helped bring into existence a disgusting hybrid [*Zwittergestalt*]. I consider it almost a brutality of feeling, and barbaric bigotry, when people erect statues of nudes here among the snowdrifts of Nordic winter, and when they ape ancient architecture, which was designed to permit a draft of air, in our climate of head cold. By contrast, it remains heart-warming to see the huge success that Japanese folk art, though transmitted only through a few connoisseurs, has achieved in Germany, and how the inner life of the Japanese nation and their tender understanding of nature has been echoed a thousand times, while antiquity—in its lack of any true relation with nature, which it turned into an awful human grimace—has, praised be God!, never touched our national life, but has eventually remained limited to the empty phrases of prep-school swagger. Is there anything more wonderful than the poetry of the bottom of the sea and its beautiful shapes; and yet Schiller, in all his classicist bigotry, has only these words for it: "But down there it is horrible!" [in the ballad *The Diver*]. In this way, our inner life is impoverished and crippled by fanatic dogmatists.[98]

The humanization of nature, together with the idealization of the human form— ambivalently taken to be the expression of the nature-induced (but still deficient) national character of the Ancient Greeks—was the topical mark of Greek mythology, which in turn was seen as feeding all other Ancient Greek art. Jacob countered with his bottom-of-the-sea aesthetics in which the personification of the non-personal was overcome by a range of ultimately superior Germanic and Oriental national aesthetics, more given to the excess that underpinned sublimity than the ideal measure that constituted the classicist conception of beauty. The passage is delightfully self-contradictory in its metaphors—the national "inner life" is still in danger of being "crippled" by classicism, and thus in danger of being deprived of its natural bodily perfection.

The transfer of Jacob's aesthetics to the production of knowledge in the epigraphic archive was marked by an analogous difficulty: among the Safaitic inscriptions in particular, the vast majority contained, or consisted entirely of, proper names of persons. The human form was not easily excised from the center of the epigraphic archive. Arguably, the decisive step was to integrate people with the material. Littmann was scrupulous in noting the contributions guides and aides made to his research, not merely in order to give due credit but also in order to avoid blame for insufficient documentation. At the same time, he carefully recorded those interactions of natives with the material which could count as contextual, as in the case of the rock piles of *il-Mrôsan*: The fact that the *Tarbā* Druze *Selâme* was so successful at finding inscriptions was, if tacitly, taken to be the result of privileged knowledge of the ways the locals handled the local rocks. *Selâme* was a name-bearing user of names who communicated with the writers of names, a person with knowledge about persons. When Littmann described the use of stone piles as guideposts, he explicitly mentioned receiving an oral explanation from one of the Druzes (though in this case he did not detail by who imparted it). This use of inscribed rocks was not understandable by way of the material alone. As would be the case with Gabra-Sellāsē in Aksum, the Syrian locals thus became objects of research, that is to say, part of the archive. Persons, their assertions, and their habits were constantly put to use as documents of "culture." The western scholars, however, were exempt from being transformed into such documents and scrutinized under the lens of scholarship. Implicitly organicist understandings of culture, which were common in the period—Jacob, a few years on, professed some degree of admiration for Leo Frobenius's (1873–1938) theory of *Kulturkreise* as a decisive step beyond the "unsystematic" work of Karl Lamprecht[99]—provided a model that allowed for easily excising, from the situation of observation, that which was alien to the organism.

Subtly, then, Littmann's research practice asserted an inequality among the people he encountered during his visit to the epigraphic archive. Arguably, the primary function of this assertion was not once more to confirm, redundantly, the superiority of Europeans over Orientals; but rather, to decenter the human form by disassembling its unity. The question of the fundamental distinctions that supposedly held between Occidentals and Orientals was therefore the correlate of an aesthetic requirement: to accommodate the rejection of the centrality of the human form with the perusal of a record that was, by dint of its reliance on proper names, inescapably human. The mechanism of this accommodation was to turn the names, as well as their users, into documents of cultural reality, including language. The main use of the inscriptions was as sources for linguistic and script-related problems.[100] Such an explication was successful if there was a shared set of cultural rules for the deployment of proper names as designators that, once bestowed, remained unalterably attached to their referent.[101] This underlying commonality ensured that the transformation of the Syrian interlocutors into documents remained by necessity incomplete: They remained bearers of names in the same manner as the scholarly observers.

Yet, with the *Tarbā* Druzes, even this imperfect, makeshift transformation was not successful. Their lack of amenability profoundly displeased Littmann. By contrast, "nature" as well as the non-human documents, although they both provided a considerable measure of difficulty, never lost the potential for aesthetic value. Rainfall continued all day—or "most of the day," according to Norris[102]—on December 7, 1904. Littmann, fearing that the trip would have to be aborted in *il-Mrôsan*, suffered what he claimed was the most serious "nervous anguish" (*nervöse Pein*) he underwent during the entire expedition.[103] Norris, it is worth adding, thought that the reasons for Littmann's state of mind were different in nature; he noted:

> This desert—nothing but one vast sea of black stone and the rain and cold and discomfort—has a depressing effect on L[ittmann] but I am in the best of spirits, feeling a sort of fierce joy in fighting nature when I see her in this aspect.[104]

The perception of implicitly personified nature as an adversary, and of struggle as a source of joy, eluded Littmann. His propensity in the perception of landscape remained toward the idyllic. The underlying tendency to write about landscape as a scene was however the same; only genres diverged.

The following day, as the group was finally able to move on, Littmann rediscovered a coveted place of inscriptions "which had previously so ravished me" and where he "spent almost all afternoon in a tiny spot where literally every stone is inscribed."[105] And on December 9, upon returning to the same spot early in the morning, poetic perception seemingly restored the order of the scene:

> I had an overwhelming spectacle of nature before me. The sun was rising in wonderful, gorgeous gold and threw its bright rays, across the white Ruḥbe and on the black Ṣafā Mountains, which seemed to float in a white sea. ... This sunrise is probably the most beautiful I have ever seen.[106]

Yet at the same time, his perception of the Druzes became increasingly less favorable. On December 10,

> the Druzes greatly irritated me; whenever we reached an area relatively devoid of boulders, they set their mares to gallop all around us, which made our horses very nervous, and then, once they were in the *waʾr*, they rode on and on without looking back. Of course, the Druze horses could get ahead much faster than ours, and thus a few times I was almost entirely without guides. After all, the Druzes had come along for their own pleasure, not for mine. That this was not the case I could not get into their skulls.[107]

It clearly irked Littmann that he was paying for services that were not delivered; but it was the disturbance of the research that angered him most. Again, Norris's perception of this type of scene was directly the opposite; for the return to *Tarbā* on December 12, he reported:

> A most enjoyably [!] day on horse back to Tarba in morning. Weather perfect, roads or rather the way good, sun in back, mountains ahead, our Druze escort racing their horses & giving exhibitions of riding glorious sight—a pity that Remington the artist could not have seen it.[108]

So where Littmann felt bullied and relinquished, Norris felt he was being offered a performance worthy of the efforts of the US favorite of frontier adventure painting, Frederic Remington. The mood of the diaries is starkly different even though they tend to agree on the events. Norris also actively provided entertainment; for instance, he instigated a shooting competition and set a prize for the winner on December 5, "and we had much fun." But it is also difficult to overlook that Norris enjoyed many of the aspects Littmann had appreciated in 1900: "After the competition they sang their war song & danced and then showed me how they charged the enemy in battle," all the while "L. obtained many inscriptions."[109] So the stark distinction between visiting and revisiting the epigraphic archive also appears to account for some of the divergence in the mood of the diaries.

Norris was not indifferent to the pleasures of epigraphy either. In October, while the expedition was in *'Arâk il-Emir* (in present day Jordan—the scholars were traveling northeast from Jerusalem), Norris described the work:

> In the afternoon we rode up the valley for some 3 miles following the E.[ast] bank of the stream until we came to a ruined building and hunted for inscriptions. This hunting for inscriptions is as fascinating as a search for gold—very exciting to think that at any minute you may find the key which will open up those great secrets of past ages which seem so near your grasp. We found none.[110]

If hunting, the sovereign pastime—and the exclusive possession of the arcane, another figure of sovereignty—provided a potential framework for the significance of epigraphy, it becomes all the more difficult to understand Littmann's distress; except that for him the processing of masses of insignificant proper name graffiti was far less exciting. Since the decipherment had already been accomplished, there were no exhilarating secrets to be discovered. Littmann's reading of the content of the inscriptions, unlike Grimme's, tended toward the banal.

On December 11, *Ḥasan Sallâm* led Littmann to "the most beautiful and important inscriptions of my entire collection, with a number of novel words. One inscription was very regularly and deeply carved and was of a more monumental character than all the others I had seen so far."[111] Yet, this demonstration of contextuality on the part of *Ḥasan Sallâm* was not enough to placate Littmann's indignation. The next day, the last leg of the trip, Littmann's aide Butrus brought him copies of inscriptions he, Butrus, had produced on a hilltop nearby. Littmann, wanting to collate the copies with the originals, went to the spot together with his aide, but they were unable to retrieve the stones. "Since the Druzes had seen [Butrus] copying there, it is very easily possible that one of them amused himself by making a mess of the stones afterward. Indeed, the spot looked as if much had just been turned over."[112]

This was the point at which Littmann began to describe the interference of the Druzes, not just as an impediment, but as malign. In the same entry he claimed that *Hasan Sallâm* had told him "lies" about the dangers to be expected in the desert, seeing as they had not encountered anyone in eight days; and he went on to complain that in the village of *Kusêb*,

> we were forced to eat, against our will, because the Druzes were so gluttonous and did not want to wait another quarter of an hour before they would have arrived home. Admittedly, one has to take into account that the law of hospitality inexorably demands that in a friendly village a man like Ḥasan has to be treated when he passes through. It would have been `aib and ḥarâm not to do this.[113]

So in spite of recognizing the Druzes' behavior as governed by normative constraints, Littmann did not refrain from moral reproach. His animus against *Hasan Sallâm* had grown too strong to remain contained. Littmann's fair copy diaries were composed during the journey, but the entries were not infrequently composed with some delay, after they had first been jotted down in pencil in a different set of notebooks.[114] Yet, in the case of the Druzes of *Tarbā*, even the distance provided by the writing procedure did not suffice to uphold the ordinary mechanism of objectification. Sheikh *Ḥasan* was neither to be decentered as an object of research nor excised from the situation. Thus, everything about the man whom Littmann had earlier praised so much became despicable.

The diary entries for the following two days—in which the caravan remained in *Tarbā*—are marked by ever more extensive invective. Since *Ḥasan* had allowed more men to accompany the scholars to the desert than had originally been agreed, Littmann decided to pay him a lump sum and tell him to take care of the distribution himself. Yet inadvertently, the morning after their return,

> he came marching in here with his vampires; everybody sat down and immediately they began to divide up [the money]. We were so infuriated that we turned our backs on the entire company and did not speak a word to any of them until they all left.[115]

And the next day, at the farewell visit to the sheikh, the bestowal of presents also was

> a rather unpleasant task. [... *Ḥasan*] himself as well as his oldest son ... brazenly begged for all sorts of things, money, weapons, knives and so on. They received more money than they deserved, but of course no weapons. Nonetheless, later on, everywhere in the Hauran it was said that we had given Ḥasan weapons.[116]

Regarding the village of *Sâle*, which was the next location they visited, Littmann—in implicit contrast to *Ḥasan* and in implicit emphasis of the inequality even among the Druze population of the southern Ḥaurān—then wrote an unusually amicable portrait of the sheikh there, "a dignified old man" who reminded him of "an elderly university professor,"[117] a class of human beings *duly* exempt from becoming an object of research.

The Druzes of *Tarbā*, by their obstinacy and (from Littmann's perspective) malignancy had forced their way out of the range of objects of epigraphic research and called, by way of coming short, moral judgment on themselves. In the case of the sheikh of *Sâle*, and in fact an entire series of subsequent encounters, Littmann seems to have attempted to compensate for the anger and revulsion that had built up during the stay in *Tarbā*. In a way, *Ḥasan Sallâm* had thus managed to destroy Littmann's more or less deliberate application of the aesthetics derived from Jacob's *Realphilologie* research project. The working principles of philological practice, though, were more resilient than theoretical positions. Littmann simply accommodated multiple perspectives on the centrality of the human form. He continued to integrate and de-center the locals by way of contextualization. At the same time, he engaged in moral assessments, which suggested a sort of universality the *realphilologisch* procedure otherwise tended to deny, on account of its subliminal aggression against the centrality of the human form. This is also to say that the philological aesthetic in question consisted in a contingent and highly peculiar constellation; it was a working aesthetic.

6. De gustibus

Most of the slurs Littmann cast on the *Tarbā* Druzes—gluttons, vampires, beggars— connoted the transgressive appropriation, or the actual ingestion, of material objects. These choices of derogatory trope might be read as further confirmation of the impression that the underlying conflict resulted from a problem of objectification. Property and consumption are salient metaphors for such entities that become integrated, as objects, into a system of purposes, into a subsection of *realia* defined by their serviceability, their openness to practical intention and manipulation. The rules supposedly governing this system had been disturbed. In a sense, though, it appears as if Littmann's dislike of the Druzes simply followed a common pattern of colonial and imperial histories, a structure of domination in which the intruding power favored particular groups at the expense of others by the measure of their availability for the establishment and maintenance of foreign rule. Ussama Makdisi has argued that the tribalist categories of nineteenth-century English and French Orientalism in particular programmed the subsequent sectarian politics of Ottoman Lebanon. The identities shaped by imperial scholarship prefigured colonization.[118] If, in a broadly Foucaultian—and Saidian—vein, one substitutes knowledge for power in the account of Littmann's belaboring of the distinction between Druzes and Bedouins, it then seems that the shift from the institutional to the epigraphic archive has not yielded much novel insight. The difference between "our" and "their" documents would ultimately appear as a simple epiphenomenon of the favoring of one group of imperial-epistemic interest, the Bedouins, at the expense of another one, the Druzes—a favoring that was only an extension of the imperial expansion of a European state (and knowledge) apparatus. If so, the epigraphic archive was only a somewhat more intricate variation of the institutional state archive as a seat of power. Such a conclusion would reproduce a standard model of historical writing, according to which a historical explanation is achieved by identifying a pursuit of political power, no matter in what state of sublimation and transmutation. Indeed, the political would be about power; history would be about the political; and archival order would be its seat.

How do Littmann's remarks on, and intimations of, the distinctness of Druzes and Bedouins speak to this problematic? It is worthwhile looking somewhat more closely at such passages in the diary in which Littmann contrasts Druzes and Bedouins. In the entry for December 4, Littmann penned a lengthy account of a punitive expedition of the Ottoman government against one of the local Bedouin tribes, as recounted by the *Tarbā* sheikh. The scene is set as follows:

> In *id-Diyâthe*, which I knew from the last expedition, we stopped for a while and looked for inscriptions, but did not find any. Here, Hasan showed me the spot at which Ḥusruf Pascha had made camp four years ago during his punitive expedition against the 'Umûr [tribe]. Dussaud had already written to me about this expedition; it had taken place almost at the same time as D[u]s[saud] and Macler had been there.[119]

Significantly, the story is offered in compensation for an unsuccessful attempt at finding inscriptions, on the occasion of a specific location that *Hasan* indicates as related to the events. The narrative is thus a contextual placeholder for the written documents that remain elusive. The story complements information to be gained from the work of the French colleagues.[120] The key portion of the narrative is the following:

> Šelâš il-'Irr [a Bedouin leader and notorious robber Littmann had met during the 1899–1900 expedition] had become too insolent and had completely plundered a very large caravan close to Damascus. ... Ḥusruf Pascha marched out with several regiments. The Druzes seem to have played a very dubious role in the entire affair. On the one hand, they did not want to entirely abandon their friends, the robbers, with whom they are usually in collusion and from whom they usually take the largest part of the loot; on the other, they wanted to be of service to the government. So they took the women and children of the Bedouins into hiding in their villages ... and at the same time acted as scouts for the soldiers in the desert. The Bedouins retreated, as they have done since the oldest times, into the Ṣafa Mountains where only they (and perhaps a few Druzes) know the trails. So Ḥusruf Pascha ... had to return to the [Ḥaurān] mountains without having achieved much. However, I know from Dussaud that the Turks took the Bedouin women and children as prisoners; and from the Druzes that Šelâš il-'Irr capitulated. ... The conclusion as to how the Turks got their hands on the Bedouin women and children is, I think, pretty simple. No Druze has given me any specific information, though. Šelâš il-

'Irr thus bowed to the government … and moved with his tribe to the Palmyrene mountains … , and in return for a small annual sum … he has pledged to leave the caravan alone.

The expressions of discontent in this passage, one-sidedly directed against the Druzes, relate to Littmann's conviction that his interlocutors did not give him a trustworthy account of the events, as the collation of their story with Dussaud's—philological routine work—demonstrated. It was not only that the Druzes kept displacing inscribed stones; they were also deeply unreliable oral sources of knowledge, which was particularly irksome when it mattered to Littmann's research, as in this case the reality of Bedouin life as the semantic key to reading the Safaitica. As a consequence, the Druzes themselves, unlike the Bedouins, were significantly less worthy of enjoying representation within scholarly knowledge.

   The notion of representation that informed this distinction was governed by the aesthetic requirements of *Realphilologie*, as is demonstrated by the comical ending Littmann imposed on the narrative. Tragic motifs of punishment, retribution, and betrayal were brought to a farcical solution that did not inspire compassion. The distinction between Druzes and Bedouins (and Ottomans) was revealed as less profound than Littmann's partisanship otherwise suggested, since all participants in the conflict were exposed as forming part of a single system of balancing interests that bound them together instead of distinguishing them.

   In a way it seems that within this system the Bedouins were meant to fill what Michel-Rolph Trouillot called the "savage slot," the fixed discursive position for the portion of humanity that supposedly stood in particular proximity to the state of nature.[121] The savage slot was part of a triad of positions. Trouillot himself differentiated between savagery, statal order, and utopia. Alternatively, and perhaps more in keeping with the context at hand, one might also propose drawing on the enlightenment triad of ancients, moderns, and savages.[122] For Trouillot, the slots were functions of the symbolic order that sustained "the West" as a system of political domination; these functions were not produced, and not even, in his view, significantly modified by scholarship. The "slot" then is another trope of discursive order as imposed by imperial power. Yet, for Littmann's 1904 perception of the Druzes, this rigid discursive template did not provide a particular slot. The Druzes were neither ancients nor moderns, neither properly under the state nor organized in a utopian community; and most certainly they were not savages since they enjoyed greater proximity to "civilization" than the Bedouin.

   Moreover, the subtlety of Littmann's treatment of the Bedouins is not fully captured if one reduces them to the position of (noble) savagery. The *Uneigentlichkeit*, the non-committal, improper, inactual quality of the assertion of the natural nobility to which Littmann's partisanship for the Bedouins was attached, has to be taken into account. The manner in which the Bedouins were tied, in his eyes, into the political game on the fringes of the Ottoman Empire was a source of irony that did not entirely escape the scholarly observer. Even to Littmann, the assumption that the savages were actually so savage was a somewhat old-fashioned and naïve perception that belonged to anachronistic armchair Orientalism.[123] Indeed, the Bedouins, having long lost the ability to write in Safaitic script, did not even provide an actually relevant context to Littmann's epigraphic work. The desire to produce knowledge by reference to and with the help of the Bedouins—and not the Druzes—was unreal and expressed an outright inclusion of a predominantly aesthetic preference into the understanding of the philological production of knowledge.

The aesthetics at work in the diary, since they were wedded to *Uneigentlichkeit* and irony, were endowed with a tendency toward the comical that is overlooked if one expects the political to be perceived as dominated by tragic motifs.[124] The comical was another mode of representation Littmann shared with Jacob, whose diatribes were often above all satiric in spirit. The string of associations by which, in the letter from July 5, 1914 quoted previously, Jacob entered into his invective against classicist aesthetics actually set out from political remarks about the Ottoman Empire where German educational ideals had supposedly stumbled over their own inherent classicism:

> [R]epeatedly I have had the opportunity to observe how the German *Gymnasium* in Constantinople, in accordance with its brainless design, imports entirely useless junk knowledge, thus creating the opinion that the Germans are impractical-pedantic muddle-heads [*Querköpfe*]. We cannot afford the classicist luxury any longer, the times are too serious for that; and how much less can the Turks! The *Gymnasium* poison we should wish upon the French. As things stand, we have been nurturing, by means of the de-nationalization of the upper classes, the misguided taste of non-indigenous artistic epigonism [*Afterkunst*], social democracy, the [Catholic] *Zentrum* party and similar things! While Britain won the world, we killed time cramming constructions of *futurum fuisse ut* and learned whiny poems by heart such as those of the phrasemonger Horace, which surely do not contain a single poetic thought, even though every year better authors go to our dustbins by the hundreds.[125]

One week into the July Crisis, Jacob identified the notion of *Bildung* with which classical philology had been bound up for more than a century as the central problem of German politics. *Bildung*—the meaning of which continued to drift in the enormous reservoir of theoretical and poetic interpretations formulated in and since the Goethe period—had come to offer a last, pedagogic refuge to classicism after the latter's actual demise in the arts. Jacob's perception of the limitations of classicism's basic plausibility, at the beginning of the twentieth century, was acute. Yet the actual field of contest remained aesthetics. The anti-classicists had never bothered to seek out a different battleground or, as for that, playground. In Jacob's eyes, classicism—with its focus on the human form, on the individual (instead of the nation), and on "humanism"—had initially perverted taste and subsequently politics. On a side note, the grammatical formalism of Latin teaching was, for Jacob, of a piece with the aesthetic idealism of classical sculpture. German geopolitics had been botched as a result of an impractical ideology of education that was neither useful nor expressive of national character. The attraction of the comical was an after-effect of the aesthetic nature of the understanding of political matters. Attacking classicism meant attacking the idealization of the human form, overturning the conception of beauty in tow with the national-pedagogical project, and questioning the monumental character of the resulting edifice, or body, of state. The subversion of the beautiful was to be achieved through the ugly, which was inherently a comical effect.[126] Among many other things, the comical was an antidote to the pathos of *Bildung*.

Littmann, to be sure, did not fully share Jacob's aesthetic politics. During the First World War, the two scholars almost fell out over Littmann's insistence on dedicating one of his publications to Howard Butler. Jacob, by contrast, had already in 1915 begun to regard the still neutral Americans as enemies of Germany. In a letter to Theodor Nöldeke, revered master of both scholars, Littmann deplored the "chauvinism" of Jacob's stance.[127] Nonetheless, Littmann, too, maintained the primacy of aesthetics over the political. When, during the war, almost all of the German Orientalists broke with Snouck Hurgronje over the "Jihad made in Germany" controversy, in which Snouck had accused the Germans of irresponsibly stoking Jihadism in the Ottoman Empire and the Islamic world in general, for their short-sighted aims against the Entente powers,[128] Littmann wrote to Nöldeke:

> My relation with Snouck has been marred for all time; in the future, only cool correctness will be possible between us; but I do not want to do him wrong, one is simply of "a different mind"—Politics is emotion, and there is no point in quarrelling over emotion. De gustibus non est disputantibus.[129]

Thus, politics, emotion, taste were still interchangeable almost a year into the war; and by way of taste, aesthetics enjoyed primacy. The vagaries of Orientalist aesthetics also spilled over into the domain of politics. Littmann's irenic interpretation of the conflict with Snouck is in itself telling: the idea of taking the "quarrel" out of "politics," in May 1915, bespeaks an almost uncanny blindness to contemporary events. In matters both Oriental and Occidental, taste was the precondition of political feeling. The aesthetic decision to prefer the Bedouins over the Druzes ultimately was of a kind with Snouck's decision to prefer the British over the Germans. Certainly, at other occasions, the First World War seemed an altogether more serious affair. Still, Littmann, while flaunting the wounds Snouck had inflicted on his national pride, found the time to crack a philologist's joke, inserting a false Latin participle (instead of a gerundive). The ridiculous asserted itself, wrecking archival order along the way.

7. Hyaena Ridens

It appears then that neither the procedure of reading nor the archival material itself, let alone a solid structure of iteration, a regime of aesthetic norms, or a political discourse that awarded stable "slots" to distinct collectives, supplied the technologically controlled level of archival order supposedly characteristic of the "house of the archon." Perhaps, though, such order might still be obtained by a discourse with the power of shaping, through normativity, the production of ordered knowledge from such admittedly unsteady resources. The prime candidate for such a discourse would be that of scientific "objectivity," which offered an epistemology regulated through person-centered virtue ethics. This discourse certainly had the power of a primal scene through which earlier and competing methodological positions would have been repressed and that could have passed for a proper founding moment of modern science. From the perspective of methodology, archival wildness would be a matter of the failing of normative orders pertaining to the organization of material, the acquisition of knowledge, and the scholarly persona.[130] I will therefore continue by outlining a number of ways in which the wild archives of epigraphy also subverted such normative ordering.

In Aksum access to whatever archival record the expedition wished to consult was problematic. Gabra-Sellāsē's support of the expedition was, at least in part, prompted by his own political motives, if Littmann's analysis of the situation was correct. The holy district of Aksum—as the center of the Ethiopian Church—was exempt from imperial taxation and punishment and accordingly unruly. For the duration of the expedition, the governor relocated from his residence in Adwa to Aksum, even having a house built for himself there, so as to impose Imperial authority. At the court in Addis Ababa, the hosting of the expedition was regarded as a demonstration of diplomatic autonomy; but it was also a demonstration of power to the Aksumites themselves. Unsurprisingly, the priesthood of Aksum disliked the presence of the expedition. The Orientalists intruded into the possessions of the church, its manuscript collection and its treasure, which were usually only accessible to select clerics. At the same time, the priests resented being ordered about by the representative of the Negus. As a consequence they were quite obstructive to the expedition. Several private proprietors of stones with inscriptions responded in similar fashion, at times going as far as burying the stones the scholars intended to look at. The German expedition, to be sure, was not the first Orientalist mission in Aksum; here, too, a parcours of *topoi* was to be followed, if a much less elaborate one than in Syria. Access required ceaseless negotiation, often involving the governor, and the constant distribution of gifts.

On April 2, 1906, a few days before the scheduled end of the expedition—the governor had already departed for business in the capital on March 20—all efforts of building goodwill in the city collapsed. Krencker had ordered digging in a private courtyard without the permission of the proprietor, who, upon arrival on the scene, protested so harshly as to make Krencker abandon the site. This episode led to riotous protests against the expedition, which the governor's deputy managed to quell without great difficulty. Nonetheless, Littmann's diary and that of the second archaeologist, Theodor von Lüpke (1873–1961), betray that the Germans were so concerned about the situation that they accepted Abyssinian soldiers from the governor's forces as protection.[131] Clearly, the scholars felt their personal safety had been compromised and therefore surrendered their autonomy in security matters. Since the planned date of departure was near, Littmann canceled all further excavations. The wild archive had bared its fangs, so to speak.

When the Aksum expedition re-entered the Italian Colonia Eritrea, nearly three weeks later, and spent the first evening in the company of Italian military officers, Littmann noted in his travel diary: "This was the first time that we fully felt we were in a European environment again. Music, excellent wine and even beer that Captain Garelli had kept ready especially for us succeeded in making us forget the time of isolation in barbarism."[132] The Abyssinians thus remained "barbarians" in spite of the various personal relations forged in Aksum, especially with Gabra-Sellāsē. On the way back, in Adwa, the expedition had re-encountered the governor who had just returned from Addis. In his diary, Littmann granted him the following words of farewell:

> For all of us, it was difficult to part: he had been a sincere friend to us, and without him we would hardly have achieved anything in Aksum. He said to us that from now on he would have nobody with whom to converse and from whom to learn; he wished us well, asked us not to forget him and hoped to see us again some time.[133]

Indeed, Littmann kept in loose touch with Gabra-Sellāsē, whose son, the politician and historian Zawde Gabra Selassie, visited him in Tübingen in 1946.[134] Photographs of the Dejazmatch and his wife from the time of the expedition adorned Littmann's study in Tübingen for decades.[135]

Yet in 1906, indebtedness, exchanges of gifts and courtesies, and assertions of "friendship" were insufficient for recognizing the governor as a fully civilized persona. After Adwa, with Gabra-Sellāsē's blessing, the expedition conducted a short two-day excavation in Jeha. There,

> Kr[encker] found ... a little altar with a fragmentary Sabaic inscription, which he ordered to be brought to the camp in secret, along with several other stones, fragments of ornaments. ... Making [the inscribed stone] disappear was not an easy job since a great number of priests and locals stood surrounding the camp, argus-eyed, watching our every movement.[136]

Wild archives were particularly vulnerable to theft, given their lack of stable indexing. While Littmann and his companions were clearly aware of the improper nature of their course of action, and while the diffident locals were clearly wary of being deceived in precisely such a fashion, nonetheless the scholars robbed the object they cherished and betrayed the trust the governor had expressed in them only the previous day. Notions of scholarly virtue did not provide the means to rein in Krencker's and Littmann's possessive desire, as they quite certainly would have done in the case of institutional European archives. Neither did scholarly virtue suffice to create unshifting, morally unambiguous relations with Ethiopians. Normative orders waned beyond the lines of European power; the scholarly persona was no exception. Indeed, transgression of normative orders may have been precisely the point of Orientalist travel.[137]

The next stop, on April 14, was the cloister of *Dabra Dammo*, which could be accessed only by means of climbing a rope. Littmann, who was not much of an athlete and had also accidentally burnt his hand on one of the preceding days, was unable to undertake this exercise and had himself hoisted up the cliff.[138] In 1910 he found out he had thus become a local laughing stock when Johannes Kolmodin (1884–1933), a young Swedish Orientalist connected with Littmann's missionary friends,[139] mentioned in correspondence that he had written down the story of the German scholar who could not climb a rope as part of a collection of Tigré anecdotes. Littmann was outraged:

I am, however, amazed to the utmost that you have *written up* humorous anecdotes about the German archaeologists and the climb to Debra Dammo. In this way, not only will the prestige of Europeans and European scholars be impaired among the natives, but the respect for academic peers will also suffer. … Did they perhaps tell you, in Debra Dammo, of our presents and that I, with a festering wound on my hand, was only able to touch the rope in the heaviest of pains?[140]

Tellingly, Littmann was most worried about the fact that the episode had been written down; it was the prospect of seeing it published he perceived as threatening to his scholarly reputation. Further, the notion that he had not been successful in gaining the unequivocal respect of the natives also appears to have piqued him. Indeed, the scholarly persona was an asset he had made much effort to maintain at least as a façade during his stay in Aksum. Littmann presented himself as an emissary of the German monarch wherever possible, for instance by the bestowal of presents in the name of Emperor Wilhelm II. Yet in the diary account, also written on site, he tended to ridicule the Aksumites, in particular the clerics, and to patronize Gabra-Sellāsē. This textual ostentation of superiority, in combination with the ostentation of deference on site, indicates the degree to which the scholarly persona had actually been compromised by the wild archival situation; and it indicates that the problem of laughter was of central importance. Concerns of security and practical failures, such as that of climbing the mountain of *Dabra Dammo*, undermined the symbolic politics of scholarly status by exposing the comical side of the Europeans. On site, once again, the normative order of the scholarly persona only worked in a deficient manner. Littmann could not control whether he looked silly to the Ethiopians or to the other members of the expedition. Only in the realm of published text was the normative order of collegiality to reign unchecked.

The scholarly persona was meant to function as a set of epistemic virtues that generated methodological order and thus constituted a subject of knowledge capable of yielding an objective account of the record of the past. In this function, the persona was unsustainable inside wild archives even in terms of its mere aesthetics. The venerable bearded men of science turned into diarrhea-plagued and flea-infested cripples who could only handle their horses with difficulty.[141] This transfiguration of the scholarly persona was a direct result of the mimetic nature of the record of the past. In the archival state of nature, it was impossible to stably separate spectator from performer, reader from document. The scholarly persona, arguably the persona of a spectator of historical time,[142] was thus disintegrated by the archival material itself, not merely by contingent circumstances. Fittingly, the archival state of nature was not one of tragedy, but of comedy.

The Aristotelian poetics of tragedy assign catharsis to the mimetic effort as a rather fixed, regular reaction. The comical, it seems, disposes of greater mobility. Its effects less predictable, it appears to be wilder than the tragic. While laughter in some form is a requirement of the comical, it is a less regulated reaction than catharsis. In a comedy, it is undetermined who laughs about, or at, whom, or what. It is a legitimate, albeit extreme, function of comedy when the comedians laugh at the audience and not vice versa. A standard element of the comical is the debunking of the only seemingly virtuous persona. Schiller, who provided some of the most important discursive blueprints of nineteenth-century German-language literary aesthetics, even emphasized that "moral indifference" was the goal of the comical, insofar as it sought to liberate the subject from passion, including moral indignation.[143] In epistemological terms, the comical resides in the becoming ridiculous of the virtuous scholarly persona in the face of the actual unfolding of the archival situation. This is the comical aspect of the wild archive, the scene, generated by its specific aesthetics, on which its event-structure unfolds so as to unveil the inherent frailty of the epistemic process. As is frequently the case, the photographic record reveals more of this situation than the textual sources. A photograph of the Aksumite crowd on the steps of St. Mary of Zion watching the ceremonies for the German visitors shows the divided attention of the audience. Part of the spectators are keenly aware of the camera, which leads many of them to cover the lower parts of their faces (Figure 3). Photography in the expedition was explicitly von Lüpke's task, but as he is visible in many of the pictures, it is never beyond doubt who operated the camera in individual situations.

To Littmann, the fluidity of the comical was unwelcome but overwhelming. It permeated his perceptions throughout, and not merely his alone. On several occasions in his Ethiopian travels Littmann encountered specimens of hyena, notorious for centuries within folklore for its "laughter."[144] Littmann—just as fascinated with exotic animals as Jacob—gleefully accepted that the hyena was a "hideous" beast.[145]

Figure 3. Crowd on the steps of St. Mary of Zion, Aksum, 1906, NL Littmann, K. 99, V, no. 771.

Figure 4. Members of Deutsche Aksum-Expedition and Italian Colonial Military with Hyena. NL Littmann, K. 98, I(B), nos. 208, 210.

The archival records of the expedition contain a photograph of one such encounter, capturing something of the aesthetics at work in the wild archival situation (Figure 4). The image shows members of the expedition with an unidentified Italian colonial official who holds a chained hyena. The Italian is bent forward to stroke the animal, thus ridiculing the beast's state of captivity that tames its wildness. The German scholars watch, detached, amused, towering over the animal. Yet, the hyena, too, bares its teeth and laughs its emblematic laughter. The comical is so little fixed it also moves to the animal, the non-human. This is a poetic regime feeding on a permeability that defies all continuity and success in the maintenance of norms, virtuous personae, and epistemic orders. In the situation of archival work, the anguish of being ridiculed by history itself could not be defeated. It appears quite possible that the surcharge of order so characteristic of present-day theoretical and methodological analyses of archival practice still distantly echoes this frightful vision of the archival wild.

To be quite clear, this is a vision in which the comical upends the stability of distinctions between self and other that are meant to provide a foundation for the inequality in status of, e.g. Europeans and Orientals. The privileging of the comical in the aesthetics of scholarly travel was a treacherous affair. While on the surface, through denigration of the ridiculous other, the comical served to uphold distance and superiority, it actually subverted this intention. In von Lüpke's visual record of the expedition, this process can be traced with some clarity, precisely because his photographs were not strongly invested in the representation of the comical. In these photographs the comical enjoyed greater mobility. For instance, this is the case in one of the images he took of one of the Aksumite steles, in which idle natives can be seen frolicking (Figure 5). This image subtly subverts the iconography he had established for the inscribed stones, which he photographed consistently with people standing next to them, so as to indicate sizes (Figure 6). This image type, however, was not merely determined by the practical purpose, which might have been better served by applying a yardstick or else by always using the same individual. Instead, the pictures show different Aksumite and Eritrean workers, spectators, and soldiers, yet never one of the Italian guards or foremen, nor indeed the German expeditioners.

Subliminally, the image type depended, it seems to me, on a much older manner of depicting inscribed monuments in landscape that is epitomized by Poussin's famous second version of the *Et in Arcadia Ego* motif (*c.* 1640, Louvre, Paris). Erwin Panofsky offered a groundbreaking analysis of the meaning of this famous painting in which he particularly highlighted Poussin's departure from the drastic baroque-era symbolism of mortality in an earlier version of this image, and the development of

Figure 5. Sunken stele with Aksumites. NL Littmann, K. 98, II, no. 281.

Figure 6. 'Ezana stone, Ge'ez side, in Aksum with Abyssinian. NL Littmann, K. 98, III, no. 502.

an iconography of subdued melancholia.[146] The painting juxtaposes the shepherds of Arcadia, the land of the innocent life of pastoral, with the *memento mori* of the tombstone inscription that gives voice either to Death himself or to a deceased traveler buried under the stone. In either case, the shepherds are the other, untouched by melancholy, which they are struggling even to decipher, as Poussin's focus on the very gesture of reading by the touch of the finger underlines.[147] The painter and the viewer of the image, by contrast, represent the position of self. Von Lüpke's repeated portrayals of Aksumites around their monuments participate in this overall motif, not least in the distribution of the positions of self and other. But his photographs also unwittingly demonstrate the weakness of the juxtaposition: the Aksumites are fully capable, as are their viewers, of plunging the entire scene into ridicule, by, say, riding astride the monuments of the kings who had also been to this shepherd country (Figure 5).

This is the trajectory along which the comical, in an almost logical combination, subverted the association of epigraphy with melancholy that was tied to the novel cultural patterns of empathy that had emerged in the eighteenth century. The distinction between self and other, the work on alterity that has often been treated as key to Orientalism in general then does not provide a defining, ordering structure for the archive of epigraphy. The distinction between "our" archive and "theirs" is prone to collapsing as well.

8. The Constantine of Abyssinia

The finding that alterity was less foundational than often presumed raises the question as to whether the distinction between self and other might not at least govern supreme in the realm of epigraphic method, in the dichotomy of autopsy and heteropsy.[148] The archive would at least generate one stable distinction between the subject of scholarly knowledge who had seen the objects of this knowledge for himself (always himself), that is to say, the traveler who had actually been to Arcadia; and the inferior knowledge of the philologist who was working from second-hand observation only. In any case, the archival materials were text; observation was not a sufficient category for grasping the manner in which knowledge was produced from them. A closer look at the history of Aksumite epigraphy provides a helpful case study for understanding the epistemic practice that marked the field.

Henry Salt (1780–1827) first came to the highlands of Ethiopia in 1805, as draughtsman of the expedition of George Annesley, Viscount Valentia, one of the many British explorers who traveled in the adjacent territories of the maritime route to India. In the report of this expedition, Salt provided the first transcript of what came to be labeled the stone of Aeizana, Aizanas, or 'Ezana, a granite stone bearing an undated monumental Greek inscription that lists the conquests of one of the otherwise rather obscure rulers of Aksum.[149] The records of the Aksumite Empire were extremely scarce, and very little was known of the history of this monarchy that had existed from around the second century CE, adopted Christianity in the fourth, and then more or less disappeared a few centuries later. The language of the inscription Salt rendered in Valentia's travelogue was Greek. The decipherment was contested. Salt revisited Aksum already in May 1810 and sought to procure an improved transcript. Facing a certain degree of hostility on the part of the local population, "which we found to be in great measure owing to the absence of the Nebrit or ruler of the disctrict," Salt was impeded from spending as much time with the document as he had hoped, yet in spite of the "rude crowd of the inhabitants" that surrounded him on the spot, he "immediately re-copied very carefully every letter and in going over it, I was gratified in finding that the greater part of the conjectures I had ventured to make on a former occasion, were confirmed."[150] The inscription also turned out to be a bilinguis of Greek and Old Ethiopic (Ge'ez), which Salt had not been able to ascertain during his first visit:

> During the time that I had been engaged in revising the Greek characters, Mr. Stuart, at my request, had been endeavouring to make out some of the smaller letters on the opposite side of the stone: and on examining what he had done, I felt immediately reassured that they were Ethiopic.[151]

The decipherment of this portion of the inscription went less smoothly than the reading of the Greek one; in fact, Salt, during the short time he and his associates spent with the stone, only grew confident enough to declare himself on the mere script in which the text was written. The party then cautiously relinquished the site and set out on the road to Adwa, but was soon intercepted by the Nebrit (or Nebrid, or Nebraïd) and his retinue, "riding hastily over the plane: and in consequence of his urgent request, we consented to alter our previous intention and return to Axum,"[152] which afforded Salt the opportunity to spend the next morning working on the Ethiopic face of the stone once again. However, Salt and his assistants remained unable to produce a conclusive transcription, for the writing

> had been so much effaced by the effects of the weather, owing to its reclined position, that we only found the last line entire, the rest of the characters which are given being taken from different parts of the inscriptions wherever they could be ascertained. Still, however, I conceive, that if a person could reside at Axum for any time, and find leisure to visit the stone at different hours of the day, he might, with great attention and perseverance, be able to make out a very considerable portion of the inscription.[153]

The methodological expectations here formulated were those summarized under the label of autopsy. The obviousness of the necessity of seeing an inscription "for oneself" (or having it looked at by one Mr. Stuart), the limited nature of the trust that was owed to fellow scholars, or to one's own previous readings, was not worthy of very much debate already at the time of Salt. And yet, the additional specifications his narrative provides, say about daylight and corrosion of surfaces, are once again indicators of the complications autopsy underwent. Epigraphic reading was quite unlike the intimate act of reading in private. Here as in the Syrian desert, one needed to ensure the benevolence of the locals in order to be able to "reside" as a foreign visitor and then spend sufficient time with the inscriptions. That the locals themselves might produce a conclusive reading was out of the question. In effect, in the few lines quoted, Salt outlined a research program that took a full century of (albeit intermittent) Aksumite studies to fully implement. It was only 101 years after Salt's first perusal of the stone, in the winter of 1906, that Littmann finally succeeded at "residing" in Aksum and visiting the stone during different times of day.

In the meantime, in two treatises from 1878 and 1880, August Dillmann (1823–1894) had undertaken to synthesize everything that was until then securely known about the older history of Ethiopia and the Aksumite Empire, and to distinguish legend from fact and reasonable conjecture.[154] Like Nöldeke—and also Wellhausen—Dillmann was a member of the school of Heinrich Ewald, in which the study of diverse Semitic languages was practiced, nominally because it was deemed useful as a contextual tool for understanding the historical reality of ancient Hebrew religion. Yet, Ewald's students veered off in all kinds of directions.[155] Unlike the others, Dillmann remained more than merely formally in the faith, and he rejected much of the more radically deconstructive Old Testament theology especially championed by

Wellhausen. Nonetheless, Dillmann's Ethiopic studies did not hold a strong claim to theological relevance. Rather, they were historical in nature and served to spell out a number of little-known aspects of the history of the periphery of the Hellenic world in late antiquity. Peripheral antiquity, to be sure, had a special significance; in a certain sense, it served to undermine notions of a self-contained ancient civilization, if only by offering a more subtle understanding of the interconnectedness of the Graeco-Roman world with not entirely obvious areas, such as the seemingly remote inland empire of Ethiopia. Moreover, especially as a result of their sixth-century invasion of the kingdom of Ḥimyar and other parts of what today is Yemen, the Aksumites also played a role in the prehistory of Islam and the competition of Judaism and Christianity in the area that preceded the time of Muhammad. Yet for the philologists of the nineteenth century, under the sway of classicism and Christian theology alike, this second aspect of the historical significance of Aksum was of subordinate interest.

In the field of Aksumite research, the stone of Aizanas (as Pauly's *Realencyclopädie* transcribed the name, following Dillmann, in 1893) acquired central importance. It was one of the few known contemporary documents, and the name of the ruler in which it had been written also occurred in a second document, a letter by Emperor Constantius II, which enabled a rough dating of the reign of the Aksumite monarch in question (the inscription does not contain dates). The stone and the letter confirmed each other's authenticity, and jointly gave credence to reports about the deeds of the Aksumites in other sources, above all that of the Greek traveler Cosmas Indicopleustes who related a lost inscription from Adulis on the western board of the Red Sea that gave a fuller account of historical events from an earlier period of Aksumite history; and other epigraphic sources from the eastern seaboard pertaining to, and in turn confirming, the various invasions the Aksumites had conducted of Southwestern Arabia.[156]

A variety of European scholars—Ethiopia was frequently visited, especially by geographic explorers who were looking for the source of the Nile—had passed through Aksum and attempted to correct Salt's failure to decipher the Ethiopic inscription on the stone, or at least to produce a copy that would have been of use to philologists in Europe. Such attempts had also expanded the source base. In the 1830s the Frankfurt naturalist Eduard von Rüppell (1794–1884) happened upon two further Geʿez inscriptions in Aksum, which also appeared to report lists of military deeds of a ruler whose name was given, in both cases, as Tazena (and variations). One of these inscriptions referred to the King as the son of a deity *Maḥrem*, who was also named in the Aizanas inscription and given in the Greek version as Ares. The second purported Tazena inscription, however, availed itself of clearly Christian language. Hence it seemed plausible to conjecture—as Dillmann did—that this was the ruler under whose government the Aksumites had converted to Christianity. Dillmann's reading gave the inscriptions a central place in the history of Christian Ethiopia. Yet, Rüppell's transcripts remained full of gaps and mistakes. The explorer, whose linguistic knowledge was insufficient, had gone on to commission two translations of his fragmentary copies, the first by an Ethiopian scholar whom he encountered in Egypt on his return journey to Europe; and the second by the Halle Orientalist Emil Roediger (1801–1874). Roediger clearly had not been much of a scholar of Geʿez, but among the handful of Semitists then working at German universities, he must have seemed the most competent. The divergent results of the two translations did not satisfy even Rüppell himself. In the 1830s and 40s, other scholars produced similarly inconclusive readings of these inscriptions, for instance the French naturalist Antoine d'Abbadie (1810–1897) and the Italian Lazarist missionary Giuseppe Sapeto (1811–1895). Dillmann was irritated:

> Among all the many European travelers who, year after year, visit Abyssinia, not a single one so far has felt called upon to produce a squeeze of these important documents, and I cannot avoid expressing here the urgent wish that this may finally be done, please, before the stones perish entirely.[157]

Some fifteen years after this outcry of heteroptic despair, of the inability to see because of someone else's failure to go and see, around the time of Dillmann's demise his appeal was finally heeded. James Theodore Bent (1852–1897) produced squeezes of the inscriptions during his 1893 journey to Ethiopia, and in the resulting travelogue, first published at the end of 1893, the Vienna Semitist David Heinrich Müller (1846–1912), a student of Nöldeke's, made a number of suggestions as to the decipherment.[158] However, Nöldeke himself rejected many of Müller's conjectures right away.[159]

Yet another decade later, the overall political situation was favorable for a renewed attempt and one which could finally be conducted under the auspices of the methodological nationalism of German philology. Almost ten years after the Ethiopians had defeated the invading Italian army in the area of Adwa, half a day's travel northeast of Aksum, the imperial government in Addis Ababa was eager to generate international relations with a variety of European powers in order to secure its recognition as an independent state. A German diplomatic mission, headed by the Orientalist Friedrich Rosen (1856–1935), was deemed a striking success in 1904–5. In the overall context of scientific academies competing for archaeological explorations, the scholarly community saw an opportunity finally to resolve the epigraphic puzzles of Aksum.[160]

In the very last days of 1905 the German members of the expedition gathered in Massawa at the Red Sea Coast of the Italian colony of Eritrea and from there traveled inland to Asmara, the capital of the colony, where the rest of the expedition team was assembled. A number of Italians were hired as foremen for the archaeological digs and as guards; and a number of young Eritreans, who had undergone schooling at the Swedish mission, were selected as "boys," personal servants and—at least in Littmann's case—occasional research assistants. From Asmara, the journey continued due south to Adwa, the first significant settlement beyond the Italian border and seat of the provincial Ethiopian government. Already on January 12, the expedition was met outside Aksum by the Dejazmach who then escorted them into town.

Littmann noted in his travel diary, among his very first impressions of the place, that he had spotted the Aizanas stone from afar upon entry into town.[161] His epigraphic research agenda was entirely dependent on Dillmann's first treatise, of which he carried either a copy or excerpt notes, or both. He also appears to have brought along excerpts or offprints of Müller's and Nöldeke's exchange. The autoptic enterprise thus was constantly in dialogue with the results of heteroptic epigraphy. On January 13, a Saturday, the expedition was formally welcomed. In the afternoon, Littmann, accompanied by the governor, made a first unsuccessful attempt to visit the older Tazena inscription, which was known to be held in the house of a deceased cleric whose sons refused to grant Littmann access. Then the scholars and governor took a "stroll" to the stone of Aizanas. The following Monday, January 15, work started there in earnest. Littmann ordered digging around the stone, and in the late afternoon made a first squeeze of the Geʿez inscription. This type of work continued in the mornings of January 16–18; in the afternoons, according to the diary, Littmann studied the squeezes in his tent. During the same days, he also began to work on the younger Tazena inscription, which was on a stone that had broken into several parts, all of which held in the treasury of the Aksumite Church. Epigraphic work continued during the week of January 22–27, amongst other activities; Littmann deplored that a number of squeezes had turned out unsuccessful and that his copies of the stones were only half-done when work had to be interrupted for Sunday. In the week from January 29 to February 3, the failed squeezes were redone. For most of the remaining period of the expedition—which departed at the beginning of April—Littmann spent only little time on epigraphic matters. For the week of February 12–17, he noted that he continued to study the squeezes and "completed" his copies in the tent. At the beginning of March the governor managed to persuade the sons of the deceased priest who owned the older Tazena inscription to grant Littmann access.[162] On March 4, there was a group visit to the stone, and it turned out that this was an inscription previously unknown to European scholarship. Littmann made squeezes. The entire negotiation was repeated and, finally, on March 16–17, Littmann obtained access to the older Tazena inscription, which in his diary he suddenly began to call the "Inscription of -zānā."[163] To be sure, Müller had already recognized from Bent's squeezes that the first portion of the name was missing and suggested that it read ʿĒzānā; a suggestion Nöldeke had accepted.[164] In a sense, then, Littmann merely corroborated an earlier heteroptic result.

Yet actually, Littmann's abandoning of the name of Tazena indicates that autopsy was paying off, and that he was arriving at a different reading of the epigraphic record. The full argument was only revealed in the 1913 expedition report. Here Littmann posited that the inscriptions previously ascribed to Tazena actually *both* referred to Aizanas, whose name, Littmann now suggested (confirming Müller's and also Nöldeke's conjectures), was best transcribed as ʿĒzānā. The seeming divergence of names was probably a mere consequence of transcribing between three different scripts (Greek, Sabaic, and Geʿez). The stone of Aizanas/ʿĒzānā described by Salt had actually turned out to be a threefold document, which held largely identical Geʿez inscriptions, one in Sabaic and the other one in unvocalized Ethiopic script. Importantly, as Littmann pointed out, the numismatic record—which was not a central autoptic concern of the expedition—supported the argument that the vast majority of the royal inscriptions of Aksum had emerged from the reign of ʿĒzānā. Various coins confirmed the long Ē in the beginning of the name instead of the "Ae" in the Greek inscriptions. It was thus ʿĒzānā who was identified as the ruler who converted his country from paganism to Christianity as he jettisoned the claim to descent from Ares that had been prominent in the older inscriptions. Another aspect of ʿĒzānā's genealogy, the mention of a brother Σαιαζανα, was repeated across the varying inscriptions, which was further evidence of the identity of the rulers celebrated in the different monuments.

Müller, by contrast, had contested that the younger pseudo-Tazena inscription, the one in the treasury of the Church of St. Mary of Zion—a text in which the soliloquizing ruler evidently made use of Christian phraseology—contained a legible name at all. Rüppell had only been able to identify two letters in the first line; d'Abbadie and Sapeto both had produced fragmentary readings on which Dillmann had drawn for his conjecture that the inscriptions documented the transition to Christianity. With reference to Bent's squeeze, Müller contested that there was a first line at all and recognized "only some crookedness and flaws in the stone, which with some fancy can be looked upon as letters, but are really nothing."[165] Littmann emphasized, in his report on the inscriptions, that he had spent a great deal of time with the original, the copies, the squeezes, and the photographs,[166] and rejected Müller's skeptical claim, replacing it with the 'Ēzānā theory.

That the correct reading was contested was a constitutive feature of the production of epigraphic knowledge. Grimme's crassly divergent reading of the entire Safaitic corpus was not an eccentric outlier, but a component of an epistemological system that arrived at agreement after often decade-long processes of the dismissal of certain readings in favor of others. Autopsy was a recognized means of gaining the upper hand in the concomitant contests. Therefore, Müller's heteroptic result was not supposed to be superior to Littmann's autoptic one. Besides, Müller was a Jewish scholar who sought to undermine the alleged documentation of the advent of Christianity in a "Semitic" nation. He went so far as to suggest that the rhetoric of what Dillmann had come to regard as the oldest Christian inscription of Ethiopia was entirely compatible with the invocation of a gentile deity of the heavens. This, too, amounted to a challenge in the continuous contest of different denominational affiliations within the framework of a single, shared tradition of *Realphilologie* on Semitic epigraphy. As a result of this tangle of competitive challenges, Littmann was under pressure to produce results, and he was lucky enough to arrive at a plausible reading—supported by copies, squeezes, and photographs—that did not simply confirm Müller's judgment that there was "really nothing," but on the contrary reached a spectacularly different understanding of the document. To be sure, the result was not so different from what Rüppell had already suspected in 1840: that the inscriptions all referred to the same ruler and that it had been this ruler who, at the time of Constantius II, had introduced Christianity to Ethiopia.[167] Yet, Rüppell had not been able to confirm his conjecture through decipherment; Littmann did not include a reference.

In the novel, autoptic understanding, everything was folded into a single name. The reading of Aksumite history was to be dominated by the referent of this name, the single most important military leader and the ruler whose government converted his territories to Christianity and even developed Ethiopic script proper as he departed from the Sabaic alphabet in his inscriptions and introduced signs of vocalization (probably following the model of Sanskrit script). As a result of the autoptic investigation, Littmann concluded that

> the time of 'Ēzānā was the great time of the Aksumite Empire. 'Ēzānā was the Constantine of Abyssinia: indeed, the example of this great ruler will have been on the mind of the King of Aksum who possibly ascended to the throne of his

fathers while that great Emperor was still among the living. 'Ēzānā fully returned the realm to the boundaries in which it had been created by the founder [namely, the second-century unnamed king commemorated in the inscription of the so-called throne of Adulis], he adopted Christianity as religion of state, and, after having himself converted to Christianity, won glorious victories over the countries along the Nile.[168]

Littmann's overall argument remained wedded to the form of a mere list of merits in which temporal sequence—as a prerequisite of narrative sequence—could not be made operational. Nonetheless, in his conjectures, Littmann did not refrain from rather far-reaching judgments on the motivations and intentions of 'Ēzānā. For instance, regarding the "oldest Christian" inscription (the second Tazena inscription in Dillmann's account), Littmann noted:

> This unique document becomes important and interesting for us precisely because it permits us to see how here a king, powerful for his time and country, who had grown up in paganism, re-interpreted the traditional formulae by additions and minor changes in such a way that the representatives of the new religion, Christianity, could not any longer take offense.[169]

The basic reading of the identity of the names in the inscriptions remains generally accepted,[170] even though one might also be of the opinion that it is harshly underdetermined by the documents, which are far and few between, undated, and might well speak of different kings with similar names. While the better-documented Ethiopian kings of the sixth century often seem to have engaged in religious wars against their Jewish neighbors, it perhaps also remains worth asking whether 'Ēzānā's purported conversion, in the fourth century, necessarily entailed that all of his subjects converted to Christianity as well. The instrumentality of the conversion and use of Christian tropes Littmann intimates in his discussion of the retained older phraseology in the newly Christian inscriptions in any case is a sign of, albeit benign, over-interpretation.

Littmann himself was already fully aware that 'Ēzānā, when he called himself king of Ḥimyar and other localities in South Arabia, was probably using merely "inherited titles [*überkommene Titel*]."[171] Recently, Glen Bowersock has suggested that one might also regard the titles of the African conquests boasted in the 'Ēzānā inscriptions as "arrogated" and empty assertions of sovereignty in a spirit of "nostalgia and irredentism."[172] Although this, too, is a highly conjectural interpretation, it does make clear that Littmann's autoptic reading was not, and not even primarily, mere decipherment of one letter after the other. Instead, autopsy was a full-blown semantic operation, which drew on contextual conjecture and outright analogy and was indissolubly bound-up with heteroptic readings. "The Abyssinian Constantine" was not merely a rhetorical trope, an illustrative metonymy extraneous to the meaning of the inscriptions, but a semantic tool inseparably entwined with the practical work of decipherment. In order to process the many lacunae the inscriptions contained, it was necessary to be able to make out words before every letter had been determined; and for this purpose, one needed to be able to tell what the text meant.

9. Beasts and Sovereigns

In the fourth volume of the expedition report, Littmann mentioned a rock graffito inscription he had seen underway, in Cohaito (a site of ancient ruins) in Eritrea. This inscription consisted of a modest scratched drawing of an elephant and the Ethiopic letters ኣነ ሐርማዝ, in transliteration: "Änä Ḥarmāz," in translation: "I [am, or: my name is] elephant [or: Ḥarmāz]." Littmann's comment: "The writer had a sense of humor: his name was 'Elephant' and therefore he drew an image of such an animal next to his name."[173] The translation is interesting since Littmann opts to read the basically ambiguous phrase as the assertion of a name. In his later work on similar Safaitic inscriptions Littmann went on to make quite different semantic conjectures. His debate with Grimme concerned, among other points, the question of whether names next to graphic representations were to be read as authorial "signatures." Moreover, he held—drawing on Rhodokanakis's reading of similar inscriptions from the Yemen corpus, which was the closest relative of the Ethiopic one—that names next to animal drawings could be read as declarations of ownership.[174]

The more obvious *non sequitur*, however, is Littmann's conjecture that the writer of the Ḥarmāz inscription was jesting when adorning his name with a drawing. This conjecture betrays a tendency to read inscriptions as records of a phenomenal space, a broad field of common and most natural experiences the epigrapher shared with the author of the document. The image–text juxtaposition of the Ḥarmāz inscription was to be understood as humorous mostly in the sense of expressing a general *joie de vivre* on the part of the author; the document concerned an enjoyment of self. In this way, "humor" entailed a framing of experience in terms of selfhood that surpassed momentary sensory perception and was culturally mediated, thus aesthetic. Ḥarmāz and Littmann, the latter contended, did not merely behold in the same manner a rock and a set of scratches on its surface. Rather, they shared a broader meaning-giving regime of perception that framed their senses of the moment and of selfhood. It was as such a self that Littmann read inscriptions, and his decision to include the Ḥarmāz graffito in his collection was at least in part documentation of his own subjectivity, and of the universal humanity with which this subjectivity was endowed. Littmann, an often ill-tempered traveler,[175] nonetheless wished to project, for his readers, an image of joyous and friendly relations with his surroundings. As was the case with the Safaitica, he tended to offer banalizing readings that deprived the inscriptions of the notion of an underlying non-obvious meaning; and this tendency aligned with his own penchant toward secrecy, toward concealment, for instance, of guilt.

The Rousseauean and Herderian categories of "popular feeling" and "national character" loomed large within Littmann's overarching image of Aksumite and Ethiopian history. 'Ēzānā's reign, for instance, was clearly connected to an epoch in which the Ge'ez people, as a "Semitic tribe" that had immigrated (thus the standard assumption) from southwestern Arabia and at first been subjected by the local Habašāt (supposedly another such tribe that had undertaken the migration previously), had shed the yoke and made themselves masters: "and when, carried along by a strengthening of national feeling, they turned the native language into a written language, naturally they chose their own [script]."[176] Wherever the nation came to language, and especially when the setting was African, race was not far, and the discourse of Ethiopians as a "mixed race," composed of "Semites," "Kushites," and "Negroes," made several appearances in Littmann's account, especially toward the beginning of the historical survey he provided in the first volume of the expedition proceedings.[177] In a general sense, such remarks dovetailed with the judgment of the archaeological finds. For instance, when Littmann characterized the monuments of Aksum as evidence for a *Mischkultur*, a "hybrid culture," at the time of 'Ēzānā, that drew on South Semitic funerary stele and Egyptian obelisks alike, the formulation suggested that racial "mixing" was an intended connotation.[178] Statements on race and on the generality of culture were structurally similar in that they drew on the same kind of autoptic authority. It was necessary to see considerable numbers of people on site in order to acquire an intuitive sense of their racial status; similarly, it was necessary to see the historical record on site in order to understand its cohesion in a cultural form, no matter how fragmented and scarce the documents actually were.

In the study of Ethiopian antiquities, it was an almost irresistible temptation to interpret nineteenth-century Ethiopian life through episodes from the Hebrew Bible. This did not perhaps amount to an unequivocal "denial of coevalness," with Johannes Fabian's formula, but rather indicated an intricate make-believe entanglement with the closed-off epochal past of antiquity. Von Lüpke's parallel diary contains similar reminiscences that sought to elucidate antiquity through present-day alterity.[179] Henry Salt, too, uses a discussion of Ethiopian dressing habits and juridical customs in order to interpret a passage in Genesis (on Joseph and Potiphar's wife).[180] Arnauld d'Abbadie (1815–1893), Antoine's younger brother, in his little-read yet highly fascinating memoir of the years he spent in Ethiopia, provides a variation on this theme when he discusses Ethiopian garments as *togae* in explicit parallel to Roman antiquity and muses on the differences in cultural habitus that are generated by wearing vestments not specifically tailored to the individual body.[181]

The decipherment of inscriptions, however, was a distinct practice from all these kinds of cultural observations. Dillmann did not say much on race, nor on the overall features of culture, not because his ideological outlook was profoundly different from Littmann's, but because he had not traveled. Epigraphers used autopsy in a different manner than as a mere marker of scholarly authority; it entailed distinctly technical skills that observational racism as practiced by many Orientalists arguably lacked. A certain awareness of methodological flaws in the merely visual observation of race was already common. In a letter Nöldeke sent to Littmann in Eritrea at the time of the expedition, he remarked:

> For a real decision of such questions [as pertaining to bodily types of human races] more is necessary than mere visual inspection, even if conducted by the best observer, but at least I would like to know your opinion, in case you have formed one by way of the observation of people from different, more or less unwashed tribes and nations. I still remember the impression the so-called Nubians (in reality Beg^wa's etc.) made on me, some 25 years ago, by their splendid *bronze* color.[182]

Nöldeke's methodological hesitation was thus immediately cast aside in order to provide space to "impression." Epigraphy did not function in the same manner.

Although an inscription such as that of Ḥarmāz tended to be treated as representing the character of such collective entities as tribe, nation, or race, concrete connections between epigraphic document and abstract cultural and/or racial generality were then often omitted since they did not *regularly* interlock with the technical procedures. Squeezes did not make "race" visible. It was the media and technical procedures of autoptic epigraphy that opened the way, in the case of the Ḥarmāz inscription, for the assertion of an overlap of cultural frames, of shared aesthetic sensibilities and subjectivities, as Littmann's little quip on the humor of Ḥarmāz illustrates. This coincidence of phenomenal spaces was bound to technical procedure; by contrast, it did not presuppose a universalist humanism on the part of the epigrapher, a set of convictions that would have been in conflict with the racist notion of alterity that was also in play in the overall situation, but precisely not tied to epigraphic autopsy.

The reading of inscribed names then was a kind of triangulation that was made possible by media technology and practical method. Both Littmann and the otherwise unknown Ḥarmāz perceived the comical quality of aligning person and elephant. As a result of the similarity of the relationship that existed between each of them and the animal, a connection between them as persons could also be established. This is significant because, *mutatis mutandis*, the same held for the names of kings as well. The animal as the point of intersection was then replaced with the (former) ruler, which suggests a certain mechanism of exchange was in place between the discursive positions of beast and sovereign.[183] In general, it is this intimate linkage of the figure of the ferocious animal with the problem of sovereignty that informs the relevance of archival wildness as a problem beyond the history of epigraphy. In many regards, the wild archive is a counter-image to sovereignty; but in this function, it also serves as an enabling condition.

When Littmann described 'Ēzānā as an equivalent, as well as an emulator, of Constantine, the latter fulfilled the function of the elephant: the object of common perception, which was, in this case, regimented less by an aesthetic sense of the comical than by a sense of historical greatness, of the historical-political sublime. The conjectures with which Littmann strove to make the historical meaning of the 'Ēzānā inscriptions intelligible drew heavily on this type of triangulation. Names were, in this context, so important because they could be taken as indexical signs of persons endowed with an aesthetic perception, a sensory apparatus, and an intentionality that allowed for the semantic operation in question.

As a consequence of this operation, in the case of Aksumite history the very quality of being historical came to hinge on the royal names. Anything to which this quality was ascribed, in this specific historical context, had to be connected to the few rulers who were known and could be roughly situated in common chronology. The history of Aksum is an interesting case of the practice of scholarly historicization in the nineteenth century. What is known about this history chiefly dates to three periods for which the intervening stretches of time are shrouded in near-complete obscurity. The three periods in question are, for the most part, dated from the outside, through other epigraphic and literary traditions that mention events or names from Aksumite contexts, mainly as regarding military operations and royal names, or matters to do with the spread of Christianity. The first of these periods is that of the throne of Adulis, for which Cosmas' alleged transcript remains the only important source. The second is the period of "Ēzānā; and the third is that of the king known as Kaleb, who invaded South Arabia in the sixth century. After the advent of Islam, outside reports on Aksum and Ethiopia cease for a number of centuries. All that remains to fill the gap are the lists of kings' names that exist in the written tradition of Ethiopia itself, if in significantly later sources, and which nineteenth-century scholarship came to consider inconsistent and purely legendary.[184] The native literary tradition only yields more informative historical documents again from the thirteenth century CE onward.

While in European contexts of tradition and documentation the quality of being historical was often assigned in terms of contextual, both figural and explanatory, cohesion with an established body of knowledge about the past, this pattern was disabled in the case of Aksum. The mere names of kings, as confirmed by epigraphic means, replaced the cohesive corpus of repeatable knowledge on which European practices of historicization commonly relied. Moreover, the inscribed names stood in a hierarchy, in which kingly names held the top position. Arguably, then, it was not merely the overall situatedness of traveling Orientalism, but the actual reading situation of epigraphy that followed the pattern of "courtly encounter," a crossing of cultural boundaries that unfolded in a hierarchical context governed by a personalized, monarchical sovereign.[185] This practice recognized, at least implicitly, a situation of equivalence that suspended the tired commonplace of "Oriental despotism"[186] and required a more complex constellation of political norms and values. The kind of social relationship that was attached to the inscriptions as documents of names relied on a solid foundation of notions about the political organization of sovereignty. This foundation was in fact shared by Littmann and his African, as well as European, interlocutors. In the autoptic situation in Aksum, it was as if the inscriptions, or more precisely the inscribed royal names, held court, and autopsy entailed vying with competitors for proximity to the sovereign. The inscriptions usurped the position of the sovereign in what Norbert Elias called the "mechanism of kingship."[187]

This pattern shaped Littmann's relations with his Ethiopian interlocutors, first of all to Gabra-Sellāsē, interactions with whom drew on two specific resources. The first of these was a shared interest in Aksumite history, which for the Dejazmach was a potential source of monarchical legitimacy (his monarch, the Negus, had named himself after Menelik, the legendary founder of the Aksumite Empire. The ancient stones continued to function as symbols of imperial power. As one of the expedition's photographs shows, the Dejazmach held his court of justice seated at the foot of the great obelisk (Figure 7). In keeping with the continuing political significance of the stones, Gabra-Sellāsē ostentatiously displayed his particular enthusiasm for epigraphy and the excavations. The second resource of establishing relations with Littmann was a sort of double triangulation vis-à-vis the existing monarchies of both Germany and Ethiopia. Both Gabra-Sellāsē and Littmann acted as envoys and quasi-courtiers on behalf of their hereditary rulers. This became especially salient on January 27–28. The 27th was Emperor Wilhelm II's birthday and a German holiday, and since the Kaiser was funding the expedition, Littmann felt particularly obliged to celebrate the occasion. He assembled his three fellow expeditioners, the Dejazmach and (for a short

Figure 7. Dejazmach Gabra-Sellāsē (center) holding his court of justice in the shadow of the great obelisk at Aksum, winter 1906. NL Littmann, K. 99, V, no. 754.

period) the high priest, as well as the Italian resident at Adwa, a military doctor by the name of Eliseo Mozzetti (1860–1942), whose task was to act as an informal go-between and political liaison for his government. Mozzetti had traveled to Aksum for the day, and apparently on his own initiative, in full awareness of the date. Littmann delivered, in Italian, a formal toast to the German monarch, in which he emphasized the Kaiser's "exalted interest" in the arts and sciences, whence the motivation to "send" scholars to excavate, and report on, the "famous royal city of Aksum." The German monarch had also "sent" several embassies to Ethiopia "to establish peace and friendship," for "our Emperor only thinks of aggrandizing his own country, not through war and the theft of land, but through peace and trade (Figures 8–9)."[188]

Subsequently, Littmann rendered his address into Amharic at the behest of the Dejazmach, who intended to send it on to Addis Ababa. The Amharic version, according to the translation provided by Voigt, contains a clause stating that "the entire German people have been pleased that the two countries Ethiopia and Germany love each other in concord."[189] This phrase, with its emphasis of reciprocal affect, is not contained in the German version Littmann noted in the diary. Gabra-Sellāsē, at any rate, responded in kind, although he postponed his reply until the following day, when he appeared again at the campsite in order to deliver a discourse he stated he had not wanted to pronounce the previous day in the presence of Mozzetti. In this address, Gabra-Sellāsē emphasized in turn that "Abyssinia and its Emperor" were aware of

Figure 8. Celebration of Kaiser's Birthday, Aksum 27 January 1906. NL Littmann, K. 98, I(B), no. 139. Seated from left: Mozzetti, Dej., Krencker, High Priest, Kaschke, Littmann.

Figure 9. Celebration of Kaiser's Birthday, Aksum 27 January 1906. NL Littmann, K. 98, I(B), no. 140. Von Lüpke (left, with cap) has joined.

the peaceful intentions of the Germans, who did not come, "like other peoples, to take away the land. For this reason, the Germans are particularly dear to the Emperor Menelik." The German expedition was an effort to tend to "the garden of friendship" between the two countries, and therefore particularly welcome to Ethiopia.[190] As Littmann had done the previous day, the Dejazmach then gave three cheers to the Kaiser, and Littmann responded with an improvised speech in celebration of Menelik that also ended with cheers.[191] The core of this exchange of orations was to confirm the status equality of the monarchs, on the basis of which a set of respectful and reciprocal relations was to be established. This matter was also of importance to the speakers because it allowed them to establish equivalence among each other.

During the January 28 visit to the expedition camp, Gabra-Sellāsē—"secondly," as Littmann puts it—also asked to see Littmann's copies of the inscriptions. Littmann describes the scene as follows:

> At first he was shown a number of photographs and drawings, for which he displayed a lively interest. Then, I read to him, word by word, the Christian Tāzēnā inscription, but only got to about the middle, since in between we constantly conversed about all kinds of things.—As presents he received 12m of black silk …, an eraser and pencil sharpener.[192]

As the bestowal of presents indicates with additional stress, the situation here described was from Littmann's perspective not one of equality. He alone was able to explain the inscriptions, even if at this point he still had not come to read the name in the inscription in question as 'Ēzānā.[193] Von Lüpke in his diary also remarked upon Gabra-Sellāsē's "vivid" interest in the inscriptions and remarked that Littmann "for hours had to dictate and translate them for him."[194] Indeed, Littmann's diary notes several occasions on which the Dejazmach asked him to dictate the inscriptions. In a long entry from February 12, Littmann describes the relations established through this repeated exercise.[195] Reading "the Aizanas inscription," Gabra-Sellāsē "several times made quite interesting remarks" on the text, for instance on the custom of making presents to visiting foreign kings, and on the alimentation of soldiers. Littmann was ready to accept these remarks as minor scholia on the inscription which also enhanced his own understanding of the meaning of the text. Things became more enlightening, however, when the conversation moved on to different topics. In particular, the Dejazmach revealed to the Germans several episodes that concerned the benevolence with which Menelik II personally responded to the governor's reports about the activities in Aksum; and the lack of benevolence with which the Italians and other European powers represented in Addis were responding to the German undertaking. It was not with respect to the scholarship of the inscriptions, but rather with respect to these matters of contemporary politics, to the situation of competition among the European powers, that Gabra-Sellāsē became a "friend" of the expedition.

Littmann ends the entry by pointing out that Gabra-Sellāsē had also commissioned excavations around some of the stele in the northeast of Aksum, and insists (underlining the phrase), with palpable concern for his scholarly reputation: "these unsystematic digs therefore do not issue from us."[196] In Littmann's account, Gabra-Sellāsē's interest in the antiquities of Aksum thus went along with an at most amateurish kind of scholarship. Since the heavy slant toward names in the inscriptions entailed that Aksumite history was a matter of persons, and, more precisely, of royal persons, Littmann's autoptic reading of the documents arguably intimated that the old rulers of Aksum conversed with him and not with the modern Aksumites; and that the latter had lost property of their own history to the visiting Orientalist. Thus, the triangulation that included the inscriptions, as opposed to the one that was based on the contemporary monarchs, served, from Littmann's point of view, to establish inequality between him and the Dejazmach. If both operations are taken to belong together, Littmann then appears to have engaged in a contradictory double procedure, of establishing equality and inequality at once, which might appear quite typical for Orientalist scholarship in the Saidian sense.

Yet, whence the desire to befriend the Dejazmach to begin with? The standard account of Orientalism knows of European desires for possession and domination that may take political, aesthetic, and also bodily, sexual forms. Arguably, however, this type of analysis does not exhaust the structures of desire that informed epigraphic autopsy. The inscription was an indirect trace of the body of the monarch, which disposed of such power as to command someone else's hand to carve letters into a stone. In a Kantorowiczian vein, one might perhaps strive to draw a distinction between the king's mortal physical body and his immortal symbolic body that represented the state in general. From Littmann's address on *Kaisers Geburtstag*, however, it is clear that he did not recognize a distinction of this type when speaking to the Ethiopians. In his discourse, he carefully omitted any reference to the state of Germany, or that of Ethiopia, as abstract entities. Instead, he emphasized the rulers' personal intentions as well as those of the multitudes of individual bodies over whom they exercised sovereignty. No doubt there is an implicit sense of condescension at work in Littmann's attitude toward the Ethiopian state, inasmuch as he seems to imply that the Ethiopian addressees of his oration would not be capable of grasping a political language of greater abstraction.

The situation was still more complicated, however. To begin with, it may be pointed out that the Ethiopian Church was marked by its adherence to the theological doctrine of "monophysitism." One of the theological indicators of the distinction of "Oriental" and other forms of Christianity, declared a heresy by the Council of Chalcedon in 451, this position entailed that Christ had only disposed of one, divine and immortal nature and not also of a human one. From the perspective of European theology, this doctrine betrayed a weakness in understanding the notion of abstract dualities of bodies. It was one of the few available clichés about Ethiopia and inevitably present when Littmann and other European scholars wrote about Ethiopian Christianity, for which they usually displayed little affection.[197] Although it appears that such disparagements remained confined to his diaries and publications and did not come to the attention of the Aksumite priesthood, the latter nonetheless rejected his presence and scholarly inquests. In part, this rejection was quite certainly the result of the traditional diffidence of Ethiopian churchmen toward European Christians who had too often sought to interfere with local dogma. Indeed, numerous nineteenth-century travelers had found it difficult to deal with the representatives of the Ethiopian Church and (once more with Salt) the "rude crowd" of the Aksumites in league with them. Littmann may have expected to encounter hostility on the part of the clergy before even arriving on site.

In addition, however, the tensions were probably also the result of his friendliness with the Dejazmach. Von Lüpke notes in his diary that already during the initial welcoming service at the Church of St. Mary of Zion, Littmann conversed "incessantly" with the governor and paid little attention to the ceremonies.[198] In general, Littmann seems to have felt that befriending the Dejazmach was far more important than his relations with the Aksumites themselves. A first grave crisis in his relations with the clergy emerged at the beginning of February when he asked to see manuscript collections that were accessible only to the high priest.[199] Already at this point, Gabra-Sellāsē needed to intervene to enable the continuation of the expedition work. The conflict with the clergy in turn enhanced Littmann's eagerness to ally with the Dejazmach, until the climax around the events of April 2.

In a personalized, non-constitutional monarchy, alliance with various groups meant partaking in a competition for proximity to the court and the throne. This rationale informed a structure of political desire that, judging from the sources, enjoyed primacy over a desire for outright imperial domination. The instrumental target of Littmann's "friendship" with Gabra-Sellāsē was to make headway in such a competition by entering an alliance with the governor. The pattern of attachment to the social system of courts—in the plural rather than in the singular, unlike in Elias's classical discussion—was widespread among scholars since the early modern period (if not earlier).[200] In the nineteenth century, presumably, the significance of court society changed, but did not disappear, when bourgeois society and the institutionalization of the university within the expanding framework of state bureaucracy re-fashioned the republic of letters.

At any rate, what the case of traveling Orientalists suggests is that even after 1900 the sociality of courts was a primary framework for staging situations of "encounter" and "contact" across cultural boundaries. Patterns similar to that of Littmann's case are discernible with regard to other travelers in Ethiopia. The eighteenth-century Scottish polymath James Bruce, whose travelogue was foundational for modern European knowledge of Ethiopia,[201] and his successor Salt both attached themselves to native kings and nobles. Arnauld d'Abbadie—who, once in Ethiopia, was quickly separated from his brother and did not on his own pursue scholarly aims—instead embarked on a career as courtier of a distinguished Ethiopian prince, the Dejazmach Wube Hayle Maryam, toward the end of the series of interregna and merely nominal emperorships that marked the history of Ethiopia in the second half of the eighteenth and the first half of the nineteenth century. The younger d'Abbadie's pursuits were indistinguishable from those of any young native notable who strove for the patronage of a prince: d'Abbadie sought to provide prudent political advice and to distinguish himself in shooting, horseback riding, hunting, and warfare. From his account, for long stretches of time, it does not seem that he was in the least concerned about returning to Europe. In his memoir, more so perhaps than if he had written an ordinary travelogue, d'Abbadie concerned himself with an analysis of the political system into which he had stumbled, and which he analyzed in terms derived from the political language of aristocracy and feudalism in France. The contiguity of courtliness in East Africa and Europe was apparently obvious to nineteenth-century European observers.

Judging from his correspondence with Mozzetti in the years following the Aksum expedition, Littmann too appears to have approved of descriptions of the political system of Ethiopia that approximated structures and events to familiar European ones. In 1909, Mozzetti criticized the former governor of Eritrea (1897–1907), Ferdinando Martini (1841–1928),

> who in one of his latest press interviews has claimed that it was not possible to even speak of 'nationalism' in the case of Abyssinia. I, on the contrary, would say that there exists a nationalism sui generis, a little different from our European one, but that it would appear to me to be a great error to affirm that the nationalist idea in Abyssinia did not exist and had never existed. Would you have put this differently? I would even add that in their more popular folktales the Abyssinians allow the idea of liberty and of independence to shine through.[202]

The counter-correspondence is lost;[203] but it does not seem, from Mozzetti's further letters, that Littmann disagreed with these notions of Abyssinian politics. The political language in place in this conversation was then not simply one of European supremacy and imperialist ambition.

In 1913, when Mozzetti, by then resident in Harar, had received complimentary copies of the volumes of the expedition report, he thanked Littmann with a long admiring letter, in which he also mentioned the response of Ethiopian notables to whom he had shown the publication:

> [S]ince Aksum is of interest to every Abyssinian, all look at [the book] with great curiosity and pleasure, expressing praise for, and also surprise about, such a great and special work with regard to the place which more than any other is connected to the history and the traditions of the country.[204]

Again, these remarks entail the equivalence of the cultural function of national history in Europe and Ethiopia, at least in the context of the uppermost stratum of society. It matters that the only name Mozzetti mentions in this passage is that of the young Tafari Makonnen (1892–1975), then Dejazmach of Harar, the later Emperor Haile Selassie. Already then, it was clear to Mozzetti, who paid close attention to political developments in Addis Ababa from afar, that Ras Makonnen had great personal and political potential. His name was that of a possible future Negus at a time when Menelik, incapacitated by a stroke since 1908, lay dying, while his designated successor, Prince Iyasu, was predictably going to be a failure as monarch.[205] Mozzetti, an avid collector with numerous scholarly interests, though tucked away in provincial Harar, nonetheless was always at court; and Littmann's involvement with the social system at hand, though peripheral, was also sustained. The durability of these contacts was considerable and biographical. The persona of the traveling philologist, in part a by-product of autopsy, was lastingly that of a courtier.

In the competitive alliance with Gabra-Sellāsē, the ability to interpret the inscriptions was a key feature and signaled the interference of the epigraphic enterprise with Littmann's courtliness. After all, what the inscriptions contained was political language, however rudimentary, which provided an opportunity for semantic transfers between epigraphic decipherment and courtly chatter. Belying Littmann's intimation that the Ethiopian court and state were less conversant in an abstract idiom of politics than he himself as a European, this kind of transfer also entailed that the political system at hand was governed by a principle of proximity that was not founded on concrete spatial relations. Littmann did not have to be in Addis to converse with the court of Menelik; and Menelik did not have to be in Aksum to converse with the inscriptions. The autoptic scholar presented himself as a go-between who mediated between the absent king and the court that was sustained, in an abstract fashion, by the mere epigraphic names.

Arguably, in his Amharic address to the Negus, with its propensity for simple syntax and list-like accounts, Littmann imitated also some of the diction in which the inscriptions extolled the efforts and achievements of 'Ēzānā and other rulers. Twice in his address, Littmann deployed the word "sent" (*geschickt*): he himself had been sent by the German monarch in order to excavate Aksum; and the German monarch had sent other ambassadors, too. The messages the Kaiser apparently sought to communicate proclaimed to be of peace and friendship. Yet, the epigraphic work, the autopsy of the documents, which enhanced the past greatness of 'Ēzānā, also communicated other things. The decipherment of the inscriptions of long-dead emperors and the excavation of royal tombs did not merely restore to the Ethiopian court a secure knowledge of an impressive national past, as Littmann surely assumed. Inadvertently, the explication of the inscriptions also conveyed forceful symbols of the mortality of the ruler and the end of empires. In light of this symbolic charge, epigraphy was prophetic; it followed the biblical motif of the writing on the wall that announced to Belshazzar that "God hath numbered thy kingdom, and finished it" (Dan. 5, 26). The structure of the desire underpinning Littmann's courtly communications was arguably split; it pertained to the living court and its mortality (its animal side) as well as to its afterlife in history (its abstract, immortal side, the actual seat of sovereignty).

This combination was not Littmann's alone. In those same years around 1900, when the German Emperor became heavily involved in the funding of archaeological research, the Assyriologist Friedrich Delitzsch (1850–1922) was invited to deliver a set of lectures with the Emperor in attendance. These lectures were controversial for their insistence that the Cuneiform archive provided the main and original context and explanation for the motifs, stories, and doctrines of the Old Testament. Hebrew antiquity was reduced to a province of Babylonian antiquity; over the course of the lectures, Delitzsch made clear that he wished to discard any theological notion of revelation with regard to the Old Testament, and indeed that he saw fit to abandon the book as a text of religious import for Christianity altogether.[206] This was in many regards the logical continuation of the anti-Judaist tendencies of deconstructive Old Testament philology throughout the nineteenth century. As Marchand has argued, the alliance of philology and racist anti-Semitism culminated in the context of the so-called Babel-Bible-Quarrel.[207] The role of the Emperor and court circles in this context was crucial; through his presence and through friendly encouragement, Wilhelm II amply demonstrated support to Delitzsch before beginning to mark his distance after the second lecture in 1903 when the polemic reached a high point. In general, the role of the Hohenzollern court in the history of German anti-Semitism has perhaps still not received sufficient attention. The linkage between Orientalist philology and the monarch, in any case, was established through inscriptions and invented inscriptions.

In Delitzsch's papers, Reinhard Lehmann found a draft *Panegyricus*, a fictitious royal inscription in German and "Assyrian" (says Lehmann), which Delitzsch composed for Wilhelm II in the context of their perceived alliance over Babylon. As a figment of literary imagination, this piece is of considerable interest. The intermediary between Delitzsch and the Kaiser, Admiral von Hollmann, had delivered a message from the monarch according to which, "as soon as you will have found a royal inscription, *as it tickled my fancy* [orig. English], do let me know!" Delitzsch responds:

> May the heart of my lord the King rejoice! I have found it. Last night, while I slept, I had a dream. Nebo, the scribe of the tablets of the universe, took me by the hand and led me out into the land between the rivers. Far extended the fields, dark was the night. Then I saw, and on the tablet of heaven he wrote with a golden stylus an inscription ... :
>
> [We,] the Kings of the lands of Assur and Akkad, the earlier as well as the later ones, greet the great King who has risen in the lands of the west, and who remembers us and resurrects us to new life. May the great gods who live in the bright heavens grant him a life of long days, an abundance of progeny, a just scepter, an eternal throne ...! And just as he has reawakened us and our fathers who were before us, to life, so may he and his children and children's children live in eternity![208]

This inscription within an inscription, the miraculous vision of a divine authoring of an epigraphic document, yet again recalls the biblical writing on the wall, even though in Delitzsch's conceit the message is supposed to be one of the eternity, not the downfall, of kingship. The authorship of the inscription is complicated since what is written on the skies by the intercession of Nebo (or Nabu), the Babylonian god of writing, is in fact a message from the forgotten rulers of Babylon to the German Emperor. The latter enjoys, the message claims, a power of resurrection and can lay claim to a government of eternity. Clearly, these motifs play with Christology. Moreover they suggest that the authorship of the message ultimately comes to rest with Wilhelm himself, since it is expressive of the "new life" he has granted. More precisely, in Delitzsch's dream, the entire universe is a tablet, and it is the work of epigraphic decipherment that reawakens the bygone kings to new life. The philologist is thus the facilitator as well as the propagator of the resurrective power of the German monarch. He makes the Kaiser legible to himself.

Mario Wimmer has argued that the notion of archival order and the "dry," technical language professional archivists in Germany developed for it especially in the interwar period expressed, in its irrepressible figurative portions, an underlying desire for being in touch with the dead. He contrasts the archivist Heinrich Otto

Meisner—who introduced a terminology of "archival bodies" into the methodology of archiving—with a contemporary thief of archival documents, a private scholar by the name of Karl Hauck. Hauck, after being apprehended as a consequence of Meisner's investigation into missing documents, confessed to the theft of thousands of autographs from the archives of the Prussian and Austrian monarchical families. In a surprisingly successful defense strategy, Hauck claimed that he was irresistibly drawn to the monarchical handwritings, especially to princely signatures, by a fetishistic homosexual desire. Indeed, Hauck himself had already become a case study in the work of Magnus Hirschfeld, who also testified as an expert witness for the defense during the trial. Wimmer interprets Hauck's desire as being chiefly directed at the dead and their reanimation (although mediated through a fetishization of writing), and identical, in terms of its figurative charge, to the desires informing Meisner's professional discourse.[209] Yet, it might also be legitimate to see in Hauck's kleptomania a more specific desire for the bodily trace of the individual, mortal monarch; and if the parallelism is to be maintained, in Meisner's normative methodology a desire for the traces of the abstract, institutional body of the monarch, the kingdom. These distinct "archival bodies" would then be affected, not merely by mortality but also by the political.

For this consideration, the exploration of the epigraphic records of the Aksumite past yields an interesting model, since it demonstrates that the twofold political aspect of such an underpinning desire could be present in a single epistemic undertaking. Leopold von Ranke, in a letter from Venice that was made notorious by Bonnie Smith, placed a sexual charge on the archival documents he perused when he labeled them as "princesses."[210] Yet, the other, the monarchical charge of the metaphor has remained consistently overlooked, perhaps because the political languages of European monarchies have become, for the most part, obsolete. If one takes such idioms into account, the task of archival research would appear to consist in being present where the documents hold court; to personalize the *realia* to which the documents grant access; to outmatch one's competitors in proximity to these personalized objects; and to convey, in various directions, a message of the frailty and mortality of sovereignty. Autopsy, as expressing a desire for proximity, and its relation with heteropsy, namely in a competitive alliance, appears to be explicable by reference to this courtly politics (and, it may be added, the situation of encounter this politics entailed). The methodological distinctness of autopsy resided in this constellation. And at the heart of the constellation in question, there would be the process of personalization that was made possible by the technical procedures and media of representation epigraphy developed over the course of the period discussed in the present chapter.

It would then seem that epigraphic (and other archival) knowledge-production established a channel of communication into and within monarchical systems that had not existed in the same form before. The ubiquity of the end of monarchy as a *topos* of political discourse in the nineteenth century may have had something to do with the expansion of such epistemic practices that deciphered the ends of kingdoms on stones the world over. Going to the epigraphic archives multiplied the writings on the wall, the messages of finitude addressed to monarchs. In turn, the increasingly frequent deployment of monumental inscriptions by European monarchies in the "historicist" style of the nineteenth century may have been, to some extent, a response in the same channel of communication. If this account appears plausible, it casts a certain measure of doubt on such accounts of the onset of archival scholarship that only ever look, in nineteenth-century European historical writing, for assertions of the potential eternity of the sovereignty of the nation.

Admittedly, the case of Delitzsch's fictitious inscription for Wilhelm II might also suggest that the rise of epigraphy within philology made the connection that was meant to hold between the king's two bodies to some extent problematic. In order to be properly in touch with his immortal body, the Kaiser required the mediation of philology. For, it was epigraphy alone that permitted him to accomplish the symbolic work of the resurrection and immortalization of the Assyrian kings. The feebleness of this mediation is manifest and also informs the comical nature of Delitzsch's message, which was designed for the monarch's exhilaration more than his exaltation. The pathos with which the inscription affirmed Hohenzollern sovereignty was in a crucial way *uneigentlich*, a meaning that departed from itself. The transfer from beast to sovereign was based on this type of departure; it was compatible with a message of the finiteness of monarchy. This is what the wildness of the archive offers to the understanding of the nexus between history and power in general.

In a carnivalistic postscript to the story of his tenure, Wilhelm II relied on philological scholarship to fashion his *uneigentlich* court life in exile after 1918. Still connected and wealthy enough to be a desirable provider and broker of research funding, he became increasingly involved with the scholars who eventually formed a sort of imperial research seminar in exile, the *Doorner Arbeitsgemeinschaft*, named after the Dutch manor to which the former monarch was confined. The *Kaiser's* longtime favorites were the classical archaeologist Wilhelm Dörpfeld (1853–1940), the theologian Alfred Jeremias (1864–1935), a Panbabylonist who had been Delitzsch's student, and the ethnographer Leo Frobenius. Common to these scholars was their penchant for grand Orientalist speculations about antiquity and the prehistory of humankind. As Christoph Johannes Franzen has shown, Frobenius's designs, in particular, permitted Wilhelm to read his own downfall as part of the universal-historical grand lines of the confrontation of an Orientalized Germany with its Occidental enemies. Frobenius also offered a cultural "morphology" in which the ritual sacrifice of kings, a motif borrowed from J. G. Frazer, could be understood as part of this confrontation.[211] Franzen highlights Wilhelm's desire to appear as a victim of forces beyond his own political making; but perhaps more importantly Frobenius offered the ex-Kaiser a manner of renewing the messianic charge of his position. As a consequence, the relationship between the monarch and his scholars was turned upside down. In their correspondence, Wilhelm consistently fashioned himself as a "student" of Frobenius. The philologists—and their imitators—had assumed full stewardship of the messianic potential of monarchy, and the archives from the possession of which they spoke were a wilderness beyond belief.

For Frobenius, modern Germans were mere representatives of a transhistorical cultural pattern (a *Paideuma*, in his terminology) that he called the "Ethiopian" one and that pertained to agricultural "plant-oriented" cultures that did not form aggressive states, but rather mystical (as opposed to ritualistic) religions. It was these cultures that murdered their kings, in recognition, and dramatic mimesis, of cyclical natural patterns.[212] On a side-note, this argument also permitted the de-Judaization of the central messianic motif of Christianity, the sacrifice of the god-king and savior. Rarely has Ethiopia been accorded a more central role in world history. The archive Frobenius interpreted was also what was written on the stones, or more precisely, what had been drawn on them, "prehistoric" rock art from Africa that provided an odd universalist reading of the diversity of all human culture. The former emperor enjoyed mirroring himself in Zimbabwean kings—"my dark colleagues," he wrote in a letter—as described and invented by Frobenius.[213] Liberated from governmental authority, Wilhelm II had entirely adopted the intellectual forms of German Orientalism.[214] The exile of the monarch came before the exile of the philologist that Auerbach, and with him Said, sought to appropriate and generalize, along with the messianic notion of the return to philology, as if the latter had been a Paradise lost.

Burdened with Gods

1. Theophoric Names

At least *prima facie*, the previous chapter has discussed the significance of the Aksumite inscriptions in different terms than the significance of the Safaitica. While Aksumite epigraphy led into the problem of monarchy and its symbolic charges, Safaitic epigraphy appeared to conjoin with primitive individuality and the savage. Yet this difference was only superficial; both archives shared underlying conditions of intelligibility. These conditions not only unified the practice of epigraphy but also pointed beyond it. In the development of the study of inscriptions in general, Semitic epigraphy held a special place since it opened the traditional notion of biblical or Hebrew antiquity to procedures and arguments developed in classics. Interference with biblical knowledge was so profound that it is almost justifiable to speak of a particular epoch in the history of scripture, perhaps the Fin-de-siècle-Bible, marked by the impact of this philological expansion. Rather than presenting a synthetic account of these developments, I will only focus on those shared conditions of intelligibility that, as I aim to show, spread far beyond the narrower confines of theology and philology. These conditions show themselves in a peculiar entanglement of naming, referential semantics, notions of religion and revelation, and of historicity. In order to gain a hold on this tangle of problems, it is worthwhile to briefly return to Littmann's and Grimme's disagreement on the interpretation of the proto-Arabic inscriptions in the Harra. This disagreement is remarkable because both authors relied on a shared, if tacit, point of reference: an older debate, dating from the 1880s, on Early Arab religious forms, the advent of monotheism, and the prehistory of Islam.

The first highly visible and significant representative of this line of thought was William Robertson Smith, whose study of Semitic norms of kinship[1] relied on contemporary British evolutionist social anthropology that drew as much on Darwin as on the progressive civilizational stage models of Scottish enlightenment philosophies of "conjectural" history.[2] As a theologian of the Old Testament, Robertson Smith was German-trained and depended on Dutch and German Protestant theological literature, especially on Abraham Kuenen and Julius Wellhausen. As an anthropologist of the Old-Semitic world, however, Robertson Smith transferred fragments of British discourse to continental Orientalism. His studies of kinship structures and of ritual practice, and in particular sacrifice, helped to refashion European concepts of religion. Wellhausen, a teacher, friend, and frequent correspondent, came to admire

Robertson Smith's work primarily in this regard. The heresy trial of several years that had ended with the Scottish theologian's suspension from his Aberdeen professorship in 1881 had provided an inspiration for Wellhausen's own almost equally scandalous relinquishment of his theology professorship in 1882. Robertson Smith was hired as secretary for the *Encyclopaedia Britannica* before he became professor of Arabic in Cambridge. Wellhausen, who enjoyed the favor of the top Prussian administrator of higher education Friedrich Althoff (1839–1908)—C. H. Becker's indirect predecessor—was granted positions in Semitic philology in Halle (1882), Marburg (1885), and finally Göttingen (1892). The work of both scholars symbolized the departure of the academic world from theological norms even in the study of religion, which in both countries, Prussia as well as the United Kingdom, was also opportune at least in some sectors of the political field.

Robertson Smith and Wellhausen—along with other authors such as the Dutch colonial scholar George Alexander Wilken (1847–1891) and furthermore Goldziher, Snouck, and Nöldeke—developed models for a history of the emergence of monotheism in which older notions of "natural" religion were reflected and refracted in various ways. The category of the cultural, for many of these scholars, represented departure from nature. The exact impact of Darwinist notions of evolution varied. For Wellhausen, the discursive patterns developing in historical writing were certainly more important.[3] Robertson Smith and Wilken in particular had included speculation on early-historical matriarchy into their studies of the emergence of religion; but the status of matriarchy continued to oscillate between necessary evolutionary stage and contingent cultural feature. Wellhausen, in his 1887 *Reste arabischen Heidentums* ("Remnants of Arab Heathendom"), developed a different, more distinctly philological agenda that started with a discussion of *Götternamen*, the names of gods, and the relation of polytheism and monotheism. He was dismissive about matriarchy, and arguably his reception of Robertson Smith's intervention sidelined the conjectural study of overall social structure. Wellhausen also already drew to some extent on epigraphic finds, especially Euting's work on the Nabataean inscriptions.[4] For Wellhausen, though, the manuscript heritage of late ancient and early Islamic Arabia provided the most important body of sources, and he remained hesitant about epigraphy. Nonetheless, the expansion of epigraphy was inexorable. For decades to come, the epigraphic debate on the "proto-Arabic" inscriptions promised the most authentic sources and the writings most proximate to nature—with rocks on the surface of rocks.

Grimme's relation to Wellhausen's work was conceptual in kind. His interpretation of the Harra as a protected "holy" district clearly drew on a problematic Wellhausen had developed, drawing partly on Snouck's work, with reference to the specific norms that governed the area around Mecca.[5] These norms constituted what European scholars called the "sanctity" of the district, the *haram*, in which numerous activities, such as hunting and bloodshed, were interdicted and in which specific rules of access held. In Wellhausen's interpretation, the regime of the *haram* could be unpacked as a compound of earlier polytheist regulations of the *cultus* around the Ka'aba. The district had emerged as the property of a pantheon of tribal deities in which Allah, but also the mother goddess Allat, already played particular roles.[6] Grimme's seemingly outré reading of the Safaitica rested on a transfer of this structure into the North Arabian desert.

Littmann's relation to Wellhausen's *Reste*, by contrast, was less straightforward. As stated, his reading of the religious import of the inscriptions was minimalist; he emphasized the mundane, individual, and even the scatological content of the inscriptions. Yet precisely in these interests, his view of Arab heathendom converged with Wellhausen's perspective on pre-monotheist forms of worship:

> The [polytheist] cult enjoys its main force of attraction at the centers of pilgrimage, through the markets and fairs connected with the place; the cult is of a cheerful character throughout, one enjoys oneself with fun and games, with women, wine, and song; also Jews and Christians are not excluded from the commerce and the amusements. ...
>
> How little the Arabs held dear their cult one sees on the occasion of the downfall of heathendom and the mass conversion to Islam. Nowhere does this downfall betray tragic qualities, much rather scurrilous ones. Conversion to Islam is much more a matter of politics than of religion.[7]

Wellhausen took issue with the notion that there was a particular penchant of "Semitic" religions toward a tyrannical, dull, legalist monotheism that would have been the result of a presumptive racial lack of imagination.[8] This notion had above all been pioneered by the French doyen of Semitics Ernest Renan (1823–1892), and was echoed in many of the nineteenth-century racist dichotomies that pitched the two "white races," "the Aryans" and "the Semites," against each other. Opposition to this Renanian idea was relatively widespread in the Germanophone Orientalism of the period, even among those who otherwise admired Renan, as was for instance the case with Goldziher, who nonetheless wrote a book-length study on Hebrew myth in order to demonstrate the vivacity of Semitic religious fantasy.[9] Nöldeke had regarded the Renanian understanding of myth as entirely erroneous already in 1860.[10] Wellhausen saw little to defend in Judaism as a doctrinal religion; yet his overall account of ancient Hebrew history, based on his philological analyses of the Old Testament, was pivoted on the historical, not the biological, emergence of the legalism of rabbinic Judaism. Before the Babylonian exile, Judaism, too, had been a "cheerful" cult.[11] So while Grimme used the Safaitica to further develop Wellhausen's notions about the cultural form of the *haram* but deviated from Wellhausen's banalizing view of polytheist cultus, Littmann adopted Wellhausen's mundane vision of "natural" Semitic heathendom but objected to Grimme's speculative theory of the holy district.

In his 1887 study, Wellhausen also laid down further patterns for the subsequent reading of Semitic inscriptions. Structurally, his entrance point to the study of "Arab heathendom," the religious forms of Arabia that preceded Islam, was the examination of such proper names that were "theophoric," that is to say, carried the semantic burden of a deity in some form or other, in accordance with paradigm cases such as e.g. *Abdallah*, "servant of Allah." The opposite category were proper names that were "atheon," free of the divine. Theophoric names occurred not only for persons but also for places. In fact, Wellhausen's main source of proper names was Yāqūt's geographical "lexicon" (*c.* 1200 CE) that had been available to European scholarship as an edited text for years.[12] The new epigraphic research was only of secondary importance to him.

He did not pay it systematic heed, in spite of the augmentation of name material it had achieved. In his eyes, the meticulous work of collection was at best auxiliary. For, the proper name that was related to the name of a deity was, as he pointed out, a core constituent of the set of practices at the heart of "religion" *tout court*. His work on theophoric names was therefore work on the very concept of religion, and not bound to quantity:

> At the same time as the cult, by way of its localization, proves the original connection between gods and demons [i.e. djinns], the cult, at least the public one at freely accessible sites, marks the decisive distinction between them. Demons only *dwell* in the sacred place, but one does not honor them. As soon as one approaches and serves them there, they are transformed into gods, in line with the transformation of the forbidden grove [*gefeiter Hag*] into a place of worship. In this way, they also depart from the obscurity of the mere general class and become individuals. Demons are usually anonymous; for gods, the name is of the utmost importance. When the latter want humans to turn their dwelling site into a place of worship, they then appear there and reveal themselves by giving their name; the name is the entire content of their revelation, which does not serve theological, but only practical interests. For, only when one knows them can one influence them and pray to them; the calling of the name of the deity signifies the cult as such ... The unnamed god is the unknown god, who cannot be served.[13]

The name then, along with place, is not merely an effective device for individuation, but provides the historical foundation for the emergence of the very notion of revelation. Moreover, on account of this foundation, scriptural monotheism, as inevitably revealed, is genealogically bound to polytheism. The latter emerges, even "with necessity,"[14] where deities are tethered to places and bear proper names. This also entails that the emergent cult of a named deity is always bound up with a specific and small social (ethnic, tribal) group.

Through the spatial mobility of people, such polytheism becomes "syncretistic," a sign of its dissolution underway toward a more generalized, nationalized godhead:

> Among the Arabs Allah indeed emerged from the decay of religious ethnicism; from the fact that the diverse deities lost the most important reason of their distinctness, namely their veneration on the part of diverse peoples, and descended to mere synonymity in which only the general concept of the deity retained meaning.[15]

Already in the pre-Islamic pantheon, "Allah" enjoys a privileged position, initially as a class name, close to a concept, that can be attributed to any tribal god. Subsequently, the class name becomes a proper name, and a general deity emerges. At first, the particular, group- and place-bound deities continue to be venerated along with the general one.[16] As long as the cult remains "natural,"[17] it retains a particularist character. When it becomes fully general—with an "international god that stands above partisanship" (224)—and therefore unnatural, when it turns into a "religion, as we actually understand it in opposition to cult" (221), monotheism is attained. In the

Arab world, Islam is the first faith to achieve this transformation and thereby impute on believers the "fear of god" (224f.).

In *Reste arabischen Heidentums*, then, Wellhausen was after a generalized theory of the conditions of the possibility of the emergence of religion *qua* monotheism. The prime place among these conditions was held by the proper name; concepts alone did not suffice for "religion," which was produced by the ability of names to individuate and personify. At the same time, the name was the precondition for revelation, for the *parousia* of the deity, and ultimately even for his embodiment. The anonymous god was unable even to take shape, nor to own a particular place, unless he revealed his name (the grammatical masculinity here mimics Wellhausen's usage). By the intellectual standards of Old Testament theology and Semitist Orientalism, since the 1880s, the name had become the central agent of the uncertain and dubious system of "religion."

Wellhausen's discussion testified to the uncertainty generated by the contrary impulses to historicize and thereby particularize religion and, at the same time, to universalize it as the referent of an abstract and globally pertinent concept.[18] One crucial weakness of his account lay in the genetic relatedness of all the instances of the concept of religion he was able to compare: the three monotheist religions and their polytheist forebears. Although Wellhausen embraced the novel field of a "comparative science of religion" (e.g. 94), if in a somewhat cavalier manner, he did not address the difficulty of finding unrelated units of comparison. With the means available to him, he was unable to overcome the countersense of forging a universal concept of religion from a merely regional paradigm. Subsequent to his efforts, it became opportune to hypostatize naming as the core of revelation, so as to anchor the floating concept of religion in this pairing. It was a subsidiary function of this exaltation of the name that inscriptions could be endowed with prophetic potential, since the decipherment of inscriptions tended to reveal, above all, names. As Littmann's and Grimme's divergent interpretations of the same corpus of inscriptions indicate, the connection between epigraphy and revelation could be spelled out in crassly different ways. As the case of the Axumitica implies, it could also align with different intellectual resources, such as the discursive patterns around monarchy, to yield a different shade of prophetic revelation. These possibilities were imposed on inscriptions as a semantic potential, to be realized in epigraphy as an aggregation of practices.

The explanation of the emergence of this semantic potential of epigraphy may depend on a broader historical context. As Markus Messling has pointed out, around 1800, the study of the Egyptian hieroglyphs in France carried republican meaning; as the origin of script, the hieroglyphs represented the first human civilization, and the rediscovery of their meaning was part of the alignment of the modern political system with originary republicanism.[19] The "symbolic" character of Old-Egyptian script— as based on a semiotic over-determination through multiple similarity relations as well as arbitrarily assigned meanings—also preoccupied Hegel. More precisely, it allowed him to temporalize his semiotic theory as a gradual move away from the "symbol"—in his terminology beholden to iconic similarity—toward merely arbitrary "signs" capable of unequivocal meaning.[20] In this context, as Warren Breckman has pointed out, Hegel also stressed the lithic nature of hieroglyph inscriptions to mark the originary failure of script to acquire freedom from the constrictions of concrete physical space, a condition the hieroglyph inscriptions shared with plastic art; the material delimited the signifying function of the sign system.[21] Wilhelm von Humboldt, who unlike other German scholars immediately accepted Champollion's decipherment, also relied on the hieroglyphs to advance a general theory of the origins of human script that subsequently fell into oblivion.[22] Such uses of epigraphy as a philosophical *topos* in the early nineteenth century do not only share the Egyptian reference but also the alignment of inscriptions with an originary state and starting point of progressive civilization. The idea that historicity was distinguished from the prehistorical by the advent of script[23] was a notion that converged with Egyptomania before the decipherment. Once the textual heritage of the ancient Egyptians became legible, the aesthetic as well as the philosophical fashion characteristically subsided. By the end of the nineteenth century, few of the previous concerns remained at all discernible in the actual practical work of epigraphers. Novel notions of the epigraphic state of nature rather redeveloped out of speculation about natural religion. This was a philosophical trope that also boasted a decidedly older, even partly Hegelian, provenance, but one that was only distantly related to the romantic-era philosophical concern for epigraphy.

In the 1880s and 90s, the theorization of religion actually formed a novel alliance with the study of inscriptions as a concrete research practice driven by concrete and limited problems and cut off from its older significance. In this process, the hypostatization of naming became crucial. The manner in which epigraphic practice was, as it were, twisted out of its intellectual history, can be instructively pursued in the case of Fritz Hommel (1854–1936). Yet another heteroptic epigrapher, Hommel retained the traditional, intimate linkage between revelation and Semitic inscriptions. Along—but in constant quarrel—with D. H. Müller,[24] he was among the main supporters of the Austrian autoptic epigrapher Eduard Glaser (1855–1908), who in the 1880s and 90s pioneered the collection and study of the so-called South Semitic inscriptions found mostly in Yemen. Within this corpus the Sabaic and Minaic inscriptions date, according to current standards, to approximately the ninth century BCE. Hommel, in his printed-autograph *Süd-Arabische Chrestomathie*, even believed they were half a millennium older.[25] The first decipherment of the Sabaica was accomplished by the Hebraist Wilhelm Gesenius (1786–1842) and his student Roediger in 1841–2, but it was only the expansion of the corpus through the travels of Joseph Halévy and then Glaser that spawned more intensive research.[26] The problems to which one thought the inscriptions would speak were similar to the ones pursued for the Thamudica and Safaitica. The general shift toward a study of the origins of monotheism in the presumably pre-biblical Semitic epigraphic record entailed novel research programs on Judaism and Christianity alike. Glaser, a Bohemian Jew who never attained a secure academic position, was widely involved in scholarly as well as political polemics; for instance, he suggested to Theodor Herzl that Jewish settlement plans be focused on Yemen, which led to public disagreement.[27] Throughout his uneven and insecure career Glaser never processed much of the material he had collected. Rhodokanakis and later Maria Höfner (1900–1992), who had also studied with Littmann, became its prime interpreters. But years before they embarked on their efforts, Hommel had also ventured into the field.[28]

Hommel was an Orientalist with training in a variety of fields, including Cuneiform, but he retained a prominent interest in the critical philology of the Old Testament that for instance his erstwhile teacher Friedrich Delitzsch increasingly sought to destroy as a field. Originally, Hommel had been a supporter of Wellhausen's work, but epigraphy, a field whose expansion was only tardily acknowledged by theologians, appeared to unsettle what had seemed a reliable method and secure opinion. The Oxford Assyriologist Archibald H. Sayce's (1846–1933) findings, in Cuneiform tablets of proper names that plausibly were identical to biblical ones had changed the rules of the game.[29] If read in the right way, the epigraphic record promised contemporary evidence of biblical events, proof of the old age of the scriptures, and even of the authenticity of the original revelation of monotheism, or so Hommel hoped. His main work of biblical criticism appeared in 1897.[30] As an intervention into theological debates, the book ultimately sought to

> reconquer, for the *Wissenschaft* of the Old Testament, a terrain that to many appears as an Eden of which they have been bereft long ago and of which they can think only with yearning ... It will be my greatest prize when I restore to the many younger theologians ... that which they already mourned as irreversibly gone— the Paradise lost of their old biblical faith.[31]

The natural happiness into which Wellhausen had suggested he was releasing religion was clearly lost on Hommel for whom the decline of faith in the letter of scripture was mournful. In pursuit of the reversal of this process, Hommel's volume built an elaborate argument around the epigraphic occurrence of personal proper names, in particular theophoric ones, in the oldest Middle Eastern epigraphic records, the Cuneiform and the Sabaic and Minaic ones.

Hommel's starting point was an early work by the theologian Eberhard Nestle (1851–1913), who had proposed a threefold periodization of groups of Hebrew names in the Old Testament.[32] Nestle had mapped these clusters of personal names to the names of the deity in the Pentateuch, which had been used since the eighteenth century as the entrance point for distinguishing the textual strata of scripture. The personal names, which occurred more frequently than the names of the deity, then supposedly facilitated the correlation of specific epochs of biblical history with the different stages of the emergence of the text. In this way, while core aspects of the philology of the Pentateuch were corroborated, the unity and basic veracity of the Pentateuch as a historical source was also vindicated. Almost needless to say, Wellhausen had dismissed the procedure and pointed to the documentary unreliability of the mere names. He insisted that their stratified similarities were consistent with the overall thesis that the legal portions of the Pentateuch had only been composed after the end of Babylonian exile. Along with a considerable portion of the historical traditions of the Old Testament, the proper names had been invented in this period that marked the transition from pre-exilic prophetic natural Hebrew religion to post-exilic legalist Judaism.[33] Hommel believed that he could intervene in this debate by showing the consistency of the periodization of the proper names in mere biblical text with the overall epigraphic record. The oldest known records provided an archive that reached back into the pre-exilic period. The similarities marking the proper names of the overall period were then meant to disprove Wellhausen's argument.[34]

Regrettably, some collateral damage to biblical history was inevitable. For instance, Hommel was convinced that the ancient Hebrews had been proto-Arabs and largely identical to the users of the South Semitic scripts. As the names in the Babylonian lists of kings indicated, or so he thought, Babylon at the time of Hammurabi presented a synthesis of Semitic and non-Semitic cultures under the government of a proto-Arab elite. Clearly, their empire had practiced a polytheistic cult; but the proto-Arabs had already been monotheists and inserted their beliefs into the polytheist cult only because of the practical requirements of empire. The Sabaica demonstrated that the lexeme "ilu" for "God" was a widespread element in the oldest documented South Semitic system of naming. This element was the equivalent of Hebrew "El," a name that indicated what the critical tradition considered the oldest, "Elohist" stratum of the Pentateuch. In both contexts, the name belonged to a generalized godhead that was revealed to be associated with fatherhood by alternative monikers.[35] Personal names were formed around the name of the godhead; the entire system was slanted toward the theophoric.

In a discussion of the etymology of the ultimate theophoric name, that of the monotheist deity, Yahweh (of the later, "Jehovist" stratum of the Old Testament), Hommel also embraced the notion that revelation was the underlying principle of the naming system itself. This etymology was introduced in the context of a discussion of name etymologies in Babylonian documents:

> As far as the two witness names *Shumu-liçi* and *Shumu-libshi* (also Shumû-ma-libshi and Shumî-libshi) … are concerned, admittedly *liçi* [sic] "may he come out" ("emerge") and *libshi* "may he be" are truly Babylonian verbal phrases, and a translation "may a son emerge," "may it be a son" might be conceivable as a personal name. But with regard to the fact that in the same bilingual list [of king's names] in which Hammu-rabi and Ammi-sadugga are explained …, the identical name Shuma-libshi [!] is paraphrased in Sumeric as *muna-tilla* "his name lives," I would like to consider the names mentioned as only formally Babylonian, and Arabic in sense. We have names such as *Ikun-ka-ilu* "God existed for you" ("suited you"?) and *Ibshi-na-ilu* "God entered into existence for us" (evinced himself for us as an existing one), which do not only provide a fitting analogy for the name *Shuma-libshi* (according to me "may his name, i.e. that of God, enter into existence"), but also form a peculiar parallel to the Hebrew name of God Yahweh (= the existing one). [… Yahweh] is a rather Arabic than Hebrew (or Kanaanite) form of the old verb *hawaja* (= Hebr. *hajah*) 'to be, to enter into existence' … In this way, witness names from Old-Babylonian contract tablets from the time of Abraham provide testimony for the traditional biblical explanation of the venerable holy [*altheilige*] name of Yahweh![36]

A few pages later, Hommel then expanded the meaning of the name Yahweh: "He exists, enters into being, reveals himself."[37] This semantic operation betrays an underlying understanding of existence as emergence and of emergence as revelation.

This understanding resided in the name of God, on which the overall system of naming hinged. In this way, epigraphy helped to achieve a theological understanding of the referentiality of scripture, for which the referentiality of personal proper names as revelation became crucial. Hommel, reactivating discursive patterns that were far older than he was presumably aware, thought he had finally found evidence that monotheism had preceded polytheism.[38] While the question of monogenetic against polygenetic accounts of the emergence of the human species had been settled in favor of monogenesis, in the study of religion—and by extension in that of culture—these patterns of argument were resurrected. The period even saw a renewed confrontation of comparative and "diffusionist" approaches as pioneered by the "cultural geographer" Friedrich Ratzel (1844–1904).[39] Wellhausen stayed relatively clear of such generalizations about human history; but, as opposed to Hommel, he considered Middle Eastern polytheism more original than monotheism.

Hommel can hardly avoid the reproach that his account was as terrifically detailed as it was terrifyingly unsound. For his argument it was crucial to "prove" the historicity of Genesis 14, a chapter that lists Abraham's wars against several neighboring nations at the time in which Amraphel was king in Sinear. The identity of Amraphel with the Babylonian ruler known best as Hammurabi had been widely assumed since Sayce and formed part of the backbone of Assyriological claims to providing historical foundations to the Bible. In order to substantiate the notion that Abraham was a historical figure, a monotheist émigré from Babylon at the time of Hammurabi, providing evidence in corroboration of this simultaneity was a necessary step. This entailed harmonizing the chronology of Genesis with the lists of the kings of Babylon. In order for this argument to appear plausible Hommel needed to stipulate that two of three known Babylonian dynasties had overlapped temporally; and in the end he had to give credence to the letter of the Bible with regard to Abraham's and Jacob's extreme longevity, in order to render the chronology consistent.[40] The contextual-philological ambition—to make the veracity of the Bible as a historical document plausible by reference to extra-textual evidence—was thus turned on its head: Hommel fell back on blind faith in the document in order to settle the meaning of the contextual sources. The neat distinction of text and context and the clear order of priority in which the inscriptions took precedence over the Pentateuch collapsed. The semantic procedure at hand was circular; the meaning of the text was revealed as referential because it had been taken as referential from the beginning.

It was as a result of this circular structure that the Bible was subsequently denied value as a historical source on equal footing with the epigraphic archive. When reviewers took Hommel to task for a "lack of truly historical method," this was what they meant.[41] Yet, the matter was more complex; some of the decisive features that shaped Hommel's circular argument also marred other scholars' efforts. In 1937, a year after Hommel's death, Hubert Grimme speculated, in a work he regarded as the culmination of his epigraphic research, that the Old-Sinaitic inscriptions provided evidence for the events narrated in Exodus and the historicity of Moses.[42] Yet, the procedural community extended across the lines of polemical conflict also to those scholars whose work epitomized "truly historical method," for instance Wellhausen.

The extreme fragmentation to which Hommel subjected his philological arguments ensured that Biblical text was not treated as a whole. In many respects, it was not read as a text any more, but as a repository of historical evidence—an archive. This mode of reading, which crucially rested on the hypostatization of naming that was driven by the insertion of epigraphy into biblical criticism, Hommel had appropriated from the deconstructive philology of his time. The recklessly speculative and uninhibited nature of his argument exposes with particular clarity features shared across the board of biblical philology in this period. In Wellhausen, too, there was a notion of revelation at work that was tied to the very notion of existence and the reading of existence as emergence.

2. Cassirer and the Name of Being

The hypostasis of theophoric names went along with a privileging of naming in general, as an abstract function of language, which was removed from its concrete conditions as a cultural practice, or so one imagined, and transferred into the realm of the merely formal. By mere association, the gods with whom the names were burdened also acquired a more formal, functional character. Moreover, in the wake of epigraphy, names and naming were also endowed with novel abstract meanings that contributed to the understanding of semantics in general. As usual, the pioneering role of the Orientalist complex of fields and pursuits was quickly eclipsed.

Ernst Cassirer took up the problem of naming in the 1920s, in the context of his work on the nature of concepts and the relationship between language and myth. The only Orientalist whose work he discussed at some length was the Indologist Max Müller. The discussion mainly served to reject Müller's general theory of myth, as the consequence of the irrepressible figural surplus in natural languages.[43] Instead, Cassirer accorded central importance to Hermann Usener's study of theophoric names in classical antiquity.[44] The findings of this work Cassirer sought to confirm through comparative readings of ethnographic literature that had appeared mainly since the 1890s and whose authors, he assumed, would not have read Usener's work.[45] This assumption may well have been correct, and in addition it was encouraged by Usener's reticence to reference theological and Orientalist works that had prepared the field he entered. Nonetheless, there was an abundance of shared context that ought not to have been so swiftly dismissed.

Key to Cassirer's interest was Usener's labor on a theoretical account of the emergence of concepts. This account radically deviated from philosophical tradition. Tradition held that concepts were formed inductively, through repeated observation and the singling out of recurrent properties. Cassirer, in a neo-Kantian vein, objected to this account since it assumed that the essential properties that were generalized into "correct" concepts were determined before the emergence of concepts, and thereby language. Yet, in order to break down an object of perception into its component properties, reliance on judgment—which by necessity presupposed concepts—was inevitable. The traditional account therefore was guilty of begging the question.[46] Even if natural reality provided a grid of object-types rigidly ordered by discrete sets of essential properties, it was impossible to derive a grid of concepts from such an ontological structure alone. The way out of the mystery of the genesis of concepts was through recognition of the nature of the "labor of naming" (*Arbeit des Benennens*),[47] an act of the arbitrary positing of meaning that was foundational for language in general. Naming thus preceded concepts.

It was in this regard that Cassirer drew on Usener's work. In a nutshell, the classicist's contribution to the theory of concept formation was to suggest that this process inevitably included a practice of naming that was to go along with an intra-linguistic tendency toward personification and a specific mode of religious experience. According to Usener, it was by way of salient momentary perceptions that primary religious concepts, such as the notion of a divine presence, emerged. Humans disposed of passively received mental contents that, if intense, were capable of dominating all attention or consciousness. When this happened, perceptions tended to generate what Usener called *Augenblicksgötter*, gods of the moment. Yet nothing much followed from these elusive events. It was only when momentary intense perceptions occurred in iterated form, in the medium of repetitive human activity, for instance in the context of labor, that something more durable could emerge. These durable perceptions, which relied on a broadening of human agency and intentionality in time, then generated a different class of deities, the gods of the particular, *Sondergötter*, who disposed of a specific area of pertinence, often an activity, such as ploughing. The gods of the particular still remained flat and abstract, mere concepts that did not interact with the particularities of the world. It was only in a third step that such gods then became substantivized and personified in a concrete, detailed, and narrative manner. They became name-bearing personal gods, capable of acting as a dialogic counterpart to humans. The figure of dialogue was important, since it signaled the interdependence of both divine and human personification. Concept formation and the formation of divine as well as human individuals were therefore inseparably linked; and what bound everything together was the proper name.

From a psychological point of view, this was a theory of the role of attention in a speculative history of the genesis of language. Attention entailed an emphasis on subjectivity; inevitably, the name emerged within a self-sufficient *Ego*. This Ego was endowed with intentionality and agency, which sufficed for the labor of naming. A distinctly social understanding of language remained remarkably absent. Supposedly, the subject-bound nature of the process sufficed to explain the centrality of personification. As a result, the history of myth—stories about deities—was inseparably interwoven with the emergence of conceptual abstraction in language. In a passage highlighted by Cassirer, Usener asked:

Can there be a doubt whether Φόβος came first or φόβος, the divine figure or the state of mind? Why is the state of mind of male instead of neutral gender, like τὸ δέος? The first creation of the word must have been inhabited by the notion of a living personal being, of the "scarer" ["*Scheucher*"], the "prompter of flight."[48]

Grammatical gender then provided a hint to the underlying mechanisms of personification.

Tacitly, this argument drew on a widespread pattern of nineteenth-century philology, of recognizing a purported natural reality of the mind in the arbitrariness of grammar, especially the assignation of gender. In fact, gender was privileged as a category that allowed shifting from syntactic-formal to semantic argument. On account of this function, grammar remained a potent participant in the theoretical debate at hand. When discussing the difficulties of translating the concept of a personal monotheist god into non-European languages, Cassirer prominently cited the work of the Africanist Carl Meinhof (1857–1944). Meinhof had in turn relied on grammatical categories developed by Wilhelm Bleek (1827–1875), who had recognized that in the family of the then so-called Bantu languages "person classes" of nouns had to be distinguished from "thing classes."[49] Under the conditions of such a grammatical structure, the process of personification had to do with the distinction of things and non-things. In the context of Ancient Greek and other Indo-European languages, by contrast, the work of distinguishing noun classes fell to the triad of gender, which seemed to rely on sexual, and therefore personifying, distinction as its primary marker. Recourse to the Bantu and similar structures then highlighted the particular status of personification in Indo-European languages. Recognizing superiority in this particularity was a matter of bias.

In Cassirer's account, the main function of evidence from other language families than the Indo-European was to indicate the presence of a stage of concept formation that supposedly *preceded* the stages Usener had distinguished. This preceding stage was best illustrated by the Polynesian expression of "mana" that had been brought to the attention of European scholarship by Max Müller with reference to the theologian, missionary, and anthropologist R. H. Codrington (1830–1922) as the "discoverer" of the term.[50] Rehearsing the wildly divergent interpretations the expression had since been given in the anthropological literature, Cassirer insisted that mana did not derive its meaning from reference to a "substance," precondition for personification, but rather was a term that expressed a focusing of attention as such, a focusing that itself indicated the presence of the momentary divine, the core of myth.[51] This was the form of predication itself rather than a distinct and defined predicate. It was an "exclamation that … signified an impression," thus an interjection that, when it had taken articulate form, had become a predicate.[52] *Mana* was "mythical-religious *ur*-predication" that brought about the very distinction between the sacred and the profane, and thereby constituted the primal "object of religious consciousness." In this way, the heightening of attention in the "mythical-religious" gave rise to the as yet "anonymous background" against which further distinctions of shapes and personified beings, a "world" of distinct objects, emerged.[53]

Although Cassirer opposed Müller's reading of the term *mana* in some respects, he retained the notion of the primitive, the basic form of religion Müller had postulated.[54] Cassirer agreed that notions akin to *mana* could be found among natives the world over. Therefore, the emergence of this type of notion had to be polygenetic. This in turn confirmed its status as a basic stage of concept formation, no matter the individual language. In this way, Cassirer concealed that Usener's and his own account relied on particular-language grammatical structures in order to stage a universalist argument. Precisely because *mana* represented the "anonymous," it thus served as the conceptual tool with which, by way of negation, the name, in accordance with Usener's schema, was hypostatized. The anonymous became a primal stage to be succeeded by "polyonymy," as a precondition for the emergence of a "higher personal god."[55]

Usener, too, rejected Max Müller's speculative comparative history of mythologies, as having "squandered the trust" of those in the same field of research. Nonetheless, like everyone else in the field, he adopted a stageist understanding of the developmental path of religion.[56] This understanding did not follow the types and categories proposed by Müller, especially in his famed Gifford Lectures of 1888–1892, but the underlying explanatory pattern, the epistemic infrastructure of the new science of comparative religion remained stable.[57] As a classicist, Usener remained alien to parts of the theological language that had governed Wellhausen's and Smith's interventions. Indeed, Usener rejected Smith—and presumably Wellhausen, too, if without justification—as "adherents of the doctrine of [Herbert] Spencer," thus as Darwinists.[58] The processual schema Usener developed, and which Cassirer later borrowed, was to be anything but an evolutionist account. Rather, the model for the speculative history of the genesis of language was supplied by state of nature and social contract theories in political philosophy. The rejection of evolutionism was a welcome pretext for avoiding the concept of revelation that had been so central to Wellhausen's discussion of theophoric names. Only in the closing of the main argument, in the context of a short description of the advent of Christian monotheism, did Usener deploy the concept in a prominent passage that departed decisively, however, from theological usage.

For Usener, there was something broadly logical about the emergence of monotheism that had to do with the establishment of general kind-concepts in response to the reiteration of the exalted singularities that in his interpretation prompted the naming of gods. Yet precisely because of the supposedly logical nature of this operation, the classicist struggled with the fact that Greco-Roman antiquity had only brought forth various forms of pantheon cults of "all gods," but no sustained notion of a unitary godhead. In order to explain this shortcoming, Usener fell back on a cliché, the positing of national-cultural life cycles; it was the fatigue of the aged and worn-out culture of classical antiquity that prevented it from drawing the logical conclusion.[59] "Only an intervening revelation was able to remove the obstacles that prevented the old polytheism to develop into monotheism." This revelation could not emerge from the oracles, the internal institutions of classical polytheism that had provided this type of service in the past, for these institutions were all bound up with the cults of individual deities and "were unable to negate themselves. … No prophetic personality could arise and pull along a populace in which the educated had become alienated from the faith of the fathers … . A Mohamed, a Zarathustra have imprinted their faiths only on youthful peoples."[60] For the Christian faith, what made the difference, what enabled it to spread across the culturally exhausted population of the ancient world more broadly, was the *Bluttaufe*, the "baptism of blood," it "received in Jerusalem," that is to say, the martyrdom of the founder.[61] The monotheism of Christianity completed the developmental logic of ancient religion as a whole, even though later on it also adopted polytheist forms, such as the trinity and the cult of the mother of god.

Usener's underlying concept of revelation was ambiguous. On the one hand, revelation was merely a form of cultural imagination, tied to specific institutions such as oracles or messianic leadership (Max Weber would later say, "charismatic," relying on some of the early literature on the comparative history of religion, among which Wellhausen's works).[62] On the other hand, only the Christian variant of revelation was able to provide a world historical caesura, in accordance with an eschatological understanding of the history of the world. On the surface, Usener's philology was secular and embraced a very typical late-nineteenth-century concept of religion as a matter partly of cultural psychology, partly of the natural history of nationhood. This national-psychological notion of the religious was, however, constructed atop an affirmative denominational undercurrent. What bridged the two meanings of revelation was the metaphor of a baptism of blood, which tied the national-psychological explication of revelation to a specific act of naming, one that was exalted by violence. Since the conceptual argument did not suffice for explaining the emergence of monotheism, Usener drew on the historical, on the epochal caesura marked by violence. The sacrificial bloodshed of the crucifixion thus became a cipher for the insertion of revelation into the sphere of historicity. Violence granted access to historicity.

The nexus of the concepts of revelation and history marked several important philosophies of history in the interwar period, among which in particular those of Hermann Cohen and Franz Rosenzweig. Arguably, even Heidegger's account of truth as *aletheia*, as a happening of "unconcealment," finds its conceptual possibility in the philological belaboring of the *Götternamen*, of epigraphic archives, and of the text of the Hebrew Bible decades earlier (in spite of the vigorous disclaimers that his own analysis of truth is as beholden to theology as the metaphysical tradition). More precisely, the philological heritage in these philosophical endeavors was an unstable amalgam of Orientalist intervention and the classicist response. The radicalism with which Wellhausen, in his Orientalist phase, had shifted revelation into the very notion of the self-naming, the unconcealment of the name, of Semitic deities undercut any pretense to retaining even a residual Christian eschatology. This conceptual solution was negated by the classicists; Usener's seemingly casual metaphor of *Bluttaufe* reasserted the privileging of Christian eschatology. The classicist hold on later philosophies of history was unchecked; the tenacity with which twentieth-century philosophers all the way to Leo Strauss or even Derrida restaged competitions of Athens and Jerusalem finds one of its roots here. Arguably, it had been the specific 1880s Orientalist challenge to classicism in the belaboring of the very concept of revelation through the names of deities that had stood at the beginning of this development. This challenge largely followed from the developments in Semitic epigraphy, biblical criticism, and the study of pre-Islamic Arabic.

Cassirer, in spite of his lopsided attention to classicism, appears to have grasped more of the conflicted structure at hand than most of his contemporaries. His solution to the problem of the emergence of monotheism intriguingly philosophized the pattern set down by Wellhausen. The key to the matter, for Cassirer, was the intertwining of the "concepts" of "being" and "ego." As for the former, it was shaped by departure from the mere copula, the being "such-and-such"—a horse, concealed, red. Inevitably language tended to generalize the copula into a concept of "existence" and emancipate it from its bond with specific properties. Discursive thought, which was rational—philosophical as well as scientific—must eventually relinquish the notion that the concept of "existence" was an actual predicate. Rather, the expression denoted relationality as such, not the property of a given substance, but the precondition of predication. By contrast, mythical-religious thought, which lacked the tools of formal abstraction, did not dispose of the critical means for de-substantializing being. It ended up exalting "being" as the highest of predicates, which enjoyed a particular role in the formulation of the unity of the divine.[63] This notion found its expression, in antiquity, across the various instances of the unknown or concealed god, of whom— Cassirer cited the Egyptologist and self-declared polymath Heinrich Brugsch—already Egyptian inscriptions had stated that he was

> Being, he himself, that which remains constant in everything ... Here all the concrete and individual names of gods are sublated in the one name of Being: the divine excludes all particular attributes from itself, it cannot be denoted by anything else any more, but only be predicated of itself.[64]

From this notion, monotheism is merely one step removed. Already in the idea of the concealed godhead, unity is established in the deity as a potential object of knowledge. According to Cassirer, this unity in the object then reverts to the subject of knowledge; the being of the unified deity produces the being of the unified person, the being of the Ego. This latter unity establishes a new "category" of subjective religious consciousness; and this consciousness is in turn reflected back upon the godhead, who becomes fully personal over the course of this back and forth. This overall process can be traced through ancient texts that contain "Ego-predication" on the part of deities. Initially, such predication is tied to a plethora of divergent aspects. Subsequently, it is reduced to assertions of self-identity, in which form it occurs in the Old Testament, where in crucial passages the godhead only speaks of himself in mere pronouns.[65] This, then, is Cassirer's way of arriving at the interpretation of the name of Yahweh, "I am he; I am the first, I also am the last" (Isaiah 48:12) whose parallels Hommel had sought to trace through inscriptions.

It is not accidental that one of the most prominent Semitist references in Cassirer's text occurs at this point. He approvingly cites the historical dynamization of the notion of the tautological god in Goldziher's *Mythos bei den Hebräern*.[66] Goldziher held that during the prophetic stage of Hebrew religious development the speculative name of God had been adopted or invented and filled with intellectual content whilst an older, more primitive religious faith and its concomitant "national thought" slackened. Goldziher also suggested that many among the Hebrew proper names that appeared theophoric actually had only been infused with Yahwist bye-meanings at this later stage.[67] It was a *historical* process that burdened names with the deity, but a process that at least according to Cassirer was inevitable, given the developmental patterns to which the symbolic form of myth was generally subjected. These patterns turned being itself into a name, thereby generating a philosophically significant variant of explanation of the meaning of "to be."

This variant of laying out the meaning of "being" was significant because it rehabilitated uses of this expression that in light of Kantian, neo-Kantian, and early logicist analyses of "being" had come to appear as mere aberrances. In fact, Cassirer's arrival at a notion of being as a name, while presented in a rhetorically casual fashion, indicates a major philosophical intervention. Like other German philosophers of the period, e.g. Husserl, Cassirer was keenly aware of, and in part responsive to, the logicist revolution in the philosophy of language that had been prompted by Gottlob Frege's works on formal logic, the philosophy of mathematics, and on matters of syntax and semantics. These works provided a formal-logical way of confirming and deepening the Kantian assertion that being had to be regarded as a precondition of predication, and not itself a predicate. Frege's predicate logic, in which existence was determined as a quantifier instead of as a predicate, offered a deflationary account that definitively ruled out the logical legitimacy of using "to be" as a predicate. Henceforth, asserting "existence" basically meant that there was at least one entity of which a given concept could truthfully be predicated; in short, that a concept was not "empty." Therefore, existence presupposed the givenness of concepts, predication, and language.

On the basis of this account, Rudolf Carnap, for instance, ridiculed Heidegger's uses of "existence" and "nothing" as gross infractions against logic.[68] It is worth mentioning, however, that Heidegger, too, spoke repeatedly of being as a "name."[69] Dissecting the "parting of the ways" in the history of twentieth-century philosophy of language, Michael Friedman has pointed to the integrative aspirations of Cassirer's notion of symbolic forms as broader determinants of semantic legitimacy.[70] This finding certainly also pertains to the very notion of naming and the name of being, and thereby referential semantics in general. It is, further, important to note that Cassirer did not merely concern himself with the great philosophical divergence, of which he was a prime witness. Simultaneously, if perhaps less consciously, he struggled to integrate the classicist and Orientalist traditions in philology. Friedman's "parting" then might not only be that of "analytic" and "continental" philosophy, but also a distant function of the division between Orientalism and classicism.

What is integrative in Cassirer's analysis of naming, through the symbolic forms of philosophical discourse on the one hand and myth on the other, is the hypostatization he derived, via classics, from the compound of biblical philology and epigraphic *Realphilologie*. As a consequence, firstly, the name of being was specifically a theophoric one; only by dint of this quality did it acquire an emphatic status within the aggregate of semantics. That the name might be conceived of as *atheon* never seems to have been a consideration for Cassirer or anyone else working on cognate notions. Once the logicist restrictions were imposed, being could be a name *only* inasmuch as it was burdened with gods. Second, if "being" was a name this entailed that it was a referential expression. That is to say that its meaning was to be sought primarily in the designation of an entity that was the bearer of the name. This reinforced an overall tendency to privilege reference in semantic explication, and it corroborated the referential interpretation of myth that had emerged with the comparative study of religion. Third, since the name of being, in the last instance, was also that of the unconcealed personal godhead, the godhead took over all functions ascribed to being as such. Yet conversely, one might also say that the godhead was exiled into this understanding of the name of being and the notion of naming. Naming then became, as Wellhausen had so precisely grasped, the key to revelation, the unconcealment of the concealed deity, that is to say, the recognition of the deity in the exile of the name. Cassirer's thought laid open—perhaps reproduced—a connection between naming and exile that had been generated, as I have argued in the previous chapter, by epigraphy.

Philological aggregation, then, subtly gained hold over a core problem of philosophical metaphysics. This problem had been known, since Kant, under the label of "ontotheology," the variant of transcendental philosophy that proposed to attain knowledge about a highest, divine being through mere conceptual reasoning, e.g. about the "concept" of "being."[71] As a consequence of Cassirer's pluralist compromise, this lineage of argument was made conditional on a notion of theophoric naming that had emerged from the interferences of deconstructive Wellhausenian textual philology and epigraphy. Philosophy thus lost a territorial claim, and Cassirer's stance registered this loss.

3. Revelation and Semantics

It was not Cassirer but rather Franz Rosenzweig and their mutual teacher Hermann Cohen who took the problem of the philosophical refashioning of naming and revelation to the most radical extremes. In his 1921 *Star of Redemption*, Rosenzweig developed a philosophical understanding of semantic meaning that required the concept of revelation as a precondition for the very possibility of bridging thought and language. He proposed an analysis of what he called the "miracle" of revelation with the help of a triad of terms, namely prophecy, testimony, and fulfillment.[72] These terms, or rather the underlying types of events, were supposed to be manifest in the historical process as a whole. With regard to this process, the particular role of the Jews was to stand outside in order to bear witness to prophecy, await its fulfillment, and thereby guarantee the unity of history. The time of history was set apart from time as mere indiscriminate drift by its directedness toward the future, a direction constituted by the messianic promise of the attainment of an ethics that would pertain to all humankind, as Cohen had also insisted.[73] This understanding of time and history was by necessity semiotic, for the underlying relations could only be grasped in terms of sign relations: prophecy was a sign of future fulfillment, testimony a sign of both. For this reason, Rosenzweig was also able to shift the argument into the area of language by claiming that the structure of revelation, as prophecy, testimony, and fulfillment, informed the correlation of thought and speech. Thought, he suggested, was not derivative of language—not merely a form of silent speech—but rather "a speech before speech," a composite of *Urworte* (a Goethean neologism, usually translated as "primal words"), which were not actual words, but *Verheißungen*, promises or prophecies, of actual words.[74] This distinction coincided with that between logic and grammar, between formal and actual, natural language.

At its most abstract, the distinction in question was based on the introduction of a modal dichotomy of the possible and the actual, so that revelation denoted the transition from the possible to its actualization: "the silent becomes audible, the secret is revealed."[75] By necessity, being actual entails being possible, but not vice versa. The gap that prevented the transition from the possible to the actual had to be bridged, and such a bridge could not be supplied by conceptual reasoning alone. In order for there to be a transition from thought to speech, from possible to actual words, a contribution from beyond the subject (including the sphere of the collective-mental) was necessary. This contribution Rosenzweig sought to grasp through the concept of the "miraculous." The miracle was *Verheißung*, promise, and its fulfilment, the sole means by which it was explicable that the name actually came to refer to its bearer, that semantics could comprise reference at all. The term *Verheißung* played on the meaning of (transitive) *heißen*, i.e. naming. For Rosenzweig, however, meaning did not stop with the transition from the potential to the actual word, but with the latter's circulation in communication. The actual word was "only a beginning" until it was received and responded to. It was therefore a projection into the future, and this future was messianic. Thought transitioned into speech under the broader promise of all-embracing communication, a state of human affairs when the Babylonian dispersion of actual languages would be lifted and universal language achieved.

Rosenzweig not only then partook in the hypostatization of the name as a referential key to semantics in general. He also inserted a modal distinction into semantics that accorded crucial importance to revelation as prophetic promise and naming. His recourse to these notions is explicable by reference to the specific register of debates to which he responded, in particular Hermann Cohen's philosophy of religion. Although in crucial respects Rosenzweig's thought developed in opposition to his teacher's, in many aspects of his conceptual infrastructure he relied on Cohen's pioneering work. This was particularly the case with regard to the notion of the monotheist deity as developed by Cohen in the last years of his life, during the First World War.[76] In this period, after his 1912 retirement from Marburg and resettlement in Berlin, where he began to teach at the independent *Hochschule für die Wissenschaft des Judentums* (Higher Institute for Jewish Studies), Cohen experienced what he came to regard as the most significant philosophical breakthrough of his life. He developed a distinction between the concepts of the unity and the uniqueness of the godhead. With the help of this distinction it became possible, he argued, to conclusively disable a pantheist understanding of monotheism, and thereby to open a novel path toward grasping the philosophical significance of Judaism as the "religion of reason."[77] The problem that had puzzled Usener with regard to the advent of Christianity—why one god specifically and not simply a cult of all gods—was thus, from Cohen's point of view, conceptual in nature.

According to Cohen, pantheist monotheism derived the unity of the divine from the notion of the unity of the cosmos. This derivation was perfectly captured in Spinoza's formula *Deus sive Natura*, whose earliest variant, Cohen claimed, had issued from the pre-Socratic philosopher Xenophanes. The latter had reputedly been the first to regard nature as an ordered whole and to transfer this unity to the notion of the divine. Famously, he had ridiculed Greek polytheism. Yet, according to Cohen the transfer from cosmic to divine unity would have required, but did not receive, a supporting argument that would have established not merely the unity, but the uniqueness of the divine, as precondition of the identity of the divine with itself. For the cosmos was constant becoming, and similarly, the divine might have appeared to be a matter of constant flux. As a consequence of this logical gap, one could discern already in the Parmenides fragments the emergence of a general philosophical notion of "being" in departure from Xenophanes' earlier notion of the unified cosmos. Parmenides located being exclusively on the side of the divine and eternal and regarded the inconstant cosmos as secondary, as mere appearance.[78]

In the oldest source texts of Hebrew antiquity, by contrast, religious speculation found a different route toward a truly monotheist concept of the uniqueness of the deity that did not, as it were, monopolize the being of the world generally. This concept was formulated in Exodus on the occasion of the "first revelation" (46) of Yahweh, who shows himself to Moses in the burning bush. In this passage, which was a prime reference for the concept of revelation and the problem of the name of the Jewish god, Moses asks by what name he should announce the deity to the nation of Israel: "And God said unto Moses, I AM THAT I AM: and he said, Thus shalt thou say unto the children of Israel, I AM hath sent me unto you" (Exodus 3:14). The passage was beset with difficulty. Translation was crucial; the Luther Bible for instance had *Ich werde sein, der ich sein werde*, "I will be who I will be." Cohen by contrast read *Ich bin, der ich bin*, which smoothly translates into the King James Version phrasing. Cohen's phrasing, however, also allows for a somewhat unorthodox interpretation, the use of the phrase "I am" *as a name* in the second clause, which one could render in English as "I am the 'I am.'"[79]

In this context Cohen also dwelled extensively on the *topos* of the etymological derivation of YHWH from the Hebrew verb root היה (*hjh*) for "to be" (46). With the advent of the YHWH name, the Hebrews broke through to full monotheism, abandoning the earlier pluraletantum of *Elohim* that had however also already tended toward singular inflections in its surrounding word forms, as Cohen intimated. The name "I am" emphasized the uniqueness, the incomparable nature of the being of the deity; it introduced, into the totality of beings, a stable, immutable distinction (*Scheidung*).[80] This distinction was that between the godhead and the world. The concept of the world was established through its *Schranken*, the "bounds," of space and time. The Hebrew tradition made clear that the godhead constituted these bounds and was outside of space and time. "Being," in the most general, substantive sense—and as opposed to the mere *Dasein* of things-in-the-world that was accessible to the senses and not to pure reason alone—was the condition of the possibility of a world of constant becoming. Hence Rosenzweig's modal distinction.

Crucially, Cohen developed his argument on the nature of monotheism throughout by discussion of the various names and bynames of the deity in the Hebrew tradition. The argument relied on three semantic language games: speculative etymologies of theophoric names; the hermeneutic, interpretive reading of passages of biblical narrative and their previous interpretations; and abstract theorization. This was a wealth of semantic procedures quite in accordance with the aggregate of philology. In his previous oeuvre, Cohen had remained much more aligned with the restrained models of "systematic" conceptual argument inherited from the German idealist tradition. Cohen's relations with philology had developed over the years through his personal relations with philologists. During Wellhausen's Marburg years (1885–1892), the philosopher had developed a close friendship with his Orientalist colleague. Cohen attentively followed, no doubt in part through Wellhausen, the progress of the field and worked some of the results of biblical criticism into his analysis.[81] Nonetheless, he insisted, not unlike the more conservative academic Lutheran theologians, e.g. Dillmann,[82] that the text of the Old Testament was unified by stable underlying religious ideas, which presented the "problems of the style of a *national spirit* in the course of its history" (44). In *Religion der Vernunft*, the deceased Halle theologian Emil Kautzsch (1841–1910), incidentally one of Littmann's teachers, was a prime target of criticism, on account of his editorship of a collective translation of the Old Testament that synthesized post-Wellhausenian biblical criticism in the form of a definitive version of the text with only a short running commentary.[83] Throughout, Cohen attacked what he regarded as faulty translations on the part of the Protestant theologians behind the effort. Yet, the underlying structure was one of heteronomy: Even though he wrote as a philosopher engaged in metaphysical argument, he found himself under an obligation to take philology into account.

As part of settling into this condition of heteronomy, it seems that for Cohen the concept of revelation accrued a role in the bringing together of the diverse and scattered language games of philological semantics. In a crucial passage he claimed that "the root of the word Yahweh establishes [the] connection with the word to be (היה) as a linguistic fact. And we will have to pay attention to how the very first revelation *clarifies* this connection with being" (46, emphasis added). Revelation therefore explicates something that mere etymological reflection on the part of, say, Moses as a competent speaker of Hebrew, could have made clear anyway. The godhead, in a revelation that offered only additional "clarification," was oddly redundant. Yet the redundancy was only seeming in nature, since the act of revelatory clarification actually guaranteed the otherwise dubious unity of the diverse procedures of explicating meaning. For Cohen, revelation was not the unveiling of the concealed—a point of subtle difference with Rosenzweig—but instead the giving of the given.[84] The very distinction between world and godhead is the precondition of *Sinn*, of assigning meaning to either god or the world.[85] In pantheism, by contrast, there would not be any outside to the whole, and it would not be possible to establish any semiotic relation, as a precondition for meaning. The semiotic relation in question, more precisely, has to be referential in nature; and reference is endowed with the exclusive ability to constitute the cohesion of the divergent forms of semantics. As Peter Gordon emphasizes, Cohen had sought, in his previous work, to develop a methodological instead of a metaphysical notion of "reality" and the Kantian "thing in itself," as mere posits of scientific method.[86] There is an underlying argument in *Religion der Vernunft* that endows Cohen's understanding of "revelation" with a similar methodological function, but in the context of semantics instead of that of knowledge: without revelation, there is no meaning. To the extent that philology builds on the presumption of imposing a *wissenschaftlich* method on semantics, Cohen's philosophy of religion then mirrors the methodological argument of his earlier epistemological work. Revelation is to semantics what reality is to physics.

This argument is present throughout Cohen's account of the notion of revelation, which he comes to define as "the creation of reason" (84). Creation in general, for Cohen, is a principle of distinction and pluralization. Being is differential, inescapably it entails other, different being. On account of this principle, the necessary, stable, and unique being of the deity entails the contingent, unstable, and merely unified (but not unique) becoming of the world (68f.). At the same time, Cohen's understanding of creation also undermines the prejudice at the root of pantheism, that all being is becoming (77), since there needs to be an Other to becoming. The concept of creation marks the inevitable differentiation of the being of the deity. The ultimate disproof of pantheism, however, is not the notion of creation in general, but that of the creation of reason in particular. Reason is, in good Aristotelian fashion, taken to be the ontological marker of humanity, so that the creation of reason coincides with that of the human. According to Cohen, the creative work of the deity pertains both to the actual production of the world and to its constant maintenance. The latter amounts to a steady making-it-anew, which is the precondition for the world to be all-encompassing becoming. The order of the world is upheld as a result of the intentionality of the godhead. Becoming in the world is only conceivable as a steady condition because this intentionality is stable. As a consequence, by necessity, the godhead himself is then exempt from being part of the world of becoming. It is only through revelation that this intentionality can become known since it is outside of the world; and it can only be understood on the part of a reasonable being. In fact, it is constitutive of reason to understand the stable and necessary that is exempt from the condition of worldly becoming. But humans are confined to the world and on their own have no access to that which is outside the world. Revelation is the means by which the eternal and immutable can nonetheless be grasped; reason is revelation. By revelation, humanity gains the ability to recognize the underlying intentional and therefore teleological structure of creation and, simultaneously, to set and pursue aims of its own. In this way, ethics are brought into the world, too. Messianism is the promise of the future perfection of ethics.

Language—the "reason of language" (*Sprachvernunft*)—played a crucial role in this process (94). The reformulation Cohen provided served as a novel foundation for the principle of "dialogue" between the godhead and humanity that subsequently was indispensable to German-Jewish philosophers of religion during the interwar period, especially Rosenzweig and Martin Buber.[87] The former's understanding of the relationship between thought and speech was actually a way of spelling out this principle, and of thereby latching onto Cohen's argument that naming constitutes semantics constitutes being. Cassirer's reservation that the theophoric name of being was only possible in the context of the symbolic form of myth therefore may, and perhaps even must be seen as an objection to Rosenzweig and Cohen on the philosophical significance of YHWH. It was then hardly surprising that after the Davos controversy between Cassirer and Heidegger in the summer of 1929, Rosenzweig sided with Heidegger and the unchecked notion of the name of being that Heidegger likewise pursued.[88] Yet even within this structure of contention, the initial unsupported posit of the name of being as a *theophoric* name, instead of an *atheon* one, remained unchallenged. This missing challenge, this unrejected inheritance, which seemed but was not the Spinozist philosophical *topos* of *deus sive natura*, constituted the manner in which the late nineteenth-century Orientalist amalgam of Semitic epigraphy and biblical criticism retained a hold across the intellectual field.

As a consequence, the entire discussion of ontotheology was shifted by its contact with the aggregate of philology. When Heidegger later took up the theme, in a critical vein that aimed to uncover what had remained "unthought" in all previous philosophers' conflations of being and the divine, the problem of "onto-theo-logy" took the form of rejecting any dependence of philosophical thought on other bodies of knowledge.[89] Primarily, Heidegger took issue with Hegel's notion of thought as always already processual, thus as always already mediated with the history of philosophy and teleologically structured as progress toward the absolute. Hegel had criticized Spinoza's notion of the absolute as accounting only for being *in* itself, but not *for* itself, as absolute subjectivity. The overall process of thought, the history of philosophy—which was the core of all history—constituted this always-becoming subjectivity. Yet, Heidegger held, Hegel's conflation of God and the absolute had remained "unthought," ununderstood. This status was an indicator of a "difference," unaccounted for in the philosophical tradition, between the "beings" produced by the history of thought, such as philosophical doctrines, and the being of thought as such. Philosophy had to cast off any beholdenness to bodies of historical knowledge in order to gain access to this difference, which alone would permit understanding the concealed relations between being, god, and thought: onto-theo-logy. The tentative recovery of the godhead in ontology was, if at all, conceivable only as a "pure" operation, stripped of all content of historical scriptural revelation.

Yet, the "unthought" in all of Heidegger's emphasis on recuperating the autonomy of "fundamental ontology" is actually the question of the root cause of its apparent heteronomy. More precisely, Heidegger lines up the usual suspects—historical knowledge, technology as subverting philosophical thought—but philology remains under the radar, and with it the territorial character of modern disciplinary knowledge, *philosophy included*. For what does the paranoid insistence on the autonomy of thought signal if not a territorial claim? The subtler accounts by the Jewish philosophers Heidegger did not deign to discuss had broached this problem. And philology, though not in the idiom of philosophy, also responded, as I will argue in the following sections.

4. Hedgehog among Hares

After Wellhausen's death in January 1918, Cohen—who was to die in April the same year—contributed a short obituary article for *Neue Jüdische Monatshefte*, a bi-weekly magazine of which Cohen was one of the editors and which addressed Jewish audiences across the liberal-Zionist divide that had become acute during the war.[90] Wellhausen had long been the figurehead of Old Testament criticism, and his sharp distinction between Hebrew prophetism and post-exilic legalistic rabbinic Judaism had driven a wedge into the previously far more unified understanding of the historical development of Jewish religion. The conservative American rabbi Solomon Schechter had famously attacked Wellhausen's work as "higher anti-Semitism" already in 1903.[91] Hence, Cohen felt the need, for a Jewish audience, to justify his relations with, and commemorative effort for, the deceased. To be sure, his attachment to Wellhausen was sincere. Given the well-known pattern of discrimination Cohen had endured for decades in academic life—in 1876 he had become the first Jew to hold a philosophy chair in a German university—it is hardly surprising that he opted to commemorate those colleagues who had befriended him.

The gist of Cohen's article was to present his relations with Wellhausen as a model of true Jewish-Gentile academic collegiality on the basis of a religious faith that was supposedly deeply felt on both sides. "Most of the time we spent the same afternoon hours reading and then walked home together, often singing musical reminiscences for each other," (180) Cohen remembered. The shared, musically framed sociability—Wellhausen's wife was a pianist, and he sang in the university choir—allowed for a frank assessment, not merely of the scientific achievements of biblical philology but also of its limitations. Wellhausen was "not so much a historian," let alone a philosopher, "but a philologist," enabled and impeded at the same time by the "self-limiting [*Selbstbeschränkung*]"—the *epokhé*—"that the precision of his scientific thought and research imposed on him with regard to all schemas for a world historical future and also to all philosophy of history" (JW, 178). As was the normative requirement for being a model philologist, this reticence was so deeply ingrained it was a veritable *Lebensader*, a main artery, "which never tired in the tracking and tracing of the tiniest detail of antiquarian matters." Yet more importantly it aligned with another impediment against "all philosophical religiosity," namely in the "force, fidelity, and security of his naïve childhood faith. This man with his clear, piercing eyes, who was perhaps never once deceived by another human being, was certainly never once beset by a doubt in God" (JW 179). In this characterization, Cohen deployed the *topos*, also used by Hommel, that connected religion with childhood. This topically naïve, undoubting faith dictated Wellhausen's preferences for those prophets, above all Amos, who most directly expressed "plain morality," but had the least to say on the grand historical perspectives of messianism. Wellhausen's speculative limitations caused the "mysterious gaps and leaps" (JW 180) that marred his oeuvre. Chief among these was his turn toward Arab history and the concomitant failure to develop any interest in the history of Judaism and in Hebrew documents younger than scripture. True faith and philological epokhé were quite sufficient as a foundation for German-Jewish academic collegiality. Yet they did not supply the tools that permitted uncovering the historical-philosophical significance of the religion of revelation. Jerusalem was to be validated by giving it equal status with (or even superiority over) Athens, to the exclusion of whatever other antiquities might appear as competitors. Hence, for Cohen, Wellhausen's Orientalist turn toward the history of Arabia and Islam was a mere aberration.

As Cohen's "farewell" to his friend indicates, the traces that led from philology into philosophy were actively concealed.[92] This concealment was important to both parties. To his friend Ferdinand Justi (1837–1907), the Marburg Persianist and folklorist of Hesse, Wellhausen wrote in 1906:

If we met the Rathkes [the Marburg professor of chemistry and his wife], this would be very nice, but no replacement for you and your wife. Toward these dear tender idealist souls I feel too much like a dirty hedge-hog [*swinegelmäßig*] and develop the urge to play the part of the barbarian and to wipe the dust off a butterfly's wing. My temperament [*Naturell*] is different from Cohen's, and I flout [*pfeife auf*] all humanist philosophy which usually only repeats what others have thought intuitively or what entire peoples and communities have experienced.[93]

Wellhausen's "barbarism" drew on a notion he expressed time and again, according to which philosophy was not based on abstract reason but on "the tradition of religion, ethos, law, language." Morality and law [*Recht*] in particular were not a product of political organization, as in the polis abstractly discussed by Plato and Aristotle, but of "more primitive communities (family, clan, folk)."[94] Intellectual achievement was always more humble than especially the philosophers were inclined to think. In terms of the competition of antiquities, the political-philosophical Greeks were to be placed on the same footing as the Hebrews, but what did this matter? In his understanding of the history of the works of the human mind, Wellhausen insisted on the prevalence of both individual intuition and communal experience, which in turn explained the rejection of the humanist universalism that Cohen, in this period, still pursued without prominent reference to Judaism. Wellhausen's notion of the foundations of thought, by contrast, was as much communitarian as it was individualist. Ultimately, it even seemed individual *Naturell* overruled tradition.

In this context, the reference to *Swinegel*, title-giving character of one of the Grimms' Low German fairy tales, is of considerable interest. The tale had actually been written by the dialect author Wilhelm Schröder in 1840 and found its way into the Grimms' collection only in a very late edition, in 1853, after a series of anonymous republications.[95] Apparently, the Grimms failed to recognize that the text was a recent fabrication the stylistic model for which they had provided themselves. *Swinegel*, the Low German word for "hedgehog," preserves the association with "hog" and impurity, also etymologically present in the English noun (but not the High German, which knows an analogon, *Schweinigel*, that, however, does not just mean the animal, but rather is a swearword for someone unclean). The plot of the tale centers on a hare, introduced as a haughty gentleman, and a disheveled pauper, the hedgehog, who, insulted by the hare, challenges the latter to a foot race. On account of the fact that the hedgehog and his wife cannot be distinguished, they are able to trick their opponent; the hedgehog stays at one end of the race course and his wife waits at the other. When the hare reaches the finish line, there is already a hedgehog present, happily pronouncing: "I am there already." The incredulous hare repeats the race over and over, back and forth, until he dies from exhaustion.

The hedgehog, thereby, is a figure of insurmountable precedence, of always-already. In the context of the tale, significantly, *Swinegel* is both name and concept; perhaps this is a faint hint that the figure parodies the workings of revelation, which is also always already there, and similarly fraudulent. Curiously, Heidegger alludes to the story centrally in his discussion of onto-theo-logy and the "always already" of fundamental, unified being and the autonomy of philosophical ontology.[96] *Swinegel*, however, is not just always already there but also a trickster and a cheat. His void claims have credibility only for the high-minded believer in purity. In reality, the hedgehog's meaning is *uneigentlich*, improper, as much as he is unclean, and can pass for a male or a female. The fairy tale concludes with two moral lessons, according to which it is, first, never a good idea to laugh at the lower classes and, second, very much advisable to marry someone of one's own class and kind. These lessons are jocular since they are built on contradictory principles: the first valorizes equality (citizenship against distinctions of class), the second inequality (essentialist distinctions of kind). Class and kind are introduced as principles of distinction that operate in different manners, namely the latter legitimately, the former illegitimately. The indistinguishability of the hedgehog and his wife is as comforting as it is unsettling. The upshot is the ironization of a political discourse that circulated around these notions: the conservative identity-based politics of nationalist majority dominance, male dominance, class privileges, and Christian supremacy, which all presupposed essential inequality; and the liberal-nationalist understanding of the political in terms of emancipation and citizenship that presupposed essential equality. *Swinegel* took none of it seriously.

Cohen, by underlining the "naivety" of Wellhausen's faith, indirectly conceded one of the latter's most basic theorems: that rabbinic Judaism was distinct from the simpler, more "natural" form of religion found among the pre-exilic Hebrews. Wellhausen had failed to understand rabbinic Judaism because it was not naïve. The naïve was always already separated from its opposite, whether this was Schiller's "sentimental" or the surrogate terms Cohen deployed. Implicitly, the philosopher found himself in a longstanding conflict with Wellhausen that provided a contrary undercurrent to their friendship. In this conflict, Cohen yielded the ancient past of Jewish religion to Wellhausen's interpretive authority and reclaimed the more recent history and, above all, the future. In the Wellhausenian configuration, the watershed between the ancient and the modern in the history of Judaism was located already in the period of Babylonian exile. Cohen, as well as Rosenzweig, and arguably a number of other Jewish thinkers of the interwar period,[97] went along with this construction.

The temporalization that this tacit adoption of Wellhausen's distinction occasioned ensured that Judaism endured or enjoyed an everlasting present in which it fulfilled, as Rosenzweig had it, the messianic role of witness to a history in which it had no part. In this manner, Rosenzweig succeeded in dismantling the progressivist philosophy of history, the aspect of Cohen's late work he least agreed with.[98] In order to underline the gulf that separated his post-war religious thought from Cohen's pre-war philosophy, he deployed the same rhetorical device as Cohen in his "farewell" to Wellhausen: he underlined the genuine naivety of the late philosopher's faith.[99] More perceptive than others among the group of intellectuals who reformulated a distinctly Jewish religious philosophy in the interwar period, Rosenzweig also realized the need to part with Wellhausen more radically.[100] In a letter he commented on Wellhausen's *Israelitische und jüdische Geschichte*: "a foundational book for current science …, a short and splendidly readable book, one of the great literary achievements of German *Wissenschaft* in the nineteenth century."[101] Yet, appreciating the literary qualities of Wellhausen on their own, as a mere matter of the past, did not do away with his scholarship. The two were indistinguishable but distinct, and wherever one ran, Wellhausen-*Swinegel* was already there.

Nonetheless, Rosenzweig's perception was keen. Wellhausen's self-understanding as a philologist deviated sharply from what Cohen's "Farewell" imputed on him and comprised notions of literary style and historical method that were not commonly part of the field of philology. To his friend, the classicist Eduard Schwartz (1858–1940), Wellhausen remarked, concerning his project of commenting on the gospels:

> I easily get done too fast; I am too round, though hopefully in a different manner than Harnack. The main regret is that I do not know Greek. This is perhaps softened by the fact that I have a general sense for linguistic matters that is whetted by non-Greek readings as much as by Greek ones, only so that the understanding of the matters at hand [*das sachliche Verständnis*] does not get difficult for me. Syntax and style, in particular, are accessible to me and interesting everywhere, with the exception of the artificially rhetorical and technical; for that I am too impatient or too stupid. I never manage to figure out a rebus; and I cannot decipher anything. Actually I am not a philologist at all, only a hermeneuticist of matters [*Sachen*] congenial to me.[102]

The notion underlying this self-description is somewhat reminiscent of Wilhelm Dilthey's explication of *Verstehen* as based on a commonality of *ingenium*, of consciousness and sensibility, between the author and exegete of a given text. Actually, though, Wellhausen's notion of hermeneutics as *less* than philology was more in keeping with a traditional understanding of the discipline, as for instance expounded in Schleiermacher's or Boeckh's lectures, who structured philology into the complementary fields of grammar, criticism, and hermeneutics. To boot, Wellhausen deployed the Diltheyesque motif of "congeniality" only to introduce a second distinction into the concept of hermeneutics at hand, to delimit an area made easily accessible by personal spirit, before any question of method even arose. Wellhausen insisted that his knowledge and sensibility only sufficed to understand syntax, style, and meaning. Hence also his feigned ignorance of Ancient Greek. He suggested that his prime attention was to textual meaning, only roughly in terms of form, but primarily in terms of factual content and context. Under the modern assumption that the sheer meaning of a text, and at best secondarily its form, was constitutive of its being part of literature, he was actually in agreement with Rosenzweig's offhand characterization. Yet Wellhausen's notion of hermeneutics—or, more precisely, of being a *Hermeneut*, a scholar with a specific natural aptitude for hermeneutics—abandoned the focus on the linguistic sphere and privileged "matters," the *Sachen*, in which the meaning actually resided. It was in the race for semantic explication that Wellhausen claimed a headstart; decidedly, this was a matter, not of understanding the ins and outs of fiction, but of access to reality as such.

This drift of methodological discourse toward *Realien* was a general feature of Wellhausen's thought on philology. For instance, several years earlier, in a critical passage about the Leipzig doyen of Arabic studies in Germany, Heinrich Leberecht Fleischer, Wellhausen had remarked to Robertson Smith: "The man just never takes into account the realia [*Sachen*] and the historical connections [*Zusammenhang*]; and from the point of view of grammar, one actually cannot make significant emendations."[103] In contrast to many of his colleagues, textual semantics (not grammar or inscriptions) remained the key concern to Wellhausen. Emendation was the ideal of philological work in the service of the meaning of text; but emendation had to be grounded in "reality." This pattern of methodological discourse indicates that Wellhausen's conflict with the philosophers was one over semantics, namely over legitimate semantic procedures. Prominent among the individualized *topoi* he developed in his writings and letters was the denigration of philosophy as based on the "hypostatization"[104] and even "adoration"[105] of abstraction. Given that abstraction is a semantic procedure—in which meanings are explained by substitution through other meanings—semantics organized the lines of conflict. Cohen found the lack of philosophical abstraction in Wellhausen's work deplorable, while Wellhausen appreciated what he considered the absence of such abstraction in the textual heritage of Hebrew antiquity.[106]

This is also to say that the *polemos* in question was not primarily one across disciplinary boundaries, a confrontation of philology and philosophy as such; nor about political orientation and identities. In his correspondence Wellhausen certainly availed himself of many opportunities to express resentment toward, or at least crack demeaning jokes about, Jews.[107] A characteristic example can be found in a letter of thanks to Nöldeke, who had sent his congratulations upon Wellhausen's appointment—on Theodor Mommsen's initiative—to a seat in the Prussian order of merit, "Pour le mérite," "in which for the time being I feel like the sow in the Jew house or alternatively—*salva venia vestra*—the other way around [i.e. the Jew in the pigsty]."[108] Through the implied inversion at the end of the phrase, the crassness of the anti-Semitic adage was both enhanced and ironized. In keeping with his self-identification with *Swinegel*, in this imagined constellation, Wellhausen adopted the role of the sow, or alternatively the Jew. On Cohen he remarked elsewhere that the Jewish philosopher was "certainly a fanatic martyr, but noble nonetheless and not as snappy as Natorp." This followed a passage about yet another visit to Marburg where, having fallen "into the hands of Cohen," he had been "forced" to philosophize, although "I broke away from the hunters [*brach durch die Lappen*], but parted in good company."[109] A widespread anecdote held that Wellhausen accepted his appointment in Göttingen only after one of the Lutheran periodicals had railed that his placement there would amount to letting loose the wild boar in the Lord's vineyard (Psalms 80:13).[110] In reality, since he was reluctant to move from Marburg to Göttingen, Althoff had him travel all the way to Berlin to explain the "necessity" of the appointment to him in person.[111] Subsequently, Wellhausen obeyed but wrote to Harnack that he would feel in Göttingen "like a *Swinegel* among the hares."[112] He always imagined himself as a wild animal, the quarry, not the hunter. He wanted to be elusive, to get away, not to arrive; to escape, not to capture.

This distinguished him from most other academics of his time; and it should perhaps have served as a warning to his readers. In an 1890 letter to Harnack, he described his political allegiance as "wild conservative." In the context of the revocation of the prohibition of the socialist party, he emphasized that his allegiance lay more with the peasants than the workers, since small-time farming constituted the last resort of individual economic independence.

The Kaiser [Wilhelm II, in the conflicted phase immediately preceding the dismissal of Bismarck] appears to have the best of convictions and also to really make an effort. But he is, it seems to me more and more, an enthusiast; and I have no faith in enthusiasts.[113]

If one wanted to cross over to the feral side of political thought, the monarchy was not a serious option, and authority and hierarchy were not all that interesting. Indeed, nothing was a terribly serious option, not even the views Wellhausen pretended to hold dear. When he was asked to deliver a university discourse on the occasion of *Kaisers Geburtstag* 1900, he presented a short address on legal forms among pre-Islamic Bedouins, "A Polity without Government," that stated as an almost irreverent political ideal the "intellectual freedom, which flourishes only in the State, which, like Noah's ark, harbors and leaves to their own devices sundry animals [*allerlei Getier*]."[114] The animal metaphors in Wellhausen's writings indicate, above all, that he was reticent to have any part in, or even just to believe in the sustained capability of, sovereignty, against which he constantly sided with its counter-concept of sorts, the animal. Given the increasing participation of the citizenry in the national-liberal unified state of Germany, however, Wellhausen's refusal of participation entailed embracing at most a hopeless agenda, a party of complete insignificance, such as that of the dwindling peasantry. His "patriotism" was, as he habitually emphasized, Prussian, not Hanoverian, unlike his teacher Ewald's, with whom he had almost fallen out over his support of Bismarck in 1866. Wellhausen was decidedly Hobbesian in his political notions. The state was the precondition of "peace and culture," as he wrote to a former Marburg colleague, the theologian Wilhelm Herrmann (1846–1922), in 1915; but it was also based on violence and injustice, to which one had no choice but to subject oneself. Self-sacrifice, the most extreme form of such subjection, no matter for what sake, was "glorious."[115] Yet this glory, or so it seems, was a matter of the individual alone; the state did not have any title to it.

Wellhausen's dislike of Judaism had to do with the hierarchical and authoritarian traits of religious law as he understood it. Against the priestly statehood of post-exilic Judaism, he leveled the charge of "theocracy" in any but flattering terms. The positive connotations—of the rule of law rather than any particular lawgiver's—this term had originally carried in Herder were entirely alien to him.[116] By 1915 he also found the universalism in Judaism offensive. Casting doubt on his own, numerous positive statements about the minor prophets from previous decades, in 1915 he wrote to Herrmann: "I distrust all psychology of peoples and do not spend time thinking about the squaring of individual and national religion, i.e. patriotism. Old Israelite religion was patriotism; Elias and Amos destroyed it, but in vain."[117] If one wants to place him within the overall field of German political discourse in the *Kaiserreich*, both the marginality and the ironized unsteadiness of his position need to be taken into account. Wellhausen was not simply, as Suzanne Marchand has suggested, a mouthpiece of 1860s national liberalism, the amalgam between, on the one hand, earlier forms of constitutionalism, nationalism, religious non-conformism, and individualism and, on the other, the terms and methods of Bismarckian conservatism and violent unification.[118] Rather, Wellhausen's political utterances were anchored in philology, not in the sense that he was a firm believer in *Wissenschaft* as the guideline of political judgment, but in terms of his notions about naming, reference, and reality as such. If it is regarded as a contribution to philological discourse about semantics, his position was not marginal, but groundbreaking. In spite of the lopsided and tangled nature of the reception process that tied him to debates about the philosophy of history, and in spite of his own evasive and ironical responses to the beginnings of this reception, the field had been demarcated by his work.

5. *Uneigentlichkeit* in Paradise

For the authors involved in interwar period debates on metaphysics, language, religion, and anthropology, the philosophy of history—understood as the barrage of enlightenment and post-enlightenment notions of history as a unified, universal, and progressive process—was a prime concern. Yet on closer scrutiny, the scholars in question all also responded to categories that were not integral to the stripped down version of the philosophy of history they were attacking. The distinction between the ancient and the modern, in particular, was conceptually incompatible with what Walter Benjamin famously labeled the "empty," "homogenous," and "linear time" of historicism.[119] Instead, this distinction was based on a typological, or in Auerbach's term, figural mode of questioning: where was the modern a figural representation of the ancient—a mirroring, the fulfillment of a promise, a parody—and where not? Arguably, the proponents of so-called historicism, in spite, or perhaps as a consequence, of the fluidity of their theoretical stance, were much less focused on a stringent notion of "linear time" than is often assumed. Rather, they sought to distance themselves from the remnants of the older aesthetic confrontations of the type of the *Querelle*. Philologists by contrast clung on to this constellation, perhaps in part because in this manner their pursuits retained contiguity with the literary field. It was unsurprising that the philological tradition then mattered to those authors who in the interwar period sought to criticize the purported basic matrix of nineteenth-century historical thought. For some thinkers, e.g. Benjamin, philology tacitly provided a resource against so-called historicism. It is a marker of the potency of philology as an episteme in Foucault's sense—as an infrastructure of scholarly knowledge—that even contemporary theorizations of history still rely on nineteenth-century *topoi* in order to reject other *topoi* from the same period.

As a consequence of the development of *Realphilologie*, the presence of figuration in philological practice had become both more subtle and more tightly tethered to the problem of naming and reference. Fritz Hommel's work on the rivers of Paradise provides a case in point. Genesis 2:10–14 lists four rivers as emerging from a common source in Eden. Elaborating on a complex philological argument to map scripture onto geographical space, Hommel was certain of having identified four physical rivers or riverbeds as referents of the names provided in scripture. To begin with, there had never been much doubt about the identification of one of the rivers, "Perat," as Euphrates, which was in accordance with ancient tradition and various languages of the ancient Middle East. Of the other three rivers, Pison, Gihon, and Hiddekel, the last one was traditionally—as for instance in Luther's translation—identified with the Tigris. The other two were left without geographical referent, or rather, with far too many. Hommel dropped the identification of Hiddekel with Tigris—which had little linguistic support—and placed the three uncertain rivers squarely in Central Arabia by identifying them with three wadis, seasonal rivers geographers had only placed on the map since the 1880s.[120] Once again in his endeavor, he drew on Glaser's speculations; only the argument about Hiddekel was Hommel's own.[121]

The geography of Paradise had been recovered, as a topic of academic scholarship proper, especially by Friedrich Delitzsch, who had relied on Assyrian epigraphy to argue for a Babylonian frame of reference.[122] The method, even when results diverged, was shared; it rested on names and their reference, and the context was the topography of the Middle East that supplied confirmation often only in the form of vague plausibility. Wellhausen had, in his harshly critical review of Hommel's *Altisraelitische Überlieferung*, already scorned the first version of the argument about Hiddekel in particular on account of the barrenness of the wadi that hardly seemed to fit with the vegetation of Eden and the etymology of the biblical name that suggested a "river of palm trees."[123] Wellhausen also provided an analysis of the actual method at work. For this purpose, he began by quoting his own words on an earlier occasion. Hommel had cited the same passage in *Altisraelitische Überlieferung*, with critical intent, but had left out a portion Wellhausen considered crucial.[124] In full the passage ran as follows:

One can calmly admit [—as Nöldeke does—] the possibility that [the Kings listed in Genesis 14] Amraphel, Arioch, Kedorlaomer and Tid'al actually once ruled over their realms, but it would in no way follow from this that what is asserted about them in Genesis 14 is true. If the subject does not exist, the assertion is obsolete on its own account, this is true. Yet one cannot turn the matter around and conclude from the reality of the subject to the truth of the assertion." [Wellhausen continued:] Hommel himself cannot deny that the acting personages, on the little Babylonian tablet on which they are mentioned, do not appear in the Dead Sea area [as is asserted in Genesis], but in Elam, and that Amraphel (*rectius* Chammurabi) is not *in league* with Kedorlaomer (*rectius* Kudurdugmal) and company, but fighting against them. But he [Hommel] is as little concerned with logic as with geology. He just continues to belabor his proper names and their etymologies.[125]

In other words, identifying the reference of proper names was logically insufficient to give biblical text meaning and therefore to judge its facticity. This very basic mistake was common to the overall development of Old Testament studies, Wellhausen pointed out, no matter whether the epigraphic record was deployed to uphold (as in Hommel's case) or even more radically to undermine the facticity of biblical text (as in the works of the Panbabylonists). The real "problem is a literary one and has to be solved in a literary manner, by the internal comparison of the strata [of the Pentateuch] with each other and with the securely known facts of Israelite history."[126] This is to say, Wellhausen rejected the more extreme aspects of the hypostatization of the proper name in defence of his own, more circumscribed philological project and his "literary-critical" method. This method, on the one hand, paid particular attention to the anchoring of the text in the "facts" of history, which in this context coincided with the *Sachen*; and on the other hand, the strata discernible in the text, which is to say, the historical process of its subsequent rewritings, the "tradition" whose study e.g. Pollock advocates, if without the arbitrary cut-off point of the more or less stabilized text Wellhausen presupposed. In this manner, the literary-critical method aimed to include, in its referential understanding of textual semantics, also the self-referential dimension tradition inserted into the meaning of cohesive texts. For Wellhausen, the meaning of text was not, in Genette's terminology, heterodiegetic; it did not belong to a world, an ontological order apart. Scripture was not a work of fiction and therefore did not enjoy autonomy over its ontology; but from this it did not follow that its relation with historical reality was as straightforward as e.g. Hommel appeared to imagine.

Needless to say, this logical demolition, which Wellhausen directed at both Hommel and Glaser,[127] did nothing to dissuade these scholars of their convictions about Genesis 14 or 2. As Thomas Kuhn already noted, patterns of scientific thought tend to be upheld against almost any criticism.[128] However, it would be rash to regard Hommel's and Glaser's obstinacy as a mere consequence of the social relations underpinning their scholarship. Neither was the motivation simply to be found in Hommel's religious desire to be of service to the Society for Promoting Christian Knowledge, as Wellhausen claimed.[129] It is true that Hommel's work had been been commissioned by the Society, a leading missionary organization, as somewhat of a counterpoint to the works of Sayce.[130] Yet there was also another reason for Hommel's and also Glaser's obstinacy. This has to do with the peculiar role of referential proper names in their arguments.

In response to Wellhausen's dismissal, Hommel first and foremost pointed to recent reports contained in Palgrave's and Lady Blunt's travelogues of palm groves in the Wadi Sirhān. Hence it was Wellhausen who was careless about the realia.[131] Moreover, Hommel insisted that there was growing evidence that a profound change had occurred to the Eastern Arabian landscape "over the millennia," which involved deforestation and desertification (*Versandung*), which had also changed the course of at least two of the Paradisian wadis.[132] Nonetheless, for Hommel, the point of the overall argument was not in the actual references of the name of Hiddekel that Wellhausen had so poignantly identified as unconvincing. When the Munich Orientalist complained about Wellhausen's "gratuitous" (*wolfeil*, 282) derision of his (and Glaser's) explications, this adjective conceded that tethering Pison, Gihon, and Hiddekel to their wadi referents was in some sense comical, just not in the cheap manner Wellhausen's formulation suggested. As it came to the rivers of Paradise, Hommel's semantic undertaking was not exhausted by the referential analysis. Even he did not go so far as to claim that Paradise had actually been located in Eastern Arabia. Another charge Wellhausen raised in his review of Hommel—that the latter's argument was dependent on the works of Sayce, who had pioneered the identification of Biblical and Babylonian names—overlooks the *uneigentlich* character the procedure assumed in the German context. Both Glaser and Hommel shared in the embrace of irony as a sign relation that was so characteristic of Wellhausen's semantics.

Glaser laconically posed the question about the names of the Edenic rivers as follows: "Where was Paradise situated? Or rather, since it was not situated anywhere: where did one imagine Paradise was situated?"[133] This manner of phrasing the problem implied particular discursive positions on myth and the nature of fiction. As far as myth was concerned, the tacit knowledge at hand, formulated since the 1870s, with E. B. Tylor as pioneer, dictated that the mythical imagination was anchored in "experience" and that any belief in an "almost boundless creative power of the human imagination" was soundly mistaken. Tylor required less than a page to point out that this psychological posit also pertained to poetics and the literary imagination:

> little by little, in what seemed the most spontaneous fiction, a more comprehensive study of the sources of poetry and romance begins to disclose a cause for each fancy, an education that has led up to each train of thought, a store of inherited materials from out of which each province of the poet's land has been shaped, and built over, and peopled.[134]

Myth therefore was a model for fiction in general; and the mooring of fiction to reality did not merely presuppose a mind that underwent perceptions, but because of the necessity of education and tradition, a location. The set of aesthetic notions behind this understanding of fiction is contiguous with, if not simply expressive of, the model of the realist novel. Did the comparative study of myth in the incipient field of the study of religion therefore constitute a body of knowledge subservient to the absolute sovereignty of a realist understanding of literature; or was it the other way around?

Tylor's evolutionism traveled on a different trajectory and constituted the main barrier that prevented a greater influence of British anthropology in German scholarship.[135] Nonetheless, both Glaser and Hommel clearly assumed that the myth of Paradise required a foundation in physical space. By dint of this assumption, they manipulated the semantic of reference. The name of Paradise referred only to an imaginary location, thus another sign, which stood in the way of a straightforward relation between name and place. In compensation, the argument assumed that the middling sign was in some sense grounded in the experience of physical space; but this grounding did not suffice to give the name meaning. The overall model for explaining the meaning of myth thus gave precedence to a broadly speaking realist poetics. Yet, realism did not suffice to provide the explanation in question. Instead, the model presupposed also an explanation of meaning by recourse to figuration: the reference of the names of the rivers of Paradise was subtly made *uneigentlich*, for the thing referred to by a name such as Pison was primarily an imaginary landscape, and only secondarily, indirectly an actual river. In logicist terms this entailed that meaning was shifted from an extensional context to an intensional one. If Hiddekel was, as Hommel claimed, an old name for the Wadi Sirhān, it would nevertheless have been impermissible to substitute *salva veritate*—say, in a modern translation of the old texts—one name for the other. For, the meaning did not solely depend on reference, or extension; but also on intension, which included the imaginary reference with which biblical Hiddekel once had been saddled and which could not be properly retrieved. Reading the intensional context as an extensional one was a transgression against the minimal semantic norms logic entailed; and this was the core of the semantic procedure Glaser and Hommel (and many others) followed.

Indeed, so did Wellhausen; when he scorned Hommel for the Hiddekel theory because the wadi in question did not contain any vegetation, this criticism was based on similar assumptions about the foundation of fiction in reality, the blurring of imaginary and realist meaning. The notion of the real that was implicit in *Realphilologie* carried the mark of transgression; the semantic on which its method rested was an illicit crossing, from name to object. This infringement was an ever-flowing source of ironical detachment, which even Glaser underlined when he posed his question, and then corrected it right away—since Paradise "was not situated anywhere." As a consequence, the reality of philology was not the one that belonged to the aesthetic of realism in literature. The entire hypostatization of the name was subservient to a project of ironization. Wellhausen's reservations did not reach so deep as to dissociate him from this project. On the contrary, he was a major contributor of irony to the overall field. Over time, the *Uneigentlichkeit* of historical reality became a prime marker of *Realphilologie*, and it belonged to this field primarily. Philosophy in any case did not adopt it. The trope of irony also underpinned the assumption of the identity of the paradisiac river with the Wadi Sirhān. The attraction of this identification rested, not on conclusive argument, but precisely on its inconclusive nature, on a paradox of identity and difference: the wadi was and was not the river Hiddekel at the same time.

This paradox deeply affected the way in which the argument related to the problem of historicity. As Glaser pointed out, in a lengthy diatribe against what he perceived as the discipline's hostility toward his work:

> It is only Arabia, to whose study a veritable army of scholars has devoted themselves since time immemorable, which defies the lifting of the veil that conceals the secrets of its past, I mean its near, not even pre-Christian past. One did not see the wood for the trees, and, preoccupied with grammatical fiddling about, one overlooked that there exists an Arabia which, like any other country of the old world of civilization is a historical individuality, worthy of our study [... He] who undertakes to travel Arabia and—horrible dictu—to unveil it [cannot] hope for approval: this is against the tradition of not allowing the gaze to stray beyond Muhammad, against the sanctity of grammar, and even against the majesty of Arabic meters.[136]

The careers of the following generation of Semitists certainly did much to change the aversion against epigraphic research and explorative travel Glaser decried. After the Babylonian frenzy of the 1890s and 1900s, there was even less justification for deploring an alleged preference of Middle-East Orientalism for Islamic instead of pre-Islamic topics, even though Arabic grammar and the study of Early Arabic poetry remained important. Beyond the competition of research programs Glaser believed to perceive, the passage is interesting for the way in which it makes its formulation of *Realphilologie* method interlock with the trope of an "unveiling" of the past. In this case, the interest resides perhaps less in the gendered sense of metaphor yet again figuring, or disfiguring, scholarly knowledge; but rather in the sense of a secure, spatial reality of the historical past that could be uncovered by the mere gesture of travel. It sufficed to be present on site in order to get a hold of the way in which myth was lodged into history.

When Wellhausen, in his quarrel with Hommel, referred to Nöldeke, he was relying on the latter's argument for the *Ungeschichtlichkeit*, the "un-historicity" of the story of Abraham's military victories in Genesis 14. Nöldeke's argument structure, although the result was the opposite, relied on the same method: The aim was to identify the referents of place names in physical space, then connect this knowledge to the army movements listed in Genesis 14, and show that under these conditions the movements in question did not make any sense. Nöldeke never traveled to the Levant, but a close look at the maps produced by modern explorers sufficed to unveil the unhistoricity of Abraham's military exploits:

> This entire campaign is then as historically improbable as it is conducive to a somewhat striking effect: a sure sign that it is fictitious. … Do not the precise indications, which make such a positive impression in favor of the historicity of the account, actually confirm its improbability?[137]

For Nöldeke, then, the method of identifying the extensions of proper names served to confirm a notion that had emerged in the eighteenth century and has been described as the "poetic" or "aesthetic" conception of scripture. This understanding of scripture as a merely poetic document had become entangled with the manner in which its historicity was established: precisely to the extent that the Bible was not a record of historical events, it became a poetic record. Moreover, the poetics Nöldeke imposed on the Pentateuch were those of literary realism. The author of Genesis, as a work of fiction, had scattered across the text of chapter 14 a set of "precise indications" that suggested the coinciding of the diegesis of the narrative with common reality. The effect in question is quite simply Roland Barthes's *effet du réel*. For Nöldeke, however, the actual work of *Realphilologie*, the meanings it sought to elucidate in the proper names, was not in the poetic side of scripture, but remained elsewhere.

In a letter to Nöldeke, Wellhausen rejected the contemporary novel outright:

> Storytelling is the art we master least. The psychological, reflexive, analytical novel is the exact opposite of true narration. Even historians do not know how to narrate any more and do not want to either. How atrocious is Treitschke's style! And how beautiful that of old Froissar[t]! But this comes from critique and source studies and the other causes that we cannot avoid. Every peasant understands it better than we educated people.[138]

The procedures and devices of literary realism and their parallel "analytical" apparatus of source criticism and "method" constituted a formidable obstacle not only in novel writing but also to historical narration. The naïve was a powerful, yet unattainable ideal. Herder, chief reference for the aesthetic of folk poetry and for reading the Bible through this lens, had proposed discussing scripture as a work of literature that expressed the national spirit of the Hebrews as well as the "oldest spirit" of humanity in general.[139] As Jonathan Sheehan has argued, when this understanding of the "poetic Bible" emerged in the eighteenth century, over the course of the intense German reception of especially English theological-political debates, it did not simply entail that the Bible was a text of fiction endowed with rhetorical qualities aiming at "effect." On the contrary, Herder especially, but also other authors in the 1780s and 90s, held that religion was by necessity poetic; and that poetry—especially the quality of the sublime—had emerged from religion in general and scripture in particular.[140] Yet, by the latter half of the nineteenth century, this subtle and intricate but also enthusiastic conviction had been submerged. In the sober eyes of readers like Nöldeke or Wellhausen, the Old Testament was to be measured on the same scale of value as the textual heritage of classical or even Nordic mythology; or indeed of other works of folk poetry in the competitive and hierarchical structure of world literature.[141] The idea of the originary status of Hebrew scripture for poetry as such had been eroded by critical philology. However, it was not a general realist poetics, a notion that all literature originated in the mind's access to naturally given reality, that replaced this older notion.

Sheehan has argued that by the early nineteenth century, an equilibrium had emerged in biblical scholarship. The troubled, multilayered and contradictory cluster of reading and translation practices that had constituted the "Enlightenment Bible" had given way to the Bible as a historical-cultural artefact. This artefact was to be studied by historians and philologists fully outside the sphere of actual religious belief. Conversely, Christian faith was to rely on the Bible only in an approximate manner, a far cry from earlier literalism. The equilibrium, however, was not altogether stable. Certainly, when Wellhausen's work was attacked by representatives of Lutheran orthodoxy, he would time and again retort that his critics were free to embrace philological ignorance and make use of scripture as they pleased. Nonetheless, it would be rash to assume that he subscribed to the insulation of religious faith as a sphere in and of itself that the conceptual separation of knowledge and belief instigated by Kant and Schleiermacher had proposed. For Wellhausen, the knowledge produced by philological scholarship was indispensable and impinged on faith. He consistently ridiculed the representatives of "cultural Protestantism," the theological movement toward an undogmatic Christianity of ethical feeling and liberal politics that retained only a loose interest in the Bible.[142] For instance, with regard to Adolf von Harnack, the leading representative of the movement after 1900, Wellhausen asserted:

> For a researcher he is actually too gifted; he knows the writing without having learned it, he skips across the difficulties, always certain of the crowd's applause. In addition, he has enviable defecation, it shoots out right away and becomes thinner with time; he does not age. Yet, there is no falsehood in him, and he is also courageous. In spite of everything, I am fond of him.[143]

The weaknesses of intellectual engagement and character that Wellhausen perceived as spoiling Harnack's work were precisely the markers of the cultural Protestant settlement of relations between science and faith: shunning the difficulties, overpublishing, and vainly enjoying public acclaim for the foul compromise, the "enviable defecation," that was liberal Protestantism. It was perhaps a more honest solution to embrace agnosticism as Nöldeke had done. Cohen, however, was right in one basic assessment: for Wellhausen there never was the option of relinquishing his faith altogether. The nineteenth-century Bible remained in disequilibrium. In Wellhausen's eyes, scripture appears to have had the primary purpose of making things difficult. The only solution was to surrender to *Uneigentlichkeit* in terms of *both* faith and knowledge. The poetics of literary realism were precisely not the point of Wellhausen's *Realphilologie*; and this is where he concurred with Hommel.

6. Wellhausen's Footnotes, or the Ironical Jesus

The transgression from intensional to extensional meaning so characteristic of the semantics of *Realphilologie* also marked Wellhausen's operating procedure. His critique of the fixation on proper names opened his discourse, it is true, to historical narrative in a manner unattainable to those philologists who sought to abandon textual semantics in favor of name semantics. Wellhausen's most remarkable works in this regard were his *Israelitische und jüdische Geschichte* ("Israelite and Jewish History") from 1894 and *Das arabische Reich und sein Sturz* (*The Arab Kingdom and Its Fall*) from 1902, the former a synthesis of ancient Hebrew history and the emergence of Judaism as the religion of law; and the latter a history of the emergence of the Muslim caliphate until its fragmentation after the Umayyad dynasty.[144] In both works, Wellhausen tried to break through to the grand narrative account of history he admired especially by Theodor Mommsen (and much less by the other iconic German historians in the nineteenth century).[145]

Arab Kingdom was in many regards the high point, as well as the end point, of Wellhausen's Orientalist research. The book was based on the transfer of interpretive tools he had developed for the context of Israelite history: paying attention to the traces of different party orientations and political interests within the corpus of source texts. The book's first chapter offers a bird's eye synthesis of the entire line of historical development which is spelled out in greater detail in the following chapters. Like *Israelite and Jewish History*, the study is based on a single main source, the "Annals" of the Persian-Arab historian aṭ-Ṭabarī (839–923 CE). From 1879, this work had been the object of that era's largest collaborative text-philological project of European Arabists; under the direction of Leiden chairholder Michael Jan de Goeje, a team of mainly German and Austrian editors had collated the extant manuscript versions of the previously unprinted annals and subsequently provided a fifteen-volume edition that was only concluded in 1901.[146] Nöldeke was one of the editors and also assisted his lifelong friend de Goeje with proofing the text, as indicated by the endless emendations and corrections noted in their correspondence over more than twenty years.[147] Wellhausen, although not involved in producing the edition, in a way became its foremost user. Nöldeke also published a historical account based on the Annals, but only regarding the Sasanian Empire in late ancient Persia, for which Tabari was also the chief source. Nöldeke published his translation of this section of the Annals as a standalone work enriched with an ample commentary and inclusion of translations of other relevant sources; characteristically, he did not offer a narrative history proper.[148]

It fell to Wellhausen to engage with the main body of the source, which discussed the early history of Islam. In terms of method, he remained committed to the rejoinder he had hurled at his critics already in the 1883 second edition of his *Prolegomena zur Geschichte Israels*: "as is common knowledge, history always has to be constructed … The difference is only whether one constructs it well or badly."[149] Construction was successful if and only if it had maximal plausibility. The narrative order of text alone was therefore insufficient for historical writing. Once again, the "simple" beauty of Froissart's chronicle was unattainable. Historical narration needed to be propped up by an apparatus that documented the solidity of the construction, the soundness of the judgment attained. This apparatus was in the annotations. For this reason, and because the textual form of the annotation remains an under-explored portion of philological writing practice, in conclusion of this chapter, I will therefore propose an analysis of Wellhausen's practice of the "construction" of historical reality, by way of his footnotes.[150]

To begin with it is crucial to understand that the footnote has a history of its own. Its foremost student, Anthony Grafton, has suggested that the footnote expresses a historical amalgamation of a mode of the performance of scholarly authority with the representation of evidence in writing. This amalgamation, when developed by eighteenth-century luminaries Pierre Bayle and Edward Gibbon, also permitted maintaining, within a scholarly text, a counter-discourse to the account above the line. It thereby became possible to include "secondary narratives": "In documenting the thought and research that underpin the narrative above them, footnotes prove that it [i.e. the narrative] is a historically contingent product, dependent on the forms of research, opportunities, and states of particular questions that existed when the historian went to work."[151] The footnote bestowed "coherent literary form"[152] also on the work of documentation. It thus represents a marriage of rhetoric and rationality that has remained, says Grafton, at the core of historical writing ever since Ranke raised the footnote to the status of cherished locale, and affective center of historical methodology. The marriage in question, however uneasy, is the sole guarantee that claims to scholarly authority—which are necessary since "construction" is inevitable—dispose of a rational basis. Modernity proves, in a distantly Weberian fashion, to be a process of rationalization.[153] Distantly, because Grafton highlights a reconciliation of the ancient (rhetoric) and the modern (documented research) that hardly constitutes a bar of the "iron cage" of modern rationality Max Weber so famously deplored.[154] The particular process of benign rationalization Grafton describes was moreover securely concluded by 1820.

Among Grafton's great merits in this field (or this little allotment) is also the rediscovery of previous authorities on the history of the footnote, such as the scholar of modern literature Michael Bernays (1834–1897), younger brother to the better-known Jewish-German classicist Jacob (Michael converted to Protestantism in order to advance his academic career). Bernays's assessment of the function of footnotes, however, subtly differs from Grafton's, as is illustrated by the following passage about Gibbon:

[The footnotes] do not provide a subordinate service to the text. In a freer movement, seemingly autonomous, they accompany the narrative [*Darstellung*]; sometimes they even seem to be supposed to turn our thoughts in other directions into more distant areas; and yet they contribute essentially to the overall impression with which the work releases us and which renews itself as often as we return to it.[155]

For Bernays, text is a matter of movement, and of impression that can also be renewed (though not formally repeated). The givenness of the text is, always already, a temporal matter; reading approximates mimesis. The reader's attention is on the author, as the central instigator of this process, who is not a neutral seat of the rationality of the text, but another actor, the protagonist: "In the notes, [Gibbon] recovers from the necessities" of his style in the main body of text, which has to carry the burden of maximal concision in the face of an overwhelming narrative complexity. In the notes "his expression changes—almost one wants to say, the expression of his face—… as soon as he engages in an intimate dialogue with the reader."[156] In the case of Barthold Georg Niebuhr, the notes permit even the reader's participation in the author's "rich and versatile inner life," which the main text entirely conceals.[157] In general, the insertion of footnotes requires an "artistic gaze"[158] that lacks a rational principle of explanation and also cannot be reduced to rhetorical convention. At the same time, the emphasis on the gaze entails that the positions of author and reader are interchangeable; they perceive the same object, and the temporality of the text generates a co-presence that facilitates actual dialogue.

In brief, Bernays stresses the aesthetic of footnotes, that is to say, he uncovers an underlying regime of the perception of textual objects that is problematic in the sense that it requires analysis. This emphasis on aesthetics, however, does not appear to be an end in itself. Rather, it serves as a gateway into a different problematic only implied by Bernays. On an abstract level, the study of annotations grants access to the problem of the historical malleability of the ways in which the givenness of objects of knowledge has been conceived in scholarship. In Grafton's account, by contrast, the figure of rationalization posits that the givenness of objects to perception is increasingly de-problematized over time. And the framework of rhetoric suggests that the problem is not so much givenness itself, which is taken to be stable, but rather its translation into an adequate textual form in light of a specific tradition of text-making. It is the advantage of the Bernaysian manner of problematization that it keeps the history of the footnote open beyond the age of Ranke; neither philology nor historical writing must then perform the somewhat ungrateful task of merely sustaining the afterlife of conclusive settlements reached in the early modern period.

The main functions of Wellhausen's footnotes in *Arab Kingdom* might be listed as follows: they offer variants, reservations, uncertainties pertaining to the events narrated in the main text; they provide semantic clarifications, including etymologies and factual explications, and, for proper names (persons and locations), they determine referents; they provide space for the discussion of issues of dating. Less frequently, they pursue what are usually taken to be the main purposes of annotations in historical writing, i.e. indicating precise passages in source texts that serve as evidence for assertions in the main text; and indicating other works of scholarly research. A common denominator of most of these functions is dialogue with the main text. Thereby, the text above the line is marked as the most plausible account by comparison to variants. The performance of the overall text is forensic in nature; the philologist-historian adopts the role of the judge who pronounces a reasoned judgment. Importantly, he is not in the position of an attorney, which is classically the position of the rhetorician. Unlike what Bernays suggests in substance for Gibbon, the authorial and readerly positions in Wellhausen's work are not placed on the same footing. Wellhausen is an author who does not need to convince the reader; rather, he needs to convince himself, and for this labor he does not require rhetorical finesse. At the same time, history remains under the skeptical caveat of "construction." Wellhausen—who despised Ranke—certainly did not aim to show *wie es eigentlich gewesen*, "how it actually was, or happened" (without caring to discuss the notorious translation difficulties marring any English rendering of this phrase);[159] but rather only *wie es uneigentlich gewesen*, namely under the ostensible proviso that it all might have been quite different.

The historian, in other words, is an unreliable narrator who owns up to his unreliability but nonetheless occasionally relieves himself of this condition by passing narrative authorship to other unreliable narrators, namely the authors of source works such as Tabari. From the point of view of the structural analysis of narrative, it is a given that each narration entails a diegesis, a world in which the narrated actions and events take place. Since the narrators in the case in question are unreliable, even when they seem to be addressing the same historical reality it is illegitimate to treat the diegeses as one. Doing so would simply mean to commit—and on a broader scale—the semantic fallacy Wellhausen criticized in Hommel's work. The notion that the meaning of different proper names for the same entity could be reduced to the same extension is illicit for the same reasons that the meaning of different narratives of the same event can also not be explicated by reference to the actual event. Wellhausen's annotations frequently aim to mark the shift from one (unreliable) diegesis to another. On the Battle of Siffin (657 CE), he remarked: "It has been described and fought with equal confusion."[160] This zeugma ties together historical reality with the diegeses of its varying descriptions; the comical effect is precisely in the absence of a syntactic boundary that would allow detailing the confusions of the descriptions in neat separation from the confusion of reality. The zeugma suggests the epistemic indigence of historical writing, the feebleness of the reasons on which one can found one's knowledge about the past. This comical effect is pervasive in Wellhausen's work.

In general, this effect is securely moored to the performative qualities of the interaction of footnote and main text, on which Wellhausen frequently relies in order to produce tension within his account. For instance, in a passage in *Israelite and Jewish History*, he chides the biblical Chronicles as the post-Exilic period product of an ossified, repetitively didactic canonization of historical knowledge in the form of a *Midrash*, a rabbinic homily, of the Books of Kings. This Midrash is

> a mere travesty of history, the clerical moralizing annihilates the aesthetic sense of truth, has no interest in things as they are, but only uses them as examples for a few meager ideas and when necessary rephrases them [*dichtet sie um*] in accordance with the latter in a starkly brazen fashion.[161]

To this harsh condemnation of a portion of scripture, Wellhausen appends a note, which points to a chapter of his *Prolegomena*, where the matter is discussed at greater length, and then undercuts the general validity of his own account of historical reality, with subtle self-irony: "Prolegomena ch. 6. More attractive specimens of the historical midrash are the Book Jonah and the Book Ruth."

In this passage Wellhausen passes judgment on a historical source, the Chronicles in the Old Testament, and rules against them, as a "mere travesty" in which a few theological ideas, and meager ones at that, dress themselves up in historical costume. There is an "aesthetic sense of truth" that is violated by this procedure. By contrast, in historical writing proper, this sense must be discernible. This is the case because it is not a garden variety set of aesthetic norms, but exclusively based on the interest in "things as they are." These three *topoi*—the figure of dress/undress, the aesthetics of truth, and things as they are—mark Wellhausen's understanding of the givenness of historical reality. This givenness is not as straightforward as the *topoi* suggest. For, it requires the counterbalance of the note: It is hardly the case that all historical knowledge that is contained in supposedly post-exilic portions of Hebrew scripture is entirely repellent. What is given is uncertain; it can always be taken away again. What the main text offers, the footnotes withdraw, and *vice versa*.

Yet another widespread Wellhausen anecdote holds that in Göttingen he supposedly nurtured the habit of going swimming in the local river on Sunday mornings and to time his exercise in such a manner that he would be able to meet churchgoers on their way home with his bathing costume over the shoulder. Rudolf Smend suspects that this is merely a legend;[162] but there is no denying that it is *ben trovata*. The philologist, or indeed the theologist, in the bathing suit makes a point about embodied scholarship and the significance of symbolic transgression in the work of philology. The subtler point, however, is that this individual counter-manifestation against the performance of congregational conformity still avoids a state of total undress, indeed any state of actual undress. The more or less respectable professor's embrace of the "natural" requires a costume and an audience; it is staged. Moreover, it symbolizes a state, not of natural nudity, but of *undress*, that is to say, it is based on a negation. What is negated is a tradition of abstractions, as a travesty of the historical that blocks access to the things as they are (or were). Wellhausen's position is that of a counter-aesthetic that requires its antagonist in order to govern any perception at all. The givenness of the *Sachen* therefore is not straightforward; the object of knowledge does not provide direct access. This is what the footnote remark on the Books of Jonah and Ruth is meant to indicate: the conclusion, from the annoying traits of the Chronicles, to the general nature of post-exilic Hebrew historical consciousness is flawed. Differentiation and ironization are always present precisely where judgment is seemingly at its most simple. Things as they are are never quite like that.

In light of this presence of antagonism within the very texture of the object-relation in Wellhausen's work, it is clear that the annotation is a medium of *polemos*. Unsurprisingly, this is quite often a matter of actual polemics, which however ought not to be mistaken for the main purpose or the driving force of the underlying tension. An instructive example can be found in a passage of the preface to the second edition of the *Prolegomena*, published shortly after Wellhausen's departure from the Greifswald faculty of theology. In the preface he carries out a trenchant anti-critique in which he attempts to respond in definitive fashion to his opponents (but which he omitted again from later editions of the work):

Clerical scholarship[1] in the field of the Old Testament appears to have the task of refuting any new discovery for fifty years, and after that to find a more or less ingenious point of view from which this discovery can be included into the creed.

_____

[1] In principle I have no objections to the polemic being raised against me from the domain of churchly practice. [... Several objections follow:] Third, I do not recognize the right of the *Neue Evangelische Kirchenzeitung* to claim that it was clear that my book was dictated by an unhistorical perspective. I do not object if they prefer to imagine David following the Chronicles and Psalms rather than Samuel, just as they prefer to regard Calvin in the light of legend rather than in that of the documents ..., but the standpoint of the church is not the historical one.[163]

The footnote here serves to insert a polemic against practical theology into a polemic against overall theological learning. The insertion prompts an interruption of the syntactic flow of the passage. Biblical scholarship, superior to pastoral care in the hierarchical structure of theology at least as an academic discipline, is separated from, but on the side of the opponents contaminated by, the requirements of practical faith in the church of the many. In the main text, Wellhausen enjoys the prerogative of the actually "historical" standpoint, which theology only ever reaches belatedly; in the note, he defines the terms of the prerogative in question as being foreign to the church as such. The muddled structure in which the necessities of pastoral practice disrupt the integrity of theological scholarship is mimicked and mocked by the placement of the footnote; the ugliness of the interrupted train of thought and sentence indicates an aesthetic shortcoming of the critical attacks. In the overall passage, Wellhausen prominently deploys an authorial voice that is characterized by reliance on the first-person singular pronoun, "I," which demarcates and defends the author's standpoint. By means of the footnote, this voice also disrupts itself, sullying the integrity of its own discourse. The note indicates the polemical descent of the counter-attack to the same, low level; the anti-critique inevitably debases itself. To this procedure of interruption—in the polemical attack, but even more so in the self-debasement—there is a comical effect. This effect in part also resides in the graphic means by the insufficient crutch of which the voice—as ironically transfigured into written form—is alone able to interrupt itself: the author has to split his voice on the printed page and relegate part of it to the bottom of the page.

In the long run the pervasiveness of this comical quality undermines the bitterness of the *polemos*, as well as the critical intention altogether. On the very next page Wellhausen inserts a footnote solely in order to crack a puerile joke that is not directed at any opponent, when he discusses the structure of the Early Arabic calendar:

[The months of] Safar and Ragab as beginnings of the semesters occur even before Muhammed's treaty with the Christians of Nagran ... For the old Arabs, almost like for German students, the semester appears to have been a similarly important unit as the year, as Ewald already remarked.[164]

In this manner, the comical overrode the enjoyment, or even the significance of the quarrel. For Wellhausen, as for other Orientalists of this period, the comical was an indispensable aesthetic quality that regimented his perspective on Arab as well as Israelite history. In the latter field in particular, he frequently used the contrast between the alleged rigidity of the post-exilic period and the "naturalness" of pre-exilic religion to generate comical effects. Such effects, though, occurred on both sides of the distinction. In the post-exilic priestly religion, they often sprang from a certain rigidity of customs. This rigidity was undermined by the deep, almost tragic irony that the customs in question upheld the pretense of rigorous national-cultural closure while they actually required foreign, namely Babylonian, rule in order to emerge at all and then to be sustained. Judaism, for Wellhausen, was the product of military defeat and foreign occupation. Violence and exile had estranged the Hebrews from their natural religious forms.

In pre-exilic religion the core of the comical is less easily grasped:

> If truth be told, Mose is the author of the 'Mosaic constitution' roughly in the same sense as Petrus was the founder of the Roman hierarchy. … Yet even if one admitted that any ancient constitution could have emerged so externally to all proper inner life of the people, even then nothing is more salient in the history of Old Israel than the extraordinary freshness and naturalness of its shoots [*Triebe*]. The acting personages throughout appear on the scene with such a necessity [*so einem Muss*] of their nature, the men of god just as much as the murderers and adulterers; they are characters [*Gestalten*] that are only accomplished in plain air.[165]

This passage expresses a serene pleasure in the creaturely that was the signature of Wellhausen's view of nations and their "proper inner life." The emphasis on the naturalness of the Israelites specifically, however, was a gesture of normalization, which deprived Hebrew antiquity of its claim to the quality of the sublime. The pre-exilic portions of the Old Testament represented nothing more—but also nothing less—than human nature. As Sheehan has noted, retrieving the sublime in scripture—in accordance with a tradition that actually went all the way back to Longinus' treaty—was key to the aesthetic reframing of the text in the late enlightenment.[166] Wellhausen ironized and subverted this process. This was the comical effect his descriptions of the pre-exilic Israelites achieved; it was not merely a function of the façade of serenity but also rested on a counter-aesthetic, a mode of perception that was based on the negation of the sublime.

Nonetheless, Wellhausen's contrariness did not exhaust itself in the aesthetic sphere. Rather, aesthetics were a marker of the problem of the givenness of historical reality. Wellhausen opposed philosophies of history; the only goal within the realm of the historical he cared to acknowledge was a notion of the free unfolding of the natural and individual. If one were to look for precedent in the history of German literature, this position is perhaps closest to a Goethean skepticism toward the category of the historical.[167] Nietzsche was a reader of his work (and Wellhausen—who was close friends with Wilamowitz since their common Greifswald period—was not ignorant of Nietzsche).[168] Nietzsche's later readers often turned to Wellhausen as well. In the interwar period, knowledge of his historical works was still widespread, and he remained a significant reference in intellectual debate.

This surprisingly broad reception did not simply follow the aesthetic peculiarities vested in the texts, but rather the problem of the givenness of the historical. This problem, however, for Wellhausen ultimately hinged on the individuality, the historical givenness, of the Christian godhead, Jesus:

> The gospels attempt to preserve the memory not only of his [Jesus'] teachings, but also of his being [Wesen]. He lives untroubled in simple and open circumstances, in the poetry of the South, not in need and lowly poverty. His gentleness is coupled with earnestness, he is also capable of anger; ironically, he lets his opponents feel his superiority ... Everything teaches him, in nature he sees the secrets of the heavenly realm ... He has not studied ... He only gives expression to what any sincere soul must feel. What he says is not strange, but evident, according to his conviction nothing else than what was written by Moses and the prophets.[1)] Yet his ravishing simplicity distinguishes him from Moses and the prophets and sets him worlds apart from the Rabbis. The historical burden that is bearing down on the Jews does not weigh on him; he is not suffocated by the mustiness of their old vestments. ... He repudiates the accidental, caricatural, necrotic and collects the eternally-valid, the humane-divine, in the burning mirror of his individuality. "Ecce homo"—a divine miracle in that time and environment.[2)] These are certainly traits that provide a correct picture.

[1)] Everything that is useful and necessary for salvation Moses and the prophets have said. 'If they hear not them, neither will they be persuaded, though one rose from the dead.' [Luke 16:31, slightly altered by Wellhausen]. In Micha 6:6–8, Psalms 73:23–28 indeed the gospel is written.

[2)] Jewish scholars wish to deny the difference, or more correctly put, the angry antagonism, in which Jesus stood toward the Pharisees; they assume, everything he said is also written in the Talmud. Yes, everything and *a lot more*. Πλέον ἥμισυ παντός [the half is more than the whole]. It was Jesus' originality to sense, and to underline with the greatest emphasis, amid a chaotic mess, the true and eternal. How close he was to, and at the same time how far from, Judaism is shown by, on the one hand, Mark 12:28–34, on the other, the Book of Esther.[169]

In this passage with its appended annotations, Wellhausen offers his creed, which by necessity has to address the problem of the "historical Jesus" that accompanied all of nineteenth-century New Testament theology. Jesus is more able to see the things as they are than anyone else. The historical travesties of rabbinic Judaism do not matter to him. Though simple—if in a romanticized Mediterranean fashion—he is also an ironist.[170] His perceptivity toward nature indicates his affinity to *Realphilologie*, as e.g. Georg Jacob envisaged the field. Both at the beginning and toward the end of the passage, Wellhausen emphasizes the source-critical caveat. The picture is only approximate, combined from a variety of traces in the gospels that only contain fragments of the memory of the living Jesus; the picture is "certainly" correct, but the certainty in question is that of the creed, not that of knowledge. This creed has its opponents: as Jesus rejects the Pharisees (the theme of the referenced passage in

Mark), so Wellhausen, in the note, antagonizes contemporary Jewish scholarship. Jesus himself rejected the weight—the (costume of) sublimity—of the historical and was exclusively oriented toward the "eternally-valid," outside of history.

The first footnote with its reference to the "gospel" allegedly contained in the minor prophet Micha and in the 73rd psalm provides indirect hints as to what Wellhausen wants to stress as the core of Jesus' teachings, namely the simple trust in God and the concomitant rejection of sacrifice that is particularly suggested by the passage in Micha. In the quotation it is through the annotations that Wellhausen attains the possibility of authorial voice. For, the account in the main text to which the footnotes are attached presents a summary voice of the evangelists. The biblical references in the first note only mimic the scholarly practice of indicating the source. Wellhausen does not even bother to identify the direct, if altered, quotation from Luke; it signals the change of genre undertaken in the passage, from scholarship to sermon. The second footnote revokes the shift worked by the first; here Wellhausen returns to the mode of historical writing as he discusses the problem of the historical Jesus' relations with the historical Pharisees, and their representation in the modern *Wissenschaft* of Judaism. The position Wellhausen attacks polemically is also one that concerns the texts and traditions, the question of relations between the Talmud and the gospels.

In the second footnote, Wellhausen also reattains the stance of being his own antagonist. The note, with its profane polemic, works as a corrective to the pathos of the "Ecce homo." This pathos constitutes a substantial transgression against the scholarly mode of discourse—namely, the rule that scholarly writing is to be placed on the intermediate level of stylistic ornamentation, the *genus medium*—in the rhetorical framework Wellhausen feigned not to have mastered. Transgression against the *genus medium* was accomplished by means of the footnote. It was this textual tool that allowed for the shifts of voice and level, the broken, *uneigentlich*, disrupted quality of the creed expressed in this concluding portion of *Israelitische und jüdische Geschichte*. The second footnote, moreover, responded to the characterization of Jesus as an ironist in the main text. Wellhausen's relation to the Talmudic argument he dismissed in the note was ironical: "Yes, everything and *a lot more*." The target of this remark was quite clearly the late Abraham Geiger's (1810–1874) discussion of the historical Jesus in the context of Judaism, and of the gospels in that of the Talmud.[171] Wellhausen ironically showed his superiority, for which purpose he also saw fit to insert a Greek proverb, borrowed from Hesiod, which he had already used as a chapter motto in *Prolegomena*.[172] Within the space of a single footnote, Geiger was relegated to the position of the Pharisees, although Wellhausen also offered a hint at reconciliation. For, the referenced passage in Mark comprises one of Jesus' most conciliatory dialogues with a Jewish learned man— "an ingenuous rabbi," as Wellhausen puts it in his commentary[173]—about the essence of the commandments. Wellhausen's philological judgment was mirrored in the words of Christ, as a form of *imitatio Christi*, if merely in ironical fashion. No wonder, then, that he clung to the motif of costume and travesty. His creed was indissolubly fettered to his irony.

A few pages further on, Wellhausen also inserts a methodological creed into this entanglement, which then gains practical-theological momentum yet again:

History is the history of society, the constitution and the law, the economy, prevailing ideas, morality, arts and sciences. Easily explicable, for only this overall sphere is subject to development, only here can one discern progress and a certain level of conformity to laws, only here can one deploy some kind of calculation and even statistics. One also cannot ignore the fact that it is only on the foundation of culture that the individual can flourish. [... Yet] All culture is insufferable [*unausstehlich*] when it does not recognize the individual and its secret. Beyond a certain limit, progress is not progress of the individual, and fortunately so. I am not merely part of the mass, a product of my time and my environment, as science announces in a tone as if this notion was reason for triumph.[174]

Wellhausen's embrace of the individual was certainly in keeping with some of the broader tendencies in the theory of the humanities, as opposed to that of natural science, in the German *fin de siècle*. Philosophers like Dilthey, and also the neo-Kantians Windelband and Rickert, insisted on the inexorable individual surplus, its obstinacy toward generalization and causal explanation that required an epistemology apart. What doctrine there was of "historicism" likewise stressed the principle of singularity as embodied in individual persons.[175]

Nonetheless, Wellhausen deviated from his peers in his use of the notion of individuality for the the purpose of ironizing *Wissenschaft* as such. The presence of irony is marked, in the otherwise seemingly serious quoted passage, by the hyperbolic trope of the "insufferability" of such forms of culture that failed to respect the boundaries of individual development. Wellhausen's individualism rejected the explanatory claims the humanities had come to connect with the figure of the individual. Indeed, from the opening of the passage it is clear that he was forward-looking and open to the anti-individualist modes of explanation the novel social sciences were championing, rather to the disadvantage of hermeneutics and historicist individualism. Yet, *Wissenschaft* in general was faulty and insufficient and hardly the most serious pursuit one could imagine since, just like anything else, it did not allow for a firm grasp of reality. History, all in all, was a subordinate pursuit; it was a matter of *idées reçues* that became a nuisance when it did not leave the "secret" of the individual alone. For this reason, all representation of historical reality for Wellhausen had to remain *uneigentlich*; the past was never fully given, and ignorance prevailed.

This position is not simply composed of the *topoi* of Pyrrhonic skepticism that had marked the theory of historical knowledge, as well as the philological ideal of *epokhé*, since the early modern period. Not only does Wellhausen place a stronger emphasis on irony than this tradition arguably suggested; more importantly, his stance is a function of the problematic of the creed, as impossible and inevitable at once, to which he therefore returns a few sentences onward:

In my core I touch upon eternity. Admittedly, I have to reach this core by myself and shape it. Above all I have to *believe* in it; believe that I do not disappear in the mill in which I am spun and ground; believe that *God* is behind and above the mechanism of the world, that he can act upon my soul, pull it upward and help it attain a selfhood of its own; that he is the bond of an invisible and eternal community of spirits.[176]

This thicket of tropes suggested that there was no true individuality, no real selfhood, that was not in some sense created, brought forth, by the support of the godhead. Agency was split in this account; it rested both with the "I" and the deity. In spite of the crudeness of the style, Wellhausen's understanding of the collaboration between the Ego and God was subtle; unlike in Cohen's philosophical speculation, the relation was not dialogic. Rather, the faith of the individual-in-emergence was blindly directed toward a *deus absconditus*. Revelation was marginalized. Much as the creed, since it was based on faith in the possibility of individuation, appeared to be aimed at a personal deity, Wellhausen left the godhead unspecified and anonymous. The text sidelined the problem of the divine nature of Jesus. For specification of the divine, Wellhausen rather just pointed to the invisibility and eternity of the "community of spirits" founded by the deity as a principle of connection.

So when it came to the question of actually embracing the hypostatization of the name he had himself promoted by his proposal for spelling out the cultural history of revelation as the self-naming of the deity, Wellhausen backed down. Instead of dialogue, there was at most a monologue. History and philology could only concern themselves with the empty "mechanism" of the world; they did not suffice to explain individuation, the flour that could not be more finely ground by the mill. The parts were all in place for revelation to occur; albeit one had to cope with, or else transgress against, its absence. The linkage between naming, revelation, being, and referential meaning remained intact; only, none of the elements concatenated in this neat manner was reliably given. As a consequence, the world in general and all semantics became elusive. Hence the endless string of ironizations.

In the end, even Wellhausen's self-fashioning, all his talk about the animal, the barbarian, and the profane, was a function of the elusiveness of the real, of the futility of philology. In the second-to-last re-edition of *Israelitische und jüdische Geschichte*, he added a note at the beginning of the concluding chapter, the one that contained his creed. In this note, he stated that he had "let the chapter stand" although he did "not fully subscribe to it any more."[177] In the last years of his life, he suffered from a long series of ailments, in particular loss of hearing, which isolated him from social contact. In 1911, he wrote to Littmann that meanwhile he merely hoped "in due time to penetrate to the feeling of a general couldn't-care-less attitude [*allgemeinen Wurstigkeit*] with regard to my health—with that, everything would be gained. One can express it in a less profane manner; but I rather content myself with the profane expression."[178] In the face of suffering, he thus formulated an ideal of detachment, which he ironically debased right away.

5

A Trade in Shadows

1. Jacob's Ladder, or Entangled History around 1900

When Georg Jacob published his first scholarly works, Wellhausen reviewed them in a rather skeptical manner: The junior scholar, in throwing himself on the neglected problem of the textual evidence of trade relations between northern Europe and the Arab world in the Middle Ages, had uncovered important materials and questions, but had been too careless with the facts.[1] Moreover, Jacob affected an unbecoming sense of the supreme importance of his obscure topic and did not seem to realize that he was "actually just playing sports."[2] Already at this point, with his usual aphoristic precision, Wellhausen had clearly identified Jacob's lack of irony as a point of divergence. This lack, I will argue in the present chapter, opens a vista on yet another manner of processing the ontological possibilities underpinning Orientalist philological semantics. The unironical Jacob, while running into various further aporias, succeeded in reestablishing a sort of attachment to the real that eluded Wellhausen. This attachment was based on the aesthetic project of the de-centering of the human form that has been broached in several preceding chapters. Jacob's resulting antihumanism is a position of interest not merely in its own right but also as a broader contribution to the genealogy of theory in the twentieth century. Indeed, I will argue that Jacob's work has the heuristic quality of uncovering many of the uncomfortable subterranean linkages that connect nineteenth-century Orientalist *Realphilologie* with aspects of the discursive matrix that currently underpins the humanities.

No doubt partly in response to Wellhausen's negative verdict, for a number of years, Jacob also expressed nothing but dislike for the Göttingen chairholder in his correspondence.[3] By 1903, however, the relationship had completely changed. Jacob was enthused by Wellhausen's history of the Caliphate,[4] which eschewed the narrowness of the text-immanent philology of the previous works on the Old Testament. All of a sudden, for Jacob, Wellhausen had come to rank among "the great," like e.g. Bismarck or the painter Hans Thoma, whose "greatness" resided in their ability "to see things as they are."[5] Jacob thus subscribed to Wellhausen's standing epistemological-semantic motto (*Die Dinge sehen, wie sie sind*). Except that for Jacob, the meaning of the phrase was subtly different, as I will seek to show.

Wellhausen, for his part, expressed pleasure with "the idealist"[6] Jacob, in whom "the researcher has not strangled the human being"[7] and who was, when they met in person, "completely different" from how Wellhausen had imagined him.[8] This rapprochement is surprising given the ample divergence of philological practice that marked both scholars' working lives. Wellhausen aimed to write self-contained national histories of *Völker* at the putative beginning of history and displayed a serious concern for the problem of the emergence of monotheism. Jacob, by contrast, studied a dizzying range of problems at a level of textual detail alien to Wellhausen's practice; but none of them were geared toward the distinction of prehistory and history, nor to the first manifestation of belief in a unique godhead. Doubtless there was also common ground. Both Wellhausen and Jacob had worked on Early Arabic poetry, and while there was disagreement in interpretive detail, they nonetheless shared a notion of the Bedouins as proximate to the state of nature and a notion of this state that was derived from Herder and demarcated a common ground of *Realphilologie* semantics and aesthetics. Nonetheless, Jacob's rejection of the interpretive model of *Altertum*—the insular account of the ancient world so important, since the times of Wolf and Boeckh, for the theorization of philology—was already discernible in his early work and only became more pronounced. His interests focused more and more on the post-ancient. Even pre-Islamic Arabia was not the synecdoche of Semitic antiquity for him that it was for Wellhausen.

In later research, Jacob devoted himself to, among other things, Turkish and Persian Sufism, Ottoman-Turkish literature, late medieval Arabic satire, the history of rhyme in world poetry,[9] and the history of silhouettes, or shadow theatre. The latter problem, which he initially pursued in the framework of Turkish and Arabic literatures, and especially the Turkish genre of the humorist Karagöz play, for which he had done fieldwork, prompted him to explore cultural forms ever further afield. Mostly bypassing India and determined to find the "origin" of the drama of silhouettes, in the years when he was approaching retirement Jacob threw himself on the study of Mandarin Chinese. Always a diligent reader of the output of literary studies in the Europeanist fields as well, in his last years, he moreover engaged in extensive analyses of the zoological and botanical vocabulary in the writings of Shakespeare, whose supreme perceptivity to natural reality he sought to demonstrate.[10] Within this dazzling array of projects, interests, and enthusiasms, one of the defining features was, as I will argue, the peculiar permeability of cultural history in Jacob's writings. This quality interlocked with the problem of the status of antiquity and historical beginnings in general; with Jacob's specific solutions for the conceptual problems of his *Realphilologie* aesthetics; and with the precise nature of relations between philology and history as core disciplines of the humanities spectrum.

One unifying thread of Jacob's disparate oeuvre was the desire to identify both natural and cultural connections between Orient and Occident. By means of such connections, he sought to outline a history of global enmeshment that would disable any argument in support of self-enclosed historical-geographical epochs and spatial containers. In his last work on Shakespeare, by implicitly assuming not only the equivalence, but in fact the fundamental equality of European and Asian poetics, Jacob even made the categories of the Oriental and Occidental disappear altogether. At the same time, however, he radically rejected notions of humanism:

We are beginning to outgrow the ideals of so-called humanism; our age stands in the developmental phase from classicism to universalism. Intellectual achievements never emerge from mere clouds and smoke [*Wolkendunst*], but require a real basis. The expansion of the foundations of our modern worldview resulted from the intrusion into the spirit of foreign cultural worlds.[11]

Orientalism, then, did represent a one-sided intrusion into other "worlds," and this intrusion even constituted its *reale Basis*. Nonetheless, such intrusion was legitimate since it allowed the Occident (the "we"-subject of the passage) to outgrow its narrow and twisted classicist understanding of the human. In Jacob's idiom, what one would nowadays tend to call cultural "transfer" was consistently labeled as "borrowing" (*Entlehnung*), in order to mark the sensitivity of the argument to problems of property, and to relativize the irreversibility of European appropriations. Universalism, whatever that meant, was the ultimate aim of this process, but an aim that was not easily attained by an act of will or by intellectual decree.

Admittedly, Jacob did not permit himself to dwell on abstractions. His general assertions were few and scattered and rarely took the form of developed argument. His discussions of cultural history moved swiftly on a sort of conceptual ladder on which one could, as it were, climb up and down, from the global toward the particular, and back; or from one side of a contradiction to the other, and back. These passages even characterized his political and personal comportment. Ardent polemicist and belligerent chauvinist in the First World War, nonetheless in the 1902 treatise he had also remarked that "the work of culture requires long periods of peace";[12] and at the end of 1916, whatever his sense of nationalist entitlement, he hoped for peace, not victory.[13] While he continued writing angry diatribes against Germany's enemies, in letters from the following years, he also frequently berated the German conservative leadership, the monarch, and the credulous public for their failure to negotiate an end to the war.[14] In the years of the republic, he remained one of the most stalwart supporters of C. H. Becker within the discipline of Oriental studies and did not express overt monarchist leanings. By 1932 his relations with his successor Theodor Menzel (1878–1939), his former student, whose appointment he had vigorously supported in 1929, had soured (Figure 10). Subsequently, Jacob did not find Menzel's membership of the Nazi party and his respective activities at the University of Kiel in 1933 deserving of praise. He witnessed Menzel's fall from grace, his forced early retirement in 1937 and the subsequent dissolution of the department for Oriental studies in Kiel, including the library Jacob had built up over twenty years, with bitterness, then resignation. All in all, the world of Jacob's world philology remained a perplexing affair that accommodated an ample number of contradictions.

It is arguably one of these contradictions that in Jacob's rejection of humanism the sign of sexuality was part of a code, not of nature, but rather its opposite. So for instance in 1931, in a letter to Littmann, in which he expressed his disdain for the classicist-humanist complex and laid out an unusually ample portion of the code in question:

Recently I have read an article somewhere about bullfights in the Rome of Leo X, the 'old evil enemy,' as Luther calls him. It is significant after all, how along with humanism the ancient Roman sadism is also revived. The devilish lust for the tormenting of creatures is the actual [*eigentliche*] idea of Romandom, as unnatural

Figure 10. Portrait photograph by Ferdinand Urbahns (1863–1944), portrait specialist in Kiel, of (from left to right) Georg Jacob, Georg Hoffmann, Theodor Menzel, Kiel 1932. NL Littmann, K. 97, folder *Kollegen, Freunde 2.*

fornication is that of Greekdom; only through the latter vice can one at all understand the art and pseudo-science of the Greeks, which always thinks past what is right, because it lives in a world of un-nature and phrase-mongering. For this reason the Greeks did not manage to invent a single thing.[15]

So homosexuality, sadistic violence, empty rhetoric in accordance with a rule-driven poetics, and the inability to make scientific inventions were all equivalent signs, interchangeable, whose referent was tacit. The mixture of aesthetic and moral notions—rhetoric stood on the same footing as "unnatural fornication" and cruelty to animals—was characteristic of Jacob's discourse. The frequently unbridled anger of his associational letter style indicates the contrarian motives underpinning his pronouncements. As much as Wellhausen's, Jacob's notions formed a counter-aesthetic. The rejection of classical antiquity and of its modern returns, as an enemy to art and nature at once, rested on a principle of the competition, even the inimical antagonism of different antiquities that Jacob shared with other Orientalists of this period. Aesthetic theorization was inherently participation in the agon. Consistency and cogency of argument were secondary values. The embarrassment of the symbolic significance of sexuality was tied into this structure.

Nonetheless, Jacob's understanding of history as a unified and permeable process also drew on an overall developmental template. This template even included the notion that a novel and presumably conclusive epoch of "universalism" was about to begin. Yet, to this directional logic, the contrarianness of Jacob's aesthetic discourse constituted an obstacle. For, if the classicist-humanist complex represented a stage in the overall historical process, and a stage that history was about to leave behind, the question of why this stage needed to be antagonized so violently became difficult to answer. Perhaps more significantly, the status of this antagonism as an actual part of the historical process (in the singular) became problematic. If the struggle of classicism with the universalist future was a function of an earlier competition of antiquities, did this competition then stand outside of historical time and enjoy the status of an ahistorical principle? If so, if there was an outside to history, how was the incipient new epoch actually going to be "universalist?" For, certainly, "universalism" entailed the recognition of the universality of the historical process, including the standpoint from which a judgement as to the universality of this process could be emitted. If this standpoint was, however, located outside of history, as part of a principle of eternal antagonism of which the new age of universalism would form part, the expectation of the advent of this age was self-defeating. These contradictions were not spelled out, let alone resolved.

The manner in which Jacob and many other scholars of the nineteenth century referred to classical antiquity was ambivalent. To begin with, antiquity represented a self-enclosed epoch within the developmental cultural history of a distinct sociogeographic space. As such, the concept of antiquity was capable of plurality. Similar epochs, with markers such as script, monumental architecture, distinct aesthetic and religious styles, and ideally a canon of texts, were possible, and indeed increasingly identified, in different locations.[16] Over the course of the nineteenth century, the Asian expansion of antiquities moved from Egypt to India, then Babylon, ancient Persia, and China, with a string of minor "high cultures" in the margins, such as Japan, or Old Java, or even Ethiopia. Gradually, this development came to provide a novel conceptual core to the meaning of the name of "Orient," in contrast with the "primitive" world. Since these antiquities stood apart from each other at least spatially, but often also chronologically, they could be set into a civilizational competition without asking complicated and often infertile questions about their interconnections.

In Nöldeke's works and letters, for instance, the competition of antiquities remained a chief theme. In spite of his tireless work on the study of ancient documents from the Middle East, he remained unshakably convinced of the superiority of classical Greece. In 1888, for instance, he commented to de Goeje on Snouck Hurgronje's declaration that Arab civilization was in many regards of equal rank to classical antiquity:

> but would Sn[ouck] care to exchange his European sense of discretion for [that of a given Arabic author]? Nay, I constantly thank Zeus "that I am Greek and no barbarian"! … How much do [the Arab medieval historians] al-Maqrizi and Ibn Khaldun surpass their European contemporaries! And yet, how fast were the Europeans to overtake the [Orientals]! One may think about Islam and the other purely Oriental religions whatever one pleases, but *in the long run* they act as appalling fetters for higher developed man.[17]

The structure here is quite similar to that which Jacob reproduces, if with reversed values. There was an overall developmental dynamism at work that was impaired by some forms of ancient heritage and promoted by others. The entire historical process was therefore subject to the multiplicity instituted by the competing forms of the ancient. To the extent that modernity hinged on its connection to the ancient, it was therefore also multiplied; multiple modernities first came about as an implication of multiple antiquities. Yet, if this was the case, why was there even supposed to be an *overall* "higher development" of universal humankind?

The hinge that connected the ancient and the modern was so stable that Jacob did not actually require solid figures of Oriental antiquity to compete with the classical civilizations he vilified. Moreover, it was chiefly aesthetic in nature. Nöldeke, although he professed to have an affective preference for ancient Greece, nonetheless was drawn to the study of early Islamic history because this epoch represented a "colossal time."[18] That is to say, it was endowed with the aesthetic quality of the sublime that was a prime organizing force in the historical writing of the nineteenth century. Jacob's preoccupation with the multiple perversions of the Greeks and the Romans represented an attempt to undermine the sublimity of the classical epoch, in a manner similar to Wellhausen's deflating of the sublimity of Hebrew antiquity. To complicate matters further, the significance of such aesthetic charges was ambiguous. They were a tool in the very practice of historicization. Yet, they also served to engineer a glissando between philological and historical modes of discourse and thereby to skate over the contradiction according to which the multiple antiquities of philology were supposed to feed into universal history's continuous line of development. The charge of the sublime with which historicity tended to be endowed always ought to be read in the context of aesthetic antagonism and competition. Moreover, where there is the sublime, the ridiculous also exists, even if it is passed over in silence. As a result of this overall constellation, the competition of antiquities always concerned the contemporary regimentation of sensory perception; inevitably, contemporary aesthetics were invaded by the philological-historical constellation.

The constellation was dynamic. The type of connection-driven cultural history Jacob espoused entailed investing hard work in the actual integration of the multiple antiquities into a common line of development. The sheer trope of such a line also marked Nöldeke's emphatic notion of "the long run." However, unlike Jacob, Nöldeke perceived a need to stabilize the contradictory tendencies at hand. Much like Wellhausen, he avoided the concrete arguments of transfer that contaminated the purity of otherwise supposedly distinct antiquities. Just as with Wellhausen, the history of Islam became un-colossal from Nöldeke's point of view when the Caliphate collapsed and multiple, less national-Arab and more hybrid states emerged.[19]

It was the ancient historian Eduard Meyer (1855–1930)—with whom most of the Orientalists discussed here entertained friendly relations—who produced the most prominent *fin de siècle* attempt at providing an integrated history of Eastern Mediterranean antiquity. Meyer aimed to end the insular treatment of the Greeks, although he failed to break entirely with the aesthetic partisanship of philhellenism, and the marginalization of Hebrew antiquity was a chief aim of his project.[20] The self-containment of classical antiquity had been a staple of German philhellenist classicism since the era of Romantic polemics in the 1810s and 20s. This notion had acted as a frame, not only for Hermann's apprehensions against Boeckh's epigraphic project; but also for the notorious Creuzer controversy of the 1810s that had already raised, in a mode of high speculation, the question of the dependence of Greek religious culture on Oriental sources.[21] In the line of development Meyer's work represented, historical time—exact location within a shared temporal framework—served as the highest unifier of antiquities; and simultaneously it worked as an anaesthetic that numbed the pains and pleasures of sensory rights and wrongs. On the whole, the contradictory structure that entailed both competitive pluralization and historicizing unification created a thorough ambivalence, between aesthetics and anaesthetics, which remained the signature of the Orientalist *Realphilologie* treatment of cultural history in the period from the 1880s onward.

The contradictory relations between aesthetics and historicization marked the seemingly peripheral field of the study of shadow theater with exceptional distinctness. Here the prospect of a connected east-western history was particularly promising, and the aesthetic hopes invested in the field reached an uncommon level of intensity. Jacob's interest in the matter went back to the 1890s, when he attempted to write a Turkish literary history with the shadow play as starting point.[22] The 1900 rectoral address, at Halle University, of the Indologist Richard Pischel (1849–1908), appears to have been a defining moment for Jacob's engagement with the field. Pischel chose this most representative setting of academic oratory to put forward an analysis of the supposed Indian origins of puppet-theater and thereby appeared to bestow on this field of study a dignity that confirmed Jacob's own sense of the importance of his concerns.[23] Moreover, Pischel provided an argumentative template that converged with Jacob's own, and he also cited his younger colleague's work as an inspiration.

According to Pischel, puppet-play was bound to fairy tales and the pleasures of childhood and had spread across the ages and the continents where it was constantly present in some form or other; for it

> appeals most strongly to the [mass of the] people because to them it owes its origin. Precisely for this reason, however, it is often a clearer mirror of the thoughts and feelings of the people than more finished poetry, and is in many cases the vehicle of old traditions. ... It is not improbable that the puppet-play is in reality everywhere the most ancient form of dramatic representation. Without doubt this is the case in India. And there, too, we must look for its home.[24]

Pischel goes on to collect the Sanskrit vocabulary for, and passages of reference to, marionette play in ancient Indian texts. He compares his findings with convergent features of European traditions of puppet theater and other forms of popular "dramatic expression." Pischel is in pursuit of a history of transfer that connects Europe and India via the Persian and Arabic language areas. One of the keys to this history, he believes, is the figure that was known in eighteenth-century German folk theater as *Hans Wurst*, *Pickelhering* or *Kasperle*, and in Italy as *Arlecchino*. This figure corresponds to the Indian *Vidūṣaka* or *Vidushaka*. The fact that *Vidushaka* is the point of origin of the character is elucidated, according to Pischel, by the many shared and specific personality traits and plot functions with which the diverse traditions endow the respective personages. Particularly important is the character's inclination to create scenes of violent "cudgelling" or "drubbing," historically "among the most popular of stage effects" (22). Since the character of the *Kasperle* is functionally entwined with puppet theater as a whole, the genealogy that places the origin of the character in India is valid for that dramatic form in its entirety. Jacob has the merit of having identified one of the intermediary links, the Turkish character of the Karagöz, who, as Jacob has also shown, is identified in some traditions as a gypsy (23f.). The gypsies, who originated in India, as a philological research tradition of the late eighteenth and nineteenth centuries had painstakingly established,[25] were therefore, in Pischel's eyes, the main agents of the transfer of puppet-play to Western Asia and eventually Europe.

Pischel's argument departed from an earlier work on the *Vidushaka*, namely Johan Huizinga's 1896 doctoral dissertation in Indo-European studies.[26] Huizinga had avoided developing a transfer argument along the lines Pischel proposed. Instead, he had argued for a mythopoetic structure inherently bound up with Indo-European linguistic patterns. One German reviewer promptly pointed out that Huizinga had failed to resolve the question of whether the figure of the *Vidushaka* was "originally Indian."[27] While Huizinga's work was useful to Pischel for its philological detail, the argument structure diverged. For most German historians, origin, genealogy, transfer, and hybridization were of greater importance. This type of argument could be established also in the form of cultural exchanges. Leipzig linguist Ernst Windisch (1844–1918), one of the most authoritative Indo-Europeanists of the period, had for instance argued that Ancient Greek drama had influenced Indian forms of theater.[28]

In general, a plethora of philological works that sought to trace the trajectories of migratory motifs and literary genres had been appearing since at least the 1840s. The model of comparative linguistics, with its tremendous pedigrees of language families, no doubt inspired this type of argument. Suzanne Marchand has proposed that the main context for this type of concern lay in the ideologically compromised doctrine of "diffusionism" pioneered by Ratzel's anthropological geography in the 1880s.[29] Yet it would seem that the tradition of literary research in question was actually older. Moreover, at least in the case of Jacob, there appears to have been relatively little convergence with Ratzel, who tended to highlight geographical determinism as providing explanations for the differentiation of humanity (also in racial terms), and whose geopolitical notions naturalized European domination. The biographical high points of Jacob's affinity with the diffusionist family of scholarly pursuits are marked by phases of admiration for the renegade Austrian art historian Josef Strzygowski (1862–1941),[30] and later on Frobenius. Yet, their bibliography hardly figures in Jacob's core works. In fact he found Ratzel's *Völkerkunde* (Ethnography) "horrendous," although he regrettably never explained his reasoning.[31] By contrast, he frequently quoted the philosopher-ethnographer Ernst Grosse (1862–1927), in particular the latter's 1894 work on "primitive" art.[32] Grosse here rejected the common racist models of explanation,[33] chided many of the determinist notions and the overall Eurocentric dismissivism of scholars in the field, including frequently Ratzel, and propounded an analysis of art forms in connection with basic forms of socioeconomic organization in hunter societies. His approach was comparativist rather than genetic. This latter feature did not impede Jacob's reception of Grosse's work, however; and in many regards the approaches actually overlapped. The key point for transfer-based cultural history was to renounce the diffusionist aim of presenting an argument on the history of humanity as a unified whole.

In a period that also saw the emergence of *Theaterwissenschaften* as an independent field of cultural study,[34] concern for the practical history of theatrical performance had increased sharply. In Halle, Jacob even struck up friendships with classicists, most prominently Wilamowitz's old friend Carl Robert (1850–1922), whose literary analyses also included practical aspects of Ancient Greek dramatic performance as drawn from archaeological evidence.[35] Jacob was invited to Robert's home where Halle classicists performed Goethe- and Greek-themed silhouette pieces, the latter based on vase painting, a specialism of Robert's.[36] In general, the study of theater was a work of affective engagement that regularly went along with amateur performance. Far from being a naïve type of historical argument as seemingly laid out by Pischel, the transfer and hybridization template of *fin de siècle* literary studies also had reflexive meaning. It entailed the contamination of disciplines, the lifting of the boundary between the classicist and Orientalist spheres of historical argument, and the blurring of the distinction between lectern and stage. For Jacob, it was clear that the classicists had conspired against him to suppress his message when at a conference his presentation, which had been supposed to include a silhouette demonstration, failed on account of technical negligence on the part of the janitor.[37] The aesthetic effect was as important as the rational argument. Many of these aspects were clearly relevant also for Huizinga, even though the latter's readiness to include historical argument in this notion of the hybridity of the world was less pronounced, if far from absent, as his later medievalist works show. Since the Orientalists regularly traveled to Leiden, Huizinga was also acquainted with many of them, including Littmann, whose works he trawled for anthropological evidence when he wrote *Homo ludens*.[38]

Karla Mallette has argued that transfer and hybridization arguments were germane to Italian and Spanish Oriental studies where they served for developing an understanding of nationhood that included and celebrated the Arab heritage of especially Sicily and Andalusia.[39] While this is a highly significant finding concerning the uses of Orientalism—or "Counter-Orientalism," as Mallette would have it—in Southern Europe, a broader historiographical perspective would nonetheless reveal that the argumentative template in question was more widely in use.[40] Pischel did not even remain alone in his use of the framework of the rectoral address for asserting the importance of studying hybridization. Much to Jacob's delight, Littmann, too, used the beginning of his 1930–1 stint as rector of the University of Tübingen for a discourse on Oriental-Occidental entanglement, in which he expressed hopes for a future *Ausgleich*, an equalizing settlement, between east and west.[41] The connectedness of human cultural forms provided a template of argument whose use was more widespread than is easily recognized today. The genre of east-western genealogy produced a rich bibliography of which Jacob was one of the keenest followers. Yet, a gaze into his annotations reveals that little of this literature has since enjoyed the privilege of canonization. By contrast, the opposite type of argument, the affirmation of the self-sufficiency of European history, was more easily assumed into disciplinary canons. There was a tacit structure of exclusion at work, of which fin-de-siècle and interwar period scholars were well aware. This structure existed across a broad range of historical and philological approaches; and it had emerged from previous patterns of exclusion and competition which had been drawn up in romantic-era philology.

In the early nineteenth century, the revolutionary fervor of the Rankean approach to historial writing had sought to discard the late-enlightenment tradition of seeking to grasp historical development across the globe in a universal vein.[42] The liberating effect of the rejection of universal history in terms of the sheer practical work of historical writing cannot be overestimated. However, the imbalances thereby created bedevil the discipline until today. The heritage of philology in this matter is often downplayed, even though Ranke had been trained as a classical philologist in Leipzig, and, good disciple that he was, he saw no merit in the absurd situation, as his teacher Hermann had put it, in which one would not be able to explain why "for instance the Bashkirians, an age-old nation, ... would not have the right to demand *Sachphilologen* for themselves."[43]

Reaffirming the irrelevance of Orientalist studies remained a pattern of the discipline of historical writing across Europe. The Belgian medievalist Henri Pirenne (1862–1935) arguably provides an instructive case for the twentieth century. Pirenne became a canonic authority of historical writing, not merely as a result of his many pioneering contributions to the emerging field of social and economic history. His status as a standard reference in the history of the discipline also hinges on his posthumous *Mahomet et Charlemagne*, in which he argued for what has become known as the "Pirenne thesis," the notion that the end of antiquity in Europe was marked by the disappearance of gold currency and diverse southern and eastern Mediterranean trade items, in the seventh to eighth centuries CE. According to Pirenne, this disappearance was the consequence of the rise of Islam, which destroyed ancient trading networks and sealed medieval Europe off from access to the eastern and southern Mediterranean sites of gold-mining. Europe had thereby been forced, as well as been permitted, to develop further *en vase clos* (in a closed chamber).[44] Marc Bloch, in his equally canonic study of "Feudal Society," echoed this view, and even this formulation.[45] He further expanded the argument about European history *en vase clos* to include, as additional separators, the various incursions Western Europe suffered along its southern, eastern, and northern rims in the ninth to tenth centuries. Pirenne's argument was cast in severe doubt already in the context of its earliest formulations in articles, years before the appearance of the monograph. His opponents argued, for instance, that one could find evidence of continuing trade relations after the emergence of Islam; or that the decline of gold and the rise of silver coinage was more complicated than Pirenne had envisaged.[46] Yet, none of the critics has been granted the same degree of canonicity. The structure that favored the isolated understanding of European history reigned unchecked. For this reign, it was irrelevant that Pirenne's argument actually challenged many traditional notions about Europe's succession to classical antiquity and shifted historical agency from Charlemagne to Muhammad.

As Ranke's and many other nineteenth-century scholars' careers demonstrate, philology and history were adjacent fields. Arguably, their formation as distinct fields was a process of interdependent differentiation, in which either side would strategically occupy the counterposition of the other. Discussion in the history of the humanities has been remarkably oblivious to this interdependence. A good example is the much-debated notion of the relation of modern historical writing to what the philosopher Karl Löwith called the "secularization of eschatology."[47] Löwith's category has the inbuilt flaw of only paying attention to the theology of *eschaton*, which translates into the future-orientation and the goal-directedness in common European philosophical notions of the historical process as a whole. Oddly, the other end of monotheist theological understandings of the time of the world, on the side of creation and Paradise and its loss, has received no comparable coverage. This is odd, because the question of whether European orientations toward various antiquities bore traces of a secularized echo of the theology of the beginnings of the world appears to be quite obvious.

It would appear that nineteenth-century philologists developed notions of temporal order in which antiquity and its diminished afterlife were dominant. Even outside of the study of actual antiquity, in the reconstruction of prehistoric linguistic forms, the expectation that historical development entailed decay and corruption of previous perfection was a widespread—and increasingly ridiculed—trope. Jacob, again and again, voiced his disdain for Praetorius's speculations about "Ice Age Hebrew," which followed precisely the pattern of language history as the loss of the last remnant from Paradise, at the collapse of the Tower of Babel.[48] By contrast, the historians of the era, as has often been noted, tended to work within a future-oriented framework where seeming openness combined with an expectation of betterment, thus a teleological orientation toward a goal and standard of improvement.

In light of this divergence, it is clear that the "secularization" of the theological understanding of world-time took the form of the division of an inheritance. Ultimately, the study of "secularized" theological notions of the historical process would have to take into account the history of the humanities as a whole. The philosophy of history, in its conversation with historical writing, does not suffice to actually tackle this problem. One of the less belabored connotations of the metaphor of secularization is, one might add, the breaking up of previously unified estates. Such disruption generated property claims that nonetheless retained a memory – however feeble—of former unity. Arguably, it is this memory that continues to drive transgression against disciplinary property claims within the humanities as a collective of heirs. In any case, a pattern of this kind appears to have marked the constant attempts of *Realphilologie*, since the times of Wolf and Boeckh, to (re-)create an amalgam of history and philology. As one of the most committed *Realphilologen* of the *realia*-producing field of Orientalism, Jacob was particularly prone to developing similar interdisciplinary tendencies. This inclination largely accounted for the contradictions between the aesthetic and anaesthetic tendencies of his work; and for the relative imbalance in favor of aesthetic discussion that marked his interventions. The ladder on which Jacob agilely climbed to and fro then actually extended between philology, as one of its ends, and history, as the other. While the ends were opposed, they were interlinked; and they were actual parts of the ladder, hence inseparable without destroying the structure as a whole.

2. The Subject of Philology

The study of shadow play, in its contradictory form of both historical anaesthetic and philological aesthetic, was not a self-enclosed domain. As a matter inseparably bound up with the problems of philological *Wissenschaft*, it found its mainspring in referential semantics, in the question of how meaning resided in the access of language to the world. For Jacob this was a matter he discussed most extensively in connection with poetry and the way in which the poetic sensibility entailed access to natural reality. Poetic sensibility was subject to a norm of excellence, which was to be met both by the individual person and by collective national tradition. While Jacob professed the inseparability of natural science and philology, the unity of knowledge he had in mind remained attuned to romantic-era developments in the understanding of scientific knowledge and nature. He was neither a positivist nor a Darwinist. He did not believe in the simplicity, the flatness of sensory access to the factual, nor did he pay much attention to "laws of nature." Further, he did not reckon that the order of natural kinds was flexible, or rather, that such flexibility was of interest to the understanding of the perception of nature.

As was the case with so many other philologists, the animal kingdom occupied a particular position in his understanding of reality. His representations of animals focused on behavioral patterns spelled out through anthropomorphism. Animals, like human individuals and national cultures, possessed a specific moral "character." In 1897, for instance, he sent to Nöldeke an excerpt from a planned, but never accomplished philological study of Arabic animal nouns:

> I would like … to share with you the passage on the jackal. The wolf is a northern animal and unthinkable in Arabia in spite of [Charles] Huber and others. זאב [se'ew] cannot be drawn upon since this [Hebrew] word also does not designate the wolf, moreover the ancient Egyptian word that Erman aligns with it, is taken to mean jackal. In addition, the jackal is utterly insolent, the wolf on the contrary a coward. In my manuscript, to Shanfara's Qasîde I confer Brehm, 2ⁿᵈ volume, 3ʳᵈ edn. p. 43, where it says of the jackal: "As soon as one of them raises his voice the others regularly fall in, and thus it may happen that from an isolated farmstead one can listen to the most peculiar music, since the sounds emerge from all directions of the compass rose." The jackal in general was the image of the famished; starving children wail the wailing of the jackal ('Iqd I p. 82 l. 5). Especially, it [the jackal] steals sheep and camel foals, but on occasion also takes a child …, for it sneaks around the campsite and attempts to intrude, sometimes here, sometimes there, for which reason one also says of a mild wind, which comes now from one direction, then from another, "it jackals" (Tarafa 12, 11). … One still cannot advance beyond Brehm when one discusses animal *lives*, which is regrettable since his material mainly consists of hunting stories.[49]

Jacob's reasons for disclaiming the existence of wolves in the Middle East appear to be obscure. The problem he belabors is primarily a lexical one that concerns the translation of nouns in poems. Shanfara and Tarafa were pre-Islamic Arab poets, the al-'Iqd an Andalusian compilation of scholarship from *c.* 900 CE. Throughout his career Jacob was dismissive of the notion of Semitic philology as a coherent field, since the languages concerned occurred, as he put it, in distinct cultural areas (*Kulturgebiete*); only a "Semitic linguistics" was possible, not a "philology."[50] Nonetheless, for the specific philological problem at hand, he relied on comparison between different Semitic languages, in this case Hebrew and Arabic, with a sideglance toward ancient Egyptian (n.b. not a Semitic language). The reasons for which Jacob opted in favor of the jackal rather than the wolf were drawn from a model, the treatment of animal behavior in Alfred Brehm's zoological studies of "animal life." This model was one of descriptive anthropomorphic animal psychology that Jacob then, as it were, collated with the philological record. In this process, the wolf turned out to be too cowardly to fit the descriptions drawn from the old poets. However, this judgment was a sideshow. More importantly, the very possibility of collating the Early Arabic texts with Brehm already provided evidence for the heightened sensibility and perfect submission to the aesthetic regime that informed the production of the Early Arabic poets. This regime was not time-bound; it aimed for the constant world of world poetry. In principle the regime also applied to Brehm, and by extension to Jacob himself, even though Brehm had made the mistake of basing his observations mainly on hunting anecdotes. Ideally, the poetic observer was not to interfere with animal lives at all; poetry was not a hunt. This also meant, however, that Jacob, unlike Wellhausen, did not embrace the figure of self as animal, not even in comical contexts. In spite of the Brehmian anthropomorphism, then, Jacob retained a strict distinction between the human and the animal. More precisely, reversing Wellhausen's private *topos*, he anthropomorphized the animal, but did not animalize the human.

As mentioned previously, for Jacob, the perception of natural reality, semantics, and aesthetics were immediately and inseparably connected. Yet, late-nineteenth-century biology marginalized the contemplative, poetic observation of the animal and therefore severed the link since it dismissed the specific notion of the subject on which Jacob's practice relied. This was a dramatic threat, for the high degree of unity invested in his notion of the subject of philological-naturalist knowledge had permitted him to give free rein to the fragmentation of the object of this knowledge. To be sure, Jacob held a notion of the systematicity of human knowledge in high regard, and he was interested in technological instruments, and even, early in his career, in physiological phonetics.[51] Nonetheless, his written work is marked above all by unbounded aggregation. His practice of *Sachphilologie* provides an almost ideal example of the philological accumulation of fragmented knowledge, which he compiled into somewhat makeshift short chapters in books with little pretense to coherent lines of argument. If the understanding of an integrating subject, of a specific philological sensibility underpinning the aggregate, was disabled, what remained was mess.

Jacob's procedure was, it bears emphasizing, not merely a matter of practice, but a research program:

> One can only understand Early Arabic poetry when one thoroughly examines the realia, otherwise one does not attain a position of one's own vis-à-vis the Arab scholastics, as following them would be tantamount to explaining the Old

Testament only in accordance with the scholastics. What a colossal step backward from [Wilhelm] Ahlwardt to [August] Fischer. [added above the line: "I have lost the courage to continue fighting in this field."] Ahlwardt still worked with a veterinarian and considered keeping a camel, for Fischer everything is made from printer's ink, Arabia is full of buffalos that are hunted with arrows from the heavy wood of Grewia, therefore by idiots.[52]

This program entailed that knowledge of natural reality was to have priority in lexical research (word semantics), as conducted by Ahlwardt (1828–1909), and not as conducted by Fischer (1865–1949)—one of the regular enemies in Jacob's correspondence—who had characteristically made a fool of himself over Grewia. Philological recourse to natural reality would also permit the bypassing of learned traditions of lexical semantics, the "scholasticism" against which Jacob railed. In this manner, *Realphilologie* was to demonstrate the superiority of properly scientific philological practice over other non-European forms of scholarship. These latter forms had allegedly neglected, or lost, their initial, natural access to the *Sachen*. Yet, the methodological advantages of the philologists of the real were squandered by their *Wortphilologie* competitors at home. Modern German Arabist philology had itself succumbed to scholasticism and in this way deprived itself of access to reality. The *polemos* at hand was a self-referential civil war. In the end, *Realphilologie* abandoned just as many connections to non-European scholarship as did *Wortphilologie*. Insofar as philological knowledge implied a dialogical structure—for instance, as a hermeneutic enterprise—it assumed the character of an echo chamber in which one only heard oneself. The desperate vehemence with which Jacob protested in the same letter against what he called the *Versauung unserer Wissenschaft*, the "screwing-up of our discipline" (with yet another porcine metaphor), perhaps points to an underlying awareness of the futility of his research program.

In these respects, Jacob's sense of the frailty of philology was arguably similar to Wellhausen's. Yet his reaction to the predicament was different. In the inconsistent manner of quotidian practice, Jacob's philology was often eager to abandon its linkage with history and embrace a radical presentism. Over the course of a spirited discussion of Ottoman politics, in a letter written during a journey to Turkey, Jacob appropriated some of the contemporary critique of historicism for tackling the malaise of the Ottoman "sick man of Europe":

Recently a cadre of the Japanese ministry of education came to visit and learn thoroughly about Turkish matters of schooling; one could see clearly that Japan shows an interest in the recovery of Turkey. I have learned a lot … from the discussions. Both the Turk and the Japanese were extraordinarily quick-witted and it was a pleasure to listen. Everything the Japanese noted the Turk tended to explain historically, in response to which the former once said: "If we had derived everything from history, for a long time yet we would not have arrived at where we are now." [… This] retort was spoken right from the bottom of my heart. The historically-grown [*Gewordene*] is absolute nonsense. That was Schopenhauer's great error: will is not the evil, but the good principle. Pitted against will—that which is in accord to reason—stand time and space, the historical, as the realm of Ahriman. With truly Satanic cunning, the historical in all possible guises seeks to deflect will from its high aim. ... Turkey essentially suffers from a surplus of historical sense. The thought imposes itself on me here everywhere; one only has to be clear that historical sense does not depend on historical knowledge.[53]

In this discussion, then, Jacob rehearsed, if somewhat coarsely, Nietzsche's criticism of Schopenhauer and of the modern obsession with history (in the second and third of the *Untimely Meditations*). National aesthetic education was not to be based on the historical—in spite of the prominence of historical research questions in Jacob's oeuvre. The principle of "will" overrode the orientation toward the past. Classicism was problematic in part because of its insufficient readiness to assert itself, its aping of historical models. The reality, the world to which Jacob's research program claimed to regain access, was inextricable from the principle of will.

Nonetheless, historical knowledge, if established in a defensible, scientific manner, could be a laudable achievement, though Jacob was far from placing historical writing on as high a pedestal as Wellhausen or Nöldeke did.[54] "Historical sense," a *topos* that sought to capture the irrational, intuitive quality of historical writing, was in principle, in Jacob's usage, a positive term. For instance, when in 1929 he surprisingly showered Arthur Rosenberg's study of the 1918 revolution with high praise, he regretted that this "outstanding historian" faced, in the faculty at Berlin, the opposition of Wilamowitz, "who does not have the slightest vestige of historial sense (according to him Bavaria had Ludwig's I salon affectations of Greekdom [*Salongriechelei*] to thank for its autonomy!!!)."[55] Rosenberg (1889–1943), an ancient historian of Jewish background who had trained with the increasingly nationalist and anti-Semitic Eduard Meyer, had defected from the political right in 1918 and joined the Independent Social Democrats, then the Communist party.[56] Littmann was so incredulous that his friend would praise a scholar of this political stripe that Jacob repeated his assessment in the next letter: Rosenberg's book was the best available, "detached and objective," although "of course I do not agree with everything."[57] Jacob clearly enjoyed the irritation he caused, in this case by dissociating "historical sense" from political affinity. But beyond their mere provocation his comments on Rosenberg express his notion that the proliferation of the historical sign system into other areas of life, such as politics, had to be halted. Historical sense was to be relevant only to its proper domain.

The liberation of "will" from its historical shackles was a prime purpose of Jacob's aesthetics and constituted the chief theoretical reason, beyond mere matters of taste, for rejecting the Greeks. From Erlangen in 1906, he wrote to Nöldeke:

By the way, our mathematician told me recently at the bowling alley that Euclidean mathematics was the dumbest fraud ever committed in his field. The pre-Columbian zero in America is a fact, I have ordered the literature and compared the calculations in the original. ... The entire talent of the Greeks is essentially a sense of forms. Yet the form is a fetter of the spirit, and we no longer have time for such things.[58]

Here spirit (*Geist*) and will stand for the same thing, the intentionality of the subject. The immediacy with which Jacob jumps from the "pure" knowledge of mathematics to aesthetic problems indicates that something is amiss in the order of thoughts the letter expresses. In spite of the embrace of will as prime principle there is no clear sense of primacy in the domains in which will or spirit manifests itself. Contrary to appearance, it is not the case that Jacob invests aesthetics with primacy over e.g. politics, let alone mathematics. For his course of argument this constitutes a problem since, given the lack of substantial content to will/spirit, the principle assumes, as it should, a purely formal character. It is the mere form of a project, the mere form of a transgression of the narrow boundaries of (historical) time and space that Jacob's discourse appears to idealize. It was therefore of crucial importance to Jacob's project to produce terms that would help to understand his tentative category of "will" that he developed ever so casually in his correspondence. It was this problem that ran like a common thread through his decades-long study of, and practical involvement with, shadow play.

3. Antihumanism on the Stage of Shadows

During his Erlangen years, in 1907, Jacob joined an artistic iniative for the resuscitation of silhouette theater in Munich, the *Schwabinger Schattenspiele*.[59] As he pointed out in various publications, recourse to specific traditions in German literature, especially the romantic period, in which the Swabians Justinus Kerner and Eduard Mörike had shown an interest in shadow plays, was a helpful factor that demonstrated the national rootedness of this genre of drama.[60] The transfer that had infused this Asian art form into European folk culture had taken place centuries earlier; it was nothing recent. Yet the passage through national culture was indispensable if the form was to regain lost ground. Indeed Jacob hoped, as he wrote to Nöldeke, that the "reanimation of German shadow theater" would prompt a renewal of German theater as a whole.[61] National theater, since the 1770s, had served as the prime site of the educational-aesthetic project of forming German national culture. This project could sound universalist overtones, as in the case of Lessing's or Schiller's treatises on the "Education of Humanity." However, the motif of national renewal preceded its universalist application. In any case, the poetics and the theorization of drama in the age of Goethe had revolved around the project of the national theater. Over the course of the nineteenth century, the project underwent several waves of renewal, but was gradually also subjected to criticism.[62] Nietzsche's individualism, while at first declaring itself to be in league with Wagner's aesthetics of the national *Gesamtkunstwerk*, arguably dealt a heavy blow to the classicist-humanist instantiation of the project. Brutally, Nietzsche undercut classicist humanism's inbuilt sense of egalitarianism, its application to all Germans, or all humans, alike. Jacob's antihumanist sense of the shadow theater embraced only some of the radical implications of the Nietzschean unraveling of the sense of cultural education built into the aesthetics of the theater. Jacob did not make room for critique of the national and didactic orientation of the overall project, but rejected the human form and the sense of idealized embodiment that was so important for competing projects of artistic reform. Therefore, his aesthetic notions represented a tendency toward compromise, as Goldziher intuited with some clarity when he remarked to Nöldeke on the ultimately "inexplicable" character of the *polemos* with the classicists: "J[acob] does not actually think that from our youth onward we should read *Šanfarâ* instead of Homer ...."[63] The *polemos*, however acerbic, was well-contained and limited in its reach. Yet arguably, this was the reason that debate did not remain locked into sterile antagonism and moved ahead in the twentieth century.

The Munich art scene was large, diverse, and densely knit. On the occasion of Paul Ernst Kahle's (1875–1964) 1911 publication of images of Egyptian shadow play figures in Becker's new journal *Der Islam*, Wassily Kandinsky wrote Kahle a letter that expressed his admiration for the figures, reproductions of which were included in the *Blaue Reiter* almanac of the same year.[64] The episode does not merely illustrate the richness of the reservoir of Orientalist knowledge which the modernist revolutionaries of the artistic and literary spheres had at their disposal. At the core of modernism, there was not merely a transfer between actual objects of art, such as the Egyptian shadow play figures and the expressionist "synaesthetic" color theory and the accompanying step into abstraction Kandinsky undertook precisely in this period; but as Jacob's theoretical efforts indicate, there was also an intellectual contiguity. Kandinsky presented his transition into abstract painting as a movement through theater reform and a modernist *Gesamtkunstwerk*. His contributions to the *Blaue Reiter* almanac, indispensable in this regard, even contained a direct juxtaposition of one of Kahle's figures with the abstract *Composition No. V* (Figure 11).[65] The history of transfers from

Figure 11. Wassily Kandinsky, *Composition V*, 1911. Heritage Image Partnership Ltd/ Alamy Stock Photo.

the exact sciences into emergent artistic modernism, and in particular abstraction, has often been told.[66] That of the transfers from humanities scholarship into artistic modernism has remained strangely obscure, even if it was arguably more extensive and more given to mutuality.

To Nöldeke, Jacob explained the aesthetics behind the Schwabing undertaking as follows:

> It is about the natural connection of poetry and painting and we hope that we will be able to do away with a number of the drawbacks [*Schattenseiten*, pun unintended] of the big theater. The most important thing is that the poet can shape his figures entirely in accordance with his own intentions and everything personal—which above all our theater lives on, even though it is a disturbance factor for true art—is eliminated.[67]

The heritage of an eighteenth-century aesthetic that emphasized unimpeded genius and regarded the brittleness of the material as the only legitimate obstacle to the realization of inner vision is clearly recognizable in this passage.[68] Unquestioningly, it was a given that any kind of aesthetics that proceeded by setting up actual rules for artistic representation was illegitimate. The guideline was artistic autonomy, as postulated in romantic literary theory in particular, with the iconoclasm of 1770s *Sturm und Drang* as a model. The distant opponent, in the form of a self-evident point of reference, was Aristotelian dramatic aesthetics as reformulated through the medium of French classicism in Germany in the first half of the eighteenth century.

Srinivas Aravamudan, in an important discussion of the literary aesthetics of Orientalism, has suggested that the flourishing of various genres of "Oriental tale" especially since the eighteenth century demonstrates that the teleological history of the "rise" of the realist novel seriously misrepresents European literary history.[69] The prose form of the novel, unarguably, was a chief genre for substantiating, if in a rough-and-ready manner, the understanding of "realism": as marked by plausible, miracle-free plots that involved empirical-psychological agents placed in environments mimetic of recognizable, typically national spaces and communities.[70] Aravamudan's revisionist discussion makes clear that Oriental tales—including those genres that emulated non-European literary forms—were integral for the development of the repertoire of anti-realist narrative devices that became constitutive of literary modernism. Even in Aravamudan's account, however, the dominance of realist aesthetics is not cast in doubt for the second half of the nineteenth century. Arguably, this is due to a general underestimation of the significance, even dominance, of other literary genres in discourses on poetics. Jacob and many others failed to even consider the novel as a relevant genre. Certainly, in a German-speaking context, but perhaps also elsewhere, the poetics of drama was of far greater significance.

To Jacob the solutions of eighteenth-century dramatic poetics—which had centered on dropping the French and then the Roman models[71] in favor of the "naturalness" of Shakespeare and Ancient Greek drama—appeared insufficient. He rejected the entire literary, theoretical, and philological field that had emerged around the idealization of Greek tragedy in particular. "Antiquity, with its doctrine of hubris [and nemesis as the forces propelling tragic conflict], is inimical to genius, i.e. to culture."[72] The tendency of tragic plot to humiliate the great was clearly offensive to Jacob. Years later, in 1918, in an effort to acquaint himself with different aspects of Greek drama, he attended a seminar on Aristophanes' *Acharnaeans* taught by his young Kiel colleague Werner Jaeger, widely regarded as Wilamowitz's most promising student.[73] The comical humiliation of the powerful in this play, which instead glorified the inventive trickster-poet, was more to Jacob's taste. To boot, at the end of the First World War, there was an obvious political context to the teaching of this particular play, whose hero privately opts out of the Athenian war with Sparta. Jacob's enjoyment of the *Acharnaeans* could not be reduced to a notion that aesthetic values had to be understood exclusively *sub specie aeternitatis*. The tragic was centered on the human form only in order to debase it; the comical did not display the same enmity toward genius and culture in general.

Jacob was not alone in having misgivings about the disturbance of the dramatic work of art through actors. For instance, the motif was prominent in the 1910 theorization of puppet theater by the British-German performer and critic Edward Gordon Craig (1872–1966). This effort, in a number of respects, bore remarkable resemblance to some of Jacob's thought. For Craig, too, the actorly body was a disturbance of artistic expression, to be replaced by a stand-in, the puppet, which would better serve the purpose of anchoring the spectatorial imagination. For this purpose, the puppet was to be oversized.[74] The French critic and actor Antonin Artaud also outlined, in an influential series of interventions from the 1930s to the 50s, which he dubbed the "theater of cruelty," a vision of stage reform that was directed against the psychological realism of the older, naturalist theater.[75] The ensemble of Artaud's appeals and manifestoes contained various discussions of Balinese dance and connoted the widespread Orientalism and "primitivism" of modernism.[76] Romantic-era *topoi* arguably permeated this entire tradition of argument. At least in the case of Craig it is possible to establish a connection to Heinrich von Kleist's 1810 meditation on the puppet theater, which received increasing attention in the years after 1900.[77] It would also be necessary, in a more full-fledged analysis, to discuss the affinity of these types of theatrical renewal to *völkisch* theater reform movements in the same period.[78] In this latter regard, Jacob's aestheticist tendency toward the delicate and un-tragic might also mark a point of divergence.

Various Orientalist colleagues—though far from all[79]—shared Jacob's fascination for silhouettes and puppets. Along with his students such as Curt Prüfer and Theodor Menzel, Littmann and their mutual friend Kahle also contributed to the literature in this marginal field.[80] Kahle was the only one who took up the study of the thirteenth-century Mamluk-era Egyptian satirist Ibn Daniyal, who had mostly written for the shadow stage and whom Jacob was the first to have brought to the attention of Orientalists, if to little effect.[81] The underlying question of a germane dramatic tradition in Arabic-language literary history dates all the way back to the Goethean problematic of the "natural forms" of literature and their uneven distribution the world over.[82] Becker's student Hellmut Ritter (1892–1971) began to work on the Karagöz tradition during his military sojourn in the Ottoman Empire during World War I. He relied on a prominent player, the director of the shadow stage at the Sultan's court, as informant and published three volumes, ever increasing in length, of Karagöz plays until the

1950s.[83] Becker himself also showed keen interest in the overall line of research. In the period before 1914, he enthusiastically staged performances at his home for the enjoyment of Hamburg society and colleagues at the Colonial Institute, which soon developed into the new university.[84] In the 1920s he formed an intimate friendship with the much younger puppeteer Harro Siegel (1900–1985).[85]

The reasons for the rejection of actors were somewhat elusive and perplexing. There were theoretical features to the problem, but also more palpable ones. Jacob explained the matter to Nöldeke in the following manner:

> Our big theater nowadays can hardly justify the funding it receives from municipalities and states; without the personal, sensual interest in actors and actresses the auditorium would always remain empty. Art hardly matters there any more; the understanding of all plasticity, which is after all an essential element of this type of stage, has been lost so thoroughly that a modern drama without a bedroom scene on stage has become a rarity. This situation can foremost be remedied by the shadow stage.[86]

So the "art-disturbing factor" that marred theatrical performance was not primarily the physical obstinacy of actors' bodies, of their expressivity and mannerisms. Rather, it was the sexual interest of audiences in the bodies of actors and actresses. The formative force of "plasticity" vested in the artistic mind was overpowered by the natural forms that drove eroticism. The readiness of theatrical performers to cater to this type of interest had supplanted art. Sexuality, then, since it was drafted into the counter-aesthetic constellation, inadvertently became the site where nature and art diverged and collided.

In what was perhaps an oblique response to this inconsistency, Jacob was willing to extend his aversion to humanity altogether, which he was able to set in opposition to nature *tout court*. In the winter of 1908, when Nöldeke sharply reproached him for a misogynist passage in a previous letter, Jacob defended himself: "It is entirely alien to me to have a much higher opinion of men than of women. The only respite is retrieving nature where humans have not yet improved on it in their manner."[87] So paradoxically, it was humanity in general that disturbed art. The connection between this resentment against the human and the aesthetics of shadow play was close, for in the very same letter, Jacob also continued with his reports from the Schwabing undertaking:

> I am not yet in agreement with everything. The silhouette in general remains too hard; blurred colored shadows in the manner of the painted porcelain of Copenhagen would be more to my liking. It is, however, the misty image [*Nebelbild*] that would capture the poet's dream inventions [*Traumgebilde*] most perfectly. Man as an actor for me constitutes a relapse from art into reality. Some reviews of the Schwabing venture spoke downright dismissively of the big stage on which human colossuses trample around.[88]

In spite of the high value placed on the natural then, in order to substantiate his dislike of human actors, Jacob was willing to play up the importance of the fantastic element in art. His devaluing of realism as a legitimate aesthetic was connected to the rejection of sovereign reason as a contributor to art. Dream constituted an aesthetic ideal to him that induced him to write an entire study of oneiric motifs.[89]

Since the renewed shadow play was to bring together poetry and painting, the unification of different arts into something akin to a Wagnerian *Gesamtkunstwerk* was a prominent aim. Yet it was significant that it was not music that was charged, in the inherent competition of the arts, with the role of prime medium of reconciliation, other than in the Wagnerian as well the early-Nietzschean contexts.[90] Jacob's vision for the arts did not aim at installing a sovereign medium on top of all the others; rather, he seems to have favored a vision in which all *polemos* was to cease as disagreements were repealed. Indeed, this was not a far cry from Littmann's dreams of setting up an irenic aesthetics of the Oriental in the form of an "Arab and Abyssinian Laocoön." Nonetheless, the frictions between the arts never quite disappeared on the plane of theory.

The project of shadow theater actually emerged alongside a competitor that soon became far more successful: the cinema. Jacob was keenly aware, especially after the First World War, of the challenge this novel integration of the painterly and the poetic entailed. Yet, silhouettes still figured as the superior aesthetic project:

> It is not actually because the silhouette theater is able to lend its objects color and language in addition to mere motion that the shadow stage is so superior to the cinema; but because it is not just a mere mirror of the world of appearances— as the old wise men and poets of the Orient often erroneously opined—much rather, by dint of the nobility of art, it strives for the highest that humankind is capable of. Above all its strength lies, as already mentioned, in its ability to unite different branches of art for the purpose of a shared effect, and thereby to extend the boundaries of the single branch.[91]

The convolutedness of this discussion indicates an embarrassment. The advent of sound and then color in film were not far off in 1925. Already the following year, the Berlin-based scissor-cut silhouette animator Lotte Reiniger (1899–1981), after three years of work, premiered one of the first ever feature-length and colored animation films, the Orientalist themed "The Adventures of Prince Ahmed" (1926),[92] which adapted episodes from the Arabian Nights based on Littmann's new multi-volume translation.[93] The swift technological changes of 1920s cinematic history voided Jacob's argument.

Jacob himself was involved, in 1934, in a project of touring with a group of amateurs who performed, with authentic Chinese silhouette figures from Jacob's own collection, a number of shorter pieces translated from Mandarin. The director of this effort was a Kiel-trained scholar of German literature, Max Bührmann (1904–1976), former academic assistant to Wolfgang Liepe (1888–1962), who had taught German literature at Kiel. Liepe had also acted as director of the town's Theater Museum, only founded by Liepe's predecessor Eugen Wolff (1863–1929) in 1924, the year after Jacob had served as rector of the university. Around the time of the opening of the museum, Jacob's then-assistant Theodor Menzel had been charged with negotiating the purchase of Karagöz figures from Turkey for the exhibition, via Johannes Kolmodin in Istanbul.[94]

Menzel was also working on shadow play. He expressed regret that Jacob was becoming "increasingly ponderous and inaccessible"[95] at the time. Wolff's eagerness to display Turkish silhouettes, however, is a clear sign that Jacob's interests were being recognized by his Germanist colleagues. A few years later, Liepe brought Chen Quan, the Chinese doctoral student and connoisseur of Sichuan shadow play, to Kiel to work on the German reception of Chinese literature.[96]

This research environment fell apart in 1933. Liepe, whose wife was Jewish, was punitively transferred to Frankfurt in 1933, after a particularly ugly conflict with another Germanist at Kiel. The Liepes emigrated to the United States in 1936.[97] After plodding on for a while under Liepe's enemy and replacement, Bührmann relinquished his academic career in order to become artistic director at the Opera of Duisburg. The performers of the 1934 tour were mainly students, including the daughter of the Berlin Sinologist Ferdinand Lessing (1882–1962), who had spent her childhood years in China and had therefore mastered the spoken language with natural ease.[98] UFA, the dominant German film production studio, apparently toyed with the idea of producing a film version of the performance of Bührmann's group, which had been favorably reviewed in the press.[99] Jacob highlighted with particular pride that the show had been performed at the Imperial Yachting Club in Kiel;[100] and that one of the friendly reviews had appeared in the Nazi daily *Völkischer Beobachter*.[101] In spite of these indicators of political palatability, the film project never came to pass in the Nazi period. It was not until 1957 that Bührmann found the opportunity to collaborate on the transformation of a performance into a short film, *Farbige Schatten*, directed by Herbert Seggelke. In this context, Bührmann was invited to travel to the People's Republic.[102] His theater continued to operate under the Orientalist name, devised by Jacob, of *San Mei Hua Pan*, or "Society of the three plum blossoms."[103]

The ensemble had toured a number of German cities in 1934, during their inaugural string of performances, which included performing in professors' homes, such as Littmann's in Tübingen, museums, and smaller theaters. Jacob, who was responsible for arranging a considerable number of the venues, accompanied Bührmann and the young student actors and even lent his voice to the role of the emperor in one of the plays. The entire project appears to have been a source of joy to the retired scholar who lived all by himself. A lifelong bachelor, he had continued to share a household with his mother and sisters, moving them along from Halle to Erlangen to Kiel, until they eventually all died on him. Questions of competition between silhouettes and the movies had disappeared, much as the pre-war hopes for the renewal of national theater through shadow play. Bührmann was actually in touch with Lotte Reiniger who, like Ferdinand Lessing, emigrated from Germany in this period.[104]

In practice, then, irenicism between the competing forms of representation won out. Indeed, in the context of his ever-expanding work on the theater of silhouettes, puppets, and masks, Jacob even softened in his judgment about Ancient Greek theater. In his *History of Shadow Play*, for instance, he conceded that the use of masks on the "big stage" of Greek theater indicated the impact of the puppet theater and its deeper antihumanist sensitivity, "not understood so far by our theorists."[105] Ironically, Reiniger, when she found an opportunity to make first-hand observations of a living culture of shadow play in the 1930s, went to Greece of all places, where a variant of the Ottoman Karagöz play remained popular.[106] And yet, Jacob's irenicism was limited. The Greeks were integrated at a low level of priority into the overall great chain of Oriental-Occidental theatrical sensitivity toward non-human actors. Abandoning the competition between shadow play and film only served to reveal the shared counter-aesthetics, the polemic opposition of both silhouettes and the cinema against other regimes of artistic perception. By the second half of the 1920s, Jacob's aesthetic ideas no longer appeared to be aimed at engendering a *Gesamtkunstwerk* reconciliation of all the arts. Rather, anti-classicism, as antihumanism, had taken center stage.

If one follows Siegfried Kracauer's classical discussion, film as a form of art is precisely based on a de-centering of the human form that coincided with the "redemption of physical reality."[107] Kracauer had little to say on animation, but maintained that film was centrally opposed to tragedy and that this opposition explained the aesthetics of cinema:

> If film is a photographic medium, it must gravitate toward the expanses of outer reality—an open-ended, limitless world which bears little resemblance to the finite and ordered cosmos set by tragedy. Unlike this cosmos, where destiny defeats chance and all the light falls on human interaction, the world of film is a flow of random events involving both humans and inanimate objects. Nor can the tragic be evoked by images of that flow; it is an exclusively mental experience which has no correspondences in camera-reality.[108]

In these remarks Kracauer uses tragedy to express the notion that different aesthetic regimes connote different understandings of reality, different ontologies. The world of tragedy is governed by destiny, it is an ordered "cosmos" whose prime material is the "interaction" of humans alone. By contrast, the world of cinema is "limitless" and contains uncontrollable "expanses" of material objects along with human bodies. It is a world of things where even the distinction—so important for the original Boeckhian formulation of *Realphilologie*—between the human-devised and the natural disappears. This disappearance, it is worth adding, also marked Jacob's understanding of *Realphilologie* whose starting point was the poetic perception of nature.

For the referential semantics of Realphilologie, the ancient trope of the "book of nature" was particularly proximate: The world could be read; it was open to semantic explication. This existential metaphor, in Hans Blumenberg's sense of a trope structuring the history of human relations with the world,[109] reoccurs in Kracauer's discussion of film:

> However purposefully directed, the motion picture camera would cease to be a camera if it did not record visible phenomena for their own sake. It fulfills itself in rendering the "ripple of the leaves." If film is an art, it is art with a difference. Along with photography, film is the only art which leaves its raw material more or less intact. In consequence, such art as goes into films results from their creators' capacity to read the book of nature. The film artist has traits of an imaginative reader, or an explorer prompted by insatiable curiosity.
>
> All this means that films cling to the surface of things.[110]

It is then the decipherment of the surface of things in the book of nature that marks the aesthetics of the cinema. The film artist is not merely a reader, but an epigrapher of natural reality. In its figures, its tropes, Kracauer's aesthetics of the "redemption" of the surface encounters philology. This encounter is not prevented by the manner in which Kracauer's analysis clings to the medium of photography and its only seeming adherence to an aesthetic of realism. For, Kracauer's point is precisely that cinema is not a realist art form in the conventional sense, because the human body and mind, and the unity and coherence of the phenomenological world of the human, do not occupy its center, as he makes clear precisely in the chapter in which he discusses the function of actors' bodies in film.

Peter Szondi's groundbreaking 1956 dissertation had meanwhile formulated the position that for "modern" drama, since the Renaissance, the exclusiveness of human interaction on stage had been the constitutive rule. If for the ancients, the tragic drama had displayed the purge after a contamination of the worlds of gods and humans, this principle had not re-emerged along with the form of written drama in the Renaissance.[111] Kracauer insisted, without overt reference to Szondi, that film differed from drama precisely by its departure from the centrality of the representation of human dialogue. This also entailed abandoning the classicist exaltation of the human. And in this rejection of the centrality and exaltation of the human in aesthetic forms as well as in the understanding of what was reality, he met with Jacob, if involuntarily. Similarly, Szondi met with earlier classicist theorists of drama in his acceptance of these notions, even though he criticized these scholars.

For Jacob, the opposition to the supremacy of tragedy entailed an antihumanist notion of the human. This notion built on his understanding of "will" or "spirit," already touched upon in the previous section. His insistence on the primacy of will did not amount to a celebration of Cartesian *ratio*, nor to a simple appropriation of the "will to power" that had marked Nietzsche's later writings, at least in the versions then known to the German reading public. Rather, it was his fascination with and work on dreams and their impact on literary form that provided the key to a further-reaching understanding of the reality of humankind and the way in which reference and semantic meaning *tout court* could be grasped.

4. The Reality of Dreams

Jacob's respective works, in particular his *Märchen und Traum* from 1923, constitute a forgotten entry into the bibliography of the literary study of the fairy tale.[112] Since the time of the Grimms, fairy tales had been the key figment in the international philological imagination of folk authenticity. By 1923, the field had moved in a direction in which German Orientalists were particularly slow to follow, perhaps on account of the laggardness of their Germanist colleagues who likewise missed this boat. With the Finnish literary scholar Antti Aarne (1867–1925) serving as somewhat of a figurehead, fairy tale and folk tale research had moved toward the broad-scale classification and comparison of plot structures.[113] Aarne's works, though written in Helsinki, were published in German, as the language continued to hold a certain sway over the humanities, especially in minority-language area universities in Russia. Despite the commonality of language, however, the reception of Aarne's publications on the German-speaking scene appears to have been feeble.[114] The complex and muddled transition into formalist and structuralist research programs in early-twentieth-century linguistics and literary studies went along with a tendency to reduce the importance of transfer studies, at least insofar as the latter aimed at identifying the origins of motifs and forms. The contradictory relationship between connective anaesthetic historicization and disconnective aesthetic presentism that continued to inform German Orientalist studies of literary texts slowly became marginal.

In defiance of these developments, Jacob's sense of the nature of a motif, such as that of dreaming, remained sharply distinct from that underpinning the typological approach. The synthetic model for the study of fairy tales "in world literature" he emulated was the Germanist Friedrich von der Leyen's (1873–1966), whose works, however, aimed at an unmethodical positing of ultimately racial (Indo-European) commonalities. In a study of the presence of fairy tale motifs in larger epic traditions, such as the Eddic one, von der Leyen systematically rejected notions of the transfer of motifs from biblical and other Jewish, e.g. Talmudic, traditions into Nordic contexts, while he recognized similar transfers of Byzantine tales and speculated about Indian origins.[115] Nonetheless, von der Leyen's approach followed methods developed by a theologian, Hermann Gunkel (1862–1932), who since the 1890s had worked on what he called the "fairy tales," episodes of wondrous narration, in the Old Testament. Gunkel's 1917 synthetic account of this work pushed Bible philology onto yet another terrain and founded a novel school of criticism that focused on literary form.[116]

In Jacob's opinion the fairy tale was defined by its reliance on the "supernatural" as a plot element, as opposed to such forms of narrative literature that only admitted *rein menschliche Verhältnisse*, exclusively human interactions (*MT* 12). A fundamental point of division in this debate was the notion of the conceptual and historical priority of myth over fairy tale, or of fairy tale over myth. The former assumption was that of the dominant nineteenth-century line of research whose most prominent representative was Jacob Grimm; the latter one was brought forward especially by Gunkel and also von der Leyen (*MT* 21). Jacob declared himself a cautious partisan of the latter approach. For him, the fairy tale assumed the status of a primal form of literature and therefore of an access route into the core of the human. The key element that had propelled the emergence of the fairy tale was, in Jacob's view, "wish" or "desire," that is to say, it was psychological in nature (*MT* 26). Granting such poetic centrality to "desire" allowed for the liberation of literature from the constraints of rationality. Jacob criticized Aarne as well as the followers of Gunkel for imposing a criterion of logical consistency on the stemmatization of fairy tale types, so that a more consistent version would be accorded greater proximity to the *Ur*-form (*MT* 27f.):

> whenever we have the opportunity to break through to what is original, most of the time its characteristic marks are inconsistency [*Sprunghaftigkeit*], feeble motivation, fantastic transformation; the subject, inhibited in its agency in many ways, often provides the only thread between adventures and experiences that are strung together loosely, without causality. In this incoherence, there is an external

affinity to dream. Yet, the affinity is not only outward; much rather it is an inner relationship in essence, for both the fairy tale and the dream are the children of wish. (*MT* 28)

Jacob's explication of desire was broadly Freudian: "the most primitive drive of the Ego" was wish fulfillment. In dreams, the subject acted as the "building master" of this pursuit that produced a loose, "contra-tectonic" construction from the after-images of desired objects (*MT* 29). Dreaming lacked the element of explicit will; all dreamt action was simply in response to drives. The most intense wishes were residual after-images from childhood; this fact explained the affinity of this period of life to the dream-derived fairy tale (*MT* 30). Nonetheless, Freud could not be spared the criticism of having gone "too far" on the "new paths" he had broken; his model only fitted certain types of dreams; and the role of erotic desire had been "immeasurably exaggerated," especially by his followers, "even if one had to admit that the water of life, the magic wand, Fortunatus' inexhaustible purse, Danaë's shower of gold, and other [motifs] can only be explained in a sexual manner" (*MT* 34f.). In order to provide a counterweight to his Freud references, Jacob accorded equal rank in oneiric research to—although he mentioned him far less frequently—the Leipzig psychiatrist Emil Kraepelin. In order to dispel the notion that he associated himself with a problematic research trend in a one-sided manner, Jacob moreover demonstrated his familiarity with other, more obscure authors in the field of dream psychology, such as the medical researcher Friedrich Hacker, the physician and sexologist Havelock Ellis, or the Norwegian philosopher John Mourly Vold.[117]

Jacob believed that there was cultural variation in the significance assigned to dreams, which in turn accounted for variation in the subjective force of dreaming between, say, Orient and Occident. It was a deep-running trait of Oriental culture to regard the erratic combinations of "half-consciousness" as "revelation of a profoundly different world of higher order" (*MT* 37f.). In the Occident, "one appears to have been, here and there, more critical; the Germanic word for 'dream' probably is connected with 'to betray'" (*MT* 38). It was perhaps the biblical corpus of dream stories that had prompted the topic to rise to greater prominence in European folk literatures. In any case, however, the relationship between dream and literature was intimate, especially in the context of drama, for "dream is after all in terms of its form a drama" (*MT* 41). The specific type of drama that displayed the greatest proximity to dreaming was, for Jacob, "Oriental shadow play," because of its "transparent, translucent, colored figures of limited mobility that act instinctively and make a ghostly impression" (*MT* 42). Shadow play also was a nighttime literary form since it required the dark. As a result of the constant movement of its images, dream moreover enjoyed an essential connection to the cinema (*MT* 44).

Certainly, the translation of dream into plotline and mimesis was not immediate; but dream, and beneath it desire, was the basis from which fiction then emerged. The difference could be captured by the adaptation of a Freudian aphorism: "In the fairy tale … the optative present of the dream is transformed into the optative perfect" (*MT* 48). The perfect tense, in the classical and Romance languages, was the tense of narration that entailed order and rationalization. In this distinction, also that between desire and will ultimately resided. Jacob believed—with particular reference to Hacker's dream protocols—that in dreams the ego was frequently split up into "subject and object," as for instance in such episodes when the dreamer saw himself as a corpse. This psychological phenomenon, which was based on the slackening of the sovereignty of consciousness, reason, and will, informed the modern reception of such doppelganger myths as that of the Egyptian *Ka*, or even that of the Ethiopian *malak*, which, however, did not resurface in Jacob's published work.

As a literary motif, the split self (*MT* 64–8) was widespread in romantic narrative. This was, for instance, prominently the case in Adelbert von Chamisso's 1814 poem *Die Erscheinung*, in which the author encounters himself writing at his desk and engages in a contentious dialogue with himself in order to figure out which one of the interlocutors is the true and authentic self. Even more prominent in terms of its cultural notoriety was the same author's fairy tale novella *Peter Schlemihl's wundersame Geschichte*, equally from 1814, whose protagonist famously sells off his own shadow (in exchange for the purse of Fortunatus). In this work, Chamisso achieved neat integration of the motifs of the split self and the shadow.[118] Jacob only referenced Peter Schlemihl in a footnote (*MT* 67 n.1), in which he also mentioned two further authors as sources for the motif of the fragmented self. The first of these was Georg Brandes, who in his famous 1870s lectures on nineteenth-century literature had relied on interpretations of Tieck, E. T. A. Hoffmann, and Chamisso, in order to illustrate how romantic reflexivity, in the form of play-within-a-play structures, could translate into a motif of existential exile (as in the case of Chamisso's Schlemihl).[119] The second authority Jacob cited was the Freudian psychoanalyst Otto Rank, who had brought together literary, mythological, and ethnographic readings of the doppelganger motif and had, just like Brandes, discussed the same two texts by Chamisso Jacob also mentioned.[120] Rank had in particular claimed the legibility of the motif of the duplicate self in terms of narcissism, homosexuality, and the beginnings of religious notions of the soul. Dream was then a doppelganger of revelation, and the history of any religion a pathology of the self.

Jacob's references indicate a vast associational space constituted by the motifs of the fragmented subject and of shadow play. To be sure, he avoided following the authorities he listed in his annotations in the matters of self-love, reflexivity, and exile. Instead, he rather stressed that the elusiveness of selfhood was closely connected to the many distortions of temporality that marked both sleeping and waking dreams. Moreover, he insisted that material differences such as Oriental climates (*MT* 73) and, more importantly, the use of hallucinogenic narcotics (*MT* 75–81) produced spatially variegated dream cultures and likewise informed the histories of religious writings, for instance the Bible as well as Islamic scriptures. All in all, dreams needed to be accorded some space in order to be able to travel at all. This space was provided by a philology of the real that could experiment with the cultivation and consumption of, say, hemp, which Jacob briefly attempted during his Greifswald years, following a journey to Morocco.[121]

In this panorama of the oneiric dissolution of the sovereign self, Jacob's notion of what constitutes the human becomes more palpable. There was a considerable degree of robust materialism and attunement to developments in the contemporary sciences involved in the approximation of *Realphilologie* and physiology. Comparatively few remnants of earlier alignments of this type prevailed, for instance the reflex of eighteenth-century climate theory. Jacob's relative lack of interest in matters of race is noteworthy in the context of the period; but even more noteworthy is his Freudianism and the alignment of literary form with a fragmented subjectivity that knows, and wholeheartedly embraces, such shades of unreason as "semi-consciousness" and "contra-tectonic" construction. Jacob's refusal to indulge in the Wellhausenian flight into irony and *uneigentlich* meanings had to do with this understanding of selfhood. The sovereignty over referential meaning vested in the exercise of irony, this Pyrrhic victory of the logos, was disabled in Jacob's account from the start. The aesthetic pronouncements Jacob scattered across his works and correspondence then actually served to state a point about the explication of meaning as the core problem of philology.

The price for Jacob's semantic procedure was what one might call interiorization. For him, too, the state of dreaming was recognizably a placeholder for the religious event of revelation. In another line of *Realphilologie* discussion, this type of event had been explicated through the hypostatization of naming and thereby through the subject as a person capable of being an addressee of dialogue. Jacob's transformation, with the help of contemporary psychology as well as romantic-period literary tropes, of the analysis of myth into that of dreaming entailed an understanding of the subject as a fragmented, only partly conscious, desire-driven compound with uncertain boundaries. The dreaming subject tended to annex formerly outward terrain; it was not dialogic. The space in which a named godhead might address it was sharply reduced. If the dream was theatrical, or cinematic, its dialogue was in fact one between different portions of the self. In crucial ways, dreaming was not moored to reality; and yet, it was supposed to provide the foundations of an aesthetic that would in turn provide the foundations of a philology of the real. This passage from dream to philology was not negotiated in careful detail. It may have seemed sufficient to Jacob that in his understanding of art—as imagined, with Grosse, from its primitive beginnings—the notion of beauty as bound to form disappeared. Strangeness, wonder, and the sublime, by contrast, remained in place. Jacob's aesthetic, inasmuch as it was also a theory of art, was wedded to the problem of post-beauty that Hegel had already posited as a marker of the romantic-modern, and the death of art, a century earlier.[122] This is another reason why Jacob's aesthetic notions were entangled with a practice of historicization: They were subliminally aligned with a tradition of aesthetic thought that recognized in itself, in the very act of theorization, a sign of the end of art.

In general, the aesthetic combinations in *Märchen und Traum* (and other works) occurred in a frame of reference that Jacob shared with younger modernist intellectuals. For instance, the parallelism of motifs that exists between Jacob's and Walter Benjamin's projects is in some regards uncanny. It constitutes a distant family resemblance that points to a shared genealogical background, a productive structure that brought forth similar traits, even if there were not any traces of direct reception. Not only did Jacob consistently rely on the romantics to formulate modernist positions and future aesthetics.[123] He also championed Freud and the blurring of the distinction between sleep and waking,[124] and showed interest in the symbolic processing of childhood, toys, ghosts, dreams, and drugs.

An obvious difference is Benjamin's deployment of a sophisticated framework of Marxist and other political thought and his overall engagement with older philosophy. And yet, the compatibility of political-economical thought with the philological tradition, indeed the contiguity of Marxist and literary "theory," is amply borne out throughout the canon. Even in Louis Althusser's work—one of whose chief endeavors was the development of antihumanism as a principle of theoretical thought—the key category of "interpellation," through which the array of ideological state apparatuses calls upon and generates the subject, is spelled out through the example of Christian religion; and in a key passage, Althusser returns to Exodus 3:14, the divine name of "I am that I am," in order to uncover the ideological foundation of subjecthood.[125] This return probably responded to Jacques Lacan's use of the same passage, within a cosmos of reference that comprised Augustine, Spinoza, and Kierkegaard; but also, and more prominently, Freud, whose recourse to philologists such as Robertson Smith forms a linkage of reception that ties twentieth-century Western Marxism and structuralism to Orientalist philology.[126]

This contiguity also pertained to the critique of "historicism." Jacob, as a militant of the philology of the real, did possess, if in little developed fashion, a set of notions about historical theory that provided relevant resources. Benjamin in turn was aware of the philological apprehension that the effect of historicization was anaesthetic, and that this effect was oddly connected to the world-historical continuum of the uses of puppets and masks. He laid out the necessity of a "critique" (his own scare quotation marks) of the nineteenth century as a "dream collective" in terms,

> not of its mechanism and cult of machinery but of its narcotic historicism, its passion for masks, in which nevertheless lurks a signal of true historical existence, one which the Surrealists were the first to pick up. To decipher this signal is the concern of the present undertaking. And the revolutionary materialist basis of Surrealism is sufficient warrant for the fact that, in this signal of true historical existence, the nineteenth century gave supreme expression to its economic basis.[127]

In the English version of this passage, the connection of a "narcotic" with a "passion" may appear puzzling; but in fact, the German original speaks of a *Maskensucht*, an "addiction to masks." The connection in question, in the quoted passage, is then simply a continuum.

Nonetheless, in this regard, Benjamin's analysis is perhaps too simple. He misses some of the antagonistic entanglement of aesthetic and anaesthetic in the compound of philology and history; and this neglect occasionally even appears to generate inconsistencies within his own project. For instance, when in "Convolute Z" of *Arcades* he discusses the theme of dolls and automatons, Benjamin quotes a passage by Huysmans, who asserts the superiority of the shop window mannequin over classical sculpture.[128] Benjamin appears to read the quotation as a diagnostic intervention into, rather than a symptom of, the collective imaginary of the nineteenth century. He fails to realize that Huysmans actually half reiterated, half parodied a philological *polemos* when he inserted the mass-produced sculpture of capitalist modernity into the aesthetic schema of competing antiquities.

A cognate imbalance of judgment is discernible in Benjamin's highly critical reception of Roger Caillois's musings on the praying mantis, a prime instance of 1930s surrealist cultural theory. Caillois, in an anti-Darwinist vein, posited that the features of the animal indicated the workings of a purposeless "mimetic drive" in nature. This drive prompted organisms to imitate and represent matters outside of themselves. The observation of natural mimesis was then semantic in kind. In the case of the praying mantis, the behavior that particularly captivated its surrealist interpreters was the propensity of the female of the species to devour the male during or after sexual intercourse. The animal, a philosophical mime, represented something otherwise concealed about the very nature of sexual difference. This "reading" extended onto the terrain of anthropological analysis, specifically of the hybrid of modern myth and psychoanalytic theorem that was the *femme fatale*. The human, as an animal, engaged in mimesis of the same underlying natural reality as did the mantis.

At Benjamin's instigation, Theodor Adorno wrote a cautiously critical review[129] of the extended version of the 1934 text that Caillois had published as a separate brochure in 1937 before it was also included in his 1938 *Le mythe et l'homme*.[130] In a letter to Benjamin, Adorno explicitly condemned the "antihistorical" and "cryptofascist" tendency of Caillois's notion of myth. This notion uncritically celebrated submission to an inherently violent nature. Instead, the aim ought to have been a historical-materialist critique of the underlying conditions that allowed violence to appear natural, although it was inherently social.[131] Benjamin, on the occasion of another 1938 contribution by Caillois, relied on even harsher formulations in order to lambast the author's "metaphysical hypostatization" of the "historically contingent character traits" of the contemporary bourgeois.[132] In *Arcades*, the reference to Caillois is not openly critical, but focuses on the alleged proximity of the mantis to automatism, and thereby to the romantic puppet motif, since its reflexes supposedly function almost in their entirety even after beheading.[133] As an animal the precise perception of whose habits would beget poetry—indeed as an animal that embodied, in its eternal gesture of preying prayer, the supposedly natural bond between religion and violence—the praying mantis rather exactly complied with models for writing the *Realphilologie* of animals. Apparently, André Breton, a latter-day Ahlwardt, even kept mantises as pets.[134] Yet, the failure Adorno and Benjamin diagnosed on the part of the surrealists to properly historicize the perception of animal nature was also their own. They did not recognize that the non-historicization of the symbolic meanings at hand was entirely consistent with the earlier partition of territories between philology and history. The harshness with which Benjamin and Adorno attacked Caillois was related to the fact that the genealogy of the theoretical idiom in which they operated was opaque. In the Francophone context, to be sure, it was not Alfred Brehm who had supplied the pattern of allegorical writing about animals, but his near-coeval, the observational entomologist Jean-Henri Fabre (1823–1915). In spite of the latter's notorious autodidacticism, the further literary models for the blending of zoology and poeticized prose were shared, perhaps all the way back to *Physiologus*. The additional step of working this textual model into the scholarly analysis of the meaning of spatially and temporally distant poetry had been made by Orientalist philologists decades before it occurred to the surrealists.

In Jacob's case, too, the passion for masks, puppets, and silhouettes belonged to the sphere of the aesthetic, as distinct from, and yet interdependent with, the anaesthetic of historicization. The complication of historical reality through the tense interconnection of aesthetics and anaesthetics was the product of Orientalist philology rather than that of surrealist modernism. More precisely, the autonomy and distinctiveness of modernism was far more questionable than one might find comfortable admitting. Following Heinz Dieter Kittsteiner, it may be permissible to see in Benjamin's motif of revolutionary awakening from the nineteenth-century sleep of dreams a case of submerged genealogical continuity with nineteenth-century historical *as well as* philological discourse.[135] While it may be somewhat uncomfortable, a figure like Georg Jacob would be part of this genealogy. Benjamin was tied to the world of academic philology by diverse connections, not merely by his thematization of the field in his writings, or his unsuccessful attempt to submit a habilitation thesis in German philology at Frankfurt University, but also by his friendship with Gershom Scholem, whose doctoral degree had been won at the University of Munich, in Semitic Philology, with Fritz Hommel as nominal supervisor.[136]

5. Semiticist Japonism in Löwith and Heidegger

The most frequented intersection of aesthetic modernism and actual Orientalism was not the Middle Eastern variant, which in art and literature had been monopolized by romanticism and mid-century academic painting. Rather, since the 1860s the avantgarde painters, with literature in tow, increasingly relied on novel patterns of Orientalist appropriation that were to eclipse the old. These new models included, for instance, the Balinese one. But the most prominent was Japonism. The dominant account of Japonism in the history of art has been about the contribution of the reception of Japanese artworks to the achievement of formal abstraction; a secondary narrative has also concerned a similar process with regard to modernist design and material cultures.[137] Both of these accounts tend to leave out the Japanese side in the dialogic structure of reception in question. Neither of them quite captures the place Japan came to enjoy in early-twentieth-century European philosophy. This development occurred in the context of the overall competition of antiquities and therefore was mediated by philological aesthetics. The philosophical variant of Japonism impinged crucially on the formation of theory outside of the spheres of art and literature.

In the second half of the 1890s Ernst Grosse became one of the prime champions and purveyors of Japonist aesthetics within the sphere of German scholarship, in the aftermath of his flirt with the "primitive."[138] Grosse's knowledge of Japanese culture was primarily obtained from a Japanese art dealer residing in Paris, Hayashi Tadamasa (1853–1906), whose impact on French modernism was also considerable.[139] After Hayashi's demise, Grosse spent the years 1908–13 in Japan, where he purchased works of art for the German government, although he apparently never acquired workable knowledge of the language.[140] In 1914 he returned to his status as a *Privatdozent*, later promoted to a titular professorship without salary, rather unusually commissioned to teach both philosophy and ethnography, at the University of Freiburg.

Jacob, given to all Orientalist enthusiasms, naturally grew into an admirer of Japanese art, as expressed for instance in his letter to Littmann dated July 5, 1914,[141] even though he later focused his Far Eastern ambitions primarily on Chinese cultural history. The Japanese provided the supreme model of a refined as well as natural and self-contained civilization that had remained untouched by the ills of Semitic monotheism, in spite of the massive cultural impact of western modernity it had experienced since the 1860s. In the Nietzschean distribution of competing antiquities, which radically opposed the dominant classicist philhellenism, the moderns were beholden to the "Judaeo-Christian" cultural tradition and separated from the Ancient Greeks by an unbridgeable gulf. The Japanese by contrast dwelled on the other side of the divide as relatively uncontaminated pagans.

One of the clearest formulations of this take on the status of Japan in German thought was put forward by the philosopher Karl Löwith (1897–1973), who had been the first of Heidegger's students to achieve a *Habilitation* degree. Because of his descent from Jewish converts to Lutheranism, his status as a *Privatdozent* in Marburg was revoked in 1934, and he went into exile, initially in Italy, with a fellowship from the Rockefeller Foundation. Narrowly escaping the first stage of racist legislation in Italy, in 1936 he transferred to Japan, where he had been appointed as a professor at Sendai University, through the intercession of Heidegger's erstwhile student Kuki Shuzo (1888–1941). From there, Löwith was once more lucky enough, in the summer of 1941, to find an opportunity to move to the U.S. In 1942–3 he wrote two articles in which he sought to explain, to a wartime American reading public, traits of the "national psychology" of the Japanese, as he put it with clear recourse to the German tradition of *Völkerpsychologie*. After another visit to Japan in 1958, he published a German article in which he brought together translated passages from the previous two texts and also updated some of his earlier observations.[142] His diaries concerning his Japanese exile were posthumously published, as well as a book-length autobiographical account written at that time.[143] Within the varied oeuvre of the philosopher, this corpus forms a hybrid between the writing forms of Orientalism—the travel diary and the essayistic, generalizing account of culture—and critical philosophical argument.[144]

Throughout, Löwith stressed the "contradictory" and "amphibian" character of Japanese culture. The Japanese inhabited, according to him, a building with two floors, whose functional differentiation was complete: one was native and familial, the other Western and more broadly social. Modernization had thus produced a fissure in cultural identity (LSS 576), yet somehow this fissure remained a mere crack in the surface:

[g]enuine Japanese life, feeling and thinking remained essentially unchanged. ... Their wonderful volcanoes, mountains, woods and streams are still the home of local deities. The family shrine in every household is a perpetual reminder of the religious customs and cults of the Greek and the Romans and paganism is still a living power, as fresh and genuine as before Christ, and one discovers on the other side that Europe is still a Christendom, inclusively its anti-Christianism. (LSS 545)

For Löwith, 1930s nationalist Japan represented a political culture that was authentically continuous with the pre-modern polity, unlike European "totalitarian states":

Japan is the only modern nation with a genuine national religion, where religion neither transcends nor interferes with but supports the social-political system. The Nazis in Tokyo envied them for this, for they realized that the cult of the Führer and the propaganda of a Nazi-millennium cannot ever compete with the originality and antiquity of Japan's Shinto cult ...

Such identity of the political and religious system is possible only in a country which has no Christian history and with a people whose individuals are not emancipated personalities, deciding upon religion and political allegiance by their own opinion and conscience. To achieve such primitive unity of the religious and political system in Europe one would have to fight Christianity which has separated the things which are God's from those which are Caesar's, creating, thus[,] the misalliance of a "Political Theology" and a "Theological Politics." The last great attempt to reconcile the duties of the good "citizen" with those of the good "man" was the "civic religion" in Rousseau's Contrat So[c]ial (IV, 8), but the result was his own confession that pagan "patriotism" and Christan "humanité" are incompatible. (LSS 549)

This political assessment reveals Löwith's emerging critique of the fusion of modern European politics with the theological heritage. This fusion took the form of the "secularized eschatology" of modern European historical thought, with its progressive understanding of the historical future. In his full-fledged formulation of this critique of modern European historicity, the 1949 *Meaning in History*, it was ancient Greece that provided the positive counter-image. A rupture within the ancient world between Athens and Jersualem had produced the particular developmental path from the prophetic and future-bound theocracy of the Hebrews of scripture into European modernity.

It is clear from Löwith's Japonist writings that the experience of his sojourn in the Far East, and specifically his political observations of wartime Japan, could equally serve to substantiate the contrast at hand. One should add the caveat that Löwith was not entirely uncritical of modern Japan, for instance of the indolent manner in which the Japanese public accommodated the extreme cruelty of the war against China. In two of the articles he mentioned how the retirement of the victorious and atrocious conqueror of Nanjing to a Shinto shrine that was devoted, of all things, to "mercy" was perceived as characteristic and apparently "compatible" with cultural norms (LSS 563, 584). Löwith also scorned attempts by nationalist Japanese philosophers to interpret Hegel through the symbols of the Japanese Empire; or to explicate Confucius' Analects with the help of Hitler's *Mein Kampf* (LSS 559). Nonetheless, he remained relatively blind to the short-term conjunctures of Japanese nationalism and the less obvious opportunistic adaptations to current politics among his Japanese philosopher friends. The only one of these whose work he accorded any intrinsic philosophical value was not Kuki, but rather Nishida Kitaro (1870–1945), whose rootedness in Zen Buddhism, from Löwith's point of view, ensured the independent character of his engagement with European thinkers.

Arguably, Löwith's overall negative perception of cultural hybridity was then driven by a sense of the rootedness of philosophical thought in culture. As a European he was convinced that he would never be able to attain more than a superficial understanding of Japanese cultural forms. Neither did the Japanese, in spite of their considerable skills in European languages and the hard work they invested in the study of western textual traditions, achieve more than a sterile reproduction (LSS 558) of European thought. The cultural divide rested on unifying, incompatible "principles" (LSS 561). For the Japanese side, these resided in intuition, feeling, and sensitivity, which provided them with an understanding of "nothingness" that diverged in a profound (yet elusive) manner from the logical-metaphysical Western understanding of being as substance and "nothing" as its negation. The Japanese, as they gave precedent to emotion and momentariness, voided the conceptual grids of European thought.

> "Even our supreme moral principle, the loyalty to the Emperor," [Nishida] points out, "has simply developed on emotional grounds." The great mistake of almost all foreigners is to think that the Japanese Emperor is either Mr. Hirohito or a god residing in Tokyo. For the Japanese he is neither the one nor the other. The concept, as Nishida points out, is emotional, not precise. (LSS 561f.)

In this manner, the Japanese, although relying on the principle of nothingness or emptiness in their national aesthetics, were able to circumvent the destructive "nihilism" of the European, especially German, philosophy Löwith repeatedly analyzed.

   In aesthetic terms, this particular culture of negativity translated into an absence of the distinction between subject and context, foreground and background, where the background represented the totality of being. Rather, summarizing what he considered Nishida's stance, but articulating some of his own emergent notions on the nature of history behind the mask of the Japanese philosopher, Löwith suggested: "What really is is eternally what it is. The whole movement of history is like the motionless movement of a waterfall, which has the clear-cut shape of a ribbon and yet is totally shapeless, changing at every moment and yet always the same" (LSS 561). These pronouncements may cause legitimate unease. They inflict an implausible degree of uniformity and essentialization on Japanese culture. They mark philosophical Japonism as a variant of Saidian Orientalism that continued to provide philosophical and theoretical tropes well into the post-war period, if one thinks for instance of Alexandre Kojève's notion of the achievement of post-histoire in Japan through national aesthetics;[145] or even of Roland Barthes's *Empire of Signs*.[146] In addition, it is unsettling that Löwith adopts a Japanese mask to express his own philosophical thought; and that he renders Japanese culture into an essence while when he speaks through his adopted mask he criticizes precisely the essentialism of European metaphysics. While superficially writing for western publics, Löwith's texts on Japan represent a conversation the philosopher was having with himself; and, further, a conversation of dubious sincerity. For, Löwith does not appear to own up, not even to himself, to the fact that his discussion of Japan is merely instrumental, and that the actual subject matter is entirely elsewhere.

   In Löwith's discussions Ancient Greek thought plays an ambivalent role. In some regards it provides foundational elements to the western tradition; in others, it stands apart from this tradition. In the first footnote to the 1960 text, Löwith attempts to sort out the "similarity" between Greek and Oriental notions of the cosmos: "By contrast, Greek cosmo-politics and its proximity to the Oriental have hardly been noticed because Greek philosophy has only ever figured as the beginning of the European and not also as a transformation of the Oriental tradition" (LSS 571). This intermediary status of ancient Greece corresponds to the romantic-era Creuzer position according to which Greek thought consisted of transfigurations of Oriental mysteries. Löwith's note bears similarity to Jacob's ambivalent perspective on the Greeks, as both secondary Orientals and founders of a tradition apart, although a vile one from Jacob's point of view and a salutary one from Löwith's. Structurally, though, both authors return to the same commonplaces, which were also frequented by other scholars.

Löwith's 1943 remarks on Japanese aesthetics, for instance, provide a mirror image to Erich Auerbach's simultaneous juxtaposition of the Homeric epics and Hebrew scripture, in the first chapter of *Mimesis*. For Auerbach, the Hebrew literary tradition was superior and altogether more formative for the European literary tradition as a whole, because of its ability to represent the depth, continuity, and unity of time. Hebrew scripture had figured out—unlike the Homeric epics—a way of nesting plot events in the temporal framework of the diegesis in a manner analogous to the pictorial relation of foreground and background. Löwith just turned the value judgment around: the Japanese renunciation of background—which was in effect somewhat similar to Auerbach's Homer—was ultimately the superior choice; and with Nietzsche (LSS 573f.) it seemed attractive, even necessary, to abandon the religious principles of the European tradition altogether, insofar as possible.

For both Löwith and Auerbach, however, the motivation of their juxtapositions was not least to counter the manner in which an anti-Semitic argument that had originated in Orientalist philology and its manner of setting antiquities in competition had sought to write the Jews out of the European tradition.[147] Löwith's Japonism, along with the notion that cultural spheres were holistic and founded on unifying principles, was above all a function of the philosophical response to anti-Semitism. It was in order to function as contrast to a unified European modernity as comprising the "Judaeo-Christian" tradition as a whole that Japan had to be a monolithic cultural unit of Zen Buddhist, non-conceptual, anti-substantialist nothingness. Löwith's writings on Japan, in spite of all the cultural detail they reproduced, were therefore far less grounded in "experience" than one might superficially be tempted to assume. Neither his actual presence in Japan nor the undoubtedly harrowing biographical experiences with German anti-Semitism dictated the patterns underpinning his interventions. Rather, he latched onto an intellectual tradition that went back decades.

It is unlikely that Heidegger took note of his former student's English-language essays on Japan. By way of a curious coincidence, however, just around the time when Löwith was returning to his wartime work in order to publish his final 1960 statement on Japanese culture, Heidegger put forward a piece of philosophical Japonism of his own, in the form of a dialogue: *Aus einem Gespräch von der Sprache. Zwischen einem Japaner und einem Fragenden*, rendered into English as "A Dialogue on Language between a Japanese and an Inquirer."[148] This dialogue was the fictionalized record of a conversation that had taken place in 1953–4 when Heidegger had received a visit from the Japanese scholar of German literature Tomio Tezuka (1903–1983).[149] Tezuka had been a student of Kuki's, who in turn had audited Heidegger's lectures in Marburg in the 1920s. Heidegger's *Gespräch* is a soundly polysemous text that, unlike many of the Platonic dialogues, gave both participating characters considerable weight, and that reveled in the indirectness of its course of argument. Nonetheless, as the starting point one can recognize the status of Kuki's attempt to grasp a principle of Japanese national aesthetics with the conceptual tools provided by European philosophy. This undertaking consists in the confrontation, but not the resolution, of difficulties of understanding across cultural divides. Such difficulties are, however, representative, from Heidegger's point of view, for the overall problem of hermeneutics. In contrast to Löwith, Heidegger pursues the arguably more interesting question of what even makes otherness and incomprehension possible in the first place. In the early portions of the dialogue, the interlocuting characters share their experiences of the difficulty of understanding Kuki's aesthetic thought. From these passages onward, it is clear that in the matter of incomprehension something more general than the cultural plurality of humankind comes to the fore. The answer to the overall question is to be sought in the philosophical problem of language rather than in aesthetics; and it has to undermine the very concept of "language."

The last portion of the dialogue, the point where the investigation comes to some kind of result, is devoted to the Inquirer's question as to the Japanese word for "language." The question is posed early on, but the Japanese resists answering it, citing a variety of apprehensions about the possibility of translating what the respective term even "means." The primary task of a dialogue with a Japanese, then, must be in semantics. After the interlocutors have established basic agreement on matters of hermeneutics, the questionable rigidity of Western concepts, and the event-character of understanding, the Japanese finally responds to the question and submits the expression *koto-ba* as the Japanese word for "language." He then explains the meaning of the expression by recourse to an etymological analysis. This analysis recognizably conforms to a specific semantic language game, one which Heidegger generally liked to embrace since it provided an alternative to a "conceptual" analysis that would have relied on extensions, qualities, and a hierarchy of subordinate and superordinate concepts. In the dialogue, the Japanese suggests that the Japanese word for language conflates *ba*, meaning leaves, especially the petals of a flower, and *koto*, rendered as "the appropriating occurrence of the lightening message of grace."[150] "Grace" (*Anmut*) is further specified as being an approximate equivalent of Ancient Greek *charis*, explicated by reference to a passage in Sophocles as "graciousness" (*OWL* 46). The Inquirer makes recourse to the same passage and points out that the ancient tragedist couples *charis* with the participle *tiktousa*, "that which brings forward and forth. Our German word *dichten, tihton* [Old High German] says the same. Thus Sophocles' lines portend to us that graciousness is itself poetical, is itself what really makes poetry" (ibid.). In the subsequent exchange, by dint of this etymological play across three languages, the expression *koto* is then further pushed in the direction of the "happening" of poetry as a bringing forth/ forward invested in grace (*Anmut*), and the combination with petals is explicated in this manner (language is the "petals that stem from *koto*," *OWL* 47). Kuki's aesthetics are then reinterpreted in light of this notion. The Inquirer further suggests his unease with the German concept of *Sprache* (language) and introduces another etymological pun, around the word *Sage* (translated as saga or Saying), which equivocates language and myth.

In an earlier passage, the dialogue contains a critique of the cinema, specifically of Kurosawa's 1950 film *Rashomon*, which the Inquirer asserts to have enjoyed. For once, the Japanese is allowed to make the more poignant criticism, when he explains that "we Japanese"—clearly an aesthetic community—"consider the presentation frequently too realistic," with the further explication of this moniker as entailing "that the Japanese world is captured and imprisoned at all in the objectness of photography ... The photographic objectification is already a consequence of the ever wider outreach of Europeanization" (*OWL* 16f.). The English translation of "objectness" levels the excessively fine distinctions of Heidegger's wordplay around *das Gegenständliche* (the objective, objectness), *das Gegenständige* (the obstinate) and *Vergegenständigung*. The latter expression is a pun on *Vergegenständlichung* (objectification) and *Verständigung* (communication, achieving mutual agreement). In the overall semantic field of objecthood, the differential effect hinges on the implication of slight divergences in the quality of the sheer resistance and obstinacy of matter. The world of objects is inserted, as an obstacle, into the very possibility of understanding and communication. The loss in translation is not entirely trivial, since it suppresses possible ontological readings of the Japanese's position that elude the interpretation the Inquirer subsequently proposes. This interpretation identifies the problem with cinematic photography in its participation in technological modernity, whose critique, needless to say, is a staple of Heidegger's writings.

As the recent publication of the philosopher's Nazi period notebooks has demonstrated, this critique carried the meaning of an anti-Semitic *polemos* that was mostly concealed in the published works.[151] The Inquirer therefore lures the Japanese into a covert antagonism toward the Jews. The trap is set by means of the notion of the modern technological takeover of aesthetic forms that in pre-modern times had constituted a regime where *charis* had occurred undisturbedly. Language itself then, from Heidegger's perspective, is destroyed by European modernity, whose most industrious protagonists are the Jews. This destruction is the cause of the difficulties of understanding that persist between modern and pre-modern cultural sensitivities. The semantic language game of etymology is important because it "brings forth" the manner in which the pre-moderns attained mutual understanding within a structure of pre-conceptual mythopoetic *Sage*. Yet, *pace* Hermann Gunkel, for Heidegger there is clearly no *Sage* in the Hebrew Bible. For, why else would the Jews be excluded from the unencumbered community of pre-moderns, the *Verständigung* that according to the dialogue prevailed among the Japanese, Old-German, and Ancient Greek? The confrontation of modernity, i.e. the Jews, with any given set of pre-moderns ultimately just collapses into the schema of competing antiquities, and more specifically the confrontation of Athens and Jerusalem that was the prime genre of this competition. It would not take much effort to show Heidegger's more or less indirect reliance on *topoi* fashioned in the nineteenth century by Renan, or even Wellhausen, specifically the notion of the legalistic rationality of Judaism as a prefiguration of the barren rationality of the purported "age of technology."[152] Heidegger would then turn out to reproduce, not merely an established structure of anti-Semitic argument, which is hardly surprising in a scholar who was, after all, a card-carrying member of the Nazi party. But moreover, in an eerily Jacobean manner, he also suggests the pertinence of both a history of (pre-modern) permeability where the "cultures" are in effortless communication and the philological constellation of an eternal, ahistorical *polemos* between the intransigent positions of Athens and Jerusalem, on the outside of history.

The problem with this reading is that Heidegger's position is, after all, more intricate and not entirely identical, I think, to that of the Inquirer. The punning around *gegenständlich–gegenständig* suggests that there is a more specific notion of the material world at work that drives forward the critique of "realism" in the dialogue. In spite of the manifest vanity with which the dialogue generally favors the position of the Inquirer—who graciously accepts the flattery of his interlocutor almost at every turn—the Japanese is in this case equipped with the subtler argument. In the passage in question, he quickly turns the discussion of realism away from technology and modernity. This also happens to be the point at which Heidegger's analysis decisively diverges from Löwith's position. The distinction Heidegger places at the bottom of the dialogue's critique of "realism" is that between the cinema and the Noh Theater. In order to get a hold on this distinction he borrows considerably from a work by the single-minded Hamburg Japanologist Oscar Benl (1914–1986).

Benl had presented a philological analysis of the Noh-actor Seami's eighteenth-century Japanese treatise on the art of theater at a session of the Mainz Academy for Sciences and Literature in 1952.[153] The extent to which Heidegger copied even verbatim formulations of supposedly general Japanese positions from Benl's analysis of this treatise has been documented in detail by Reinhard May.[154] Notably, the significance of the flower and its petals in Heidegger's dialogue appears to depend on Benl's interpretation of his source text, in which the blossom, in its ability to surprise perception by its unexpectedness, fragility, and transitoriness, is the chief symbol for the effect that constitutes the aesthetics of the theater.[155] In Seami's treatise the ability to surprise mandates that aesthetic teachings remain secret, so that the theorization of poetry does not destroy its ability to generate a surprise effect on the audience. The treatise was actually written, Benl suggests, as a work of instruction whose circulation was meant to remain limited to a family of well-known and successful actors of the Noh stage. The text is remarkable also for laying out instructions for the induction of children and youths into the craft of acting. In such education, the unimpaired acting out of children was regarded as mandatory, whilst authority and command were considered detrimental. The subtle manner in which Benl's discussion speaks to notions of educational reform in twentieth-century Germany is remarkable, and probably constituted one of the less obvious attractions of his work even for Heidegger.

In the dialogue, the discussion of Noh and the aesthetics of theater focuses on the emptiness of the stage, the lack of background that allows for the maximal effect of even the most ephemeral gesture. The chief task of Japanese theatrical aesthetics is to grasp what is meant by the notion of gesture, the explication of the gestural sign. The Inquirer at this point proposes: "Gesture is the gathering of a bearing" (*OWL* 18). This leads to another exchange of puns and culminates in the Japanese's explication: "the gathering which originally unites within itself what we bear to it and what it bears to us" (*OWL* 19), onto which is added the corollary that the "gathering" is also the origin of the meaning of the gestural sign in question. At the core of this, then, is a notion that the aesthetic of the Noh play resides in a meaning-producing confluence or coincidence that seems at most partially accessible to the intentionality and agency of a subject. This confluence is even a pre-condition for the emergence of the subject in question. The Heideggerian position, then, appears to be one that does not aim at reconstituting the subject, the self, through aesthetics, but rather at abolishing it altogether. Unlike Jacob, Heidegger does not bother with a fragmentation of selfhood and psychological interiorization; and unlike Wellhausen, he does not pursue—at all— an avenue of ironic sovereignty over semantics. Rather, Heidegger aims to recast the understanding of the very ontological structure at hand, so that it is reenabled to figure as the precondition of meaning. What constitutes the aesthetic of the Noh stage is that it leaves space for that which is "borne to us," for what the situation lets emerge. By contrast, the cinematic representation of reality presupposes a surfeit of planning and design, and not merely one of technology, so that there is too little space for the necessary "letting be," or *Gelassenheit*, with another Hedeggerian keyword.

Heidegger's speculations about the aesthetics of the Noh Theater align effortlessly with a more general web of thoughts he had been developing for years, on emptiness. It is this emptiness, also associated with boredom—a standing feature of Orientalist travel writing[156] and a staple of Heidegger's analyses of "being in the world"[157]—that he recovers regularly in his Orientalist references. The emptiness in question, he insists, does not entail the "nihilist," metaphysical meaning of a substance of "nothingness," but rather merely the precondition of "being" as a situational happening altogether (*OWL* 19–21). And yet, the antagonism, the *polemos* against modern technology and the Jews, never appears to become boring. In his notebooks from 1939, he remarks about T. E. Lawrence's *Seven Pillars of Wisdom*, whose German translation had appeared in 1936:[158]

The first, boldest book of the great silencing and withholding [*Verschweigung*]. He who only reads descriptions in it and indulges in its telling of "stories" and even discovers just the most recent Karl May in it, who even thinks that Arabia and the Arabs are its subject matter and an episode of the World War is made historical in it, who finally seeks "psychology" in it or the "experiences" of the author, does not have the least inkling and does not see a single one of the seven pillars of wisdom. What happens here is the overcoming of the machination [*Machenschaft*] of Being [*Seyn*] in the form of a knowing, noninvolved endurance of its [the machination's] enforcements and enchantments [*Verzwingungen und Verzauberungen*]—all from the inkling of the foreclosure of other possibilities of Being [*des Seins*], for which [inkling] any essential future human being has to become a *dichtend-denkend* [poetizing-thinking] Inquirer, who rejects all auxiliaries and destroys, already by his hard diffidence alone, all surrogate figurations [*Ersatzgebilde*] of humankind that have been calculated from those of the past.[159]

There can be little doubt that Lawrence, whose substantial interest in Arabia and the Arabs was acute, would have been unable to recognize his intentions in this characterization, which combined semantic density with syntactic acrobatics and was not beyond embracing recognizable Nazi era diction, as in the otherwise unmotivated choice of adjective in "hard diffidence." Nonetheless, quoting the passage is worthwhile, even at full length, because it contains many of the expectations with which Heidegger read Orientalist works, be it philology proper, as in the case of Benl, or travelogues, as in the case of Lawrence. In both contexts, Heidegger admired a quality of withholding and concealment, an abnegation of subjectivity, that could be wielded, as a weapon, against "calculating," technological (and Jewish) modernity and its alleged "machination." This latter concept also includes, as the passage makes clear twice over, the ordinary forms of historicization, of making things historical. For Heidegger, the aim of Orientalism was hardly to provide positive knowledge, let alone tell tall tales of adventures and experiences. Much rather, the Orientalist was to renounce psychology, experience, subjecthood, and historicity, and to embrace instead the amalgamation of thought and poetry. In this way, he was to contribute to a destructive work that would lay the foundations of a renewed, future, and empty humanity. Yet, how much emptiness and letting-be was possible in a constellation that remained at rock bottom legible as sheer anti-Semitism? This *polemos* sustained the substance of a subject, a self that Heidegger had managed to reduce to mere resentment—but not any further. This is what the anti-Semitism of the "black notebooks" makes abundantly clear; and this is also why Orientalist philology, as the chief mediator between anti-Semitism, classicism, and theoretical thought, cannot be written out of Heidegger's way of thinking.

6. The Shadow of the Last Man

The endpoint of German philosophical Japonism, however, does not lie with Heidegger. Rather it lies with Günther Anders (1902–1992), who likewise visited Japan—in the very same summer when Löwith also returned to the country—and composed his own amalgam of travelogue and philosophical analysis as a result of this journey.[160] Anders, *alias* Günther Stern, erstwhile husband of Hannah Arendt, had once studied philosophy with Cassirer and Heidegger in Marburg and written his dissertation with Husserl in Freiburg. His intention to submit a *Habilitation* thesis in Frankfurt came to nothing, and in the following years he worked as a journalist. It was possibly this activity that allowed him to develop a lucid and concrete style of philosophizing whose feigned simplicity has, oddly and yet predictably, not helped his reception. There can be little argument, however, that it was Anders and not Heidegger who offered German- and English-language reading publics the most elaborate philosophical analysis of the "nuclear age," that is to say, the philosophy of history after the atom bomb.[161]

The diary of the journey to Japan—which has not been translated into English— borrows the form of the literary-scholarly travelogue, but only in order to destroy it. In the opening paragraph, Anders scorns the "aroma of the 'Far East'" so common in the genre, and renounces all talk of "exotics or picturesque attractions, temples or Noh plays, Zen Buddhists or Tea ceremonies, pagodas or artful gardens, Chinese lanterns and geishas, and even fishermen and rice farmers" (*MB* 7). The nuclear age, he insists, has "annulled" all cultural distance and all difference of space. Even the roundness of the globe, from the altitude of the airplane that carries him across the Arctic to Japan, has become a matter of individual perception rather than of abstract calculation. Technology has collapsed the difference between globe and landscape. There is no independent aesthetic of the phenomenal space around the subject left (*MB* 16f.). The sudden arrival of a future unity of humankind, which had seemed unattainable before 1945, has done away with earlier distinctions and *polemoi*. Humankind as such is now "antiquated," and in such antiquity all competition and all plurality has been eliminated.[162] The "exotic" is over. Antihumanism has become, not an aesthetic agenda, but a description of the reality of humankind. More precisely, the regime of perception has not gained access to nature, but replaced it.

Nonetheless, to Anders Japan presents a novel environment. He sums up his first walk in the streets of Tokyo as follows:

> Outside at night, prompted by curiosity. After two minutes, I find myself in a seedy quarter of narrow streets, the air is warm and buttery, reminiscence of a vieux quartier, but even the shadiest figures dressed as neatly as a pin. The contents of the bowels of the sea lie all around, fancy fish and species of algae. For the Japanese the world is apparently not only visible, but edible. Inky, oily, bitter, medicine-like smells. Dead ends. Things resembling a brothel. Methods of attraction not nearly as terrorist as in Europe. After ten minutes the Japanese crowd stops being surprising. "People look like Japanese," become a "physiognomical point-zero." I am being looked at, without malice, but with slight hesitation; in fact I am the only non-Japanese ... (*MB* 23).

Even though the telegraphic style, the images of disgust and attraction, and the lines from the phrasebook of touristic emptiness parody the tropes of exoticism, Anders still sneaks in a few markers of generalized distance: For instance, the national aesthetics of Japan cater to the sense of taste as well as to that of vision. Then again, such may be the privilege of the traveler; and here and elsewhere, Anders seems to regard cultural difference as a residual category rather than as an essential one and also displays awareness of the mutuality of "Othering." Nonetheless, the entanglement of aesthetics and the explication of meaning remains, at this point, unchallenged.

The journey had been occasioned by an invitation to participate in the 1958 *Fourth World Conference against Atomic and Hydrogen Bombs and for Disarmament* in Tokyo, whose activities also included visits to other Japanese cities and to Hiroshima and Nagasaki. In Hiroshima, at night, at a hotel bar, Anders engages in a conversation about the destruction of the city with two Japanese guests, whom he seeks to convince—he insists, successfully—of his notion that after the nuclear destruction, the destruction itself, more precisely its memory, has also been destroyed, by the reconstruction of the city. He argues that the remaining monument, the Genbaku Dome, as a *pars pro toto* and inadequate (indexical) sign, is insufficient and that the only way of preserving the memory of the "immeasurability" of the damage would have been to preserve the entire site of the destroyed city (*MB* 108–12). "The whole as a sign for the whole?" one of his interlocutors asks incredulously. But Anders retorts that even an entirely destroyed Hiroshima would only have been a partial sign, a synecdoche, namely "of the entire possible annihilation" (*MB* 112). The nuclear age has command over the very nature of the sign relations at hand, whose transitive logic is broken. In a traditional semiotic setting, if the destroyed Hiroshima was a signifier of the nuclear epoch, and the Genbaku Dome a signifier of the destroyed Hiroshima, then the Dome would also have to be able to work as a signifier of the epoch. This simple transfer of meanings, however, is disabled, or so Anders insists. It is the bomb, the technological device with the power to end humanity and thereby historical time, that has finally established full and complete sovereignty over semantic meaning, with which it can do whimsical things. The historical destruction of Hiroshima is no longer categorically distinct from the merely possible destruction of the world at large, because, along with other particular semiotic systems, the bomb has destroyed historical time.

In Nagasaki the delegation of activists is given a show of the "museum" of remains of the catastrophe, the account of which Anders uses to further clarify his understandings of the aesthetics of the nuclear age. The "first-rate pieces," as he calls them with desperate sarcasm, constitue a "surrealist exhibition" (MB 145). For,

> what makes surrealist images so shocking: that they do not simply mix together things of a different kind, but rather that things from different modes of being are forced to grow together, and that modes of being are even interchanged—here one can learn that the art of surrealism had been absolutely adequate for the age ... It had not invented those hybrids, but discovered them. In its own way, it was entirely realist. (ibid.)

One of the exhibits is a glass bottle that has melted together with a human hand. Bottle and hand, Anders suggests, illustrate the problem of the distinct "modes of being" (*Seinsweisen*). From the phenomenological point of view the bottle is essentially defined by its design for a purpose, whereas the hand, a part of the body, is a natural entity that is constitutively un-designed and un-purposeful. Anders follows up this observation with an impromptu definition of nihilism, for which it is constitutive "not that it sees everything as null and void [*nichtig*], but that it sees everything as capable of being annihilated in the same manner" (*MB* 146).[163] The capacity of annihilation thus unifies formerly divergent ontologies, in a manner anticipated by the surrealist transgression against the boundaries of the modes of being. Ontological productivity, since it requires its own order, its own range of objects and kinds, is canceled, in the age of the bomb. Nihilism is the cancelation of ontological pluralism. The command over semantics vested in the bomb is therefore one over referential meaning above all. Once again, the linkage between the notion of subjecting semantics to historical agency and the very understanding of reality comes to the fore. There is not any subject left that would be capable of ironizing meaning in the Wellhausenian way. Equally, there is not any unshakeable order of objects in place that would be capable of ordering meaning. Therefore, the bomb itself, a novel technical object, becomes the ultimate condition of meaning.

So the redefinition of nihilism is the aim behind Anders's critique of the "exotic," and he then uses the updated notion of nihilism to analyze the breakdown of the historicity of meaning. In an earlier passage, he describes at length the embarrassment created by one of the European delegates of the conference who, at a formal dinner, decides to read a self-written poem to the participants in a language of which Anders is the only other speaker present. Anders is therefore asked to provide a rough translation of the text into English, which then is translated again into Japanese (*MB* 49–54). In his analysis of the episode, along with a vivid evocation of both his own and the Japanese translator's profound embarrassment, Anders points out the following lessons:

> Poetry is poetry only in its own language. It cannot be translated into another one any more than "I" into "he," or "my pain" into "his pain." It is the Arcanum among the modes of linguistic expression.
>
> Yet today "my pain" is "the pain of all of us." For we are all *in the same boat* [orig. English]. That is to say, what needs to be said today concerns all of us, because all of us … can hit anyone else and be hit by anyone else; not only, as in the case of poetry, the few who share a language. …
>
> We have to learn how to speak in our own language *in a translatable manner*, nay, even for the purpose of being translated …
>
> In world literature there have always been linguistic creations (and not just short-format maxims or fables, but real texts) that were strong enough to uphold, when translated into whatever language, their force and their truth. Epictet is translatable. Among the contemporary German philosophers, none is. (*MB* 52–4)

The force by which the world has become a unified reality is once again the indiscriminate destructive potential that unifies the possible meanings and subjects any language to the necessity of expressing pain, agency, normativity in newly universal fashion. The world of world literature, with its hierarchical structure in which equivalence rules only at the top, supplies Anders with a model for this novel mode of signification. The resulting "instrumental language" will have to be "laconic" (*MB* 54). That is to say, in spite of its instrumentality, it will not be completely liberated from aesthetic norms, such as that of laconism. The notion of a technological mode of signification to correspond to the technological leveling of differences in the world is apparently not what Anders is after. Unlike proponents of coeval attempts at achieving a scientific account of communication—be it in cybernetics or the self-styled communication science—Anders does not show any interest in a notion of meaning as a unified code that would reduce reading to the variables of encryption, decipherment, interference, and feedback. Rather, his agenda is about universalizing discourse by means of an aesthetic of the nuclear age. Thus, however reduced, there is still an aesthetic education of humankind in store.

What might such an aesthetic look like? The last exhibit of the Nagasaki exhibition Anders describes provides a number of hints, and opens a few connections to previous models. The object in question is elusive, a photograph of the shadow of a man on a wall, but without a man that could be casting it: a "Peter Schlemihl-shadow," separated from its owner by the power of the bomb:

> So in the morning of [August] 9, [1945] someone had been leaning on this wall, unaware. And then the lightning struck. And instantaneously the wall was incandescent and the man burnt to ashes.
>
> Yet, what was not incandescent was the part of the wall the man had been covering in the last fraction of his last second. This piece was caught in the

flashlight image. As a negative. This piece he had saved. In this negative, he had saved himself. For it is the only trace that has remained of his days on earth. And the only one that will remain thereof.

What then will remain of us?

This is what will remain of the last man: his outline on an object that his body, in the instant of the flash of lightning, happens to be covering. That will be the last image of the last man. If one can call it an image. Because witnesses who might find it or recognize it—well, they will not exist. Only other images of shadows on other walls. But they will be blind and will not recognize each other. (*MB* 148)

This then is the aesthetic of nuclear shadow play the author has traveled to Japan to retrieve. After trading in some of the old features for new ones, the meaning of the shadow has changed. The individual shadow, which is fused with the monumentality of an inscription on a wall, and in this way separated, with unimaginable finality and through unimaginable violence, from the human body that originally cast it, foreshadows the death of humanity. This indexical signifier, which emerges through the annihilation of its signified, represents the ultimate displacement and decentering of the human form: into the surface of a wall, permanently; rather than onto it, passingly. The allusion to philosophical tradition is, needless to say, to Plato's cave; the negative image, the dream of the real replaces the real. The bomb completes the logic of annihilation, following the German politics of extermination in the Second World War; where the Nazis had expanded the agency of murder into the mortality of anyone, the bomb has one mode of signification for all humanity, which is the possible annihilation of everyone, at once.[164]

Yet Anders, who deplores that the surrealists "often presented [their] hybrids with such gusto for the ghastly" (*MB* 145), cannot avoid exposure to the same question: Are the theatrics with which he writes about the Nagasaki exhibits not also a recognizable strategy of endowing their representation with a taste for the horrific? Does he not insert them, therefore, into a specific aesthetic framework that goes beyond the instrumental laconism, the minimalist poetics he has previously considered to be the only remaining legitimate possibility? Moreover, it is problematic that his novel definition of nihilism—as part of a logic of historical escalation—was achieved by means of contrasting the catastrophe of Japanese victimization with the catastrophe of Jewish victimization. Auschwitz gained its full universality only by way of a passage to Hiroshima and Nagasaki. In his writings on the atomic philosophy of history, Anders mentioned the Shoah openly and not infrequently. Yet, it was only later, from the mid-1960s onward, that he came to write more extensively about it in its own right.[165] The structure of distribution and balancing—of the ever so subtle contest of victimization—that marks this development indicates the continuing, if waning, presence of the contest of Athens and Jerusalem across his writings.

The last portions of the book are dedicated to the journey back to his final destination, Rome, with a first layover in Bangkok. In the respective passages, Anders is particularly attentive to ruins and the traditional aesthetics of history. In Bangkok he even insists on the extensive residual functioning of the notion of the exotic: "This now is really the 'Far East'" (*MB* 193). As in Tokyo, he gets lost walking around in the city, and this time it is only by sheer luck (or so he says) that he finds his way back to the hotel. He visits the Wat Arun "pyramid," the "most colossal man-made, the most hybrid thing I have ever seen," not a building, but itself a landscape (*MB* 195). The significance of this description emerges only during his sojourn in Rome, which Anders states is his first ever visit there, in fulfilment of a lifelong desire until then thwarted by the years of existential struggle and exile (*MB* 202f.). Diligent tourist, Anders then sets out to visit the well-known ruins. Regarding the Colosseum, he remarks:

> Looks damned "Asian," despotic and barbarian. Always it is only the testimony of power that survives. Darwinism of things.
>   How fed up I am with the colossal. When I climbed (when was it? Yesterday? A week ago?) through the man-made building-stone mountains of the Wat Aroon, and through the man-made gorges, and down the man-made rock faces, and onto the man-made towering summits ... then I felt I had had enough of the colossal for a lifetime. This here is smaller, but also only colossal. Not sufficient to re-Europeanize me. Where is Horace? Where Tibull? (*MB* 204)

He scorns the indiscriminate "beauty" of ruins that does not hold reckoning with the question of whether the original building was beautiful at all; and he observes the other tourists, and reminisces about his adolescent self, with melancholic detachment, as they cavort, and he along with them, among the debris of classical antiquity and pay empty homage to an aesthetic from the nineteenth century (or even before). "Finding beauty in ruins in a time of real ruins goes beyond the power" of his eyes (*MB* 205). And still, the residuum of beauty he longs for is in the Latin poets, although poetry, too, has been destroyed.[166]

As previously discussed, the cipher of the "colossal" was a clear marker of the competition of antiquities that was so central to the *polemos* of classical and Orientalist philologies. Anders plays with this template when he laconically recognizes the superiority of the Bangkok temples over the Colosseum. Yet, with the category of the colossal—a category that merely represents brute power, he insists—not only the competition, but also the very notion of historicity goes out of the window. The end of history is also the end of the relevance of the past. The agency that brought forth the colossal—the earlier monsters and hybrids that preceded surrealism—has been voided by the present. The new society will be, if anything, cosmopolitan-universal.

In order to illustrate this prospect, Anders gives a lengthy description of the representatives of the recently decolonized nations to the Tokyo congress, whose easy interactions, conducted in perfect "European" politeness, and in "European" (broadly, Western) forms of political discourse, provincialize Europe (*MB* 158).

> While I, the European, even today, after so many weeks, am still breathless and captivated by my flight over the Arctic, they have adopted—with a lack of timidity that makes me breathless once more—the technology supplied by Europe as the most natural thing in the world, and they make use of it as if this abrupt restart were the most natural continuation of their own tradition. Testingly I look into their faces. Somewhere, I think, there must be a sign of the irruption into their history

(or their lack of history [*Geschichtslosigkeit*]), as a fissure; some physiognomic discrepancy has to prove that they are "broken humans." Yet nothing of the kind. Probably my expectation is simply a child of speculation, namely the speculative philosophy of history of German romanticism, in which I also still partake; as a child of the axiom—untainted by any empiricism—that "real history" forms an "organic continuum," that history, under no circumstances, "facit saltus." Humbug. (*MB* 159f.)

This remarkable "Humbug," with which Anders discards the entire tradition of modern German thought, from Lavaterian physiognomy to Hegelian and Marxist philosophies of history, nonetheless still requires encounter with "the Orient," and indeed, quite literally, all of it. For it is the assembly of representatives of all the formerly colonized nations that is, to Anders, so eye-opening. While he once again pleads for abandoning the term "exotic," nonetheless he remarks on the non-European delegates:

> Hardly possible for people to look *less broken*. For the most part, they are even expressly handsome—some because they *still* partake in the strength and elegant raciness of the animalic; others, because—certainly in the first generation—they *already* reflect the beauty of intellectual passion; and others, finally, in particular delegates of the old nations of culture [*Kulturvölker*], because they have a tradition of wisdom behind them that has made their faces friendly. We Eurasians by comparison look washed up and screwed up. We certainly do not occupy a place of honor in this global gallery. (*MB* 160)

Clearly, it was hard to relinquish the idiom, even the aestheticization of competitive difference, in which the racist *topos* of the "animalic" and the Orientalist one (in the Saidian sense) of "wisdom" figured so prominently. Anders struggled to describe the emergent "family" of humankind, in which the others were kind enough to include the Europeans without "a word of resentment or vengefulness" (*MB* 162). This novel spirit of familial belonging is nothing less than a refoundation of humanism; for Anders, it finally lifts the condition of exile, in which he has been living since 1933: "For long years I have felt (simply because I had to wander from country to country) as a *'no man's land'* [orig. English]. For the first time I feel at home: namely as a 'child of our earth'" (*MB* 163). This realization—of a new home in nuclear universalism—is the most hopeful note Anders dares to offer his readers: At least under the nihilist threat of the bomb, the condition of exile has also finally been abolished.

All in all, the structure of theoretical critique has been progressive, no doubt: Some of the more problematic *topoi* Anders still deployed have been abandoned. Nonetheless, the preponderance of negation, in Anders's thought, has retained its significance. The negative that resided in that culmination of the colossal, the atom bomb, was far more important for laying out the normativity that was to take hold, progressively, of the present, than any positive determinations. The present time in question was moreover extended, bereft of the dimensions of the past and the future, and thereby also constituted by negation. For, the past was irrelevant and annihilation the only conceivable future. The dependence of all of these negatives on the idiom of

Orientalist philology is significant. In light of the history of Orientalist preoccupations, it is sobering that the aesthetic of Anders's ultimate humanism comes to rest, precisely, in a shadow; and that he continues to trust in aesthetics in spite of himself, in spite of the denials he emits. The antihumanism of the bomb, and the post-mortem humanism Anders sought to retrieve from its debris, was then entangled with what the Orientalist philology of the real had earlier brought to the table. The genealogical lines of tradition that generated these twentieth-century notions extend back into the nineteenth. The mid-twentieth-century topography of both humanism and antihumanism, the parcours of critical theory from the 1930s into the 1970s, had already been laid out earlier. It followed in the grid of philology's history of meaning.

The course of intellectual history has not treated Anders kindly. As cogent as his arguments were, as striking as their lucidity was, they have remained marginal. The bomb continues to define global politics, but is met with public indifference. Anders had captured many traits of this neglect; and yet, both his more optimistic and his more pessimistic notions have been belied—at least until the world goes under in nuclear war after all. The resilience of mess and the force of forgetting have had the upper hand. A different future still arrived, and passed; and Hiroshima and Nagasaki have been thoroughly historicized. The bomb has not managed to assume sovereignty over the explication of meaning. And the very notion that any technological device—any product of the human mind, any *cognitum*—could have done so, was a battered heirloom, passed down through the generations ever since the time of the reckless gambit of August Boeckh's *Realphilologie*.

Conclusion: *Logos*, to Have and Have Not

In the preceding chapters, I have laid out some aspects of a history of semantics in philology. In this conclusion, I will provide two summation arguments, (1) regarding the overall trajectory of philological semantics and the concomitant historical ontology; and (2) regarding the more specific positions and plot elements of a history of these semantics, including its interfaces with a history of meaning beyond the bounds of disciplinary scholarship. I will then (3) offer a few remarks on the enduring significance of the history of philological meaning.

1. The redefinition, or perhaps simply refashioning, of the disciplinary territory of the philologies in Germany around 1800 took place under the promise of providing better, more reliable access especially to the explication of such linguistic meanings that were obscured by temporal or cultural distance. In this manner, a domain of epistemic procedures in its own right was to emerge that would stand apart from quotidian forms of knowledge about meanings. That is to say, the project of a scientific renewal of philology entailed introducing an epistemological rupture, with the term coined by Bachelard.

In order to make possible the required rupture within knowledge about meaning, philologists imposed a hierarchy among existing semantic procedures. Amid the given and ineradicable multitude of semantic "games" (using Wittgenstein's term), philological scholarship tended to rely one-sidedly on preferred procedures. Yet philological practice could not, and did not seek to, overcome the pre-given condition of dispersed plurality among semantic language games. Most prominently, the ambition to render semantics scientific privileged the explication of meaning by identification of "things in the world" to which language referred, or, in short, reference. Reference meant setting two preconditions for there to be meaning, the givenness of objects as potential referents, and the general access of language to "the world." On account of this second precondition, philologists also subscribed to extending epistemological rupture to the problem of intentionality, that is to say, the subject's mental access to the world, as mediator between words and things. Philology was about objectification as much as it was about subjectification. In both these domains, scholars privileged particular pathways and established novel routes, which the preceding chapters have sought to map out: from the world access and objectification that underpinned reference to revelation to irony and absurdity, and to the disintegrated subjectivity of dreams. In an odd affinity to its own subfield of grammar, for the purpose of achieving and sustaining epistemological rupture, philology established combinatory rules of objects and subjects of knowledge. Yet, unlike in grammar, these rules never seemed to become more than just provisionally stable.

The notion that philology was the pursuit of a somehow novel project of scienticization produced a pressure to develop a theoretical account of methods and innovation in the field. The resulting theorization was understood to be a temporary stand-in for systematization, the creation of a coherent and stable set of abstract principles to govern the scientific discipline within an overall edifice of scientific thought. Theorizing, by contrast, was more like striking up a tent. Only, the tent of philology tended to come down with even the slightest gust of wind. The main reason for this shortfall, as Friedrich Schlegel and Hegel diagnosed early on, was philology's inability to be more than an "aggregate" of knowledge, to curb the indomitable sprawl of unconnected objects of philological knowledge. Since Boeckh's influential intervention, theorization and aggregation in fact became interdependent. Although Boeckh had initially set out to resolve the perceived problem of aggregation, he ended up contributing to its proliferation. He expected to delimit the range of possible objects of philological knowledge with the help of only two concepts. One of these was the *Erkenntnis des Erkannten*, the understanding of the previously understood, which defined the domain of philological study as comprising anything that had been touched upon by human intentionality. The other one was the concept of *Altertum*, the epoch of classical antiquity as a self-sufficient cultural totality, which tacitly required a normative standard, most plausibly of an aesthetic kind, to sustain its unity. The notion of classical antiquity quickly disintegrated as research into its Oriental surroundings expanded and encroached on its territory, generating an ever greater aggregation of novel and un-classical objects of knowledge. This development had precisely been legitimized by Boeckh's general notion that anything that had been accessed by the human mind was to be an object of philological knowledge. As a long-term consequence of this incurable flaw, the concept of "theory," in philology and its successor disciplines, came to jettison any claim to philosophical systematicity. This development only strengthened the interdependence of theorization and aggregation, since the theory of philology, as it cut its moorings to any general theory of mind and world, had nothing else to work with but the datum of philological practice. This interdependence means that the historical study of philology may not bypass Orientalism, which was the prime agent of aggregation.

The privileging of reference and the steady increase of aggregation had far-reaching consequences for the scholarly understanding of reality and the manner in which language was supposed to have access to it. Piecemeal, through philological theorizing and the working practice of aggregation, a novel sense of plurality was imposed on the notion of the real. Across cognate formations of knowledge, the meaning of "world" began to diverge, as in the composites of world philology, world history, world literature, or world poetry, all in use in nineteenth- and twentieth-century Germany. The history of philological semantics became a matter of historical ontology. As is the case in other contexts of science and scholarship, the production of knowledge gives rise to novel objects and kinds of such objects, for instance abstract or imperceptible entities, or technological tools. Beyond this rather simple form of adding to a presumptively still unified reality, many forms of science and scholarship also add discrete classes of concepts with underlying spheres of objects of reference. These can differ between disciplinary territories, and their mutual compatibility is often uncertain. This is why territoriality is a decisive force in the history of scholarship. Territory is not merely about institutional power and distribution conflicts and jealous ownership. Rather, it is about ranges of objects of knowledge, realities inseparably enmeshed with epistemic structures. The object of physical knowledge is physics, not nature as a whole, and the object of historical knowledge is history, not the past—that is to say, the given body of knowledge as much as the province of reality underpinning it. In philology, work that was conducted on far-out, marginal fields of scholarship tended to operate on its own terms and lose compatibility with the presumptive core of disciplinary knowledge. This was perhaps the most basic problem that was addressed by the charge of "aggregation": an argument of distance tipping over into categorical incompatibility through forgetfulness, negligence, and the accumulation of small differences. The argument about aggregation was an argument about ontological problems. It entailed recognizing that something as odd as the fracturing of aggregation might actually happen to the notion of the real as entwined with scientific knowledge. So the overall impulse of scienticization within semantics conditioned the instability of intuitive, tacit knowledge about the nature of reality and the world as sources of meaning.

2. In the first chapter the confrontation of strategies of personification and objectification in the sequence of conflicts over the name of philology since the 1820s exposed the chief trajectory along which semantics became subject to historical change. The history of philology proved, before anything else, to be the history of a name within a historically malleable practice of naming; and from there, an exercise in historical ontology. Other candidates for re-stabilizing philology, either through a rigid conceptual approach to semantics or through grammar, turned out to be indissolubly bound up with a disorderly field of semantic practices.

In the second chapter, discussion of the suicide of Enno Littmann's informant Naffa' wad 'Etmân conducted a probe into the divergence of concepts of "world" as marking philological work on poetry. The positioning of explications of meaning within an entire range of divergent understandings of world grants access to the ontological productivity of philological semantics. At the same time, it provides an inroad into the problem of the relationship between philological knowledge and violence as an agential power of disposition over reality. Philologists, I have argued, processed violence as a type of event or structure within its ontological bounds in a particular manner that amounts to a form of appropriation. This appropriation, somewhat paradoxically, staked a claim to the ownership of imperial violence on the part of philologists proper, but a claim that entailed the power of making violence an entirely marginal type of event. Naffa''s suicide, as a violent act that was at least in some measure provoked by his unfortunate encounter with philologists, failed this pattern. It was not marginal to its author and could not be. As an "informant" Naffa' had been objectified, a condition he could not fully escape. In its linkages with practices of objectification, the problem of violence was an important marker for the distinctive ontological productivity of philological studies. Yet, it was also a marker of tensions within philological semantics that came to the fore around the difficulties Littmann and his peers experienced when attempting to account for Naffa''s suicide. World and violence, as accessible reality and extreme form of access to it, did not therefore provide a durable foundation to the philology of the real.

In the third chapter, the analysis of epigraphy as a working practice, with Enno Littmann as the guiding figure, targeted concrete practices of objectification in *Realphilologie*, beyond the general problem of world-making world access. Philological knowledge proved to be contiguous with archival knowledge, as gained from the perusal of written records of the past. This contiguity obliges the study of the semantic world-access of philology to address the problem of "order" in the records, as the decisive concept and simultaneously the master trope of archival theories. In its various guises— procedural, ontological, normative-moral, or iterative—"order" promises conclusive control over referential meaning. Yet in none of these guises does such control actually emerge. Instead, the semantics at work in the study of inscriptions rather indicate that the archival work of epigraphy took the form of scenes, of staged performance. One of the templates of scenes that emerged in epigraphy was that of the state of nature of human society, and of a natural state of writing, as providing a foundational reality to the explication of meaning. Another template was that of courtly encounter, which provided the frame for privileging a specific type of linguistic expression, the regal proper name as endowed with prophetic-messianic significance. This duality of templates, by no means a dichotomy, indicates that scenes followed patterns of genre none of which may be regarded as foundational to the others. Only a different kind of primacy was almost expressed in practice. Given that the epigraphic attention to regal proper names was one of the guises of the project of rendering semantics scientific, epigraphic work came to the brink of asserting the primacy of philological knowledge over the political theology of monarchy. In short, there are traces of a political theology of philology. Political language was caught up in the shifting historical ontology of philological semantics.

The privileging of the proper name was a genuine contribution to semantic practice on the part of Semitist epigraphy. It was only here that the transfer of the semantics of naming into the field of religious revelation could occur. In the fourth chapter, Julius Wellhausen figured as a hesitant pioneer of the hypostatization of proper name semantics. In this endeavor, he was seconded by more enthusiastic scholars from the field of epigraphy, such as Hommel, Glaser, and Grimme. The field was prepared for reinterpreting the very concept of "being" through the notion of the name of the deity as the substance of revelation. It fell to philosophers to refashion these semantic provisions into a modernist metaphysical tradition in its own right, centered on the "name of being." Along various lines of reception and conflict, Cassirer, Cohen, and Rosenzweig were of particular significance for this development. Certainly, their discussion echoed earlier Spinozist and other theological ideas, but it was also informed and mediated by modern philological scholarship, namely Usener and Wellhausen. As a consequence of this mediation, the problem of the name of being also proved to be intimately bound up with philological anti-Semitism in the context of the competition of Greek and Hebrew antiquity and its Orientalist extensions around 1900. Wellhausen, although he had been crucial for the emergence of this tangle, struggled to extricate himself from it. He attempted to resolve the problems around reference as revelation by retreating to a semantic of *Uneigentlichkeit*, a pervasive deployment of irony. This shift of the semantic subject toward the refuge of irony also indicated that the obscurities marring reference in light of the "name of being" prompted philological concern to focus on other semantic games. Irony is not a matter of reference, specifically.

Yet, Orientalist semantics also provided a possibility for relinquishing the claim to sovereignty over the explication of meaning vested in irony. In the fifth chapter analysis of the works of Georg Jacob suggested that philology, in reaction to the menace of ironical discourse, could still proceed by dropping the pretense to philological subjecthood as sovereign over the explication of meaning. Jacob theorized about aesthetic questions in order to attain an understanding of subjecthood in which intentionality was adrift and plural. The tensions that persisted in Jacob's aesthetics, particularly palpable around the complex of shadow theater, indicate the larger contradictions the *Realphilologie* tradition accrued after 1900. Chief among these tensions was the implicit conflict between the historical argument of global connectedness, on which Jacob relied to demonstrate the universal appeal of shadow theater to the human mind; and the combative particularism and contrarian tendencies that shaped his views of self-contained aesthetic cultures. Moreover, Jacob bestowed decisive prominence on the poetic observation of nature, along the lines of a romantic natural philosophy that had long become entirely anachronistic. Yet, this preference collided with his exaltation of a dream-subject that was only feebly intentional. In a similar vein, his rejection of the classicist exaltation of the human body and the rational mind generated an antihumanist affect that was powerful but also internally conflicted. Throughout, Jacob's notions about aesthetics and history were founded in tacit views about semantics. The resources Jacob's work bundled into aporias once again point to the significance of philological semantics for subsequent intellectual traditions. This significance could be traced through the relevance of the work on shadows for artistic modernism, as well as through a variety of forays into mid-twentieth-century philosophical thought. Various screens—intermediary doctrines such as psychoanalysis or philosophical Japonism—obscured the genealogical connection to Orientalism and Semitics. Philology itself became a shadowy memory. As a tentative end point to this development, Anders's philosophy of the atomic age remained bound up with the "Oriental" location of Japan in ways that preserved the traditional confrontation of Athens and Jerusalem. Similarly, Anders's views continued to belabor the contradiction between the aesthetics of philology and the anaesthetics of history, as previously traced in the works of Jacob. Anders's theory of the atom bomb emerges as another, if perhaps the ultimate conceivable, attempt at installing, through ontological productivity, a sovereign over the explication of meaning: the technological device that can put an end to humankind and therefore all natural language. In a sense, this means coming full circle: The philological embrace of colonial violence as agential world access turns into a rejection of violence as the unmaking of the world. And yet, these contrary trajectories emanate from the same source. Their interdependence signals that it would be inappropriate to regard the tentative plotline the chapter lays out as that of a civilizing process of sorts in which an earlier accommodation of violence was abandoned.

The overall departure of nineteenth-century philology from previous traditions is palpable not least in the disappearance of the existential metaphor of the book of nature and the legibility of the world, as Blumenberg called it. The philological involvement with meaning was far more anarchic than hermeneutic theory, with its orderly dialogue between unified experiential sovereign-subjects, would suffer. Philological practice produced precisely the deleterious undermining of semantic sovereignty that theories of hermeneutics have consistently sought to conceal. The uneven, fractured, aggregate ontology of philology also makes the history of semantics incompatible with other theories of reading. Philology was bound up with the notion of an illegible world. This notion remained, as it were, in the screened-off background of the stage of knowledge, but it made for a powerful presence. It connected scholarly discourse to the condition of modernity, whose self-understanding as an epoch of ontological uncertainty profoundly relies on the record of philology. In this manner, philology has provided crucial contributions to the anti-systematic patterns of philosophical thought that continue to exist under the names of "literary" and "critical theory."

It is this nexus of positions that continues to provide some of the most crowded commonplaces of present-day humanities thought. Decisive portions of contemporary critical theory have been formulated in continuity with the history of philology. These lines of continuity often have the disadvantage of not being clearly inscribed, or, on account of their greater age, having been overwritten. The dependence of critical theory discourse on Marxism, Freudian psychoanalysis, ethnography, and linguistic and semiotic structuralism has certainly attracted more attention. Nonetheless, themes that emanated from the travails of referential semantics, such as irony, antihumanism, and political theologies have remained crucial concerns in theory debates that extend into the present. The genealogical linkage of critical theory to the disorderly semantics of the philology of the real is therefore of prime importance for understanding the history of knowledge production in the contemporary humanities. By contrast, other theory fields, for instance historical theory, function in accordance with different inherited programs. The more self-enclosed, far less interdisciplinary character of historical theory is arguably a function of the rather more stable territoriality of historical writing as a discipline. In the ambit of "theory" particularity and difference exist, which opens a space for historical analysis.

If taken to form the plotline of a history of meaning the chapters suggest the following unstable combinatory rules of objects and subjects in semantics. Names combine with territories and *polemoi*. World access combines with the agency of violence. Referential objectification undermines possibilities of order and combines with the bounded spontaneity of archival scenes and their actors. The name of being combines with revelation, then with irony. The response to irony is to revolt against the semantic sovereignty of any subject-position that stands in the way of referential realism. This revolt combines with a dissolution of the real into aesthetic forms, and finally the dissociation of violence and world access. The territoriality of philology forms a field of mutually exclusive positions as well as a plotline of transformations. Many things were happening at once, few positions were truly abandoned. The history of meaning does not fit into a neat chronological arrangement.

3. In concluding this parcours, I will outline a few theses on the further significance of the arguments here presented:

a. Along with the legibility of the world, philology cast doubt on the notion of a universal essence of humanity that would have consisted in the exclusive access of the species to linguistic meanings. From the spectrum of responses to the shifting semantics in German Orientalism, a seditious aesthetic anti-classicism emerged and informed a set of antihumanist resentments against the representational primacy of both the human body and the human subject. These notions broke the ground for further theoretical developments. As a consequence, linguistic meaning ceased to provide the foundation for a solid and unified mode of mutual understanding that would have been at once exclusive to and constitutive of human nature. The Aristotelian definition of the human being as the *zoon logon echon*, the species of animal defined by its endowment with language, speech, and reason,[1] ceased to apply, precisely because the "having" of "logos" acquired a doubtful, dispersed character. Outside of philosophy, the notion of "logos" became dubious much earlier than within that field. And across the plural mess of semantics, the philological project unfolded its own fragmented ontological production of the subjects and objects of knowledge about meaning. As a consequence of this shift the notion of the subject as the sovereign of intentionality and reason remains stubbornly irretrievable.

b. The most basic historical definition of the political in the classical textual tradition hinges directly on the human command of *logos*; it is merely an alternative spelling out of the meaning of this definition when Aristotle also determines the human species as the *zoon politikon*, the animal that communicates in language about public affairs and thereby forms states.[2] Thus, undermining the quality of *logon echein* also entailed a fundamental shift in European political thought. Admittedly, the Aristotelian notion of the *zoon politikon* had been under revision for centuries. Since the time of Hobbes— needless to say, this is a brutally inadequate sketch—and his notion of the state of nature as war of all against all a mechanist political anthropology of unsociability had come to dominate over the teleological anthropology of natural statehood in the Aristotelian tradition. Nonetheless the philological bungling of the hold on the meaning of *logon echein* was significant because it ended the autonomy and self-sufficiency of political thought in defining the terms of the general anthropology underpinning politics. After philology, the Aristotelian idiom was opaque before it ever even came to address the sphere of the political. The scienticization of semantics produced an infrastructure of critique that unmade one of the key tenets of the tradition of European political thought.

c. The analysis of the understanding of the political among the philologists has helped to recover some of the historical unease about the uncertainty of *logos*, about sovereignty over the explication of meaning. If it is a beloved etymological cliché that philologists are "lovers" of words, it must be added that they have been anything but lovers of *logos* in the other meanings of this Ancient Greek concept, of reason, order, and even rhetorical ability. Since the inauguration of philological theory in the lectures and writings of Wolf, Schleiermacher, Schlegel, and Boeckh, philologists prompted rather than comprehended the erosion of *logon echein*. Perhaps it has been because of this relative lack of comprehension that it also fell to philological scholarship, mainly of the classicist persuasion, to formulate novel doctrines of "humanism" every couple of decades. Thus far, none of these programs for the aesthetic education of polities has proven intellectually, or even just institutionally, sustainable. They are, however, indicators of the territorial, possessive structure of scholarly disciplines in which modern understandings of the political also tend to be embroiled. Werner Hamacher has argued that the point of Aristotle's linkage of speech and state was really in uncovering the manner in which justice is founded on language, on the boundless movement of meanings and the unchecked ability to refer to reference (*Verweisung*).[3] This ultimate optimism of the politics of deconstructionist thought, which one might equally trace in the writings of Derrida, is arguably too oblivious of the bond between scholarship and politics, too eager to concede to political thought a degree of autonomy it has long ceased to enjoy (if, in fact, it ever did). Carl Schmitt's famous assertion that "all significant concepts of the modern theory of the state are secularized theological concepts …"[4] might be taken to indicate nothing more than the extent to which the political has been transformed by its own scholarly theorization. In this process, political thought lays claim to parts of the theological heritage, but never the whole. In the same manner, other disciplines, perhaps mainly in the humanities spectrum, acquired dominion over parts of the theological estate. Although political thought is not simply an academic discipline, it is partly so, and, according to Schmitt, partakes in the condition of carving out post-theological domains. Understood correctly the condition is one of holding on firmly to certain historically acquired patterns of discourse. Such tenacity might be an underlying prerequisite of disciplinary territoriality. And it might constitute an insurmountable limit to the ability of humanities scholarship to critique injustices in the distribution of the ownership of, and the access to, language and knowledge. Disciplinary territories emerge as partial surrogates when it is impossible to "have" the totality of *logos*; and philology was, in some regards, the precondition for this impossibility.

d. The conflicted, territorial structure of disciplines has inscribed itself into the realities produced by scholarship. It will not simply disappear, though its institutional upkeep might well end. Arguments for taking disciplinarity seriously are a prerequisite for understanding the historical import of philology. First, the changes wrought by philology are an inalienable part of natural language systems worldwide, in speech as much as in writing. The notion of the ontological productivity of philology is to be taken seriously: these products added to the real. Second, the basic claim of philology around 1800—so basic it was barely spelled out—remains hard to dispute. If humanities scholars cannot explain meanings better than other agencies of the production of semantic knowledge, they might as well shut down the entire operation; and anyone doubting the very possibility of such improvement would have to explain why the claim is flawed, in principle, and not just in terms of the shortcomings of some body of scholarship or other. This challenge continues to be pertinent. Third, an intellectual world without philology, its wavering about reference and its strange, antihumanist anthropology, as wrought from the ability to proliferate the explication of meaning, might eventually revert to the anthropology of the *zoon logon echon*. Probably, such a process would favor the unsociable rather than the naturally sociable variant of this anthropology, but in any case it would favor the epistemic space of the political. This development might seem to be already palpable in the ruminations of the *homo oeconomicus* and the many attempts to reform this abstract homunculus into something more amenable to this or that mathematical contraption. It is perhaps even more manifest in the ubiquitous movements, in political spheres the contemporary world over, to sever ties to scholarship and reaffirm at least an illusion of autonomous agency. All of these tendencies seem to dovetail with an idiom of empowerment, a reconquest of sovereignty far beyond the narrower precinct of Wellhausenian irony. Things mean what they mean because we say so, in earnest, and who is to challenge us? It might be worthwhile to keep a door open for other kinds of semantics and the concomitant pluralism of theories.

e. The dominant historical interpretation continues to regard Orientalist philology as a form of *logon echein*, a pursuit of the ownership of a foreign, "Oriental" language in the service of empire. Rather similar conditions apply to many of the contributions Orientalist philology made to the political languages Germany and other European nation states developed for themselves, their minorities, and their immediate neighbors abroad. The most striking of these is probably the contribution of Orientalism to the shaping of modern anti-Semitism, in its intricate interweaving of antiquity, theology, and race. This overall line of argument on Orientalism as an *-ism*, an ideological structure, is an elegant way of developing further the Aristotelian formula, through yet another semantic exercise that uncovers the tacit meanings of political domination within it. Nonetheless, in my view, this interpretation of the history of Orientalist philology is incomplete, precisely because philological work undermines as much as establishes the possibility of "having" a language, even in the sense of imperial domination. The ties that tethered Orientalist philology to colonial empires were more pluriform and pertained to various types of semantic explication, especially those in which violence, historicity, and such arenas of aesthetic conflict as "world literature" were prominent. It might be important, not only to criticize the destructive effects these semantics had but also to shine a light on the *non sequiturs* among them and the constant pressure of their undoing by their own work.

f. As the current conjuncture in pertinent research underlines, space—as well as need—for a critique of Orientalist philology remains ample, and perhaps more so than ever. Nonetheless, the role of Orientalism in the actual genealogy of critical theory also ought to be taken into account. Scholars of diverse backgrounds and orientations appear to agree that Orientalism, while a target of critique, is also among the preconditions of the terms in which such critique is formulated. The question of whether there is an escape from historical entanglement with philology and Orientalism is up for debate. Yet since it is precisely the unsteadiness of modern philological semantics that informs practices of critique, prospects for such an escape appear less than obvious. Equally, from this point of view, prospects for the tendency to posit normative understandings of "philology" without deepened attention to the complex history of the field hardly appear promising.

Reading more and more of the works and letters of Georg Jacob, it began to intrigue me increasingly that, for all his obsessive rejection of Greek antiquity and all his enthusiasm for the play of silhouettes, he never addressed Plato's allegory of the cave. This first and foremost instance of the denigration of shadows, even of an imagined science of shadows, cannot have failed to provoke Jacob's dismay. Perhaps, however, the prospect of having to argue for remaining in the cave and continuing with the *uneigentlich* science of shadows was too harsh a requirement even for Jacob. The problem may have been with the notion, very much at the core of the allegory, that one ultimately would have to dwell "in truth" as a single abode. Yet, giving up this notion of exalting only one abode over all others meant something sobering for the deployment of critique as an exit strategy, a way out of the cave as the habitation of errancy. Perhaps it is legitimate to see in Jacob's silence on the Platonic allegory more than an uncaring omission: A silent concession that the enclosed cave and the open country under the sun are part of the same landscape and that no *polemos* will succeed to discard one or the other.

Notes

Introduction

1   See Gaston Bachelard, *La formation de l'esprit scientifique: Contribution à une psychanalyse de la connaissance objective* (Paris: Vrin, 1938).

2   Jacob to Nöldeke, March 21, 1914, Nachlass Theodor Nöldeke, Universitätsbibliothek Tübingen, Md. 782 (subsequently NL Nöldeke), A4, Nr. 224. Translations are my own unless otherwise noted. Emphases are in the original text unless otherwise noted.

3   Georg Jacob, "Ḥamâm," *Der Islam* 5 (1915): 247f.; idem, "Tauben und Flughühner," *Der Islam* 6 (1916): 99f.; see moreover Manfred Ullmann, *Flughühner und Tauben*, (München: Bayerische Akademie der Wissenschaften, 1982).

4   Denis Sinor, "Remembering Paul Pelliot," *Journal of the American Oriental Society* 119, no. 3 (1999): 471.

5   As highlighted by Rosalie L. Colie, *Paradoxia Epidemica: The Renaissance Tradition of Paradox* (Princeton, NJ: Princeton University Press, 1966), xiii with hints to further literature, and generally with recourse to Johan Huizinga, *Homo Ludens: Proeve eener bepaling van het spel-element der cultuur* [1938], Verzamelde Werken 5 (Haarlem: Tjeenk Willink, 1950), especially ch. 1 on interrelations between seriousness and play.

6   Jacob also discussed extensively the history of Arabic as well as European-language discussions and translations of Al-Shanfara's poem, which had risen to the status of a prime example of Early Arabic poetry at the latest with Antoine-Isaac Silvestre de Sacy's inclusion of the piece—along with a translation Jacob considered extremely flawed—in his *Chrestomathie arabe*, 3 vols. (Paris: Imprimerie Impériale, 1806, 2nd edn. 1826–27), a reader of Arabic texts that became foundational for modern Arabic studies. See Georg Jacob, *Schanfarà-Studien 2: Parallelen und Kommentar zur Lâmîja, Schanfarà-Bibliographie* (Munich: Bayerische Akademie der Wissenschaften, 1915).

7   Georg Jacob, *Schanfaras Lamijat-al-'Arab, auf Grund neuer Studien neu übertragen* (Kiel: Mühlau, 1915), 8.

8   Hans Blumenberg, *Die Lesbarkeit der Welt* (Frankfurt a.M.: Suhrkamp, 1981).

9   Blumenberg, *Lesbarkeit*, ch. 16 discusses this process under the heading of the "romanticization" of the world, as pursued by some of the German romantics around 1800.

10   See on the context Andreas W. Daum, *Wissenschaftspopularisierung im 19. Jahrhundert: Bürgerliche Kultur, naturwissenschaftliche Bildung und die deutsche Öffentlichkeit 1848–1914* (Munich: Oldenbourg, 2nd edn. 2002).

11   Alfred Brehm, *Brehms Tierleben: Allgemeine Kunde des Tierreichs*, 4th edition, 13 vols. ed. Otto Zur Strassen (Leipzig, Vienna: Bibliographisches Institut, 1911–1918).

12   In accordance with Blumenberg, *Lesbarkeit*, 171–179. See Giambattista Vico, *The New Science* [3rd edn. 1744], transl. Thomas Goddard Bergin, Max H. Fisch (Ithaca, NY: Cornell University Press, 1948), Book II; see also Jürgen Trabant, *Vico's New Science of Ancient Signs*, transl. Sean Ward (London: Routledge, 2004).

13 Georg Jacob, *Schanfarà-Studien, 1: Der Wortschatz der Lâmîja nebst Übersetzung und beigefügtem Text* (Munich: Bayerische Akademie der Wissenschaften, 1914), 16f. n. 6.

14 The concluding chapter of Blumenberg, *Lesbarkeit,* on the genetic "code" and its replication through the "reading" practice of evolution, marks these points with particular clarity.

15 Wilhelm Dilthey, *Einleitung in die Geisteswissenschaften,* Gesammelte Schriften 1, ed. Bernhard Groethuysen (Leipzig: Teubner, 1922), XVI.

16 According to the terminology Dilthey deploys in *Der Aufbau der geschichtlichen Welt in den Geisteswissenschaften,* Gesammelte Schriften 7, ed. Bernhard Groethuysen (Leipzig: Teubner, 1927), 217.

17 Paul Ricœur, "The Model of the Text: Meaningful Action Considered as a Text," *New Literary History* 5, no. 1 (1973): 91–117.

18 See the poignant critique offered in James Clifford, "On Ethnographic Authority," *Representations* 1, no. 2 (1983): 118–46,

19 The most impressive survey to date of approaches to conceptual history and historical semantics in some form or other has been provided by Ernst Müller, Falko Schmieder, *Begriffsgeschichte und historische Semantik: Ein kritisches Kompendium* (Frankfurt a.M.: Suhrkamp, 2016). The volume also indirectly illustrates the reticence of theorists to ascribe historicity to semantics as such.

20 Ludwig Wittgenstein, *Philosophische Untersuchungen—Philosophical Investigations* [1953] (Oxford: Blackwell, 2001). The above remarks refer in particular to the early portions of the work; at this level of generality, it seems futile to offer a list of the respective numbered sections.

21 Jacob, *Schanfaras Lamîjat,* 5f.

22 Michel Foucault, *L'Archéologie du Savoir* (Paris: Gallimard, 1969); Franco Moretti, *Distant Reading* (London: Verso, 2013).

23 A model case of such transcripts can be found in the papers of David Magie, Mudd Manuscript Library, Princeton University, which would merit further study than can be accomplished in the present book.

24 Immanuel Kant, *Der Streit der Fakultäten* [1798], Akademie-Ausgabe 7 (Berlin: Reimer, 1907).

25 On the context, see William Clark, *Academic Charisma and the Origins of the Research University* (Chicago: University of Chicago Press, 2006).

26 See e.g. the précis by Michael Holquist, "Why We Should Remember Philology," *Profession* (2002): 72–9.

27 See below 41.

28 Michel Foucault, *The Order of Things: An Archaeology of the Human Sciences* [*Les mots et les choses,* 1966] (New York: Vintage, 1994).

29 Ibid., 294–300.

30 Edward W. Said, *Orientalism* [1978] (New York: Vintage, 1994).

31 John Darwin, *Unfinished Empire: The Global Expansion of Britain* (London: Allen Lane, 2012).

32 See Edward W. Said, *Culture and Imperialism* (New York: Knopf, 1993).

33 Paul Ricœur, *Freud and Philosophy: An Essay on Interpretation* [1965] (New Haven, CT: Yale University Press, 1970), 32–6, although the exact phrase that has become proverbial is actually not the author's.

34 Siraj Ahmed, *The Archaeology of Babel: The Colonial Foundation of the Humanities* (Stanford, CA: Stanford University Press, 2017), 29–37 and first chapter.

35 Ibid., 37.

36   Bernard S. Cohn, "The Command of Language and the Language of Command" [1985], in *Colonialism and Its Forms of Knowledge: The British in India* (Princeton: Princeton University Press, 1996), 16–56.

37   Ibid., 19.

38   Nicholas A. Germana, *The Anxiety of Autonomy and the Aesthetics of German Orientalism* (Rochester, NY: Camden House, 2017).

39   See, however, Philippe Bornet, Svetlana Gorshenina, eds., *Orientalismes des marges: Éclairages à partir de l'Inde et de la Russie* (Lausanne: Université de Lausanne, 2014). The analysis of category-defying cases of Orientalisms has been a longstanding concern; as a model for this line of argument, see Ann Thomson, *Barbary and Enlightenment: European Attitudes toward the Maghreb in the Eighteenth Century* (Leiden: Brill, 1987).

40   Robert Irwin, *For Lust of Knowing: The Orientalists and Their Enemies* (London: Allen Lane, 2005).

41   Raymond Schwab, *The Oriental Renaissance: Europe's Discovery of India and the East, 1689–1880* [1950] (New York: Columbia University Press, 1984).

42   Tuska Benes, *In Babel's Shadow: Language, Philology and the Nation in Nineteenth-Century Germany* (Detroit: Wayne State University Press, 2008).

43   Thus the (partial) title of ch. 11 of Hans W. Frei, *The Eclipse of Biblical Narrative: A Study in Eighteenth and Nineteenth Century Hermeneutics* (Princeton, NJ: Princeton University Press, 1974). See also Azade Seyhan, *Representation and Its Discontents: The Critical Legacy of German Romanticism* (Berkeley: University of California Press, 1992); Martha B. Helfer, *The Retreat of Representation: The Concept of Darstellung in German Critical Discourse* (Albany: State University of New York Press, 1996).

44   See e.g. Martin Jay, *Downcast Eyes: The Denigration of Vision in Twentieth-Century French Thought* (Berkeley: University of California Press, 1993).

45   See e.g. Anthony Giddens, *The Consequences of Modernity* (Stanford, CA: Stanford University Press, 1990), ch. III.

46   Hugo von Hofmannsthal, "Ein Brief" [1902], *Sämtliche Werke 31: Erfundene Gespräche und Briefe*, ed. Ellen Ritter (Frankfurt a.M.: Fischer, 1991), 45–55.

47   See e.g. Hartmut Rosa, *Social Acceleration: A New Theory of Modernity* [2013], transl. Jonathan Trejo-Mathys (New York: Columbia University Press, 2016); the argument is indebted to Reinhart Koselleck, *Futures Past: On the Semantics of Historical Time* [1979], transl. Keith Tribe (New York: Columbia University Press, 2004).

48   For a perspective from the history and philosophy of science, see Gregor Schiemann, *Hermann von Helmholtz's Mechanism: The Loss of Certainty, a Study on the Transition from Classical to Modern Philosophy of Nature* [1997], transl. Cynthia Klohr (Dordrecht: Springer, 2009).

49   As introduced by Ian Hacking, *Historical Ontology* (Cambridge, MA: Harvard University Press, 2002).

50   On the concept, see Hans-Jörg Rheinberger, *On Historicizing Epistemology: An Essay*, transl. David Fernbach (Stanford, CA: Stanford University Press, 2010).

51   For partial histories of the field, see the still indispensable pan-European handbook on the history of Arabic studies by Johann Fück, *Die Geschichte der arabischen Studien in Europa bis in den Anfang des 20. Jahrhunderts* (Leipzig: Harrassowitz, 1955); for the history of the study of Islam, see also Jean-Jacques Waardenburg, *L'Islam dans le miroir de l'occident: Comment quelques orientalistes occidentaux se sont penchés sur l'Islam et se sont formés une image de cette religion. Goldziher, Snouck Hurgronje, Becker, Macdonald, Massignon* (Paris:

Mouton, 3rd edn. 1969); and for Germany, Ludmilla Hanisch, *Die Nachfolger der Exegeten: Deutschsprachige Erforschung des Vorderen Orients in der ersten Hälfte des 20. Jahrhunderts* (Wiesbaden: Harrassowitz, 2003); Sabine Mangold, *Eine "weltbürgerliche Wissenschaft": Die deutsche Orientalistik im 19. Jahrhundert* (Stuttgart: Steiner, 2004); Ursula Wokoeck, *German Orientalism: The Study of the Middle East and Islam from 1800 to 1945* (London: Routledge, 2009); Ian Almond, *History of Islam in German Thought: From Leibniz to Nietzsche* (London: Routledge, 2010).

52 Apart from the historical compendium by Ernst Windisch, *Geschichte der Sanskrit-Philologie und indischen Altertumskunde*, 1–3 (Berlin: de Gruyter, 1917–21), see Dorothy Figueira, *Translating the Orient: The Reception of Śākuntala in Nineteenth-Century Europe* (Albany: State University of New York Press, 1991); Douglas McGetchin et al., eds., *Sanskrit and "Orientalism": Indology and Comparative Linguistics in Germany, 1750–1958* (Delhi: Manohar, 2004); Indra Sengupta, *From Salon to Discipline: University and Indology in Germany, 1821–1914* (Heidelberg: Ergon, 2005); Bradley Herling, *The German Gita: Hermeneutics and Discipline in the Early German Reception of Indian Thought, 1778–1831* (London: Routledge, 2006); Pascale Rabault-Feuerhahn, *L'archive des origines: Sanskrit, philologie, anthropologie dans l'Allemagne du XIXe siècle* (Paris: Editions du Cerf, 2008); Douglas McGetchin, *Indology, Indomania, Orientalism: Ancient India's Rebirth in Modern Germany* (Madison, WI: Fairleigh Dickinson University Press, 2009); Nicholas Germana, *The Orient of Europe: The Mythical Image of India and Competing Images of German National Identity* (Newcastle: Cambridge Scholars Publishing, 2009). An early, indispensable quarry of information and important document of disciplinary self-knowledge is moreover Theodor Benfey, *Geschichte der Sprachwissenschaft und orientalischen Philologie in Deutschland seit dem Anfange des 19. Jahrhunderts, mit einem Rückblick auf frühere Zeiten* (Munich: Cotta, 1869).

53 Suzanne Marchand, *German Orientalism in the Age of Empire: Religion, Race, and Scholarship* (Cambridge: Cambridge University Press, 2009).

54 See on this in particular Maurice Olender, *The Languages of Paradise: Race, Religion, and Philology in the Nineteenth Century* [1989] (Cambridge, MA: Harvard University Press, 2nd edn. 2008), for an integrative account. For an important perspective on the complexity of Aryanist racism in the British Empire, see Tony Ballantyne, *Orientalism and Race: Aryanism in the British Empire* (Basingstoke: Palgrave, 2002).

55 For a prominent example, see Susannah Heschel, *Abraham Geiger and the Jewish Jesus* (Chicago: University of Chicago Press, 1998).

56 The most extensive survey of contemporary Arabic responses to European Orientalism I am aware of is the unpublished dissertation by Ronen Raz, *The Transparent Mirror: Arab Intellectuals and Orientalism, 1798–1950* (PhD Dissertation, Princeton University, 1997).

57 Vishwa Adluri; Joydeep Bagchee, *The Nay Science: A History of German Indology* (Oxford: Oxford University Press, 2014).

58 Adluri, Bagchee, *Nay Science*, ch. 4–5.

59 A classical model for this view on linguistics is Hans Aarsleff, *The Study of Language in England, 1780–1860* (Princeton, NJ: Princeton University Press, 1967). See also the important argument in Benes, *In Babel's Shadow*, which identifies a lineage linking nineteenth-century philological understandings of language to 1960s antihumanist

theory, but like Foucault privileges comparative linguistics at the expense of other genealogical connections.

60 On Semitic languages see Robert Hetzron, ed., *The Semitic Languages* (London: Routledge, 1997); and Stefan Weninger, ed., *Semitic Languages: An International Handbook* (Berlin: de Gruyter, 2011); from the ambit of the studies discussed in the present book, see Carl Brockelmann, *Grundriss der vergleichenden semitischen Grammatik*, 2 vols. (Berlin: Reuther & Reichard, 1908–13).

61 Sheldon Pollock, *Language of the Gods in the World of Men: Sanskrit, Culture, and Power in Pre-Modern India* (Berkeley: University of California Press, 2006).

62 Sanjay Subrahmanyam, *Courtly Encounters: Translating Courtliness and Violence in Early Modern Eurasia* (Cambridge, MA: Harvard University Press, 2012).

Chapter 1

1 See e.g. Louis Aragon et al., *Essais de critique génétique*, afterword by Louis Hay (Paris: Flammarion, 1979); Almuth Grésillon, *Eléments de critique génétique: Lire les manuscrits modernes* (Paris: Presses Universitaires de France, 1994).

2 As an instructive case study, see Stephen G. Alter, *William Dwight Whitney and the Science of Language* (Baltimore: Johns Hopkins University Press, 2005).

3 Edward W. Said, "The Return to Philology," in *Humanism and Democratic Criticism* (New York: Columbia University Press, 2004), 57–84. See further Hans Ulrich Gumbrecht, *The Powers of Philology: Dynamics of Textual Scholarship* (Urbana: University of Illinois Press, 2003); Christian Benne, *Nietzsche und die historisch-kritische Philologie* (Berlin, New York. de Gruyter, 2005); Sheldon Pollock, "Future Philology? The Fate of a Soft Science in a Hard World," *Critical Inquiry* 35, no. 4 (2009): 931–61, Jürgen Paul Schwindt, ed., *Was ist eine philologische Frage? Beiträge zur Erkundung einer theoretischen Einstellung* (Frankfurt a.M.: Suhrkamp, 2009), Sean Gurd, ed., *Philology and Its Histories*, Columbus: Ohio State University Press, 2010; Werner Hamacher, *Minima Philologica*, transl. Catherine Diehl, Jason Groves (New York: Fordham University Press, 2015); Andrew Hui, "The Many Returns of Philology: A State of the Field Report," *Journal of the History of Ideas* 78, no. 1 (2017): 137–56.

4 As is the working definition, and arguably the plight, of James Turner, *Philology: The Forgotten Origins of the Modern Humanities* (Princeton, NJ: Princeton University Press, 2014).

5 Paul de Man, "The Return to Philology" [1982], in *The Resistance to Theory* (Minneapolis: University of Minnesota Press, 1986), 21–6. See also the discussion of the convergence of Said and de Man in Geoffrey Galt Harpham, "Roots, Races, and the Return to Philology," *Representations* 106 (2009), spring: 34–62.

6 De Man, "Return," 24, where the portrayal of Brower's agenda is not entirely faithful if one compares William H. Pritchard, "Teaching: Reuben A. Brower," *The American Scholar* 54, no. 2 (1985): 239–47, and, as a first-hand account, Reuben A. Brower, "Reading in Slow Motion" [1959], in idem, Richard Poirier, eds., *In Defense of Reading* (New York: E. P. Dutton, 1962), 3–21.

7 See e.g. the closing remarks in Paul de Man, "The Concept of Irony," in *Aesthetic Ideology*, ed. Andrzej Warminski (Minneapolis: University of Minnesota Press, 1996), 163–84, where the author notes the "curious," inimical linkage between historical narrative and the flight of meaning in irony.

8   Jan Ziolkowski, "What Is Philology?" *Comparative Literature Studies* 27, no. 1
    (1990): 4. Ziolkowski also saw the then-current "clash" of "literary theory"
    and "philology" "memorably anticipated" (ibid.) by the Wilamowitz-Nietzsche
    controversy.

9   See Richard Utz, *Chaucer and the Discourse of German Philology: A History of
    Reception and an Annotated Bibliography of Studies, 1798–1948* (Turnhout: Brepols,
    2002).

10 Emil Staiger, *Die Kunst der Interpretation* (Zurich: Atlantis, 1955).

11 See esp. I. A. Richards, *Practical Criticism* (London: Kegan Paul, 1929). On
    Richards's approach, see also the sharply critical account by René Wellek, *A
    History of Modern Criticism*, 4, no. 1 (New Haven, CT: Yale University Press,
    1986), pt. 1, ch. 7. See also Barbara Herrnstein Smith, "What Was 'Close Reading'?
    A Century of Method in Literary Studies," *Minnesota Review* 87 (2016): 57–75,
    which however does not opt to pursue the transnational genealogy of the formula
    in its title.

12 Paul de Man, *Blindness and Insight: Essays in the Rhetoric of Contemporary Criticism*
    (New York: Oxford University Press, 1971).

13 See especially the chapters on Nietzsche in Paul de Man, *Allegories of Reading:
    Figural Language in Rousseau, Nietzsche, Rilke, and Proust* (New Haven, CT: Yale
    University Press, 1982).

14 Pollock, "Future Philology?," 933.

15 Nietzsche, *Morgenröthe* [1887], Kritische Studienausgabe (KSA) 3 (Berlin: de
    Gruyter, 1988²), Vorrede, §5 (transl. modified from J. M. Kennedy's, 1911).

16 For Nietzsche on philology, see James I. Porter, *Nietzsche and the Philology of
    the Future* (Stanford, CA: Stanford University Press, 2000); see further Benne,
    Nietzsche. On the tradition of Pyrrhonism, see moreover Markus Völkel,
    *"Pyrrhonismus" und "fides historica": Die Entwicklung der deutschen historischen
    Methodologie unter dem Gesichtspunkt der historischen Skepsis* (Frankfurt a.M.:
    Lang, 1987); Richard H. Popkin, *The High Road to Pyrrhonism* (Indianapolis:
    Hackett, 2nd edn. 1993).

17 According to Porter, *Nietzsche*, ch. 3. It bears mention that de Man may well be
    read as suppressing attempts to temporalize reading, see e.g. his respective remarks
    in "Kant and Schiller," in *Aesthetic Ideology*, ed. Andrzej Warminski (Minneapolis:
    University of Minnesota Press, 1996) 133f.

18 Nietzsche, *Morgenröthe*, § 5.

19 Since Schleiermacher at the latest, the notion that the understanding of language
    generally and reading in particular was an "art" had become topical, see his
    Hermeneutik und Kritik, ed. Manfred Frank (Frankfurt a.M.: Suhrkamp, 1977),
    80f. This novel terminology emerged in a field of theoretical qualifications
    of the reading process that was highly active, as Ulrich Johannes Schneider,
    Die Vergangenheit des Geistes: Eine Archäologie der Philosophiegeschichte
    (Frankfurt a.M.: Suhrkamp, 1990), has shown.

20 De Man, *Return*, 25.

21 De Man, "Kant and Schiller," 155.

22 See the damning remarks on de Man's allegedly merely insidious interest in
    irony, in Edward W. Said, "Reflections on American 'Left' Literary Criticism," in
    The World, the Text, and the Critic (Cambridge, MA: Harvard University Press,
    1984), 163.

23 Said, "Return," 58. See also Vera Tolz's alternative hypothesis as to the indirect formation of Said's approach, by way of Soviet-educated Lebanese scholars, through the tradition of Russian Orientalism, which was bent on accommodating national minorities and hybridity within the frame of an inland empire and critical of the Western European ostentation of superiority over Asia; this intriguing proposal certainly merits further research, Vera Tolz, *Russia's Own Orient: The Politics of Identity and Oriental Studies in the Late Imperial and Early Soviet Periods* (Oxford: Oxford University Press, 2011), here esp. ch. 2.

24 Said, "Return," 60.

25 Ibid., 61.

26 See e.g. the strikingly casual mention of "the great philologists such as Erich Auerbach, E. R. Curtius, and Leo Spitzer" in Harpham, "Roots," 35.

27 On Spitzer, see Hans Ulrich Gumbrecht, *Leo Spitzers Stil* (Tübingen: Narr, 2001); idem, *Vom Leben und Sterben der großen Romanisten* (Munich: Hanser, 2002); also James V. Catano, *Language, History, Style: Leo Spitzer and the Critical Tradition* (London: Routledge, 1988); on Auerbach, see Seth Lerer, *Literary History and the Challenge of Philology: The Legacy of Erich Auerbach* (Stanford, CA: Stanford University Press, 1988); Kader Konuk, *East West Mimesis: Erich Auerbach in Turkey* (Stanford, CA: Stanford University Press, 2010); and most pertinently to the concerns of the present chapter, James I. Porter, "Erich Auerbach and the Judaizing of Philology," *Critical Inquiry* 35, no. 1 (2008): 115–47, which expounds the political implications of Auerbach's unique perspective in the context of the anti-Semitism of 1920s and 30s German philology.

28 Said, "Return," 66.

29 Sheldon Pollock, "Philology and Freedom," *Philological Encounters* 1 (2016): 13f.

30 Pollock, "Philology and Freedom," 19.

31 The importance of the theory of writing and script, in part of the history of early-nineteenth-century philology, has been demonstrated by Markus Messling, *Pariser Orientlektüren: Zu Wilhelm von Humboldts Theorie der Schrift* (Paderborn: Schöningh, 2008). Consideration of the actual practices of writing, however, remains lacking.

32 Gottlob Frege, "Über Begriff und Gegenstand" [1892], in *Funktion, Begriff, Bedeutung: Fünf logische Studien*, ed. Günther Patzig (Göttingen: Vandenhoeck & Ruprecht, 2nd edn. 2008), 47–60.

33 Reinhart Koselleck, "Einleitung," in *Geschichtliche Grundbegriffe: Historisches Lexikon zur politisch-sozialen Sprache in Deutschland*, ed. idem, Werner Conze and Otto Brunner, 1 (Stuttgart: Klett Cotta, 1972), XIII–XXVII.

34 Naming as a *Herrenrecht* expressive of power, Nietzsche, *Zur Genealogie der Moral: Eine Streitschrift* [1887], KSA 5 (Berlin: de Gruyter, 2nd edn. 1988), 260, § 2.

35 Reinhart Koselleck et al., "Geschichte," in *Geschichtliche Grundbegriffe*, 2 (Stuttgart: Klett Cotta, 1979), 593–717.

36 Gottlob Frege, "Über Sinn und Bedeutung" [1892], in *Funktion*, 23–46.

37 See Claude Lévi-Strauss, *La pensée sauvage* (Paris: Plon, 1962), ch. 7. It may also be opportune to point to Benjamin's repeated reliance on the biblical myth of the origin of language in Paradise. Naming then becomes a metaphor for a semantics that cannot be freed from figuration and representation in the form of a (primal) scene, see Walter Benjamin, *Ursprung des deutschen Trauerspiels* [1928], ed. Rolf Tiedemann (Frankfurt a.M.: Suhrkamp, 1978), 15–20.

38   Sebastiano Timpanaro, *La genesi del metodo di Lachmann* (Florence: Le Monnier, 1963).
39   A more comprehensive and equally indispensable pedigree of this line of early modern philology is laid out by Anthony Grafton, *Defenders of the Text: The Traditions of Scholarship in an Age of Science* (Cambridge, MA: Harvard University Press, 1991).
40   See, for instance, Markus Messling, Ottmar Ette, eds., *Wort Macht Stamm: Rassismus und Determinismus in der Philologie* (Munich: Fink, 2013); and Maurice Olender, *Race and Erudition* (Cambridge, MA: Harvard University Press, 2009).
41   Michel Foucault, "Nietzsche, la généalogie et l'histoire," in *Hommage à Jean Hippolyte*, ed. Suzanne Bachelard et al. (Paris: Presses Universitaires de France, 1971), 145–172.
42   James I. Porter, "'Don't Quote Me on That!': Wilamowitz Contra Nietzsche in 1872 and 1873," *Journal of Nietzsche Studies* 42 (2011): 80.
43   As is clear from Rohde to Nietzsche June 5, 1872, *Friedrich Nietzsches Briefwechsel mit E. Rohde*, ed. E. Förster-Nietzsche, F. Schöll (Leipzig: Insel, 2nd edn. 1903), 318, which is the first mention of Wilamowitz's pamphlet in the correspondence. Nietzsche's approval is in the response from June 8, ibid., 320, and another corroboration follows in the letter from June 18, ibid., 327.
44   Erwin Rohde, *Afterphilologie: Zur Beleuchtung des von dem Dr. phil. Ulrich von Wilamowitz-Moellendorff herausgegebenen Pamphlets: ,Zukunftsphilologie!'. Sendschreiben eines Philologen an Richard Wagner* (Leipzig: E. W. Fritzsch, 1872), 40.
45   Ulrich von Wilamowitz-Moellendorff, *Erinnerungen 1848–1914* [1928] (Leipzig: Koehler, 2nd edn. 1932), 129.
46   Ulrich von Wilamowitz-Moellendorff, *Zukunftsphilologie! Zweites Stück. Eine erwidrung auf die rettungsversuche für Fr. Nietzsches "geburt der tragödie"* (Berlin: Borntraeger, 1873).
47   Nietzsche to Rohde October 25, 1872, *Nietzsche-Rohde Briefwechsel*, 354.
48   Wilamowitz, *Erinnerungen*, 130.
49   Nietzsche to Rohde, July 16, 1872, *Nietzsche-Rohde Briefwechsel*, 335.
50   Rohde to Nietzsche, late July 1872, *Nietzsche-Rohde Briefwechsel*, 343.
51   Nietzsche to Rohde, August 2, 1872, *Nietzsche-Rohde Briefwechsel*, 344.
52   Nietzsche, *Genealogie der Moral*, § 7.
53   Richard Wagner, *Das Judenthum in der Musik* (Leipzig: J. J. Weber, 1869), 36.
54   Richard Wagner, *Zukunftsmusik: Brief an einen französischen Freund* (Leipzig: J. J. Weber, 1861).
55   Nietzsche to Rohde, June 8, 1872, *Nietzsche-Rohde Briefwechsel*, 321.
56   Nietzsche to Rohde, May 5, 1873, *Nietzsche-Rohde Briefwechsel*, 406.
57   Rohde, *Afterphilologie*, 12 [emphasis added].
58   Nietzsche, *Wir Philologen* [1875], Nachgelassene Fragmente 1875–1879, KSA 8 (Berlin: de Gruyter, 2nd edn. 1988), § 123.
59   With the formula introduced by Johannes Fabian, *Time and the Other: How Anthropology Makes Its Object* (New York: Columbia University Press, 1983).
60   Taking a cue, if perhaps somewhat inexactly, from Helge Jordheim, "Philology of the Future, Futures of Philology: Interdisciplinarity, Intertemporality, and *Begriffsgeschichte*," in Hans Lauge Hansen, ed., *Disciplines and Interdisciplinarity in Foreign Language Study* (Copenhagen: Museum Tusculanum, 2004), 35–50.
61   Using the translation offered by Gregory Fried, *Heidegger's Polemos: From Being to Politics* (New Haven, CT: Yale University Press, 2000), 21.

62　See Heidegger, *Einführung in die Metaphysik* [1935], Gesamtausgabe 40 (Frankfurt a.M.: Klostermann, 1983), 47.

63　In the beginning of *Geburt der Tragödie* [1872], KSA 1 (Berlin: de Gruyter, 2nd edn. 1988), §4, Nietzsche speaks of "eternal contradiction, the father of things" ("… des ewigen Widerspruchs, des Vaters der Dinge").

64　Fried, *Heidegger's Polemos*, 21.

65　Hermann Diels, *Die Fragmente der Vorsokratiker* [1903], 5th edn. Walther Kranz (Hildesheim: Weidmann, 1934). For the overall context, see Glenn W. Most, "Die Vorsokratiker in der Forschung der Zwanziger Jahre," in Hellmut Flashar, Sabine Vogt, eds., *Altertumswissenschaft in den 20er Jahren: Neue Fragen und Impulse* (Stuttgart: Steiner, 1995), 87–114.

66　Ulrich von Wilamowitz-Moellendorff, *Zukunftsphilologie! Eine erwidrung auf Friedrich Nietzsches "geburt der tragödie"* (Berlin: Borntraeger, 1872), 4–5.

67　Friedrich August Wolf, *Encyclopädie der Philologie: Nach dessen Vorlesungen im Winterhalbjahre von 1789–1799*, ed. S. M. Stockmann (Leipzig: Expedition des Europäischen Aufsehers, 1831); see also his programmatic *Darstellung der Alterthums-Wissenschaft nach Begriff, Umfang, Zweck und Werth* (Berlin: Realschulbuchahndlung, 1807); on Wolf's foundational role for the discipline, see Constanze Güthenke, "'Enthusiasm Dwells Only in Specialization': Classical Philology and Disciplinarity in Nineteenth-Century Germany," in Pollock et al., eds., *World Philology*, 264–84.

68　The main texts were reprinted in Gottfried Hermann, *Über Herrn Professor Böckhs Behandlung der griechischen Inschriften* (Leipzig: Gerhard Fleischer, 1826). It was in the preface to this compilation, pp. 3–10, that Hermann first provided a concentrated formulation of the two positions regarding the primacy of things or language. It had been Boeckh's student M. H. Eduard Meier who, in defense of his teacher, had introduced this theoretical problem into the polemic, ibid., 101, which had otherwise mainly addressed personal animosities and the reading of individual inscriptions.

69　For a nineteenth-century codification of the terms see Conrad Bursian, *Geschichte der classischen Philologie in Deutschland von den Anfängen bis zur Gegenwart*, 2 vols. (Munich: Oldenbourg, 1883), 2, book 4, ch. 2. On the controversy and its context see Ernst Vogt, "Der Methodenstreit zwischen Hermann und Böckh und seine Bedeutung für die Geschichte der Philologie," in Hellmut Flashar et al., eds., *Philologie und Hermeneutik im 19. Jahrhundert: Zur Geschichte und Methodologie der Geisteswissenschaften* (Göttingen: Vandenhoeck & Ruprecht, 1979), 103–21; Wilfried Nippel, "Philologenstreit und Schulpolitik: Zur Kontroverse zwischen Gottfried Hermann und August Böckh," in Wolfgang Küttler et al., eds., *Geschichtsdiskurs 3: Die Epoche der Historisierung* (Frankfurt a.M.: Fischer, 1997), 244–53; Christine Hackel, *Die Bedeutung August Boeckhs für den Geschichtstheoretiker Johann Gustav Droysen: Die Enzyklopädie-Vorlesungen im Vergleich* (Würzburg: Königshausen & Neumann, 2006); Thomas Poiss, "Zur Idee der Philologie: Der Streit zwischen Gottfried Hermann und August Boeckh," in Kurt Sier and Eva Wöckener-Gade, eds., *Gottfried Hermann (1772–1848): Internationales Symposium in Leipzig, 11–13 Oktober 2007* (Tübingen: Narr, 2010), 143–63.

70　As laid out in the beginning chapter of Boeckh's posthumously published *Enzyklopädie und Methodologie der philologischen Wissenschaften*, ed. Ernst Bartuschek (Leipzig: Teubner, 1877).

71   Schleiermacher, *Hermeneutik und Kritik*, 77.
72   It is not then quite precise to assume that the relation between theory and philology
     was inimical in the nineteenth century, cf. e.g. Nikolaus Wegmann, "The Future
     of Philology—an Update," in Hannes Bajohr et al., eds., *The Future of Philology:
     Proceedings of the 11th Annual Columbia University German Graduate Student
     Conference* (Newcastle/Tyne: Cambridge Scholars Publ., 2014), 25–7.
73   Friedrich Schleiermacher, "Über den Begriff der Hermeneutik mit Bezug auf
     F. A. Wolfs Andeutungen und Asts Lehrbuch" [1829], in *Hermeneutik und Kritik*,
     ed. Manfred Frank (Frankfurt a.M.: Suhrkamp, 1977), 312f.
74   See e.g. the lemma *Theorie* in Rudolf Eisler, *Kant-Lexikon* (Berlin: Mittler & Sohn,
     1930).
75   As is indirectly confirmed by Philipp Felsch, *Der lange Sommer der Theorie:
     Geschichte einer Revolte* (Munich: Beck, 2015), who appeals to a variety of
     extraneous cultural connotations in order to substantiate his notion that the
     1960s and 70s constituted a particular epoch in the conceptual history of
     "theory."
76   Friedrich Ast, *Grundlinien der Grammatik, Hermeneutik und Kritik* (Landshut: Jos.
     Thomann, 1808), §75; Schleiermacher, "Begriff der Hermeneutik," 328.
77   Rohde, *Afterphilologie*, 11 (with the quotation: "Il est impossible, de ranger les
     pieces, à qui n'a une forme du total en sa teste").
78   G. W. F. Hegel, *Enzyklopädie der philosophischen Wissenschaften*, ed.Wolfgang
     Bonsiepen and Hans-Christian Lucas (Hamburg: Meiner, 1992), §16; see further
     Phänomenologie des Geistes, ed. Wolfgang Bonsiepen and Reinhard Heede
     (Hamburg: Meiner, 1980), 9; see also the important annotation in Porter, *Nietzsche*,
     310, n. 119 regarding the history of the metaphor.
79   See Friedrich Schlegel, "Zur Philologie, I" [1797], in *Fragmente zur Poesie und
     Literatur* 1, ed. Hans Eichner, KFSA 16 (Paderborn: Schöningh, Zürich: Thomas,
     1981), nos. 14, 60, 62. Schleiermacher used the term frequently in his lectures; it
     is well known that he developed his thought in dialogue with Schlegel's and that
     Boeckh adopted many of Schlegel's positions from Schleiermacher indirectly (see
     Schlegel, KFSA 16, XVI-XIX).
80   Schlegel, "Zur Philologie I," no. 5.
81   Friedrich Schlegel, "Zur Philologie II" [1797], in *Fragmente zur Poesie und Literatur*
     1, ed. Hans Eichner, KFSA 16 (Paderborn: Schöningh, Zürich: Thomas, 1981),
     no. 77.
82   Immanuel Kant, *Kritik der reinen Vernunft* [B 1787], *Akademie-Ausgabe* 3 (Berlin:
     Reimer, 1904), 538.
83   Leibniz introduces the term right away in §2 of *Monadologie* [1714], ed. Hartmut
     Hecht (Stuttgart: Reclam, 1998), where it marks a composite of substances. It
     is worth adding that according to Johann Christoph Adelung, *Grammatisch-
     kritisches Wörterbuch der hochdeutschen Mundart* (Vienna: Bauer, 1811), 1,
     182f., an "aggregate is an accumulation [*Haufen*] of plural things that have been
     brought together. Especially (1) in arithmetic where the aggregate is the sum. (2)
     In physics [i.e. natural philosophy] the aggregate is a combination, into a whole,
     of several such parts that themselves consist of notably different parts, and a
     thing combined in such a manner; an accumulation; a clustering." The second
     definition is remarkable because it suggests that aggregation means a second-order
     accumulation whose principles of combination differ from those effective in the
     first order.

84   See Dietrich von Engelhardt, *Hegel und die Chemie: Studien zur Philosophie und Wissenschaft der Natur um 1800* (Wiesbaden: Harrassowitz, 1976); John William Burbridge, *Real Process: How Logic and Chemistry Combine in Hegel's Philosophy of Nature* (Toronto: University of Toronto Press, 1996); For the broader context see Timothy Lenoir, *The Strategy of Life: Teleology and Mechanics in Nineteenth-Century German Biology* (Dordrecht: Reidel, 1982); Peter Hanns Reill, *Vitalizing Nature in the Enlightenment* (Berkeley: University of California Press, 2005); and Jonathan Sheehan, Dror Wahrman, *Invisible Hands: Self-Organization and the Eighteenth Century* (Chicago: University of Chicago Press, 2015).

85   E.g. Boeckh, *Enzyklopädie*, 40.

86   August Boeckh, *Metrologische Untersuchungen über Gewichte, Münzfüße und Maße des Alterthums in ihrem Zusammenhange* (Berlin: Veit, 1838).

87   The use of the term "system" was uncontroversial and ordinary still in the 1880s, when Bursian, *Geschichte*, 2, 703, described Boeckh's stance.

88   See esp. Joachim Dyck, *Athen und Jerusalem: Bibel und Poesie in der Tradition ihrer Verknüpfung* (Munich: Beck, 1977).

89   It is this contradictory structure that makes problematic the one-sided emphasis on specialization as fragmentation that drives e.g. the argument of Turner, *Philology*.

90   Michel Bréal, *Semantics: Studies in the Science of Meaning* [1897], transl. Nina Cust (New York: Henry Holt, 1900), 99.

91   See Marc Décimo, *Sciences et Pataphysique, 2: Comment la linguistique vint à Paris—De Michel Bréal à Ferdinand de Saussure* (Dijon: Les presses du réel, 2014), 70, who refers to Bréal's obituary by Salomon Reinach, *Revue archéologique* 1916 (5e série, tôme III), no. 1: 145 (with reference to Reisig's "semasiology").

92   Karl Christian Reisig, *Vorlesungen über lateinische Sprachwissenschaft*, ed. Friedrich Haase (Leipzig: Lehnhold'sche Buchhandlung, 1839), part 2.

93   Adolf Zauner, *Die romanischen Namen der Körperteile: Eine onomasiologische Studie* (Erlangen: Junge & Sohn, 1902).

94   Bréal, *Semantics*, 6f.

95   Ibid., 11f.

96   Important perspectives on this problematic in the context of Orientalism are provided by Pascale Rabault-Feuerhahn, Céline Trautmann-Waller, eds., *Itinéraires orientalistes entre France et Allemagne*, theme issue, *Revue germanique internationale* 7 (2008); Bénédicte Savoy, *Nofretete, eine deutsch-französische Affäre 1912–1931* (Cologne: Böhlau, 2011).

97   Michel Foucault, "Le cycle des grenouilles" [1962], *Dits et écrits I* (Paris: Gallimard, 1994), 204. See also Andrew Hugill, *Pataphysics: A Useless Guide* (Cambridge, MA: MIT Press, 2012), esp. 185–9.

98   On the wider cultural significance of grammar in the history of European scholarship, which I will not explore here, see Michel de Certeau, Dominique Julia, Jacques Revel, *Une politique de la langue: La Révolution française et les patois* (Paris: Gallimard, 1975); Linda C. Mitchell, *Grammar Wars: Language as Cultural Battlefield in 17th and 18th Century England* (Aldershot: Ashgate, 2001).

99   Heinrich Leberecht Fleischer, *Kleinere Schriften, gesammelt, durchgesehen und vermehrt, vols. 1–2: Beiträge zur arabischen Sprachkunde* [1863–1876] (Leipzig: Hirzel, 1885–88); Carl Paul Caspari, *A Grammar of the Arabic Language. Translated from the German and edited with numerous additions and corrections by William Wright*, 2 vols. (Cambridge: Cambridge University Press, 1859–62); Albert Socin, *Arabische Grammatik: Paradigmen, Litteratur, Chrestomathie und Glossar*

(Karlsruhe: Reuther 1885). On Wright see Bernhard Maier, *Semitic Studies in Victorian Britain: A Portrait of William Wright and his World through his Letters* (Würzburg: Ergon, 2011).

100 Carl Paul Caspari, *Arabische Grammatik*, revised and ed. by August Müller (Halle: Buchhandlung des Waisenhauses, 1876).

101 Albert Socin, *Arabische Grammatik*, revised and ed. by Carl Brockelmann (Berlin: Reuther, 5th edn. 1904).

102 Hermann Reckendorf, *Die syntaktischen Verhältnisse des Arabischen* (Leiden: Brill, 1898); and idem, *Arabische Syntax* (Heidelberg: Winter, 1921).

103 Theodor Nöldeke, *Zur Grammatik des classichen Arabisch* [1897]. *Im Anhang: die handschriftlichen Ergänzungen in dem Handexemplar Theodor Nöldekes, bearbeitet und mit Zusätzen versehen von Anton Spitaler* (Darmstadt: Wissenschaftliche Buchgesellschaft, 1963).

104 On the older history of Arabic grammars in Europe, see Fück, *Arabische Studien*, passim; Carolyn G. Killean, "The Development of Western Grammars of Arabic," *Journal of Near Eastern Studies* 43, no. 3 (1984): 223–30; Hartmut Bobzin, "Guillaume Postel (1510–1581) und die Geschichte der arabischen Nationalgrammatik," in Michael G. Carter, Kees Versteegh, eds., *Studies in the History of Arabic Grammar*, 2 (Amsterdam: Benjamins, 1990), 57–71; Hartmut Bobzin, "Geschichte der arabischen Philologie in Europa bis zum Ausgang des achtzehnten Jahrhunderts," in Wolfdietrich Fischer, ed., *Grundriss der Arabischen Philologie, 3: Supplement* (Wiesbaden: Reichert, 1992), 155–87.

105 On the study of Arabic grammar writing see Georges Bohas et al., *The Arabic Linguistic Tradition* (London: Routledge, 1990); Kees Versteegh, *Arabic Grammar and Qur'ānic Exegesis* (Leiden: Brill, 1993); and for Arabic theoretical views on language, idem, *Landmarks in Linguistic Thought III: The Arabic Linguistic Tradition* (London: Routledge, 1997).

106 Matthew Lumsden, *A Grammar of the Arabic Language According to the Principles Taught and Maintained in the Schools of Arabia* (Calcutta: F. Dissent, 1813), especially 48–50 on the author's acceptance of the very basics of the Arab grammatical tradition.

107 Antoine-Isaac Silvestre de Sacy, *Grammaire arabe* [1810] (Paris: Imprimerie Royale, 2nd edn. 1831), I, préface, X.

108 As he more explicitly laid out in his *Principes de grammaire générale, mis à la portée des enfans, et propres à servir d'introduction à l'étude de toutes les langues* (Paris: Delance et Lesueur, 2nd edn. 1803).

109 Heinrich Ewald, *Grammatica critica linguae arabicae*, 2 vols. (Leipzig: Libraria Hahniana, 1831).

110 As laid out in the posthumous Wilhelm von Humboldt, *Über die Verschiedenheit des menschlichen Sprachbaues und ihren Einfluß auf die geistige Entwicklung des Menschengeschlechts* [1836], ed. Donatella di Cesare (Paderborn: Schöningh, 1998); Fück, *Arabische Studien*, 167, notes the Humboldtian influence on Ewald and the contrast with Silvestre de Sacy's orientation toward Port-Royal.

111 Heinrich Ewald, *Ausführliches Lehrbuch der hebräischen Sprache des Alten Bundes* (Leipzig Hahn'sche Verlagsbuchhandlung, 5th edn. 1844), 27f.

112 As pointed out by both Fück, *Arabische Studien*, 200, and Killean, "Development," 226.

113 From a mission context, P. Donat Vernier, SJ, *Grammaire arabe composée d'après les sources primitives*, 2 vols. (Beyrouth: Imprimerie Catholique, 1891–2); and in the context of British colonial administration in India, Mortimer Sloper Howell, *A Grammar of the Classical Arabic Language, Translated and Compiled from the Works of the Most Approved Native or Naturalized Authorities*, 7 vols. (Allahabad: North-Western Provinces Government Press, 1880–1911).

114 The distinction was drawn explicitly by Fleischer, *Beiträge* 1, 2.

115 I have previously discussed parts of the following questions in "Suchen und Finden: Notizführung und Grammatik bei Theodor Nöldeke," in Thomas Brandstetter, Thomas Hübel, Anton Tantner, eds., *Vor Google: Eine Mediengeschichte der Suchmaschine im analogen Zeitalter* (Bielefeld: Transcript, 2012), 173–201.

116 For recent perspectives, see Rudolf Sellheim, "Theodor Nöldeke (1836–1930): Begründer der modernen Orientalistik," *Die Welt des Orients* 37 (2007): 135–44; Bernhard Maier, *Gründerzeit der Orientalisten: Theodor Nöldekes Leben und Werk im Spiegel seiner Briefe* (Würzburg: Ergon, 2013).

117 Theodor Nöldeke, *Geschichte des Qorâns*, Göttingen: Dieterichsche Buchhandlung, 1860; 2nd revised edition by Friedrich Schwally, 3 vols. (Leipzig: Dieterich, 1909–38). For more recent perspectives on this genre of historical-critical philology and its underlying questions see Angelika Neuwirth, *Koranforschung—Eine politische Philologie? Bibel, Koran und Islamentstehung im Spiegel spätantiker Textpolitik und moderner Philologie* (Berlin: de Gruyter, 2014). The Parisian prize was awarded *ex aequo* to Nöldeke, the Austrian Aloys Sprenger and the Italian Michele Amari.

118 Examples of such notes are preserved at Universitätsbibliothek Tübingen, Nachlass Theodor Nöldeke, Md. 783 (working papers).

119 Nöldeke, *Zur Grammatik*, 17. The referenced work is Jaromír Košut, *Fünf Streitfragen der Basrenser und Kûfenser über die Abwandlung des Nomen aus Ibn el-Anbârî's Kitâb al Inṣâf fî masâ'il al-ḫilâf baina an naḥwîyîn al-Baṣrîyîn wa-'l-Kûfîyîn, nach der Leydener Handschrift* (Vienna: Gerold, 1878), a dissertation defended at Leipzig with Fleischer.

120 Nöldeke to de Goeje, June 11, 1898, Briefwisseling de Goeje, Leiden Universiteitsbibliotheek, BPL 2389.

121 Nöldeke, *Zur Grammatik*, 15.

122 For instance in a letter to de Goeje, June 9, 1902, Briefwisseling de Goeje.

123 See Stephen G. Alter, *Darwinism and the Linguistic Image: Language, Race, and Natural Theology in the Nineteenth Century* (Baltimore: Johns Hopkins University Press, 1999); also Joseph Errington, *Linguistics in a Colonial World: A Story of Language, Meaning, and Power* (Malden, MA: Blackwell, 2008), ch. 4.

124 Nöldeke, *Zur Grammatik*, 132, note no. 5 to page 20 of the original publication. The quoted work is the posthumous Gerardo Meloni, *Saggi di filologia semitica. A cura degli amici, con dieci tavole in autografia* (Rome: Casa Editrice Italiana, 1913).

125 Nöldeke, *Zur Grammatik*, 20, n. 1.

126 For a sharp critique of the claim to systematicity in the methodolgy of these authors, see Roy Harris, "Introduction: Comparative Philology: A 'Science' in Search of Foundations," in *Foundations of Indo-European Comparative Philology, 1800–1850*, ed. Roy Harris (London: Routldege, 1999), 1, 1–18. The narrow sense of "scienticity"—as well as the narrowly linguistic understanding of "philology"—in this account is, however, somewhat unhelpful for a sounder historical understanding.

127 Nöldeke, *Zur Grammatik*, 18, n. 4 on Jakob Barth, *Nominalbildung in den semitischen Sprachen* (Leipzig: Hinrichs, 2nd edn. 1894).
128 Caspari-Müller, *Arabische Grammatik*, IV.

Chapter 2

1 Ann Laura Stoler, *Along the Archival Grain: Epistemic Anxieties and Colonial Common Sense* (Princeton, NJ: Princeton University Press, 2009).
2 See Thomas Zitelmann, "Enno Littmann (1875–1958): Äthiopische Studien und deutscher Orientalismus," in Steffen Wenig et al., eds., *In Kaiserlichem Auftrag: Die Deutsche Aksumexpedition (DAE) unter Enno Littmann, 1: Die Akteure und die wissenschaftlichen Unternehmungen der DAE in Eritrea* (Aichwald: Linden Soft, 2006), 99–110.
3 Littmann to Nöldeke August 16, 1916, Staatsbibliothek Berlin, Preußischer Kulturbesitz, NL 246 (Teilnachlass Theodor Nöldeke, subsequently Teil-NL Nöldeke), K. 1.
4 E.g. Littmann to Nöldeke January 27, 1920, ibid.
5 Enno Littmann, "Erinnerungen an Naffaʿ wad ʿEtmân," in *Ein Jahrhundert Orientalistik: Lebensbilder aus der Feder von Enno Littmann*, ed. Rudi Paret, Anton Schall (Wiesbaden: Harrassowitz, 1955), 14–25, first published *Der Neue Orient* 2 (1918): 587–91. See also the short discussion, almost entirely based on Littmann's account, in James De Lorenzi, *Guardians of the Tradition: Historians and Historical Writing in Ethiopia* (Rochester, NY: University of Rochester Press, 2015), 130–2.
6 Max Müller, however, wrote an obituary (including edited letters) for one of his Japanese students of Sanskrit, "Kenju Kasawara" (also Kasahara Kenju, 1851–1883) who had died of tuberculosis, but who had not actually served as a collaborator; see Müller, *Biographical Essays* (London: Longmans, Green & Co. 1884), 211–27.
7 In the transliteration of the name, I follow Littmann's habits, which were however inconsistent; he often rendered the glottal stops simply as inverted commas.
8 Enno Littmann, "Das Verbum der Tigresprache," *Zeitschrift für Assyriologie und verwandte Gebiete* 13 (1898): 133–78 and 14 (1899): 1–102.
9 As Littmann mentions in the preface to *Publications of the Princeton Expedition to Abyssinia*, 4 vols. (in 5 tomes) (Leiden: Brill, 1910–15) (subsequently *PEA*), 3, p. VII.
10 *PEA* I and III contain Tigré texts, prose and poetry; II contains annotated English-language translations of the prose texts by Littmann; IV (vols. A and B) provides annotated German-language translations of the poetry.
11 Manuscripts survive in the collection of the papers of Richard Sundström at Uppsala University Library, Kat 479a, NC 1567–8.
12 Carlo Conti Rossini, "Canti popolari tigrai," *Zeitschrift für Assyriologie und verwandte Gebiete* 17 (1903): 23–52 (pt. 1); 18 (1904–5): 320–86 (pt. 2); 19 (1905–6): 288–341 (pt. 3).
13 *PEA* III, VIIf.
14 *PEA* IV A, X.
15 *PEA* I, XI–XIII; III, VIII; IV A, VIIIf.

16   *PEA* III, XI-XXIV. Contrary to the announcement made in the preface to IV A,
      Littmann did not include a German translation of Naffa''s Tigré preface from III
      in IV B.
17   Littmann, "Naffa'", 16.
18   For instance in Enno Littmann, *Abessinien* (Hamburg: Hanseatische Verlagsanstalt,
      1935), 36, where Naffa' is anonymized and referred to as "my Abyssinian
      informant" (*Gewährsmann*).
19   K. G. Rodén to Littmann, May 5, 1909 (Italian postcard), Nachlass Enno Littmann,
      Staatsbibliothek Berlin, Preußischer Kulturbesitz, NL 245 (subsequently NL
      Littmann), K. 45, *Fall Naffa'*.
20   Salamon wad Ḥemad and 'Etmân wad 'Ečâl to Littmann, May 19, 1909, NL
      Littmann, K. 45, *Fall Naffa'*. The translation from the Tigré I owe to Maria Bulakh
      and Saleh Idris. Rodén mentions, in a postcard to Littmann, May 5, 1909 (Swedish
      postcard), NL Littmann, K. 45, that 'Etmân had been "notified" of the situation,
      which is odd since according to his own letter to Littmann, it was rather he who
      had notified the missionaries.
21   Afework Gebre Yesus to Littmann, May 1909, NL Littmann, K. 45, folder *Fall
      Naffa'*. I thank Yonas Addise for the translation of the letter.
22   Richard Sundström to Littmann, May 20, 1909, NL Littmann, K 45.
23   Naffa' wad 'Etmân to Littmann, April 14, 1909 (postal mark, Livorno), NL
      Littmann, K. 45, folder *Fall Naffa'*. It is worth noting that the stamps were lifted
      from this document, probably by Littmann himself, for someone's collection.
24   Sundström to Littmann, May 24, 1909, ibid.
25   Rodén to Littmann, May 21, 1909, ibid. Sundström concurred June 7.
26   Rodén to Littmann, October 27, 1909 asked what had happened to the body but
      apparently remained without answer, since he raised the question again, March 30,
      1910, both letters NL Littmann, K. 28, folder *Rodén*.
27   Rodén to Littmann, March 30, 1910, NL Littmann, K. 28, folder *Rodén*.
28   As is clear from the present tense in *PEA* I, XII where Littmann points out that
      Naffa''s father "is a bard, a *ṣābṭāy*, i.e. a rhapsodist."
29   Notebook *Aussprüche Naffas*, NL Littmann, K. 88.
30   For contextualization, which incidentally reveals the stereotypical nature of
      numerous of Naffa''s "spontaneous" remarks and their rootedness in an implicit
      exchange of demand and response between him and Littmann, see Michael
      Harbsmeier, "Schauspiel Europa: Die außereuropäische Entdeckung Europas im
      19. Jahrhundert am Beispiel afrikanischer Texte," *Historische Anthropologie* 2, no.
      3 (1994): 331–50. Foundational for the study of the perception of Europeans on
      the part of the colonized in Northeast African context remains Timothy Mitchell,
      Colonising Egypt (Cambridge: Cambridge University Press, 1988).
31   Littmann, "Naffa'," 14.
32   Ibid., 14–15.
33   As is for instance expressed in Littmann's correspondence with Georg Jacob, e.g.
      Jacob to Littmann, June 25, 1935, NL Littmann, K. 15, folder *Jacob, G. (15)*. In a
      letter to Snouck Hurgronje of September 14, 1935, Littmann details the censorship
      to which even his attempt to write in an "entirely objective-historical" manner
      about the present conflict had fallen victim, Nalatenschap Christiaan Snouck
      Hurgronje, Leiden University Library, Or. 8952A, 633. See also Zitelmann, "Enno
      Littmann."
34   Littmann, *Abessinien*, 24.

35 Littmann, "Naffaʿ," 15. The medical researcher in question was Martin Bartels (1875–1947), who, after a sojourn in Peru and rather peripatetic deployment during the war, partly in Turkey, became head of an ophthalmological hospital in Dortmund and specialized on miners' diseases of the eye.

36 Mary Louise Pratt, *Imperial Eyes: Travel Writing and Transculturation* (New York: Routledge, 2nd edn. 2008).

37 Littmann, *Abessinien*, 8. Craven Howell Walker's work had been published with Sheldon Press.

38 As classically expounded in Gayatri Chakravorty Spivak, "Can the Subaltern Speak?" in *Colonial Discourse and Post-Colonial Theory: A Reader*, ed. Patrick Williams, Laura Chrisman (New York: Harvester Wheatsheaf, 1993), 66–111.

39 Littmann, "Naffaʿ," 16–17.

40 Naffaʿ to Littmann, April 14, 1909, NL Littmann, K. 88, folder *Fall Naffaʿ*. No speaker of Tigré, I am relying on the translation kindly supplied by Maria Bulakh and Saleh Idris.

41 Littmann, "Naffaʿ," 18.

42 Ibid., 18–19.

43 For an introduction to the history of this field, see Egbert Klautke, *The Mind of the Nation: Völkerpsychologie in Germany, 1851–1955* (New York: Berghahn, 2013).

44 Tycho von Wilamowitz-Moellendorff, *Die dramatische Technik des Sophokles*, ed. Ernst Kapp, with a contribution by Ulrich von Wilamowitz-Moellendorff and an appendix by William M. Calder and Anton Bierl (Hildesheim: Weidmann, 1996). See here e.g. the conclusion of the chapter on Antigone, 47–50, which states the point with great clarity and also makes clear that the interpretive tradition Tycho von Wilamowitz's anti-psychologism sought to attack comprised all German theory of drama since the Goethe period.

45 See also Littmann, *PAE* I, XIII; in the eulogy he wrote for his own funeral, and which was published as an "Autobiographical Sketch," in *The Library of Enno Littmann*, ed. Maria Höfner (Leiden: Brill, 1959), XIII–XX, in the very closing lines, he repeated it once more, signaling his intent to have the explanation of the event buried with him.

46 Navigazione Generale Italiana to Otto Joel, September 22, 1909, NL Littmann, K. 45, *Fall Naffaʿ*.

47 Littmann, "Naffaʿ," 18.

48 Salamon wad Ḥemad and ʿEtmân wad ʿEčâl to Littmann, May 19, 1909, NL Littmann, K. 45, *Fall Naffaʿ*.

49 See, for instance, the remarks in Littmann, "Naffaʿ," 17 and the passages in Enno Littmann, Aksum Tagebuch, Entries January 12, March 14, 1906, NL Littmann, K. 88, which has been edited by Rainer Voigt, "Enno Littmanns Tagebuch der Abessinischen Expedition (Deutsche Aksum-Expedition), 29. Dezember 1905–7. April 1906," in Wenig, *In Kaiserlichem Auftrag*, 1, 173, 193. The remaining second portion of the diary, April 7–26, 1906, has also been edited by Voigt in Steffen Wenig, ed., *In Kaiserlichem Auftrag, 2: Altertumskundliche Untersuchungen der Deutschen Aksum Expedition in Tigray/Äthiopien* (Wiesbaden: Reichert, 2011), 109–34.

50 So, for instance, in letters to Carl Heinrich Becker, April 29, 1907 and March 30, 1909, Geheimes Staatsarchiv Preußischer Kulturbesitz, VI. HA, Nachlass Carl Heinrich Becker (subsequently NL Becker), No. 4579 (Littmann).

51 Becker to Littmann, November 9, 1909, NL Becker, No. 4579 (Littmann).

52   Littmann to Veit, March 1, 1909, NL Littmann, K. 46, folder *An Veit*. See also
      Littmann's obituary in *Der Islam* 4 (1913): 330f.

53   Naffaʿ to Littmann, April 14, 1909, NL Littmann, K. 88, folder *Fall Naffaʿ*.

54   Littmann, "Naffaʿ," 19.

55   Littmann, *Abessinien*, 36.

56   Littmann had previously published this anecdote, as related to him by his "former
      servant Naffaʿ," in a short note "Bemerkungen über den Islam in Nordabessinien,"
      Der Islam 1 (1910): 71.

57   Littmann to Veit, April 23, 1911, NL Littmann, K. 46, folder *An Veit*.

58   Littmann to Veit, May 31, 1911, NL Littmann, K. 46, folder *An Veit*.

59   Littmann to Jacob, December 13, 1923, NL Littmann, K. 46, *An Jacob 8*.

60   Littmann to Nöldeke, March 25, 1912, Teil-NL Nöldeke, K. 1.

61   Jonathan Lamb, *Preserving the Self in the South Seas, 1680–1840* (Chicago:
      University of Chicago Press, 2001).

62   For this concept see Islam Dayeh, "The Potential of World Philology," *Philological
      Encounters* 1 (2016): 396–418.

63   Littmann to Veit, February 1, 1910, NL Littmann, K. 46, folder *An Veit*: "Februar
      rückt näher schon, in stummer Ruh liegt Babylon—d.i. Straßburg …".

64   Homi K. Bhabha, "Of Mimicry and Man," in *The Location of Culture* (London,
      New York: Routledge, 1994), 85–92.

65   Littmann to Veit, August 2, 1911, NL Littmann, K. 46, folder *An Veit*.

66   *PEA* IV A, no. 27, p. 44f. "Du bist aber ja verkrüppelt:/sonst suchte ich Dich zur
      Hilfe." Littmann's translation seeks to emulate the original meter; he adds in the
      commentary to this: "Distich 10 is an address to the son Tegar who has a crippled
      arm and cannot help his father. The second half literally means: 'You I would seek
      for every labor.'"

67   *PEA* IV A, no. 18, 31–33.

68   Littmann, "Naffaʿ," 15.

69   Enno Littmann, "Preliminary Report of the Princeton Expedition to Abyssinia,"
      Zeitschrift für Assyriologie und verwandte Gebiete 20 (1907): 162–4.

70   *PEA* IV A, no. 27, 44: "Da ackern wir jetzt so weiter/mit Pflügen und Hölzern
      am Joche./Denn der Leib verlangt ja nach Nahrung/[wie] der Held nach Sterben
      und Töten." I hasten to add that my translation of "Hölzer" with "drawbars" is
      questionable and avail myself of the opportunity to own up to the deplorable limits
      of my linguistic competence; recourse to the original texts would of course have
      been preferable.

71   A similarly vague association is expressed in the annotations to *PEA* IV, no. 312, 496.

72   Preface *PEA* IV A, IXf. Presumably, however, he also relied on Low German
      dictionaries, since his ephemeral experiences of farm life are not likely to have
      furnished him with all the terms required.

73   Georg Jacob, *Altarabisches Beduinenleben* (Berlin: Mayer & Müller, 1897), here
      Preface, p. V on Littmann's collaboration.

74   Littmann to Theodor Nöldeke October 13, 1915, Teil-NL Nöldeke, K. 1.

75   Gotthold Ephraim Lessing, *Laokoon. Briefe antiquarischen Inhalts*, ed. Wilfried
      Barner (Frankfurt a.M.: Deutscher Klassikerverlag, 2007).

76   See the foundational account in Peter Szondi, *Poetik und Geschichtsphilosophie I:
      Antike und Moderne in der Ästhetik der Goethezeit* (Frankfurt a.M.: Suhrkamp,
      1974). For a more concrete account of how Orientalism fits into the resulting

literary aesthetics, see Andrea Polaschegg, *Der andere Orientalismus: Regeln deutsch-morgenländischer Imagination im 19. Jahrhundert* (Berlin, New York: de Gruyter, 2004).

77   See, for instance, Enno Littmann, "Abessinische und semitische Poesie," *Zeitschrift der Deutschen Morgenländischen Gesellschaft* 84 (1930): 224; or the mention of the point in Enno Littmann, "Leben und Arbeit," ed. H. H. Biesterfeldt, *Oriens* 29/30 (1986): 97.

78   For pastoral Paul Alpers, *What is Pastoral?* (Chicago: University of Chicago Press, 1996); Mathilde Skoie, Sonia Bjørnstad Velázquez, eds., *Pastoral and the Humanities: Arcadia Re-inscribed* (Exeter: Bristol Phoenix, 2006). On political histories of the uses of landscape, especially in colonial context, see W. J. T. Mitchell, ed., *Landscape and Power* (Chicago: University of Chicago Press, 2nd edn. 2002).

79   Pratt, *Imperial Eyes*, 7.

80   Homi K. Bhabha, *The Location of Culture* (New York: Routledge, 1994).

81   E.g. in Bhabha, "The Other Question: Stereotype, Discrimination and the Discourse of Colonialism," in *Location of Culture*, 66–84.

82   E.g. Bachelard, *Formation*, 10f.

83   Theodor Nöldeke, "Tigre-Lieder," *Zeitschrift für Assyriologie und verwandte Gebiete* 31 (1917–18): 7.

84   Ibid., 10f.

85   Ibid., 11f. Littmann, *Abessinien*, 94f. borrows this remark of Nöldeke's (without attribution), and spins the fantasy further: "… and Goethe would have had a deep impression of the force of the passions that express themselves in [the poems], and of their dramatic representation."

86   See on this type of procedure Jérôme David, *Spectres de Goethe: Les métamorphoses de la "littérature mondiale"* (Paris: Les Prairies ordinaires, 2011).

87   Becker to Littmann, August 17, 1926, NL Littmann, K. 2.

88   As theorized by Emily Apter, *Against World Literature: On the Politics of Untranslatability* (London, New York: Verso, 2013).

89   In a letter to a Swedish Ethiopicist colleague, Johannes Kolmodin, from May 24, 1913, Littmann acknowledged Naffa''s exhaustive knowledge of the "history of the Tigré tribes," whereas his familiarity with that of neighboring tribes was supposedly patchy, Uppsala University Library, Papers of Johannes Axel Kolmodin, Q 15:9, fol. 84f. Littmann did not make an explicit point of this historical knowledge in the same manner Nöldeke did.

90   Littmann to Nöldeke, May 14, 1916, Teil-NL Nöldeke, K. 1.

91   Theodor Nöldeke, "Tigre-Lieder," *Zeitschrift für Assyriologie und verwandte Gebiete* 31 (1917–18): 2, 7.

92   Conti Rossini, *Canti*, 3, 330–8, nos. 156–65. In the introductory portion, *Canti*, 1, 25f., Conti Rossini stresses that he collected the poems with the greatest "impartiality," yet with preference for those that "best reflect the intolerant, independent, proud Abyssinian spirit"; and that he collected other poems that referred to recent events only sparingly.

93   Nöldeke, "Tigre-Lieder," 8.

94   Friedrich Schiller, "Über naive und sentimentalische Dichtung" [1795–6], in idem, *Theoretische Schriften*, ed. Rolf-Peter Janz (Frankfurt a.M.: Deutscher Klassikerverlag, 2008), 726 n. 6.

95   Nöldeke, "Tigre-Lieder," 22f.

96   Ibid.

97   Nöldeke, "Tigre-Lieder," 10.

98   Werner Munzinger, *Ostafrikanische Studien* (Schaffhausen: Fr. Hurtersche
      Buchhandlung, 1864); see now Wolbert G. C. Smidt, "Werner Munzinger Pascha:
      An Orientalist and Ethnographer-Turned-Politician in the Ethiopian-Egyptian
      Borderlands," in idem, Sophia Thubauville, eds., *Cultural Research in Northeastern
      Africa: German Histories and Stories* (Frankfurt a.M.: Frobenius Institut, 2015),
      105–25.

99   Littmann to Nöldeke, July 6, 1916, Teil-NL Nöldeke, K. 1.

100   See, for instance, Charles Sanders Peirce, "What is a Sign?" [1894] in *The Essential
      Peirce: Selected Philosophical Writings*, 2 (Bloomington: Indiana University Press,
      1998), 4–10, §3. It may be worthwhile pointing out that in the terms the present
      book proposes, the semiotic tradition, as a tool of analysis, was a specific semantic
      language game that, in its eighteenth- and twentieth-century guises both preceded
      and succeeded, or at least complemented, the games of *Realphilologie*.

101   Dipesh Chakrabarty, *Provincializing Europe* (Princeton, NJ: Princeton University
      Press, 2nd edn. 2007).

102   As e.g. in Littmann to Nöldeke, May 8, 1918, Teil-NL Nöldeke, K. 2; the same *topos*,
      "historischer Sinn," was also habitually applied to Julius Wellhausen, as e.g. in
      Littmann to Nöldeke, June 20, 1915, Teil-NL Nöldeke, K. 1.

103   Erich Auerbach, "Philologie der Weltliteratur," in *Weltliteratur: Festgabe für Fritz
      Strich zum 70. Geburtstag*, ed. Walter Muschg, Emil Staiger (Berne: Francke, 1952),
      40. For an initiative to develop the field laid out by the term, see Pollock et al.,
      World Philology and Dayeh, "Potential."

104   Auerbach, "Philologie der Weltliteratur," 41.

105   See Apter, *Against World Literature*, 175–90, who forcefully argues for the need,
      in "world literature," to clarify the meaning of "world," and extends the argument
      to "philology" as well. See also Pascal David's entry on "Welt," in *Dictionary of
      Untranslatables*, ed. Barbara Cassin et al. (Princeton, NJ: Princeton University Press,
      2014), 1217–24; see further Gayatri Chakravorty Spivak, *Death of a Discipline* (New
      York: Columbia University Press, 2003), here ch. 3 on the idea of "planetarity,"
      which helps in understanding the alterity and the pressure to create subalterns that
      is contained, if often silenced, in the current, "global" notion of the world.

106   It may be worthwhile pointing out the present study's divergence from the
      explication of the phenomenon that Andrew Zimmerman, *Anthropology and
      Antihumanism in Imperial Germany* (Chicago: University of Chicago Press, 2001),
      has put forward. I agree with Zimmerman that the linkages between imperialism
      and the history of the humanities are indissoluble and their character was
      therefore globally interconnected (p. 3). I disagree with the one-sided location of
      antihumanism in the ambit of anthropology as pivoted against the "humanist"
      humanities and as imitative of models in the natural sciences (e.g. evolutionism). In
      my opinion, this view offers too simple a perspective on the intellectual genealogy
      at hand. I also have reservations about the purely theological-philosophical and
      heavily Francocentric genealogy of antihumanism—as emerging from the dual
      root of the refusal of recognizing any positive determination of human nature and
      of embracing an atheism that cannot rely on a concept of human nature to fill the
      void—proposed by Stefanos Geroulanos, *An Atheism that Is Not Humanist Emerges
      in French Thought* (Stanford, CA: Stanford University Press, 2010). The humbler
      infra-structural question of semantics eludes this otherwise highly instructive

account. Mark Greif has presented another epochal analysis of antihumanism, with a different focal area, the United States, and an argument that highlights the collective experience of generations in the intersecting production of "thought" and literature: *The Age of the Crisis of Man: Thought and Fiction in America 1933–1973* (Princeton, NJ: Princeton University Press, 2015). The phenomenological foundation of this argument, which presupposes a strong concept of experience as the system governing intellectual work, renders it partial against what it analyzes; this partisanship I find problematic.

107   Michel Foucault, *Archéologie*, 166–73. See on the context of Foucault's use of the phrase Wouter Goris, "Das historische Apriori bei Husserl und Foucault: Zur philosophischen Relevanz eines Leitbegriffs der historischen Epistemologie," *Quaestio* 12 (2012): 291–342.

108   Spivak, "Can the Subaltern Speak?" 74.

109   Frantz Fanon, *Les damnés de la terre* (Paris: Maspero, 1961), pt. I, "De la violence."

110   Jacques Derrida, "La structure, le signe et le jeu dans le discours des sciences humaines," in *L'écriture et la différence* (Paris: Seuil, 1967), 409–28.

111   Littmann to Nöldeke, March 15, 1912, Teil-NL Nöldeke, K. 1.

112   Littmann to Nöldeke, March 25, 1912, Teil-NL Nöldeke, K. 1.

113   On Peters see Arne Perras, *Carl Peters and German Imperialism 1856–1918: A Political Biography* (Oxford: Oxford University Press, 2004).

114   Nöldeke to Littmann, February 16, 1911, NL Littmann, K. 23. It is unclear whether Nöldeke was here referring to the geographer Heinrich Kiepert (1818–1899) or the latter's son Richard (1846–1918), also a geographer.

115   Susanne Zantop, *Colonial Fantasies: Conquest, Family and Nation in Precolonial Germany 1770–1870* (Durham, NC: Duke University Press, 1997); on German "pre-coloniality" see also the more teleological account of George Steinmetz, *The Devil's Handwriting: Precoloniality and the German Colonial State in Qingdao, Samoa, and Southwest Africa* (Chicago: The University of Chicago Press, 2008).

116   Christian Geulen, "'The Final Frontier …' Heimat, Nation und Kolonie um 1900: Carl Peters," in Birthe Kundrus, ed., *"Phantasiereiche:" Zur Kulturgeschichte des deutschen Kolonialismus* (Frankfurt a.M.: Campus, 2003).

117   Roger Chickering, *We Men Who Feel Most German: A Cultural Study of the Pan-German League, 1886–1914* (Boston: Allen & Unwin, 1984).

118   As, for instance, expressed in a letter by Nöldeke to his coeval friend, the Leiden professor Michael Jan de Goeje, April 26, 1885, Briefwisseling de Goeje.

119   Nöldeke to Littmann, September 23, 1911, NL Littmann, K. 23.

120   As is clear from Nöldeke to Littmann, August 8 and 22 and September 15, 1911, NL Littmann, K. 23.

121   On the history of racism in Germany see especially Christian Geulen, *Wahlverwandte: Rassendiskurs und Nationalismus im späten 19. Jahrhundert* (Hamburg: Hamburger Edition, 2004).

122   Nöldeke discusses these activities in various letters to de Goeje, March 8, April 26, 1885, June 29, 1892, *Briefwisseling de Goeje*. For the overall context see Helmut Walser Smith, *The Butcher's Tale: Murder and Anti-Semitism in a German Town* (New York: W. W. Norton, 2002); Christoph Nonn, *Eine Stadt sucht einen Mörder: Gerücht, Gewalt und Antisemitismus im deutschen Kaiserreich* (Göttingen: Vandenhoeck & Ruprecht, 2002).

123   For instance, Nöldeke to Eduard Meyer, October 28–29, 1923, Berlin-Brandenburgische Akademie der Wissenschaften, Nachlass Eduard Meyer, 130.

124 Marchand rightly discerned this tendency in Littmann's correspondence, *German Orientalism*, 222f.

125 See e.g. W. E. B. Du Bois, *The Souls of Black Folk: Essays and Sketches* (Chicago: McClurgh & Co., 1903), p. vii.

126 Andrew Zimmerman, *Alabama in Africa: Booker T. Washington, the German Empire, and the Globalization of the New South* (Princeton, NJ: Princeton University Press, 2010). See also Sebastian Conrad, *Globalisierung und Nation im deutschen Kaiserreich* (Munich: Beck, 2nd edn. 2010), here ch. 2, for a perspective on the connected history of German programs of work education.

127 Judith Butler, *Gender Trouble: Feminism and the Subversion of Identity* (New York: Routledge, 1990), 143.

128 Untitled poem in Jacob's handwriting, dated May 26, 1917, NL Littmann, K. 14, folder Jacob, G. (5).

129 As he wrote to Nöldeke, September 15, 1920, Teil-NL Nöldeke, K. 2.

130 Enno Littmann, "Tigré-Erzählungen," *Zeitschrift der Deutschen Morgenländischen Gesellschaft* 65 (1911): 707f.

131 For mentions with further comments on the myth, beyond the aforementioned article, see especially Littmann, *PEA* IV B, no. 442, 477, 561 and 591 (pp. 650–2, 694–7, 854f., 891).

132 Littmann, *PEA* IV B, no. 479, p. 701: *dobera glabra*.

133 Littmann, *PEA* IV B, nos. 436, p. 642; 588, p. 888; also no. 595, here p. 895f.

134 Littmann, *PEA* II, proper name etymologies nos. 404, p. 170; 472, p. 172, and 725, p. 179.

135 Littmann, *PEA* II, 132.

136 Littmann, *PEA* II, 139, 143; ibid., 16n. Littmann mentions that the eating of hard butter was an abomination to the Tigré-speaking tribes; and butter is also included in a list of taboo foods, ibid., 239.

137 Littmann, *PEA* IV B, no. 561, p. 850.

138 Littmann, *PEA* II, 313.

139 Littmann, *PEA* IV B, no. 649, p. 1000; and no. 555, p. 843.

140 Wu Xiaoqiao, "Chen Quan," in *Internationales Germanistenlexikon 1800–1950*, ed. Christoph König (Berlin, New York: de Gruyter, 2003), 1, 326f. The dissertation was Chuan Chen, *Die chinesische schöne Literatur im deutschen Schrifttum* (Glückstadt, Hamburg: Augustin, 1933). The colleague who had recruited Chen as a doctoral student was Wolfgang Liepe, see Georg Jacob, Hans Jensen, *Das chinesische Schattentheater* (Stuttgart: Kohlhammer, 1933), IXf.

141 Littmann, "Naffa'," 22.

142 Giorgio Agamben, "In Playland: Reflections on History and Play," in *Infancy and History: Essays on the Destruction of Experience* [1978], transl. Liz Heron (London: Verso, 1993), 65–87.

143 Agamben, "Playland," 71.

Chapter 3

1 See, for instance, Alf Lüdtke, Sebastian Jobs, eds., *Unsettling History: Archiving and Narrating in Historiography* (Frankfurt a.M.: Campus, 2010); Mario Wimmer, *Archivkörper: Eine Geschichte historischer Einbildungskraft* (Paderborn: Konstanz University Press, 2012); Pieter Huistra, Herman Paul, Johan Tollebeek, eds.,

"Historians in the Archive: Changing Historiographical Practices in the Nineteenth Century," theme issue, *History of the Human Sciences* 26, no. 4 (2013); Daniela Saxer, *Die Schärfung des Quellenblicks: Forschungspraktiken in der Geschichtswissenschaft 1840–1914* (Munich: Oldenbourg, 2014). All in all, this literature has been rather unclear, however, about sorting out relations of archival practice to other types of epistemic practice constitutive of historical writing, first and foremost writing practice itself.

2   Foucault, *Archéologie*, 177f.

3   As explored by Arlette Farge, Michel Foucault, *Le désordre des familles: Lettres de cachet des archives de la Bastille au XVIIIe siècle* (Paris: Gallimard, 1982); see further Arlette Farge, *Le goût des archives* (Paris: Seuil, 1997).

4   See the important précis by Jacques Le Goff, "Documento/Monumento," in *Storia e memoria* (Turin: Einaudi, 1982), 443–56.

5   Foucault, *Archéologie*, Preface.

6   Lara Jennifer Moore, *Restoring Order: The Ecole des Chartes and the Organization of Archives and Libraries in France, 1821–1870* (Duluth, MN: Litwin Books, 2008).

7   Jacques Derrida, *Mal d'Archive: Une impression freudienne* (Paris: Galilée, 1995).

8   In important ways, *Mal d'Archive* continues another one of Derrida's discussions of Freud, in "Freud et la scène de l'écriture," in *L'écriture*, 293–340.

9   This point is further developed—perhaps beyond the bounds of understanding—in Wolfgang Ernst, *Das Rumoren der Archive: Ordnung aus Unordnung* (Berlin: Merve, 2002); and idem, *Im Namen von Geschichte: Sammeln—Speichern—(Er)Zählen. Infrastrukturelle Konfigurationen des deutschen Gedächtnisses* (Munich: Fink, 2003).

10   Derrida, *Mal*, 60.

11   Carolyn K. Steedman, *Dust: The Archive and Cultural History* (Brunswick, NJ: Rutgers University Press, 2001).

12   Ernst Posner, *Archives in the Ancient World* (Cambridge, MA: Harvard University Press, 1972).

13   Kasper R. Eskildsen, "Leopold Ranke's Archival Turn: Location and Evidence in Modern Historiography," *Modern Intellectual History* 5 (2008): 425–53.

14   Further to the classical piece by Arnaldo Momigliano, "Ancient History and the Antiquarian" [1950], in *Studies in Historiography* (London: Weidenfeld and Nicholson, 1966), 1–39, see now, above all, Peter N. Miller, *Peiresc's Orient: Antiquarianism as Cultural History in the 17th Century* (Farnham: Ashgate, 2012); idem, *Peiresc's Mediterranean World* (Cambridge, MA: Harvard University Press, 2015).

15   On Niebuhr see Josef Wiesehöfer, Stephan Conermann, eds., *Carsten Niebuhr (1733–1815) und seine Zeit: Beiträge eines interdisziplinären Symposiums 7–10. Oktober 1999* (Stuttgart: Steiner, 2002). On Niebuhr's significance in the context of ethnology and ethnography in enlightenment Germany, see Han F. Vermeulen, *Before Boas: The Genesis of Ethnography and Ethnology in the German Enlightenment* (Lincoln, NE: University of Nebraska Press, 2015), ch. 5.

16   For a survey of the history of Egyptology, see now Jason Thompson, *Wonderful Things: A History of Egyptology*, 2 vols. (Cairo: American University in Cairo Press, 2015). See also Fredrik Thomasson, *The Life of Johan David Åkerblad: Egyptian Decipherment and Orientalism in Revolutionary Times* (Leiden: Brill, 2013), for a wide-ranging perspective into the antiquarian contexts of scholarly travel in Egypt around 1800.

17   As according to Saxer, *Schärfung*.

18   See e.g. Stefan Rebenich, "Vom Nutzen und Nachteil der Großwissenschaft. Altertumswissenschaftliche Unternehmungen an der Berliner Akademie und Universität im 19. Jahrhundert," in Annette Baertschi, Colin G. King, eds., *Die modernen Väter der Antike: Die Entwicklung der Altertumswissenschaften an Akademie und Universität im Berlin des 19. Jahrhunderts* (Berlin: de Gruyter, 2009), 397–422. It may be worth pointing out that the idiom of the "archival body" discussed in Wimmer, *Archivkörper*, might derive in part from the corpora of inscriptions.

19   Enno Littmann, *Publications of the Princeton University Archaeological Expeditions to Syria in 1904–5 and 1909, Division IV, Semitic Inscriptions, Section A: Nabataean Inscriptions* (Leiden: Brill, 1914), nos. 100–7.

20   Farge, *Le goût*.

21   This was hardly a novel type of conflict, see e.g. Fredrik Thomasson, "Justifying and Criticizing the Removals of Antiquities in Ottoman Lands: Tracking the Sigeion Inscription," *International Journal of Cultural Property* 17, no. 3 (2010): 493–517 for eighteenth and early nineteenth-century perspectives on a number of cases, including that of the Elgin Marbles.

22   See Wimmer, *Archivkörper* for an account of the possessive desires governing, arguably, the archive in general.

23   As shown especially by Moore, *Restoring Order*; and Philipp Müller, "Archives and History: Towards a History of 'the Use of State Archives' in the Nineteenth Century," *History of the Human Sciences* 26, no. 4 (2013): 27–49.

24   Thus for instance, and influentially, Bruno Latour, "Drawing Things Together," in Michael Lynch, Steve Woolgar, eds., *Representation in Scientific Practice* (Cambridge, MA: MIT Press, 1990), 19–69.

25   Obliquely alluding to Michael Harbsmeier's usage in *Wilde Völkerkunde*; see also his "Spontaneous Ehtnographies: Towards a Social History of Travellers' Tales," *Studies in Travel Writing* 1, no. 1 (1997): 216–38.

26   Philippe Lacoue-Labarthe, *Poétique de l'histoire* (Paris: Galilée, 2002).

27   Laqueur, Thomas W., "Bodies, Details, and the Humanitarian Narrative," in *The New Cultural History*, ed. Lynn Hunt (Berkeley: University of California Press, 1989), 176–204; idem, "Mourning, Pity, and the Work of Narrative in the Making of 'Humanity,'" in *Humanitarianism and Suffering: The Mobilization of Empathy*, ed. Richard Ashby Wilson, Richard D. Brown (Cambridge: Cambridge University Press, 2009), 31–57.

28   A locus classicus in this important line of interpretation is Fritz Saxl, "The Classical Inscription in Renaissance Art and Politics: Bartholomaeus Fontius, Liber Monumentorum Romanae Urbis, et Aliorum Locorum," *Journal of the Warburg and Courtauld Institutes* 4, no. 1–2 (1940–1): 19–46. See moreover Armando Petrucci, *Public Lettering: Script, Power, and Culture* [1980], transl. Linda Lappin (Chicago: University of Chicago Press, 1993).

29   Jonathan Lamb, *The Rhetoric of Suffering: Reading the Book of Job in the Eighteenth Century* (Oxford: Oxford University Press, 1995).

30   Davide Rodogno, *Against Massacre: Humanitarian Interventions in the Ottoman Empire, 1815–1914* (Princeton, NJ: Princeton University Press, 2012).

31   Ingeborg Huhn, *Johann Gottfried Wetzstein: Orientalist und preußischer Konsul im osmanischen Syrien (1849–1861)* (Berlin: Klaus Schwarz Verlag, 2016).

32   Marchand, *German Orientalism*, 554–63.

33   For this use of the concept of "scene" see Philippe Lacoue-Labarthe, Jean-Luc Nancy, *Scène* (Paris: Bourgois, 2013).

34 See the preliminary account of the 1861–62 journey Melchior de Vogüé, "Voyage de MM. Waddington et le comte Melchior de Vogüé en Syrie," in *Comptes rendus de l'Académie des Inscriptions et Belles-Lettres* 7, no. 7 (1863): 23–29.

35 See the accounts of the decipherment in Enno Littmann, *Thamūd und Ṣafā: Studien zur altnordarabischen Inschriftenkunde* (Leipzig: Borckhaus 1940), 94f. and Hubert Grimme, *Texte und Untersuchungen zur ṣafatenisch-arabischen Religion. Mit einer Einführung in die ṣafatenische Epigraphik* (Paderborn: Schöningh, 1929), 13.

36 Johann Gottfried Wetzstein, *Reisebericht über Hauran und die Trachonen* (Berlin: Reimer, 1860).

37 Melchior de Vogüé, *Syrie centrale*, 2 (Paris: Noblet & Baudry, 1877).

38 Joseph Halévy, *Essai sur les inscriptions du Safa* (Paris: Imprimerie Nationale, 1882); Franz Praetorius, "Bemerkungen über die Ṣafa-Inschriften," *Zeitschrift der Deutschen Morgenländischen Gesellschaft* 36, no. 3–4 (1882): 661–3.

39 Enno Littmann, *Zur Entzifferung der Safa-Inschriften*, Leipzig: Harrassowitz, 1901.

40 *Publications of the Princeton University Archaeological Expeditions to Syria in 1904-5 and 1909, Division IV, Semitic Inscriptions, Section C: Safaitic*, by Enno Littmann (Leiden: Brill, 1943) (subsequently *PPUAES*).

41 Grimme 1929; for instance René Dussaud, ed., *Les relevés du Capitaine Rees dans le désert de Syrie* (Paris: Geuthner, 1929).

42 *Publications of an American Archaeological Expedition to Syria 1899-1900, Part IV: Semitic Inscriptions*, by Enno Littmann (New York: Century Co., 1904) (subsequently *PAAES*).

43 NL Littmann, K. 87, Syrian Journey 1899–1900, Diary VI, fol. 31 (May 18, 1900).

44 This also illustrates how intricate the relations between stocks of archival material and the notion of being with or without history were in practice, even though in methodological discourse these matters were discussed in terms of sharp dichotomies, see Mario Wimmer, "Die Lagen der Historik," *Österreichische Zeitschrift für Geschichtswissenschaften* 18, no. 2 (2007): 106–25; on the problem of the nexus of writing and history generally see still Jack Goody, *The Domestication of the Savage Mind* (Cambridge: Cambridge University Press, 1977); Eric Wolf, *Europe and the People Without History* (Berkeley: University of California Press, 1982); Zimmerman, *Anthropology*, ch. 2.

45 NL Littmann, K. 87, Syrian Journey 1899–1900, Diary VI, fol. 29 (May 17, 1900).

46 Littmann, *Thamūd und Ṣafā*.

47 Grimme, *Texte und Untersuchungen*, 7f., Littmann, *Thamūd und Ṣafā*, 5.

48 A list of Grimme's rather ephemeral Oriental journeys (to North Africa and Palestine) is contained in Franz Taeschner, "Nachruf Hubert Grimme," *Zeitschrift der Deutschen Morgenländischen Gesellschaft* 96 (1943): 382.

49 Nicolaus Rhodokanakis, *Der Grundsatz der Öffentlichkeit in den südarabischen Urkunden* (Wien: Hölder, 1915).

50 NL Littmann, K. 87, Syrian Journey 1899–1900, Diary I, fol. 10.

51 See NL Littmann, K. 87, Syrian Journey 1899–1900, Diary II, fol. 29f.; Diary III, foll. 6, 13f.

52 After de Vogüé and Waddington, Eduard Sachau had traveled in Syria in the 1880s, and Max van Berchem in the 1890s.

53 Theodor Mommsen, "Über Plan und Ausführung eines Corpus Inscriptionum Latinarum" [1847], in *Tagebuch der französisch-italienischen Reise 1844/1845*, ed. G. and B. Walser (Berne: P. Lang, 1976), 223–52.

54 NL Littmann, K. 87, Syrian Journey 1899–1900, Diary IV, fol. 41.

55 Littmann, "Leben und Arbeit," 96.

56 Thus in NL Littmann, K. 87, Syrian Journey 1899–1900, Diary I, p. 3, October 20, 1899.

57 Littmann, "Leben und Arbeit," 44.

58 Littmann, "Leben und Arbeit," 56f.

59 For a different approach to the *Gegenständlichkeit* of literary text see now the contribution by Christian Benne, *Die Erfindung des Manuskripts: Zu Theorie und Geschichte literarischer Gegenständlichkeit* (Berlin: Suhrkamp, 2015). The approach of the present book appears to diverge from Benne's, especially with regard to the plurality of the quality in question, its interdependency with the historicization of semantics, and its ties to the problem of archival theory and practice (the latter oddly does not figure at all in Benne's account, which is regrettably short on discussions from the field of historical theory).

60 See Ali Behdad, *Belated Travelers: Orientalism in the Age of Colonial Dissolution* (Durham, NC: Duke University Press, 1994).

61 NL Littmann, K. 87, Syrian Journey 1899–1900, diary V, fol. 20.

62 See e.g. the remarks in Littmann, "Leben und Arbeit," 65.

63 NL Littmann, K. 87, Syrian Journey, diary V, fol. 45.

64 NL Littmann, K. 87, Syrian Journey, diary V, fol. 44.

65 Littmann, *Aksum Tagebuch*, ed. Voigt, 1, 174.

66 Nöldeke to de Goeje, April 11, 1908, *Briefwisseling de Goeje*.

67 Drawing on my *Topography of a Method: François Louis Ganshof and the Writing of History* (Tübingen: Mohr, 2014), here Part II.

68 For this latter term, see Frank Ankersmit, *Sublime Historical Experience* (Stanford, CA: Stanford University Press, 2005).

69 In the diary, Littmann abbreviated the title, and referred to the person, as "Dedsch." or "Dedj." most of the time; his transliterations remained inconstant.

70 Littmann, *Aksum Tagebuch*, ed. Voigt, 1, 191.

71 On Norris see *The Class of 1895 Princeton University: 25th Year Record*, ed. Andrew C. Imbrie, John Hamilton Thacher (Princeton, NJ: Princeton University Press, 1920), 177f. and his correspondence with Imbrie in Princeton University Library, Class of 1895, Records, AC 130, Folders 7–8 (F. Norris 1–2).

72 NL Littmann, K. 87, Syrisches Tagebuch 1904–5, Notebook II, December 2–4, 1904.

73 NL Littmann, K. 87, Syrisches Tagebuch 1899–1900, Notebook VI, May 15, 1900. The portrait photograph was also reproduced in the official travelogue of the expedition Howard C. Butler, Frederick A. Norris, Edward R. Stoever, *Publications of the Princeton University Archaeological Expeditions to Syria in 1904–5 and 1909, Division I: Geography and Itinerary* (Leiden: Brill, 1930), 23. The narrative was prepared by Stoever, not one of the original participants, with the help of Norris's diaries. Norris himself did not even review the resulting account. Butler, although his name figures first on the cover, had been dead for eight years when the volume appeared. The inevitable abridgements introduced by Stoever led to many errors and misrepresentations, for instance in the *Tarba* episode the notion that Hasan Sallam did not accompany the group into the Harra. I therefore did not make use of this published narrative.

74 Ibid., May 16, 1900.

75 NL Littmann, K. 87, Syrisches Tagebuch 1904–5, Notebook II, December 4, 1904. The inconsistencies in the spelling of Arabic names are Littmann's.

76   NL Littmann, K. 87, Syrisches Tagebuch 1904–5, December 6, 1904.

77   Ernst Bernheim, *Lehrbuch der historischen Methode* [1889] (Leipzig: Duncker &
      Humblot, 5th-6th edn. 1905); Charles Victor Langlois, Charles Seignobos,
      Introduction aux études historiques [1898], ed. M. Rébérioux (Paris: Editions Kimé,
      1992); see on this also Trüper, *Topography*, 51–73.

78   Littmann, *Thamud und Safa*, 23.

79   Littmann, *Thamud und Safa*, 98.

80   Littmann, *Thamud und Safa*, 103; Grimme, *Texte und Untersuchungen*, 142–50.

81   Enno Littmann *PPUAES*, Div. IV, Sec. C, Safaitic, 90f. No. 350f.

82   See the discussion ibid. of *PAAES*, Pt. IV, nos. 121–7a.

83   Grimme, *Texte und Untersuchungen*, 132f.

84   Littmann to Nöldeke, August 28, 1905: "I hold them both in very high esteem and
      have learned much from both of them, but I always feel so abandoned when I hear
      P. swearing at J. and J. swearing at P., and—with a pure conscience—am forced to
      agree with both to a certain extent." Teil-NL Nöldeke, K. 1.

85   On the neogrammarians see still Kurt R. Jankowsky, *The Neogrammarians: A Re-
      Evaluation of their Place in the History of Linguistic Science* (The Hague: Mouton,
      1972); Kurt Růžička, *Historie und Historizität der Junggrammatiker* (Berlin:
      Akademie Verlag, 1977); and Eveline Einhauser, *Die Junggrammatiker: Ein Problem
      für die Sprachwissenschaftsgeschichtsschreibung* (Trier: WVT, 1989); see also Benes,
      In Babel's Shadow, passim on the relations between comparative linguistics and
      Orientalism.

86   John E. Joseph, *Saussure* (Oxford: Oxford University Press, 2012).

87   On this constellation, see Lisa Medrow, *Moderne Tradition und religiöse
      Wissenschaft: Islam, Wissenschaft und Moderne bei I. Goldziher, C. Snouck
      Hurgronje und C. H. Becker* (Paderborn: Schöningh, 2018).

88   Georg Jacob, *Beiträge zur Erkenntnis des Derwisch-Ordens der Bektaschis* (Berlin:
      Mayer & Müller, 1908).

89   Thus e.g. in the preface ibid., p. VI. See also Becker's account of Jacob's
      program, "Georg Jacob als Orientalist," in *Festschrift Georg Jacob zum 70. Geburtstag
      26. Mai 1932 gewidmet von Freunden und Schülern*, ed. Theodor Menzel (Leipzig:
      Harrassowitz, 1932), 1–8.

90   See Littmann, "Leben und Arbeit," 19. Jacob had hired Littmann to proofread the
      text and compose the index of his study of the Bedouins.

91   Jacob, *Altarabisches Beduinenleben*, XIII.

92   Jacob, *Beduinenleben*, XIV.

93   Next to Szondi, *Poetik*, see as a more recent survey also Ritchie Robertson,
      "Ancients, Moderns and the Future: The *Querelle* in Germany from Winckelmann
      to Schiller," in *Ancients and Moderns in Europe: Comparative Perspectives*, ed. Paddy
      Bullard, Alexis Tadié (Oxford: Voltaire Foundation, 2016), 257–76.

94   See, for instance, Enno Littmann, "Georg Jacob," in *Ein Jahrhundert Orientalistik*, 99.

95   See Lorraine Daston, Peter Galison, *Objectivity* (New York: Zone, 2007), chs. 1–2.
      In the context of travel literature, the history of the nineteenth-century fortunes
      of the enlightenment-era eyewitnessing-based notion of objectivity remains
      to be fully integrated with the account offered by Daston and Galison; see the
      synthetic account by Jürgen Osterhammel, *Die Entzauberung Asiens: Europa und
      die asiatischen Reiche im 18. Jahrhundert* (Munich: Beck, 1998); and for the more
      remote early modern context, Justin Stagl, *A History of Curiosity: The Theory of
      Travel 1550–1800* (Chur: Harwood, 1995).

96   Johann Joachim Winckelmann, "Gedanken über die Nachahmung der griechischen Werke in der Malerei und Bildhauerkunst" [1755], in *Werke*, 2 (Stuttgart: Hoffmann'sche Verlagsbuchhandlung, 1847), esp. §§ 45–52.

97   Winckelmann, "Gedanken," § 10.

98   NL Littmann, K. 14, Letter Jacob to Littmann, July 5, 1914.

99   Jacob to Littmann, November 2, 1926, NL Littmann, K. 15, folder "Jacob, G. (9);" on Frobenius, see Suzanne Marchand, "Leo Frobenius and the Revolt against the West," *Journal of Contemporary History* 32, no. 2 (1997): 153–70.

100 Enno Littmann, *Zur Entzifferung der Safâ-Inschriften* (Leipzig: Harrassowitz, 1901).

101 Across all possible worlds, if one cares to apply the vocabulary of Saul Kripke, *Naming and Necessity* (Oxford: Blackwell, 1980). Lévi-Strauss, *Pensée sauvage*, ch. 6 has numerous examples of proper names in differently structured language games; see also the instructive discussions in István Rév, "The Necronym," *Representations* 64 (1998): 76–108, and Thomas Schestag, "Namen nehmen: Zur Theorie des Namens bei Carl Schmitt," *Modern Language Notes* 122 (2007): 544–62.

102 Princeton University, Department of Art and Archaeology—Visual Resources, Archaeological Archives, Howard C. Butler Archive - Syria, F. Norris Diaries: Diary A: July 27 to December 31, 1904, entry December 7.

103 NL Littmann, K. 87, Syrian Diary 1904–5, Notebook II, December 7, 1904.

104 Norris, Diary A, December 7, 1904.

105 NL Littmann, K. 87, Syrian Diary 1904–5, Notebook II, December 8, 1904.

106 Ibid., December 9, 1904.

107 Ibid., December 10, 1904.

108 Norris, Diary A, December 12, 1904.

109 Norris, Supplementary Diary C, October 1 to December 21, 1904, Entry December 5.

110 Norris, Diary A, October 16, 1904.

111 NL Littmann, K. 87, Syrian Diary 1904–5, Notebook II, December 11, 1904.

112 Ibid., December 12, 1904.

113 Ibid.

114 As is to be concluded from the ensemble of manuscripts preserved in his archives.

115 Ibid., Notebook III, December 13, 1904.

116 Ibid., December 14, 1904.

117 Ibid., December 15, 1904.

118 Ussama Makdisi, *The Culture of Sectarianism: Community, History, and Violence in Nineteenth Century Ottoman Lebanon* (Berkeley: University of California Press, 2000).

119 Dussaud's letter, unfortunately, is missing in Littmann's papers (K. 7, folder *Dussaud*).

120 René Dussaud, Frédéric Macler, *Voyage archéologique au Ṣafâ et au Djebel ed-Drûz* (Paris: Leroux, 1901); idem, "Rapport d'une mission dans les régions désertiques de la Syrie moyenne," *Nouvelles Archives des Missions Scientifiques et Littéraires* 10 (1903): 412–744. Dussaud and Littmann had met in Strasbourg in 1898 or 1899 and amicably exchanged results of their epigraphic research throughout their lives.

121 Michel-Rolph Trouillot, "Anthropology and the Savage Slot: The Poetics and Politics of Otherness," in *Global Transformations: Anthropology and the Modern World* (Basingstoke: Palgrave Macmillan, 2003), 7–28.

122 See e.g. François Hartog, *Anciens, Modernes, Sauvages* (Paris: Galaade, 2005).

123   Most immediately expressed, perhaps, in the first pages of Reinhart Dozy's work on
      Muslim Spain, *Histoire des Musulmans d'Espagne jusqu'à la conquête de l'Andalousie
      par les Almoravides (711–1110)*, 4 vols. (Leiden: Brill, 1861).
124   As is indeed the contention of the analysis in Lacoue-Labarthe, *Poétique*.
125   Jacob to Littmann, July 5, 1914, NL Littmann, K. 14. The passage quoted here
      immediately follows the end of this quotation. Years later, in a letter to Nöldeke
      (August 2, 1924, Teil-NL Nöldeke, A4), Jacob admitted that his hatred of *Bildung*
      was founded in his own dissatisfactory experience with secondary education in his
      native Königsberg.
126   In keeping with Karl Rosenkranz, *Aesthetik des Häßlichen*, Königsberg: Gebr.
      Bornträger, 1853.
127   Littmann to Nöldeke May 6, 1915, Teil-NL Nöldeke, K. 2.
128   See Wolfgang G. Schwanitz, "'Djihad, Made in Germany': Der Streit um den
      Heiligen Krieg 1914–1915," *Sozial.Geschichte* 18, no. 2 (2003): 7–34.; for context see
      also Lionel Gossman, *The Passion of Max von Oppenheim: Archaeology and Intrigue
      in the Middle East from Wilhelm II to Hitler* (Cambridge: Open Book Publishing,
      2014).
129   Littmann to Nöldeke, May 19, 1915, Teil-NL Nöldeke, K. 2.
130   For a discussion of this concept that has given rise to some debate in recent years,
      see, as an entry point, Herman Paul, "What Is a Scholarly Persona? Ten Theses on
      Virtues, Skills, and Desires," *History and Theory* 53 (2014): 348–71.
131   Littmann, *Aksum Tagebuch*, ed. Voigt, 1, 197f.; Reiner Koppe, "Das Reisetagebuch
      von Theodor von Lüpke," in Wenig, *In Kaiserlichem Auftrag*, 1, 224–26.
132   NL Littmann, K. 88, Ethiopian journey, Aksum, Diary IV, fol. 24 (April 20, 1906).
      As far as "barbarism" is concerned, it is perhaps worthwhile to point out the
      rhetorical possibility of reverting the relation, which was arguably not much more
      than a matter of wordplay; Georg Jacob, at any rate, in 1930 remembered about his
      years in Berlin around 1890 that it was only in the Museum of Ethnography that "I
      felt I was among human beings again," Jacob to Littmann, April 24, 1930 (postcard),
      NL Littmann, K. 14, folder Jacob, G. (12).
133   NL Littmann, K. 88, Ethiopian journey, Aksum, Diary IV, fol. 7v (April 11, 1906).
134   As is mentioned in Thomas Zitelmann "Körperschaft und Reich: Nordostafrika
      als Interessenfeld und Projektionsfläche kolonialer Ethnologien," *Paideuma* 42
      (1996): 48.
135   As can be seen on photographs of his working rooms included in Höfner, *Library*.
136   NL Littmann, K. 88, Ethiopian journey, Aksum, Diary IV, fol. 9v–10r. (April 12–13,
      1906).
137   See on this my "Epistemic Vice: Scholarly Transgression in the Travels of Julius
      Euting," in Christiaan Engberts, Herman Paul, eds., *Scholarly Personae in the
      History of Orientalism, 1870–1930*, (Leiden: Brill, 2019), 64–98.
138   NL Littmann, K. 88, Ethiopian journey, Aksum, Diary IV, fol. 13v, 14r. (April 14,
      1906).
139   See Elisabeth Özdalga, ed., *The Last Dragoman: The Swedish Orientalist Johannes
      Kolmodin as Scholar, Activist and Diplomat*, Istanbul: Swedish Institute, 2006.
140   Enno Littmann to Johannes Kolmodin December 20, 1910, Uppsala University
      Library, Papers of Johannes Axel Kolmodin Q15:9, fol. 72f. A draft is also preserved
      in NL Littmann, K. 18. It should be added that Kolmodin quickly managed to
      defuse Littmann's anger (letter from December 28, 1910, NL Littmann, K. 18,
      folder Kolmodin), and that relations between the scholars remained amicable until

1918, when Kolmodin had taken up diplomatic functions in Turkey and withdrew to some extent from scholarly activity, at least in the Ethiopicist field (until he returned to Ethiopia in diplomatic service in 1931). Littmann was so pleased about his Swedish colleague's pro-German stance during the war that he offered Kolmodin his Ethiopicist research materials in case he, Littmann, was called to arms and died in battle, as he expected in a letter from October 26, 1915, Kolmodin papers, fol. 88.

141   See Littmann, "Leben und Arbeit," 37. There are also other indications; for instance, Frederick Norris recounts how Littmann fell off his horse and suffered a laceration of the forehead in practice runs in Jerusalem, Norris Diary A, September 27, 1904.

142   As I have argued in my "Dispersed Personae: Subject-Matters of Scholarly Biography in Nineteenth-Century Oriental Philology," *Asiatische Studien—Etudes Asiatiques* 67 (2013): 1338f.

143   Schiller, "Naive," 743–5; see also the note "Tragödie und Komödie," in *Theoretische Schriften*, ed. Janz, 1047f. that drafted some of this passage and from which the expression "moral indifference" is here lifted.

144   Markus Krajewski, Harun Maye, eds., *Die Hyäne: Lesarten eines politischen Tiers* (Zurich: Diaphanes, 2010).

145   On December 31, 1905, Littmann noted "the first time I saw this hideous animal in the wild," Littmann, *Aksum Tagebuch*, ed. Voigt, 1, 164.

146   Erwin Panofsky, "Et in Arcadia Ego: Poussin and the Elegiac Tradition," in *Philosophy and History: Essays Presented to Ernst Cassirer*, ed. R. Klibansky, H. J. Paton (Oxford: Clarendon Press, 1936), 223–54.

147   As pointed out by Petrucci, *Public Lettering*, 44.

148   This and the following section is adapted from my "Heteropsy and Autopsy in Nineteenth-Century Aksumite Epigraphy," *Storia della Storiografia* 66 (2015): 121–42.

149   George, Viscount Valentia, *Voyages and Travels to India, Ceylon, the Red Sea, Abyssinia, and Egypt, in the Years 1802, 1803, 1804, 1805, and 1806*, 3 vols. (London: William Miller, 1809), here vol. 3, plate 16, after p. 180, and on the inscription (transcription and translation), and Aksumite history more generally, 179–201. The stone was first described in modern scholarly style by Enno Littmann, *Deutsche Aksum Expedition* [subsequently DAE], 4, *Sabäische griechische und altabessinische Inschriften* (Berlin: Reimer, 1913), here nos. 4, 6, 7. This volume has been superseded by Etienne Bernard et al., eds., *Recueil des inscriptions de l'Ethiopie des périodes pré-axoumite et axoumite*, 3 vols. (Paris: Académie des Inscriptions et Belle-Lettres, 1991–2000).

150   Henry Salt, *A Voyage to Abyssinia, & Travels Into the Interiors of that Country, Executed Under the Orders of the British Government in the Years 1809 & 1810* [1814] (Philadelphia: M. Carey 1816), 317f.

151   Ibid., 319f.

152   Ibid., 323. Salt's spelling of the title is inconsistent.

153   Ibid., 324.

154   August Dillmann, *Über die Anfänge des Axumitischen Reiches*, Abhandlungen der Königlichen Akademie der Wissenschaften zu Berlin 1878 (Berlin: Akademie, 1879), 177–238; and idem, *Zur Geschichte des aksumitischen Reichs im vierten bis sechsten Jahrhundert*, Abhandlungen der Königlichen Akademie der Wissenschaften zu Berlin 1880 (Berlin: Akademie, 1881), 1–51 (this volume does not have continuous pagination).

155   For an overview of research programs see Marchand, *German Orientalism*, 167–86.
      For the most notorious of Ewald's students, the later anti-Semitic agitator Paul de
      Lagarde, see Ulrich Sieg, *Deutschlands Prophet: Paul de Lagarde und die Anfänge
      des modernen Antisemitismus* (Munich: Beck, 2007).
156   For the current state of debate on the history of Aksum, see Glen W. Bowersock,
      The Throne of Adulis: Red Sea Wars on the Eve of Islam (Oxford: Oxford University
      Press, 2013). For an older, in parts divergent, synthesis of Aksumite history see
      also still Stuart Munro-Hay, *Aksum: An African Civilization of Late Antiquity*
      (Edinburgh: Edinburgh University Press, 1991). See further Yuri M. Kobishchanov,
      Axum [1966] (University Park: Pennsylvania State University Press, 1979).
157   Dillmann, *Anfänge*, 211.
158   See James Theodore Bent, *The Sacred City of the Ethiopians, Being a Record of Travel
      and Research in Abyssinia in 1893* [1893] (London: Longmans, 2nd edn. 1896),
      with a chapter by D. H. Müller on the inscriptions of Yeha and Aksum. Müller also
      published his results separately and in extended form as *Epigraphische Denkmäler
      aus Abessinien*, Denkschriften der Kaiserlichen Akademie der Wissenschaften zu
      Wien, Philosophisch-historische Klasse, 43, no. 3 (Wien: F. Tempsky, 1894).
159   Theodor Nöldeke, "Review D. H. Müller, Epigraphische Denkmäler aus
      Abessinien," *Zeitschrift der Deutschen Morgenländischen Gesellschaft* 48 (1894):
      367–79.
160   Nöldeke was a driving force and had settled on Littmann as the appropriate
      scholar to undertake the expedition (and to become his successor) already in 1903,
      Nöldeke to Littmann, September 30, 1903, NL Littmann, K. 23. Littmann had
      already expressed his desire to go to Ethiopia in a letter to Nöldeke dated March 14,
      1902, Teil-NL Nöldeke, K. 1.
161   Littmann, *Aksum Tagebuch*, ed. Voigt, 1, 173.
162   Significantly, in the publication of results, Littmann states that this was achieved in
      part through the mediation of the governor and in part through direct negotiations
      he undertook with the owners himself; the diary suggests that the governor's
      intervention had been crucial, see entries from March 4 and for the working week
      of March 12–17, 1906, Littmann, *Aksum Tagebuch*, ed. Voigt, 1, 190, 193.
163   Entry March 17, 1906, Littmann, *Aksum Tagebuch*, ed. Voigt, 1, 193.
164   Nöldeke, "Review," 376.
165   Müller, in Bent, *Sacred City*, 264.
166   Littmann, DAE, 4, 35.
167   Eduard von Rüppell, *Reise in Abyssinien*, 2, Frankfurt a.M.: Schmerber, 1840, 284f.
168   Littmann, DAE, 1, 48.
169   Littmann, DAE, 4, 35.
170   Francis Breyer, "Die Inschriften 'Ēzānās," in Wenig, *In Kaiserlichem Auftrag*, 2,
      339–52; Bowersock, *Throne*, ch. 5.
171   Littmann, DAE, 1, 51.
172   Bowersock, *Throne*, 64.
173   Littmann, DAE, 4, 70.
174   Rhodokanakis, *Grundsatz der Öffentlichkeit*; Littmann, *PPUAES*, Div. IV, Semitic
      Inscriptions, Sec. C: Safaitic, VIIIf.
175   See the observations on internal conflict among the explorers in Hans von Lüpke,
      "Die Zeit in Aksum—Innenansichten," in Wenig, *In Kaiserlichem Auftrag*, 2,
      151–68; and Steffen Wenig, "Addendum zu Hans v. Lüpkes *Die Zeit in Aksum*," in
      ibid., 169–76.

176 Littmann, DAE 1, 47.
177 Especially Littmann, DAE 1, 45.
178 Littmann, DAE 1, 51.
179 Von Lüpke, *Reisetagebuch*, ed. Koppe, e.g. entry January 13, 1906, 212 (von Lüpke's reminiscence is to the three Magi).
180 Salt, *Voyage*, 316f.
181 Arnauld d'Abbadie, *Douze ans de séjour dans la Haute-Ethiopie* [1868], vol. 1, ed. Jeanne-Marie Allier (Città del Vaticano: Biblioteca Apostolica Vaticana, 1980), here ch. 2.
182 Nöldeke to Littmann, April 21, 1906, NL Littmann, K. 23, Nöldeke. The context of Nöldeke's "impression" probably relates to a display of Africans at a German zoo.
183 As according to Derrida's final set of lectures, *Séminaire: La bête et le souverain*, 2 vols. (Paris: Galilée, 2008–12).
184 Refuting the validity of these lists was a chief concern of Dillmann's; it appears that it was mainly the considerable amount of futile work Rüppell had conducted on the matter in his *Reise in Abyssinien*, 2, §§11–12, 335–403, that convinced Dillmann of the necessity of doing away with this autochthonous tradition. Littmann, in his survey of Aksumite history in DAE, 1, 37–40, repeated much of this argument.
185 Once again with reference to Subrahmanyam, *Courtly Encounters*.
186 For a survey, see Michael Curtis, *Orientalism and Islam: European Thinkers on Oriental Despotism in the Middle East and India* (Cambridge: Cambridge University Press, 2009).
187 See Norbert Elias, *Die höfische Gesellschaft: Untersuchungen zur Soziologie des Königtums und der höfischen Aristokratie* (Darmstadt: Luchterhand, 1969).
188 Littmann, *Aksum Tagebuch*, ed. Voigt, 1, 182.
189 Littmann, *Aksum Tagebuch*, ed. Voigt, 1, 183.
190 Littmann, *Aksum Tagebuch*, ed. Voigt, 1, 183.
191 Littmann, *Aksum Tagebuch*, ed. Voigt, 1, 183f.
192 Littmann, *Aksum Tagebuch*, ed. Voigt, 1, 184.
193 This indicates, incidentally, that the diary, even though its full text is preserved in fair copy only (with a few notebooks representing previous stages for individual episodes also preserved), was nonetheless composed piecemeal on site, during the journey.
194 Von Lüpke, *Reisetagebuch*, ed. Koppe, January 28, 1906, 216.
195 Littmann, *Aksum Tagebuch*, ed. Voigt, 1, 187f.
196 Littmann, *Aksum Tagebuch*, ed. Voigt, 1, 188.
197 Reproducing a longstanding constellation of interdenominational conflict, as a result of which, for instance, the clergy of Ethiopia had managed, in the late sixteenth century to suppress the ongoing association of the royal family with the Jesuit missionaries who were seeking to missionize the already Christian country. The travelogues of the early modern period were regularly quoted as scholarly works (not merely as historical sources) by scholars such as Dillmann and Littmann. The same was true for Hiob Ludolf, *Historia Aethiopica, sive brevis et succincta descriptio regnis Habessinorum* (Frankfurt/M.: Joh. Dav. Zunner, 1681). There was no clear rupture between modern and early modern scholarship in this field.
198 Von Lüpke, *Reisetagebuch*, ed. Koppe, January 13, 1906, 212.
199 Littmann, *Aksum Tagebuch*, ed. Voigt, 1, 185. Von Lüpke, *Reisetagebuch*, ed. Koppe, February 4, 1906, 216 also mentions this episode.

200   In the history of science, the classical account of this social environment remains
      Mario Biagioli, *Galileo, Courtier: The Practice of Science in the Culture of Absolutism*
      (Chicago: University of Chicago Press, 1994).
201   James Bruce of Kinnaird, *Travels to Discover the Source of the Nile, in the Years
      1768, 1769, 1770, 1771, 1772, and 1773*, 5 vols. (London: Robinson, 1790).
202   Mozzetti to Littmann, August 31, 1909, NL Littmann, K. 23, Mozzetti.
203   On account of the destruction of Mozzetti's possessions and collections, after his
      return to Italy, in the Battle of Caporetto in 1917, as he relates in his post-war letters
      to Littmann, ibid.
204   Mozzetti to Littmann, October 31, 1913, ibid.
205   In a letter to Littmann from June 21, 1913, ibid. Mozzetti describes the young
      prince in highly unfavorable terms.
206   Klaus Johanning, *Der Bibel-Babel-Streit: Eine forschungsgeschichtliche Studie*
      (Frankfurt a.M.: Lang, 1988); Reinhard G. Lehmann, *Friedrich Delitzsch und der
      Babel-Bibel-Streit* (Fribourg: Universitätsverlag, Göttingen: Vandenhoeck und
      Ruprecht, 1994).
207   Marchand, *German Orientalism*, 236–51.
208   Lehmann, *Delitzsch*, 284f.
209   Wimmer, *Archivkörper*. See also his "On Sources: Mythical and Historical Thinking
      in Fin-de-Siècle Vienna," *Res: Anthropology and Aesthetics* 63–4 (2013), spring/
      autumn: 108–24.
210   Bonnie Smith, "Gender and the Practices of Scientific History: The Seminar and
      Archival Research," *American Historical Review* 100, no. 4 (1995): 1150–76.
211   Christoph Johannes Franzen, "Einleitung," in idem, Karl-Heinz Kohl, Marie-Luise
      Recker, eds., *Der Kaiser und sein Forscher: Der Briefwechsel zwischen Wilhelm II.
      und Leo Frobenius (1924–1938)* (Stuttgart: Kohlhammer, 2012), 37–48.
212   Leo Frobenius, *Erythräa: Länder und Zeiten des heiligen Königsmordes* (Berlin,
      Zurich: Atlantis, 1931), ch. 13. For the "Aithiopian" theme, see esp. idem, *Und
      Afrika sprach ..., 3: Unter den unsträflichen Aethiopen* (Berlin: Vita Deutsches
      Verlagshaus, 1913).
213   Wilhelm II to Frobenius June 25, 1929, Franzen et al., *Der Kaiser*, no. 67. See also
      ibid., "Einleitung," 19.
214   As something of an oblique contribution to the research program laid out in
      Sebastian Conrad, Jürgen Osterhammel, eds., *Das Kaiserreich transnational:
      Deutschland in der Welt 1871–1914* (Göttingen: Vandenhoeck und Ruprecht, 2004),
      where in spite of the presence of the imperial monarchy in the title a transnational
      perspective on this form of government and its cultural meanings has remained
      absent.

Chapter 4

1   William Robertson Smith, *Kinship and Marriage in Early Arabia* (Cambridge:
      Cambridge University Press, 1885).
2   See Bernhard Maier, *William Robertson Smith: His Life, his Work and his Times*
      (Tübingen: Mohr Siebeck, 2009).
3   As already Friedemann Boschwitz, *Julius Wellhausen: Motive und Maßstäbe seiner
      Geschichtsschreibung* [1938] (Darmstadt: Wissenschaftliche Buchgesellschaft, 1968)
      has argued.

4 Julius Euting, *Nabatäische Inschriften aus Arabien* (Berlin: Reimer, 1885).

5 Christiaan Snouck Hurgronje, *Mekka*, 2 vols. (Leiden: Nijhoff, 1888–9), and *Mekka: Bilderatlas* (The Hague: Nijhoff, 1888). Snouck's work has been subject to controversial discussion, see Peter Sjoerd van Koningsveld, *Snouck Hurgronje en de Islam: Acht artiekelen over leven en werk van een oriëntalist uit het koloniale tijdperk* (Leiden: Rijksuniversiteit, 1988); Jan Just Witkam, *Honderd jaar Mekka in Leiden. 1885–1985* (Leiden: Rijksuniversiteit, 1985); Jan Just Witkam et al., *Christiaan Snouck Hurgronje (1857–1936): Orientalist* (Leiden: Universiteitsbibliotheek, 2007).

6 Julius Wellhausen, *Reste arabischen Heidentums* [1887] (Berlin: Georg Reimer, 2nd edn. 1897), 72, 78.

7 Wellhausen, *Reste*, 220.

8 E.g. Wellhausen, *Reste*, 219.

9 Ignaz Goldziher, *Der Mythos bei den Hebräern und seine geschichtliche Entwickelung* (Leipzig: F. Brockhaus, 1876). See also idem, *Tagebuch*, ed. Alexander Scheiber (Leiden: Brill, 1978), a mixed autobiography and diary that reveals the depth of Goldziher's engagement with Judaism and Islam in opposition to the Christianity of his period. See further Peter Haber, *Zwischen jüdischer Tradition und Wissenschaft: Der ungarische Orientalist Ignác Goldziher (1850–1921)* (Cologne: Böhlau, 2006).

10 Nöldeke to de Goeje, April 29, 1860, *Briefwisseling de Goeje*, admitted differences in degree of elaboration between, among others, Semitic and "Indogermanic" mythologies, but rejected Renan's postulate that the Semites had been monotheists originally. In general, a significant portion of German philological scholarship tended to be critical of Renan's racialized posits about the rigid legalism of "the Semites" as opposed to the creative production of mythological narrative in the religious forms of "Aryan" peoples. See Ernest Renan, *Etudes d'histoire religieuse* (Paris: Michel Lévy Frères, 1857); Olender, *Languages of Paradise*; Marchand, *German Orientalism*, 124–30.

11 See e.g. the passage on sacrifice in Wellhausen, *Prolegomena*, 79–85.

12 Wellhausen, *Reste*, 10–13. The edition used by European Orientalists was one of the earliest large-scale philological undertakings, Ferdinand Wüstenfeld, ed. *Jacut's Geographisches Wörterbuch*, 6 vols. (Leipzig: F. A. Brockhaus, 1866–73).

13 Wellhausen, *Reste*, 213.

14 Wellhausen, *Reste*, 215.

15 Wellhausen, *Reste*, 217.

16 It may be worth mentioning that Hubert Grimme, *Mohammed, 2: Einleitung in den Koran. System der koranischen Theologie* (Münster: Aschendorff, 1895), 36 cites this explanation approvingly.

17 Wellhausen, *Reste*, 219.

18 See the classical discussion by Talal Asad, *Genealogies of Religion: Disciplines and Reasons of Power in Christianity and Islam* (Baltimore: Johns Hopkins University Press, 1993). See also Brent Nongbri, *Before Religion: A History of a Modern Concept* (New Haven, CT: Yale University Press, 2013).

19 Markus Messling, *Champollions Hieroglyphen: Philologie und Weltaneignung*, (Berlin: Kadmos, 2012).

20 G. W. F. Hegel, *Vorlesungen über die Aesthetik*, ed. E. Moldenhauer, K. M. Michel (Frankfurt a.M.: Suhrkamp, 1970), I, 448–66, II, 375 (this latter passage lays out Hegel's use of "hieroglyphic" as a theoretical term); see also Kathleen Dow Magnus, *Hegel and the Symbolic Mediation of Spirit* (Albany: State University of New York Press, 2001).

21   Warren Breckman, *Adventures of the Symbolic: Post-Marxism and Radical Democracy* (New York: Columbia University Press, 2013), 35–41.

22   Messling, *Pariser Orientlektüren*, developing further a line of argument initiated by Jürgen Trabant, *Traditionen Humboldts* (Frankfurt a.M.: Suhrkamp, 1990).

23   The history of this idea is complicated; see the pertinent remarks on the cognate idea of literacy as a distinguishing mark of the European in Michael Harbsmeier, "Writing and the Other: Travellers' Literacy, or Towards an Archaeology of Orality," in Karen Schousboe, Mogens Trolle Larsen, eds., *Literacy and Society* (Copenhagen: Akademisk Forlag, 1989), 197–228. Arguably, as far as the concept of history is concerned, the idea is fully present already in Hegel's *Vorlesungen über die Philosophie der Geschichte*, ed. E. Moldenhauer, K. M. Michel (Frankfurt a.M.: Suhrkamp, 1986), where it comes to the fore most clearly in the passage on Ancient China (1. Teil, 1. Abschnitt): for Hegel, historical writing begins where *Nachrichten*, i.e. written traditions, are present; it is also clear that history is the self-realization of reason and that this self-realization requires the gradual development of a phonetic alphabet, whence the lagging behind of China. Humboldt's position, as reconstructed by Messling, *Pariser Orientlektüren*, here esp. ch. 4, subtly deviates from Hegel's linear model of the history of writing; after Champollion's decipherment, it became clear that the hieroglyphs were not an image-script, but had phonetic components. Therefore Humboldt began to integrate the history of writing systems with the (speculative) history of languages in terms of their *innere Sprachform*. This term meant an overall pattern of linguistic production that was rooted in cultural practice, shaped grammatical regularities, and therefore accounted for the diversity of human languages. Over the course of the nineteenth century, the nexus between historicity and script was trivialized until it was condensed, in Francophone historical writing, into the blunt decree: "L'histoire se fait avec des textes," on which see Trüper, *Topography*, 16–19, 388–91.

24   See e.g. Fritz Hommel, *Die südarabischen Altertümer (Eduard Glaser Sammlung) des Wiener Hofmuseums und ihr Herausgeber Professor David Heinrich Müller: Offene Darlegung an die kaiserlich österreichische Akademie der Wissenschaften* (Munich: Hermann Lukaschik, 1899); also in idem, *Aufsätze und Abhandlungen arabistisch-semitologischen Inhalts*, 2 (Munich: Hermann Lukaschick, 1900), 129–65.

25   Fritz Hommel, *Süd-Arabische Chrestomathie* (Munich: Franz'sche Hofbuchhandlung, 1893), 1.

26   Hommel, *Chrestomathie*, 3.

27   On Glaser see Walter Dostal, *Eduard Glaser—Forschungen im Yemen: Eine quellenkritische Untersuchung in ethnologischer Sicht* (Vienna: Akademie, 1990); Peter Rohrbacher, "'Wüstenwanderer' gegen 'Wolkenpolitiker'—Die Pressefehde zwischen Eduard Glaser und Theodor Herzl," *Österreichische Akademie der Wissenschaften, Philosophisch-Historische Klasse, Anzeiger* 142 (2007): 103–16.

28   Fritz Hommel, *Eduard Glasers historische Ergebnisse aus seinen südarabischen Inschriften*, Beilage, Allgemeine Zeitung, No. 291 (München: Cotta, 1889).

29   A. H. Sayce, *Fresh Light from the Ancient Monuments: A Sketch of the Most Recent Confirmations of the Bible, From Recent Discoveries in Egypt, Palestine, Assyria, Babylonia, Asia Minor* (London: The Religious Tract Society, 1883). Structurally, the type of argument had been laid out already by the more speculative writer Ernest de Bunsen (son of the Romantic-era Orientalist Christian von Bunsen) to whose *The Chronology of the Bible Connected with Contemporaneous Events in the History*

of the Babylonians, Assyrians, and Egyptians (London: Longmans & Green, 1874.)
Sayce had contributed a short preface.

30 Fritz Hommel, *Die Altisraelitische Überlieferung in inschriftlicher Beleuchtung: Ein Einspruch gegen die Aufstellungen der modernen Pentateuchkritik* (Munich: G. Franz'sche Buchhandlung, 1897).

31 Hommel, *Altisraelitische Überlieferung,* 316f.

32 Eberhard Nestle, *Die israelitischen Eigennamen nach ihrer religionsgeschichtlichen Bedeutung* (Haarlem: De Erven F. Boon, 1876).

33 Julius Wellhausen, "Review of Fritz Hommel, Die altisraelitische Überlieferung in inschriftlicher Beleuchtung," *Göttingische Gelehrte Anzeigen* 159, no. 2 (1897): 608–16.

34 Hommel, *Altisraelitische Überlieferung,* Vf., see also 43f.

35 Hommel, *Altisraelitische Überlieferung,* 78–98.

36 Hommel, *Altisraelitische Überlieferung,* 100–2.

37 Hommel, *Altisraelitische Überlieferung,* 115.

38 See on the early modern hunt for *Ur*-religion Jan Assmann, *Moses the Egyptian: The Memory of Egypt in Western Monotheism* (Cambridge, MA: Harvard University Press, 1997), esp. chs. 3–4; Urs App, *The Birth of Orientalism* (Philadelphia: University of Pennsylvania Press, 2010), esp. ch. 5, also on the visual record of this pursuit Paola von Wyss-Giacosa, *Religionsbilder der frühen Aufklärung: Bernard Picarts Tafeln für die "Cérémonies et Coutumes religieuses de tous les Peuples du Monde"* (Wabern/Berne: Benteli, 2006).

39 See on this Marchand, *German Orientalism,* 227–51, who suggests that the matter was one of cultural Darwinism and its limited reception, as well as of the resurgence of a quasi-ideological argument structure of "diffusionism," directed against the "comparativism" of e.g. Max Müller. The question of the applicability of these categories in the detailed reading of the texts remains to be discussed further.

40 Hommel, *Altisraelitische Überlieferung,* 119–46, here 126f. and 140 for the patriarchs' ages.

41 E.g. Carl Siegfried "Review of Hommel, Altisraelitische Überlieferung," *Theologische Literaturzeitung* 23, no. 2 (1898): 35.

42 Hubert Grimme, *Altsinaitische Forschungen: Epigraphisches und Historisches* (Paderborn: Schöningh, 1937). The author's assessment of the merits of his work can be found in a letter to Littmann, July 13, 1940, NL Littmann, K. 11, *Grimme*.

43 Ernst Cassirer, "Sprache und Mythos: Ein Beitrag zum Problem der Götternamen," [1923] in *Wesen und Wirkung des Symbolbegriffs* (Darmstadt: Wissenschaftliche Buchgesellschaft, 1956), 75–9. The text he took issue with was F. Max Müller, "On the Philosophy of Mythology: A Lecture Delivered at the Royal Institution in 1871," in *The Essential Max Müller on Language, Mythology and Religion,* ed. Jon R. Stone (New York: Palgrave, 2002), 145–66.

44 Hermann Usener, *Götternamen: Versuch einer Lehre von der religiösen Begriffsbildung* (Bonn: F. Cohen, 1896).

45 Cassirer, *Sprache und Mythos,* 92, here with regard to the work of the missionary Andreas Jakob Spieth, *Die Religion der Eweer in Süd-Togo* (Göttingen/Leipzig: Vandenhoeck & Ruprecht/J.C. Hinrichs, 1911).

46 Cassirer, *Sprache und Mythos,* 94; also Ernst Cassirer, *Philosophie der symbolischen Formen I: Die Sprache* (Berlin: Bruno Cassirer, 1923), 244f.

47 Cassirer, *Sprache und Mythos,* 99. See also idem, *Symbolische Formen I,* 2, 247–50, where the underlying philosophical point is developed with reference to Lotze's *Logik.*

48   Usener, *Götternamen*, 375; Cassirer, *Sprache und Mythos*, 111.

49   Cassirer, *Sprache und Mythos*, 132–34.

50   Robert Henry Codrington, *The Melanesians: Studies in their Anthropology and
      Folk-Lore* (Oxford: Clarendon, 1891), 118–20. As Codrington points out, the
      concept had in fact been in use since Max Müller's Hibbert Lectures of 1878, which
      had referenced Codrington's correspondence to the author, see F. Max Müller,
      Lectures on the Origin and Growth of Religions as Illustrated by the Religions of India
      (London: Longmans, Green, 1878), 53–5.

51   Later, Lévi-Strauss stripped *mana* even of the basic phenomenal meaning Cassirer
      suggested and used the term as chief example for the introduction of the notion of
      an empty or "floating signifier," see his *Introduction to the Work of Marcel Mauss*
      [1950], transl. Felicity Baker (London: Routledge & Kegan Paul, 1987), 63.

52   Cassirer, *Sprache und Mythos*, 134.

53   Cassirer, *Sprache und Mythos*, 130.

54   The concept of the "primitive" was a by-product of evolutionary theories of
      human society, see still J. W. Burrow, *Evolution and Society: A Study in Victorian
      Social Theory* (Cambridge: Cambridge University Press, 1970). See also Angus
      Nicholls, "A Germanic Reception in England: Friedrich Max Müller's Critique
      of Darwin's 'Descent of Man,'" in *The Literary and Cultural Reception of Charles
      Darwin in Europe*, ed. Thomas F. Glick, Elinor Shaffer (London: Bloomsbury,
      2014), 78–100.

55   Usener, *Götternamen*, 334. Cassirer took over the concept of polyonymy, *Sprache
      und Mythos*, 135.

56   Usener, *Götternamen*, 324.

57   On Müller as a foundational figure for the comparative study of religion see
      Lourens van den Bosch, *Friedrich Max Müller: A Life Devoted to the Humanities*
      (Leiden: Brill, 2002).

58   Usener, *Götternamen*, 264.

59   Usener, *Götternamen*, 344–7.

60   Usener, *Götternamen*, 348.

61   Usener, *Götternamen*, 348.

62   For the link between Weber and Wellhausen, see especially Max Weber, *Die
      Wirtschaftsethik der Weltreligionen: Das antike Judentum, Schriften und Reden
      1911–1920*, ed. Eckart Otto, Max-Weber-Gesamtausgabe I, 21, 1–2 (Tübingen:
      Mohr Siebeck, 2005). See also Daniel Weidner, "'Geschichte gegen den Strich
      bürsten': Julius Wellhausen und die jüdische 'Gegengeschichte,'" *Zeitschrift für
      Religions- und Geistesgeschichte* 54, no. 1 (2002): 40, with further reference to
      Jacob Taubes, "Die Entstehung des jüdischen Paria-Volkes," in *Max Weber:
      Gedächtnisschrift der Ludwig-Maximilians-Universität München zur hundertsten
      Wiederkehr seines Geburtstages*, ed. Karl Englisch et al. (Berlin: Duncker &
      Humblot, 1966), 185–94.

63   Cassirer, *Sprache und Mythos*, 137f.

64   Cassirer, *Sprache und Mythos*, 138. The context of this reference was the emerging
      problem of the reinterpretation of Moses as an "Egyptian," which Freud was to
      propose in his last work, on the supposed oedipal constitution of Judaism, *Der
      Mann Moses und die monotheistische Religion: Drei Abhandlungen* (Amsterdam:
      Allert de Lange, 1939). Freud's imitation of the discursive forms of philology is
      striking in these essays; the work mimicks the historical argument patterns of
      Realphilologie.

65   Cassirer, *Sprache und Mythos*, 139.

66   The respective passage is in Goldziher, *Mythos*, 359–61.

67   Goldziher, *Mythos*, 348–57.

68   Rudolf Carnap, "Überwindung der Metaphysik durch logische Analyse der Sprache" [1932], in *Scheinprobleme in der Philosophie und andere metaphysikkritische Schriften*, ed. Thomas Mormann (Hamburg: Meiner, 2004), 81–109.

69   Heidegger, *Einführung in die Metaphysik*, 56.

70   Michael Friedman, *A Parting of the Ways: Carnap, Cassirer, Heidegger* (Chicago: Open Court, 2000).

71   Kant, *Kritik der reinen Vernunft* [B787], Akademie-Ausgabe 3, 420.

72   Franz Rosenzweig, *Der Stern der Erlösung* [1921], *Gesammelte Schriften* II, ed. Reinhold Mayer (The Hague: Nijhoff, 1976), 103–23.

73   See the still poignant analysis in Karl Löwith "Martin Heidegger und Franz Rosenzweig: Ein Nachtrag zu Sein und Zeit" [1958], in *Sämtliche Schriften*, 8, ed. Klaus Stichweh (Stuttgart: Metzler, 1984), 72–100.

74   Rosenzweig, *Stern*, 122.

75   Rosenzweig, *Stern*, 122.

76   For the intellectual relation, especially the many points of contestation, see in particular Leora Batnitzky, *Idolatry and Representation: The Philosophy of Franz Rosenzweig Reconsidered* (Princeton, NJ: Princeton University Press, 2000), and Myriam Bienenstock, *Cohen face à Rosenzweig: Débat sur la pensée allemande* (Paris: Vrin, 2009). For the intellectual landscape of German-Jewish thought in this period, see Ulrich Sieg, *Jüdische Intellektuelle im Ersten Weltkrieg: Kriegserfahrungen, Weltanschauungen und kulturelle Neuentwürfe* (Berlin: Akademie, 2001).

77   Hermann Cohen, "Einheit oder Einzigkeit Gottes?" in *Jüdische Schriften*, ed. Bruno Strauß, 1 (Berlin: Schwentker & Sohn, 1924), 87–99.

78   Hermann Cohen, *Religion der Vernunft aus den Quellen des Judentums* [1919], ed. Bruno Strauß (Frankfurt a.M.: J. Kauffmann, 1929), 47f.

79   On this phrase and its deeper historical links with the philosophical discussion of subjecthood, see also the important chapter by Hendrik Birus, "'Ich bin, der ich bin': Über die Echos eines Namens," in Stéphane Moses, Albrecht Schöne, eds., *Juden in der deutschen Literatur* (Frankfurt a.M.: Suhrkamp, 1986), 25–53. In light of Birus's account, it would seem that what novelty there was in the exegesis of the phrase in the period discussed in the present study was indeed chiefly related to the changing sense of the semantics of naming.

80   Cohen, *Einheit*, 91.

81   The indispensable role of the reception of Wellhausen has been emphasized already by Hans Liebeschütz, "Hermann Cohen and his Historical Background," *Leo Baeck Institute Year Book* 13 (1968): 3–33.

82   See e.g. the posthumous lectures August Dillmann, *Handbuch der alttestamentlichen Theologie*, ed. G. Kittel (Leipzig: Hirzel, 1895), here e.g. 15.

83   Emil Kautzsch, *Die Heilige Schrift des Alten Testaments*, Tübingen: Mohr, 1894.

84   Cohen, *Einheit*, 96.

85   Cohen, *Einheit*, 94.

86   Peter E. Gordon, *Rosenzweig and Heidegger: Between Judaism and German Philosophy* (Berkeley: University of California Press, 2003), 42–6.

87   Martin Buber, *Ich und Du* (Leipzig: Insel, 1923).

88   Gordon, *Rosenzweig*. See further also Peter E. Gordon, *Continental Divide: Heidegger, Cassirer, Davos* (Cambridge, MA: Harvard University Press, 2010).

89   Martin Heidegger, "Die onto-theo-logische Verfassung der Metaphysik," in *Identität und Differenz* [1957], Gesamtausgabe I.11 (Frankfurt a.M.: Klostermann, 2006), 51–79.

90   Hermann Cohen, "Julius Wellhausen: Ein Abschiedsgruß," *Neue Jüdische Monatshefte* 1918, no. 8, January 25, 178–81; also in Hermann Cohen, *Jüdische Schriften* 2, ed. Bruno Strauß (Berlin: Schwetschke, 1924), 463–8.

91   Solomon Schechter, "Higher Criticism—Higher Anti-Semitism" [1903], in *Seminary Address and Other Papers* (Cincinnati: Ark Publishing, 1915), 35–9.

92   It may be opportune to point out in passing that such concealment should precisely not be taken as justification for discounting the entwinement of philology and philosophy in the nineteenth and twentieth centuries, as is a key tenet of Turner, *Philology*. Turner is no doubt right to emphasize the long-lasting tensions between the fields; but especially philology's thrust toward theorization in the nineteenth century, and philosophy's increasing engagement with problems of meaning, entailed interdependence, albeit tacit and conflicted.

93   Wellhausen to Justi, July 19, 1906, in Wellhausen, *Briefe*, ed. Rudolf Smend (subsequently *Briefe*), 487.

94   Wellhausen to Eduard Schwartz, February 15, 1907, *Briefe*, 499–501.

95   See e.g. the monograph edition Wilhelm Schröder, *Het Wetloopen tüschen den Haasen un den Swinegel up der Buxtehuder Heid* (Düsseldorf: Arnz & Co., 1855). On the author as well as the problem of the provenance of the tale, see the article by Karl Ernst Wilhelm Krause in *Allgemeine Deutsche Biographie* 32 (1891), 533–4. That Wellhausen's repeated uses of *Swinegel* in his correspondence refer to the tale is confirmed by a letter to Rudolf von Jhering, April 24, 1892, *Briefe*, 283.

96   Heidegger, "Onto-theo-logische Verfassung," 69. Derrida picked up on the reference, see Jan Bauke-Ruegg, "Gott und Kontingenz bei Derrida: Hasensprünge und Igeleien, oder: Das Spiel der différance," in *Vernunft, Kontingenz und Gott: Konstellationen eines offenen Problems*, ed. Philipp Stoellger, Ingolf U. Dalferth (Tübingen: Mohr, 2000), 355–82.

97   For the broader context see Daniel Weidner, "Geschichte gegen den Strich." Moreover see Jerry Z. Muller, "A Zionist Critique of Jewish Politics: The Early Thought of Leo Strauss," in *Against the Grain: Jewish Intellectuals in Hard Times*, ed. Ezra Mendelssohn, Stefani Hoffman, Richard I. Cohen (New York: Berghahn, 2014), 17–31.

98   See Batnitzky, *Idolatry*, ch. 1.

99   See e.g. the emphasis on the "high naivety" of Cohen's last work in Rosenzweig's "Einleitung," in Cohen, *Jüdische Schriften* 1, LXIIIf.

100   On the "antihistoricist" tradition in German-Jewish philosophical discourse, see David N. Myers, *Resisting History: Historicism and its Discontents in German-Jewish Thought* (Princeton, NJ: Princeton University Press, 2003); and also still David Biale, *Gershom Scholem: Kabbalah and Counter-History* (Cambridge, MA: Harvard University Press, 2nd edn. 1982) and Amos Funkenstein, "History, Counterhistory, and Narrative," in *Perceptions of Jewish History* (Berkeley: University of California Press, 1993), 22–49. On the mimetic relation of Jewish religious philosophy to Protestant theology see also David N. Myers, "Hermann Cohen and the Quest for Protestant Judaism," *Leo Baeck International Yearbook* 46 (2001): 195–214, and for the political context of this tendency of thought Christian Wiese, "'The

Best Antidote to Anti-Semitism'? *Wissenschaft des Judentums*, Protestant Biblical Scholarship, and Anti-Semitism in Germany before 1933," in Andreas Gotzmann, Christian Wiese, eds., *Modern Judaism and Historical Consciousness: Identities, Encounters, Perspectives* (Leiden: Brill, 2007), 146–92.

101   Franz Rosenzweig, *Briefe und Tagebücher*, ed. Rachel Rosenzweig, Edith Rosenzweig-Scheinemann, 2 (The Hague: Martinus Nijhoff, 1979), 1170.

102   Wellhausen to Eduard Schwartz, September 27, 1908, *Briefe*, 531. Rudolf Smend has stressed the importance of this self-description also in *Julius Wellhausen, ein Bahnbrecher in drei Disziplinen* (Munich: Carl Friedrich von Siemens Stiftung, 2006), 27.

103   Wellhausen to Robertson Smith, January 21, 1885, *Briefe*, 167.

104   Wellhausen to Nöldeke, October 2, 1905, *Briefe*, 464.

105   Wellhausen to Eduard Schwartz, April 7, 1907, *Briefe*, 513.

106   Wellhausen to Nöldeke, October 2, 1905, *Briefe*, 464.

107   The question of whether he "was" an anti-Semite has been much debated, see Rudolf Smend, "Wellhausen und das Judentum," *Zeitschrift für Theologie und Kirche* 79 (1982): 249–82. Perhaps it would be helpful not to regard the term as one of personal identity; the presence of respective tropes in his letter discourse is undeniable; as is the reality of Wellhausen's cordial relations with Jewish colleagues and his dislike of political anti-Semitism and the "code" of the ethno-nationalist (*völkisch*) right, as it emerged in the 1880s and 90s, see Shulamit Volkov, "Antisemitism as a Cultural Code: Reflections on the History and Historiography of Antisemitism in Imperial Germany," *Yearbook of the Leo-Baeck-Institute* 23 (1978): 25–45. In a way, a telling episode can be found in a letter by the then very aged Adolf Erman to Littmann, December 31, 1932, in which Erman complained that the "silly" anti-Semitic agitation had spoilt enjoyment of "all the good Jew jokes," NL Littmann, K. 8, folder *Erman, A.* Erman, it should be added, took pride in having a Jewish grandparent.

108   Wellhausen to Nöldeke, July 11, 1901, *Briefe*, 399.

109   Wellhausen to Harnack, May 26, 1907, *Briefe*, 517.

110   See on this episode Rudolf Smend, "Julius Wellhausen und seine Prolegomena zur Geschichte Israels," in *Epochen der Bibelkritik: Gesammelte Studien*, 3 (Munich: Chr. Kaiser Verlag, 1991), 175.

111   Wellhausen to Althoff and Wellhausen to Ferdinand Justi, both April 5, 1892, *Briefe*, 282f.

112   Wellhausen to Harnack, April 25, 1892, *Briefe*, 284, the phrase he put in Low German: "als ein Swinegel mang die Hasen."

113   Wellhausen to Harnack, February 12, 1890, *Briefe*, 251.

114   Julius Wellhausen, *Ein Gemeinwesen ohne Obrigkeit: Rede zur Feier des Geburtstages seiner Majestät des Kaisers und Königs am 27. Januar 1900 im Namen der Georg-Augusts-Universität* (Göttingen: Dieterich'sche Buchhandlung, 1900), 15.

115   Wellhausen to Wilhelm Herrmann, April 21, 1915, *Briefe*, 633.

116   See on this Johann Gottfried Herder, *Vom Geist der Ebräischen Poesie: Eine Anleitung für die Liebhaber derselben, und der ältesten Geschichte des menschlichen Geistes* [1782–3], Sämtliche Werke, ed. B. Suphan, 11–12 [1879] (Hildesheim: Olms, 1967), 2, ch. V; the intermediary intellectual history is laid out in Wolfgang Hübener, "Die verlorene Unschuld der Theokratie," in *Religionstheorie und politische Theologie, 3: Theokratie*, ed. Jacob Taubes (Munich: Fink, 1987), 29–64.

117   Wellhausen to Wilhelm Herrmann, April 14, 1915, *Briefe*, 633.

118 Marchand, *German Orientalism*, 178–86.
119 Walter Benjamin, *Über den Begriff der Geschichte*, ed. Gérard Raulet (Berlin: Suhrkamp, 2010).
120 Fritz Hommel, "Vier neue arabische Landschaftsnamen im Alten Testament nebst einem Nachtrag über die vier Paradiesflüsse in altbabylonischer und altarabischer Überlieferung," in *Aufsätze und Abhandlungen arabistisch-semitologischen Inhalts*, III.1 (Munich: G. Franz, 1901), 273–343.
121 Eduard Glaser, *Skizze der Geschichte und Geographie Arabiens von den ältesten Zeiten bis zum Propheten Muḥammad*, 2 (Berlin: Weidmann, 1890), 314–57.
122 Friedrich Delitzsch, *Wo lag das Paradies? Eine biblisch-assyriologische Studie mit zahlreichen assyriologischen Beiträgen zur biblischen Länder- und Völkerkunde* (Leipzig: J. C. Hinrichs, 1881), 45–83.
123 Julius Wellhausen, Review of "Fritz Hommel, Die altisraelitische Überlieferung in inschriftlicher Beleuchtung," *Göttingische Gelehrte Anzeigen* 159 (1897): 613.
124 Hommel, *Altisraelitische Überlieferung*, 199f. The contested passage is in Julius Wellhausen, *Die Composition des Hexateuchs und der historischen Bücher des Alten Testaments* [1885] (Berlin: Reimer, 3rd edn. 1899), 312.
125 Wellhausen, "Review Hommel," 615. In the review, Wellhausen omitted his own reference to Theodor Nöldeke, "Die Ungeschichtlichkeit der Erzählung Gen. XIV," in *Untersuchungen zur Kritik des Alten Testaments* (Kiel: Schwers'sche Buchhandlung, 1869), 156–72.
126 Wellhausen, "Review Hommel," 614.
127 To Robertson Smith, Wellhausen remarked: "I am afraid that he [Glaser] will spoil a lot of his finds through his and his friend Hommel's speculations. He does not have a trace of judgment," June 5, 1890, *Briefe*, 256.
128 Thomas S. Kuhn, *The Structure of Scientific Revolutions* (Chicago: The University of Chicago Press, 1962).
129 Wellhausen, "Review Hommel," 614.
130 A hint on Hommel's title page points to the Society as publisher of the English version that appeared at the same time as the German.
131 Hommel, "Vier neue arabische," 282f.
132 Hommel, "Vier neue arabische," 336–8.
133 Glaser, *Skizze*, 318.
134 Edward Burnett Tylor, *Primitive Religion: Researches into the Development of Mythology, Philosophy, Religion, Art, and Custom* (London: John Murray, 1871), I, 247.
135 See Marchand, *German Orientalism*, 227–36. See also for the broader intellectual context Angus Nicholls, "Against Darwin: Teleology in German Philosophical Anthropology," in *Historical Teleologies in the Modern World*, ed. Henning Trüper, Dipesh Chakrabarty, Sanjay Subrahmanyam (London: Bloomsbury, 2015), 89–113.
136 Glaser, *Skizze*, 316.
137 Nöldeke, *Ungeschichtlichkeit*, 162f.
138 Wellhausen to Nöldeke, October 2, 1905, *Briefe*, 464.
139 Herder, *Vom Geist*.
140 Jonathan Sheehan, *The Enlightenment Bible: Translation, Scholarship, Culture* (Princeton, NJ: Princeton University Press, 2005), 148–81. On the history of Old Testament scholarship, see the collaborative history Magne Sæbø, with Peter Machinist, Jean Louis Ska, eds., *Hebrew Bible/Old Testament: The History of Its Interpretation*, 3.1 *The Nineteenth Century: A Century of Modernism and*

Historicism, 3.2 *The Twentieth Century: From Modernism to Post-Modernism* (Göttingen: Vandenhoeck & Ruprecht, 2013–15). For the uses of scripture in German literature, see the detailed analysis by Daniel Weidner, *Bibel und Literatur um 1800* (Munich: Fink, 2010).

141 For Wellhausen's appreciation of the "wonderful prose" of the Icelandic sagas—and lack of appreciation for the poetic forms of old Germanic and German literature, see his letters to Nöldeke, October 2, 1905 and to Eduard Schwartz, February 15, 1907, *Briefe*, 463, 500.

142 Gangolf Hübinger, *Kulturprotestantismus und Politik: Zum Verhältnis von Liberalismus und Protestantismus im wilhelminischen Deutschland* (Tübingen: Mohr, 1994).

143 Wellhausen to Adolf Jülicher, May 24, 1911, *Briefe*, 575.

144 Julius Wellhausen, *Israelitische und jüdische Geschichte* (Berlin: Reimer, 1894); idem, *Das arabische Reich und sein Sturz* (Berlin: Reimer, 1902). I have not had the opportunity to collate the English translation of the latter work by Margaret Graham Weir (Calcutta: University of Calcutta, 1927).

145 On his idealization of and intellectual debt to Mommsen see especially still Lothar Perlitt, *Vatke und Wellhausen: Geschichtsphilosophische Voraussetzungen und historiographische Motive für die Darstellung der Religion und Geschichte Israels durch Wilhelm Vatke und Julius Wellhausen* (Berlin: Töpelmann, 1965).

146 *Annals of the Prophets and Kings: Annales quos scripsit Abu Djafar Mohammed Ibn Djarir At-Tabari*, ed. Michael Jan de Goeje (Leiden: Brill, 1879–1901). On the history of the edition, see Arnoud Vrolijk, "The Leiden Edition of Tabari's Annals: The Search for the Istanbul Manuscripts as Reflected in Michael Jan de Goeje's Correspondence," *Quaderni di studi arabi* 19 (2001): 71–86; see further Franz-Christoph Muth, *Die Annalen von aṭ-Ṭabarī im Spiegel der europäischen Bearbeitungen* (Frankfurt a.M.: Lang, 1983). On the extraordinary research environment at Leiden, see Willem Otterspeer, ed. *Leiden Oriental Connections 1850–1940* (Leiden: Brill, 1989).

147 The correspondence is at Leiden University Library, Briefwisseling de Goeje.

148 Theodor Nöldeke, *Geschichte der Perser und Araber zur Zeit der Sasaniden. Aus der arabischen Chronik des Tabari übersetzt und mit ausführlichen Erläuterungen und Ergänzungen versehn* (Leiden: Brill, 1879).

149 Julius Wellhausen, *Prolegomena zur Geschichte Israels* (Berlin: Reimer, 1883), 389; second revised edition of *Geschichte Israels I* (Berlin: Reimer, 1878).

150 I have previously discussed this theme in my "Wie es uneigentlich gewesen: Zum Gebrauch der Fußnote bei Julius Wellhausen," *Zeitschrift für Germanistik*, N.F. 23, no. 2 (2013), 329–42.

151 Anthony Grafton, *The Footnote: A Curious History* (London: Faber & Faber, 1997), 23n.

152 Grafton, *Footnote*, 232.

153 Grafton, *Footnote*, 4.

154 In the concluding pages of *Die Protestantische Ethik und der "Geist" des Kapitalismus* [1904–5, 1920], Max Weber Gesamtausgabe I/9 and 18, ed. Wolfgang Schluchter, Ursula Bube (Tübingen: Mohr Siebeck, 2014–16).

155 Michael Bernays, "Zur Lehre von den Citaten und Noten" [1892], in *Schriften zur Kritik und Litteraturgeschichte*, IV (Berlin: Behr, 1899), 306.

156 Bernays, Zur Lehre, 310.

157 Bernays, Zur Lehre, 336.

158 Bernays, Zur Lehre, 326.
159 For the difficulties of the translation, see still Peter Novick, *That Noble Dream: The "Objectivity Question" and the American Historical Profession* (Cambridge: Cambridge University Press, 1988), 26–31. I do not entirely concur with Novick, however, that "eigentlich" entails commitment to philosophical essentialism; or rather, the intellectual background would still require further discussion. On the possible status of the phrase as a classicist quotation from Thucydides, see also Ronald S. Stroud, "'Wie es eigentlich gewesen' and Thucydides 2.48.3," *Hermes* 115, no. 3 (1987): 379–382. An intermediary, and perhaps more important, ancient reference might actually be Lucian's treatise "How to write history," with its insistence on impartiality and unadorned style; see e.g. Matthew Kempshall, *Rhetoric and the Writing of History, 400–1500* (Manchester: Manchester University Press, 2011), 489–91; and for the context in eighteenth-century German historical writing, Daniel Fulda, *Wissenschaft aus Kunst: Die Entstehung der modernen Geschichtsschreibung in Deutschland 1760–1860* (Berlin: de Gruyter, 1996), 146–55. Ranke's contemporaries were arguably aware of this connection; Friedrich August Pauly's translation, "Wie man Geschichte schreiben soll," *Lucian's Werke*, 6 (Stuttgart: Metzler, 1827), 653, appears to echo Ranke's 1824 phrase when he indicates that history ought to figure out "was denn eigentlich vorgieng." Christoph Martin Wieland, in his more influential translation, had rendered the same phrase quite differently, as "Verlauf der Sachen," "the course of matters," see *Lucians von Samosata Sämmtliche Werke*, transl. C. M. Wieland, 4, [1789] (Vienna: Haas, 1798), 98.
160 Wellhausen, *Arabisches Reich*, 51.
161 Wellhausen, *Israelitische und jüdische Geschichte*, 192.
162 Rudolf Smend, "Wellhausen und seine Prolegomena," 171.
163 Wellhausen, *Prolegomena*, VII.
164 Wellhausen, *Prolegomena*, VIII.
165 Wellhausen, *Prolegomena*, 436f.
166 Sheehan, *Enlightenment Bible*, 158.
167 Nicholas Boyle, "Geschichtsschreibung und Autobiographik bei Goethe (1810–1817)," *Goethe-Jahrbuch* 110 (1993): 163–72 sorted out the divergent and confusing remarks Goethe made on the category of the historical. Michael Jäger, *Fausts Kolonie: Goethes kritische Phänomenologie der Moderne* (Würzburg: Königshausen & Neumann, 2004) provides a far-reaching interpretation of Goethe's work in the context of eighteenth- and early-nineteenth-century philosophies of history.
168 Andreas Urs Sommer, *Friedrich Nietzsches der "Der Antichrist": Ein philosophisch-historischer Kommentar* (Basel: Schwabe, 2000), 245–66.
169 Wellhausen, *Israelitische und jüdische Geschichte*, 350f.
170 On the notion of divine irony, as a purportedly indirect and frivolous product of romanticism, see the polemical remarks in Hegel, *Ästhetik*, I, 93–99, esp. 95.
171 Heschel, *Geiger*.
172 Wellhausen, *Prolegomena*, 175.
173 Julius Wellhausen, *Das Evangelium Marci übersetzt und erklärt* (Berlin: Reimer, 1903), 104.
174 Wellhausen, *Israelitische und jüdische Geschichte*, 355.
175 On the role of the individual in nineteenth-century humanities theorizing, see Sabina Loriga, *Le petit x: De la biographie à l'histoire* (Paris: Seuil, 2010).

176 Wellhausen, *Israelitische und jüdische Geschichte*, 355f.
177 Here relying on Wellhausen, *Israelitische und jüdische Geschichte* (Berlin, Leipzig: Vereinigung Wissenschaftlicher Verleger, 8th edn. 1921), 358n.
178 Wellhausen to Littmann, December 29, 1911, *Briefe*, 583.

Chapter 5

1   Julius Wellhausen, "Rezension Georg Jacob, Welche Handelsartikel bezogen die Araber des Mittelalters aus den nordisch-baltischen Ländern?" *Deutsche Literaturzeitung* 13 (1892), 589f.
2   Wellhausen to Heinrich Ulmann, February 14, 1892, *Briefe*, 276.
3   E.g. Jacob to Nöldeke, June 11, 1897, NL Nöldeke, A4, with a lengthy diatribe against *Reste arabischen Heidenthums* and Wellhausen's tendency to ignore available research literature.
4   As is mentioned specifically in Jacob to Nöldeke, January 13, 1905, NL Nöldeke A4.
5   Jacob to Nöldeke, March 31, 1903, NL Nöldeke, A4.
6   Wellhausen to Nöldeke, October 27, 1908, *Briefe*, 533.
7   Wellhausen to Littmann, December 29, 1911, *Briefe*, 583.
8   Wellhausen to Nöldeke, November 25, 1910, *Briefe*, 567.
9   Georg Jacob, *Reimstudien* (Kiel: Typescript Published by the Author, 1934, version March 9); the question constitutes a continuing philological problem, see on its broader bibliography and implications Wolfgang Behr, *Reimende Bronzeinschriften und die Entstehung der chinesischen Endreimdichtung* (Bochum: Projekt Verlag, 2008), 596–615.
10 Georg Jacob, *Shakespeare-Studien*, ed. Hans Jensen (Glückstadt: Augustin, 1938).
11 Georg Jacob, *Östliche Kulturelemente im Abendland* (Berlin: Mayer & Müller, 1902), 13; see also his *Der Einfluß des Morgenlands auf das Abendland vorzüglich während des Mittelalters* (Hannover: Lafaire, 1924), a thoroughly revised and extended version of the previous treatise.
12 Jacob, *Östliche Kulturelemente*.
13 Jacob to Littmann, December 29, 1916, NL Littmann, K. 14, folder *Jacob, G. (5)*.
14 For instance Jacob to Littmann, July 12, 1917, NL Littmann, K. 14, folder *Jacob, G. (5)*.
15 Jacob to Littmann, March 27, 1931, NL Littmann, K. 15, folder *Jacob, G. (13)*.
16 For an overview of different manifestations of this phenomenon, see Gábor Klaniczay, Michael Werner, Otto Gecser, eds., *Multiple Antiquities—Multiple Modernities: Ancient Histories in Nineteenth-Century European Cultures* (Frankfurt a.M.: Campus, 2011). The basic point, the shattering of the formerly unified sense of the ancient, can already be found in Werner Kaegi, "Voltaire und der Zerfall des christlichen Geschichtsbildes," in *Historische Meditationen* (Zurich: Fretz & Wasmuth, 1942), 221–48.
17 Nöldeke to de Goeje, February 12, 1888, *Briefwisseling de Goeje*.
18 Nöldeke to de Goeje, March 2, 1873, *Briefwisseling de Goeje*.
19 As he emphasizes in a letter to de Goeje, March 2, 1873, *Briefwisseling de Goeje*. See also his characterization of the Caliph Mansur, as a personified turning point

in Islamic history, Theodor Nöldeke, "Der Chalif Mansûr," in *Orientalische Skizzen* (Berlin: Paetel, 1892), 111–52.

20 Eduard Meyer, *Geschichte des Alterthums*, 5 vols. (Stuttgart, Berlin: Cotta, 1884–1902). On Meyer in general see William M. Calder III, Alexander Demandt, eds., *Eduard Meyer: Leben und Leistung eines Universalhistorikers* (Leiden: Brill, 1990); Arnaldo Momigliano, "Introduction to a Discussion of Eduard Meyer," in *A. D. Momigliano: Studies on Modern Scholarship*, ed. G. W. Bowersock, T. J. Cornell (Berkeley: University of California Press, 1994), 209–22. Marchand, *German Orientalism*, 206–11.

21 Marchand, *German Orientalism*, esp. 66–71.

22 Georg Jacob, *Türkische Litteraturgeschichte in Einzeldarstellungen, 1: Das türkische Schattentheater* (Berlin: Mayer & Müller, 1900). Traveling scholars had repeatedly observed the practice; the first extensive scholarly treatment of the Turkish variant appears to have been Felix von Luschan, "Das türkische Schattenspiel," *Internationales Archiv für Ethnographie* 2 (1889): 1–9, 81–90, 125–44.

23 As is for instance indicated by an extensive summary of Pischel's talk in Jacob to Nöldeke, July 10, 1900, NL Nöldeke, A4.

24 Richard Pischel, *The Home of the Puppet-Play: An Address on Assuming the Office of Rector of the Königliche Vereinigte Friedrichs-Universität, Halle-Wittenberg, on the 12th July 1900*, transl. Mildred C. Tawney (London: Luzac & Co., 1902), 5. Jacob gratefully remembered this address years later, as is clear from his letter to Littmann, August 27, 1916, NL Littmann, K. 14, folder *Jacob, G. (5)*.

25 The defining synthesis of this research was August Friedrich Pott, *Die Zigeuner in Europa und Asien: Ethnographisch-linguistische Untersuchung, vornehmlich ihrer Herkunft und Sprache, nach gedruckten und ungedruckten Quellen* (Halle a.d.S.: Ed. Heynemann, 1844); nineteenth-century Arabists contributed discussions of the transition of this ethnic group into the Middle East, see e.g. Michael Jan de Goeje, *Bijdrage tot de Geschiedenis der Zigeuners* (Amsterdam: C. G. van der Post, 1875); Littmann wrote a short monograph on remnants of Arabic vocabulary and grammar in the languages of Middle Eastern Roma, *Zigeuner-Arabisch: Wortschatz und Grammatik der arabischen Bestandteile in den morgenländischen Zigeunersprachen, nebst einer Einleitung über das arabische Rotwälsch und die Namen der morgenländischen Zigeuner* (Bonn: Schroeder, 1920).

26 Johan Huizinga, *De Vidushaka in het indisch toneel* [1897], Verzamelde Werken 1 (Haarlem: Tjeenk Willink, 1948). See on the agenda of Huizinga's early Indologist work Willem Otterspeer, *Orde en Trouw: Over Johan Huizinga* (Amsterdam: De Bezige Bij, 2006), English transl. *Reading Huizinga* (Amsterdam: Amsterdam University Press, 2010).

27 Kurt Klemm, "Inder bis zur Gegenwart: Litteraturgeschichte," *Jahresberichte der Geschichtswissenschaft* 21 (1898): 59.

28 Ernst Windisch, *Der griechische Einfluss im indischen Drama* (Berlin: A. Asher, 1882).

29 As Marchand suggests, *German Orientalism*, 234f. See Friedrich Ratzel, *Anthropo-Geographie, oder Anwendung der Grundzüge der Erdkunde auf die Geschichte* (Stuttgart: Engelhorn, 1882).

30 Jacob to Nöldeke, January 31, 1904; March 25, 1905; July 7 and September 7, 1907, NL Nöldeke, A4. The last-mentioned letter confirms that Jacob visited Strzygowski in Graz. According to the first-mentioned letter, Jacob's enthusiasm hinged, not on the standard work Josef Strzygowski, *Orient oder Rom: Beiträge zur Geschichte*

der spätantiken und frühchristlichen Kunst (Leipzig: Hinrichs'sche Buchhandlung, 1901), but rather on the author's follow-up study *Kleinasien: Ein Neuland der Kunstgeschichte* (Leipzig: Hinrichs'sche Buchhandlung, 1903). See Marchand, *German Orientalism*, 403–10; see further Suzanne Marchand, "The Rhetoric of Artifacts and the Decline of Classical Humanism: The Case of Josef Strzygowski," *History and Theory* 33, no. 4 (1994): 106–30.

31   Jacob to Nöldeke, April 13, 1900, NL Nöldeke, A4.

32   Ernst Grosse, *Die Anfänge der Kunst* (Freiburg i.Br.: Mohr, 1894); English transl. *The Beginnings of Art* (New York, London: Appleton, 1914). Jacob has high praise for the work in a letter to Nöldeke, February 2, 1898, NL Nöldeke, A4; as well as in *Märchen und Traum mit besonderer Berücksichtigung des Orients*, Hannover: Lafaire, 1923, 21n.

33   On Grosse's views on race, see also his "Kunst und Race," in *Kunstwissenschaftliche Studien* (Tübingen: Mohr Siebeck, 1900), 113–66.

34   On the emergence of *Theaterwissenschaft* as a novel epistemic formation, see Hans-Christian von Herrmann, *Das Archiv der Bühne: Eine Archäologie des Theaters und seiner Wissenschaft* (Munich: Fink, 2005).

35   As for instance in Carl Robert, *Oidipus: Geschichte eines poetischen Stoffs im griechischen Altertum* (Berlin: Weidmannsche Buchhandlung, 1915). The volume was dedicated to the memory of Tycho von Wilamowitz.

36   Jacob to Littmann, February 18, 1909, NL Littmann, K. 14, folder *Jacob, G. (1)*. The question of the relation of black-figure vase-painting to the art history of shadows in Europe might mark an interesting addition to the themes addressed in Victor I. Stoichita, *A Short History of the Shadow* (London: Reaktion Books, 1997).

37   Jacob to Nöldeke, March 31, 1903, NL Nöldeke, A4.

38   Huizinga, *Homo Ludens*, 112, 116n.

39   Karla Mallette, *European Modernity and the Arab Mediterranean: Toward a New Philology and a Counter-Orientalism* (Philadelphia: University of Pennsylvania Press, 2010).

40   See, for instance, Andrea Celli, *Dante e l'Oriente: Le fonti islamiche nella storiografia novecentesca* (Rome: Carocci, 2013), which also demonstrates the participation of Germanophone scholarship in one of the most important focal points of debate about cross-Mediterranean literary heritage, concerning the sources of the works of Dante.

41   Enno Littmann, "Abendland und Morgenland," in *Reden bei der Rektoratsübergabe am 30. April 1930 im Festsaal der Universität Tübingen* (Tübingen: Universität, 1930), 20.

42   As Ernst Schulin already emphasized in his anatomy of this shift in *Die weltgeschichtliche Erfassung des Orients bei Hegel und Ranke* (Göttingen: Vandenhoeck & Ruprecht, 1958).

43   Hermann, *Böckhs Behandlung*, 9.

44   Henri Pirenne, *Mahomet et Charlemagne* (Paris: Alcan, 1937), conclusion.

45   Marc Bloch, *La société féodale*, 2 vols. (Paris: Albin Michel, 1939–1940), here vol. I, 94.

46   The Austrian historian Erna Patzelt, a student of Alfons Dopsch who was the chief proponent of a continuity-based account of the transition from the ancient world into the Middle Ages, attacked Pirenne's earlier articles on the matter already in her *Die fränkische Kultur und der Islam, mit besonderer Berücksichtigung der nordischen Entwicklung: Eine universalhistorische Studie* (Baden: Rohrer, 1932); see further

Robert S. Lopez, "Mohammed and Charlemagne: A Revision," *Speculum* 18 (1943): 14–38. Even Pirenne's disciple and successor François Louis Ganshof argued against the hypothesis, see his "Note sur les ports de Provence du VIIIe au Xe siècle," *Revue historique* 183 (1938): 28–37.

47 Karl Löwith, *Meaning in History: The Theological Implications of the Philosophy of History* (Chicago: University of Chicago Press, 1949).

48 E.g. Jacob to Littmann, February 11 and 16, 1927, NL Littmann, K. 15, folder 10, "Jacob, G. 1927." Many of the phrases in Jacob's repeated letter invectives against Praetorius—as well as against August Fischer, Carl Brockelmann, Albert Socin, Friedrich Althoff and others—recur verbatim over decades.

49 Jacob to Nöldeke, January 23, 1897, NL Nöldeke, A4. Nöldeke's take on the Arabic name of the jackal, which stresses above all the onomatopoetic "howl" inscribed in the word, is in his "Tiernamen mit Reduplikation," in *Beiträge zur semitischen Sprachwissenschaft* (Strasbourg: Trübner, 1904), 110.

50 Jacob to Littmann, June 26, 1933, NL Littmann, K. 15, folder 14, "Jacob, G. 1933–34." The letter in general discusses Jacob's concerns about the institutional threat to the discipline under the new anti-Semitic regime.

51 As is evident from letters: Jacob to Nöldeke, January 9, 1905 (on systematicity), June 30, 1904 (on the use of an "episcope" for rendering the colors of Oriental carpets), and November 2, 1897 (on phonetics), NL Nöldeke, A4.

52 Jacob to Nöldeke, Easter Sunday 1910, NL Nöldeke, A4.

53 Jacob to Nöldeke, September 15, 1906, NL Nöldeke, A4.

54 For Nöldeke's attitude toward historical writing, see my own "Dispersed Personae," here 1332–40.

55 Jacob to Littmann, September 13, 1929 (postcard), NL Littmann, K. 14, folder Jacob, G. (12).

56 On Arthur Rosenberg, who died in exile in New York City, see Mario Keßler, *Arthur Rosenberg: Ein Historiker im Zeitalter der Katastrophen* (Cologne: Böhlau, 2003); see also still Francis L. Carsten, "Arthur Rosenberg: Ancient Historian into Leading Communist," *Journal of Contemporary History* 8, no. 1 (1973): 63–75.

57 Jacob to Littmann, September 17, 1929, NL Littmann, K. 14, folder Jacob, G. (12).

58 Jacob to Nöldeke, July 24, 1906, NL Nöldeke, A4.

59 Ironically, Jacob's own historical account, in his *Die Geschichte des Schattentheaters im Morgen- und Abendland* (Hanover: Lafaire, 2nd edn. 1925), remained the most magisterial account of the history of this art form in Germany (and elsewhere); see now also the Stuttgart exhibition catalogue Jasmin Ii Sabai Günther, Inés de Castro, eds., *Die Welt des Schattentheaters: Von Asien bis Europa* (Munich: Hirmer, 2015). The *Schwabinger Schattenspiele* existed from 1907 until 1912 under the directorship of Alexander von Bernus (1880–1965), who toward the end of this period became involved with the theosophical society and the overall followership of Madame Blavatsky, whose contribution to modernist Orientalism was, needless to say, tremendous. Jacob's relative indolence toward religion appears to have kept him from developing similar leanings. Scripts for the Schwabing performances were contributed by noted authors such as the George circle regular Karl Wolfskehl, *Wolfdietrich und die Rauhe Els* (Munich: Schwabinger Schattenspiele, 1907); idem, *Thors Hammer. Silhouetten von Emil Preetorius* (Munich: Schwabinger Schattenspiele, 1908); and the later Nazi propaganda writer Will Vesper, *Der Blinde: Ein Narrenspiel* (Munich: Schwabinger Schattenspiele 1907).

60 More extensively discussed in the first edition, Georg Jacob, *Geschichte des Schattentheaters* (Berlin: Mayer & Müller, 1907), 120–37.

61 Jacob to Nöldeke, April 23, 1907, NL Nöldeke, A4.

62 On the notion of national theater in fin-de-siècle Munich modernism, see still Peter Jelavich, *Munich and Theatrical Modernism: Politics, Playwriting, and Performance 1890–1914* (Cambridge, MA: Harvard University Press, 1985).

63 Goldziher to Nöldeke August 12, 1895, NL Nöldeke, A2.

64 See Nina Frankenhauser, Anette Krämer, "Das arabische Schattentheater und die ägyptischen Figuren der Sammlung Kahle," in Sabai Günther, de Castro, eds., *Welt des Schattentheaters* (Munich: Hirmer, 2015), 29–33; and Brigitte Salmen, ed. *Der Almanach "Der Blaue Reiter": Bilder und Bildwerke in Originalen* (Murnau: Schlossmuseum, 1998), 147, with quotation from the letter. The unique shapes and iconography of the figures Kahle bought in Egypt continue to prompt debate, see Marcus Milwright, "On the Date of Paul Kahle's Egyptian Shadow Puppets," *Muqarnas: An Annual of the Visual Culture of the Islamic World* 28 (2011): 43–68; while Kahle thought the figures dated back to the Mamluk period (thirteenth to fourteenth centuries CE), Milwright suggests they were only made in the seventeenth to eighteenth centuries.

65 Kandinsky, Franz Marc, eds., *Der Blaue Reiter* (Munich: Piper, 2nd edn. 1914), 112 and following plate. The nine Egyptian figures are scattered across the volume, but particularly prominent among the illustrations of Kandinsky's synaesthetic *Gesamtkunstwerk* essay "Über Bühnenkomposition" and his accompanying demonstration of how such a work of art would have to be imagined on the stage, "Der gelbe Klang," which concludes the volume. Kahle's permission for reprint is mentioned in the list of illustrations (136).

66 See prominently Arthur I. Miller, *Einstein, Picasso: Space, Time, and the Beauty that Causes Havoc* (New York: Basic Books, 2001).

67 Jacob to Nöldeke, April 23, 1907, NL Nöldeke, A4.

68 See Jochen Schmidt, *Die Geschichte des Genie-Gedankens in der deutschen Literatur, Philosophie und Politik, 1750–1945*, 2 vols. (Heidelberg: Winter, 3rd edn. 2004).

69 Srinivas Aravamudan, *Enlightenment Orientalism: Resisting the Rise of the Novel* (Chicago: University of Chicago Press, 2012).

70 Relying loosely on terms introduced by Ian Watt, *The Rise of the Novel: Studies in Defoe, Richardson and Fielding* (London: Chatto & Windus, 1957); on the Germanophone side, the philosophy of history of the form of the novel had been pioneered by Georg Lukács, *Die Theorie des Romans: Ein geschichtsphilosophischer Versuch über die Formen der großen Epik* (Berlin: Cassirer, 1920). Watt's argument rose to greater prominence in the context of Empire with the help of Benedict Anderson, *Imagined Communities: Reflections on the Origin and Spread of Nationalism* (London: Verso, 2nd edn. 1991); and Homi K. Bhabha, ed., *Nation and Narration* (London: Routledge, 1990).

71 Wilfried Barner, in an important study, has traced this process across the dramatic works of Lessing and pointed to the overwhelming importance of the model of Senecan, i.e. Roman, stoic tragedy precisely until the 1760s when reliance on the model ceased abruptly; see his *Produktive Rezeption: Lessing und die Tragödien Senecas* (Munich: Beck, 1973).

72 Jacob to Nöldeke, April 1, 1898, NL Nöldeke, A4. A very similar phrase recurs in Georg Jacob, *Reimstudien* (Kiel: The Author, Typescript, 1934), 2f.

73 Jacob to Nöldeke, June 5, 1918, NL Nöldeke, A4.

74   I have not managed to establish reception in either direction; see Edward Gordon
      Craig, "The Actor and the Über-Marionette," *The Mask* 1, no. 2 (1908): 3–15.

75   Antonin Artaud, *The Theater and its Double* [1938], transl. M. C. Richards
      (New York: Grove Press, 1958).

76   On the overall phenomenon, see Erhard Schüttpelz, *Die Moderne im Spiegel des
      Primitiven: Weltliteratur und Ethnologie (1870–1960)* (Munich: Fink, 2005).

77   See on this connection László F. Földényi, *Marionetten und Übermarionetten*
      (Berlin: Matthes & Seitz, 2011). Literary studies turned to Kleist's essay especially
      with Ottokar Fischer, "Mimische Studien zu Heinrich von Kleist," *Euphorion*
      16 (1909): 747–772; and Hanna Hellmann, *Heinrich von Kleist: Darstellung des
      Problems* (Heidelberg: Winter, 1911).

78   See on this Sven Neufert, *Theater als Tempel: Völkische Ursprungssuche in Drama,
      Theater und Festkultur 1890–1930* (Würzburg: Königshausen & Neumann, 2018).

79   Goldziher, for instance, mocked Jacob's "love affair with the Turkish
      Hanswurstiaden" and hoped for his eventual recovery from this aberration, in a
      letter to Nöldeke, November 14, 1900, NL Nöldeke, A2.

80   See Enno Littmann, *Arabische Schattenspiele. Mit Anhängen von Georg Jacob*
      (Berlin: Mayer & Müller, 1901); idem, *Das Malerspiel: Ein Schattenspiel aus
      Aleppo nach einer armenisch-türkischen Handschrift* (Heidelberg: Carl Winters
      Universitätsbuchhandlung, 1918); Curt Prüfer, *Ein ägyptisches Schattenspiel*
      (Erlangen: E. Th. Jacob, 1906); idem, "Das Schiffsspiel: Ein Schattenspiel aus Cairo,"
      Münchener Beiträge zur Kenntnis des Orients 2, no. 2 (1906): 154–69; Paul E. Kahle,
      Zur Geschichte des arabischen Schattenspieles in Ägypten (Halle: Universität, 1909);
      idem, "Islamische Schattenspielfiguren aus Egypten, 1. Teil," *Der Islam* 1 (1910):
      264–99; idem, "Islamische Schattenspielfiguren aus Egypten, 2. Teil," *Der Islam*
      2 (1911): 143–95; Theodor Menzel, *Meddah, Schattentheater und Orta ojunu:
      Eine kritische Übersicht der jüngeren Forschung nebst neuen Beiträgen*, ed. Ottokar
      Menzel (Prague: Orientalisches Institut, 1941).

81   See Muhammad Ibn Daniyal, *Three Shadow Plays*, ed. Paul Kahle (Cambridge: Gibb
      Memorial Trust, 1992). Moreover Paul Kahle, ed., *Der Leuchtturm von Alexandria:
      Ein ägyptisches Schattenspiel aus dem mittelalterlichen Ägypten, mit Beiträgen
      von Georg Jacob* (Stuttgart: Kohlhammer, 1930); see further Roberto Tottoli, ed.,
      *Orientalists at Work: Some Excerpts from Paul E. Kahle's Papers upon Ibn Dāniyāl
      Kept in the Department of Oriental Studies of the University of Turin* (Alessandria:
      Edizioni dell'Orso, 2009); Derek Hopwood, "From the Shadow Plays of Ibn
      Daniyal to the Poetry of Philip Larkin: Mustafa Badawi as Editor and Translator,"
      in *Studying Arabic Literature: Mustafa Badawi, Scholar and Critic*, ed. Roger Allen,
      Robin Ostle (Edinburgh: Edinburgh University Press, 2015), 55–66; on the state
      of research on Mamluk Egypt shadow play, see Li Guo, *The Performing Arts in
      Medieval Islam: Shadow Play and Popular Poetry in Ibn Daniyal's Mamluk Cairo*
      (Leiden: Brill, 2012).

82   As developed, not accidentally, in the comments on the "West-Eastern Diwan,"
      in which Goethe muses on the "natural" order of literary forms—in what became
      the canonic triad in German literary studies, of lyrical poetry, epic poetry, and
      drama—and their uneven distribution in literary traditions the world over, see
      Johann Wolfgang von Goethe, "Dichtarten. Naturformen der Dichtung. Nachtrag,"
      in *Noten und Abhandlungen zu besserem Verständnis des West-östlichen Divan*.
      Goethes Werke, Weimarer Ausgabe 7, Weimar: Böhlau, 1887, 117–21.

83   Hellmut Ritter, *Karagös, Folge 1: Die Blutpappel u.a.* (Hanover: Lafaire, 1924); idem,
        Karagös, Folge 2: Der Ausflug nach Jalowa u.a. (Hanover: Lafaire, 1941); idem,
        Karagös, Folge 3: Die Beschneidung u.a. Mit Beiträgen von Andreas Tietze (Hanover:
        Lafaire, 1953). See Annette Krämer, "Das osmanisch-türkische Schattentheater
        'Karagöz' und die Sammlung Tuğtekin des Linden-Museums," in Sabai Günther, de
        Castro, eds., *Welt des Schattentheaters* (Munich: Hirmer, 2015), 124–45.

84   Becker to Jacob March 5, 1910, NL Becker, No. 2044 (Georg Jacob); among the
        pieces performed was a shadow play that the specialist of contemporary Islamic
        culture and languages Karl Süssheim had rendered in his article "Die moderne
        Gestalt des türkischen Schattenspiels (Qaragöz)," *Zeitschrift der Deutschen
        Morgenländischen Gesellschaft* 63 (1909): 739–73. On Süssheim, see Barbara
        Flemming, Jan Schmidt, *The Diary of Karl Süssheim (1878–1947)* (Stuttgart: Steiner,
        2002). On the context of Becker's aesthetic convictions, see also my own "Matte
        farbige Schatten: Zugehörigkeiten des Gelehrtenpolitikers Carl Heinrich Becker,"
        Österreichische Zeitschrift für Geschichtswissenschaften 25, no. 3 (2014): 177–211.

85   See correspondence in NL Becker, No. 4750.

86   Jacob to Nöldeke, October 15, 1907, NL Nöldeke, A4.

87   Jacob to Nöldeke, February 5, 1908, NL Nöldeke, A4.

88   Ibid.

89   Jacob, *Märchen und Traum.*

90   See on this problem, Philippe Lacoue-Labarthe, *Musica ficta: Figures de Wagner*
        (Paris: Bourgois, 1991).

91   Jacob, *Geschichte des Schattentheaters* [1925], 213. It is worth mentioning that Jacob
        was not alone in recognizing the competition of forms; Theodor Menzel, when he
        asked Johannes Kolmodin to purchase Karagöz figures in Turkey for the new Kiel
        Theater Museum in 1924, expressed the hope that it might be possible to acquire
        the entire inventory of a retiring performer, since the "age of the cinematograph"
        heavily impinged on the "primitive artistic practice of the Karagöz," Menzel to
        Kolmodin, April 7, 1924, Kolmodin papers, Q 15:9, fol. 143f.

92   See Evamarie Blattner, Dorothee Kimmich, eds., *Lotte Reiniger im Kontext der
        europäischen Medienavantgarde* (Tübingen: Stadtmuseum, 2011); Barbara Lange et
        al., eds., *Animationen: Lotte Reiniger im Kontext der Mediengeschichte* (Tübingen:
        Kunsthistorisches Institut, 2012).

93   Enno Littmann, *Die Erzählungen aus den tausendundein Nächten: Zum ersten Mal
        nach dem arabischen Urtext der Calcuttaer Ausgabe vom Jahre 1839*, 6 vols. (Leipzig:
        Insel, 1921–28).

94   Menzel to Kolmodin, April 7, 1924, Kolmodin papers Q 15:9, fol. 143f.

95   Menzel to Kolmodin, September 17, 1924, Kolmodin paper Q 15:9, fol. 147f.

96   See above 93.

97   See Mechthild Kirsch, "Wolfgang Liepe," in König, ed., *Internationales
        Germanistenlexikon*, 2, 1094.

98   Jacob to Littmann, November 12, 1934, NL Littmann, K. 15, folder 14 "Jacob,
        G. 1933–34."

99   Jacob to Littmann, October 18, 1934, NL Littmann, K. 15, folder 14 "Jacob,
        G. 1933–34."

100   Jacob to Littmann, November 13, 1934, NL Littmann, K. 15, folder 14 "Jacob,
        G. 1933–34."

101   Jacob to Littmann, October 18, 1934, NL Littmann, K. 15, folder 14 "Jacob, G.
        1933–34."

102 Max Bührmann, *Studien über das chinesische Schattenspiel: Erfahrungen aus einer Reise nach China* (Lüdenscheid: Volkshochschule, 1963), 38f. See also idem, *Das farbige Schattenspiel: Besonderheit, Technik, Führung* (Bern: Haupt, 1955).

103 The progress of this undertaking was the object of ample correspondence between Jacob and Littmann in 1934; I refrain from referencing individual letters, but point also to Jacob's typescript report of the journey that in the collection of Littmann's papers is currently contained in a folder of "unidentified letters," NL Littmann, K. 1. This document, authored by the younger players around Christmas 1934, after the tour had ended, states Jacob's authorship of the name and his functions as "godfather" (*Taufpate*) and "gleefully growling patron saint."

104 The contact is evident from the inventory of the Bührmann collection of shadow play figures—which includes Jacob's—at *Theatermuseum Düsseldorf*. Reiniger's attempts to emigrate, together with her husband, the film producer Carl Koch, were unsuccessful; temporary visas forced them to switch countries several times in the 1930s; after a stint in wartime Italy they returned to Germany in 1943-4, then moved to London permanently in 1949.

105 Jacob, *Geschichte des Schattentheaters*, 211.

106 See Lotte Reiniger, *Schattentheater, Schattenpuppen, Schattenfilm* (Tübingen: Texte-Verlag, 1981).

107 Siegfried Kracauer, *Theory of Film: The Redemption of Physical Reality* (Oxford: Oxford University Press, 1960).

108 Kracauer, *Theory of Film*, x.

109 As for instance laid out in Hans Blumenberg, *Schiffbruch mit Zuschauer: Paradigma einer Daseinsmetapher* (Frankfurt a.M.: Suhrkamp, 1979).

110 Kracauer, *Theory of Film*, x.

111 Peter Szondi, *Theorie des modernen Dramas* (Frankfurt a.M.: Suhrkamp, 1956).

112 Georg Jacob, *Märchen und Traum, mit besonderer Berücksichtigung des Orients* (Hannover: Lafaire, 1923), no. 1 of a planned but never realized larger collective oeuvre of *Beiträge zur Märchenkunde des Orients* (Contributions to the Study of the Oriental Fairy Tale) Jacob was to co-edit with Theodor Menzel.

113 Antti Aarne, *Verzeichnis der Märchentypen, mit Hülfe von Fachgenossen ausgearbeitet* (Helsinki: Suomalainen Tiedeakatemia, 1910); idem, *Finnische Märchentypen: Verzeichnis der bis 1908 gesammelten Aufzeichnungen* (Hamina: Suomalainen Tiedeakatemia, 1911). The English translation and revision by the American folklorist Stith Thompson appeared as *The Types of the Folktale: A Classification and Bibliography—Antti Aarne's Verzeichnis der Märchentypen, translated and enlarged by Stith Thompson* (Helsinki: Suomalainen Tiedeakatemia, 1961). This publication became known as the Aarne-Thompson Index and gained international canonicity. A pioneering, if far less systematic and international comparative collection of folk motifs was the lifelong project of Harvard rhetoric professor and American folklorist James Francis Child (1825–1896), which culminated in the collection *English and Scottish Popular Ballads*, 10 vols. (Boston: Houghton, 1882–98). Child had studied with Jacob Grimm in his youth, but the specificity of developments in US folklore research must not be overlooked in this overall history. Stith Thompson (1885–1976) had been a student of Child's successor, the folklorist George Lyman Kittredge (1860–1941), at Harvard.

114 Littmann possessed a copy of Aarne's *Verzeichnis*, as is evident from Höfner, *Library*; Jacob references Aarne in *Märchen und Traum*, 27, 51.

115   Friedrich von der Leyen, *Das Märchen in den Göttersagen der Edda* (Berlin: Georg Reimer, 1899), §§ 4, 5, 15.

116   Hermann Gunkel, *Das Märchen im Alten Testament* (Tübingen: Mohr, 1917).

117   Friedrich Hacker, *Systematische Traumbeobachtungen mit besonderer Berücksichtigung der Gedanken* (Leipzig: Engelmann, 1911); Havelock Ellis, *Die Welt der Träume*, ed. Hans Kurella (Würzburg: Kabitzsch, 1911; simultaneous English edition: *The World of Dreams* (London: Constable, 1911); John Mourly Vold, *Über den Traum: Experimental-psychologische Untersuchungen*, ed. Otto Klemm, 2 vols. (Leipzig: Barth, 1910–12).

118   Adelbert von Chamisso, *Peter Schlemihl's wundersame Geschichte* (Nürnberg: Schrag, 1814). It is worth mentioning that the story assumed wider cultural significance for the formulation of Jewish identity, see e.g. on Heine Regina Grundmann, *"Rabbi Faibisch, was auf Hochdeutsch heißt Apollo": Judentum, Dichtertum, Schlemihltum in Heinrich Heines Werk* (Stuttgart: Metzler, 2008).

119   Georg Brandes, *Die Hauptströmungen der Litteratur des neunzehnten Jahrhunderts 2: Die romantische Schule in Deutschland*, transl. Adolf Strodtmann [1873] (Charlottenburg: Barsdorf, 8th edn. 1900), ch. 10, 164–95.

120   Otto Rank, "Der Doppelgänger," *Imago* 3, no. 2 (1914): 102f.

121   In *MT* 76, n. 1 Jacob mentions an experiment with the cultivation of hemp seeds he had been gifted in Morocco, "but already the first harvest did not produce an effect any more." This also means, of course, that he had attempted consumption with greater success previously, even if his subsequent descriptions of the effect, as based on various passages in especially European nineteenth-century literatures, do not appear to indicate extensive phenomenological familiarity.

122   Hegel, *Ästhetik*, II, 127–41. See the lucid remarks on Hegel's *romantische Kunstform* and Freud by Odo Marquard, "Die Bedeutung der Theorie des Unbewußten für eine Theorie der nicht mehr schönen Kunst," in *Poetik und Hermeneutik III: Die nicht mehr schönen Künste. Grenzphänomene des Ästhetischen*, ed. Hans Robert Jauss (Munich: Fink, 1968), 375–92.

123   As Benjamin did e.g. in his doctoral dissertation *Der Begriff der Kunstkritik in der deutschen Romantik* [1920], Gesammelte Schriften I.1, ed. Rolf Tiedemann, Hermann Schweppenhäuser (Frankfurt a.M.: Suhrkamp, 1974).

124   See Walter Benjamin *Passagen*, convolute K, Gesammelte Schriften V.1, ed. Rolf Tiedemann (Frankfurt a.M.: Suhrkamp, 1982), 492.

125   Louis Althusser, "Idéologie et appareils idéologiques d'Etat" [1970], in *Sur la reproduction* (Paris: Presses Universitaires de France, 2011), 263–306, section: "Un exemple: l'idéologie religieuse chrétienne."

126   See Jacques Lacan, "Introduction to the Names-of-the-Father Seminar" [1963], text established by Jacques-Alain Miller, transl. Jeffrey Mehlman, *October* 40 (1987): 81–95. Freud's discussion of Robertson Smith is in *Totem und Tabu: Einige Übereinstimmungen im Seelenleben der Wilden und der Neurotiker* [1913], Gesammelte Werke 9 (Frankfurt a.M.: Fischer, 1999), here ch. 4.

127   Benjamin, *Passagen* V.1, 493, here quoted after idem, *The Arcades Project*, transl. Howard Eiland, Kevin McLaughlin (Cambridge, MA: Belknap Press, 1999), 391.

128   Benjamin, *Passagen*, V.2, 848f.

129   Theodor W. Adorno, "Besprechung von Roger Caillois, La mante religieuse," *Zeitschrift für Sozialforschung* 7 (1938): 410f.

130   Roger Caillois, *La mante religieuse: Recherche sur la nature et la signification du mythe* (Paris: Aux Amis des Livres, 1937); also in *Le mythe et l'homme* (Paris:

Gallimard, 1938). See Rosa Eidelpes, "Roger Caillois' Biology of Myth and the Myth of Biology," *Anthropology and Materialism* 2 (2014) [URL: http://am.revues.org/84]; and on the wider literary history of mantis, see Thomas Schestag, *Mantisrelikte: Maurice Blanchot, Jean-Henri Fabre, Paul Celan* (Basel: Urs Engeler, 1999).

131   Adorno to Benjamin September 22, 1937, Theodor W. Adorno, Walter Benjamin, *Briefwechsel 1928–1940*, ed. Henri Lonitz (Frankfurt a.M.: Suhrkamp, 1994), 277; see also Anson Rabinbach, *In the Shadow of Catastrophe: German Intellectuals between Apocalypse and Enlightenment* (Berkeley: University of California Press, 2001), ch. 5, n. 70.

132   Walter Benjamin, "Review of Roger Caillois, L'aridité et al." [1938], in idem, *Kritiken und Rezensionen*, ed. Hella Tiedemann Bartels, Gesammelte Schriften III (Frankfurt a.M.: Suhrkamp, 1972), 549–52.

133   Benjamin, *Passagen*, V.2, 850f. The overall fascination of the Parisian scene with (what Freud had regarded as the fetish of) the head, and of headlessness, also marked Caillois's association with Georges Batailles's revue *Acéphale* (1936–9).

134   Eidelpes, "Caillois' Biology," §14.

135   Heinz Dieter Kittsteiner, "Erwachen aus dem Traumschlaf: Walter Benjamins Historismus" [1984], in *Listen der Vernunft: Motive geschichtsphilosophischen Denkens* (Frankfurt a.M.: Fischer, 1998), 150–81.

136   Gershom Scholem, *From Berlin to Jerusalem: Memories of my Youth*, transl. Harry Zohn (New York: Schocken, 1980), 119, 138f. In Bayerische Staatsbibliothek München, Ana 335, Nachlass Fritz Hommel, there is a single letter by Scholem dated July 18, 1924, written for Hommel's 70th birthday and retirement, along with which Scholem also sent offprints of his works and in which he included a paragraph of self-justification for his emigration to Palestine, which perhaps demonstrates that at this point he had not severed all ties to the discipline of Semitist Orientalism in Germany.

137   See, for instance, Gabriel Weisberg, Yvonne Weisberg, *Japonisme: An Annotated Bibliography* (New York: Garland, 1990); Toshio Watanabe, *High Victorian Japonisme* (Berne: Lang, 1991); Vera Wolff, *Die Rache des Materials: Eine andere Geschichte des Japonismus* (Zürich, Berlin: Diaphanes, 2015).

138   As most amply evidenced by his illustrated work *Die ostasiatische Tuschmalerei* (Berlin: Cassirer, 1922).

139   See Brigitte Koyama-Richard, *Japon rêvé: Edmond de Goncourt et Hayashi Tadamasa* (Paris: Hermann, 2001). Hayashi was the second intellectually influential intermediary, after the Parisian art dealer Siegfried (or Samuel) Bing (1838–1905), who had been the prime instigator of artistic Japonism from the mid-1870s onward; see his *Japanischer Formenschatz*, 6 vols. (Leipzig: Seemann, 1888–91).

140   See the letters of Grosse to his student Otto Kümmel, who was mainly responsible for building a collection of Japanese Art in Berlin in the years after 1900, in Hartmut Walravens, ed., *"Und der Sumeru meines Dankes würde wachsen": Beiträge zur ostasiatischen Kunstgeschichte in Deutschland* (Wiesbaden: Harrassowitz, 2010). A letter to Kümmel from May 14, 1896, ibid., 14, mentions Grosse's "studies" with Bing, Hayashi, and the collector of Japonica Charles Gillot, which followed a lecture course he had given on the topic in Freiburg; these events mark the beginning of Grosse's Orientalist turn. Kümmel, whose influence in Germany was more sustained than Grosse's, remains notorious for his support of Nazism, his denunciation of colleagues, and his involvement in the looting of art from occupied Europe in the 1940s.

141 See above 123, 131.

142 Karl Löwith, "Japan's Westernization and Moral Foundation" [1942–3] in *Sämtliche Schriften* 2, ed. Klaus Stichweh, Marc B. de Launay (Stuttgart: Metzler, 1983), 541–55; idem, "The Japanese Mind: A Picture of the Mentality that We Must Understand if We Are to Conquer" [1943], ibid., 556–70; idem, "Bemerkungen zum Unterschied von Orient und Okzident" [1960], ibid., 571–601. (Henceforth referenced as LSS + page no.). Several other articles also indirectly address his Japanese experiences, for an introduction to this work see Wolfang Schwentker, "Karl Löwith und Japan," *Archiv für Kulturgeschichte* 76 (1994): 415–49.

143 Karl Löwith, *Mein Leben in Deutschland vor und nach 1933*, ed. F. R. Hausmann (Stuttgart: Metzler, 2007); idem, *Reisetagebuch 1936 und 1941: Von Rom nach Sendai, von Japan nach Amerika*, ed. Klaus Stichweh (Marbach: Deutsche Schillergesellschaft, 2001). See in particular also the perceptive afterword by Adolf Muschg, which very clearly works out the Orientalist discourse underpinning Löwith's observations during his journey to Japan.

144 I have discussed the systematic place of Orientalist themes in Löwith's philosophy of history and his critique of Heidegger in my "Löwith, Löwith's Heidegger, and the Unity of History," *History and Theory* 53, no. 1 (2014): 45–68.

145 Alexandre Kojève, *Introduction à la lecture de Hegel* [2nd edn. 1962] (Paris: Gallimard, 1997), 434–7. See on this also Jacob Taubes, "Ästhetisierung der Wahrheit im Posthistoire," in *Streitbare Philosophie: Margherita von Brentano zum 65. Geburtstag*, ed. Gabriele Althaus, Irmingard Staeuble (Berlin: Metropol, 1988), 41–51.

146 Roland Barthes, *L'empire des signes* (Geneva: Skira, 1970). See also the incisive analysis of Barthes's and Kristeva's writings on Maoist China in Lisa Lowe, *Critical Terrains: French and British Orientalisms* (Ithaca, NY: Cornell University Press, 1991), ch. 4.

147 As Porter, "Erich Auerbach," has shown for the case of Auerbach.

148 The text appeared in the collection *Unterwegs zur Sprache* (Pfullingen: Neske, 1959), 83–155, Heidegger Gesamtausgabe I, 12, ed. F. W. von Herrmann (Frankfurt a.M.: Klostermann, 1985) ; the English translation appeared in *On the Way to Language*, transl. Peter D. Hertz (New York: Harper & Roe, 1971), 1–56.

149 A German translation of Tezuka's own account of his visit with Heidegger, which details the extensively fictitious character of the dialogue, is contained in the indispensable contribution by Reinhard May, *Heideggers verborgene Quellen: Sein Werk unter chinesischem und japanischem Einfluss* [1989] (Wiesbaden: Harassowitz, 2nd edn. 2014); English translation by Graham Parkes, *Heidegger's Hidden Sources: East Asian Influences on his Work* (London: Routledge, 1996).

150 Heidegger, *On the Way to Language*, 45 (henceforth in-text as OWL + page no.).

151 See Peter Trawny, *Heidegger und der Mythos der jüdischen Weltverschwörung* (Frankfurt a.M.: Klostermann, 2014).

152 Martin Heidegger, "Die Frage nach der Technik [1955]," in *Die Technik und die Kehre* (Stuttgart: Cotta, 1962), 5–36.

153 Oscar Benl, *Seami Motokiyo und der Geist des Nô-Schauspiels*, Abhandlungen der Klasse der Literatur 1952, No. 5 (Mainz: Akademie, 1952).

154 May, *Heideggers verborgene Quellen*.

155 Benl, *Seami*, 89f.

156 See, in particular, Behdad, *Belated Travelers*, ch. 3.

157   See the account in Martin Heidegger, *Die Grundbegriffe der Metaphysik: Welt—
      Endlichkeit—Einsamkeit* [1930, 1975] (Frankfurt a.M.: Klostermann, 3rd edn.
      1983), §§ 19–38.

158   T. E. Lawrence, *Die sieben Säulen der Weisheit*, transl. Dagobert von Mikusch
      (Munich, Leipzig: List, 1936).

159   Martin Heidegger, *Überlegungen VII–XI (Schwarze Hefte 1938/39)*, ed. Peter
      Trawny (Frankfurt a.M.: Klostermann, 2014), XI, 97. The episode perhaps marks
      the importance of further work on Heidegger's Orientalist readings; his unfortunate
      habit of not disclosing his readings and the lack of critical commentary in the
      Gesamtausgabe, which remains proudly unphilological, combine to make this task
      difficult; for instance, as to my knowledge, the question of whether Heidegger was
      familiar with the work, or the collections, of his fellow Freiburg philosopher Ernst
      Grosse has not been discussed, yet would be of obvious interest to the matter of
      philosophical Japonism.

160   Günther Anders, *Der Mann auf der Brücke: Tagebuch aus Hiroshima und Nagasaki*
      [1959] (Berlin, W.: Union Verlag, 2nd edn. 1965).

161   See Ludger Lütkehaus, *Philosophieren nach Hiroshima: Über Günther Anders*
      (Frankfurt a.M.: Fischer, 1992); and Paul van Dijk, *Anthropology in the Age of
      Technology: The Philosophical Contribution of Günther Anders* (Amsterdam: Rodopi,
      2000).

162   See especially Günther Anders, "Über die Bombe und die Wurzeln unserer
      Apokalypse-Blindheit," in *Die Antiquiertheit des Menschen* [1956], 1 (Munich: Beck,
      2010), 233–324.

163   Echoing notions that are laid out more comprehensively in Anders, "Über die
      Bombe," §§19–21.

164   Anders, "Über die Bombe," §3.

165   E.g. Günther Anders, *Wir Eichmannsöhne: Offener Brief an Klaus Eichmann*
      (Munich: Beck, 1964); idem, *Besuch im Hades*, 2 vols. (Munich: Beck, 1979).

166   Lütkehaus, *Philosophieren*, ch. III, points out Anders's tendency toward
      performative self-contradiction precisely in this regard, where he seemed to have
      echoed Adorno's dictum regarding the impossibility of poetry "after Auschwitz,"
      but in his further oeuvre, and indeed in his overall occasion-bound approach to
      philosophizing, was actually on a different trajectory.

Conclusion

1   Aristotle, *Politica*, Works of Aristotle, ed. W. D. Ross, 10, transl. Benjamin Jowett
    (Oxford: Clarendon, 1921), Book I, Chapter 1, 1252b–53a.

2   Ibid.

3   Werner Hamacher, *Sprachgerechtigkeit* (Frankfurt a.M.: Fischer, 2018), 7–49.

4   Carl Schmitt, *Political Theology: Four Chapters on the Concept of Sovereignty*, transl.
    George Schwab (Cambridge, MA: Massachussetts Institute of Technology Press,
    1985), 36.

Bibliography

Unpublished Sources

Berlin, Berlin-Brandenburgische Akademie der Wissenschaften, Archiv
Nachlass Eduard Meyer.
Berlin, Geheimes Staatsarchiv Preußischer Kulturbesitz
VI. HA, Nachlass Carl Heinrich Becker.
Berlin, Staatsbibliothek zu Berlin, Preußischer Kulturbesitz, Handschriften
NL 245: Nachlass Enno Littmann.
NL 246: Teilnachlass Theodor Nöldeke.
Leiden, Universiteitsbibliotheek
Briefwisseling Michael Jan de Goeje, BPL 2389,
Nalatenschap Christiaan Snouck Hurgronje: BPL Or 8952.
München, Bayerische Staatsbibliothek, Handschriften
Nachlass Fritz Hommel: Ana 335.
Princeton NJ, Princeton University, Department of Art and Archaeology—Visual Resources,
Archaeological Archives
Howard C. Butler Archive—Syria.
Princeton, NJ, University Library
Class of 1895, Records, AC 130.
Princeton, NJ, Mudd Manuscript Library
David Magie Papers.
Tübingen, Universitätsbibliothek, Handschriften
NL Theodor Nöldeke, Md 782.
NL Theodor Nöldeke (working papers), Md 783.
Uppsala Universitetsbibliotek
Johannes Alexander Kolmodin Papers, Q15.
Collection Richard Sundström, Kat 479a, NC 1567/8.

Bibliography

Aarne, Antti. *Verzeichnis der Märchentypen, mit Hülfe von Fachgenossen ausgearbeitet.*
Helsinki: Suomalainen Tiedeakatemia, 1910.
Aarne, Antti. *Finnische Märchentypen: Verzeichnis der bis 1908 gesammelten*
Aufzeichnungen. Hamina: Suomalainen Tiedeakatemia, 1911.
Aarne, Antti; Thompson, Stith. *The Types of the Folktale: A Classification and*
Bibliography – Antti Aarne's Verzeichnis der Märchentypen, translated and enlarged by
Stith Thompson. Helsinki: Suomalainen Tiedeakatemia, 1961.
Aarsleff, Hans. *The Study of Language in England, 1780–1860.* Princeton, NJ: Princeton
University Press, 1967.

Abbadie, Arnauld d'. *Douze ans de séjour dans la Haute-Ethiopie* [1868], vol. 1, ed. Jeanne-Marie Allier. Città del Vaticano: Biblioteca Apostolica Vaticana, 1980.

Adelung, Johann Christoph. *Grammatisch-kritisches Wörterbuch der hochdeutschen Mundart*. Vienna: Bauer, 1811.

Adluri, Vishwa; Bagchee, Joydeep. *The Nay Science: A History of German Indology*. Oxford: Oxford University Press, 2014.

Adorno, Theodor W. "Besprechung von Roger Caillois, La mante religieuse." *Zeitschrift für Sozialforschung* 7 (1938): 410f.

Adorno, Theodor W.; Benjamin, Walter. *Briefwechsel 1928–1940*, ed. Henri Lonitz. Frankfurt a.M.: Suhrkamp, 1994.

Agamben, Giorgio. "In Playland: Reflections on History and Play." In *Infancy and History: The Destruction of Experience* [1978], transl. Liz Heron, 65–87. London: Verso, 1993.

Ahmed, Siraj. *Archaeology of Babel: The Colonial Foundation of the Humanities*. Stanford, CA: Stanford University Press, 2017.

Almond, Ian. *History of Islam in German Thought: From Leibniz to Nietzsche*. London: Routledge, 2010.

Alpers, Paul. *What is Pastoral?* Chicago: University of Chicago Press, 1996.

Alter, Stephen G. *Darwinism and the Linguistic Image: Language, Race, and Natural Theology in the Nineteenth Century*. Baltimore: Johns Hopkins University Press, 1999.

Alter, Stephen G. *William Dwight Whitney and the Science of Language*. Baltimore: Johns Hopkins University Press, 2005.

Althusser, Louis. "Idéologie et appareils idéologiques d'Etat" [1970]. In *Sur la reproduction*, 263–306. Paris: Presses Universitaires de France, 2011.

Anders, Günther. "Über die Bombe und die Wurzeln unserer Apokalypse-Blindheit." In *Die Antiquiertheit des Menschen* [1956], vol. 1, 233–324. Munich: Beck, 2010.

Anders, Günther. *Der Mann auf der Brücke: Tagebuch aus Hiroshima und Nagasaki* [1959]. Berlin (W): Union Verlag, 2nd edn. 1965.

Anders, Günther. *Wir Eichmannsöhne: Offener Brief an Klaus Eichmann*. Munich: Beck, 1964.

Anders, Günther. *Besuch im Hades*, 2 vols. Munich: Beck, 1979.

Anderson, Benedict. *Imagined Communities: Reflections on the Origin and Spread of Nationalism*. London: Verso, 2nd edn. 1991.

Ankersmit, Frank R. *Sublime Historical Experience*. Stanford, CA: Stanford University Press, 2005.

App, Urs. *The Birth of Orientalism*. Philadelphia: University of Pennsylvania Press, 2010.

Apter, Emily. *Against World Literature: On the Politics of Untranslatability*. London, New York: Verso, 2013.

Aragon, Louis, et al. *Essais de critique génétique*, afterword by Louis Hay. Paris: Flammarion, 1979.

Aravamudan, Srinivas. *Enlightenment Orientalism: Resisting the Rise of the Novel*. Chicago: University of Chicago Press, 2012.

Aristotle. *Politica*, transl. Benjamin Jowett. Works of Aristotle, ed. W. D. Ross, 10. Oxford: Clarendon, 1921.

Artaud, Antonin. *The Theater and its Double* [1938], transl. M. C. Richards. New York: Grove Press, 1958.

Asad, Talal. *Genealogies of Religion: Disciplines and Reasons of Power in Christianity and Islam*. Baltimore: Johns Hopkins University Press, 1993.

Assmann, Jan. *Moses the Egyptian: The Memory of Egypt in Western Monotheism*. Cambridge, MA: Harvard University Press, 1997.

Ast, Friedrich. *Grundlinien der Grammatik, Hermeneutik und Kritik*. Landshut: Jos. Thomann, 1808.

Auerbach, Erich. "Figura," *Archivium Romanicum* 22 (1938): 436–89.

Auerbach, Erich. *Mimesis: Dargestellte Wirklichkeit in der abendländischen Literatur*. Berne: Francke, 1946.

Auerbach, Erich. "Philologie der Weltliteratur." In *Weltliteratur: Festgabe für Fritz Strich zum 70. Geburtstag*, ed. Walter Muschg, Emil Staiger, 39–50. Berne: Francke, 1952. English transl. by Jane O. Newman, "The Philology of World Literature." In *Time, History, and Literature: Selected Essays of Erich Auerbach*, ed. James I. Porter, 253–66. Princeton, NJ: Princeton University Press, 2014.

Bachelard, Gaston. *La formation de l'esprit scientifique: Contribution à une psychanalyse de la connaissance objective*. Paris: Vrin, 1938.

Ballantyne, Tony. *Orientalism and Race: Aryanism in the British Empire*. Basingstoke: Palgrave, 2002.

Barner, Wilfried. *Produktive Rezeption: Lessing und die Tragödien Senecas*. Munich: Beck, 1973.

Barth, Jakob. *Nominalbildung in den semitischen Sprachen*. Leipzig: Hinrichs, 2nd edn. 1894.

Barthes, Roland. *L'empire des signes*. Geneva: Skira, 1970.

Batnitzky, Leora. *Idolatry and Representation: The Philosophy of Franz Rosenzweig Reconsidered*. Princeton, NJ: Princeton University Press, 2000.

Bauke-Ruegg, Jan. "Gott und Kontingenz bei Derrida: Hasensprünge und Igeleien, oder: Das Spiel der différance." In *Vernunft, Kontingenz und Gott: Konstellationen eines offenen Problems*, ed. Philipp Stoellger, Ingolf U. Dalferth, 355–82. Tübingen: Mohr, 2000.

Becker, Carl Heinrich. "Georg Jacob als Orientalist." In *Festschrift Georg Jacob zum 70. Geburtstag 26. Mai 1932 gewidmet von Freunden und Schülern*, ed. Theodor Menzel, 1–8. Leipzig: Harrassowitz, 1932.

Behdad, Ali. *Belated Travelers: Orientalism in the Age of Colonial Dissolution*. Durham, NC: Duke University Press, 1994.

Behr, Wolfgang. *Reimende Bronzeinschriften und die Entstehung der chinesischen Endreimdichtung*. Bochum: Projekt Verlag, 2008.

Benes, Tuska. *In Babel's Shadow: Language, Philology and the Nation in Nineteenth-Century Germany*. Detroit: Wayne State University Press, 2008.

Benfey, Theodor. *Geschichte der Sprachwissenschaft und orientalischen Philologie in Deutschland seit dem Anfange des 19. Jahrhunderts, mit einem Rückblick auf frühere Zeiten*. Munich: Cotta, 1869.

Benjamin, Walter. *Der Begriff der Kunstkritik in der deutschen Romantik* [1920]. Gesammelte Schriften I.1, ed. Rolf Tiedemann, Hermann Schweppenhäuser. Frankfurt a.M.: Suhrkamp, 1974.

Benjamin, Walter. *Ursprung des deutschen Trauerspiels* [1928], ed. Rolf Tiedemann. Frankfurt a.M.: Suhrkamp, 1978.

Benjamin, Walter. "Review of Roger Caillois, *L'aridité et al.*" [1938]. In idem, *Kritiken und Rezensionen*, ed. Hella Tiedemann Bartels, Gesammelte Schriften III, 549–52. Frankfurt a.M.: Suhrkamp, 1972.

Benjamin, Walter. *Passagen-Werk*. Gesammelte Schriften, V, 1–2, ed. Rolf Tiedemann. Frankfurt a.M.: Suhrkamp, 1982. English translation: *The Arcades Project*, transl. Howard Eiland, Kevin McLaughlin. Cambridge, MA: Belknap Press, 1999.

Benjamin, Walter. *Über den Begriff der Geschichte*, ed. Gérard Raulet. Berlin: Suhrkamp, 2010.

Benl, Oscar. *Seami Motokiyo und der Geist des Nô-Schauspiels*. Abhandlungen der Klasse der Literatur 1952, No. 5. Mainz: Akademie, 1952.

Benne, Christian. *Nietzsche und die historisch-kritische Philologie*. Berlin, New York: de Gruyter, 2005.

Benne, Christian. *Die Erfindung des Manuskripts: Zu Theorie und Geschichte literarischer Gegenständlichkeit*. Berlin: Suhrkamp, 2015.

Bent, James Theodore. *The Sacred City of the Ethiopians, Being a Record of Travel and Research in Abyssinia in 1893* [1893]. London: Longmans, 2nd edn. 1896.

Bernard, Etienne, et al. (eds.), *Recueil des inscriptions de l'Ethiopie des périodes pré-axoumite et axoumite*, 3 vols. Paris: Académie des Inscriptions et Belle-Lettres, 1991–2000.

Bernays, Michael, "Zur Lehre von den Citaten und Noten" [1892]. In *Schriften zur Kritik und Litteraturgeschichte*, IV, 255–347. Berlin: Behr, 1899.

Bernheim, Ernst. *Lehrbuch der historischen Methode* [1889]. Leipzig: Duncker & Humblot, 5th—6th edn. 1905.

Bhabha, Homi K. "Of Mimicry and Man." In *The Location of Culture*, 85–92. New York: Routledge, 1994.

Bhabha, Homi K. "The Other Question: Stereotype, Discrimination and the Discourse of Colonialism." In *The Location of Culture*, 66–84. New York: Routledge, 1994.

Bhabha, Homi K. ed. *Nation and Narration*. London: Routledge, 1990.

Biagioli, Mario. *Galileo, Courtier: The Practice of Science in the Culture of Absolutism*. Chicago: University of Chicago Press, 1994.

Biale, David. *Gershom Scholem: Kabbalah and Counter-History*. Cambridge, MA: Harvard University Press, 2nd edn. 1982.

Bienenstock, Myriam. *Cohen face à Rosenzweig: Débat sur la pensée allemande*. Paris: Vrin, 2009.

Bing, Siegfried. *Japanischer Formenschatz*. 6 vols. Leipzig: Seemann, 1888–91.

Birus, Hendrik. "'Ich bin, der ich bin': Über die Echos eines Namens." In Stéphane Moses, Albrecht Schöne, eds. *Juden in der deutschen Literatur*, 25–53. Frankfurt a.M.: Suhrkamp, 1986.

Blattner, Evamarie; Kimmich, Dorothee, eds. *Lotte Reiniger im Kontext der europäischen Medienavantgarde*. Tübingen: Stadtmuseum, 2011.

Bloch, Marc. *La société féodale*. 2 vols. Paris: Albin Michel, 1939–1940.

Blumenberg, Hans. *Schiffbruch mit Zuschauer: Paradigma einer Daseinsmetapher*. Frankfurt a.M.: Suhrkamp, 1979.

Blumenberg, Hans. *Die Lesbarkeit der Welt*. Frankfurt a.M.: Suhrkamp, 1981.

Bobzin, Hartmut. "Guillaume Postel (1510–1581) und die Geschichte der arabischen Nationalgrammatik." In Michael G. Carter, Kees Versteegh, eds. *Studies in the History of Arabic Grammar*, 2, 57–71. Amsterdam: Benjamins, 1990.

Bobzin, Hartmut. "Geschichte der arabischen Philologie in Europa bis zum Ausgang des achtzehnten Jahrhunderts." In *Grundriss der Arabischen Philologie, 3: Supplement*, ed. Wolfdietrich Fischer, 155–87. Wiesbaden: Reichert, 1992.

Boeckh, August. *Metrologische Untersuchungen über Gewichte, Münzfüße und Maße des Alterthums in ihrem Zusammenhange*. Berlin: Veit, 1838.

Boeckh, August. *Enzyklopädie und Methodologie der philologischen Wissenschaften*, ed. Ernst Bartuschek. Leipzig: Teubner, 1877.

Bohas, Georges, et al. *The Arabic Linguistic Tradition*. London: Routledge, 1990.

Bornet, Philippe; Gorshenina, Svetlana, eds. *Orientalismes des marges: Eclairages à partir de l'Inde et de la Russie*. Lausanne: Université de Lausanne, 2014 (Études de Lettres 296, no. 2–3).

Bosch, Lourens van den. *Friedrich Max Müller: A Life Devoted to the Humanities*. Leiden: Brill, 2002.

Boschwitz, Friedemann. *Julius Wellhausen: Motive und Maßstäbe seiner Geschichtsschreibung* [1938]. Darmstadt: Wissenschaftliche Buchgesellschaft, 1968.

Bowersock, Glen W. *The Throne of Adulis: Red Sea Wars on the Eve of Islam*. Oxford: Oxford University Press, 2013.

Boyle, Nicholas. "Geschichtsschreibung und Autobiographik bei Goethe (1810–1817)." *Goethe-Jahrbuch* 110 (1993): 163–7.

Brandes, Georg. *Die Hauptströmungen der Litteratur des neunzehnten Jahrhunderts 2: Die romantische Schule in Deutschland*, transl. Adolf Strodtmann [1873]. Charlottenburg: Barsdorf, 8th edn. 1900.

Bréal, Michel. *Semantics: Studies in the Science of Meaning* [1897], transl. Nina Cust. New York: Henry Holt, 1900.

Breckman, Warren. *Adventures of the Symbolic: Post-Marxism and Radical Democracy*. New York: Columbia University Press, 2013.

Brehm, Alfred. *Brehms Tierleben: Allgemeine Kunde des Tierreichs*, 4th edn, 13 vols. ed. Otto zur Strassen. Leipzig, Vienna: Bibliographisches Institut, 1911–18.

Breyer, Francis. "Die Inschriften 'Ēzānās." *In Kaiserlichem Auftrag: Die Deutsche Aksum-Expedition 1906 unter Enno Littmann*, 2, ed. Steffen Wenig et al., 339–52. Wiesbaden: Reichert, 2011.

Brockelmann, Carl. *Grundriss der vergleichenden semitischen Grammatik*. 2 vols. Berlin: Reuther & Reichard, 1908–13.

Brower, Reuben A. "Reading in Slow Motion [1959]. In idem, *In Defense of Reading*, ed. Richard Poirier, 3–21. New York: E. P. Dutton, 1962.

Bruce of Kinnaird, James. *Travels to Discover the Source of the Nile, in the Years 1768, 1769, 1770, 1771, 1772, and 1773*. 5 vols. London: Robinson, 1790.

Buber, Martin. *Ich und Du*. Leipzig: Insel, 1923.

Bührmann, Max. *Das farbige Schattenspiel: Besonderheit, Technik, Führung*. Bern: Haupt, 1955.

Bührmann, Max. *Studien über das chinesische Schattenspiel: Erfahrungen aus einer Reise nach China*. Lüdenscheid: Volkshochschule, 1963.

Bunsen, Ernest de. *The Chronology of the Bible Connected with Contemporaneous Events in the History of the Babylonians, Assyrians, and Egyptians*. London: Longmans & Green, 1874.

Burbridge, John William. *Real Process: How Logic and Chemistry Combine in Hegel's Philosophy of Nature*. Toronto: University of Toronto Press, 1996.

Burrow, J. W. *Evolution and Society: A Study in Victorian Social Theory*. Cambridge: Cambridge University Press, 1970.

Bursian, Conrad. *Geschichte der classischen Philologie in Deutschland von den Anfängen bis zur Gegenwart*. 2 vols. Munich: Oldenbourg, 1883.

Butler, Howard C. "Report of an American Archaeological Expedition to Syria, 1899–1900." *American Journal of Archaeology* 4, no. 4 (1900): 415–40.

Butler, Howard C.; Norris, Frederick A.; Stoever, Edward R. *Publications of the Princeton University Archaeological Expeditions to Syria in 1904–5 and 1909, Division I: Geography and Itinerary*. Leiden: Brill, 1930.

Butler, Judith. *Gender Trouble: Feminism and the Subversion of Identity*. New York: Routledge, 1990.

Caillois, Roger. *La mante religieuse: Recherche sur la nature et la signification du mythe*. Paris: Aux Amis des Livres, 1937; also in *Le mythe et l'homme*. Paris: Gallimard, 1938.

Calder, William M. III; Demandt, Alexander, eds. *Eduard Meyer: Leben und Leistung eines Universalhistorikers*. Leiden: Brill, 1990.

Bibliography

Carnap, Rudolf. "Überwindung der Metaphysik durch logische Analyse der Sprache" [1932]. In *Scheinprobleme in der Philosophie und andere metaphysikkritische Schriften*, ed. Thomas Mormann, 81–109. Hamburg: Meiner, 2004.

Carsten, Francis L. "Arthur Rosenberg: Ancient Historian into Leading Communist." *Journal of Contemporary History* 8, no. 1 (1973): 63–75.

Caspari, Carl Paul. *A Grammar of the Arabic Language. Translated from the German and edited with numerous additions and corrections by William Wright*. 2 vols. Cambridge: Cambridge University Press, 1859–62.

Caspari, Carl Paul. *Arabische Grammatik*, revised and ed. by August Müller. Halle: Buchhandlung des Waisenhauses, 1876.

Cassirer, Ernst. "Sprache und Mythos: Ein Beitrag zum Problem der Götternamen" [1923]. In *Wesen und Wirkung des Symbolbegriffs*, 71–167. Darmstadt: Wissenschaftliche Buchgesellschaft, 1956.

Cassirer, Ernst. *Philosophie der symbolischen Formen I: Die Sprache*. Berlin: Bruno Cassirer, 1923.

Catano, James V. *Language, History, Style: Leo Spitzer and the Critical Tradition*. London: Routledge, 1988.

Celli, Andrea. *Dante e l'Oriente: Le fonti islamiche nella storiografia novecentesca*. Rome: Carocci, 2013.

Certeau, Michel de; Julia, Dominique; Revel, Jacques. *Une politique de la langue: La Révolution française et les patois*. Paris: Gallimard, 1975.

Chakrabarty, Dipesh. *Provincializing Europe*. Princeton, NJ: Princeton University Press, 2nd edn. 2007.

Chamisso, Adelbert von. *Peter Schlemihl's wundersame Geschichte*. Nürnberg: Schrag, 1814.

Chen, Chuan. *Die chinesische schöne Literatur im deutschen Schrifttum*. Glückstadt, Hamburg: Augustin, 1933.

Chickering, Roger. *We Men Who Feel Most German: A Cultural Study of the Pan-German League, 1886–1914*. Boston: Allen & Unwin, 1984.

Child, James Francis. *English and Scottish Popular Ballads*. 10 vols. Boston: Houghton, 1882–98.

Clark, William. *Academic Charisma and the Origins of the Research University*. Chicago: University of Chicago Press, 2006.

Clifford, James. "On Ethnographic Authority." *Representations* 1, no. 2 (1983): 118–46.

Codrington, Robert Henry. *The Melanesians: Studies in their Anthropology and Folk-Lore*. Oxford: Clarendon, 1891.

Cohen, Hermann. "Einheit oder Einzigkeit Gottes?" In *Jüdische Schriften*, ed. Bruno Strauß, 1, 87–99. Berlin: Schwentker & Sohn, 1924.

Cohen, Hermann. "Julius Wellhausen: Ein Abschiedsgruß." *Neue Jüdische Monatshefte* 1918, no. 8, 25 January: 178–81; also in Hermann Cohen. *Jüdische Schriften* 2, ed. Bruno Strauß, 463–8. Berlin: Schwetschke, 1924.

Cohen, Hermann. *Religion der Vernunft aus den Quellen des Judentums* [1919], ed. Bruno Strauß. Frankfurt a.M.: J. Kauffmann, 1929.

Cohn, Bernard S. "The Command of Language and the Language of Command." In *Colonialism and Its Forms of Knowledge: The British in India*, 16–56. Princeton, NJ: Princeton University Press, 1996.

Colie, Rosalie L. *Paradoxia Epidemica: The Renaissance Tradition of Paradox*. Princeton, NJ: Princeton University Press, 1966.

Conrad, Sebastian. *Globalisierung und Nation im deutschen Kaiserreich*. Munich: Beck, 2nd edn. 2010.

Conrad, Sebastian; Osterhammel, Jürgen, eds. *Das Kaiserreich transnational: Deutschland in der Welt 1871–1914*, Göttingen: Vandenhoeck & Ruprecht, 2004.

Conti Rossini, Carlo. "Canti popolari tigrai." *Zeitschrift für Assyriologie und verwandte Gebiete* 17 (1903): 23–52 (pt. 1); 18 (1904–5): 320–86 (pt. 2); 19 (1905–6): 288–341 (pt. 3).

Craig, Edward Gordon. "The Actor and the Über-Marionette." *The Mask* 1, no. 2 (1908) 3–15.

Curtis, Michael. *Orientalism and Islam: European Thinkers on Oriental Despotism in the Middle East and India*. Cambridge: Cambridge University Press, 2009.

Darwin, John. *Unfinished Empire: The Global Expansion of Britain*. London: Allen Lane, 2012.

Daston, Lorraine; Galison, Peter. *Objectivity*. New York: Zone, 2007.

Daum, Andreas W. *Wissenschaftspopularisierung im 19. Jahrhundert: Bürgerliche Kultur, naturwissenschaftliche Bildung und die deutsche Öffentlichkeit 1848–1914*. Munich: Oldenbourg, 2nd edn. 2002.

David, Jérôme. *Spectres de Goethe: Les métamorphoses de la 'littérature mondiale.'* Paris: Les Prairies ordinaires, 2011.

David, Pascal. "Welt." In *Dictionary of Untranslatables: A Philosophical Lexicon*, ed. Barbara Cassin et al., 1217–24. Princeton, NJ: Princeton University Press, 2014.

Dayeh, Islam. "The Potential of World Philology." *Philological Encounters* 1 (2016): 396–418.

Décimo, Marc. *Sciences et Pataphysique, 2: Comment la linguistique vint à Paris— De Michel Bréal à Ferdinand de Saussure*. Dijon: Les presses du réel, 2014.

Delitzsch, Friedrich. *Wo lag das Paradies? Eine biblisch-assyriologische Studie mit zahlreichen assyriologischen Beiträgen zur biblischen Länder- und Völkerkunde*. Leipzig: J. C. Hinrichs, 1881.

De Lorenzi, James. *Guardians of the Tradition: Historians and Historical Writing in Ethiopia*. Rochester, NY: University of Rochester Press, 2015.

Derrida, Jacques. "La structure, le signe et le jeu dans le discours des sciences humaines." In *L'écriture et la différence*, 409–28. Paris: Seuil, 1967.

Derrida, Jacques. "Freud et la scène de l'écriture." In *L'écriture et la différence*, 293–340. Paris: Seuil, 1967.

Derrida, Jacques. *Mal d'Archive: Une impression freudienne*. Paris: Galilée, 1995.

Diels, Hermann. *Die Fragmente der Vorsokratiker*. Berlin: Weidmann, 1903; 5th edn. by Walther Kranz. Hildesheim: Weidmann, 1934.

Dijk, Paul van. *Anthropology in the Age of Technology: The Philosophical Contribution of Günther Anders*. Amsterdam: Rodopi, 2000.

Dillmann, August. *Über die Anfänge des Axumitischen Reiches*. Abhandlungen der Königlichen Akademie der Wissenschaften zu Berlin 1878, 177–238. Berlin: Akademie, 1879.

Dillmann, August. *Zur Geschichte des aksumitischen Reichs im vierten bis sechsten Jahrhundert*. Abhandlungen der Königlichen Akademie der Wissenschaften zu Berlin 1880, 1–51. Berlin: Akademie, 1881.

Dillmann, August. *Handbuch der alttestamentlichen Theologie*, ed. G. Kittel. Leipzig: Hirzel, 1895.

Dilthey, Wilhelm. *Einleitung in die Geisteswissenschaften*. Gesammelte Schriften 1, ed. Bernhard Groethuysen. Leipzig: Teubner, 1922.

Dilthey, Wilhelm. *Der Aufbau der geschichtlichen Welt in den Geisteswissenschaften*. Gesammelte Schriften 7, ed. Bernhard Groethuysen. Leipzig: Teubner, 1927.

Dostal, Walter. *Eduard Glaser—Forschungen im Yemen: Eine quellenkritische Untersuchung in ethnologischer Sicht.* Vienna: Akademie, 1990.

Dozy, Reinhart. *Histoire des Musulmans d'Espagne jusqu'à la conquête de l'Andalousie par les Almoravides (711–1110).* 4 vols. Leiden: Brill, 1861.

Du Bois, W. E. B. *The Souls of Black Folk: Essays and Sketches.* Chicago: McClurgh & Co., 1903.

Dussaud, René, ed. *Les relevés du Capitaine Rees dans le désert de Syrie.* Paris: Geuthner, 1929.

Dussaud, René; Macler, Frédéric. *Voyage archéologique au Ṣafâ et au Djebel ed-Drûz.* Paris: Leroux, 1901.

Dussaud, René; Macler, Frédéric. "Rapport d'une mission dans les régions désertiques de la Syrie moyenne." *Nouvelles Archives des Missions Scientifiques et Littéraires* 10 (1903): 412–744.

Dyck, Joachim. *Athen und Jerusalem: Bibel und Poesie in der Tradition ihrer Verknüpfung.* Munich: Beck, 1977.

Eckermann, Johann Peter. *Gespräche mit Goethe in den letzten Jahren seines Lebens.* Frankfurter Ausgabe II 39. Frankfurt a.M.: Deutscher Klassiker Verlag, 1999.

Eidelpes, Rosa. "Roger Caillois' Biology of Myth and the Myth of Biology." *Anthropology and Materialism* 2 (2014). [URL: http://am.revues.org/84].

Einhauser, Eveline. *Die Junggrammatiker: Ein Problem für die Sprachwissenschaftsgeschichtsschreibung.* Trier: Wissenschaftlicher Verlag Trier, 1989.

Eisler, Rudolf. *Kant-Lexikon.* Berlin: Mittler & Sohn, 1930.

Elias, Norbert. *Die höfische Gesellschaft: Untersuchungen zur Soziologie des Königtums und der höfischen Aristokratie.* Darmstadt: Luchterhand, 1969.

Elliesie, Hatem, et al. "Der Littmann-Nachlass im Archiv der Österreichischen Akademie der Wissenschaften." In *Tigre Studies in the Twenty-First Century*, ed. Rainer Voigt, 1–12. Cologne: Rüdiger Köppe, 2015.

Ellis, Havelock. *Die Welt der Träume*, ed. Hans Kurella. Würzburg: Kabitzsch, 1911; English edition: *The World of Dreams.* London: Constable, 1911.

Engelhardt, Dietrich von. *Hegel und die Chemie: Studien zur Philosophie und Wissenschaft der Natur um 1800.* Wiesbaden: Harrassowitz, 1976.

Ernst, Wolfgang. *Das Rumoren der Archive: Ordnung aus Unordnung.* Berlin: Merve, 2002.

Ernst, Wolfgang. *Im Namen von Geschichte: Sammeln–Speichern–(Er)Zählen. Infrastrukturelle Konfigurationen des deutschen Gedächtnisses.* Munich: Fink, 2003.

Errington, Joseph. *Linguistics in a Colonial World: A Story of Language, Meaning, and Power.* Malden, MA: Blackwell, 2008.

Eskildsen, Kasper R. "Leopold Ranke's Archival Turn: Location and Evidence in Modern Historiography." *Modern Intellectual History* 5 (2008): 425–53.

Euting, Julius. *Nabatäische Inschriften aus Arabien.* Berlin: Reimer, 1885.

Ewald, Heinrich. *Grammatica critica linguae arabicae.* 2 vols. Leipzig: Libraria Hahniana, 1831.

Ewald, Heinrich. *Ausführliches Lehrbuch der hebräischen Sprache des Alten Bundes.* Leipzig: Hahn'sche Verlagsbuchhandlung, 5th edn. 1844.

Fabian, Johannes. *Time and the Other: How Anthropology Makes Its Object.* New York: Columbia University Press, 1983.

Fanon, Frantz. *Les damnés de la terre.* Paris: Maspero, 1961.

Farge, Arlette. *Le goût des archives.* Paris: Seuil, 1997.

Farge, Arlette; Foucault, Michel. *Le désordre des familles: Lettres de cachet des archives de la Bastille au XVIIIe siècle.* Paris: Gallimard, 1982.

Felsch, Philipp. *Der lange Sommer der Theorie: Geschichte einer Revolte*. Munich: Beck, 2015.

Figueira, Dorothy M. *Translating the Orient: The Reception of Śākuntala in Nineteenth-Century Europe*. Albany: State University of New York Press, 1991.

Fischer, Ottokar. "Mimische Studien zu Heinrich von Kleist." *Euphorion* 16 (1909): 747–72.

Fleischer, Heinrich Leberecht. *Kleinere Schriften, gesammelt, durchgesehen und vermehrt*, vols. 1–2: *Beiträge zur arabischen Sprachkunde* [1863–1876]. Leipzig: Hirzel, 1885–88.

Flemming, Barbara; Schmidt, Jan. *The Diary of Karl Süssheim (1878–1947)*. Stuttgart: Steiner, 2002.

Földényi, László F. *Marionetten und Übermarionetten*. Berlin: Matthes & Seitz, 2011.

Foucault, Michel. "Le cycle des grenouilles" [1962]. In *Dits et écrits I*, 203–5. Paris: Gallimard, 1994.

Foucault, Michel. *The Order of Things: An Archaeology of the Human Sciences* [1966]. New York: Vintage, 1994.

Foucault, Michel. *L'Archéologie du Savoir*. Paris: Gallimard, 1969.

Foucault, Michel. "Nietzsche, la généalogie et l'histoire." In *Hommage à Jean Hippolyte*, ed. Suzanne Bachelard et al., 145–72. Paris: Presses Universitaires de France, 1971.

Frankenhauser, Nina; Krämer, Annette. "Das arabische Schattentheater und die ägyptischen Figuren der Sammlung Kahle." In *Die Welt des Schattentheaters: Von Asien bis Europa*, ed. Jasmin Ii Sabai Günther, Inés de Castro, 18–37. Munich: Hirmer, 2015.

Franzen, Christoph Johannes. "Einleitung." In idem, *Der Kaiser und sein Forscher: Der Briefwechsel zwischen Wilhelm II. Und Leo Frobenius (1924–1938)*, ed. Karl-Heinz Kohl, Marie-Luise Recker, 17–75. Stuttgart: Kohlhammer, 2012.

Franzen, Christoph Johannes; Kohl, Karl-Heinz; Recker, Marie-Luise, eds. *Der Kaiser und sein Forscher: Der Briefwechsel zwischen Wilhelm II. und Leo Frobenius (1924–1938)*. Stuttgart: Kohlhammer, 2012.

Frege, Gottlob. "Über Sinn und Bedeutung" [1892]. In *Funktion, Begriff, Bedeutung: Fünf logische Studien*, ed. Günther Patzig, 23–46. Göttingen: Vandenhoeck & Ruprecht, 2nd edn. 2008.

Frege, Gottlob. "Über Begriff und Gegenstand" [1892]. In *Funktion, Begriff, Bedeutung: Fünf logische Studien*, ed. Günther Patzig, 47–60. Göttingen: Vandenhoeck & Ruprecht, 2nd edn. 2008.

Frei, Hans W. *The Eclipse of Biblical Narrative: A Study in Eighteenth and Nineteenth Century Hermeneutics*. Princeton, NJ: Princeton University Press, 1974.

Freud, Sigmund. *Totem und Tabu: Einige Übereinstimmungen im Seelenleben der Wilden und der Neurotiker* [1913]. Gesammelte Werke 9, ed. Anna Freud. Frankfurt a.M.: Fischer, 1999.

Freud, Sigmund. *Der Mann Moses und die monotheistische Religion: Drei Abhandlungen*. Amsterdam: Allert de Lange, 1939.

Fried, Gregory. *Heidegger's Polemos: From Being to Politics*. New Haven, CT: Yale University Press, 2000.

Friedman, Michael. *A Parting of the Ways: Carnap, Cassirer, Heidegger*. Chicago: Open Court, 2000.

Frobenius, Leo. *Und Afrika sprach …, 3: Unter den unsträflichen Aethiopen*. Berlin: Vita Deutsches Verlagshaus, 1913.

Frobenius, Leo. *Erythräa: Länder und Zeiten des heiligen Königsmordes*. Berlin, Zurich: Atlantis, 1931.

Fück, Johann. *Die Geschichte der arabischen Studien in Europa bis in den Anfang des 20. Jahrhunderts*. Leipzig: Harrassowitz, 1955.

Fulda, Daniel. *Wissenschaft aus Kunst: Die Entstehung der modernen Geschichtsschreibung in Deutschland 1760–1860*. Berlin: de Gruyter, 1996.

Funkenstein, Amos. "History, Counterhistory, and Narrative." In *Perceptions of Jewish History*, 22–49. Berkeley: University of California Press, 1993.

Ganshof, François Louis. "Note sur les ports de Provence du VIIIe au Xe siècle." *Revue historique* 183 (1938): 28–37.

Germana, Nicholas A. *The Orient of Europe: The Mythical Image of India and Competing Images of German National Identity*. Newcastle: Cambridge Scholars Publishing, 2009.

Germana, Nicholas A. *The Anxiety of Autonomy and the Aesthetics of German Orientalism*. Rochester, NY: Camden House, 2017.

Geroulanos, Stefanos. *An Atheism that Is Not Humanist Emerges in French Thought*. Stanford, CA: Stanford University Press, 2010.

Geulen, Christian. "'The Final Frontier …' Heimat, Nation und Kolonie um 1900: Carl Peters." In *"Phantasiereiche:" Zur Kulturgeschichte des deutschen Kolonialismus*, ed. Birthe Kundrus, 35–55. Frankfurt a.M.: Campus, 2003.

Geulen, Christian. *Wahlverwandte: Rassendiskurs und Nationalismus im späten 19. Jahrhundert*. Hamburg: Hamburger Edition, 2004.

Giddens, Anthony. *The Consequences of Modernity*. Stanford, CA: Stanford University Press, 1990.

Glaser, Eduard. *Skizze der Geschichte und Geographie Arabiens von den ältesten Zeiten bis zum Propheten Muḥammad*, 2. Berlin: Weidmann, 1890.

Goeje, Michael Jan de, ed. *Annals of the Prophets and Kings: Annales quos scripsit Abu Djafar Mohammed Ibn Djarir At-Tabari*. Leiden: Brill, 1879–1901.

Goeje, Michael Jan de. *Bijdrage tot de Geschiedenis der Zigeuners*. Amsterdam: C. G. van der Post, 1875.

Goethe, Johann Wolfgang von. "Dichtarten. Naturformen der Dichtung. Nachtrag." In *Noten und Abhandlungen zu besserem Verständnis des West-östlichen Divan*. Goethes Werke, Weimarer Ausgabe 7, 117–21. Weimar: Böhlau, 1887.

Goldziher, Ignaz. *Der Mythos bei den Hebräern und seine geschichtliche Entwickelung*. Leipzig: F. Brockhaus, 1876.

Goldziher, Ignaz. *Tagebuch*, ed. Alexander Scheiber. Leiden: Brill, 1978.

Goody, Jack. *The Domestication of the Savage Mind*. Cambridge: Cambridge University Press, 1977.

Gordon, Peter E. *Rosenzweig and Heidegger: Between Judaism and German Philosophy*. Berkeley: University of California Press, 2003.

Gordon, Peter E. *Continental Divide: Heidegger, Cassirer, Davos*. Cambridge, MA: Harvard University Press, 2010.

Goris, Wouter. "Das historische Apriori bei Husserl und Foucault: Zur philosophischen Relevanz eines Leitbegriffs der historischen Epistemologie." *Quaestio* 12 (2012): 291–342.

Gossman, Lionel. *The Passion of Max von Oppenheim: Archaeology and Intrigue in the Middle East from Wilhelm II to Hitler*. Cambridge: Open Book Publishing, 2014.

Grafton, Anthony. *Defenders of the Text: The Traditions of Scholarship in an Age of Science*. Cambridge, MA: Harvard University Press, 1991.

Grafton, Anthony. *The Footnote: A Curious History*. London: Faber & Faber, 1997.

Greif, Mark. *The Age of the Crisis of Man: Thought and Fiction in America 1933–1973*. Princeton, NJ: Princeton University Press, 2015.

Grésillon, Almuth. *Eléments de critique génétique: Lire les manuscrits modernes*. Paris: Presses Universitaires de France, 1994.

Grimme, Hubert. *Mohammed*, 2: *Einleitung in den Koran. System der koranischen Theologie*. Münster: Aschendorff, 1895.

Grimme, Hubert. *Texte und Untersuchungen zur ṣafatenisch-arabischen Religion. Mit einer Einführung in die ṣafatenische Epigraphik*. Paderborn: Schöningh, 1929.

Grimme, Hubert. *Altsinaitische Forschungen: Epigraphisches und Historisches*. Paderborn: Schöningh, 1937.

Grosse, Ernst. *Die Anfänge der Kunst*. Freiburg i.Br.: Mohr, 1894; English transl. *The Beginnings of Art*. New York, London: Appleton, 1914.

Grosse, Ernst. "Kunst und Race." In *Kunstwissenschaftliche Studien*, 113–66. Tübingen: Mohr Siebeck, 1900.

Grosse, Ernst. *Die ostasiatische Tuschmalerei*. Berlin: Cassirer, 1922.

Grundmann, Regina. "*Rabbi Faibisch, was auf Hochdeutsch heißt Apollo:" Judentum, Dichtertum, Schlemihltum in Heinrich Heines Werk*. Stuttgart: Metzler, 2008.

Gumbrecht, Hans Ulrich. *Leo Spitzers Stil*. Tübingen: Narr, 2001.

Gumbrecht, Hans Ulrich. *Vom Leben und Sterben der großen Romanisten*. Munich: Hanser, 2002.

Gumbrecht, Hans Ulrich. *The Powers of Philology: Dynamics of Textual Scholarship*. Urbana, IL: University of Illinois Press, 2003.

Gunkel, Hermann. *Das Märchen im Alten Testament*. Tübingen: Mohr, 1917.

Gurd, Sean, ed. *Philology and Its Histories*. Columbus, OH: Ohio State University Press, 2010.

Güthenke, Constanze. "'Enthusiasm Dwells Only in Specialization': Classical Philology and Disciplinarity in Nineteenth-Century Germany." In *World Philology* ed. Sheldon Pollock, et al., 264–84. Cambridge, MA: Harvard University Press, 2015.

Haber, Peter. *Zwischen jüdischer Tradition und Wissenschaft: Der ungarische Orientalist Ignác Goldziher (1850–1921)*. Cologne: Böhlau, 2006.

Hackel, Christine. *Die Bedeutung August Boeckhs für den Geschichtstheoretiker Johann Gustav Droysen: Die Enzyklopädie-Vorlesungen im Vergleich*. Würzburg: Königshausen & Neumann, 2006.

Hacker, Friedrich. *Systematische Traumbeobachtungen mit besonderer Berücksichtigung der Gedanken*. Leipzig: Engelmann, 1911.

Hacking, Ian. *Historical Ontology*. Cambridge, MA: Harvard University Press, 2002.

Halévy, Joseph. *Essai sur les inscriptions du Safa*. Paris: Imprimerie Nationale, 1882.

Hamacher, Werner. *Minima Philologica*, transl. Catherine Diehl, Jason Groves. New York: Fordham University Press, 2015.

Hamacher, Werner. *Sprachgerechtigkeit*. Frankfurt a.M.: Fischer, 2018.

Hanisch, Ludmilla. *Die Nachfolger der Exegeten: Deutschsprachige Erforschung des Vorderen Orients in der ersten Hälfte des 20. Jahrhunderts*. Wiesbaden: Harrassowitz, 2003.

Harpham, Geoffrey Galt. "Roots, Races, and the Return to Philology." *Representations* 106 (2009), spring: 34–62.

Harris, Roy. "Introduction: Comparative Philology: A 'Science' in Search of Foundations." In *Foundations of Indo-European Comparative Philology, 1800–1850*, ed. Roy Harris, 1, 1–18. London: Routledge, 1999.

Hartog, François. *Anciens, Modernes, Sauvages*. Paris: Galaade, 2005.

Hegel, Georg Wilhelm Friedrich. *Phänomenologie des Geistes* [1805]. Gesammelte Werke 9 , ed. Wolfgang Bonsiepen and Reinhard Heede. Hamburg: Meiner, 1980.

Hegel, Georg Wilhelm Friedrich. *Enzyklopädie der philosophischen Wissenschaften.* Gesammelte Werke 20, ed.Wolfgang Bonsiepen and Hans-Christian Lucas. Hamburg: Meiner, 1992.

Hegel, Georg Wilhelm Friedrich. *Vorlesungen über die Aesthetik*, ed. E. Moldenhauer, K. M. Michel. Frankfurt a.M.: Suhrkamp, 1970.

Hegel, Georg Wilhelm Friedrich. *Vorlesungen über die Philosophie der Geschichte*, ed. E. Moldenhauer, K. M. Michel. Frankfurt a.M.: Suhrkamp, 1986.

Heidegger, Martin. *Die Grundbegriffe der Metaphysik: Welt–Endlichkeit–Einsamkeit* [1930, 1975]. Frankfurt a.M.: Klostermann, 3rd edn. 1983.

Heidegger, Martin. *Einführung in die Metaphysik* [1935]. Gesamtausgabe I.40. Frankfurt a.M.: Klostermann, 1983.

Heidegger, Martin. "Die Frage nach der Technik [1955]." In *Die Technik und die Kehre*, 5–36. Stuttgart: Cotta, 1962.

Heidegger, Martin. "Die onto-theo-logische Verfassung der Metaphysik." In *Identität und Differenz* [1957], Gesamtausgabe I.11, 51–79. Frankfurt a.M.: Klostermann, 2006.

Heidegger, Martin. "Aus einem Gespräch von der Sprache. Zwischen einem Japaner und einem Fragenden." In *Unterwegs zur Sprache*, 83–155. Pfullingen: Neske, 1959. (Heidegger Gesamtausgabe I, 12, ed. F. W. von Herrmann, Frankfurt a.M.: Klostermann, 1985). English translation by Peter D. Hertz, *On the Way to Language*, 1–56. New York: Harper & Roe, 1971.

Heidegger, Martin. *Überlegungen VII–XI (Schwarze Hefte 1938/39)*, ed. Peter Trawny. Frankfurt a.M.: Klostermann, 2014.

Helfer, Martha B. *The Retreat of Representation: The Concept of Darstellung in German Critical Discourse.* Albany, NY: State University of New York Press, 1996.

Hellmann, Hanna. *Heinrich von Kleist: Darstellung des Problems.* Heidelberg: Winter, 1911.

Herder, Johann Gottfried. *Vom Geist der Ebräischen Poesie: Eine Anleitung für die Liebhaber derselben, und der ältesten Geschichte des menschlichen Geistes* [1782–3]. Sämtliche Werke, ed. B. Suphan, 11–12 [1879]. Reprint Hildesheim: Olms, 1967.

Herling, Bradley. *The German Gita: Hermeneutics and Discipline in the Early German Reception of Indian Thought, 1778–1831.* London: Routledge, 2006.

Hermann, Gottfried. *Über Herrn Professor Böckhs Behandlung der griechischen Inschriften.* Leipzig: Gerhard Fleischer, 1826.

Herrmann, Hans-Christian von. *Das Archiv der Bühne: Eine Archäologie des Theaters und seiner Wissenschaft.* Munich: Fink, 2005.

Heschel, Susannah. *Abraham Geiger and the Jewish Jesus.* Chicago: University of Chicago Press, 1998.

Hetzron, Robert, ed. *The Semitic Languages.* London: Routledge, 1997.

Heussi, Karl. *Die Krisis des Historismus.* Tübingen: Mohr, 1932.

Hofmannsthal, Hugo von. "Ein Brief" [1902]. In *Sämtliche Werke 31: Erfundene Gespräche und Briefe*, ed. Ellen Ritter, 45–55. Frankfurt a.M.: Fischer, 1991.

Höfner, Maria, ed. *The Library of Enno Littmann.* Leiden: Brill, 1959.

Holquist, Michael. "Why We Should Remember Philology." *Profession* (2002): 72–9.

Hommel, Fritz. *Die aethiopische Übersetzung des Physiologus nach je einer Londoner, Pariser und Wiener Handschrift.* Leipzig: J. C. Hinrichs'sche Buchhandlung, 1877.

Hommel, Fritz. *Eduard Glasers historische Ergebnisse aus seinen südarabischen Inschriften.* Beilage, Allgemeine Zeitung, No. 291. Munich: Cotta, 1889.

Hommel, Fritz. *Süd-Arabische Chrestomathie.* Munich: Franz'sche Hofbuchhandlung, 1893.

Hommel, Fritz. *Die Altisraelitische Überlieferung in inschriftlicher Beleuchtung: Ein Einspruch gegen die Aufstellungen der modernen Pentateuchkritik.* Munich: G. Franz'sche Buchhandlung, 1897.

Hommel, Fritz. *Die südarabischen Altertümer (Eduard Glaser Sammlung) des Wiener Hofmuseums und ihr Herausgeber Professor David Heinrich Müller: Offene Darlegung an die kaiserlich österreichische Akademie der Wissenschaften.* Munich: Hermann Lukaschik, 1899 (also in idem. *Aufsätze und Abhandlungen arabistisch-semitologischen Inhalts*, 2, 129–65. Munich: Hermann Lukaschick, 1900).

Hommel, Fritz. "Vier neue arabische Landschaftsnamen im Alten Testament nebst einem Nachtrag über die vier Paradiesflüsse in altbabylonischer und altarabischer Überlieferung." In *Aufsätze und Abhandlungen arabistisch-semitologischen Inhalts*, III.1, 273–343. Munich: G. Franz, 1901.

Hopwood, Derek. "From the Shadow Plays of Ibn Daniyal to the Poetry of Philip Larkin: Mustafa Badawi as Editor and Translator." In *Studying Arabic Literature: Mustafa Badawi, Scholar and Critic*, ed. Roger Allen, Robin Ostle, 55–66. Edinburgh: Edinburgh University Press, 2015.

Howell, Mortimer Sloper. *A Grammar of the Classical Arabic Language, Translated and Compiled from the Works of the Most Approved Native or Naturalized Authorities.* 7 vols. Allahabad: North-Western Provinces Government Press, 1880–1911.

Hübener, Wolfgang. "Die verlorene Unschuld der Theokratie." In *Religionstheorie und politische Theologie, 3: Theokratie*, ed. Jacob Taubes, 29–64. Munich: Fink, 1987.

Hübinger, Gangolf. *Kulturprotestantismus und Politik: Zum Verhältnis von Liberalismus und Protestantismus im wilhelminischen Deutschland.* Tübingen: Mohr, 1994.

Hugill, Andrew. *Pataphysics: A Useless Guide.* Cambridge, MA: MIT Press, 2012.

Hui, Andrew. "The Many Returns of Philology: A State of the Field Report." *Journal of the History of Ideas* 78, no. 1 (2017): 137–56.

Huhn, Ingeborg. *Johann Gottfried Wetzstein: Orientalist und preußischer Konsul im osmanischen Syrien (1849–1861).* Berlin: Klaus Schwarz Verlag, 2016.

Huistra, Pieter; Paul, Herman; Tollebeek, Johan, eds. "Historians in the Archive: Changing Historiographical Practices in the Nineteenth Century." Theme issue. *History of the Human Sciences* 26, no. 4 (2013).

Huizinga, Johan. *De Vidushaka in het indisch toneel* [1897]. Verzamelde Werken 1. Haarlem: Tjeenk Willink, 1948.

Huizinga, Johan. *Homo Ludens: Proeve eener bepaling van het spel-element der cultuur* [1938]. Verzamelde Werken 5. Haarlem: Tjeenk Willink, 1950.

Humboldt, Wilhelm von. *Über die Verschiedenheit des menschlichen Sprachbaues und ihren Einfluß auf die geistige Entwicklung des Menschengeschlechts* [1836], ed. Donatella di Cesare. Paderborn: Schöningh, 1998.

Ibn Daniyal, Muhammad. *Three Shadow Plays*, ed. Paul Kahle. Cambridge: Gibb Memorial Trust, 1992.

Imbrie, Andrew C.; Thacher, John Hamilton, eds. *The Class of 1895 Princeton University: 25th Year Record.* Princeton, NJ: Princeton University Press, 1920.

Irwin, Robert. *For Lust of Knowing: The Orientalists and Their Enemies.* London: Allen Lane, 2005.

Jacob, Georg. *Altarabisches Beduinenleben. Nach den Quellen geschildert.* Berlin: Mayer & Müller, 2nd edn. 1897. Reprint Hildesheim: Olms, 2004.

Jacob, Georg. *Türkische Litteraturgeschichte in Einzeldarstellungen, 1: Das türkische Schattentheater.* Berlin: Mayer & Müller, 1900.

Jacob, Georg. *Östliche Kulturelemente im Abendland.* Berlin: Mayer & Müller, 1902.

Jacob, Georg. "Das Weinhaus nebst Zubehör nach den Γazelen des Hāfiz: Ein Beitrag zu
    einer Darstellung des altpersischen Lebens." In *Orientalische Studien: Theodor Nöldeke
    zum siebzigsten Geburtstag*, ed. Carl Bezold, 2, 1055–76. Gießen: Töpelmann, 1906.

Jacob, Georg. *Geschichte des Schattentheaters*. Berlin: Mayer & Müller, 1907.

Jacob, Georg. *Beiträge zur Erkenntnis des Derwisch-Ordens der Bektaschis*. Berlin: Mayer &
    Müller, 1908.

Jacob, Georg. *Schanfarà-Studien, 1: Der Wortschatz der Lâmîja nebst Übersetzung und
    beigefügtem Text*. Sitzungsberichte, Philosophisch-philologische und historische
    Klasse, 1914, no. 8. Munich: Bayerische Akademie der Wissenschaften, 1914.

Jacob, Georg. *Schanfarà-Studien 2: Parallelen und Kommentar zur Lâmîja, Schanfarà-
    Bibliographie*. Sitzungsberichte, Philosophisch-philologische und historische Klasse,
    1915, no. 4. Munich: Bayerische Akademie der Wissenschaften, 1915.

Jacob, Georg. *Schanfaras Lamijat-al-'Arab, auf Grund neuer Studien neu übertragen*. Kiel:
    Mühlau, 1915.

Jacob, Georg. "Hamâm." *Der Islam* 5 (1915): 247f.

Jacob, Georg. "Tauben und Flughühner." *Der Islam* 6 (1916): 99f.

Jacob, Georg. *Märchen und Traum mit besonderer Berücksichtigung des Orients*. Hannover:
    Lafaire, 1923.

Jacob, Georg. *Der Einfluß des Morgenlands auf das Abendland vorzüglich während des
    Mittelalters*. Hannover: Lafaire, 1924.

Jacob, Georg. *Die Geschichte des Schattentheaters im Morgen- und Abendland*. Hannover:
    Lafaire, 2nd edn. 1925.

Jacob, Georg. *Reimstudien*, Typescript, Kiel: The Author, 1934 (version 9 March).

Jacob, Georg. *Shakespeare-Studien*, ed. Hans Jensen. Glückstadt: Augustin, 1938.

Jacob, Georg; Jensen, Hans. *Das chinesische Schattentheater*. Stuttgart: Kohlhammer, 1933.

Jäger, Michael. *Fausts Kolonie: Goethes kritische Phänomenologie der Moderne*. Würzburg:
    Königshausen & Neumann, 2004.

Jankowsky, Kurt R. *The Neogrammarians: A Re-Evaluation of their Place in the History of
    Linguistic Science*. The Hague: Mouton, 1972.

Jay, Martin. *Downcast Eyes: The Denigration of Vision in Twentieth-Century French
    Thought*. Berkeley: University of California Press, 1993.

Jelavich, Peter. *Munich and Theatrical Modernism: Politics, Playwriting, and Performance
    1890–1914*. Cambridge, MA: Harvard University Press, 1985.

Johanning, Klaus. *Der Bibel-Babel-Streit: Eine forschungsgeschichtliche Studie*. Frankfurt
    a.M.: Peter Lang, 1988.

Jordheim, Helge. "Philology of the Future, Futures of Philology: Interdisciplinarity,
    Intertemporality, and *Begriffsgeschichte*." In *Disciplines and Interdisciplinarity in Foreign
    Language Study*, ed. Hans Lauge Hansen, 35–50. Copenhagen: Museum Tusculanum, 2004.

Joseph, John E. *Saussure*. Oxford: Oxford University Press, 2012.

Kaegi, Werner. "Voltaire und der Zerfall des christlichen Geschichtsbildes." In *Historische
    Meditationen*, 221–48. Zurich: Fretz & Wasmuth, 1942.

Kahle, Paul E. *Zur Geschichte des arabischen Schattenspieles in Ägypten*. Halle: Universität,
    1909.

Kahle, Paul E. "Islamische Schattenspielfiguren aus Egypten, 1. Teil." *Der Islam* 1 (1910):
    264–99.

Kahle, Paul E. "Islamische Schattenspielfiguren aus Egypten, 2. Teil." *Der Islam* 2 (1911):
    143–95.

Kahle, Paul E. ed. *Der Leuchtturm von Alexandria: Ein ägyptisches Schattenspiel aus dem
    mittelalterlichen Ägypten, mit Beiträgen von Georg Jacob*. Stuttgart: Kohlhammer, 1930.

Kandinsky[, Wassily]; Marc, Franz, eds. *Der Blaue Reiter*, 2nd edn. Munich: Piper, 1914.

Kant, Immanuel. *Kritik der reinen Vernunft* [B 1787]. Akademie-Ausgabe 3. Berlin: Reimer, 1904.

Kant, Immanuel. *Der Streit der Fakultäten* [1798]. Akademie-Ausgabe 7, 1–115. Berlin: Reimer, 1907.

Kautzsch, Emil. *Die Heilige Schrift des Alten Testaments*. Tübingen: Mohr, 1894.

Kempshall, Matthew. *Rhetoric and the Writing of History, 400–1500*. Manchester: Manchester University Press, 2011.

Keßler, Mario. *Arthur Rosenberg: Ein Historiker im Zeitalter der Katastrophen*. Cologne: Böhlau, 2003.

Killean, Carolyn G. "The Development of Western Grammars of Arabic." *Journal of Near Eastern Studies* 43, no. 3 (1984): 223–30.

Kirsch, Mechthild. "Wolfgang Liepe." In *Internationales Germanistenlexikon 1800–1950*, ed. Christoph König, 2, 1094. Berlin, New York: de Gruyter, 2003.

Kittler, Friedrich A. *Aufschreibesysteme 1800/1900*. Munich: Fink, 1985.

Kittsteiner, Heinz Dieter. "Erwachen aus dem Traumschlaf: Walter Benjamins Historismus" [1984]. In *Listen der Vernunft: Motive geschichtsphilosophischen Denkens*, 150–81. Frankfurt a.M.: Fischer, 1998.

Kittsteiner, Heinz Dieter. "Kants Theorie des Geschichtszeichens: Vorläufer und Nachfahren." In *Geschichtszeichen*, ed. idem, 81–115. Cologne: Böhlau, 1999.

Klaniczay, Gábor; Werner, Michael; Gecser, Otto, eds. *Multiple Antiquities—Multiple Modernities: Ancient Histories in Nineteenth-Century European Cultures*. Frankfurt a.M.: Campus, 2011.

Klautke, Egbert. *The Mind of the Nation: Völkerpsychologie in Germany, 1851–1955*. New York: Berghahn, 2013.

Kleist, Heinrich von. "Über das Marionettentheater" [1810]. In *Sämtliche Werke und Briefe*, 3, 555–63. Frankfurt a.M.: Deutscher Klassiker Verlag, 1990.

Klemm, Kurt. "Inder bis zur Gegenwart: Litteraturgeschichte." *Jahresberichte der Geschichtswissenschaft* 21 (1898), I.

Kobishchanov, Yuri M. *Axum* [1966]. University Park: Pennsylvania State University Press, 1979.

Kojève, Alexandre. *Introduction à la lecture de Hegel* [2nd edn. 1962]. Paris: Gallimard, 1997.

Koningsveld, Peter Sjoerd van. *Snouck Hurgronje en de Islam: Acht artiekelen over leven en werk van een oriëntalist uit het koloniale tijdperk*. Leiden: Rijksuniversiteit, 1988.

Konuk, Kader. *East West Mimesis: Erich Auerbach in Turkey*. Stanford, CA: Stanford University Press, 2010.

Koppe, Rainer, ed. "Das Reisetagebuch von Theodor von Lüpke." *In Kaiserlichem Auftrag: Die Deutsche Aksum-Expedition 1906 unter Enno Littmann*, 1, ed. Steffen Wenig et al., 201–38. Aichwald: Linden Soft, 2006.

Koselleck, Reinhart. "Einleitung." In *Geschichtliche Grundbegriffe: Historisches Lexikon zur politisch-sozialen Sprache in Deutschland*, ed. idem, Werner Conze and Otto Brunner, 1, XIII–XXVII. Stuttgart: Klett Cotta, 1972.

Koselleck, Reinhart. *Futures Past: On the Semantics of Historical Times* [1979], transl. Keith Tribe. New York: Columbia University Press, 2004.

Koselleck, Reinhart, et al. "Geschichte." In *Geschichtliche Grundbegriffe*, 2, 593–717. Stuttgart: Klett Cotta, 1979.

Košut, Jaromír. *Fünf Streitfragen der Basrenser und Kûfenser über die Abwandlung des Nomen aus Ibn el-Anbârî's Kitāb al Inṣāf fī masā'il al-ḫilāf baina an naḥwīwyīn al-Baṣrīyīn wa-'l-Kūfiyīn, nach der Leydener Handschrift*. Vienna: Gerold, 1878.

Koyama-Richard, Brigitte. *Japon rêvé: Edmond de Goncourt et Hayashi Tadamasa*. Paris: Hermann, 2001.

Kracauer, Siegfried. *Theory of Film: The Redemption of Physical Reality*. Oxford: Oxford University Press, 1960.

Krajewski, Markus; Maye, Harun, eds. *Die Hyäne: Lesarten eines politischen Tiers*. Zurich: Diaphanes, 2010.

Krämer, Annette. "Das osmanisch-türkische Schattentheater 'Karagöz' und die Sammlung Tuğtekin des Linden-Museums." In *Die Welt des Schattentheaters: Von Asien bis Europa*, ed. Jasmin Ii Sabai Günther, Inés de Castro, 124–45. Munich: Hirmer, 2015.

Krause, Karl Ernst Wilhelm. "Wilhelm Schröder." In *Allgemeine Deutsche Biographie* 32 (1891): 533–4.

Kripke, Saul A. *Naming and Necessity*. Oxford: Blackwell, 1980.

Kuhn, Thomas S. *The Structure of Scientific Revolutions*. Chicago: The University of Chicago Press, 1962.

Lacan, Jacques. "Introduction to the Names-of-the-Father Seminar" [1963], text established by Jacques-Alain Miller, transl. Jeffrey Mehlman. *October* 40 (1987): 81–95.

Lacoue-Labarthe, Philippe. *Musica ficta: Figures de Wagner*. Paris: Bourgois, 1991.

Lacoue-Labarthe, Philippe. *Poétique de l'histoire*. Paris: Galilée, 2002.

Lacoue-Labarthe, Philippe; Nancy, Jean-Luc. *Scène*. Paris: Bourgois, 2013.

Lamb, Jonathan. *The Rhetoric of Suffering: Reading the Book of Job in the Eighteenth Century*. Oxford: Oxford University Press, 1995.

Lamb, Jonathan. *Preserving the Self in the South Seas, 1680–1840*. Chicago: University of Chicago Press, 2001.

Lange, Barbara, et al., eds. *Animationen: Lotte Reiniger im Kontext der Mediengeschichte*. Tübingen: Kunsthistorisches Institut, 2012.

Langlois, Charles-Victor; Seignobos, Charles. *Introduction aux études historiques* [1898], ed. M. Rébérioux. Paris: Editions Kimé, 1992.

Laqueur, Thomas W. "Bodies, Details, and the Humanitarian Narrative." In *The New Cultural History*, ed. Lynn Hunt, 176–204. Berkeley: University of California Press, 1989.

Laqueur, Thomas W. "Mourning, Pity, and the Work of Narrative in the Making of 'Humanity.'" In *Humanitarianism and Suffering: The Mobilization of Empathy*, ed. Richard Ashby Wilson, Richard D. Brown, 31–57. Cambridge: Cambridge University Press, 2009.

Latour, Bruno. "Drawing Things Together." In *Representation in Scientific Practice*, ed. Michael Lynch, Steve Woolgar, 19–69. Cambridge, MA: Massachussetts Institute of Technology Press, 1990.

Lawrence, T. E. *Die sieben Säulen der Weisheit*, transl. Dagobert von Mikusch. Munich, Leipzig: List, 1936.

Le Goff, Jacques. "Documento/Monumento." In *Storia e memoria*, 443–56. Turin: Einaudi, 1982.

Lehmann, Reinhard G. *Friedrich Delitzsch und der Babel-Bibel-Streit*. Fribourg: Universitätsverlag, and Göttingen: Vandenhoeck & Ruprecht, 1994.

Leibniz, Gottfried Wilhelm. *Monadologie* [1714], ed. Hartmut Hecht. Stuttgart: Reclam, 1998.

Lenoir, Timothy. *The Strategy of Life: Teleology and Mechanics in Nineteenth-Century German Biology*. Dordrecht: Reidel, 1982.

Lerer, Seth. *Literary History and the Challenge of Philology: The Legacy of Erich Auerbach*. Stanford, CA: Stanford University Press, 1988.

Lessing, Gotthold Ephraim. *Laokoon. Briefe antiquarischen Inhalts*, ed. Wilfried Barner. Frankfurt a.M.: Deutscher Klassikerverlag, 2007.

Lévi-Strauss, Claude. *Introduction to the Work of Marcel Mauss* [1950], transl. Felicity Baker. London: Routledge & Kegan Paul, 1987.

Lévi-Strauss, Claude. *La pensée sauvage*. Paris: Plon, 1962.

Leyen, Friedrich von der. *Das Märchen in den Göttersagen der Edda*. Berlin: Georg Reimer, 1899.

Li Guo. *The Performing Arts in Medieval Islam: Shadow Play and Popular Poetry in Ibn Daniyal's Mamluk Cairo*. Leiden: Brill, 2012.

Liebeschütz, Hans. "Hermann Cohen and his Historical Background." *Leo Baeck Institute Year Book* 13 (1968): 3–33.

Littmann, Enno. "Das Verbum der Tigresprache." *Zeitschrift für Assyriologie und verwandte Gebiete* 13 (1898): 133–78 and 14 (1899): 1–102.

Littmann, Enno. *Zur Entzifferung der Safa-Inschriften*. Leipzig: Harrassowitz, 1901.

Littmann, Enno. *Arabische Schattenspiele. Mit Anhängen von Georg Jacob*. Berlin: Mayer & Müller, 1901.

Littmann, Enno. *Publications of an American Archaeological Expedition to Syria 1899–1900, Part IV: Semitic Inscriptions*. New York: Century Co., 1904.

Littmann, Enno. "Preliminary Report of the Princeton Expedition to Abyssinia." *Zeitschrift für Assyriologie und verwandte Gebiete* 20 (1907): 151–82.

Littmann, Enno. "Bemerkungen über den Islam in Nordabessinien." *Der Islam* 1 (1910): 68–71.

Littmann, Enno. "Tigré-Erzählungen." *Zeitschrift der Deutschen Morgenländischen Gesellschaft* 65 (1911): 697–708.

Littmann, Enno. *Publications of the Princeton Expedition to Abyssinia*. 4 vols. (in 5 tomes). Leiden: Brill, 1910–15.

Littmann, Enno. *Deutsche Aksum Expedition, 4, Sabäische griechische und altabessinische Inschriften*. Berlin: Georg Reimer, 1913.

Littmann, Enno. "Ein nordabessinisches Heldenlied." *Zeitschrift für Assyriologie und verwandte Gebiete* 27 (1913): 112–20.

Littmann, Enno. "Friedrich Veit." *Der Islam* 4 (1913): 300f.

Littmann, Enno. *Publications of the Princeton University Archaeological Expeditions to Syria in 1904–5 and 1909, Division IV, Semitic Inscriptions, Section A: Nabataean Inscriptions*. Leiden: Brill, 1914.

Littmann, Enno. "Erinnerungen an Naffa' wad 'Etmân." In *Ein Jahrhundert* Orientalistik: Lebensbilder aus der Feder von Enno Littmann, ed. Rudi Paret, Anton Schall, 14–25. Wiesbaden: Harrassowitz, 1955. [Originally: *Der Neue Orient* 2 (1918): 587–91].

Littmann, Enno. *Das Malerspiel: Ein Schattenspiel aus Aleppo nach einer armenisch-türkischen Handschrift*. Heidelberg: Carl Winters Universitätsbuchhandlung, 1918.

Littmann, Enno. *Zigeuner-Arabisch: Wortschatz und Grammatik der arabischen Bestandteile in den morgenländischen Zigeunersprachen, nebst einer Einleitung über das arabische Rotwälsch und die Namen der morgenländischen Zigeuner*. Bonn: Schroeder, 1920.

Littmann, Enno. *Die Erzählungen aus den tausendundein Nächten: Zum ersten Mal nach dem arabischen Urtext der Calcuttaer Ausgabe vom Jahre 1839*. 6 vols. Leipzig: Insel, 1921–8.

Littmann, Enno. "Abendland und Morgenland." In *Reden bei der Rektoratsübergabe am 30. April 1930 im Festsaal der Universität Tübingen*, 13–29. Tübingen: Universität, 1930.

Littmann, Enno. "Abessinische und semitische Poesie." *Zeitschrift der Deutschen Morgenländischen Gesellschaft* 84 (1930): 207–25.

Littmann, Enno. *Abessinien*. Hamburg: Hanseatische Verlagsanstalt, 1935.

Littmann, Enno. "Georg Jacob" [1937]. In *Ein Jahrhundert Orientalistik: Lebensbilder aus der Feder von Enno Littmann*, ed. Rudi Paret, Anton Schall, 96–109. Wiesbaden: Harrassowitz, 1955.

Littmann, Enno. *Thamūd und Ṣafā: Studien zur altnordarabischen Inschriftenkunde*. Leipzig: Brockhaus, 1940.

Littmann, Enno. *Publications of the Princeton University Archaeological Expeditions to Syria in 1904–5 and 1909, Division IV, Semitic Inscriptions, Section C: Safaitic*. Leiden: Brill, 1943.

Littmann, Enno. *Ein Jahrhundert Orientalistik: Lebensbilder aus der Feder von Enno Littmann*, ed. Rudi Paret, Anton Schall. Wiesbaden: Harrassowitz, 1955.

Littmann, Enno. "Leben und Arbeit," ed. H. H. Biesterfeldt. *Oriens* 29/30 (1986): 1–101.

Lopez, Robert S. "Mohammed and Charlemagne: A Revision." *Speculum* 18 (1943): 14–38.

Loriga, Sabina. *Le petit x: De la biographie à l'histoire*. Paris: Seuil, 2010.

Lowe, Lisa. *Critical Terrains: French and British Orientalisms*. Ithaca, NY: Cornell University Press, 1991.

Löwith, Karl. "Japan's Westernization and Moral Foundation" [1942–3]. In *Sämtliche Schriften* 2, ed. Klaus Stichweh, Marc B. de Launay, 541–55. Stuttgart: Metzler, 1983.

Löwith, Karl. "The Japanese Mind: A Picture of the Mentality that We Must Understand if We Are to Conquer" [1943]. *Sämtliche Schriften*, 2, 556–70, Stuttgart: Metzler, 1983.

Löwith, Karl. *Meaning in History: The Theological Implications of the Philosophy of History*. Chicago: University of Chicago Press, 1949.

Löwith, Karl. "Martin Heidegger und Franz Rosenzweig: Ein Nachtrag zu Sein und Zeit" [1958]. In *Sämtliche Schriften*, 8, ed. Klaus Stichweh, 72–100. Stuttgart: Metzler, 1984.

Löwith, Karl. "Bemerkungen zum Unterschied von Orient und Okzident" [1960]. In *Sämtliche Schriften*, 2, 571–601. Stuttgart: Metzler, 1983.

Löwith, Karl. *Reisetagebuch 1936 und 1941: Von Rom nach Sendai, von Japan nach Amerika*, ed. Klaus Stichweh. Marbach: Deutsche Schillergesellschaft, 2001.

Löwith, Karl. *Mein Leben in Deutschland vor und nach 1933*, ed. Frank Rutger Hausmann. Stuttgart: Metzler, 2007.

Lucian. "Wie man Geschichte schreiben müsse." In *Lucians von Samosata Sämmtliche Werke*, transl. Christoph Martin Wieland [1789], 4, 73–142. Vienna: Haas, 1798.

Lucian. "Wie man Geschichte schreiben soll." In *Lucian's Werke*, transl. Friedrich August Pauly, 6, 635–84. Stuttgart, Metzler, 1827.

Ludolf, Hiob. *Historia Aethiopica, sive brevis et succincta descriptio regnis Habessinorum*. Frankfurt a.M.: Joh. Dav. Zunner, 1681.

Lüdtke, Alf; Jobs, Sebastian, eds. *Unsettling History: Archiving and Narrating in Historiography*. Frankfurt a.M.: Campus, 2010.

Lumsden, Matthew. *A Grammar of the Arabic Language According to the Principles Taught and Maintained in the Schools of Arabia*. Calcutta: F. Dissent, 1813.

Lüpke, Hans von. "Die Zeit in Aksum—Innenansichten." *In Kaiserlichem Auftrag: Die Deutsche Aksum-Expedition 1906 unter Enno Littmann*, 2, ed. Steffen Wenig et al., 151–68 Wiesbaden: Reichert, 2011.

Luschan, Felix von. "Das türkische Schattenspiel." *Internationales Archiv für Ethnographie* 2 (1889): 1–9, 81–90, 125–44.

Lütkehaus, Ludger. *Philosophieren nach Hiroshima: Über Günther Anders*. Frankfurt a.M.: Fischer, 1992.

Magnus, Kathleen Dow. *Hegel and the Symbolic Mediation of Spirit*. Albany, NY: State University of New York Press, 2001.

Maier, Bernhard. *William Robertson Smith: His Life, his Work and his Times*. Tübingen: Mohr Siebeck, 2009.

Maier, Bernhard. *Semitic Studies in Victorian Britain: A Portrait of William Wright and his World through his Letters*. Würzburg: Ergon, 2011.

Maier, Bernhard. *Gründerzeit der Orientalisten: Theodor Nöldekes Leben und Werk im Spiegel seiner Briefe*. Würzburg: Ergon, 2013.

Makdisi, Ussama. *The Culture of Sectarianism: Community, History, and Violence in Nineteenth Century Ottoman Lebanon*. Berkeley: University of California Press, 2000.

Mallette, Karla. *European Modernity and the Arab Mediterranean: Toward a New Philology and a Counter-Orientalism*. Philadelphia: University of Pennsylvania Press, 2010.

Man, Paul de. *Blindness and Insight: Essays in the Rhetoric of Contemporary Criticism*. New York: Oxford University Press, 1971.

Man, Paul de. *Allegories of Reading: Figural Language in Rousseau, Nietzsche, Rilke, and Proust*. New Haven, CT: Yale University Press, 1982.

Man, Paul de. "The Return to Philology" [1982]. In *The Resistance to Theory*, 21–6. Minneapolis: University of Minnesota Press, 1986.

Man, Paul de. *Aesthetic Ideology*, ed. Andrzej Warminski. Minneapolis: University of Minnesota Press, 1996.

Man, Paul de. "Kant and Schiller." In *Aesthetic Ideology*, ed. Andrzej Warminski, 129–62. Minneapolis: University of Minnesota Press, 1996.

Man, Paul de. "The Concept of Irony." In *Aesthetic Ideology*, ed. Andrzej Warminski, 163–84. Minneapolis: University of Minnesota Press, 1996.

Mangold, Sabine. *Eine "weltbürgerliche Wissenschaft:" Die deutsche Orientalistik im 19. Jahrhundert*. Stuttgart: Steiner, 2004.

Marchand, Suzanne. "The Rhetoric of Artifacts and the Decline of Classical Humanism: The Case of Josef Strzygowski." *History and Theory* 33, no. 4 (1994): 106–30.

Marchand, Suzanne. *Down from Olympus: Archaeology and Philhellenism in Germany 1750–1970*. Princeton, NJ: Princeton University Press, 1996.

Marchand, Suzanne. "Leo Frobenius and the Revolt against the West." *Journal of Contemporary History* 32, no. 2 (1997): 153–70.

Marchand, Suzanne. *German Orientalism in the Age of Empire: Religion, Race, and Scholarship*. Cambridge: Cambridge University Press, 2009.

Marquard, Odo. "Die Bedeutung der Theorie des Unbewußten für eine Theorie der nicht mehr schönen Kunst." In *Poetik und Hermeneutik III: Die nicht mehr schönen Künste. Grenzphänomene des Ästhetischen*, ed. Hans Robert Jauss, 375–92. Munich: Fink, 1968.

May, Reinhard. *Heideggers verborgene Quellen: Sein Werk unter chinesischem und japanischem Einfluss* [1989]. Wiesbaden: Harrassowitz, 2nd edn. 2014. English translation by Graham Parkes, *Heidegger's Hidden Sources: East Asian Influences on his Work*. London: Routledge, 1996.

McGetchin, Douglas T. *Indology, Indomania, Orientalism: Ancient India's Rebirth in Modern Germany*. Madison, WI: Fairleigh Dickinson University Press, 2009.

McGetchin, Douglas T. et al., eds. *Sanskrit and "Orientalism": Indology and Comparative Linguistics in Germany, 1750–1958*. Delhi: Manohar, 2004.

Medrow, Lisa. *Moderne Tradition und religiöse Wissenschaft: Islam, Wissenschaft und Moderne bei I. Goldziher, C. Snouck Hurgronje und C. H. Becker*. Paderborn: Schöningh, 2018.

Meinecke, Friedrich. *Die Entstehung des Historismus*. 2 vols. Munich, Berlin: Oldenbourg, 1936.

Meloni, Gerardo. *Saggi di filologia semitica. A cura degli amici, con dieci tavole in autografia*. Rome: Casa Editrice Italiana, 1913.

Menzel, Theodor. *Meddah, Schattentheater und Orta ojunu: Eine kritische Übersicht der jüngeren Forschung nebst neuen Beiträgen*, ed. Ottokar Menzel. Prague: Orientalisches Institut, 1941.

Messling, Markus. *Pariser Orientlektüren: Zu Wilhelm von Humboldts Theorie der Schrift*. Paderborn: Schöningh, 2008.

Messling, Markus. *Champollions Hieroglyphen: Philologie und Weltaneignung*. Berlin: Kadmos, 2012.

Messling, Markus, Ottmar Ette, eds. *Wort Macht Stamm: Rassismus und Determinismus in der Philologie*. Munich: Fink, 2013.

Meyer, Eduard. *Geschichte des Alterthums*. 5 vols. Stuttgart, Berlin: Cotta, 1884–1902.

Miller, Arthur I. *Einstein, Picasso: Space, Time, and the Beauty that Causes Havoc*. New York: Basic Books, 2001.

Miller, Peter N. *Peiresc's Orient: Antiquarianism as Cultural History in the Seventeenth Century*. Farnham: Ashgate, 2012.

Miller, Peter N. *Peiresc's Mediterranean World*. Cambridge, MA: Harvard University Press, 2015.

Milwright, Marcus. "On the Date of Paul Kahle's Egyptian Shadow Puppets." *Muqarnas: An Annual of the Visual Culture of the Islamic World* 28 (2011): 43–68.

Mitchell, Linda C. *Grammar Wars: Language as Cultural Battlefield in 17th and 18th Century England*. Aldershot: Ashgate, 2001.

Mitchell, Timothy. *Colonising Egypt*. Cambridge: Cambridge University Press, 1988.

Mitchell, W. J. T., ed. *Landscape and Power*. Chicago: University of Chicago Press, 2nd edn. 2002.

Momigliano, Arnaldo. "Ancient History and the Antiquarian" [1950]. In *Studies in Historiography*, 1–39. London: Weidenfeld and Nicholson, 1966.

Momigliano, Arnaldo. "Introduction to a Discussion of Eduard Meyer." In *A. D. Momigliano: Studies on Modern Scholarship*, ed. G. W. Bowersock, T. J. Cornell, 209–22. Berkeley: University of California Press, 1994.

Mommsen, Theodor. "Über Plan und Ausführung eines Corpus Inscriptionum Latinarum" [1847]. In *Tagebuch der französisch-italienischen Reise 1844/1845*, ed. G. and B. Walser, 223–52. Berne: Lang, 1976.

Moore, Lara Jennifer. *Restoring Order: The Ecole des Chartes and the Organization of Archives and Libraries in France, 1821–1870*. Duluth, MN: Litwin Books, 2008.

Moretti, Franco. *Distant Reading*. London: Verso, 2013.

Most, Glenn W. "Die Vorsokratiker in der Forschung der Zwanziger Jahre." In *Altertumswissenschaft in den 20er Jahren: Neue Fragen und Impulse*, ed. Hellmut Flashar, Sabine Vogt, 87–114. Stuttgart: Steiner, 1995.

Müller, David Heinrich. *Epigraphische Denkmäler aus Abessinien*. Denkschriften der Kaiserlichen Akademie der Wissenschaften zu Wien, Philosophisch-historische Klasse, vol. 43, no. 3. Vienna: F. Tempsky, 1894.

Müller, Ernst; Schmieder, Falko. *Begriffsgeschichte und historische Semantik: Ein kritisches Kompendium*. Frankfurt a.M.: Suhrkamp, 2016.

Müller, F. Max. "On the Philosophy of Mythology: A Lecture Delivered at the Royal Institution in 1871." In *The Essential Max Müller on Language, Mythology and Religion*, ed. Jon R. Stone, 145–66. New York: Palgrave, 2002.

Müller, F. Max. *Lectures on the Origin and Growth of Religions as Illustrated by the Religions of India*. London: Longmans, Green, 1878.

Müller, F. Max. "Kenju Kasawara." In *Biographical Essays*, 211–27. London: Longmans, Green & Co. 1884.

Muller, Jerry Z. "A Zionist Critique of Jewish Politics: The Early Thought of Leo Strauss." In *Against the Grain: Jewish Intellectuals in Hard Times*, ed. Ezra Mendelssohn, Stefani Hoffman, Richard I. Cohen, 17–31. New York: Berghahn, 2014.

Müller, Philipp, "Archives and History: Towards a History of 'the Use of State Archives' in the Nineteenth Century." *History of the Human Sciences* 26, no. 4 (2013): 27–49.

Munro-Hay, Stuart. *Aksum: An African Civilization of Late Antiquity*. Edinburgh: Edinburgh University Press, 1991.

Munzinger, Werner. *Ostafrikanische Studien*. Schaffhausen: Fr. Hurtersche Buchhandlung, 1864.

Muth, Franz-Christoph. *Die Annalen von aṭ-Ṭabarī im Spiegel der europäischen Bearbeitungen*. Frankfurt a.M.: Lang, 1983.

Myers, David N. "Hermann Cohen and the Quest for Protestant Judaism." *Leo Baeck International Yearbook* 46 (2001): 195–214.

Myers, David N. *Resisting History: Historicism and its Discontents in German-Jewish Thought*. Princeton, NJ: Princeton University Press, 2003.

Nestle, Eberhard. *Die israelitischen Eigennamen nach ihrer religionsgeschichtlichen Bedeutung*. Haarlem: De Erven F. Boon, 1876.

Neufert, Sven. *Theater als Tempel: Völkische Ursprungssuche in Drama, Theater und Festkultur 1890–1930*. Würzburg: Königshausen & Neumann, 2018.

Neuwirth, Angelika. *Koranforschung—Eine politische Philologie? Bibel, Koran und Islamentstehung im Spiegel spätantiker Textpolitik und moderner Philologie*. Berlin: de Gruyter, 2014.

Nicholls, Angus. "A Germanic Reception in England: Friedrich Max Müller's Critique of Darwin's 'Descent of Man.'" In *The Literary and Cultural Reception of Charles Darwin in Europe*, ed. Thomas F. Glick, Elinor Shaffer, 78–100. London: Bloomsbury, 2014.

Nicholls, Angus. "Against Darwin: Teleology in German Philosophical Anthropology." In *Historical Teleologies in the Modern World*, ed. Henning Trüper, Dipesh Chakrabarty, Sanjay Subrahmanyam, 89–113. London: Bloomsbury, 2015.

Nietzsche, Friedrich. *Geburt der Tragödie* [1872]. Kritische Studienausgabe (KSA) 1. Berlin: de Gruyter, 2nd edn. 1988.

Nietzsche, Friedrich. *Morgenröthe* [1887]. KSA 3. Berlin: de Gruyter, 2nd edn. 1988.

Nietzsche, Friedrich. *Zur Genealogie der Moral: Eine Streitschrift* [1887]. KSA 5. Berlin: de Gruyter, 2nd edn. 1988.

Nietzsche, Friedrich. *Wir Philologen* [1875]. Nachgelassene Fragmente 1875–79, KSA 8. Berlin: de Gruyter, 2nd edn. 1988.

Nietzsche, Friedrich. *Briefwechsel mit E. Rohde*, ed. E. Förster-Nietzsche, F. Schöll. Leipzig: Insel, 2nd edn. 1903.

Nippel, Wilfried. "Philologenstreit und Schulpolitik: Zur Kontroverse zwischen Gottfried Hermann und August Böckh." In *Geschichtsdiskurs 3: Die Epoche der Historisierung*, ed. Wolfgang Kuttler et al., 244–53. Frankfurt a.M.: Fischer, 1997.

Nöldeke, Theodor. *Geschichte des Qorâns*. Göttingen: Dieterichsche Buchhandlung, 1860; 2nd revised edition by Friedrich Schwally, 3 vols. Leipzig: Dieterich, 1909–38.

Nöldeke, Theodor. "Die Ungeschichtlichkeit der Erzählung Gen. XIV." In *Untersuchungen zur Kritik des Alten Testaments*, 156–72. Kiel: Schwers'sche Buchhandlung, 1869.

Nöldeke, Theodor. *Geschichte der Perser und Araber zur Zeit der Sasaniden. Aus der arabischen Chronik des Tabari übersetzt und mit ausführlichen Erläuterungen und Ergänzungen versehn.* Leiden: Brill, 1879.

Nöldeke, Theodor. "Altaramäische Inschriften aus Teimâ (Arabien)." *Sitzungsberichte der Königlich-Preußischen Akademie der Wissenschaften* 35 (1884): 813–20.

Nöldeke, Theodor. "Der Chalif Mansûr." In *Orientalische Skizzen*, 111–52. Berlin: Paetel, 1892.

Nöldeke, Theodor. "Review D. H. Müller, Epigraphische Denkmäler aus Abessinien." *Zeitschrift der Deutschen Morgenländischen Gesellschaft* 48 (1894): 367–79.

Nöldeke, Theodor. *Zur Grammatik des classichen Arabisch* [1897]. *Im Anhang: die handschriftlichen Ergänzungen in dem Handexemplar Theodor Nöldekes, bearbeitet und mit Zusätzen versehen von Anton Spitaler.* Darmstadt: Wissenschaftliche Buchgesellschaft, 1963.

Nöldeke, Theodor. "Tiernamen mit Reduplikation." In *Beiträge zur semitischen Sprachwissenschaft*, 107–23. Strasbourg: Trübner, 1904.

Nöldeke, Theodor. "Tigre-Lieder" *Zeitschrift für Assyriologie und verwandte Gebiete* 31 (1917–18): 1–25.

Nongbri, Brent. *Before Religion: A History of a Modern Concept*. New Haven, CT: Yale University Press, 2013.

Nonn, Christoph. *Eine Stadt sucht einen Mörder: Gerücht, Gewalt und Antisemitismus im deutschen Kaiserreich*. Göttingen: Vandenhoeck & Ruprecht, 2002.

Novick, Peter. *That Noble Dream: The "Objectivity Question" and the American Historical Profession*. Cambridge: Cambridge University Press, 1988.

Oexle, Otto Gerhard. *Geschichtswissenschaft im Zeichen des Historismus: Studien zur Problemgeschichte der Moderne*. Göttingen: Vandenhoeck & Ruprecht, 1996.

Olender, Maurice. *The Languages of Paradise: Race, Religion, and Philology in the Nineteenth Century* [1989]. Cambridge, MA: Harvard University Press, 2nd edn. 2008.

Olender, Maurice. *Race and Erudition*. Cambridge, MA: Harvard University Press, 2009.

Osborne, Henry Fairfield. "Howard Crosby Butler." In *Dictionary of American Biography*, 3, 361. New York: Scribner's Sons, 1929.

Osterhammel, Jürgen. *Die Entzauberung Asiens: Europa und die asiatischen Reiche im 18. Jahrhundert*. Munich: Beck, 1998.

Otterspeer, Willem. *Orde en Trouw: Over Johan Huizinga*. Amsterdam: De Bezige Bij, 2006; English translation *Reading Huizinga*. Amsterdam: Amsterdam University Press, 2010.

Otterspeer, Willem, ed. *Leiden Oriental Connections 1850–1940*. Leiden: Brill, 1989.

Özdalga, Elisabeth, ed. *The Last Dragoman: The Swedish Orientalist Johannes Kolmodin as Scholar, Activist and Diplomat*. Istanbul: Swedish Institute, 2006.

Panofsky, Erwin. "Et in Arcadia Ego: Poussin and the Elegiac Tradition." In *Philosophy and History: Essays Presented to Ernst Cassirer*, ed. R. Klibansky, H. J. Paton, 223–54. Oxford: Clarendon Press, 1936.

Patzelt, Erna. *Die fränkische Kultur und der Islam, mit besonderer Berücksichtigung der nordischen Entwicklung: Eine universalhistorische Studie*. Baden: Rohrer, 1932.

Paul, Herman. "What Is a Scholarly Persona? Ten Theses on Virtues, Skills, and Desires." *History and Theory* 53 (2014): 348–71.

Peirce, Charles Sanders. "What is a Sign?" [1894]. In *The Essential Peirce: Selected Philosophical Writings*, 2, 4–10. Bloomington: Indiana University Press, 1998.

Perlitt, Lothar. *Vatke und Wellhausen: Geschichtsphilosophische Voraussetzungen und historiographische Motive für die Darstellung der Religion und Geschichte Israels durch Wilhelm Vatke und Julius Wellhausen*. Berlin: Töpelmann, 1965.

Perras, Arne. *Carl Peters and German Imperialism 1856–1918: A Political Biography*. Oxford: Oxford University Press, 2004.

Petrucci, Armando. *Public Lettering: Script, Power, and Culture* [1980], transl. Linda Lappin. Chicago: University of Chicago Press, 1993.

Pirenne, Henri. *Mahomet et Charlemagne*. Paris: Alcan, 1937.

Pischel, Richard. *The Home of the Puppet-Play: An Address on Assuming the Office of Rector of the Königliche Vereinigte Friedrichs-Universität, Halle-Wittenberg, on the 12th July 1900*, transl. Mildred C. Tawney. London: Luzac & Co., 1902.

Poiss, Thomas. "Zur Idee der Philologie: Der Streit zwischen Gottfried Hermann und August Boeckh." In *Gottfried Hermann (1772–1848): Internationales Symposium in Leipzig, 11.-13. Oktober 2007*, ed. Kurt Sier, Eva Wockener-Gade, 143–63. Tübingen: Narr, 2010.

Polaschegg, Andrea. *Der andere Orientalismus: Regeln deutsch-morgenländischer Imagination im 19. Jahrhundert*. Berlin, New York: de Gruyter, 2004.

Pollock, Sheldon. *Language of the Gods in the World of Men: Sanskrit, Culture, and Power in Pre-Modern India*. Berkeley: University of California Press, 2006.

Pollock, Sheldon. "Future Philology? The Fate of a Soft Science in a Hard World." *Critical Inquiry* 35, no. 4 (2009): 931–61.

Pollock, Sheldon. "Philology and Freedom." *Philological Encounters* 1 (2016): 4–30.

Pollock, Sheldon, Benjamin A. Elman, Ku-ming Kevin Chang, eds. *World Philology*. Cambridge, MA: Harvard University Press, 2015.

Popkin, Richard H. *The High Road to Pyrrhonism*. Indianapolis: Hackett, 2nd edn. 1993.

Porter, James I. *Nietzsche and the Philology of the Future*. Stanford, CA: Stanford University Press, 2000.

Porter, James I. "Erich Auerbach and the Judaizing of Philology." *Critical Inquiry* 35, no. 1 (2008): 115–47.

Porter, James I. "'Don't Quote Me on That!': Wilamowitz Contra Nietzsche in 1872 and 1873." *Journal of Nietzsche Studies* 42 (2011): 73–99.

Posner, Ernst. *Archives in the Ancient World*. Cambridge, MA: Harvard University Press, 1972.

Pott, August Friedrich. *Die Zigeuner in Europa und Asien: Ethnographisch-linguistische Untersuchung, vornehmlich ihrer Herkunft und Sprache, nach gedruckten und ungedruckten Quellen*. Halle a.d.S.: Ed. Heynemann, 1844.

Praetorius, Franz. "Bemerkungen über die Ṣafa-Inschriften." *Zeitschrift der Deutschen Morgenländischen Gesellschaft* 36, no. 3–4 (1882): 661–3.

Pratt, Mary Louise. *Imperial Eyes: Travel Writing and Transculturation*. New York: Routledge, 2nd edn. 2008.

Pritchard, William H. "Teaching: Reuben A. Brower." *The American Scholar* 54, no. 2 (1985): 239–47.

Prüfer, Curt. *Ein ägyptisches Schattenspiel*. Erlangen: E. Th. Jacob, 1906.

Prüfer, Curt. "Das Schiffsspiel: Ein Schattenspiel aus Cairo." *Münchener Beiträge zur Kenntnis des Orients* 2, no. 2 (1906): 154–69.

Rabault-Feuerhahn, Pascale. *L'archive des origines: Sanskrit, philologie, anthropologie dans l'Allemagne du XIXe siècle*. Paris: Editions du Cerf, 2008.

Rabault-Feuerhahn, Pascale. "Orientalistenkongresse: Mündliche Formen der philologischen Zusammenarbeit—Funktionen, Probleme und historische

Entwicklung." In *Symphilologie: Formen der Kooperation in den Geisteswissenschaften*, ed. Stefanie Stockhorst et al., 101–21. Göttingen: Vandenhoeck & Ruprecht, 2016.

Rabault-Feuerhahn, Pascale; Trautmann-Waller, Céline, eds. *Itinéraires orientalistes entre France et Allemagne*. Theme issue. *Revue germanique internationale* 7 (2008).

Rabinbach, Anson. *In the Shadow of Catastrophe: German Intellectuals between Apocalypse and Enlightenment*. Berkeley: University of California Press, 2001.

Rank, Otto. "Der Doppelgänger." *Imago* 3, no. 2 (1914): 97–164. Republished: *Der Doppelgänger: Eine psycho-analytische Studie*. Vienna: Internationaler Psychoanalytischer Verlag, 1925.

Ratzel, Friedrich. *Anthropo-Geographie, oder Anwendung der Grundzüge der Erdkunde auf die Geschichte*. Stuttgart: Engelhorn, 1882.

Raz, Ronen. *The Transparent Mirror: Arab Intellectuals and Orientalism, 1798–1950*. PhD Dissertation. Princeton University, 1997.

Rebenich, Stefan. "Vom Nutzen und Nachteil der Großwissenschaft. Altertumswissenschaftliche Unternehmungen an der Berliner Akademie und Universität im 19. Jahrhundert." In *Die modernen Väter der Antike: Die Entwicklung der Altertumswissenschaften an Akademie und Universität im Berlin des 19. Jahrhunderts*, ed. Annette Baertschi, Colin G. King, 397–422. Berlin: de Gruyter, 2009.

Reckendorf, Hermann. *Die syntaktischen Verhältnisse des Arabischen*. Leiden: Brill, 1898.

Reckendorf, Hermann. *Arabische Syntax*. Heidelberg: Winter 1921.

Reill, Peter Hanns. *Vitalizing Nature in the Enlightenment*. Berkeley: University of California Press, 2005.

Reinach, Salomon. "Michel Bréal." *Revue archéologique* 1916 (5e série, tôme III), no. 1: 139–50.

Reiniger, Lotte. *Schattentheater, Schattenpuppen, Schattenfilm*. Tübingen: Texte-Verlag, 1981.

Reisig, Karl Christian. *Vorlesungen über lateinische Sprachwissenschaft*, ed. Friedrich Haase. Leipzig: Lehnhold'sche Buchhandlung, 1839.

Renan, Ernest. *Etudes d'histoire religieuse*. Paris: Michel Lévy Frères, 1857.

Rév, István. "The Necronym." *Representations* 64 (1998): 76–108.

Rheinberger, Hans-Jörg. *On Historicizing Epistemology: An Essay*, transl. David Fernbach. Stanford, CA: Stanford University Press, 2010.

Rhodokanakis, Nicolaus. *Der Grundsatz der Öffentlichkeit in den südarabischen Urkunden*. Sitzungsberichte der Kaiserlichen Akademie der Wissenschaften Wien, Philosophisch-historische Klasse, 177, No. 2. Vienna: Hölder, 1915.

Richards, I[van] A[rmstrong]. *Practical Criticism*. London: Kegan Paul, 1929.

Ricœur, Paul. *Freud and Philosophy: An Essay on Interpretation* [1965]. New Haven, CT: Yale University Press, 1970.

Ricœur, Paul. "The Model of the Text: Meaningful Action Considered as a Text." *New Literary History* 5, no. 1 (1973): 91–117.

Ritter, Hellmut. *Karagös, Folge 1: Die Blutpappel u.a.* Hanover: Lafaire, 1924.

Ritter, Hellmut. *Karagös, Folge 2: Der Ausflug nach Jalowa u.a.* Hanover: Lafaire, 1941.

Ritter, Hellmut. *Karagös, Folge 3: Die Beschneidung u.a.* mit Beiträgen von Andreas Tietze. Hanover: Lafaire, 1953.

Robert, Carl. *Oidipus: Geschichte eines poetischen Stoffs im griechischen Altertum*. Berlin: Weidmannsche Buchhandlung, 1915.

Robertson, Ritchie. "Ancients, Moderns and the Future: The *Querelle* in Germany from Winckelmann to Schiller." In *Ancients and Moderns in Europe: Comparative Perspectives*, ed. Paddy Bullard, Alexis Tadié, 257–76. Oxford: Voltaire Foundation, 2016.

Rodogno, Davide. *Against Massacre: Humanitarian Interventions in the Ottoman Empire, 1815–1914*. Princeton, NJ: Princeton University Press, 2012.

Rohde, Erwin. *Afterphilologie: Zur Beleuchtung des von dem Dr. phil. Ulrich von Wilamowitz-Moellendorff herausgegebenen Pamphlets: ‚Zukunftsphilologie!'. Sendschreiben eines Philologen an Richard Wagner*. Leipzig: E. W. Fritzsch, 1872.

Rohrbacher, Peter. "'Wüstenwanderer' gegen 'Wolkenpolitiker'—Die Pressefehde zwischen Eduard Glaser und Theodor Herzl." *Österreichische Akademie der Wissenschaften, Philosophisch-Historische Klasse, Anzeiger* 142 (2007): 103–16.

Rosa, Hartmut. *Social Acceleration: A New Theory of Modernity* [2013], transl. Jonathan Trejo-Mathys. New York: Columbia University Press, 2016.

Rosenkranz, Karl. *Aesthetik des Häßlichen*. Königsberg: Gebr. Bornträger, 1853.

Rosenzweig, Franz. *Der Stern der Erlösung* [1921], *Gesammelte Schriften* II, ed. Reinhold Mayer. The Hague: Nijhoff, 1976.

Rosenzweig, Franz. "Einleitung." In Hermann Cohen, *Jüdische Schriften*, 1, ed. Bruno Strauß, XIII–LXIV. Berlin: Schwetschke, 1924.

Rosenzweig, Franz. *Briefe und Tagebücher*, ed. Rachel Rosenzweig, Edith Rosenzweig-Scheinemann, 2. The Hague: Martinus Nijhoff, 1979.

Rüppell, Eduard von. *Reise in Abyssinien*. 2 vols. Frankfurt a.M.: Schmerber, 1838–40.

Růžička, Kurt. *Historie und Historizität der Junggrammatiker*. Berlin: Akademie Verlag, 1977.

Sabai Günther, Jasmin Ii; Castro, Inés de, eds. *Die Welt des Schattentheaters: Von Asien bis Europa*. Munich: Hirmer, 2015.

Said, Edward W. *Orientalism* [1978]. New York: Vintage, 1994.

Said, Edward W. "Reflections on American 'Left' Literary Criticism." In *The World, the Text, and the Critic*, 158–77. Cambridge, MA: Harvard University Press, 1984.

Said, Edward W. *Culture and Imperialism*. New York: Knopf, 1993.

Said, Edward W. "The Return to Philology." In *Humanism and Democratic Criticism*, 57–84. New York: Columbia University Press, 2004.

Salmen, Brigitte, ed. *Der Almanach 'Der Blaue Reiter': Bilder und Bildwerke in Originalen*. Murnau: Schlossmuseum, 1998.

Salt, Henry. *A Voyage to Abyssinia, & Travels Into the Interiors of that Country, Executed Under the Orders of the British Government in the Years 1809 & 1810* [1814]. Philadelphia: M. Carey, 1816.

Savoy, Bénédicte. *Nofretete, eine deutsch-französische Affäre 1912–1931*. Cologne: Böhlau, 2011.

Saxer, Daniela. *Die Schärfung des Quellenblicks: Forschungspraktiken in der Geschichtswissenschaft 1840–1914*. Munich: Oldenbourg, 2014.

Saxl, Fritz. "The Classical Inscription in Renaissance Art and Politics: Bartholomaeus Fontius, Liber Monumentorum Romanae Urbis et Aliorum Locorum." *Journal of the Warburg and Courtauld Institutes* 4, no. 1–2 (1940–1): 19–46.

Sayce, A[rchibald] H[enry]. *Fresh Light from the Ancient Monuments: A Sketch of the Most Recent Confirmations of the Bible, From Recent Discoveries in Egypt, Palestine, Assyria, Babylonia, Asia Minor*. London: The Religious Tract Society, 1883.

Schechter, Solomon. "Higher Criticism—Higher Anti-Semitism" [1903]. In *Seminary Address and Other Papers*, 35–9. Cincinnati: Ark Publishing, 1915.

Schestag, Thomas. *Mantisrelikte: Maurice Blanchot, Jean-Henri Fabre, Paul Celan*. Basel: Urs Engeler, 1999.

Schestag, Thomas. "Namen nehmen: Zur Theorie des Namens bei Carl Schmitt." *Modern Language Notes* 122 (2007): 544–62.

Schiemann, Gregor. *Hermann von Helmholtz's Mechanism: The Loss of Certainty, a Study on the Transition from Classical to Modern Philosophy of Nature* [1997], transl. Cynthia Klohr. Dordrecht: Springer, 2009.

Schiller, Friedrich. "Über naive und sentimentalische Dichtung" [1795–6]. In idem, *Theoretische Schriften*, ed. Rolf-Peter Janz, 706–810. Frankfurt a.M.: Deutscher Klassiker Verlag, 2008.

Schiller, Friedrich. "Tragödie und Komödie." In *Theoretische Schriften*, 1047f. Frankfurt a.M.: Deutscher Klassiker Verlag, 2008.

Schlegel, Friedrich. "Zur Philologie I, II." In *Fragmente zur Poesie und Literatur* 1, ed. Hans Eichner. Kritische Friedrich Schlegel Ausgabe, 16. Paderborn: Schöningh, Zürich: Thomas, 1981.

Schleiermacher, Friedrich Daniel Ernst. *Hermeneutik und Kritik*, ed. Manfred Frank. Frankfurt a.M.: Suhrkamp, 1977.

Schleiermacher, Friedrich Daniel Ernst. "Über den Begriff der Hermeneutik mit Bezug auf F. A. Wolfs Andeutungen und Asts Lehrbuch" [1829]. In *Hermeneutik und Kritik*, ed. Manfred Frank, 309–46. Frankfurt a.M.: Suhrkamp, 1977.

Schmidt, Jochen. *Die Geschichte des Genie-Gedankens in der deutschen Literatur, Philosophie und Politik, 1750–1945*. 2 vols. Heidelberg: Winter, 3rd edn. 2004.

Schmitt, Carl. *Political Theology: Four Chapters on the Concept of Sovereignty*, transl. George Schwab. Cambridge, MA: Massachussetts Institute of Technology Press, 1985.

Schneider, Ulrich Johannes. *Die Vergangenheit des Geistes: Eine Archäologie der Philosophiegeschichte*. Frankfurt a.M.: Suhrkamp, 1990.

Scholem, Gershom. *From Berlin to Jerusalem: Memories of my Youth*, transl. Harry Zohn. New York: Schocken, 1980.

Schröder, Wilhelm. *Het Wetloopen tüschen den Haasen un den Swinegel up der Buxtehuder Heid*. Düsseldorf: Arnz & Co., 1855.

Schulin, Ernst. *Die weltgeschichtliche Erfassung des Orients bei Hegel und Ranke*. Göttingen: Vandenhoeck & Ruprecht, 1958.

Schüttpelz, Erhard. *Die Moderne im Spiegel des Primitiven: Weltliteratur und Ethnologie (1870–1960)*. Munich: Fink, 2005.

Schwab, Raymond. *The Oriental Renaissance: Europe's Discovery of India and the East, 1689–1880* [1950]. New York: Columbia University Press, 1984.

Schwanitz, Wolfgang G. "'Djihad, Made in Germany': Der Streit um den Heiligen Krieg 1914–1915." *Sozial.Geschichte* 18, no. 2 (2003): 7–34.

Schwentker, Wolfgang. "Karl Löwith und Japan." *Archiv für Kulturgeschichte* 76 (1994): 415–49.

Schwindt, Jürgen Paul, ed. *Was ist eine philologische Frage? Beiträge zur Erkundung einer theoretischen Einstellung*. Frankfurt a.M.: Suhrkamp, 2009.

Sellheim, Rudolf. "Theodor Nöldeke (1836–1930): Begründer der modernen Orientalistik." *Die Welt des Orients* 37 (2007): 135–44.

Seyhan, Azade. *Representation and Its Discontents: The Critical Legacy of German Romanticism*. Berkeley: University of California Press, 1992.

Sheehan, Jonathan. *The Enlightenment Bible: Translation, Scholarship, Culture*. Princeton, NJ: Princeton University Press, 2005.

Sheehan, Jonathan; Wahrman, Dror. *Invisible Hands: Self-Organization and the Eighteenth Century*. Chicago: University of Chicago Press, 2015.

Sieg, Ulrich. *Jüdische Intellektuelle im Ersten Weltkrieg: Kriegserfahrungen, Weltanschauungen und kulturelle Neuentwürfe*. Berlin: Akademie, 2001.

Sieg, Ulrich. *Deutschlands Prophet: Paul de Lagarde und die Anfänge des modernen Antisemitismus*. Munich: Beck, 2007.

Siegfried, Carl. "Review of Hommel, Altisraelitische Überlieferung." *Theologische Literaturzeitung* 23, no. 2 (1898): 33–5.

Silvestre de Sacy, Antoine-Isaac. *Principes de grammaire générale, mis à la portée des enfans, et propres à servir d'introduction à l'étude de toutes les langues*. Paris: Delance et Lesueur, 2nd edn. 1803.

Silvestre de Sacy, Antoine-Isaac. *Chrestomathie arabe, ou extraits de divers écrivains arabes, tant en prose qu'en vers*. 3 vols. Paris: Imprimerie Impériale, 1806.

Silvestre de Sacy, Antoine-Isaac. *Grammaire arabe à l'usage des élèves de l'Ecole spéciale des langues orientales vivantes*. 2 vols. Paris: Imprimerie Impériale, 1810, 2nd edn. 1831.

Sinor, Denis. "Remembering Paul Pelliot." *Journal of the American Oriental Society* 119, no. 3 (1999): 467–72.

Skoie, Mathilde; Bjørnstad Velázquez, Sonia, eds. *Pastoral and the Humanities: Arcadia Re-inscribed*. Exeter: Bristol Phoenix, 2006.

Smend, Rudolf. "Wellhausen und das Judentum." *Zeitschrift für Theologie und Kirche* 79 (1982): 249–82.

Smend, Rudolf. "Julius Wellhausen und seine Prolegomena zur Geschichte Israels." In *Epochen der Bibelkritik: Gesammelte Studien*, 3, 168–85. Munich: Chr. Kaiser Verlag, 1991.

Smend, Rudolf. *Julius Wellhausen, ein Bahnbrecher in drei Disziplinen*. Munich: Carl Friedrich von Siemens Stiftung, 2006.

Smidt, Wolbert G. C. "Die äthiopischen und eritreischen Mittler." *In Kaiserlichem Auftrag: Die Deutsche Aksum-Expedition 1906 unter Enno Littmann*, 1, ed. Steffen Wenig et al., 145–57. Aichwald: Linden Soft, 2006.

Smidt, Wolbert G. C. "Werner Munzinger Pascha: An Orientalist and Ethnographer-Turned-Politician in the Ethiopian-Egyptian Borderlands." In *Cultural Research in Northeastern Africa: German Histories and Stories*, ed. Wolbert G. C. Smidt, Sophia Thubauville, 105–25. Frankfurt a.M.: Frobenius Institut, 2015.

Smith, Barbara Herrnstein. "What Was 'Close Reading'? A Century of Method in Literary Studies." *Minnesota Review* 87 (2016): 57–75.

Smith, Bonnie. "Gender and the Practices of Scientific History: The Seminar and Archival Research." *American Historical Review* 100, no. 4 (1995): 1150–76.

Smith, Helmut Walser. *The Butcher's Tale: Murder and Anti-Semitism in a German Town*. New York: Norton, 2002.

Smith, William Robertson. *Kinship and Marriage in Early Arabia*. Cambridge: Cambridge University Press, 1885.

Snouck Hurgronje, Christiaan. *Mekka*. 2 vols. Leiden: Nijhoff, 1888–9.

Snouck Hurgronje, Christiaan. *Mekka: Bilderatlas*. The Hague: Nijhoff, 1888.

Socin, Albert. *Arabische Grammatik: Paradigmen, Litteratur, Chrestomathie und Glossar*. Karlsruhe: Reuther 1885, 5th rev. edn. by Carl Brockelmann, Berlin: Reuther, 1904.

Sommer, Andreas Urs. *Friedrich Nietzsches der 'Der Antichrist': Ein philosophisch-historischer Kommentar*. Basel: Schwabe, 2000.

Spieth, Andreas Jakob. *Die Religion der Eweer in Süd-Togo*. Göttingen/Leipzig: Vandenhoeck & Ruprecht/J.C. Hinrichs, 1911.

Spivak, Gayatri Chakravorty. "Can the Subaltern Speak?" In *Colonial Discourse and Post-Colonial Theory: A Reader*, ed. Patrick Williams, Laura Chrisman, 66–111. New York: Harvester Wheatsheaf, 1993.

Spivak, Gayatri Chakravorty. *A Critique of Postcolonial Reason: Toward a History of the Vanishing Present*. Cambridge, MA: Harvard University Press, 1999.

Spivak, Gayatri Chakravorty. *Death of a Discipline*. New York: Columbia University Press, 2003.

Stagl, Justin. *A History of Curiosity: The Theory of Travel 1550–1800*. Chur: Harwood, 1995.

Staiger, Emil. *Die Kunst der Interpretation*. Zurich: Atlantis, 1955.

Steedman, Carolyn K. *Dust: The Archive and Cultural History*. Brunswick, NJ: Rutgers University Press, 2001.

Steinmetz, George. *The Devil's Handwriting: Precoloniality and the German Colonial State in Qingdao, Samoa, and Southwest Africa*. Chicago: The University of Chicago Press, 2008.

Stoichita, Victor I. *A Short History of the Shadow*. London: Reaktion Books, 1997.

Stoler, Ann Laura. *Along the Archival Grain: Epistemic Anxieties and Colonial Common Sense*. Princeton, NJ: Princeton University Press, 2009.

Stroud, Ronald S. "'Wie es eigentlich gewesen' and Thucydides 2.48.3." *Hermes* 115, no. 3 (1987): 379–82.

Strzygowski, Josef. *Orient oder Rom: Beiträge zur Geschichte der spätantiken und frühchristlichen Kunst*. Leipzig: Hinrichs'sche Buchhandlung, 1901.

Strzygowski, Josef. *Kleinasien: Ein Neuland der Kunstgeschichte*. Leipzig: Hinrichs'sche Buchhandlung, 1903.

Subrahmanyam, Sanjay. *Courtly Encounters: Translating Courtliness and Violence in Early Modern Eurasia*. Cambridge, MA: Harvard University Press, 2012.

Süssheim, Karl. "Die moderne Gestalt des türkischen Schattenspiels (Qaragöz)." *Zeitschrift der Deutschen Morgenländischen Gesellschaft* 63 (1909): 739–73.

Szondi, Peter. *Theorie des modernen Dramas*. Frankfurt a.M.: Suhrkamp, 1956.

Szondi, Peter. *Poetik und Geschichtsphilosophie I: Antike und Moderne in der Ästhetik der Goethezeit*. Frankfurt a.M.: Suhrkamp, 1974.

Sæbø, Magne, with Peter Machinist, Jean Louis Ska, eds. *Hebrew Bible/Old Testament: The History of Its Interpretation, 3.1 The Nineteenth Century: A Century of Modernism and Historicism, 3.2 The Twentieth Century—From Modernism to Post-Modernism*. Göttingen: Vandenhoeck & Ruprecht, 2013–5.

Taeschner, Franz. "Nachruf Hubert Grimme." *Zeitschrift der Deutschen Morgenländischen Gesellschaft* 96 (1943): 380–92.

Taubes, Jacob. "Die Entstehung des jüdischen Paria-Volkes." In *Max Weber: Gedächtnisschrift der Ludwig-Maximilians-Universität München zur hundertsten Wiederkehr seines Geburtstages*, ed. Karl Englisch et al., 185–94. Berlin: Duncker & Humblot, 1966.

Taubes, Jacob. "Ästhetisierung der Wahrheit im Posthistoire." In *Streitbare Philosophie: Margherita von Brentano zum 65. Geburtstag*, ed. Gabriele Althaus, Irmingard Staeuble, 41–51. Berlin: Metropol, 1988.

Thomasson, Fredrik. "Justifying and Criticizing the Removals of Antiquities in Ottoman Lands: Tracking the Sigeion Inscription." *International Journal of Cultural Property* 17, no. 3 (2010): 493–517.

Thomasson, Fredrik. *The Life of Johan David Åkerblad: Egyptian Decipherment and Orientalism in Revolutionary Times*. Leiden: Brill, 2013.

Thomson, Ann. *Barbary and Enlightenment: European Attitudes toward the Maghreb in the Eighteenth Century*. Leiden: Brill, 1987.

Timpanaro, Sebastiano. *La genesi del metodo di Lachmann*. Florence: Le Monnier, 1963; English translation *The Genesis of Lachmann's Method*, ed. and transl. Glenn W. Most. Chicago: University of Chicago Press, 2010.

Tolz, Vera. *Russia's Own Orient: The Politics of Identity and Oriental Studies in the Late Imperial and Early Soviet Periods*. Oxford: Oxford University Press, 2011.

Tottoli, Roberto, ed. *Orientalists at Work: Some Excerpts from Paul E. Kahle's Papers upon Ibn Dāniyāl Kept in the Department of Oriental Studies of the University of Turin*. Allessandria: Edizioni dell'Orso, 2009.

Trabant, Jürgen. *Traditionen Humboldts*. Frankfurt a.M.: Suhrkamp, 1990.

Trabant, Jürgen. *Vico's New Science of Ancient Signs*, transl. Sean Ward. London: Routledge, 2004.

Trawny, Peter. *Heidegger und der Mythos der jüdischen Weltverschwörung*. Frankfurt a.M.: Klostermann, 2014.

Troeltsch, Ernst. *Der Historismus und seine Probleme, 1: Das logische Problem der Geschichtsphilosophie* [1922]. Kritische Gesamtausgabe 16.1-2, ed. F. W. Graf. Berlin: de Gruyter, 2008.

Trouillot, Michel-Rolph. "Anthropology and the Savage Slot: The Poetics and Politics of Otherness." In *Global Transformations: Anthropology and the Modern World*, 7–28. Basingstoke: Palgrave Macmillan, 2003.

Trüper, Henning. "Suchen und Finden: Notizführung und Grammatik bei Theodor Nöldeke." In *Vor Google: Eine Mediengeschichte der Suchmaschinen im analogen Zeitalter*, ed. Thomas Brandstetter, Thomas Hübel, Anton Tantner, 173–201. Bielefeld: Transcript, 2012.

Trüper, Henning. "Wild Archives: Unsteady Records of the Past in the Travels of Enno Littmann." *History of the Human Sciences* 26, no. 4 (2013): 128–48.

Trüper, Henning. "Dispersed Personae: Subject-Matters of Scholarly Biography in Nineteenth-Century Oriental Philology." *Asiatische Studien—Etudes Asiatiques* 67 (2013): 1325–60.

Trüper, Henning. "Wie es uneigentlich gewesen: Zum Gebrauch der Fußnote bei Julius Wellhausen." *Zeitschrift für Germanistik*, N.F. 23, no. 2 (2013): 329–42.

Trüper, Henning. "Löwith, Löwith's Heidegger, and the Unity of History." *History and Theory* 53, no. 1 (2014): 45–68.

Trüper, Henning. "Matte farbige Schatten: Zugehörigkeiten des Gelehrtenpolitikers Carl Heinrich Becker." *Österreichische Zeitschrift für Geschichtswissenschaften* 25, no. 3 (2014): 177–211.

Trüper, Henning. *Topography of a Method: François Louis Ganshof and the Writing of History*. Tübingen: Mohr Siebeck, 2014.

Trüper, Henning. "Heteropsy and Autopsy in Nineteenth-Century Aksumite Epigraphy." *Storia della Storiografia* 66 (2015): 121–42.

Trüper, Henning. "Epistemic Vice: Transgression in the Arabian Travels of Julius Euting." In *Scholarly Personae in the History of Orientalism, 1870–1930* ed. Christiaan Engberts, Herman Paul, 64–98. Leiden: Brill, 2019.

Turner, James. *Philology: The Forgotten Origins of the Modern Humanities*. Princeton, NJ: Princeton University Press, 2014.

Tylor, Edward Burnett. *Primitive Religion: Researches into the Development of Mythology, Philosophy, Religion, Art, and Custom*. London: John Murray, 1871.

Ullmann, Manfred. *Flughühner und Tauben*. Munich: Bayerische Akademie der Wissenschaften, 1982.

Usener, Hermann. *Götternamen: Versuch einer Lehre von der religiösen Begriffsbildung*. Bonn: F. Cohen, 1896.

Utz, Richard. *Chaucer and the Discourse of German Philology: A History of Reception and an Annotated Bibliography of Studies, 1798–1948*. Turnhout: Brepols, 2002.

Valentia, George Viscount. *Voyages and Travels to India, Ceylon, the Red Sea, Abyssinia, and Egypt, in the Years 1802, 1803, 1804, 1805, and 1806.* 3 vols. London: William Miller, 1809.

Vermeulen, Han F. *Before Boas: The Genesis of Ethnography and Ethnology in the German Enlightenment.* Lincoln, NE: University of Nebraska Press, 2015.

Vernier, P.; Donat, SJ. *Grammaire arabe composée d'après les sources primitives.* 2 vols. Beyrouth: Imprimerie Catholique, 1891–2.

Versteegh, Kees. *Arabic Grammar and Qurʾānic Exegesis.* Leiden: Brill, 1993.

Versteegh, Kees. *Landmarks in Linguistic Thought III: The Arabic Linguistic Tradition.* London: Routledge, 1997.

Vesper, Will. *Der Blinde: Ein Narrenspiel.* Munich: Schwabinger Schattenspiele, 1907.

Vico, Giambattista. *The New Science* [3rd edn. 1744], transl. Thomas Goddard Bergin, Max H. Fisch. Ithaca, NY: Cornell University Press, 1948.

Vogt, Ernst. "Der Methodenstreit zwischen Hermann und Böckh und seine Bedeutung für die Geschichte der Philologie." In *Philologie und Hermeneutik im 19. Jahrhundert: Zur Geschichte und Methodologie der Geisteswissenschaften* ed. Hellmut Flashar et al., 103–21. Göttingen: Vandenhoeck & Ruprecht, 1979.

Vogüé, Melchior de. "Voyage de MM. Waddington et le comte Melchior de Vogüé en Syrie." *Comptes rendus de l'Académie des Inscriptions et Belles-Lettres* 7, no. 7 (1863): 23–9.

Vogüé, Melchior de. *Syrie centrale.* 2 vols. Paris: Noblet & Baudry, 1877.

Voigt, Rainer, ed. "Enno Littmanns Tagebuch der Abessinischen Expedition (Deutsche Aksum-Expedition), 29. Dezember 1905–7. April 1906." *In Kaiserlichem Auftrag: Die Deutsche Aksum-Expedition 1906 unter Enno Littmann,* 1 ed. Steffen Wenig et al., 161–99. Aichwald: Linden Soft, 2006.

Voigt, Rainer, ed. "Enno Littmanns Tagebuch der Abessinischen Expedition (Deutsche Aksum-Expedition), 7.-26. April 1906 und der Heimreise." *In Kaiserlichem Auftrag: Die Deutsche Aksum-Expedition 1906 unter Enno Littmann,* 2 ed. Steffen Wenig et al., 109–34. Wiesbaden: Reichert, 2011.

Vold, John Mourly. *Über den Traum: Experimental-psychologische Untersuchungen,* ed. Otto Klemm. 2 vols. Leipzig: Barth, 1910–12.

Völkel, Markus. *"Pyrrhonismus" und "fides historica": Die Entwicklung der deutschen historischen Methodologie unter dem Gesichtspunkt der historischen Skepsis.* Frankfurt a.M.: Lang, 1987.

Volkov, Shulamit. "Antisemitism as a Cultural Code: Reflections on the History and Historiography of Antisemitism in Imperial Germany." *Yearbook of the Leo-Baeck-Institute* 23 (1978): 25–45.

Vrolijk, Arnoud. "The Leiden Edition of Tabari's Annals: The Search for the Istanbul Manuscripts as Reflected in Michael Jan de Goeje's Correspondence." *Quaderni di studi arabi* 19 (2001): 71–86.

Waardenburg, Jean Jacques. *L'Islam dans le miroir de l'Occident: Comment quelques orientalistes occidentaux se sont formés une image de cette religion: Goldziher, Snouck Hurgronje, Becker, Macdonald, Massignon.* Paris: Mouton, 3rd edn. 1969.

Wagner, Richard. *Zukunftsmusik: Brief an einen französischen Freund.* Leipzig: J. J. Weber, 1861.

Wagner, Richard. *Das Judenthum in der Musik.* Leipzig: J. J. Weber, 1869.

Walravens, Hartmut, ed. *"Und der Sumeru meines Dankes würde wachsen": Beiträge zur ostasiatischen Kunstgeschichte in Deutschland.* Wiesbaden: Harrassowitz, 2010.

Watanabe, Toshio. *High Victorian Japonisme.* Berne: Lang, 1991.

Watt, Ian. *The Rise of the Novel: Studies in Defoe, Richardson and Fielding.* London: Chatto & Windus, 1957.

Weber, Max. *Die Wirtschaftsethik der Weltreligionen: Das antike Judentum, Schriften und Reden 1911–1920,* ed. Eckart Otto. Max-Weber-Gesamtausgabe I, 21, 1–2. Tübingen: Mohr Siebeck, 2005.

Weber, Max. *Die Protestantische Ethik und der 'Geist' des Kapitalismus* [1904–5, 1920]. Max Weber Gesamtausgabe I/9 and I/18, ed. Wolfgang Schluchter, Ursula Bube. Tübingen: Mohr Siebeck, 2014–16.

Wegmann, Nikolaus. "The Future of Philology—an Update." In *The Future of Philology: Proceedings of the 11th Annual Columbia University German Graduate Student Conference* ed. Hannes Bajohr et al., 24–43. Newcastle/Tyne: Cambrige Scholars Publ., 2014.

Weidner, Daniel. "'Geschichte gegen den Strich bürsten': Julius Wellhausen und die jüdische 'Gegengeschichte.'" *Zeitschrift für Religions- und Geistesgeschichte* 54, no. 1 (2002): 32–61.

Weidner, Daniel. *Bibel und Literatur um 1800.* Munich: Fink, 2010.

Weisberg, Gabriel; Weisberg, Yvonne. *Japonisme: An Annotated Bibliography.* New York: Garland, 1990.

Wellek, René. *A History of Modern Criticism,* 4.1. New Haven, CT: Yale University Press, 1986.

Wellhausen, Julius. *Prolegomena zur Geschichte Israels.* Berlin: Reimer, 1883 (2nd rev. edn. of *Geschichte Israels I.* Berlin: Reimer, 1878).

Wellhausen, Julius. *Die Composition des Hexateuchs und der historischen Bücher des Alten Testaments* [1885]. Berlin: Reimer; 3rd edn. 1899.

Wellhausen, Julius. *Reste arabischen Heidentums* [1887]. Berlin: Georg Reimer; 2nd edn. 1897.

Wellhausen, Julius. "Rezension Georg Jacob, Welche Handelsartikel bezogen die Araber des Mittelalters aus den nordisch-baltischen Ländern?" *Deutsche Literaturzeitung* 13 (1892): 589f.

Wellhausen, Julius. *Israelitische und jüdische Geschichte.* Berlin: Reimer, 1894, Berlin: 8th edn. Leipzig: Vereinigung wissenschaftlicher Verleger, 1921.

Wellhausen, Julius. "Review of Fritz Hommel, Die altisraelitische Überlieferung in inschriftlicher Beleuchtung." *Göttingische Gelehrte Anzeigen* 159, no. 2 (1897): 608–16.

Wellhausen, Julius. *Ein Gemeinwesen ohne Obrigkit: Rede zur Feier des Geburtstages seiner Majestät des Kaisers und Königs am 27. Januar 1900 im Namen der Georg-Augusts-Universität.* Göttingen: Dieterich'sche Buchhandlung, 1900.

Wellhausen, Julius. *Das arabische Reich und sein Sturz.* Berlin: Reimer, 1902.

Wellhausen, Julius. *Das Evangelium Marci übersetzt und erklärt.* Berlin: Reimer, 1903.

Wellhausen, Julius. *Briefe,* ed. Rudolf Smend. Tübingen: Mohr Siebeck, 2013.

Wenig, Steffen, et al., eds. *In Kaiserlichem Auftrag: Die Deutsche Aksum-Expedition 1906 unter Enno Littmann,* 1: *Die Akteure und die wissenschaftlichen Unternehmungen der DAE in Eritrea.* Aichwald: Linden Soft, 2006; 2: *Altertumskundliche Untersuchungen der DAE in Tigray/Äthiopien.* Wiesbaden: Reichert, 2011.

Wenig, Steffen. "Addendum zu Hans v. Lüpkes Die Zeit in Aksum." *In Kaiserlichem Auftrag: Die Deutsche Aksum-Expedition 1906 unter Enno Littmann,* 2 ed. Steffen Wenig et al., 169–76. Wiesbaden Reichert, 2011.

Weninger, Stefan, ed. *Semitic Languages: An International Handbook.* Berlin: de Gruyter, 2011.

Wetzstein, Johann Gottfried. *Reisebericht über Hauran und die Trachonen.* Berlin: Reimer, 1860.

Wiese, Christian. "'The Best Antidote to Anti-Semitism'? *Wissenschaft des Judentums,* Protestant Biblical Scholarship, and Anti-Semitism in Germany before 1933." In *Modern Judaism and Historical Consciousness: Identities, Encounters, Perspectives,* ed. Andreas Gotzmann, Christian Wiese, 146–92. Leiden: Brill, 2007.

Wiesehöfer, Josef; Conermann, Stephan, eds. *Carsten Niebuhr (1733–1815) und seine Zeit: Beiträge eines interdisziplinären Symposiums 7–10. Oktober 1999.* Stuttgart: Steiner, 2002.

Wilamowitz-Moellendorff, Tycho von. *Die dramatische Technik des Sophokles,* ed. Ernst Kapp, with a contribution by Ulrich von Wilamowitz-Moellendorff and an appendix by William M. Calder and Anton Bierl. Hildesheim: Weidmann, 1996.

Wilamowitz-Moellendorff, Ulrich von. *Zukunftsphilologie! Eine erwidrung auf Friedrich Nietzsches "geburt der tragödie."* Berlin: Borntraeger, 1872.

Wilamowitz-Moellendorff, Ulrich von. *Zukunftsphilologie! Zweites Stück. Eine erwidrung auf die rettungsversuche für Fr. Nietzsches "geburt der tragödie."* Berlin: Borntraeger, 1873.

Wilamowitz-Moellendorff, Ulrich von. *Erinnerungen 1848–1914* [1928]. Leipzig: Koehler, 2nd edn. 1932.

Wimmer, Mario. "Die Lagen der Historik." *Österreichische Zeitschrift für Geschichtswissenschaften* 18, no. 2 (2007): 106–25.

Wimmer, Mario. *Archivkörper: Eine Geschichte historischer Einbildungskraft.* Paderborn: Konstanz University Press, 2012.

Wimmer, Mario. "On Sources: Mythical and Historical Thinking in Fin-de-Siècle Vienna." *Res: Anthropology and Aesthetics* 63–4 (2013), spring/autumn: 108–24.

Winckelmann, Johann Joachim. "Gedanken über die Nachahmung der griechischen Werke in der Malerei und Bildhauerkunst" [1755]. *Werke,* 2. Stuttgart: Hoffmann'sche Verlagsbuchhandlung, 1847.

Windisch, Ernst. *Der griechische Einfluss im indischen Drama.* Berlin: A. Asher, 1882.

Windisch, Ernst. *Geschichte der Sanskrit-Philologie und indischen Altertumskunde,* 1–3. Berlin: de Gruyter, 1917–21.

Witkam, Jan Just. *Honderd jaar Mekka in Leiden. 1885–1985.* Leiden: Rijksuniversiteit, 1985.

Witkam, Jan Just; Vrolijk, Arnoud; Velde, H. van de. *Christiaan Snouck Hurgronje (1857–1936): Orientalist.* Leiden: Universiteitsbibliotheek, 2007.

Wittgenstein, Ludwig. *Philosophische Untersuchungen—Philosophical Investigations* [1953]. Oxford: Blackwell, 2001.

Wokoeck, Ursula. *German Orientalism: The Study of the Middle East and Islam from 1800 to 1945.* London: Routledge, 2009.

Wolf, Eric. *Europe and the People without History.* Berkeley: University of California Press, 1982.

Wolf, Friedrich August. *Darstellung der Alterthums-Wissenschaft nach Begriff, Umfang, Zweck und Werth.* Museum der Alterthums-Wissenschaft 1. Berlin: Realschulbuchahndlung, 1807.

Wolf, Friedrich August. *Encyclopädie der Philologie: Nach dessen Vorlesungen im Winterhalbjahre von 1789–1799,* ed. S. M. Stockmann. Leipzig: Expedition des Europäischen Aufsehers, 1831.

Wolff, Vera. *Die Rache des Materials: Eine andere Geschichte des Japonismus.* Zürich, Berlin: Diaphanes, 2015.

Wolfskehl, Karl. *Wolfdietrich und die Rauhe Els.* Munich: Schwabinger Schattenspiele, 1907.

Wolfskehl, Karl. *Thors Hammer*, Silhouetten von Emil Preetorius. Munich: Schwabinger Schattenspiele, 1908.

Wu Xiaoqiao. "Chen Quan." In *Internationales Germanistenlexikon 1800–1950*, ed. Christoph König, 1, 326f. Berlin, New York: de Gruyter, 2003.

Wüstenfeld, Ferdinand, ed. *Jacut's Geographisches Wörterbuch.* 6 vols. Leipzig: F. A. Brockhaus, 1866–73.

Wyss-Giacosa, Paola von. *Religionsbilder der frühen Aufklärung: Bernard Picarts Tafeln für die 'Cérémonies et Coutumes religieuses de tous les Peuples du Monde.'* Wabern/Berne: Benteli, 2006.

Zantop, Susanne. *Colonial Fantasies: Conquest, Family and Nation in Precolonial Germany 1770–1870.* Durham, NC: Duke University Press, 1997.

Zauner, Adolf. *Die romanischen Namen der Körperteile: Eine onomasiologische Studie.* Erlangen: Junge & Sohn, 1902.

Zimmerman, Andrew. *Anthropology and Antihumanism in Imperial Germany.* Chicago: University of Chicago Press, 2001.

Zimmerman, Andrew. *Alabama in Africa: Booker T. Washington, the German Empire, and the Globalization of the New South.* Princeton, NJ: Princeton University Press, 2010.

Ziolkowski, Jan. "What Is Philology?" *Comparative Literature Studies* 27, no. 1 (1990): 1–12.

Zitelmann, Thomas. "Körperschaft und Reich: Nordostafrika als Interessenfeld und Projektionsfläche kolonialer Ethnologien." *Paideuma* 42 (1996): 37–51.

Zitelmann, Thomas. "Enno Littmann (1875–1958): Äthiopische Studien und deutscher Orientalismus." In *Kaiserlichem Auftrag: Die Deutsche Aksum-Expedition 1906 unter Enno Littmann*, 1 ed. Steffen Wenig et al., 99–110. Aichwald: Linden Soft, 2006.

Index